THE FRENCH CINEMA BOOK

Max Linder in *Au secours!* (Abel Gance, 1923)

THE FRENCH CINEMA BOOK

Edited by
Michael Temple and Michael Witt

bfi Publishing

For *La Rosière de Pessac*

First published in 2004 by the
British Film Institute
21 Stephen Street, London W1T 1LN

The British Film Institute is the UK national agency with responsibility for encouraging the arts of film and television and conserving them in the national interest.

Cover design by Ketchup
Cover illustration (front): *Le Mépris* (Jean-Luc Godard, 1963) © Studio Canal Image – Compagnia Cinematografica Champion; (back) *La Passion de Jeanne d'Arc* (Carl Theodor Dreyer, 1928), Société Genérale de Films; *Le Ballon rouge* (Albert Lamorisse, 1956), Films Montsouris; *Beau travail* (Claire Denis, 1999), La Sept-Arte/SM Films/Tanaïs Productions

Set by Fakenham Photosetting Limited, Fakenham, Norfolk
Printed in the UK by St Edmundsbury Press, Bury St Edmunds, Suffolk

British Library Cataloguing-in-Publication Data
A catalogue record for this book is available from the British Library

ISBN 1–84457–012–6 (pbk)
ISBN 1–84457–011–8 (hbk)

Contents

Acknowledgments

We would like to thank Andrew Lockett for inviting us to edit this book, and for his valuable suggestions at key moments in its development; Richard Abel, Dudley Andrew, Thomas Elsaesser, the late Jill Forbes, Noel King, Jonathan Rosenbaum, Bill Rout and Ginette Vincendeau for their helpful advice in the early planning stage; Colin Crisp for his invaluable support and practical assistance throughout; and all the contributors for the enthusiasm and expertise they brought to the project. We are also grateful to Aäton (Grenoble) and P.O.L. (Paris) for supplying illustrations; to Richard Abel for making available rare documents from his personal collection; to Muriel Tinel for her photographic skills; and to Sophia Contento for her exhaustive searches through the BFI picture archive.

One of the pleasures of working on this project has been the accompanying collaboration with the National Film Theatre in London. Our thanks therefore to all those who have contributed to the success of the Rethinking French Cinema events at the NFT in recent years; Stacey Abbott, Thalia Cassimatis, Angela English, Julie Pearce and Hilary Smith.

Finally, we would like to express our heartfelt thanks to the many friends and family members who have given us their love and support, especially Isa Temple, Muriel Tinel, Alexandra Witt, Julie Witt, Jack, Ella and Violet.

Notes on Contributors

Richard Abel is Robert Altman Collegiate Professor of Film Studies at the University of Michigan. His recent books include *The Red Rooster Scare* (California University Press, 1999) and, co-edited with Rick Altman, *The Sounds of Early Cinema* (Indiana University Press, 2001). He is currently editing the *Encyclopedia of Early Cinema* for Routledge and writing *The 'Imagined Community' of US Cinema, 1910–1914* for California University Press.

Nicole Brenez teaches Cinema Studies at the University of Paris-I and is the curator of experimental and avant-garde film at the Cinémathèque française. She has published *Shadows* (Nathan, 1995), *De la figure en général et du corps en particulier* (De Boeck, 1998) and co-edited with Christian Lebrat *Jeune, dure et pure! Une histoire du cinéma d'avant-garde et expérimental en France* (Mazzotta/Cinémathèque française, 2000).

Vicki Callahan is Associate Professor of Film Studies at the University of Wisconsin-Milwaukee. She is currently completing a book on the films of Louis Feuillade, *Zones of Anxiety: Movement, Musidora, and the Crime Serials of Louis Feuillade*, to be published by Wayne State University Press.

Ian Christie has published widely in the fields of Russian, British, avant-garde and early cinema, as well as writing on such film-makers as Eisenstein, Powell and Pressburger, Scorsese, Gilliam and Buñuel. He is co-editor of *Film Studies*, vice-president of Europa Cinemas and Anniversary Professor of Film and Media History at Birkbeck College, London.

Laurent Creton is Professor of Film Studies at the University of Paris-III. He has published exten-

sively on the economics of the cinema industry, including *Économie du cinéma, perspectives stratégiques* (Nathan, 1994), *Cinéma et marché* (Armand Colin, 1997), *Le Cinéma à l'épreuve du système télévisuel* (CNRS, 2003).

Colin Crisp became interested in the French cinema when teaching at the ANU in Canberra, where he could draw on the vast library of films then available from the French embassy. Before his recent retirement, he was Associate Professor of Film and Media Studies at Griffith University in Brisbane, which he joined when it opened in 1975.

Monica Dall'Asta teaches Film Studies at the University of Bologna, Italy. She has written widely on serials and popular cinema in the silent period, and is the author of a study of the 'muscle-men genre' in Italian silent cinema, *Un Cinéma musclé* (Yellow Now, 1992). Her current research is on French film theory and the work of Jean-Luc Godard.

Elizabeth Ezra is Senior Lecturer in French at the University of Stirling. She is the author of *Georges Méliès* (Manchester, 2000) and *The Colonial Unconscious: Race and Culture in Interwar France* (Cornell, 2000); co-editor, with Sue Harris, of *France in Focus: Film and National Identity* (Berg, 2000); and editor of *European Cinema* (Oxford, 2003).

Christopher Faulkner is Professor of Film Studies at Carleton University, Ottawa. He is the author of three books on Jean Renoir and numerous articles on French cinema. His most recent book, with Olivier Curchod, is *La Règle du jeu: scénario original de Jean Renoir* (Nathan, 1999). Currently, he is completing a reception study of *La Règle du jeu*.

Naomi Greene is Professor Emeritus of French and Film Studies at the University of California at Santa Barbara. She has translated Marc Ferro's *Cinéma et histoire* and written *Pier Paolo Pasolini: Cinema of Heresy* (Princeton University Press, 1990) and *Landscapes of Loss: The National Past in Postwar French Cinema* (Princeton University Press, 1999).

Sue Harris is Senior Lecturer in French Studies at Queen Mary, University of London. She has a wide range of research interests in French cinema and the performance arts. Her publications include *Bertrand Blier* (Manchester University Press, 2001) and, co-edited with Elizabeth Ezra, *France in Focus: Film and National Identity* (Berg, 2000).

Anne Jäckel is Visiting Research Fellow at the University of the West of England. She has written on European cinema and film policies in journals such as *Media Culture and Society*, *European Journal of Communications* and *International Journal of Cultural Policy*. She is the author of *European Film Industries* (BFI, 2003).

Laurent Jullier teaches film aesthetics at the University of Metz. He is the author of *Précis d'analyse de la bande-son* (Armand Colin, 1995), *Les Images de synthèse* (Nathan, 1998), *L'Analyse de séquences* (Nathan, 2002), *Qu'est-ce qu'un bon film?* (La Dispute, 2002) and *Cinéma et cognition* (L'Harmattan, 2002).

Lucy Mazdon is Senior Lecturer in Film Studies at the University of Southampton. She is the author of *Encore Hollywood: Remaking French Cinema* (BFI, 2000), and the editor of *France on Film: Reflections on Popular French Cinema* (Wallflower, 2001) and of a special issue of *French Cultural Studies* devoted to French television (2002).

Alison McMahan wrote the award-winning *Alice Guy Blaché, Lost Cinematic Visionary* (Continuum, 2002). From 1997 to 2001 she taught early cinema and new media at the University of Amsterdam. She currently holds a Mellon Fellowship in Visual Culture at Vassar College and is writing a book on the work of Tim Burton.

Michelle Millar is the author of a doctoral thesis entitled 'Alice Guy Blaché and the Development of Early Cinema' (University of London, 2000). A Wingate Scholar from 2001 to 2002, she has published on the work of Alice Guy in *French Cultural Studies* and is currently completing a book re-evaluating the commercial foundations of early cinema.

Charles O'Brien is Assistant Professor of Film Studies at Carleton University, Ottawa. He has published widely in the areas of film historiography, film technology, national cinema and French film history. He is currently completing a book entitled *Cinema's Conversion to Sound* for Indiana University Press.

Alastair Phillips teaches Film Studies in the Department of Film, Theatre and Television at the University of Reading. He is the author of *City of Darkness, City of Light: Émigré Filmmakers in Paris 1929–1939* (Amsterdam University Press, 2004) and the co-editor, with Ginette Vincendeau, of the forthcoming *Journeys of Desire: European Actors in Hollywood* (BFI).

Keith Reader is Professor of Modern French Studies at the University of Glasgow. He has written extensively for journals such as *French Studies*, *French Cultural Studies*, *Modern and Contemporary France*, *Contemporary French Civilisation* and *L'Esprit créateur*. His recent books include *Robert Bresson* (Manchester University Press, 2000).

Gregory Sims taught French Studies at the University of Melbourne until 2003. His recent research has centred on French cinema of the Occupation period, French fascist film theory and criticism from 1930 to 1945 and the modernisation of cinema architecture in post-war France. He is currently working as a wine consultant in Berlin.

Alison Smith teaches European Film Studies at Liverpool University. She is the author of *Agnès Varda* (Manchester University Press, 1998) and the co-editor, with Diana Holmes, of *100 Years of European Cinema: Entertainment or Ideology?* (Manchester University Press, 2000). Her current research interests include the French cinema of the 1970s, and the films of Patrice Chéreau and Jacques Rivette.

Michael Temple teaches French at Birkbeck College, London. He is the author of *The Name of the Poet* (Exeter University Press, 1995), editor of *Meetings with Mallarmé* (Exeter University Press, 1998) and co-editor of *The Cinema Alone: Jean-Luc Godard 1985–2000* (Amsterdam University Press, 2000), and is currently writing *Jean Vigo* for Manchester University Press.

Ginette Vincendeau is Professor of Film Studies at the University of Warwick. She has published widely on French cinema and is the editor of *The Encyclopedia of European Cinema* (BFI/Cassell, 1995). Among her recent books are *Stars and Stardom in French Cinema* (Continuum, 2000) and *Jean-Pierre Melville: An American in Paris* (BFI, 2003).

James S. Williams teaches French and comparative literature at the University of Kent. He is the author of *The Erotics of Passage: The Later Work of Marguerite Duras* (Liverpool University Press, 1997) and co-editor of *Gay Signatures: Theory, Fiction and Film, 1945–1995* (Berg, 1998), *The Cinema Alone: Jean-Luc Godard 1985–2000* (Amsterdam University Press, 2000) and *Gender and French Cinema* (Berg, 2001).

Michael Witt teaches Cinema Studies at the University of Surrey Roehampton. He is the co-editor, with Michael Temple and James S. Williams, of *For Ever Godard* (Black Dog Publishing, 2004) and is currently writing *Jean-Luc Godard, Cinema Historian* for Indiana University Press.

GENERAL INTRODUCTION
Rethinking French Cinema

Michael Temple and Michael Witt

This book is designed to provide the film student and film enthusiast with an accessible, structured and innovative history of French cinema from its origins to the present day. A collective project, it comprises twenty-one individual chapters by specialists from around the world, and three historical survey chapters written by the editors. In terms of structure and scope, *The French Cinema Book* has three main objectives. First, to give the reader a clear understanding of the major developments in French cinema from the end of the 19th to the early 21st century. Second, to propose a fresh conceptual framework for the historical appreciation of French cinema by students and filmgoers alike. Third, to explore as fully as possible the fascinating range and diversity of films, people, trends and practices that together make up France's rich film culture. In order to accomplish these aims, the editors made three strategic decisions that have informed the conception and realisation of the project over the last few years. First, we believe in an equal commitment to all periods of French film-making, not just the traditionally favoured decades of the 1930s, 1960s and contemporary cinema. This is why a third of the book is devoted to the silent period, which in spite of the work of Richard Abel and a handful of other writers (many of them contributors to this book) remains relatively unknown, even within the field of film studies. Second, we believe in an open understanding of what 'cinema' is, rather than the predominant focus on feature films by recognised directors or with recognisable stars. This is again especially relevant to the early period, but throughout the book the contributors have included where relevant a discussion of popular, experimental and documentary films, as well as work by lesser-known film-makers. One could potentially expand these fields of enquiry much further to include neglected topics such as newsreels, shorts,

industrial films and home movies, but the basic research in these areas still remains largely to be done. Finally, we believe that the appreciation of French cinema history should not be restricted by the limited range of subtitled materials that are distributed, broadcast or released on video or DVD outside France. We recognise that as students, teachers and researchers we face a very real problem, since one can easily fall into the trap of thinking that 'French cinema' is truly represented by the small proportion of films selected for commercial exhibition abroad and distributed on video or DVD, which are then taught in classrooms, written about by critics and eventually come to constitute its 'history'. As editors of this book, we have therefore encouraged the contributors freely to choose the films, film-makers and traditions most applicable to their ideas and arguments, while at the same time bearing in mind this problem of the availability of materials. We hope that by suggesting new fields of enquiry and profiling a range of fresh names, titles and topics, this collection will perhaps inspire teachers and researchers like ourselves – but above all, programmers, distributors and exhibitors – to be more ambitious and more demanding in this regard (see 'Sources for Buying Videos and DVDs' on p. 273).

The reader will see that *The French Cinema Book* is divided into three chronological parts: 1890–1930 (Chapters 1–7); 1930–60 (Chapters 8–14); and 1960–2004 (Chapters 15–21). This corresponds broadly to the periodisation suggested by many historical surveys. We have chosen to retain these accepted historical divisions, although a number of contributors raise interesting questions about how different the map of French cinema might look if these boundaries were redrawn (see Chapters 11, 14 and 18). For each of these three chronological sections, the editors have written a brief introductory

Josette Andriot in 1913 as the vengeance figure Protéa

Julien Duvivier making *The Great Waltz* in Hollywood in 1938

François Truffaut shooting the final sequence of *Les Quatre cents coups*, 1959

Baise-moi (Virginie Despentes and Coralie Trinh-Ti, 2000)

survey, presenting the consensual view of the main trends, films and personalities of the period. This is intended to give the reader a clear narrative background, against which the originality of the individual chapters will be distinctly highlighted. There then follows for each period a sequence of seven chapters, under the headings of 'People', 'Business', 'Technology', 'Forms', 'Representations', 'Spectators' and 'Debates'. This is the simple conceptual model that we are proposing to our readers as a fresh way of thinking about French cinema and its history, one that we believe poses important questions and interesting challenges for students and teachers, as well as suggesting prospective lines of enquiry for researchers. So let us now say a few words about

each of these seven topics, and outline some of the ways in which the contributors have addressed them.

PEOPLE: Who are the men and women who make French cinema happen? The three chapters devoted to *People* respond to this question by exploring the role of human agency and the power of working communities in the film-making process. The long tradition (see Chapters 1, 8 and 15) and enduring prevalence of 'auteurism' as a critical perspective for thinking about cinema has tended to reduce the notion of French 'film people' to directors, a tendency complemented in recent years by growth in the study of stars. While numerous directors and stars are represented and discussed in this book, we invited the writers of the *People* chapters to open up the category of 'film-maker' to embrace the diversity of human energies and relations that together 'make films'. In Chapter 1, Richard Abel provides a detailed account of early French cinema in terms of the diverse personnel – scientists, inventors, artists, entrepreneurs and producers, as well as actors and directors – whose actions established cinema as a cultural institution and film-making as a practice between the 1890s and the coming of sound. In Chapter 8, Alastair Phillips questions the definition of classic 'French' cinema by focusing on the contribution made by émigré personnel to film production between 1930 and 1960, and he discusses in detail the cases of the cinematographer Curt Courant, the set designer André Andrejew, the director Julien Duvivier and the producer Pierre Braunberger. In Chapter 15, Alison Smith argues against the familiar auteurist perspective on post-New Wave cinema, and examines through case studies the importance of three frequently neglected roles in the film-making process, namely producers (Marin Karmitz), cinematographers (Agnès Godard) and scriptwriters (Jean-Claude Carrière).

BUSINESS: What is the industrial culture in which French cinema has evolved? In responding to this question, the three *Business* chapters explore the socio-economic infrastructure, including issues of investment, plant, distribution and markets, the role of governmental intervention in production and consumption, and the framework of venture capitalism in which 'the business' takes place. In Chapter 2, Michelle Millar examines the commercial strategies of the main French film companies as they competed for control of the domestic market at the turn of the century, charts the massive international expansion of the industry in the 1900s and reviews the complex commercial events that led to Pathé's loss of dominance and ultimate withdrawal from the US market by the end of the decade. In Chapter 9, Colin Crisp shows how the shock of the conversion to sound, and the restructuring to which the film industry was subjected during the Occupation, combined to establish an industrial structure that conditioned the way in which the films of the period were made and ultimately enabled France to compete with Hollywood in the post-war era. In

Chapter 16, Laurent Creton and Anne Jäckel argue that although the modern industry is strengthened by governmental support and regulation, it is also important to consider the special place held by cinema in French culture, the development of innovative business strategies and the emergence of new players on the scene.

TECHNOLOGY: To what extent have technological factors determined the course of French cinema? The three *Technology* chapters address this basic question by focusing on the relationship between cinema and scientific culture, for example the diverse research that first gave birth to the cinematograph, or the subsequent artistic and commercial responses to technological advances. In Chapter 3, Alison McMahan situates the invention of cinema in the broader scientific context of motion studies, examines the proliferation of experiments with sound recording and reproduction in the so-called 'silent' era and relates the parallel histories of film and animation to subsequent developments in digital cinema. In Chapter 10, Charles O'Brien confronts the conventional deterministic view of film style as a direct product of technological change by showing how techniques first industrialised elsewhere, such as multiple-camera shooting, colour and widescreen, were imported and adapted into French cinema between 1930 and 1960. In Chapter 17, Laurent Jullier and Lucy Mazdon relate French technological invention to the enduring realist tradition associated with André Bazin, examining a range of developments in camera technology, the techniques of the New Wave, experimentation with 16mm synchronised sound in the early 1960s, developments in remotely controlled technologies such as the Louma crane and the little discussed work of France's digital film studios.

FORMS: What types of films constitute French cinema, and what formal 'languages' do they deploy? Adopting a primarily aesthetic perspective, these chapters propose significant revisions to the accepted formal canons and invite us to rethink categories such as the 'dominant' and the 'marginal', the 'popular' and the 'avant-garde', the 'progressive' and the 'conservative'. In Chapter 4, Ian Christie engages with a wide variety of forms and genres of the early period – single-shot films, trick films, comic films, documentaries, historical films, serials, the avant-garde, dramatic narratives – in order to question the linear account of early film history as a 'steady technical-cum-expressive development'. In Chapter 11, Ginette Vincendeau explores the aesthetics of 'the art of spectacle' in mainstream feature films of the classical period, drawing attention to neglected popular genres such as musicals and 'filmed theatre', alongside a range of more familiar examples taken from the Poetic Realist and 1950s noir traditions. In Chapter 18, Nicole Brenez redraws the map of modern French cinema by placing the marginalised political and experimental film-making traditions at the heart of her discussion, alongside a range of higher-profile auteur films from the post-New Wave era.

REPRESENTATIONS: What have French films shown us of France, its society, its concerns and the changing lives of its citizens? Given the vast range of possible approaches to this question, the contributors were invited to select themes and motifs that they consider especially symptomatic of changes in French society during their respective periods. In Chapter 5, Vicki Callahan argues that at the start of the 20th century, cinema was uniquely equipped to reflect a period of rapid cultural mutation, and that the shifting representation of the female body can be read as a kind of 'signpost for changing identities' throughout the early period. In Chapter 12, Keith Reader proposes a topographical and geographical approach to the discussion of cinema's representation of urban and provincial French society between 1930 and 1960. In Chapter 19, Naomi Greene focuses on the representation of Paris in films from the New Wave to the *cinéma du look* and *cinéma de banlieue* of the 1980s and 1990s, arguing that the changing images of the capital reflect the wider social and economic changes that have produced modern France.

SPECTATORS: How has the filmgoing experience evolved in France? Who saw which films, where and in what conditions? The questions addressed in the *Spectators* chapters (the reception of films, patterns of filmgoing, the changing socio-cultural profile of audiences) have remained largely unexplored until now. In Chapter 6, Elizabeth Ezra argues that the growth in filmgoing as a regular part of the urban experience in turn-of-the-century France

established cinema as a vital cultural force and set in motion a 'cinemising' process whereby a codified set of spectatorial conventions was introduced and gradually reinforced. In Chapter 13, Gregory Sims describes geographical and demographic variations in audiences during the 'golden age of spectatorship', and examines the impact of the arrival of sound, the competition from television and other new forms of leisure, and the post-war modernisation of cinemas. In Chapter 20, Sue Harris charts the protracted decline in cinemagoing during the 1960s, and the modest revival since the mid-1990s, and discusses issues of government intervention, the deregulation of television, the growth in the domestic audiovisual market, the expansion of marginal areas of film production and the nationwide reorganisation of the exhibition infrastructure.

DEBATES: How has cinema been represented and debated in French culture? The three *Debates* chapters look at the rich tradition of French film-thinking, and explore how the experience of cinema has been analysed and contested by a variety of critical voices. In Chapter 7, Monica Dall'Asta explores the work of the 'First Wave' of critics-turned-film-makers of the 1920s (including Jean Epstein and Louis Delluc), and highlights three key theoretical concepts from the period: *photogénie*, 'pure cinema' and Surrealism. In Chapter 14, Christopher Faulkner argues that throughout the classical period, the key debates about sound and realism in the 1930s, censorship during the Occupation and film criticism and history in the 1950s have been concerned equally with underlying questions about French national identity. In Chapter 21, James S. Williams examines the personal itinerary of writer Serge Daney, whose major contribution to film-thinking remains largely unknown outside France, as a way of charting wider trends and changes in post-New Wave film theory: from the cinephilia of the 1960s to the political theory of the 1970s, from discussion of television in the 1980s to the issues of gender and sexuality raised in his late autobiographical works.

It will be clear from this outline that *The French Cinema Book* does not claim to be an encyclopaedia of French cinema, nor does it promise a complete chronological survey of French film history. As editors, we are acutely conscious of just how much work remains to be done in all periods and all areas of French cinema studies. What our collection proposes is a model that combines the virtues of consensus with the pleasures of innovation, offering a clear narrative account of the major historical developments in French cinema, as well as new areas of enquiry, neglected topics, unknown people, fresh ideas and hundreds of films, both familiar and forgotten. We therefore invite the reader to explore the collection in a number of ways. The first approach is of course to read the book from cover to cover in an unbroken flow of enthusiasm and enjoyment. It may be preferable, however, to start with the three brief surveys that introduce the periods 1890–1930, 1930–60 and 1960–2004, before looking at the more specialised chapters by individual contributors. Equally, the book can be approached section by section, if the reader is especially interested, for example, in silent cinema, the classic age or the modern era. Alternatively, the reader may wish to study a particular topic across the different periods, for example to see how 'People', 'Forms' or 'Debates' have evolved over time. On a practical note, and in the interests of readability, we have asked the contributors to avoid academic jargon and to exclude footnotes. Thus, the short references given in the body of the text can be found in the lists of works cited at the end of each chapter. In addition, the book also provides four separate lists of suggested 'Further Reading'. The first, a choice of general titles on French cinema, is given after this introduction. The three others appear at the end of each chronological section (i.e. after Chapters 7, 14 and 21). At the end of the book, there is also a list of 'Further Reading on Films and Film People'. Finally, as editors, we very much hope that you find *The French Cinema Book* informative, enjoyable and inspiring.

GENERAL FURTHER READING

Armes, R. (1985) *French Cinema*, London, Secker and Warburg. (Narrative survey from the 1890s to the 1980s.)

Bandy, M. ed. (1983) *Rediscovering French Film*, New York, Museum of Modern Art. (Collection of texts by film-makers and essays covering the 1890s to the 1950.)

Ezra, E. and Harris, S. eds (2000) *France in Focus: Film and National Identity*, Oxford, Berg. (Collection of essays addressing the relationship of cinema to questions of national identity.)

Flitterman-Lewis, S. (1990) *To Desire Differently: Feminism and the French Cinema*, New York, Columbia University Press. (Study of women film-makers from the 1920s to the 1980s, with particular reference to Germaine Dulac, Marie Epstein and Agnès Varda.)

Hayward, S. (1993) *French National Cinema*, London, Routledge. (Narrative survey from the 1890s to the early 1990s.)

Hayward, S. and Vincendeau, G. eds (2000) *French Film: Texts and Contexts*, London, Routledge. (Collection of essays analysing individual films from the 1930s to the 1990s.)

Hughes, A. and Williams, J. eds (2001) *Gender and French Cinema*, Oxford, Berg. (Collection of essays examining the representation of gender in selected films from the 1920s to the 1990s.)

Lanzoni, R. (2002) *French Cinema: From its Beginnings to the Present*, New York, Continuum. (Narrative survey with emphasis on cinema since 1945.)

Powrie, P. and Reader, K. (2002) *French Cinema: A Student's Guide*, London, Arnold. (Introductory textbook, with a survey of selected theorists and sample student essays.)

Sherzer, D. (1996) *Cinema, Colonialism, Postcolonialism: Perspectives from the French and Francophone World*, Austin, University of Texas Press. (Collection of essays discussing selected colonial and post-colonial films.)

Vincendeau, G. (1996) *The Companion to French Cinema*, London, BFI/Cassell. (Reference book with approximately 200 entries on institutions, movements, genres and people.)

Vincendeau, G. (2000) *Stars and Stardom in French Cinema*, New York, Continuum. (History of the French star system followed by studies of selected stars from the 1900s to the 1990s.)

Williams, A. (1992) *Republic of Images: A History of French Filmmaking*, Cambridge, MA, Harvard University Press. (Narrative survey with emphasis on the period from the 1890s to the 1950s.)

PART ONE

1890–1930

Introduction 1890–1930
Hello Cinema!

Michael Temple and Michael Witt

An art was born before our eyes. We met Lumière and Méliès, we could have known Edison or Reynaud. (Sadoul 1949: 5)

The study of French cinema's origins and early years is not solely a task for the film historian. It also provides a profitable exercise in the art of cultural memory. The year 1895 is commemorated as marking the beginning of cinema in France and across the world. Most of us, if we were asked 'When did cinema begin?', would probably recall this date. We might even be more precise and reply '28 December 1895'. This is, after all, the date when approximately thirty people came to the Salon Indien at the Grand Café, Boulevard des Capucines, Paris, and paid to see a curious demonstration that had been advertised in the following terms:

> This machine, invented by Messrs Auguste and Louis Lumière, allows one to gather, by series of instantaneous prints, all the movements that, during a given time, have succeeded one another before the lens, and then to reproduce those movements, by projecting, life-size, before an entire hall, their images on a screen. Entrance ticket one franc. Ten animated views will be presented.

What these pioneering film spectators actually paid to see was not a film in the sense that we would recognise today, but rather a series of short 'animated views', each about fifty seconds long, showing such everyday subjects as:

1. Exit from the Lumière factory in Lyons
2. Trick-riding
3. Fishing for goldfish
4. Disembarkation of the congress of photography at Lyons
5. Blacksmiths
6. The gardener
7. The meal
8. Jumping the blanket
9. Cordeliers Square in Lyons
10. The sea

These views may not look much like movies, but they were certainly moving pictures, as lifelike as photographs, and showing real people in the real world. As for the paying public, they may well have been sceptical or surprised, inspired or indifferent. But the point is that they had gathered in a public place to see a commercial projection of motion pictures. One hundred years later, in 1995, many different film cultures, in France and elsewhere, celebrated the centenary of cinema in respect of this occasion in Paris on 28 December 1895, which successive generations have collectively come to acknowledge as the beginning of cinema.

Our memory is not false. However, film historians have sought to complement this memorable story of cinema's origins in a number of ways. First, they point out that the Lumières' picture-show in fact has a long prehistory that is both technical and cultural. From a technical point of view, the *cinématographe*, as the brothers decided to call their invention, was a particularly ingenious synthesis of research into motion-picture technology carried out by several generations of scientists and amateur inventors. It brought together a number of different devices for the photographic recording of movement and the projection of moving images onto a screen, which had been invented, demonstrated and discussed in Europe and the USA ever since the arrival of photography in the 1830s (see Chapter 3). The cinematograph was simple, portable and reversible (it could both take the pictures and project them). From a cultural point of view, the prehistory goes back even further. Film archaeologists have argued that the desire to create convincing and entertaining illusions of the world in motion is probably as old as humanity itself, and certainly they have been able to demonstrate that at least 300 years of 'the great art of light and shadow' – i.e. cultural practices such as magic-lantern shows, slide-shows and various optical toys (thaumatropes, zootropes, phenakistiscopes, praxinoscopes) – had prepared the general public for cinema as a spectacle and not just as a technical invention (Mannoni 2000).

The second way in which film historians have tried to qualify our memory of cinema's beginnings is to argue that in terms of formal content, and commercial exploitation, the Lumière cinematograph may be better understood as one of the final episodes of film's prehistory rather than as the original moment of the story of cinema proper. Formally, we can recognise the Lumière views, to a certain degree, as the kind of moving pictures that we see in films today. In terms of content, the world is there, alive and beautiful. The images are often carefully composed in terms of framing, light, depth, movement and the timing of the action that is represented. Moreover, from a commercial point of view, we know that at first the Lumière franchise was tremendously profitable and successful as an entertaining spectacle. The Lumière company trained newly recruited agents as cameramen and projectionists, who then travelled the globe, filming scenes from everyday life and organising picture-shows. This was not just in France and its neighbouring European countries, but all across Eastern Europe, North Africa, the Far East, Latin America and, of course, the USA – where in fact Thomas Edison's kinetoscope (a kind of peep-show version of cinema for one spectator at a time) had preceded the Lumière machine by a number of years. However, when the public's enthusiasm for these animated views of everyday life had begun to wane, it soon became clear that something else was needed to take the cinematograph beyond the brief lifespan that the Lumières had predicted for their invention ('This is not a career with a future,' they are reported to have told their ambitious trainees). What was required for the cinematograph to become cinema, for these animated views to become entertaining films that the paying public would

want to come and see, again and again, was variety and novelty, spectacle and stories. Without this double development, both formal and commercial, it is unlikely that the cinema would have survived for long, and certainly it would not have become the art and the industry whose centenary we celebrated in 1995.

The Lumières were probably not the right sort of people to take this next step towards establishing a modern entertainment industry. They did not consider themselves artists or showmen. They already owned a successful business in the manufacture of photographic (and now cinematographic) equipment and materials, and their personal interests (to which they soon returned) lay much more in the domain of practical scientific research than in the uncertain world of theatre and spectacle. It is the marvellous figure of Georges Méliès who has been traditionally identified as taking the first step from the cinematograph as scientific curiosity to the cinema as spectacle and narrative entertainment. With his background as an artist and a showman in the theatre and especially in the world of magic and illusion, Méliès surely had very different designs and ambitions for the cinematograph than the Lumières, and although he initially did little more than reproduce their genre of motion picture postcards and everyday views, soon he was developing a whole range of trick films and narrative fantasies, in the process establishing much of what we now think of as film language, especially in terms of montage and special effects.

Between 1896 and 1905, this new style of cinema brought him considerable commercial success, and in order to make his 'transformation views' and other spectacular shorts more freely, he even took the big step of building France's first ever film studio, or 'workshop of cinematographic poses' as he called it, at Montreuil-sous-Bois in 1897. Surviving photographs and drawings show a glass and metal construction designed to similar proportions and specifications as Méliès's theatre of illusions, the Robert-Houdin in Paris, including a corresponding assortment of trapdoors, mobile decor and stage-machinery, which enabled him to re-create his magical feats and fantastic performances with all the new possibilities and marvellous techniques of cutting, editing, colouring, multiple exposure and stop-motion. Here he produced such intense wonders as *Escamotage d'une dame chez Robert-Houdin* (1896), *Un Homme de têtes* (1898), *L'Homme-orchestre* (1900), *L'Homme à la tête en caoutchouc* (1901) and *Le Mélomane* (1903), as well as longer narrative fantasy films, *Le Voyage dans la lune* (1902) and *Le Voyage à travers l'impossible* (1904), reconstituted actualities, *L'Affaire Dreyfus* (1899) and *Le Sacre d'Édouard VII* (1902), and even a selection of publicity films. These extremely labour-intensive films, which Méliès personally constructed with his own hands at almost every stage of their creation, have come to represent one of the foundation-stones of French film culture, along with the hundreds of extant views and other works produced by the Lumière company.

In terms of cultural memory, these two names, Lumière and Méliès, were for many years cited as the mythical founding fathers of the documentary and fiction traditions in French cinema. Without dismissing the importance of such an influential idea, many historians have sought to provide a more rounded picture of early French cinema, firstly by questioning the historical validity of applying to this period such concepts as documentary and fiction, which clearly come from a later stage in film's evolution, and secondly by showing that the Lumière catalogue and the Méliès corpus are both much richer and more diverse than such categorical labels would indicate. Perhaps more importantly, however, they have demonstrated the crucial role played by businessmen like Charles Pathé and Léon Gaumont, who not only came to cinema with a business model that was bigger and bolder than anything the Lumières or Méliès would have dreamed of risking but who also established techniques of production that would develop the forms and genres of cinema significantly beyond what Méliès's individual vision and limited means could achieve. Whereas by 1905 the latter's commercial position had considerably weakened, and his artistic inspiration had perhaps begun to fail, the companies established in the late 1890s by Pathé and Gaumont were rapidly expanding on both industrial and creative fronts, and this strong growth and diversification would continue right up to the outbreak of World War I. Along with companies such as Éclair, Éclipse and Lux, the two largest French film companies, symbolised by the Pathé cockerel and the Gaumont daisy, would collectively dominate the global market until 1914. It is hard to imagine today that by around 1910 French companies provided something like two out of every three films shown in the world!

This period of expansion sees the emergence of a number of important economic and artistic trends that together form a model of pre-war French film culture. First, Pathé and Gaumont were able to acquire serious venture capital from private investors and banks. This capital allowed them to invest heavily in infrastructure and to build their businesses at every level of the burgeoning film industry, from the manufacture of equipment and materials through production, distribution and exhibition. Their ambitious strategies have led some to claim that the French, and Pathé in particular, invented the system known as vertical integration, where a single company aims to control every phase of the film business, from making the cameras to projecting the pictures on the screen. What is clear is that both Pathé and Gaumont had started their businesses in the manufacture and sale of equipment, and this was to remain an important aspect of their commercial activities for many years to come. At the level of film production, what we see emerging is a set of working practices that by 1914 had evolved into a real dream-factory. By modern standards, Pathé and Gaumont were very much hands-on executives, but they developed in their studios new techniques of rationalisation and delegation that make Méliès's working methods seem artisanal by comparison. Their whole attitude was different and much closer to the philosophy of a movie executive. They estimated on a daily basis how many metres of film could be produced, at what cost in relation to each metre's selling price, and the number of spectators who would pay to see it. They devolved responsibility for film-making to production managers (Alice Guy at Gaumont and Ferdinand Zecca at Pathé), who in turn began to train and supervise teams of personnel with increasingly precise functions as directors, writers, cameramen, etc.

At the same time as these working roles became more rationalised and categorised, so the types of films produced were evolving into an increasingly

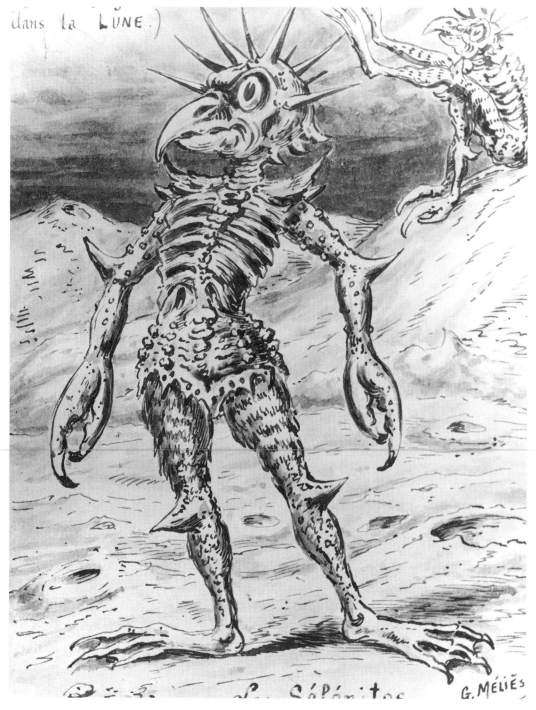

Drawing by Méliès for *Le Voyage dans la lune* (1902)

coherent system of diverse genres. Alongside the earliest film forms such as the Lumière view, the Méliès trick film, fantasy and reconstituted actuality, we can see that by 1903, for example, Pathé is already proposing to the public a wide range of biblical subjects (*La Vie et la passion de Jésus Christ*), historical themes (*L'Épopée napoléonienne*), literary adaptations (*Don Quichotte*) and social dramas (*Les Victimes de l'alcoolisme*). This trend towards more distinctive and respectable genres would develop strongly over the next decade, as film companies tried to appeal more explicitly to a bourgeois audience. Often cited as symptomatic of this process is the Film d'Art company's *L'Assassinat du duc de Guise* (Calmettes and Le Bargy, 1908), insofar as it featured well-known actors from the Comédie-Française performing in a historical drama with high production values and even a specially commissioned score by composer Camille Saint-Saëns.

In a different vein, comedies also evolved during this period from slapstick and chase films towards comic series clearly defined around a single character, whose name the public would recognise and follow. Thus among France's first stars are comics such as child actors Bout-de-Zan and Willy, as well as André Deed, Prince Rigadin and most famously Max Linder, often considered to be the cinema's first worldwide star. A similar interaction of commercial logic and formal innovation can be seen in the 1910s with the appearance of serial formats, examples of which are Victorin Jasset's *Nick Carter* and *Zigomar*, as well as Louis Feuillade's celebrated *Fantômas*. Marking a mid-point in the development from the very short formats of the early years and the longer standard length of the classic feature film, the serial brings together a number of other significant features from pre-war French cinema. It represents the regular and rationalised production of a distinct format with clear genre rules and recognisable stars, which is aimed at a public whose tastes the industry is trying both to follow and foresee.

Finally, in the areas of distribution and exhibition, two important developments occur in the years preceding World War I. As regards distribution, in 1908 Pathé caused great surprise in the industry when he announced that he would henceforth no longer be selling films by the metre directly to the loose network of independent exhibitors that

had developed since the 1890s. Instead he switched to a system of rental distribution, over which he could exert much tighter control regarding which films were to be shown, and in what conditions. This move also meant that increasingly films would be shown in Pathé-owned cinemas, for example the Omnia-Pathé, which had opened in Paris in 1906. Gaumont and the other French companies steadily followed Pathé's lead, switching from sale to rental and establishing their own cinema chains. By 1911 the 3,000-seat Gaumont Palace was proudly proclaimed as 'the biggest cinema in the world'! The change in distribution system was therefore linked to the growing trend in the exhibition sector, where the informal, temporary and polyvalent sites of the early years (fairgrounds, cafés, theatres, shops) had been gradually replaced by more formal, fixed and single-purpose venues. The new cinemas were theatre-like buildings designed specifically for the exhibition and consumption of motion pictures. They were significantly more appealing to the middle classes, whom the film business had by now successfully added to its original popular audience.

Writing in the early 1960s, the great French film historian Georges Sadoul stated that, whereas 'in 1910 the hegemony of French cinema was perhaps more complete than the hegemony of Hollywood in 1950', by the end of World War I, 'French cinema, once master of the world, had fallen from a great height' (Sadoul 1962: 17, 23). It is difficult to argue with this general assessment, unless it be to add that France's reversal of fortune during the 1910s was perhaps neither so sudden nor as catastrophic as a purely military reading of events might at first suggest. Certainly, by the end of the conflict, the USA had replaced France both as industrial world leader and in terms of its influence on film culture. In particular, the six months of temporary paralysis experienced by all sectors of the French film industry in late 1914 and early 1915 had provided the opportunity for American imports to flood the French market, setting a pattern of Hollywood dominance that remains unbroken to the present day (except, ironically, for the four years of German occupation during World War II). However, most historians, including Sadoul, would recognise that not only had France's global power probably already started to wane in the early 1910s but also that given the sheer scale of the USA's domestic market and general industrial might, it was inevitable that one day hegemony would pass from Paris to Hollywood.

They have also pointed out that, in their different ways, the two French majors, Pathé and Gaumont, responded quite positively to the difficult and unforeseen events of the war. Resuming production in France as soon as politically possible, Gaumont continued the string of pre-war hits started by *Fantômas* (1913–14), with the serials *Les Vampires* (1915), *Judex* (1916), *La Nouvelle mission de Judex* (1917) and *Tih Minh* (1918), all directed by Louis Feuillade, who indeed pursued his success with this format well into the 1920s. In addition to assuring the survival of Gaumont during and beyond the war (Feuillade later claimed somewhat excessively that his serials had single-handedly saved the industry), these classic serials have become one of the most treasured features of France's national film heritage. Following an alternative strategy, Charles Pathé put his faith in the American-based company, Pathé-Exchange, which duly rewarded him by producing Louis Gasnier's massively popular series of Pearl White adventures and (somewhat ironically, given the historical power shift that was happening) exporting them back to France as the highly profitable *Les Mystères de New York* (1915–18). Indeed, writing some twenty years later, Pathé even maintained that, short of being in the arms trade, his company had performed very well in wartime, distributing annual dividends to shareholders of 4 per cent on average. But the simple fact that both French majors did more than just survive the war should not obscure the long-term trend, namely that from the 1920s they each progressively abandoned any serious ambitions to maintain their earlier vertically integrated dominance at home or abroad. Different branches of their respective empires were scaled down, sold off or merged with other interested parties. On a personal level, Léon Gaumont and Charles Pathé had both retired from affairs by 1930, although the companies that bear their names, and the symbols of the Cockerel and the Daisy, are still doing business in the 21st century.

A much more beneficial change, however, had also taken place during the war years. For it is from this time that most observers date the artistic renewal and cultural definition of French cinema that has come to be known as 'the First Wave' (Abel 1984). In cultural terms, cinema in the 1920s was redefined as Art. Exposed to American films during the war, a new generation of artists and intellectuals began for the first time to take a serious interest in cinema, both as popular art (this is when Chaplin forever became 'Charlot') and as a potentially new cultural force to revive, or simply replace, the moribund visual and literary art forms of the 19th century. From the mid-1910s, the novelist Colette, the music critic Émile Vuillermoz, the poets Guillaume Apollinaire and Blaise Cendrars, and the art historian Élie Faure established an intellectual trend for open-minded critical engagement with film that was followed in the next ten years by Jean Cocteau, Louis Aragon, Robert Desnos, Philippe Soupault and many more, thus making the 1920s what is now considered to be one of the richest periods in French film theory (see Chapter 7). From this marvellous decade of cultural (or 'cinephile') activity, film historians have highlighted the contributions of a number of key individuals. First, the Italian Ricciotto Canudo, who is generally considered to have invented the notion of cinema as the prestigious 'Seventh Art', which French film culture adopted and celebrated from this time (Abel 1988: 58–66, 291–303). He also founded in 1921 the CASA or 'Club des Amis du Septième Art', thereby initiating the whole film-club and cinephile movement, whose influence in France and elsewhere has since been so profound. Second, the critic Louis Delluc, whose spiritual conversion to cinema on first seeing Cecil B. DeMille's *The Cheat* has come to symbolise the broad cultural transformation that was taking place in French intellectual and artistic circles throughout this period. His writings (*Cinéma et cie*, 1919; *Photogénie*, 1920) and cinephile activism (*Le Journal du ciné-club*; the magazine *Cinéa*) also mark the beginnings of French film theory's love-hate relationship with American cinema, insofar as Delluc was looking to Hollywood for a double inspiration that would enable 'French cinema to be real cinema', while at the same time allowing 'French cinema to be really French'. Before his early death, Delluc had made the transition from criticism to film-making (*Le Silence*, 1920; *Fièvre*, 1921), and his example was followed by the third key figure, Jean Epstein, who combined important critical and theoretical writing (see Chapter 7) with film-making in the mainstream and the avant-garde (*Mauprat*, 1926; *La Belle Nivernaise*, 1924; *La Chute de la maison Usher*, 1928). This passage between criticism and film-making is, of course, a trend most commonly associated with the late 1950s emergence of the New Wave, but it is equally a prominent feature of 20s film culture. Important figures such as Germaine Dulac (*La Fête espagnole*, 1919; *La Souriante Madame Beudet*, 1922), Abel Gance (*J'accuse!*, 1918; *La Roue*, 1923; *Napoléon*, 1927) and Marcel L'Herbier (*Eldorado*, 1921; *L'Inhumaine*, 1924; *L'Argent*, 1928) were all to some extent theorists as well as film-makers, and they certainly contributed through word and image to the cultural redefinition of cinema that took place in France during this decade. However, what is more significant in the long term than the names and works of these exemplary individuals is the whole set of cultural practices, institutions and discourses that together reinvented the meaning and standing of cinema for modern culture. At least six new trends appeared at this time, which together form what some historians have called an 'alternate cinema network' (Abel 1984; Gauthier 1999). These tendencies may be summarised as follows:

- Film criticism: the publication in newspapers and magazines of personally signed articles discussing the artistic merits or faults of individual films, rather than merely rehearsing publicity material or plot summary.
- Film theory: the critical discussion of particular films or aspects of cinema leading to the establishment of a coherent set of principles and beliefs that describe or prescribe what cinema is or should be.
- Film history: the emergence of narrative accounts of cinema's origins and technical, commercial and artistic development to the present day, based on documentary research and personal testimony.
- Film magazines and film journals: the regular publication of organs exclusively devoted to the world of cinema and addressed to a popular or intellectual readership drawn from the filmgoing public.

- Film clubs: the social and pedagogical commitment to improving appreciation and spreading knowledge of cinema as an art, featuring screenings of rare films, old films, banned films or anthologised film extracts, combined with lectures, presentations and discussion.
- Film exhibitions: the public display in galleries and museums of images, documents, objects and other materials drawn from the film world and illustrating its diverse relations with the other major arts.

This is an impressive record for one decade. But the important theoretical and cultural contribution that France has made to our modern conception of cinema as the Seventh Art should not overshadow the period's equally interesting range of film forms and genres, which it would be remiss to ignore, but impossible to represent, as we draw this introductory essay to a close.

The variety and wealth of films from the 1920s will be discussed at length in Chapters 1, 4 and 5, so here let us refer briefly to three strands of French film art from these years: the Popular, the Quality and the Experimental. Among the traditionally popular formats, comedy gradually moved away from the star-based series of the pre-war years, although Max Linder achieved considerable success with an extended sketch film, *Le Roi du cirque* (1925), before his tragic suicide the same year. Generally the comic form evolved into longer features, often drawing inspiration from the theatre, as in Raymond Bernard's successful adaptation of his father Tristan's boulevard comedy, *Le Petit café* (1919). Elsewhere, the Russian émigrés at Albatros films produced a number of comedies, for example Ivan Mosjoukine's *Le Brasier ardent* (1923), as well as René Clair's early hit, *Paris qui dort* (1924), and his silent masterpiece *Un Chapeau de paille d'Italie* (1927). Other well-known directors who successfully tried their hand at comedy were Julien Duvivier (*Le Mystère de la Tour Eiffel*, 1927), Jacques Feyder (*Les Nouveaux Messieurs*, 1929) and Jean Renoir (*Tire au flanc*, 1928). Another popular format that survived and prospered after the war was the serial, which Feuillade continued to explore with the crime serial *Barrabas* (1920), before moving to more sentimental territory with *Les Deux gamines* (1921), *L'Orpheline* (1921) and *Parisette* (1922). Other directors pursued this thematic transformation of the format during this period, adding classic literary adaptations and historical subjects to the staple regime of crime and melodrama: Henri Diamant-Berger's *Les Trois mousquetaires* (1921) and Henri Fescourt's *Mandarin* (1924) were particularly successful examples of these two new themes. The *cinéroman*, as the serial came to be known, was not so much a genre as an intricate commercial and artistic system, where regular team-based production supplied a steady flow of episodic films, via a friendly distribution network, to spectators whose appetite and interest was in turn stimulated by the serialisation of the same narrative in the popular press. The Société des cinéromans, as the name suggests, even specialised in this format, which also lent itself to parodic recuperation by more highbrow directors such as Epstein (*Les Aventures de Robert Macaire*, 1925).

The second strand comprises what Richard Abel (1984) simply refers to as 'commercial narrative films', which we might also call the 'quality mainstream', insofar as it brings together films that at the time were conceived and promoted as quality products, combining artistic ambition with commercial appeal to the cultivated as well as the popular audience. This desire for a French cinema of quality draws on a tradition dating back to the *film d'art,* and it foreshadows the famous 'tradition of quality' that later emerged in the 1940s and 1950s. A number of distinct genres may be grouped together under this heading of 'quality'. First, there is the theatrical respectability and emotion offered by the bourgeois melodrama, such as Gance's *La Dixième symphonie* (1919), Raymond Bernard's *La Maison vide* (1921) and *Triplepatte* (1922), and Léon Poirier's *Jocelyn* (1922) and *Geneviève* (1923). Second, the realist drama provides both the moral purpose and the social authenticity inherited from nineteenth-century naturalism, as in Henri Pouctal's *Travail* (1918), André Antoine's *La Terre* (1921), as well as Feyder's *Crainquebille* (1923), *Visages d'enfants* (1924) and *Gribiche* (1926). The qualities of authenticity and heritage can also be found in the big-budget historical reconstructions, among the best known of which are Bernard's *Le Miracle des loups* (1924) and *Le Joueur d'échecs* (1927), both pro-

duced by the specialist Société des films historiques; Léonce Perret's *Koenigsmark* (1923) and *Madame Sans-Gêne* (1925); Marco de Gastyne's *La Merveilleuse vie de Jeanne d'Arc* (1928); and the Albatros productions *Kean* (1923) and *Casanova* (1927), directed by Alexandre Volkoff, Victor Tourjansky's *Michel Strogoff* (1926) and last but not least, Gance's *Napoléon*. Whereas the historical drama took the audience to a lavish and familiar past, the colonial film offered the qualities of displacement and exoticism, as in Feyder's *L'Atlantide* (1921), Fescourt's *La Maison du Maltais* (1927) and Renoir's *Le Bled* (1929). Finally, the modern studio spectacular, such as L'Herbier's *L'Inhumaine, Le Vertige* (1926) and *L'Argent*, or Duvivier's *Le Tourbillon de Paris* (1928) and *Au bonheur des dames* (1929), combined the qualities of high production values, elaborate design and costumes, and a dramatic sense of modern luxury.

The third strand is the grand explosion of experimental cinema during the 1920s, which is usually divided into two distinct groups. First, those film-makers and cultural activists, traditionally labelled the 'impressionist' avant-garde, whose careers combined their experimental ambitions (especially regarding narrative structure, psychological realism and the formal specificities of film language) with work in mainstream commercial cinema. Here we rediscover, in their more experimental vein, the films of Delluc (*La Femme de nulle part*, 1922), Dulac (*La Coquille et le clergyman*, 1927; *L'Invitation au voyage*, 1927; *Thèmes et variations*, 1928) and Epstein (*Coeur fidèle*, 1923; *6½ x 11*, 1926; *La Glace à trois faces*, 1927). Similarly, the works of Gance (*Au secours!*, 1923; *La Roue*) and L'Herbier (*Don Juan et Faust*, 1923; *Feu Mathias Pascal*, 1925) contain passages of dazzling technical audacity and experimental virtuosity, but the artists themselves would not have considered their films to be aimed at the kind of intellectual elite normally associated with the term avant-garde. The second group is more radical, more extreme and more provocative, but also much less interested in dialogue with the commercial mainstream and in cinema as a popular art form. Here we can recall a number of experimental classics, such as Luis Buñuel's *Un chien andalou* (1928) and *L'Âge d'or* (1930); Marcel Duchamp's *Anémic cinéma* (1926);

Fernand Léger's *Ballet mécanique* (1924); and Man Ray's *Le Retour à la raison* (1923), *Emak Bakia* (1927), *L'Étoile de mer* (1928) and *Les Mystères du château du dé* (1929). Lastly, we can identify in this period a number of early experimental works by film-makers who would later become well known as auteurs, such as Claude Autant-Lara (*Construire un feu*, 1929); Alberto Cavalcanti (*La Petite Lily*, 1927); Clair (*Entr'acte*, 1924); Jean Cocteau (*Le Sang d'un poète*, 1930); Duvivier (*La Machine à refaire la vie*, 1924); Jean Grémillon (*Photogénie mécanique*, 1924); Renoir (*La Fille de l'eau*, 1925; *Charleston*, 1926); and Jean Vigo (*À propos de Nice*, 1929).

In conclusion, as editors of *The French Cinema Book* we are all too aware that, despite the pioneering work of film historians in France and elsewhere, this whole early period of French cinema history from the 1890s to 1930 remains relatively unknown to the majority of film lovers, film students, film scholars and film programmers around the world. So we would like to end this introductory essay with an appeal to artists, archivists, critics, curators, researchers, students and teachers to work together, precisely in the spirit of the 1920s, in order to spread the appreciation, knowledge and love of French cinema in all its forms and phases from the prehistoric world of Étienne-Jules Marey to the volcanic future of 'the cinematograph seen from Etna' by Jean Epstein (Epstein 1926).

WORKS CITED

Abel, R. (1984) *French Cinema: The First Wave, 1915–1929*, Princeton, NJ, Princeton University Press.

Abel, R. (1988) *French Film Theory and Criticism: A History/Anthology 1907–1939*, vol. 1: 1907–29, Princeton, NJ, Princeton University Press.

Epstein, J. (1926) *Le Cinématographe vu de l'Etna*, Paris, Les Écrivains Réunies.

Gauthier, C. (1999) *La Passion du cinéma: cinéphiles, ciné-clubs et salles spécialisées à Paris de 1920 à 1929*, Paris, AFRHC/Écoles des Chartes.

Mannoni, L. (2000) *The Great Art of Light and Shadow: Archaeology of the Cinema*, Exeter, University of Exeter Press.

Sadoul, G. (1949) *Histoire du cinéma mondial*, Paris, Flammarion.

Sadoul, G. (1962) *Le Cinéma français 1890–1962*, Paris, Flammarion.

1 PEOPLE 1890–1930
The Men and Women Who Made French Cinema

Richard Abel

This chapter presents a history of French cinema through the people who worked in or for the new industry during the silent period. Besides exploring the contribution of key individuals, it seeks to suggest ways of rethinking the relationship among them as well as between them and the topics addressed in subsequent chapters in the 1890–1930 period. The discussion follows the transformation of moving pictures into 'cinema'. Organised chronologically and divided into nine sections, it focuses on those who made significant changes in the cinema as a cultural institution and/or in film-making as a practice, or did most to consolidate and stabilise it as an institution or practice at particular historical moments.

PRELUDE: PRIOR TO 1894

Of the numerous strands of scientific, technological and cultural practice that intersected in the late 19th century to produce moving pictures, there were two in which the French especially excelled: the analysis of movement and the optical synthesis of movement. For the first, Étienne-Jules Marey was undoubtedly the crucial figure. A professor of physiology at the Collège de France in Paris, Marey originated a graphic method of recording the movements of humans, animals and objects. Initially, his research led him to develop electrical and mechanical devices to record physiological movement in and of the human body: e.g. blood circulation, heat changes, respiration, locomotion. After seeing Eadweard Muybridge's serial photographs of moving figures, published in France in 1878, and meeting the photographer in Paris in 1881, Marey turned to single-plate chronophotography as a much more precise method. His first device, a 'photographic gun', was modelled on an apparatus that astronomer Pierre-Jules-César Janssen had used to record a

solar eclipse in 1874. Once Marey's publicly funded centre, the Station Physiologique, opened in Paris in 1882, he constructed a number of single-plate cameras to advance his research. In 1888, Marey again improved his recording methods by designing a camera that substituted Eastman paper roll film for glass plates; the first series of photographs taken by this apparatus (a pigeon in flight, a hand opening and closing) was presented later that year to the Académie des sciences. Within another year, he was using transparent celluloid negative film. During his career, Marey amassed thousands of glass plates and nearly 800 short chronophotographic films, many images from which were reproduced in his encyclopaedic work, *Le Mouvement* (1894).

Marey was committed to analytical research, so it was left to others to work on the optical synthesis of movement. In France, the crucial figure was Émile Reynaud. Trained in industrial and optical design, Reynaud assisted Abbé Moigno's illustrated lectures on popular science in Paris. This magic-lantern work led him to tinker with improving the Zoëtrope and Phénakistoscope, popular toys of synthesised motion. Patenting his Praxinoscope in 1877, he decided to market a toy Praxinoscope Theatre, in which a band of images reflected by a spinning mirror was viewed through a proscenium arch. His next step was to develop a projecting Praxinoscope, and in 1888 he patented a Théâtre Optique, which used a long band of coloured images painted on gelatine squares linked by leather straps and metal strips, with holes to engage pins on a cranked revolving drum (analogous to a bicycle chain). In 1892, Reynaud contacted Gabriel Thomas, director of the Musée Grévin in Paris, who had already explored, albeit unsuccessfully, an option to project Marey's motion studies as visual spectacle. Thomas contracted with Reynaud to present five half-hour shows a day (twelve on Sundays and holidays) in the museum's Cabinet Fantastique, providing the narration himself for the stories of his first three bands – *Pauvre Pierrot*, *Clown et ses chiens* and *Un Bon bock* – accompanied by a piano player and singer. The shows quickly became popular, and over the next eight years (as he created at least one new set of images a year), Reynaud gave 12,800 performances to half a million museum visitors. By 1894, it was clear that the Parisian public seeking entertainment would pay to view lengthy bands of sequential moving images (not yet fixed on celluloid) projected mechanically, and repeatedly, on a large luminous screen.

BEGINNINGS: 1894–6

In 1894, the strands of scientific, technological and cultural practice began to come together. One of Marey's collaborators, Georges Demenÿ, founder of a 'rational gymnastics', was perhaps the first to link the recording and projecting of moving images. In 1892, at the International Exhibition of Photography in Paris, Demenÿ exhibited his Phonoscope, an apparatus for viewing some of the chronophotograph series he had made at the Station Physiologique: e.g. images of himself saying 'Je vous aime'. Against Marey's wishes, he set up a company to promote the Phonoscope, especially for amateurs and families to present 'animated portraits'. He also developed a camera for taking moving images, using 60mm celluloid film and an intermittent device, a roller (mounted on a rotating gear) that advanced just enough film to make precise exposures. After Marey fired him in 1894, Demenÿ opened his own laboratory in Paris, patented his improved camera as the Chronophotographe and began filming the first of a hundred short subjects: e.g. street scenes, boxers, dancers, passing trains, a baby's first steps. His attempts to market both apparatuses, however, through Georges de Bedts (Paris agent for European Blair, suppliers of celluloid film) and Léon Gaumont, proved unsuccessful. Under-financed and lacking a sound business sense, Demenÿ had to cede all his patents to Gaumont in 1896, after which he resumed his research on physical education and, in 1902, was appointed Professor of Applied Physiology at Joinville. Yet his designs (recently discovered) for a combined camera-projector and a large projec-

tor (with a claw intermittent movement) intended for publicly exhibiting moving pictures would soon be realised by others, including de Bedts and, most significantly, the Lumière brothers.

In the early 1890s, the Lyons family firm of Lumière was one of Europe's most important suppliers of photographic film and supplies. In late 1894, Louis Lumière discussed Demenÿ's designs on a visit to the latter's new laboratory in Paris; about the same time, he and Auguste Lumière took note of Edison's popular kinetoscopes (which used 35mm film), perhaps in the concession that Michel and Eugène Werner had opened near the Musée Grévin. This conjunction spurred the brothers to design their own apparatus, an elegant, lightweight, sophisticated machine that not only recorded and projected but also printed moving images on 35mm film. Patented in February 1895, the Cinématographe (their father Antoine suggested the name 'Domitor') was demonstrated at professional meetings in France and Belgium throughout the year, and Jules Carpentier, a scientific instrument-maker in Paris, was engaged to manufacture twenty-five machines. Anxious to promote the Cinématographe, Antoine Lumière organised afternoon and evening showings in the Grand Café's Salon Indien, on the Paris Boulevard des Capucines, beginning on 28 December 1895. That day, photographer Clément Maurice sold tickets and Charles Moisson (an engineer who constructed the first model) ran the Cinématographe, showing films such as *Sortie d'usine*, *Arroseur et arrosé* and *Repas de bébé*. So successful was the show that Clément Maurice continued to give performances for several months thereafter, and Carpentier was ordered to make 200 more machines. Instead of selling their apparatus – as de Bedts did his patented Kinétographe in early 1896 – the Lumières leased franchises in France, its colonies and elsewhere to agents who would pay a daily fee for the services of an operator and machine. Consequently, the company trained dozens of operators – among them Félix Mesguich, Alexandre Promio and Gabriel Veyre – to conduct pioneering exhibitions of the portable Cinématographe around the world, and ship the results of their film-making back to Lyons for inclusion in a growing catalogue of films. Their apparent aim was to use the machine

Workers outside the Lumière factory in Lyons

ENTERTAINERS AND ENTREPRENEURS: 1896–1903

One witness to that first Grand Café show was Georges Méliès, owner-manager of the Robert-Houdin Théâtre in Paris, where he directed his own popular magic acts and *féeries*. Méliès immediately saw the Cinématographe as a new technology of amusement that could augment his own performances. Within months, he had purchased a projector from Robert Paul in England (since Lumière would not sell him one), used its design to construct his own camera, begun to shoot short subjects in imitation of Lumière and projected them as an added attraction in his theatre. In the spring of 1897, sensing the public's interest in this new spectacle attraction, he erected a glass-house studio on family property in Montreuil in order to make 'transformation views'; the following autumn, the Robert-Houdin was regularly showing moving pictures that now bore his trademark, Star-Film. Méliès also began selling his trick films for exhibition at the music halls and *cafés-concerts* in Paris as well as at the annual or twice yearly fairs in the provinces, quickly beating such competitors as the inventor-entrepreneurs, Georges Mendel and A.-F. Parnaland. Soon he was able to produce moving-picture adaptations of his and others' *féeries* that ran for ten or fifteen minutes, some of which, like *Cendrillon* (1899), were sold in hand-coloured prints as far away as the USA and featured as headline vaudeville acts. Unlike the Lumières and others, Méliès remained above all an entertainer and owner of a small family business, a position that did not change even after the worldwide success of *Le Voyage dans la lune* (1902). In order to prevent others from duping his popular films (no copyright protection existed), he hired sales agents in England, Germany and Spain and, in 1903, sent his brother Gaston to open a Star-Film office in New York. The following year, Méliès produced a total of forty-five films (many of them lengthy *féeries*) in what turned out to be the apogee of his career.

Although he did not witness the Grand Café shows, Léon Gaumont did have an indirect connection to the Lumières. He had served briefly as a ledger clerk for Carpentier in 1881, before working his way up to be manager of a reputable Paris photographic supply firm – its clients included psychologist Jean Charcot, politician René Waldeck-Rousseau and writer Émile Zola. In 1895, with the backing of entrepreneurs such as Gustave Eiffel, the ambitious Gaumont seized an opportunity to buy the company (after the previous owners quarrelled) and set out to manufacture and market optical and photographic equipment on a larger scale. Acquiring Demenÿ's patents, Gaumont had his chief engineer, L.-R. Decaux, design an improved 'Chronographe' that used 35mm film, and gave his young office manager, the equally ambitious Alice Guy, whose family fortune had been lost in Chile when she was sixteen, the task of producing short films for its promotion. So successful were Guy's *actualités*, comic films (often drawn from postcards), dance films and other short fictional subjects such as *La Concierge* (1899) that Gaumont began to market the films in France and then hired a sales agent for England. Gaumont's personal interest remained focused on technological developments, and not only in cameras and projectors – one of which won a top award at the 1900 Paris Exposition – but in colour cinematography and image–sound synchrony. In 1902, he presented his own speaking image to the French Photographic Society by synchronising a 'Chrono' projector with a phonographic cylinder. He then promoted this 'Chronophone' system through performances at the Musée Grévin and other Paris venues, using *phonoscènes* that Guy produced of celebrated Paris music-hall performers.

Although he had no connection with the Lumières, Charles Pathé did share their interest in Edison's kinetoscope. The son of Alsatian butchers, and a Protestant (in a largely Catholic country) with an unusually keen desire to gain wealth, Pathé had initially made money exhibiting and selling Edison phonographs at the fairs near Paris, which led him and his brother Émile to open a supply shop in Vincennes. When the kinetoscope appeared in 1895, Charles bought several made by Paul in London and installed them at the same fairs. Realising the need for a ready supply of films, he joined with Henri Joly, a former gymnastics instructor at Joinville (where Demenÿ had sometimes filmed)

who had already designed his own version of the kinetoscope, to construct a camera using intermittent movement and 35mm film. This partnership was brief, but Pathé retained rights to the camera and began to exploit the films it could produce at the fairs. In 1897, Claude Grivolas, the new owner of Continsouza and Bunzli's precision tool factory at Chatou, approached him with a financial offer to transform Pathé-Frères into a joint-stock company, in alliance with his own firm. The phonograph branch of the business, run by Émile, generated most of the company's profit at first, while Charles supervised the work of Continsouza and Bunzli in perfecting marketable cameras, projectors and negative and positive film stock. As work progressed, Charles realised the growing commercial value of films in exhibition and, in 1900, hired Ferdinand Zecca, a Paris *café-concert* writer of comic and dramatic monologues, to supervise the production of a wider range of films than was available from Méliès or Gaumont. Once Pathé-Frères films began to circulate throughout France and elsewhere, several met with great success, from *Histoire d'un crime* (1901) to *Ali Baba* (1902). By 1902, Charles was constructing a glass-house studio and related laboratories in Vincennes and preparing to make his company's films a major fairground attraction.

If only a few people led the development of apparatuses for recording and projecting moving pictures as well as the production of films in this early period, those involved in developing exhibition venues were more numerous and more dispersed. In Paris, for instance, at the Musée Grévin, Thomas had convinced Reynaud to use celluloid for his bands of images by 1896 and then switched to showing Gaumont films, including *phonoscènes*. In managing major music halls such as the Olympia, Parisiana and Folies Bergère, Émile and Vincent Isola (originally from Algeria) became regular clients for Méliès and Pathé films, as did Georges Froissart, who showed films at *cafés-concerts*, such as the Eldorado. The Lumières operated two small cinemas through 1897, with Clément Maurice managing one that continued at the Grand Café. As the most popular source of amusement for France's largely rural population, the fairs were even more important than the urban venues, because, much like weekly newspaper supplements, they disseminated news, fashions and 'scientific wonders' throughout the provinces. Touring these fairs were a number of small family businesses with portable theatres (perhaps seating as many as 500 people) that offered entertainments, including, shortly after they became available, moving pictures. The families worked regional circuits, encamping in designated public spaces for several weeks: e.g. Pierre Unik to the west and north of Paris, Alexandre Camby to the east, Charles and Schélmo Katorza around Nantes. The Dulaar family, originally from Belgium, was one of the largest, with several brothers each managing a separate theatre in their circuit around Lyons. From his experience with the fairs around Paris, Pathé had come to know these businesses well, and he quickly turned this to his advantage, becoming their principal source of projectors and films.

INDUSTRIALISATION: 1903–7

Between 1903 and 1907, the cinema in France underwent a process of industrialisation, several years earlier than in any other country, including the USA. The Lumières played no role in that process, having limited their attention to the production of film stock after 1900. Nor did Méliès, whose influence waned, even though some of his expensive *féeries*, such as *Le Voyage à travers l'impossible* (1904) and *Le Raid Paris–Monte Carlo en deux heures* (1905), had long runs in Paris music halls. Instead, that industrialisation, increasingly dependent on fiction films, was led by Pathé, followed at a distance by Gaumont, with the assistance of new business associates and employees.

Confirming his famous line, 'I may not have invented the cinema, but I did industrialise it' (Pathé 1970: 36), Charles Pathé augmented the cinema division of Pathé-Frères in a series of bold moves designed to increase profits and dividends, sometimes drawing on contacts with 'outsider' figures like himself. At Joinville-le-Pont, next to Vincennes, he invested in a maze of factories that employed nearly 1,000 workers (many of them women) for manufacturing, perforating, developing, printing and splicing film stock. At Vincennes, another factory (also employing women) specialised in stencil-colouring prints, a process that soon became a Pathé-Frères trademark. A new Continsouza factory built and serviced the apparatuses the company marketed,

especially projectors and studio cameras – 200 apparatuses were being turned out per month by 1905. Within another year, the mass production of positive film stock for sale had risen to an astonishing 40,000 metres per day. This production capacity was based on constructing more studios in Vincennes, Joinville-le-Pont and Montreuil, with Zecca supervising a loosely organised 'director unit' system of film-makers hired to specialise in making one or more kinds of films. A former crowd-scene manager at several Paris theatres, Lucien Nonguet, specialised in *actualités* and historical reconstructions such as *La Révolution en Russie* (1905); Gaston Velle, in trick films and *féeries* such as *La Poule aux oeufs d'or* (1905); a former Lumière cameraman, Georges Hatot, in comedies and chase films such as *Dix femmes pour un mari* (1905); a former publicity agent, André Heuzé, also in comedies and chase films; a former actor for André Antoine, Albert Capellani, in sentimental dramas such as *La Loi du pardon* (1906); and Zecca himself in realist dramas such as *Au pays noir* (1905). By 1906, this veritable image factory was so standardised that at least half a dozen film titles were being produced in hundreds of prints for sale each week.

These phenomenal sales came partly from Pathé's efforts to monopolise the fairs, but the French market overall was relatively small compared to the potential market worldwide. His boldest move, then, was to establish sales offices for Pathé-Frères films and apparatuses across the globe between 1904 and 1907. A German Jew by the name of Sigmund Popert was apparently the crucial advance man in this process of 'globalisation': a top salesman for the phonograph division, Popert was sent first into England and Germany to market the company's films, and his success then prompted forays into Austria, Russia, Italy and Spain. Following the trajectory he mapped out, Pathé-Frères sales offices spread through the 'First World' of developed countries and client states such as Russia, sometimes creating the very markets they then saturated. These included Moscow (February 1904), New York (August 1904), Brussels (October 1904), Berlin (March 1905), Vienna (July 1905), Chicago (August 1905), St Petersburg (December 1905), Amsterdam (January 1906), Barcelona (February 1906) and Milan (May 1906). Within another year,

Pathé-Frères had monopolised Central Europe and was opening up the colonised areas of Asia, South America and Africa. Among the many agents responsible for creating this first 'cinema empire' were Jacques Berst in the USA (the nickelodeon boom made it Pathé's largest market) and Serge Sandberg, a Jewish émigré from Lithuania, who ran the offices in Moscow, Vienna, Berlin and Budapest. Engineer Franz Dussaud's prophecy – that cinema would be 'the schoolhouse, newspaper, and theatre of tomorrow' (Pathé 1970: 37) – seemed on the verge of fulfilment, and Pathé's success was trumpeted in the first trade journal that promoted the new industry, *Phono-Ciné-Gazette* (1905–8), whose editor, Edmond Benoît-Lévy, was a Paris lawyer and educator (whose parents also came from Alsace) closely associated with the company.

More cautious than his rival, Gaumont typically imitated Pathé's moves, once they proved successful. After 1903, he too encouraged Guy to produce more and more fiction films, ranging from historical dramas such as *L'Assassinat du courrier de Lyon* (1904) to comic sketches such as *Le Bébé embarrassant* (1905) or serial-gag films such as *Le Matelas alcoolique* (1906), and which British Gaumont (now an independent firm) agreed to market not only in England but in the USA. By 1905, Gaumont had achieved a secure enough position in the industry to construct, next to the Buttes-Chaumont park in Paris, a 'glass cathedral' studio (then the largest in Europe), with mercury vapour lamps (the first in France) to supplement the sunlight in winter, and an adjacent factory capable of printing up to 10,000 metres of positive film stock per day. He also began to hire more personnel, from Étienne Arnaud and Louis Feuillade, whom Guy trained as scriptwriters and directors, to set designer Henri Ménessier and his assistant, Ben Carré. Guy herself took on the task of producing even longer films such as *La Vie du Christ* (660 metres, 1906). The Gaumont company prospered to the point that, in December 1906, it could be reorganised as a joint-stock company, allied with a major bank linked to the French electrical industry. By then, as Gaumont films and apparatuses had followed Pathé's (in smaller numbers) into the French fairgrounds, music halls and *cafés-concerts*, the cinema division was far outstripping the original photography branch of the business.

MONOPOLY PLANS AND COMPETITION: 1907–11

Pathé and Gaumont remained the dominant figures in the French cinema industry, yet they faced competition after 1906–7, spurred not only by their success but by Charles's determination to risk even further expansion. In short, Pathé sought to exploit his manufacturing and marketing capacity to create something like a monopoly that could control every stage from producing to exhibiting films, at least within France. His initial move, in partnership with Benoît-Lévy, Dussaud and lawyers Maurice Guégan and Émile Maugras, was to set up an affiliated company with the long-range project of building a circuit of permanent cinemas that would shift exhibition away from the fairs, where exhibitors had no need to constantly renew their supply of films. The first of these, the Omnia-Pathé, opened right across the street from the Musée Grévin in late December 1906, and was soon followed by others not only in Paris (there were fifty by the end of 1907) but as far away as Lyons, Marseilles, Bordeaux and Toulouse. His second move was to begin renting rather than selling films and to grant concessions to half a dozen satellite companies, covering France, Belgium, Holland and North Africa, which would distribute Pathé-Frères films exclusively to these cinemas; while Pathé himself controlled the company distributing films in and around Paris, Benoît-Lévy and Sandberg were among those running the others. Certain parts of this plan – the circuit of cinemas, the renting of films – were quite successful, but the satellite companies soon proved unworkable and unwieldy, so that Pathé-Frères eventually had to pull back and manage its own film distribution as well as rent films to cinemas other than its own. The monopoly plans may have failed (perhaps inevitably), but they did convince Pathé that his empire's success depended on controlling film distribution and exhibition as much as on investing in production.

In the meantime, Pathé continued to augment other parts of his company. A new studio was opened near Nice, in the south of France. Continsouza increased the output of apparatuses, with new models of the Pathé camera and projector, and Arthur Roussel developed a KOK projector (using

28mm films) for schools, churches and homes. As the weekly production of film titles and positive film stock continued to grow, Henri Fourel, head of the colouring department, and a machinist named Méry mechanised and refined Pathé's trademark stencil-colour process. Laboratory space was allotted for an educational film division, where Dr Jean Comandon began research on microscopic cinematography. The earliest weekly newsreel, *Pathé-Journal*, was introduced, its half-hour episodes premiering at a Paris cinema bearing that name. New film-makers joined the company: Spanish cameraman Segundo de Chomón, to make trick films and work on others such as the company's most widely sold film, the third version of its *Vie et passion de N.S. Jésus Christ* (1907); Paris theatre director Georges Monca and playwright Camille de Morlhon, to direct adaptations from historical to contemporary dramas. Several Pathé actors became stars, with each developing a comic type for one of three very profitable comic series: André Deed in *Boireau*, Charles Prince in *Rigadin* and Max Linder in *Max*. Provoked in part by Benoît-Lévy, Pathé began to promote films of higher quality, or *films d'art*, but now by helping set up satellite companies and then contracting to distribute their films. The first of these, Film d'Art, financed by businessman Paul Lafitte, involved directors, writers and actors from the prestigious Comédie-Française in dramatic films such as *L'Assassinat du duc de Guise* (1908). Another was SCAGL, whose rights to adapt contemporary authors were brokered by the popular novelist Pierre Decourcelle. Given the use of a Pathé studio, Capellani agreed to head a production team that was soon releasing one hit after another, from *L'Arlésienne* (1908) to *L'Assommoir* (1909). So successful was this strategy that similar satellite companies were established in Italy, Russia, Germany, the USA and elsewhere to ensure that Pathé-Frères had culturally specific films that were attractive on both the international market and different national markets.

Once again, Gaumont cautiously followed Pathé's lead. In the summer of 1908, long after others such as Gabriel Kaiser had begun constructing cinemas or converting existing venues, he opened his own Cinéma-Palace on the Paris boulevards. Slowly others were added there and in other cities, and by 1910 the circuit had reached Bordeaux. Gaumont also retained the practice of selling films, which improved his firm's position at the fairs; only in 1909 did he set up a satellite company to rent films. Two years after *Pathé-Journal* appeared, he introduced his own weekly newsreel, *Gaumont-Actualités*. Perhaps most importantly, Gaumont personally supervised the transition from a single film-maker, Guy (who accompanied her new husband, Herbert Blaché, when he sailed to the USA as the firm's representative), to a director-unit system of production, headed now by Feuillade. In this system, the company's chief comic actor, Romeo Bosetti, specialised in chase films and then developed several comic series that could compete with Pathé's. Another minor theatre actor, Léonce Perret, was hired to write and direct a variety of comedies and dramatic films. Taken on initially to assist Arnaud, caricaturist Émile Cohl was soon making a series of original animation films. Feuillade himself wrote and directed films that ranged across the spectrum, from realist dramas and biblical or historical films to the comic series *Bébé* (1910–12). By the time Gaumont agreed to rent films, he was making good on a promise to release at least half a dozen new films each week. That success sustained his commitment to the 'Chronophone' system, with the latest model demonstrated to professional societies in 1910.

The demand for films generated by Pathé, Gaumont and Méliès (who soon left film-making to resume staging *féerie* spectacles for his Paris theatre) now attracted other entrepreneurs, artists and educators to the industry. Pathé's former partner, Joly, founded a production company, Lux, hiring as writer-directors a former melodrama actor, Gérard Bourgeois, and a young caricaturist and journalist, Jean Durand. Even Théophile Pathé, a younger brother of Charles and Émile, set up a short-lived production company under his own name, hiring as his film-maker the former Lumière cameramen Promio. Much more successful were Paris lawyers Charles Jourjon and Marcel Vandal, who founded the production company of Éclair, erecting a glasshouse studio in Épinay-sur-Seine, renovating the Parnaland laboratories and hiring Victorin Jasset, a popular director of spectacles at the Hippodrome and various *cafés-concerts* in Paris, to produce a regular schedule of fiction films. Their strategy was to make a series of films built around a single character, and the formula first seized on was a detective series starring Pierre Bressol as Nick Carter, based loosely on popular American dime novels – and that series' success soon led to others. André Debrie, head of a precision-tool factory in Paris, added a line of high-quality machines for perforating and printing film stock to his company's output and then designed a compact, lightweight camera marketed as the Debrie Parvo, which soon became standard for location shooting. Under the leadership of G.-Michel Coissac, the Catholic publisher, La Bonne Presse, opened an office in Paris for selling projectors and selected programmes of films as 'teaching aids' and 'illuminated sermons'. Soon Coissac was running a co-operative exchange that rivalled those supplying the fairs and publishing the first French manual of film projectionists, all of which led Benoît-Lévy to organise similar efforts to incorporate films into French public education.

CONSOLIDATION AND PROLIFERATION: 1911–14

In the early 1910s, certain changes in the industry brought several familiar figures into greater prominence and allowed others to emerge and make their mark. Now that his far-flung company had reached what seemed the limits of its expansion, Pathé focused on strategies that could sustain its operations and profitability. He convinced his partners to invest in mass-producing negative and positive film stock, in order to make the company a leading supplier of material as well as apparatuses in Europe. He also increasingly cut back on direct financial involvement in production and concentrated on distributing and exhibiting the output of a dozen satellite firms. When the company's position on the burgeoning American market began to slip by 1910, Pathé targeted Central and Eastern Europe for increased distribution. These moves gave greater autonomy to satellites such as SCAGL, where Capellani supervised Monca, René Leprince and others, and pushed Pathé film-makers such as Morlhon to set up his own production company (Valetta), along with those involved in its popular comic series: Bosetti (Comica), Linder, Prince. They also spurred film-makers at rival companies to

increase their output. These included not only Feuillade, Perret, Durand and others at Gaumont (which opened another studio near Nice) or Jasset (joined by Émile Chautard and Maurice Tourneur) at Éclair but also Henri Pouctal at Film d'Art, reorganised by Charles Delac (originally from Algeria) with Louis Nalpas (from Anatolia) as head of production, and Louis Mercanton, Joë Hammon (who created a cowboy character, Arizona Bill) and others at Éclipse, which had grown slowly since 1906 and finally capitalised on Mercanton's direction of Sarah Bernhardt in *Queen Elizabeth* (1912). Moreover, directors such as Charles Burguet and even stars like Suzanne Grandais at Gaumont set up small companies for making films. In short, Pathé's decision to decentralise film production set in motion the proliferation of a 'cottage industry' of established and new production companies, largely in and around Paris, which has characterised French cinema ever since.

Distribution was much more concentrated, but here too Pathé and Gaumont left plenty of space for new entrepreneurs. Out of the ashes of Cinéma-Halls, a company that had tried and failed to run a circuit of cinemas in Paris, Maurice Astaix and François Lallement (former Méliès employees), along with Paul Kastor (co-owner of several Paris cinemas), founded AGC, which first acquired exclusive rental rights to the output of Film d'Art and Éclipse and then shared rights to Éclair films with a smaller company. It also gained rights to distribute a range of Italian, American and British films in France. The son of an engineering contractor in the Vendée, Louis Aubert bought out a small firm in Paris that sold and rented films and turned it into the fourth largest rental company by acquiring exclusive rights to distribute the Danish films of Nordisk and the Italian films of Cinès, most notably *Quo Vadis?* (1913). Less concentrated was the exhibition sector, where a boom in cinema construction coincided with the emergence of luxury cinemas or 'palaces'. One of the first of these opened in November 1911, the 5,000-seat Gaumont-Palace (the former Hippodrome, which Cinéma-Halls had earlier tried to run as a cinema), managed by Edgar Costil as the new flagship of Gaumont's circuit. In partnership with Benoît-Lévy, Sandberg and others, Pathé erected the greatest number of luxury cinemas throughout Paris, from the Pathé-Palace to the 2,200-seat Tivoli Cinéma. But the boom quickly attracted others. Léon Brézillon (who would found and head the French Trade Association of Film Theatre Owners in 1912) turned the Palais de Fêtes music hall into a 2,200-seat cinema, and former actor Jacques Castillan ran the Colisée, the first cinema built on the Champs-Élysées, which, though much smaller, successfully catered to Parisian high society. For his part, Aubert extended his business by building up a small chain of neighbourhood cinemas in Paris.

One of the more significant changes marking French cinema in the early 1910s was the development of multi-reel and then feature-length films. For the most part, well-established film-makers led this transformation, which affected all sectors of the industry. Through SCAGL, Capellani became the most crucial figure, especially in his adaptations of famous nineteenth-century stage plays and novels: e.g. *Le Courrier de Lyon* (1911), *Notre Dame de Paris* (1911), *Les Mystères de Paris* (1912) and *Les Misérables* (1912), which ran for 3,500 metres or twelve reels. At Film d'Art, Delac and Nalpas made multi-reel films the company's exclusive province, with Albert Calmettes directing Gabrielle Réjane in *Madame Sans-Gêne* (1911) and Pouctal directing Bernhardt in *La Dame aux camélias* (1912), as well as competing with Capellani in such big historical productions as the 4,000-metre *Les Trois Mousquetaires* (1913). At Éclair, Jasset exploited popular crime novels for a series of sensational melodramas, notably those starring Alexandre Arquillière: *Zigomar* (1911), *Zigomar contre Nick Carter* (1912) and *Zigomar, peau d'anguille* (1913). At Gaumont, Perret and Feuillade mined this genre as well, especially in Perret's three *Main de fer* films (1912–13) and Feuillade's five *Fantômas* films (1913–14). Other film-makers explored the multi-reel format in contemporary bourgeois melodramas, as in Monca's *Le Petit chose* (1912), for SCAGL, and Morlhon's *La Broyeuse des coeurs* (1913), for Valetta. Feuillade and Perret did likewise for Gaumont: the former in *La Tare* (1911), an early title in the *Scènes de la vie telle qu'elle est* series that was featured on the Gaumont-Palace's inaugural programme; the latter with eight-reel productions, *L'Enfant de Paris* (1913) and *Le Roman d'un mousse* (1914), both of which premiered

in two hour-long parts, with an interval, much like a theatre performance.

Finally, the cinema gained enough influence during this period to justify an independent (more or less) trade press and to attract the attention of major newspapers. In 1908, Georges Dureau, who already had published a trade journal aimed at the fairground exhibitors, began to edit the bi-weekly *Ciné-Journal*, the principal specialised journal devoted to the industry; at first Dureau ignored Pathé-Frères and, reciprocally, the company did not place ads in his journal. By 1911, Dureau had rivals such as Charles Le Fraper, who edited *Le Courrier cinématographique*, and then E. L. Fouquet, who edited *Le Cinéma*, which merged with Georges Lordier's *L'Écho du cinéma* (when Lordier, who owned several small Paris cinemas, founded his own production company, Les Grands Films Populaires, taking over the bankrupt Lux studio and granting Aubert distribution rights) to become the only bi-weekly aimed mainly at exhibitors and even spectators. By 1913, the four largest Paris dailies were printing weekly columns – or pages, in the case of *Le Journal* – devoted to moving pictures, while *Comoedia*, uniquely specialising in the arts, had a daily column, which included synoptic reviews. Even the noted literary historian and drama critic, René Doumic, felt compelled to write a partially admiring essay in the prestigious journal he edited, *La Revue des deux mondes*.

DISRUPTION AND RECOVERY: 1914–18

The outbreak of war in August 1914 crippled the French cinema industry and provoked a number of unanticipated changes. Exhibition venues were closed for several months; exports were cut off to Central and Eastern Europe; production was halted and only gradually resumed in early 1915. After losing its offices and laboratories in the USA to a fire in the spring of 1914, Éclair sold its studio facilities once the war erupted – and was never again a major producer in France. Key personnel such as Capellani, Perret and Linder were lured away from Pathé-Frères and Gaumont to the USA, joining Louis Gasnier (head of Pathé's growing American output), Tourneur, Chautard and others from Éclair's American affiliate already well established in the

American industry. Gaumont and Pathé made diametrically opposed decisions in meeting the challenges of the war. Gaumont quickly resumed production, relying first on Feuillade's talent and efficiency to gather together a team in southern France and then hiring a number of new writer-directors such as Brussels-born Jacques Feyder and Raymond Bernard, the son of a popular playwright. At Film d'Art, where he had taken over for Delac (mobilised for the war), Nalpas did likewise, adding Abel Gance as a new writer-director. Although Pathé continued to support SCAGL (where the famous theatre director, André Antoine, joined Monca, Leprince and others), Valetta and other satellites by distributing their films, he turned primarily to his American affiliate, now reorganised as Pathé-Exchange, to shore up his company's fortunes. In short, he gambled on making Pathé-Exchange films the core of Pathé-Frères's weekly programme of releases, in France and elsewhere. The gamble paid off largely through the success of the serials starring Pearl White, Ruth Roland and others, the first of which was released in late 1915 and given the 'Frenchified' title, *Les Mystères de New York*.

Given the demand for films and the general lack of French titles, wave after wave of American films, which were already inundating the French market before the war, now flooded the cinemas. Pathé was hardly alone in opening the floodgates. A Jewish émigré from Tunisia, Jacques Haïk, who had set up Western Import in early 1914, not only secured rental rights to the popular Keystone films but distributed those starring Charlie Chaplin in a series called *Charlot*. Later AGC would win out in a battle for the rights to Chaplin's Essanay and Mutual films. Charles Mary, a cinema-owner and distributor of pre-war German films, took over the rights to Famous Players/Jesse Lasky features from Aubert, and one of his widely celebrated hits was Cecil B. DeMille's *The Cheat*; Éclipse would later buy out his agency and distribute Triangle features, including the *Rio Jim* Westerns of William S. Hart. Even Gaumont finally succumbed to this obvious source of revenue, and in 1917 negotiated a contract to distribute Paramount's features. The war period was hardly propitious for constructing new cinemas, but Aubert was prosperous enough to make an exception. In May 1915, now in partnership with Sand-berg, he finally opened his long-planned Nouveautés-Aubert-Palace (its 1,500 seats making it the largest cinema on the Grand Boulevards), the first of a circuit of Aubert-Palaces that would extend throughout Paris and other major cities.

Now that American films dominated their home market, the French faced this question: what exactly was 'French' about their 'national' cinema, a question first posed by publisher Henri Diamant-Berger in his new bi-weekly trade journal, *Le Film*, in 1916. One answer came from Feuillade, who, with Gaumont's blessing, set out to compete with Pathé's American serials by abandoning crime thriller series such as *Les Vampires* (1915–16) and, with scenarios written by novelist Arthur Bernède, producing instead 'avenger' adventure serials that drew on nineteenth-century traditions of French storytelling and updated the figure of the chivalric hero. Backed by a trade-press campaign strongly stressing its 'Frenchness' and complemented by Bernède's fictionalisation published in *Le Petit Parisien*, *Judex* (1917) was so popular that Feuillade quickly put another *Judex* serial into production. Another answer was to reinvent the bourgeois melodrama so as to avoid any reference to the war. The trick was to tell stories of threats, sexual and/or financial, to the French family, with the focus on misperceived female characters, perhaps acknowledging the ideological significance of women on the homefront. Such stories depended on the appeal of female stars, and at least five came forward to ensure a profitable series of films: Gabrielle Robinne, for SCAGL; Maryse Dauvray, for Valetta; Emmy Lynn, for Film d'Art; Mistinguett for André Hugon's Films Succès; and most popular of all, Suzanne Grandais, directed by Mercanton and René Hervil, for Éclipse. Tellingly, another female star, Musidora, who had played the chief villain in *Judex*, sought to produce her own films, but had to do so 'in exile' in Italy.

In *Le Film*, along with several newspapers, a sustained body of film theory and criticism now also began to emerge. Colette was the first writer of some importance to engage in film criticism, although she reviewed films irregularly for the new journal in 1916 and 1917, before leaving to write scenarios for her friend, Musidora. But her review of *The Cheat*, in August 1916, was ground-breaking. In June 1917, a young drama critic, Louis Delluc, became *Le Film*'s regular reviewer, and one year later he was writing a weekly column for *Paris-Midi*. Delluc used his columns to promote the work of French film-makers such as Antoine, Gance and Jacques de Baroncelli, a Paris journalist who had set up his own company in 1917, as well as that of selected American (Chaplin, Hart, Thomas Ince, D. W. Griffith) and Swedish film-makers (Victor Sjöström, Mauritz Stiller). He also supported several young writers such as Louis Aragon and Jean Cocteau who were discovering the cinema and whose ideas to some extent he shared. Perhaps his most lasting contribution, however, was to develop certain concepts such as *photogénie* in order to apprehend what he saw as 'the birth of an extraordinary art' (Delluc 1918). Delluc's principal rival during the war was Émile Vuillermoz, the most important French music critic of the day, who began writing a bi-weekly column of film criticism in the influential Paris daily, *Le Temps*, in November 1916. Although he too promoted some of the same film-makers as Delluc (together they expressed a prototypical auteur theory of cinema), Vuillermoz was more tied to a Symbolist aesthetic in his own efforts to theorise this new art form.

'QUALITY CINEMA' AND ITS DIVERSE PROPONENTS: 1919–24

By 1919, the French confronted conditions no better, and perhaps even worse, than they had two or three years before. Despite its best defensive efforts, as Diamant-Berger put it, 'France was in danger of becoming a colony of the American cinema' (Sadoul 1974: 45). As soon as the war ended, one after another the major American companies set up their own offices in Paris: first came Paramount and Fox-Film, then United Artists and First National, and finally Universal. Goldwyn and Metro signed exclusive contracts, respectively, with Gaumont and Aubert. By 1922, Adolph Osso was even heading a production unit for Paramount that would release one of the most popular French films of the 1922–3 season, an epic historical project entitled *Les Opprimés*, directed by former actor Henry Roussell. How would the French respond?

Pathé provided one model by reorganising and refining the structural changes initiated before the war. As early as 1917, he had declared impractical any notion that the French could re-establish a production system comparable to that of the Americans – specifically rejecting a proposal from Sandberg and Nalpas to modernise French studio facilities and create a consortium of French film producers. Instead, he made the primary objective of Pathé-Cinéma (the company's new core) the production and marketing of negative and positive film stock for France and the rest of Europe. Pathé cameras and projectors continued to set the standard for such apparatuses in Europe; in addition to the KOK projector, now widely used in schools throughout Europe and North America, Pathé had his laboratories develop a new camera and projector for amateurs, Pathé-Baby (using 9.5mm film). In short, the company would focus on exploiting technological advances in the hardware and material base that the cinema required. In 1920, a further reorganisation established a separate company, Pathé-Consortium, whose chief mission was to assume control over film distribution and exhibition. Significantly absent was any reference to production, confirming rumours that Pathé was abandoning not only satellites such as SCAGL but film production altogether.

Despite being dropped by Paramount, Gaumont used the profits from Feuillade's new avenger serials, *Tih Minh* (1918) and *Barrabas* (1920) to fund the development of several young talented film-makers. The result, under the guidance of Costil (now a producer), was 'Séries Pax', a remarkable series of medium-budget films written and directed by former theatre director Léon Poirier and poet Marcel L'Herbier, including the latter's *L'Homme du large* (1920) and *Eldorado* (1921). Some recently recruited film-makers, such as Gance and Feyder, secured independent financing to strike out on their own; others such as Baroncelli worked first for Film d'Art (now managed by Delac, with Vandal as a new partner) and then again on his own or, in the case of former journalist Germaine Dulac, for Films André Legrand and then Film d'Art, most notably on *La Souriante Madame Beudet* (1922). With far more financial resources than Delac and Vandal (whose consortium plans came to nought), Aubert began to put in place his own consortium, taking over the rental rights of AGC (including Film d'Art) and adding production facilities at a studio he had built outside Paris, for

Tih Minh (Louis Feuillade, 1918)

such film-makers as René Le Somptier and Hervil and Mercanton (from Éclipse, now defunct). With C. F. Tavano as producer, Aubert now embarked on making films, after a costly project he had risked distributing, Feyder's *L'Atlantide* (1921), made a huge profit, running for a full year at the Madeleine Cinema he controlled in Paris, a record broken only by *Ben-Hur* in 1927. The Madeleine was only one of many luxury cinemas erected in the capital and other French cities after the war. Still active, Benoît-Lévy financed some of these, including the Madeleine and the Salle Marivaux; Linder, returning from the USA, put up the money for another, the Ciné-Max-Linder. Pathé, Gaumont and Aubert all expanded their circuits, with Aubert now leasing some of the largest and most prestigious cinemas, from the Tivoli Cinema to the Madeleine.

Much like Aubert, Sandberg was also committed to building a consortium that allied production with studio ownership and distribution, and part of his strategy was to produce distinctly French serials. The format that Feuillade had developed in *Judex*

was taken up by new film companies, by Phocéa (in Marseilles) and most notably by the Société des cinéromans, a crucial component of Sandberg's plan to rebuild the French film industry, with its home base at the Ciné-Studio, newly constructed at La Victorine outside Nice. Phocéa capitalised on the undimmed star status of Grandais in several serials, the last of which, *L'Essor* (1920), came out just weeks after her sudden death in a car accident. Financed by Sandberg, who also supported 'Films Louis Nalpas' projects, Cinéromans engaged Édouard-Émile Violet (a former Gaumont film-maker), René Navarre (the star of *Fantômas*), Bernède (Feuillade's scriptwriter) and another *feuilleton* novelist, Gaston Leroux, to produce two serials a year, marketed in conjunction with their fictionalisation in several Paris dailies, especially *Le Matin*. Together with Gaumont, Cinéromans and Phocéa sought to standardise French film production and distribution. Financial resources would be concentrated in integrated multiple-film projects requiring a coherent production schedule, rather than be dispersed over half a dozen to a dozen separate films, whose production would be much less regularised. In Sandberg's case, moreover, it was assumed that their distribution would be guaranteed through SIC Éclair, another company he had formed out of the bankruptcy of Éclair.

Despite his declarations, Pathé himself could not refrain from giving selective support to film production. This could be direct, as in the case of independent projects such as Gance's four-part *J'accuse* (1919) and three-part *La Roue* (1922). It also could be indirect (and violate the company's reorganisation), as in the distribution contract linking Pathé-Cinéma with a new company that Decourcelle founded, SEC (replacing SCAGL), which set out to make serials and 'superproductions' modelled on the initial success of Pouctal's four-part adaptation, *Travail* (1920). SEC made French serials, often written by Decourcelle for Burguet and other film-makers, the core of its programme of releases. In sharp conflict with Pathé, but imitating his moves, Denis Richard, the new head at Pathé-Consortium, boldly plunged his company into film production as well. Most notably, he arranged to finance Diamant-Berger's serial adaptation of *Les Trois mousquetaires*, the first of several planned projects. Not only did the film's budget reach a grand total of 2.5 million francs (unheard of at the time) but a large sum was also allotted to promote its press previews and then its premiere, which launched Pathé-Consortium's 1921–2 season. Yet this massive serial (each of its twelve parts was feature-length) achieved an astonishing success: over the course of three months, it set a record by playing in more than 1,000 cinemas, nearly half of all those operating in France, and by grossing at least six times its cost. Although there is no question that these serials helped to revive the French industry, their success was compromised by the internal struggle within the Pathé companies, a financial crisis in 1921 (which affected Sandberg adversely) and mounting criticism in the press which discredited many of them as 'bad cinema', an unhealthy indulgence, even a form of drug addiction.

The serial thus became the focus of a crisis of 'quality' – a term often defined not aesthetically but morally, socially, even medically. Could a standardised commodity like the serial ever be a quality product? And how could it be representative of a 'healthy' national cinema? The answer came in early 1922, when the managing director of *Le Matin*, Jean Sapène, a self-made man, much like Pathé and Gaumont, who emulated the German magnate, Alfred Hugenberg, took control of Cinéromans, merging the industries of the cinema and the press. Sapène shifted the company's operations to Paris (first renting one of Pathé's studios) and set up an even more systematic production schedule (four serials per year, standardised at eight episodes each), with Nalpas (who had fallen out with Sandberg) to serve as executive producer, Bernède to head a new scenario department (the first in France) and Henri Fescourt, whose serial, *Mathias Sandorf*, had been a hit for Nalpas the previous year, to lead the first of several film-making teams. Sapène also contracted with the four major Paris dailies to publish one fictionalisation each per year, worked out a distribution deal with Pathé-Consortium and negotiated with the Lutetia-Fournier cinema chain in Paris to showcase the company's serials. In short, Sapène built up a powerful conglomerate around Cinéromans, whose technical efficiency, from production to exhibition, offered the model of a rational, predictable, profitable business operation. As Fescourt later put it, the Cinéromans serials 'offered exhibitors the guarantees of a long series of weeks of huge returns from a faithful mass public hooked on the formula', permitting them to 'resist the foreign film salesmen' (Fescourt 1959: 359). But Sapène also made sure that, from Fescourt's *Rouletabille chez les bohemiens* (1922) to *Mandrin* (1924), nearly all costume adventures centred on male heroes from the period of 1750 to 1850, they achieved what the readers of *Mon ciné*, a new fan magazine, had called for in a survey on French serials: a popular cinema of quality, artistic but accessible to all (Roelens 1979).

A very different conception of quality cinema was promoted by the ciné-club movement that emerged in Paris in the early 1920s. Although many writers, artists, film-makers and intellectuals were involved, several were especially crucial. Tireless in promoting the cinema as a new, international art form, now through his own films such as *Fièvre* (1921) as well as books and journals such as *Cinéa*, Delluc set a precedent with public *conférences* (lectures, screenings, discussions) at several cinemas in 1920–1. The Italian-born writer, Ricciotto Canudo, systematised this format by forming the 'Club des Amis du Septième Art' or CASA, a group of cinephiles who met regularly to screen and discuss films. Under his direction, beginning in November 1921, CASA sponsored special exhibitions on film art at the most important annual show of new painting, the Salon d'Automne. Originating in the exhibitions was the idea for an 'anthology of cinema' or film styles, exemplified in selected excerpts from the best films of the year, one of which in 1923 was Gance's *La Roue*. In early 1923, a young friend of Delluc's and already an astute film critic for the Paris daily, *L'Humanité*, and the prestigious monthly *Mercure de France*, Léon Moussinac, established a rival organisation, the 'Club Français du Cinéma'. After Canudo and Delluc died within five months of one another, Moussinac helped René Blum carry on the work of CASA, including a programme honouring Delluc, at which Jean Epstein, another Jewish émigré (from Poland) and author of the brilliant *Bonjour Cinéma* (1921), showed a short montage work, *Photogénie*. Even more importantly, Moussinac persuaded Henri Clouzot, director of the Musée Galliera (devoted to decorative arts), to mount a full-scale exposition on French film art that extended from May through October 1924. The high point was a month-long series of lectures and screenings in June, presented by, among others, Moussinac, L'Herbier and Dulac.

NEW PLAYERS STEP OUT OF THE SHADOWS: 1924–9

Having played central roles in building and sustaining the French film industry over more than two decades, Pathé and Gaumont left the stage as active leaders during the 1920s. Although he still sat on many of his companies' boards of directors, Pathé now worked behind the scenes supporting others. For his part, Gaumont shut down 'Séries Pax' in 1922; after Feuillade died in 1925, he reduced his company's activities to exhibition and distribution, with the latter contracted exclusively to an American studio, MGM. The arena was left to Sapène, Aubert and a host of new figures. Although the Cinéromans's serials and films of Pierre Colombier, Fescourt, L'Herbier, Dulac and others kept his con-

sortium viable, Sapène too began to redirect his energies. In 1927, he relinquished control of Pathé-Consortium, sold off several cinema circuits and directly intervened in Cinéromans's production, partly with the aim of making his wife, Claudia Victrix, a star. He also took the duplicitous position, as records in the American National Archives reveal, of leading a campaign to impose a quota on American film imports, while at the same time undermining that campaign in exchange for the release of Victrix's films in the USA. These tactics backfired, and Sapène was ready to abandon Cinéromans by 1928. Aubert also began to take a less active role in his consortium, but not until his joint production and distribution contracts with Erich Pommer at UFA ended badly: Paramount and MGM gained control of UFA by 1926, and UFA opened its own distribution agency, ACE, in Paris. Thereafter, administration of the Aubert-Palace circuit was ceded to others, and the filmmakers in his company's orbit gained more autonomy, from veterans such as Roussell and Baroncelli to the new team of Jean Benoît-Lévy and Marie Epstein as well as Julien Duvivier, whose successes for Film d'Art included *Tourbillon de Paris* (1928) and *Au bonheur des dames* (1929). By 1929, Aubert's interests shifted to politics, and he was elected deputy to the National Assembly from the Vendée region of his childhood.

Of the new figures who now assumed crucial roles, several 'outsiders' continued to promote a distinctly French cinema. One of those, a Jewish Russian émigré, Alexandre Kamenka, had assumed control of Films Ermolieff in 1922, and turned it into Films Albatros, with its own distributor, Armor. Albatros first traded on the strength of its Russian colony: actor Ivan Mosjoukine, set designer Ivan Lochakoff, costume designer Boris Bilinsky and film-makers Victor Tourjansky and Alexandre Volkoff, whose *Kean* (1924) was especially notable. By 1925, Kamenka was hiring French film-makers to anchor his growing production schedule, from Epstein and Feyder to newcomers Jean Grémillon and René Clair. Starting with *Un Chapeau de paille d'Italie* (1927), Clair arguably reinvented French film comedy. Scriptwriter Charles Spaak later described Kamenka as the greatest French producer of the 1920s. Another Russian émigré, a little-known steel industrialist named Jacques Grinieff, financed the Société des Films Historiques (SFH), whose objective was 'to render visually the whole history of France' (Antoine 1972: 211). Its initial effort, Bernard's epic *Le Miracle des loups* (with architect Robert Mallet-Stevens as set designer), became the first film to premiere at the Paris Opéra, in November 1924. SFH expanded its range beyond France with Bernard's next epic, *Le Joueur d'échecs* (1927), but returned to its origins with several films by Jean Renoir: *Le Tournoi* and *Le Bled* (both 1929). A third figure, another Jewish Russian émigré named Bernard Natan, had a film laboratory called Rapid-Film, which was so profitable by 1924 that he could expand into publicity films and then film production at his newly constructed Studios Réunis in Paris, where Marco de Gastyne shot *La Merveilleuse vie de Jeanne d'Arc* (1929). In 1929, with Charles Pathé's tacit approval, Rapid-Film merged with Pathé-Cinéma, and Natan moved up to preside over a new giant, Pathé-Natan.

Given the dominance of the Americans and, secondarily, the Germans, many in the French industry forged links with producers in either one country or the other. Noë Bloch, a former associate of Kamenka, became the head of Ciné-France in 1923, linking Pathé-Consortium with the Westi Corporation in Berlin in an ambitious European consortium that initiated epic projects such as Gance's *Napoléon* (1927), Tourjansky's *Michel Strogoff* (1926) and Fescourt's four-part *Les Misérables* (1925–6). When Westi suddenly went bankrupt in 1925, and Ciné-France collapsed, Grinieff stepped in to finance *Napoléon*'s completion, a move that quickly led to him founding the Société Générale du Film (SGF), with Henry de Cazotte. Although SGF primarily supported French historical films, its production teams, as in *Napoléon*, included personnel from France, Germany and beyond. *Casanova* (1927) reunited many of the Russian émigrés: Bloch, Volkoff, Mosjoukine, Lochakoff and Bilinsky. *La Passion de Jeanne d'Arc* (1928) was written and directed by Danish film-maker Carl Dreyer, starred the French stage actress Renée Jeanne Falconetti and imported its cinematographer and set designer from Germany. Backed by Édouard Corniglion-Moliner of the KCM financial group, Perret and Robert Hurel, by contrast, exploited their

connections with Paramount. Both had worked in the company's production office in France, the former most notably in directing a spectacular version of *Madame Sans-Gêne* (1925) starring Gloria Swanson. Based on the success of Perret's next Paramount production, *La Femme nue* (1926), starring Louise Lagrange, the two men set up a French consortium, Franco-Film, which involved buying Sandberg's Ciné-Studio (where Rex Ingram had been shooting films) in order to produce the projects of Films Léonce Perret and other smaller companies. In 1929, Franco-Film bought out Aubert and then was itself subsumed within a larger consortium that KCM established when Gaumont sold his shares in his company – and retired.

Several new figures also joined Moussinac and others in expanding the ciné-club movement. As a result of Moussinac's Musée Galliera exhibition, CASA and the Club Français du Cinéma merged into the Ciné-Club de France. At the same time, Charles Léger organised a younger group of cinephiles in Paris (among them Marcel Carné, Jean Dréville and Jean Mitry) into La Tribune Libre. Léger and Moussinac together arranged screenings of selected French films at the famous 1925 Exposition des Arts Décoratifs et Industries Modernes in Paris. The clubs were so successful that others proliferated in the capital and across France, including Jean Vigo's Amis du Cinéma in Marseilles. The most controversial was the attempt by Moussinac, Jean Lods and others, in 1927, to create a mass movement through Les Amis de Spartacus, which showed banned Soviet films and older 'classics' at the Cinéma du Casino de Grenelle and the Belleviloise, a workers' co-operative cinema. As the group's membership multiplied and attendance soared, rivalling commercial cinemas and making a mockery of government censorship, Paris police chief Jean Chiappe threatened to disrupt its screenings – and Spartacus had no recourse in 1928 but to disband. Within a year, however, certain members organised an International Congress on Independent Cinema in Switzerland as well as a Congress of Ciné-Clubs in Paris, out of which would emerge the first Fédération des Ciné-Clubs. All this activity was supported by a host of new journals and books. Jean Tedesco transformed *Cinéa* into *Cinéa-Ciné-pour-tous*, the premier independent journal of the decade. René Jeanne oversaw the publication of dozens of lectures and essays in a booklet series, *L'Art cinématographique* (1926–9). Dréville edited several film journals, including the deluxe *Cinégraphie* (1927–8). Canudo's influence continued in the publication of his collected essays, *L'Usine aux images* (1927), and Moussinac and Epstein published important selections from their theoretical and critical writings.

Two other components of the ciné-club movement were crucial to this expansion. In November 1924, Tedesco opened the Vieux-Colombier (the former site of Jacques Copeau's theatre in Paris) as a specialised cinema. He not only scheduled regular repertory programmes but showed avant-garde work, such as Fernand Léger's *Ballet mécanique* (1924) and Dmitri Kirsanoff's *Ménilmontant* (1926), and hosted series of lectures and discussions. By 1926, he was premiering new features and specialising in documentaries by André Sauvage and Grémillon, including *Tour au large* (1927). Inspired by Tedesco, former Gaumont actors Armand Tallier and Laurence Myrga opened their own Studio des Ursulines in January 1926. Their programmes also included avant-garde work, from Clair's *Entr'acte* (1924) to Dulac's *La Coquille et le clergyman* (1927) and Man Ray's *L'Étoile de mer* (1928), as well as examples of pre-war cinema and unreleased features. At one point, the Studio des Ursulines became an exclusive venue for Epstein's independent films, *6½ x 11* (1926) and *La Glace à trois faces* (1927). The success of these cinemas soon led to others, with perhaps as many as a dozen operating in Paris by the end of the decade. Jean Mauclaire opened the most attractive of these, Studio 28, in January 1928. It was there that Epstein's *La Chute de la maison Usher* (1928) had its premiere, as did Luis Buñuel's *Un Chien andalou* (1929) and *L'Âge d'or* (1930), the latter of which provoked a destructive attack by right-wing groups.

But who could supply the increasing demand for these films? In 1922, after leaving Gaumont, L'Herbier had set up Cinégraphic as a co-operative workshop for film-making. Not only did Cinégraphic produce L'Herbier's own *L'Inhumaine* (1924) but it also supported the work of young film-makers, such as Claude Autant-Lara's *Fait-divers* (1924). Although it proved premature, lasting

no more than two years, Cinégraphic did influence later production strategies. Tedesco turned the loft above the Vieux-Colombier into a film laboratory and studio, where Renoir made *La Petite marchande d'allumettes* (1928). Mauclaire, Tallier and others sponsored experimental films, among them Dulac's abstract composition, *Thèmes et variations* (1928). Sandberg even returned to financing productions such as Epstein's *Finis terrae* (1929). The Vicomte de Noailles, who had provided office space for Cinégraphic, was one of several wealthy patrons who dabbled in underwriting such films: his included Buñuel's *L'Âge d'or*. Both Tedesco and Tallier also found themselves having to distribute programmes of films to other cinemas and ciné-clubs throughout France, Belgium and Switzerland, as did Robert Aaron, the editor of the new deluxe journal, *La Revue du cinéma* (1928–31). The most important of these figures, however, was Pierre Braunberger, the son of a Paris doctor who had worked as Irving Thalberg's assistant in Hollywood before returning to France to help Renoir produce his ambitious failure, *Nana* (1926). Braunberger founded a small production company, Néro-Film, which supported several short films and features, among them Alberto Cavalcanti's *En rade* (1927). Yet his real achievement was to set up Studio-Film in 1929, the first company to amass a wide range of avant-garde films for systematic distribution. Braunberger later would play a similar role in co-producing the early work of several New Wave film-makers.

WORKS CITED

Antoine, A.-P. (1972) *Antoine, père et fils*, Paris, René Julliard.

Delluc, L. (1918) 'Le Cinquième Art', *Le Film*, 113, 13 May, 2.

Fescourt, H. (1959) *La Foi et les montagnes*, Paris, Paul Montel.

Pathé, C. (1970) *De Pathé-Frères à Pathé Cinéma*, Lyons, Serdoc.

Roelens, M. (1979) '*Mon-Ciné* (1922–1924) et le mélodrame', *Les Cahiers de la cinémathèque*, 28, 201–14.

Sadoul, G. (1974) *Histoire générale du cinéma*, vol. 4, Paris, Denoël.

2 BUSINESS 1890–1930
A Re-Examination of Key Milestones in the Development of the Industry

Michelle Millar

The study of early French film history has concentrated on its artistic, technological and sociological aspects, while the historical account of its commercial components has been less exhaustive. Commercial analysis has proved problematic partly for practical reasons. By the time that film history was accepted into the academic portfolio, much of the relevant commercial documentation concerning the early years of the industry was difficult to trace, remained uncatalogued or had simply vanished. Yet until we gain a fuller and more accurate picture of the commercial and competitive forces influencing the growth of the incipient film industry, we will not truly understand the formation and development of early cinema in France. By shaping convincing theories and coherent narratives from incomplete commercial data, historians who undertake the analysis of the early economic and competitive development of the film industry run the risk of oversimplifying or simply drawing erroneous conclusions. This chapter draws on forensics – a methodology more usually associated with disciplines such as law and finance – to examine the interplay of commercial forces with technological and artistic factors as the French film industry expanded nationally and internationally in the early years of the 20th century. This approach involves the use of techniques such as data-mining, link analysis, network analysis and timeline charts to identify patterns from disparate early film industry records (bills, catalogues, exhibition records, legal agreements, etc.). To take just one example, the cross-mapping of names of boards of directors and stockholders of corporations can reveal unexpected connections and hidden alliances. Adapted data acquisition and analysis software capable of processing large quantities of uneven information is also used to map networks of relationships visually.

Together, such techniques allow the historian to examine and test existing historical narratives.

Besides reviewing a range of historical assumptions and perspectives regarding the birth and development of the French film industry, the chapter employs forensics to illuminate two crucial areas of early cinema history: first, the commercial strategies of the major companies in France as they competed for control of the domestic market at the turn of the 20th century; and second, Pathé's loss of domination of the American market towards the end of the 1900s. The repercussions of the power play between Pathé and Edison in the USA would have a profound impact on the developing industry. It is central to our understanding of early French film history and constitutes the principal focus of the discussion that follows.

REVIEWING EARLY FRENCH CINEMA HISTORY

The year 1895 or 1896 is commonly advanced as the date of cinema's birth in France. However, if one marks the beginning of cinema as 1895/6, then little distinction is being made between the 'moving picture' (i.e. the technology) and the 'moving story' (i.e. the art form). The tendency to fail to differentiate between the moving picture and the moving story has not only confused the historical account of their evolution, it has also obscured the importance of the commercial forces driving the formation of the film industry. The first moving pictures were shown primarily as demonstrations of the new technology. In business terms, this means that at the inception of the film industry, despite the earlier commercial success of magic-lantern moving stories, it was the motion picture equipment that was initially considered to have primary commercial value, as opposed to the motion picture itself. It was not long, however, before the manufacturers would recognise that the potential revenues and financial returns from a strip of film could far exceed the potential earnings from sales of equipment. The commercialised exhibition of the filmstrip became an unprecedented mass-market entertainment phenomenon, and its financial impact upon the fledgling industry – which had initially modelled itself after the photographic camera equipment market – was incalculable. The industry's creative and commercial energies turned to increasing the value of the celluloid filmstrip, thereby initiating the development of motion-picture skits and sketches, and ultimately the moving story or 'movie' (i.e. a dramatic narrative with a beginning, middle and end, whose plot moves its characters towards a dénouement). It is the movie that would become the key commodity driving the commercial wheel of the film industry forward.

The invention of this new film industry has often been attributed to certain leading manufacturers in France and the USA, namely Auguste and Louis Lumière and Thomas Edison respectively. However, an analysis of the chronology and key commercial events at the time of the invention of the motion-picture camera reveals a different story. It was rather their marketing prowess that made it possible for the Lumières and Edison to steal the commercial thunder of those less powerful inventors and scientists to whose work they had access. These include Étienne-Jules Marey and Émile Reynaud, of whose work the Lumières and Edison were aware through their attendance at the 1889 Paris Exposition, where both Marey's and Reynaud's work was readily accessible. The Lumières also knew about the perforated film band utilised by Léon Bouly in his Cinématographe; Bouly's patent expired on 16 March 1895, following which the Lumières adopted the name for their own camera/projector. According to Leo Sauvage, it appears that the Lumière brothers, whose family owned a successful photographic equipment company in Lyons, were encouraged to start working seriously on their own motion-picture camera and projector after viewing a pirated version of Edison's kinetoscope in Paris in 1894 (Sauvage 1985: 172–5). There exists a similarly popular misconception that the Lumières, in France, and Edison, in the USA, were the first to

record images on celluloid, a distinction that more likely belongs to Louis Aimé Augustin Le Prince (French by birth, but resident in England and the USA) and to William Friese-Greene in the UK, who independently of each other began to record images on celluloid as early as 1889, when celluloid became commercially available.

The general proclamation of the year 1895 as 'the beginning of cinema' also blurs the distinction between the invention of the motion-picture camera/projector and its formal commercialisation. It is often stated that 1895 marks the first public demonstration of projected motion-picture camera and projector technology. However, although the Lumières are generally acclaimed to have first projected a motion picture on celluloid publicly on 22 March 1895, technically it would appear that Jean Acme Le Roy was the first to do this. The first private showing of his projected 'Pictures in Life Motion' using his 'Marvelous Cinematograph' was on 5 February 1894 before approximately twenty people at the back of Riley Brothers' opticians at 16 Beekman Street, Manhattan; his first public showing took place the following year, on 22 February 1895, at the opera house in Clinton, New Jersey. Unlike the Lumières and others, Le Roy failed to apply for a patent for his camera. More accurately stated, then, the Lumières were the first to formally commercialise the new projected medium.

EXPANSION AND COMPETITION

Not long after the Lumière brothers' first formal public exhibition on 28 December 1895, the race to capitalise on the projection of celluloid filmstrips was already under way worldwide. The potential revenues that could be reaped from possible international filmstrip sales quickly became apparent. In France, Léon Gaumont and Company and Georges Méliès's Star-Film entered the arena as the Lumières' principal competition, followed within a couple of years by Pathé-Frères. The comparative ease with which this new mass-market commodity could be reproduced and transported rapidly opened up the international marketplace to the French. As early as 1897–8, for example, Gaumont was already offering its filmstrips for sale in the British market. By 1903, Pathé had begun to open offices in London, New York and Moscow, while Méliès established an office in New York. Conversely, the French also found themselves subject to potentially formidable competition both at home and abroad from the Italians, Danes, Germans and British, among others. It was essential that the French move aggressively to secure their position both domestically and internationally. Certain key commercial decisions soon differentiated the competition. By 1900, Pathé, Gaumont and Méliès vied for dominance in the French market, the Lumières having effectively defaulted the race by passing up fiction-film production in favour of equipment manufacture. A use of forensics to track a host of financial performance measures to analyse these companies' respective commercial strategies reveals the significant impact of the level and timing of capitalisation on the direction and timing of production and distribution. Most telling is the fact that although Gaumont had commenced production in France and expanded into distribution abroad earlier than Pathé-Frères, Pathé would overtake Gaumont both domestically and internationally within just a matter of a few years.

Léon Gaumont and Company was formally established in 1895 with 200,000 francs of capital but, despite the rapid growth of the industry, had only received a further capital injection of 300,000 francs from its investors by 1906. By contrast, in December 1897 Pathé-Frères, initially set up to sell phonograph equipment, was transformed into a joint-stock company. This was a consequence of an injection of up to 1 million francs in capital stock and its partnerships with Claude Grivolas, a precision-tool factory owner, financier Jean Neyret and the Crédit Lyonnais bank. Méliès, meanwhile, had elected to internally finance expansion of Star-Film principally through film sales. By 1903–4, the strongly capitalised Pathé had already begun to outstrip Gaumont, as well as Méliès, in both international and domestic sales and the number of satellite offices. With the burgeoning popularity of the filmstrip, the French film producers realised that, with a monopoly on product, they could also control distribution and exhibition. Pathé was the first company worldwide to introduce the concept of film rental, thereby ensuring that the producer maintained control over the product. As there was insufficient domestic anti-competitive legislation or

enforcement to pose any legal obstacles, not only did Pathé and Gaumont quickly move to establish their own distribution networks, they also soon vigorously undertook the construction of their own cinemas to exhibit their product. It is often said that the French, specifically Pathé, introduced the concept of vertical integration, i.e. the bringing together of production, distribution and exhibition under a single corporate structure. However, this present-day concept, used to describe the acquisition, merging and integration of differentiated, though integrally related, operations in order to create synergies, efficiencies or cost savings, is perhaps less applicable to the Pathé of the early 1900s. While the Pathé company was no doubt organised as a business in the most profitable manner possible, its overriding primary objective was the monopolistic dominance of the new and fast-growing industry. As for Gaumont, it modelled itself on Pathé and soon began to vie with its larger French counterpart.

THE FRENCH FILM COMPANIES IN THE USA

By 1907, France had become the largest producer of movies in the world. In part this was due to the early commercial and technological prowess of the Lumières, Pathé and Gaumont, but their success also owed a great deal to the artistic endeavours of pioneer film-makers such as Alice Guy at Gaumont, Georges Méliès at Star-Film and later Ferdinand Zecca at Pathé. Ironically, this French domination of the international market – including the largest single market of all, the USA – was not solely a result of their own commercial efforts and artistic endeavours. For they also benefited substantially from Thomas Edison's monopolistic actions and exploitation of equipment patents. Edison's litigation against other American film producers inhibited American film output; most other American producers could ill afford the legal threat and expense of protracted legal battles with Edison. As a result, American film-makers were slower to start the production of narrative movies; indeed most historians date fiction films in the USA from 1903–4, coincidentally at a time when American film companies had legally won some freedom from Edison's grasp. With their vast production reserves, fuelled by their international sales, the French were

Open-air Pathé set (1910s)

legally unconstrained and freely distributed their wares in an American market hungry for product. As documented in a letter dated 20 February 1911 from George Eastman to Wm S. Gifford (preserved in the George Eastman House Collections in New York), by 1907 Pathé alone was responsible for between a third and a half of the film product distributed in the USA. Charles Musser has estimated that in total the Europeans were responsible for approximately two-thirds of the American film distribution market (Musser 1990: 488). If Pathé accounted for one-third, then the other non-American players, particularly Gaumont, accounted for the other third.

Many crucial questions regarding the most significant power play in the early film industry – between the French and the Americans in the USA – have been left unanswered by historians. As suggested earlier, this is in some measure due to missing or incomplete documentation and data. A forensic examination of material relating to this period reveals a fresh picture of the forces causing the shift in power within the American film industry from the French companies to the Edison consortium, and a new understanding of the motivations, relationships, decisions and strategies affecting the struggle between the French and American industries at this crucial moment in early cinema history. In the early 1900s, so pivotal was the commercial battle for supremacy between the Americans and French that the victor – the Americans – still dominates the international film industry today. One key historical question that remains to be answered is how and why, within such a short period of time, Pathé, the world's most powerful studio in 1907, so quickly relinquished its hold on the American film market, an outcome that would ultimately have profound consequences for the future of the French film industry in its totality. It is easy to understand why Edison would soon turn his attention from domestic rivals to foreign producers. Pathé alone was selling film in the USA at a rate of at least 30 to 40 million feet per year. If one multiplies the average price of this footage with an average price of 10 cents per foot, Pathé's estimated total sales were $3.5 million. Even at the most conservative projection of profits as a percentage of sales, Pathé's estimated profits based upon this total would be staggering when compared to Edison's profits from film sales of $116,912.23 for the financial year ended 29 February 1908. It is hardly surprising, then, that Edison should have set out to systematically crush the French competition in the USA, in the first instance through the formation of the Motion Picture Patents Company, a consortium of film companies or 'Licensees' allowed to utilise equipment whose patents were held by the MPPC.

THE EDISON CONSORTIUM

It would have been a dangerous supposition for Edison to presume he could maintain sway over the American film industry simply through litigation to enforce his patents, given that Pathé, the industry powerhouse, could easily absorb the legal costs and indefinitely prolong the proceedings. In order for Edison's risky strategy to succeed, it was crucial to split the ranks of the three leading French fiction-film producers, Pathé, Gaumont and Méliès. First he co-opted Méliès by offering him Licensee status in the MPPC. His aim was no doubt to do the same with either Gaumont or Pathé, thereby disrupting a potential French consortium. The overriding aim of limiting competition from outside the USA was openly discussed by Edison with his American MPPC Licensees. George Spoor of Essanay, among others, wrote to George Scull of Edison raising his objections to the granting of a licence to even such an apparently weak choice as Méliès. Edison, however, had recognised that although Méliès was the weak link in the French franchise in terms of output, his name was a brand that was well known to American and international audiences. By co-opting him, Edison strategically neutralised the possibility of Méliès acting as mediator between the competitive rivals Pathé and Gaumont, who, combined, were the French and

American market leaders at this time. So in fact Edison's early offer to Méliès of Licensee status in the MPPC was astute. It effectively removed Méliès from the French equation and, as an added benefit, perhaps allayed any possible anti-trust or anti-competitive concerns. But Edison still had to contend with the potential combined force of Pathé and Gaumont. Strategically, Edison decided to attempt to draw onto his side the largest French producer, the company capable of wielding the greatest power against him. Beguiling Pathé with attractive offers of partnership, Edison drew Pathé into negotiations and marginalised Gaumont. No doubt Edison was aware of Pathé and Gaumont's antagonistic relationship, and his move to exclude Gaumont could only have fuelled their rivalry, to the American's advantage.

While Edison's divisive approach would appear to have been robustly effective, Pathé was still a significant force to be reckoned with. A fundamental question remains to be answered: why did Pathé, the undisputed industry leader, capitulate in the negotiations and become a Licensee? It would only be a matter of months, during this key period from 1907 to 1908, before the power in the American film industry – and, as a long-term consequence, in the international marketplace – would shift from Pathé (and the French) to the Edison consortium (and the Americans). A cursory reconstruction of Pathé–Edison negotiations and a cross-matching of meeting times, travel itineraries, correspondence and dates of legal rulings show patterns emerging that hint at the possible motivations behind Pathé's and Edison's decisions. It would seem that Pathé had been undeterred by an earlier legal ruling – encompassing two decisions, only one of which was favourable to Edison – handed down in March 1907. Edison's subsequent approach to Pathé with a distribution and production deal, which the latter turned down, further indicates that Pathé's legal position and leverage had remained strong, regardless of the ruling. The conventional explanation for Pathé's capitulation is that after a few years of litigation, the first significant adverse ruling – from the Chicago Court of Appeals in October 1907 – caused Pathé to fold its hand. Yet there were other avenues of appeal available to Pathé, many further legal tests of Edison that could be conducted in states other than Illinois, and so forth. Pathé and Edison had been involved in ongoing patent litigation since 1904, and a company of Pathé's wealth could easily have afforded a long legal battle.

PATHÉ, EASTMAN AND EDISON

What has perhaps been overlooked is that Pathé's return to the negotiating table may not have been principally due to Edison, but to the real power behind the national and international scenes – George Eastman. Whereas Edison attempted to maintain his hold over the American film industry through extensive litigation to enforce his camera equipment patents, Eastman absolutely dominated the film-stock market and could effect change throughout the industry to suit his purposes. It appears to have been Eastman who initially persuaded Edison to drop litigation against Pathé, then cajoled him in spring 1907 to join forces with the French company in order to eliminate any adversarial forces that might hinder the expansion of Eastman's market. Edison initially took Eastman's advice to pursue Pathé, but Pathé balked at the terms of Edison's offer to become the French company's distributor in the USA. Eastman engineered the next move: it is likely that he, rather than Edison, as is historically accepted, was the catalyst behind the licensing strategy. In a letter dated 2 December 1907 to one M. B. Phillip preserved in the George Eastman House Collections, Eastman acknowledges his role in the impending Licensee agreements. Importantly, Eastman promised Pathé that if the French company became a Licensee, his company would cease to supply Pathé's non-American competitors with film stock. When Eastman reneged on his offer, Pathé withdrew from negotiations with Edison.

It is often suggested that Pathé signed on with the initial Edison Licensees, but no contract has been found yet to support this contention. The earliest archived agreement in which Pathé's name appears is dated 8 February 1908, but this document is merely an unsigned draft. In his letter of 11 February 1908 to George Eastman preserved in the MPPC Collection at the Edison National Historic Site in New Jersey, Jacques Berst, Pathé's general manager, states that the only reason Pathé would accept a licence and 'thereby permit Edison to make

an enormous amount of profit with the royalty, would be to keep foreign competition out. I, therefore, do not see why you should give these European people favours in regard to our market.' When Pathé withdrew, Eastman pulled out as well. This turn of events is yet another example of Pathé's continuing leverage in its negotiations with Edison, as well as its indispensable importance to Eastman as the latter's biggest volume customer. That the Edison–Pathé and Edison–Eastman contracts were finally signed on the same day, 20 May 1908, further attests to Pathé's importance – Eastman and Pathé were both indispensable to Edison's monopolistic designs. In other words, Edison had insufficient influence over either Eastman or Pathé in May 1908 to effect their signing; it took Pathé's signature to bring Eastman to the table.

The coincidental date of Eastman and Pathé's entry into the Edison consortium invites two remaining questions: what power did Pathé actually wield, and why did it finally sign on as Licensee? As already mentioned, Eastman offered little inducement to Pathé by reneging on its promise to restrict supply to Pathé's non-American competition. In fact, Pathé chose not to take what would have seemed a logical and potent step: to align itself with the American Biograph and Mutoscope Company ('Biograph') and the agent George Kleine, who had joined forces in 1908 as 'Biograph-Kleine' to offer an alternative to those exchanges and distributors who chose not to succumb to the legal threat exerted by Edison's Film Service Association (FSA), a consortium of American film exhibitors and distributors organised by Edison in early 1908 to exclusively exhibit and distribute his Licensees' product. Pathé's added weight behind the Biograph-Kleine consortium would have rivalled Edison and his Licensees. Not only did Pathé have the finances to fight any lawsuits on behalf of those connected with a prospective consortium, Biograph also held its own camera patents (upheld in the March 1907 ruling), and Kleine had the necessary complement of distributor/exhibitor relationships. From the Biograph-Kleine perspective, the quantity and popularity of Pathé's product would have made it worth sacrificing Kleine's other non-American producers, including Gaumont, if required by Pathé. But for reasons yet to be explained by historians,

Pathé did not pursue this seemingly attractive option. Instead, Edison moved to co-opt both Biograph and Kleine. As a result, it became crucial for Pathé to find a means to close off George Kleine, the American distributor of its French competitors.

Perhaps it was Pathé's inability to offset this implicit, or perhaps explicit, threat – that Edison could effectively opt to look to Kleine and its relatively extensive foreign customer base to augment supply – that finally induced Pathé to sign on as Licensee. It is clear from a review of the progressive changes to the original Edison Licensee agreements of 31 January 1908, and to subsequent draft proposals to Pathé and Eastman that significant negotiations were under way between Pathé, Eastman, and Edison regarding Pathé's competitors. The number of Licensees was originally envisaged as seven in total, including Pathé, but the Edison–Eastman contract of 20 May 1908 indicated that additional Licensees might now be added. The final limitation of the potential number of total Licensees to nine is telling. If Pathé were the seventh signatory, this leaves the three remaining major players on the scene – Biograph, Kleine and Gaumont – to fill the two outstanding slots. Given the most imminent threat posed by the Biograph-Kleine trust, Edison most probably had them in mind as the two final Licensees. When they did finally sign, the restriction of Kleine to two foreign customers – Gaumont and Urban-Éclipse, whose weekly film footage of new subject matter for the American market was strictly limited to 2,000 and 1,000 feet respectively – indicates that Edison compromised with Pathé. The full explanation of Pathé's decision to become a Licensee may only come to light with the eventual cataloguing of the entire Pathé archives. Meanwhile, what is evident is that the unusual complexity of detail in the 18 December 1908 MPPC–Edison–Pathé agreement, which superseded the 20 May 1908 contract, attests to elaborate negotiations between Pathé and Edison.

THE FRENCH FILM INDUSTRY IN THE 1910s

Despite its fall from dominance in the American market, Pathé maintained a formidable position at home and in all foreign markets except the USA

during this period. When Eastman lobbied the International Congress of Film Producers during its annual meeting held in Paris in early February 1909 to form a European consortium modelled on that of Edison's Licensees, Pathé successfully resisted (Eastman had unsuccessfully proposed the same idea the previous year as well). Despite Pathé's and the other major European film producers' reliance on Eastman's superior film stock, Eastman could not wield the same power as it had in the USA. But the long-term consequences to Pathé, both international and domestic, of its decision to become a Licensee cannot be underestimated. When Pathé relinquished its pre-eminent position in the USA, it opened the door for its competitors to challenge the company not only in the international marketplace but also at home. By agreeing to share more equitably the American market with the other Licensees, Pathé's potential growth and profitability were curtailed. In addition, the burgeoning American Independents soon began to erode Pathé's market share in the USA, along with that of the other Edison Licensees. The individual Licensees, and soon thereafter the Independents – not to mention other non-American film companies – also moved aggressively to expand their distribution internationally. Furthermore, Pathé faced increasing competition from the growing number of French film companies. By 1914, prior to the beginning of World War I, Urban-Éclipse, Société Lux, Éclair, Film d'Art and Gaumont constituted the largest and most successful members of this group; the total number of French film companies was around thirty. Pathé at this point was one of four major French distributors – Gaumont, Aubert and AGC were the others – of domestic and foreign product in France, including films from the USA, Italy, Denmark and Sweden. Despite their status as France's leading exhibitors, Gaumont and Pathé could no longer exclude or marginalise foreign product by pushing through their own films. The ratio of film footage exhibited in the French capital by mid-1914, for example, was four to one in favour of foreign product, a disconcerting indication of the direction of French audience taste.

Pathé – and, by extension, the French – would be most dramatically affected by two critical events, commencing with the anti-competitive legal proceedings instituted by the American government in the first half of the 1910s against the MPPC and its Licensees, including Pathé. As a result of the negative ruling, General Film, the distribution and exhibition network set up by Edison to distribute the Licensees' product, was broken up. Pathé, like the other Licensees, now had to start afresh to secure American distribution on a new playing field dominated by the American Independents. The second critical event was the outbreak of World War I in August 1914 and the consequential halt of film production in Europe. It seems reasonable to surmise that the level of production at Pathé's New Jersey studio was insufficient to allow the company to compete with the increasingly successful Independents in the American market. Neither Pathé nor Gaumont had sufficient product to fight off the foreign competition from non-French producers at home, let alone in the USA. Perhaps if Pathé and/or Gaumont had decided to establish a new studio in Hollywood alongside the American Independents, the French would have been able to regain some of their former glory within the American marketplace, and might as a result have been in a position to repatriate more product to France and Europe after the war. But to establish whether either company at this time was indeed in a viable financial position to do so would require access to company balance sheets and financial records for the period, which are currently unavailable or not archived.

By the end of World War I, the French faced a fast-changing marketplace in which they no longer set the pace. The French market was flooded with American product, whose hallmark was a driving, straightforward narrative line, typically with an emphasis on action and a happy ending. It was a form that international audiences increasingly embraced. The French, particularly Pathé and Gaumont, may still have controlled exhibition in France but they were faced with ever-increasing audience demand for American movies. Besides, there was a dearth of French product. By 1918–19, approximately three-quarters of all films exhibited in France were American. Initially, French distributors, again mainly Pathé and Gaumont, handled the American business directly, but then American studios such as Paramount, Universal and Fox soon creamed off the best of their product and established their own distribution offices in Paris, setting up alliances among the French distributors. On the other side of the Atlantic, where French films had remained popular prior to the war, they now experienced increasing difficulties finding an audience as the French studios struggled to establish significant distribution pipelines. Ironically, despite Gaumont's pre-eminent technological lead from as early as 1902 in the manufacture of sound film, it was the emergence of the talkies from 1927 onwards that definitively closed the vast American market to the French industry. Gaumont, Pathé and Méliès had all failed to establish a major studio presence in the emerging capital of the film industry in the USA – Hollywood – and so, with the coming of sound, the French companies were not in a position to produce English-language films. Never again would French cinema find a significant mainstream audience in the USA.

WORKS CITED

Musser, C. (1990) *The Emergence of Cinema: The American Screen to 1907*, vol. 1: 'History of the American Cinema', New York, Charles Scribners.

Sauvage, L. (1985) *L'Affaire Lumière*, Paris, L'Herminier.

3 TECHNOLOGY 1890–1930
The Drive to Mechanisation and Digitisation

Alison McMahan

The technological history of French cinema in this early period is often limited to accounts of cinema's invention in the 1890s and its later transition to sound in the 1920s. This chapter proposes three alternative approaches to the subject. First, it situates the invention of cinema in relation to the science of motion studies, in particular the technological devices intended to study flight. Second, it demonstrates that the relationship between recorded sound and recorded pictures long predates the arrival of optical sound and the talkies in the late 1920s. Finally, it examines in parallel the early histories of cinema and animation, particularly in the light of digitisation at the dawn of the 21st century. These three approaches share a common premise: namely that the history of cinema can be seen as part of a broad industrial drive to mechanisation, the drive to measure, quantify and ultimately automate every aspect of life. Looked at in this way, cinema, flying machines, motion studies, sound recording and animation are inextricably linked, as all were products of this general movement towards mechanisation and, eventually, digitisation.

MOTION PICTURES AND MOTION STUDIES

The pioneers of the science of motion studies, such as Étienne-Jules Marey and Eadweard Muybridge, had one goal in mind: to produce a visual record of motion, whether it be a man walking or a woman lifting a child, in order to be able to break each motion down and study it. The results of such analysis would facilitate the training of soldiers and provide an aid to the practice of medicine. Scientists who specialised in motion studies were also interested in the movement of the planets, the flight of birds and the movement of air currents. The overall goal of motion studies was to make visible

forces that are not immediately evident to the human eye. Once made visible, the information had to be stored so that it could be re-created, or re-played, for further study. At first scientists such as Marey sought to reproduce captured motion graphically. Marey invented the Cardiographe, which traced the contractions of the human heart, the Thermographe, which registered changes in body temperature, the Pneumographe, which registered changes in respiration, and the Polygraphe, designed for use in hospitals, which combined the transcription of pulse rate, heart rate, respiration and muscular contraction. He created devices to record graphically the walk of a person, another for the gait of a horse and yet another to record the movement of insect wings and the flight of birds. The idea that was popular in most aerodynamic circles in 1870, when Marey conducted his first bird studies, was the concept of the ornithopter, or a flying device modelled on birds, although some favoured the idea of a rotating blade that would screw upwards, as in a helicopter. But great minds like Leonardo da Vinci and Otto Lilienthal had favoured ornithopters. And in order to build an ornithopter it was necessary to study the flight of birds.

In 1872, Alphonse Penaud, one of the unsung heroes of aerodynamics (he invented the helicopter in 1876, though he was never able to build one), co-operated with Marey to construct a mechanical bird (Marey had previously built a mechanical insect). It is not clear how successful this model was, but apparently more work must have been required, since Penaud then suggested that instead of recording the flight of birds graphically, they should be photographed, using the 'photographic rifle' recently invented by astronomer Pierre-Jules César Janssen. Janssen was a member of a team that travelled to Japan in 1874 to witness the passage of Venus across the face of the sun, an event that only occurs twice each century. He spent two years preparing a photographic device to register the event. The 'rifle' registered images on a light-sensitive wheel. His second version was able to register forty-eight images in seventy-two seconds and successfully took pictures of Venus crossing the face of the sun. These images enabled him to prove one of his theories, that the solar corona was in fact an attribute of the sun itself and not an effect of looking at the sun through the Earth's atmosphere. Janssen's rifle was used to photograph solar eclipses for many years.

At first Marey was reluctant to switch to photography for his motion studies. However, the publication of Muybridge's photographic series of racehorses, taken with a sequence of still cameras lined up on a course rigged with camera cables that were triggered by the horse's movement, encouraged him to move in this direction. In 1883 Marey was awarded funds by the French government to establish a centre for motion studies with his associate, Georges Demeny. At first Marey used single large fixed plates on which a series of images would be imprinted; however, the overlap in these images made it difficult to decipher the motions he wished to study. But on 29 October 1888 he presented the chronophotographe sur bande mobile, a motion-picture camera that could register up to twenty images a second. Because the roll of paper was unperforated, it was impossible to make the images equidistant, which rendered it unreliable in the capture and projection of true motion-picture images. But this did not concern Marey, because his interest was the study of locomotion and not motion-picture projection. By 1890, however, celluloid (the result of

research by inventors all over the world but primarily commercialised by George Eastman) had become widely available. Marey patented his camera for use with celluloid on 3 October 1890. Now he and Demeny began to produce motion pictures in earnest, always with the purpose of studying locomotion. Unlike Muybridge, Marey was sensitive to public opinion and so avoided photographing women; most of his films feature nude male athletes going through various athletic moves such as jumping, leaping, using a baton, etc., and one film was made of ocean waves. Until 1892 Marey studied his images of locomotion by cutting them out and then attaching them equidistantly inside a Zoëtrope, a cylindrical device with slits in it. When the user rotated the cylinder and watched through the slits, the images inside the cylinder appeared to move. By May of 1892 Marey began to recognise the need for real projection, and he started to work on a chronophotographic projector in earnest. By November of 1892 many of his colleagues considered that the projector he had developed resolved the problems of projecting movement. However, Marey's projector, like his camera, did not use a perforated-film system, which made it difficult to assure a steady movement.

Demeny continued to work on the improvement of his master's inventions, and he was also eager to commercialise them. In 1891 Demeny gave a demonstration of his Phonoscope at the Musée Grévin. The Phonoscope was a projector designed to reproduce the living manner of a subject as s/he pronounced short phrases. The images were taken with Marey's Chronophotographe and then laboriously transferred to a glass disc, from which they could be projected or observed through the Phonoscope peephole. Demeny also gave some thought to synchronising his Phonoscope images with a phonograph but apparently never pursued this. His original intention was to use the device to teach deaf-mutes how to speak, but he also hoped to commercialise it. However, Marey was not interested in this aspect of their joint research. After he parted company with Marey in 1894, Demeny formed a company to promote the Phonoscope and the other devices he had patented. Marey, aware that his Chronophotographe was necessary for the success of the Phonoscope (the two had to be linked

Chronophotography of a fencer by Étienne-Jules Marey (1890)

for projection), re-patented it in June 1893. But Demenÿ got around the problem by patenting his own *caméra chronophotographique*, which was Marey's camera but with one improvement: by using an oval-shaped reel the film could be unwound in a more regular manner. This solution was not completely satisfactory, however, as the speed varied when the film unwound, but it solved the problem of having to deal with Marey. By then approaching Gaumont and co-operating with him in the development of a motion-picture camera and projector, Demenÿ crossed over from developing devices that studied movement to perfecting cameras that projected movement. Gaumont purchased the rights to Demenÿ's patents for the Phonoscope (patented in 1891) and the Biographe (patented in 1893) after Demenÿ had tried in vain to interest the Lumière brothers in them. Demenÿ's patent of 10 October 1893 became the basis for the Gaumont 60mm camera, also called a Chronophotographe, which was perfected in the first few months of 1896. According to the memoirs of Alice Guy Blaché, the first woman film-maker, who had started out as a secretary for Léon Gaumont, it was during this period, sometime before May 1896, that she wrote, produced and directed her first fiction film. She does not specify which camera she used, but it is most likely to have been the Demenÿ–Gaumont 60mm camera (Guy 1976: 25).

At the same time, the Lumière brothers were busy working on a Cinématographe of their own invention. The Lumière camera used 35mm film and they had solved the problem of stabilising the film as it unwound by perforating the celluloid with sprocket holes along the edges and using these to hold the film in place with a registration claw while each individual frame was exposed. Because the Lumières solved the registration problem and were credited as the first to project films to a paying public (although the Skladanowky brothers in Germany had done this somewhat earlier), and because their 35mm format is still the principal cinematographic format to this day, they are usually regarded as the inventors of the motion picture. While the December 1895 date remains a convenient marker for the beginning of moving-picture history as we know it, the fact is that many inventors, including Marey, Demenÿ, Reynaud and Gaumont, among others, were all trying to solve the problem of capturing and projecting motion with moving images, a process that had begun with the desire of scientists to solve the problem of flight. The motion-picture cameras appeared just in time to film the first successful flights of dirigibles and aeroplanes. The same motion studies that had produced the cameras had demonstrated the futility of ornithopters and helped scientists conduct studies in drag, velocity and wind tunnels that would lead eventually to flight.

SOUND BEFORE SOUND

In histories of the cinema, progress towards colour film with synchronised sound is often interpreted as an unstoppable evolution towards increased realism. This insistence on perceiving the history of cinema as a steadily evolving technology has led film historians to overlook a vital chapter in the history of synchronised sound. In fact, the drive to colour and especially synchronised sound is another manifestation of the impetus to full mechanisation. Synchronisation and the optical soundtrack resulted not from audience demand for increased realism but from capitalist and industrial pressures to homogenise product and control distribution and exhibition. To put it another way, movies were never silent, they were only imperfectly mechanised. The earliest known synchronised film to exist is the *Dickson Experimental Sound Film*, made in late 1894 or early 1895, or perhaps even earlier. The film has been known to film scholars and archivists for many years, but in spite of its title no one was sure that it had ever really had a soundtrack. The successful restoration of the film in 1999 resulted in perfect synchronisation between Dickson's violin, as he plays an air from Pietro Mascagni's *Cavalleria Rusticana*, and the sound of the two dancing men's feet on the wooden boards. Although Dickson succeeded in recording the sound and image of his film simultaneously, it is doubtful that the film was ever shown in its synchronised form. The post-synchronised sound films such as the *phonoscènes* made for the Gaumont Chronophone, on the other hand, were recorded and filmed separately, but were exhibited regularly, properly synchronised, to paying audiences. And the Chronophone was not alone: in the USA there was the Cameraphone, the Cort-Kitsee Device and the Synchronophone. In

Auguste Lumière demonstrating speed of 'blue plaque' photographic film

England there was the Cinematophone, the Viva-phone and the Animatophone. In Germany, there was Messter's Biophon, Alfred Dusker produced a Cinephon, Karl Geeyr built the Ton-biograph for the company Deutsche Mutoskop und Biograph GmbH and Guido Seeber developed the See-berophon, later using Messter's synchronophon as a technical model for the German Bioscop. Accord-ing to Michael Wedel (1998), after the demise of Messter's Tonbilder, synchronised music films con-tinued to be produced in Germany from 1914 to 1929 on the Beck system, the Lloyd-Lachman Device and the Notofilm system.

The proliferation of devices is matched by placid expectation in the editorials: for example, from around 1906 to the mid-1910, *The Moving Picture World* discussed widespread synchronised sound film production and distribution as if it were just over the horizon, an inevitable and natural occur-rence. If we retell the history of cinema in light of these early synchronised sound systems, would it not be more logical to claim that the cinema of attractions – these spectacle films without a sound-track – was really a poor man's sound cinema? What if the attractions aesthetic was just one stylistic option in a sound cinema that was imperfectly mechanised? To begin with, a certain type of 'attrac-tions' film – those that most resemble filmed vaude-ville acts – and early synchronised sound films shared the same aesthetic. Consider the *phonoscènes* made for the Gaumont Chronophone: these were usually filmed versions of opera performances or of popular songs from the *cafés-concerts*. They are shot proscenium style, with the camera taking the point of view of a spectator seated in the centre of an auditorium, between five and ten rows back. The performers are mostly seen in long shot, i.e. from head to toe, and much of the stage and backdrop are included in the frame. In rare cases the camera moves a little closer so that the performer is seen from ankle to head, although much of the backdrop is still visible. And on very rare occasions the per-former is shot in a medium shot or even a medium close-up. Occasionally, some kind of vignette is used to produce a close-up effect, or the actor is shown in close-up without the vignette. In other words, a comparison of post-synchronised sound films and many of the cinema of attractions films, especially those 'attractions' films whose diegesis evidently calls for sound, reveals that the only difference lies in the origin of their soundtracks: either mechanised or non-mechanised. Clearly, certain types of silent films, such as those with diegetic sound events like explosions or dance films, were meant to be shown with sound added at the exhibition venue. These films displayed a low level of mechanisation, which might be enhanced by the addition of printed speeches for the narrator or arrangements or orches-tral scores for the musicians. Seen in this light, early silent films and early sound films are part of the same continuum in a period of cinema's history when mechanisation was the driving force behind technological changes. In other words, films pro-duced with various degrees of mechanisation, at the level of both colour and sound, existed side by side.

All of these post-synchronised sound systems fell out of favour at about the same time, in the mid-1910s. This supports my argument that by then these systems represented imperfect mechanisation and so were gradually replaced by double systems (sound recorded with picture but played back on a separate track) and optical sound systems (soundtrack incor-porated into the image band). The Gaumont Company continues to serve as an example: Léon Gaumont was slow to lose his faith in his Chrono-phone system. He promoted it tirelessly for over twenty years, from the first presentation in 1902 to 15 June 1922, when he gave a public demonstration of the improvements at the Gaumont Theatre, to which the press responded enthusiastically. However, in 1925 the Gaumont Company formed a partnership with the Danish Electrical Fono Films Company that represented Peterson and Poulsen. Their aim was to exploit a double-band system called 'Gaumont, Peterson & Poulsen' and their research resulted in the projection of the first synchronised feature film in France on 13 October 1928, Marcel Vandal's *L'Eau du nil*. However, the double-band system proved not to be commercially feasible and was abandoned in favour of optical sound, in which the Gaumont Company invested heavily from 1929 onwards. Léon Gaumont himself retired in August 1929.

I have chosen to concentrate on sound tech-nology, but a similar argument can be made for the progressive mechanisation of colour. At first, colour was applied by hand onto each individual 35mm frame with a paintbrush – a job done primarily by women working in factory settings. Soon stencil processes, in which three different layers of colour were applied progressively to each filmstrip, were developed by companies such as Pathé. Tinting and toning, which applied colour to the entire negative or to the silver elements only, were also widely adopted, usually only on selected films in each manufacturer's catalogue, with cheaper black-and-white prints always remaining an option, until completely mechanised colour became the standard.

ANIMATION, CINEMA AND DIGITAL CINEMA

The history of animation is usually kept separate from the history of cinema, or it becomes a sub-section of that story. However, when cinema and animation are looked at, not in isolation but in terms of what roles they play in the movement towards mechanisation, it soon becomes clear that animation is not a sub-species of cinema, but rather that both were born out of the same drive to capture, store and replay motion at will. Cinema and animation were always much more intricately related than is commonly accepted. It appears that their paths diverged after 1907, when live-action trick films using stop-motion, such as those made by Georges Méliès, fell out of favour, though live-action films continued to rely on the techniques of animation for their special-effects sequences. When we look closely at the history of certain nineteenth-century mechanised media, such as the case of Émile Reynaud, it is clear that what we now call 'digitisation' was already the goal. Reynaud was making animated bands for his Praxinoscope as early as 1877. The Praxinoscope was based on earlier optical devices like the Zoëtrope, but used a cluster of revolving mirrors to project the series of images that were animated by the movement of a revolving drum. In 1879 Reynaud refined his invention by superimposing the moving drawings onto the scenery of a little proscenium theatre. The whole device was no bigger than a doll's house and could only be enjoyed by one or two people at a time. From 1892 to 1900 he rear-projected more elaborate bands, which he now called *pantomimes lumineuses*, onto a screen by means of a complicated mirror-and-lens system. The images were hand-painted on long strips of

transparent celluloid and fitted into a leather band with perforations next to each frame; in other words, his apparatus in many ways prefigured that of cinematic projection, though all of the images were hand-drawn and coloured by Reynaud himself. He also supplied narration and vocal sound effects during his performances, along with music played by a phonograph or live musicians. This was animation with almost no mechanisation.

The production of animation itself gradually became more mechanised. At first artists like Émile Cohl, who began making animated films for Gaumont and Lux in 1908–9, and his American counterpart, Windsor McCay, had to produce every drawing for an animated film by hand. The laboriousness of this process was often highlighted in the films themselves, and live action and animation were combined in order to achieve the standard one-reel length while remaining within budget. As a result the animator himself, or at least his hand, appeared in the cartoon, which was often framed with opening and closing live-action scenes. In 1910 the philosophy of Taylorism, or scientific management, was gaining widespread popularity in the USA. Frederick Taylor had proposed a 'science of systems' or work efficiency for factories in the 1880s, which Louis Brandeis had applied with great success to the railroads in 1910. This period coincided with the establishment of many animation studios in the USA, and John Bray, an animator with a regular production contract with Paramount studios, patented a series of inventions and, most importantly, a system of scientific management for animation studios. The idea was to automate the process so that a maximum number of unskilled labourers could be used for smaller tasks, and to plan the work of the skilled labour in such a way that their time was used most profitably. Bray established a strict hierarchical chain of command, spelled out the daily tasks for everyone on his staff, penalised those who did not finish the assigned work and rewarded with bonuses those who finished ahead of time. This was in sharp contrast to the earlier workshop arrangements, but since animation studios were just getting established, the system of scientific management became the norm, and remains so to this day (even though scientific management fell out of fashion in other industries by the late 1910s). This concept of the scientific management of the animation studio spread to Paris in 1921 thanks to the animator Lortac (real name Robert Collard), who had observed the process at work in New York. Two-dimensional animation suffered in Europe during World War I, although some animators such as Lortac managed to survive by producing commercials and public service films. Many French artists joined the French film-making community in Fort Lee, New Jersey, which was the centre of American film-making before the emergence of Hollywood. Émile Cohl migrated to the USA in 1913, where he worked with other French expatriates such as Victorin Jasset and Étienne Arnaud at the Éclair Studio. According to Donald Crafton, Cohl was responsible for disassociating animation from the trick-film genre (Crafton 1993: 61). Unfortunately, the only films that survive from his years in the USA are *He Poses for His Portrait* (1913), which used speech balloons, and *Bewitched Matches* (1913), a stop-motion film with matches as characters, an effect that was copied by René Clair in *Entr'acte* in 1924. Cohl's work also influenced another Surrealist film-maker, Fernand Léger, who included an animated Charlie Chaplin cutout in *Ballet mécanique* (1923–4). In spite of these efforts, Europe in general failed to produce a viable animation industry, though many individual artists managed to produce works of great beauty and ingenuity, such as Lotte Reiniger and her work with shadow puppets in Germany from 1918 to 1936.

However we choose to look at the relationship between cinema and animation during the last hundred years or so, there is no question that their paths were joined at the beginning of their history and that they are coming together again in the 21st century. The nineteenth-century drive towards mechanisation has become the drive to digitisation. There are three basic modern techniques for creating a digital character: key framing, motion capture and simulation. Each technique varies in the amount of control it gives the animator and in how much work the computer does on its own. More control means less mechanisation in the animation process. The term key framing comes from traditional two-dimensional animation, in which the animator specifies key positions for the object or character being animated. Originally, another animator, but now a computer, would then fill in the missing frames by interpolating between one position and another. In motion capture, vision-based sensors record the actions of a human or animal subject in three dimensions. A computer then uses the data to animate a character. Simulation employs the laws of physics to generate the motion of figures and other objects. Virtual humans are usually represented as a collection of rigid body parts.

Key framing, as already indicated, is a classic technique of hand-drawn animation, and was the principal method applied to the charming looping movements on Phénakistiscopes, Phantasmascopes, Zoëtropes and Praxinoscopes. When Muybridge made his celebrated series of images of a horse galloping, he was simply making a Zoëtrope band with photographs instead of hand-drawn images. As for Marey and Demenÿ, they used an early version of motion capture: Demenÿ or other test subjects would wear black body socks marked with white dots so that only the dots were recorded by the camera as the subject moved. Reynaud also applied a form of digitisation similar to motion capture. In 1896 he adapted Marey's Chronophotographe to make a motion-picture camera-projector and produced a handful of films. The first of these was a classic vaudeville act by two clowns, Footit and Chocolat (black or in blackface), loosely based on an episode of William Tell: Chocolat has an apple on his head and takes bites out of it; Footit shoots it off with a water rifle, soaking Chocolat in the process. Once Reynaud had the film – shot at sixteen frames a second – he took a few frames from one part and a few frames from another. These short selected sequences were then reproduced on the transparent celluloid, improved by drawing and colouring applied by hand and then strung into a sequential loop by joining them within a perforated flexible metal band. Reynaud repeated this process with two other early digitisations, one entitled *Le Premier cigare (mimodrame comique)*, in which a university student tries his first cigar and finds it comically sickening, and another vaudeville act featuring a pair of clowns, called *Les Clowns Prince (scène comique)*, made in 1898, which was never shown to the public. Unfortunately, none of these early efforts survive. A similar method was used in 1899–1900, by the Brothers Bing of Nuremberg, along with other German toy firms, Planck, Bub and Carette, and the French Lapierre Company, all of whom made cartoons for use in toy viewers based on live-action films. These toy cartoon animators invented a form of 'rotoscoping', tracing from live-action films, such as *L'Arroseur arrosé* (1898), Méliès's *The Serpentine Dance* (1901), Ernst Planck's *Skiers, Jumping Clowns, Clown and Dog* and *Rider* (all by Ernst Planck, all 1910). Rotoscoping continued to be important in animation films until the advent of digital motion capture. Films such as Disney's *Snow White* (1943) relied on rotoscoping extensively, though the animators were reluctant to admit to it.

A closer examination of trick-film techniques shows that they can be considered a mechanical version of modern computer simulation techniques. These techniques were then applied to animation using puppetry and models (adjustable figures built around armatures). Trick films made before 1908 by artists such as Méliès, working in his own studio, and Ferdinand Zecca and Segundo de Chomón, working for Pathé, included processes such as stop-substitution (stopping the camera and replacing a beautiful princess with an old hag, or a horse with a toy); filming in slow motion, so that when projected at normal speed the film would appear speeded up; combining such fast-motion with a regular speed sequence through superimposition, so that some characters moved at comically fast speeds and others at a normal pace; cutting alternate frames out of a sequence to speed it up; shooting with the camera hanging upside down, so that the film when projected normally would play the action backwards; fade in and fade out of a figure in superimposition to simulate the apparition and disappearance of a ghostly figure; and the use of props such as removable limbs, miniature sets and miniature props. The list is much longer, but this gives an indication of the creativity of the film manufacturers working in live-action cinema before 1910. Similar tricks were adopted in Europe and applied to stop-motion animation, often using animatronic figures and puppets, which can be remotely controlled with cables, for example. Ladislas Starevitch, who was born in

Poland but did most of his work in France, made animated films using the carcasses of real insects such as grasshoppers and beetles, as well as the corpses of birds and other animals. He later began to work with puppets and continued to make animated films into the sound era. What makes Starevitch's films so powerful, even today, is the convincing emotional performance of his insect carcasses and later of his puppets and models. The techniques of imbuing an otherwise lifeless figure with a lifelike performance is applied in simulated animation figures to this day. Historians generally focus on the influence of early trick films on animation films in terms of content. But we must not forget that animation itself is a product of stop-motion, as each drawing is substituted by the next, shot on another bit of film, until the whole gives the impression of movement. It is at this point that we see cinema and animation going in apparently separate ways: stop-motion lost its popularity after the first decade or so of the 20th century, though it was still used for special effects; but animation continued to be based on the stop-motion principle. Now the two paths, relatively separate for most of the century, are coming back together as the drive towards mechanisation reaches its peak and is replaced by the drive to digitisation. In digitisation, as we have seen in films such as *L'Anglaise et le duc* (Éric Rohmer, 2001), *Le Pacte des loups* (Christophe Gans, 2001) and *Vidocq* (Pitof, 2001), cinema and animation are coming back together, forcing us to reconsider the true nature of both arts.

WORKS CITED

Crafton, D. (1993) *Before Mickey: The Animated Film 1898–1928*, Chicago, University of Chicago Press.

Guy, A. (1976) *Autobiographie d'une pionnière du cinéma (1873–1968)*, Paris, Denoël/Gonthier.

Wedel, M. (1998) 'Schizophrene Technik, Sinnliches Glück: Die Filmoperette und der synchrone Musikfilm 1914–1929', in Uhlenbrok, K. ed., *Musikspektakelfilm, Musiktheater und Tanzkultur im deutschen Film 1922–1937*, Munich, edition text+kritik, 85–104.

4 FORMS 1890–1930
The Shifting Boundaries of Art and Industry

Ian Christie

Film, whether hybrid or homogeneous, assumes all sorts of forms: the fantastic film, the sentimental film, the comic or dramatic film, buffoonery and acrobatics, the 'artistic' film and the serial, the scientific film, the police film, the 'historical' film, the moralising film, everything from the real to the imaginary, and sometimes 'enhanced by natural colours' . . . (Haugmard 1913: 79)

Consider two films from opposite ends of the period covered by this chapter: Louis Lumière's *Arroseur et arrosé* (1895–6) and Marcel L'Herbier's *L'Argent* (1928). A single-shot gag and a dramatic film that aspires to emulate the scope of a classic novel. One apparently simple; the other visibly complex. It is tempting to see the history of cinema, at least up to the 1930s, largely as a matter of 'progress', of filmmakers learning how to express and audiences to understand more sophisticated material. And yet, on closer examination, even these two bookends are not what they might seem. The Lumière film that we know today is in fact a 1896 remake of the previous year's *Le Jardinier et le petit espiègle*, proving that even the earliest demonstration films were not innocent of direction and, as in this case, often derived from existing popular graphic art. Thirty years later, L'Herbier had already devised elaborate mobile camera effects for his ambitious updating of Zola's novel when the impact of Hollywood's talkies made it desirable also to introduce sound, which he did with ambient noise recordings. The result was a film apparently overloaded by formal experimentation, yet already anachronistic in the light of the newer 'realisms' that were being promoted by documentarists and by the makers of the first synchronised sound dramas. Lumière's and L'Herbier's films can stand as boundary markers for the period still generally known as 'silent', even though the former certainly had piano accompaniment at its public premiere and the latter, as we have seen, was at least partly sonorised. On one level, the history of filmic form is unavoidably a history of invention and technical development. The Lumières' filming took place within narrowly defined technical constraints, such as the 18-metre length of filmstrip that could be exposed and the availability of sunlight, while their work was shown in a wide variety of improvised venues, as well as in variety theatres and fairgrounds. By 1928, in France as elsewhere, films routinely lasted over eighty minutes and were composed of hundreds of shots, most made with controlled artificial light. They were shown in thousands of cinemas, which ranged from simple halls to 'palaces' as lavishly appointed as opera houses, with musical accompaniment that varied from a solitary piano or gramophone to a full orchestra, while synchronised sound was beginning to be added, to create the distinctive ensemble of the feature film that is still the normal currency of cinema today.

If we ask what motivated or drove this development, the answer will usually invoke a mixture of commercial competition, innovation and artistic self-assertion, held together by an overarching concept of national cinema – in this case 'French'. Tacitly, such answers focus on French *production*, largely ignoring the fact that this falls dramatically across the period in question as a proportion of the total programming of French cinemas or of tickets bought, from over 90 per cent to less than 10 per cent. This is a general phenomenon of the 1920s, when all European countries saw their national production lose ground sharply to American imports, but the crucial difference for France was the loss of its early global lead, followed by a redefinition of its export market in terms of the avant-garde and identifiable 'Frenchness'. The idea of a steady technical-cum-expressive development of cinema across most of the silent period is what David Bordwell (1997) has aptly characterised as the 'basic story' of cinema history, supported by a 'standard version' of its aesthetic distinctiveness. But it was French critics, from the 1940s onwards, who began to question the adequacy of such a linear, positivistic view. First, Georges Sadoul (1946) greatly enlarged the scope of previous histories by devoting the first volume of his *Histoire générale du cinéma* to the precursors of Lumière, thus placing film per se in a longer continuum of optical invention and spectacle. Then André Bazin (1967), reacting both to Sadoul's account of pre-cinema and to the diverse contemporary trends of the 1940s represented by Welles's and Wyler's use of deep focus and Italian neo-realism, began in 1946 to sketch a normative view of cinema as essentially realist. For Bazin, the period of experiment and invention that preceded the Lumières' breakthrough indicated that the idea of cinema as a 'total' reproduction of reality heralded, and effectively guided, its actual invention. He then challenged the prevailing view that cinema's claim to artistic status depended on its growing ability to manipulate the recording of reality, arguing that such revered landmarks as German Expressionist cinema and the Soviet montage school should be considered instead deviations from cinema's intrinsically realist mission. Sadoul, meanwhile, established what has since become perhaps the most pervasive interpretative myth of cinema's origins: the dichotomy, or rather complementarity, of Lumière and Méliès, as progenitors of, respectively, documentary realism and theatrical fiction.

These are not the only French positions to have shaped both popular and academic film history. Surrealism, less as an artists' movement than as a polemical outlook, has had a pervasive influence out of all proportion to the film work of actual Surrealists. Indeed it is no exaggeration to say that the prevailing canon of world as well as French cinema history has been strongly marked by Surrealist taste, from the promotion of Méliès as an early exemplar of the 'marvellous' in its naive state and the cult of Feuillade's serials, up to the polarisation of attitudes towards French avant-garde film in the 1920s. Paul Hammond conveyed this polemical tone well in his introduction to a collection of Surrealist writings on cinema:

Not only did the Surrealists hold bourgeois art and culture in disdain, they found the aestheticism of the Gance faction, which limited itself to a palace revolution in technical novelty (and held American popular films, and the home-grown Feuillade productions in contempt), academic, contemptible. (Hammond 1978: 2)

Somewhat like the notorious Surrealist world map of 1929, in which such sites of the fantastic as Easter Island and Mexico loomed much larger than the homelands of conventional art, our inherited map of French cinema is distorted by a set of historic prejudices. And given the Surrealists' enduring hostility to everything French that they considered 'bourgeois', their few favoured French film-makers tended to be cast as mavericks or outsiders, while the self-professed experimenters and innovators were excoriated for their pretension.

No account of the evolution of forms up to 1930 can avoid engaging with these dominant narratives and valuations, even if to challenge them. In doing so, it can draw upon the work of the new early cinema movement that, since the early 1980s, has set itself against teleological argument ('the forerunner of . . .') and mythic claims of originality ('the first close-up . . .'), in favour of systematic empirical study of films from before 1913 in the context of their production and contemporary reception. It must also take particular note of the radical reinterpretation of cinema history proposed by Noël Burch, which was guided in large part by a close study of early French cinema as a mainstay of what he termed the 'primitive mode of representation' and of the 1920s French avant-garde, particularly L'Herbier, as a later site of resistance to the spread of a global 'institutional mode of representation' centred in Hollywood (Burch 1990: 186, 74). Here again is a stimulus to see form as doubly dialectical: a material product of competition and also an analytical 'product' of debate and polemic.

AN INVENTION WITH A PAST

In an interview at the time of *Le Mépris* (1963), which featured Louis Lumière's 'the cinema is an invention without a future' on the wall of a Cinecittà viewing theatre, Jean-Luc Godard jokingly emphasised the interrelationship of these two emblematic figures: 'Méliès is the greatest, but without Lumière he would have languished in obscurity' – a pun on 'lumière' also meaning 'light' (Godard 1972: 200). However familiar it has become, the traditional Lumière–Méliès dichotomy is distinctly misleading if we want to understand the evolution of film forms in a historical perspective. For neither of these were really inventors of forms, much less rivals, but rather adapters of the traditions in which they were already working. Unlike the earliest moving pictures, which were vaudeville acts filmed in 1894 on the stage of Edison's sunlit New Jersey studio, nicknamed the 'Black Maria', the first Lumière subjects were informed by the conventions of naturalistic photography: street scenes, family and domestic groupings, picturesque characters and places. They were also chosen with a photographer's awareness of how movement within the frame – a train approaching, people coming forward as a crowd or singly, a man vaulting onto a horse or being tossed in a blanket – would enhance their appeal. Audiences enjoyed their dynamism and their 'naturalness', especially in such atmospheric details as the rippling of waves and the smoke rising from a blacksmith's forge. Some of these were the same effects that Impressionist painting sought to capture, but instead of a new painterly language that demanded the spectator's active involvement, the Lumière 'views' remained overwhelmingly within existing photographic conventions. It is therefore anachronistic to speak of them as 'early documentaries', implying a kinship with the didactic conventions of future documentary; instead, as Pinel, Burch and Gunning have urged, we should accept Louis Lumière's disclaimer of artistic intention, and accept his genre scenes as an extension of the amateur photography movement that his company served. But this is not to say they were 'naïve' or entirely spontaneous. On the contrary, many have had specific sources identified from within the many other contemporary narrative and entertainment forms.

Most of the more than 2,000 titles that would eventually make up the Lumière catalogue appear to be single, unbroken shots, although recent research reveals that many have 'invisible' internal elisions, in order to compress their action. Moreover, these views, lasting just under a minute, were never shown singly, but usually in groups of eight or more (Ger-

stenkorn 1999). The basic Lumière form should perhaps therefore be regarded as a programme; and as the company's operators and franchisees spread out around the world, they developed a distinctive pattern of showing both 'stock' items from the back-catalogue and new material, often filmed near the place of exhibition. Such sequences or suites, capable of being varied to meet audience or occasional needs, evoke many similar cultural forms of the late 19th century, from the variety theatre and *café-concert* programme, to the 'album' formats increasingly used by composers following Schumann and Liszt, in France notably Debussy and Satie, and of course the typical magic-lantern slide-show. This last was the immediate precursor of the early moving-picture show, and at least until the early 1900s lantern slides would be included in many programmes, not only in travelling fairs but also in city theatre venues and even as part of the spectacular Lumière presentation at the 1900 Exposition Universelle in Paris. Other types of theatrical presentation common in late nineteenth-century Paris would also influence the course of moving-picture development, although in some cases not immediately. The shadow puppet theatre of the Cabaret du Chat Noir and the tradition of graphic caricature in popular magazines both influenced the pioneer animator Émile Cohl. The *cafés-concerts* produced many early film personnel, including Pathé's first head of production, Ferdinand Zecca, and their star acts were later reproduced in Gaumont's synchronised *phonoscènes*. Émile Reynaud's hand-painted *pantomimes lumineuses*, shown at the Musée Grévin wax museum from 1892, were the ancestors of later one-reel film comedies. However, it would be over ten years before scenic painting, or exterior shooting, would make possible the filmic presentation of an elaborate comic scene such as his *Autour d'une cabine, ou mésaventures d'un copurchic aux bains de mer* (1894).

The clearest case of moving pictures being used to enhance an existing form of entertainment is that of Georges Méliès, who was running the Robert-Houdin magic theatre when the Lumière cinematograph made its debut. Like the English theatrical illusionists who had influenced him, Méliès used an elaborate combination of optical and mechanical devices to present 'theatrical compositions' such as 'The Fairy of the Flowers' and 'American Spiritualistic Mediums, or the Recalcitrant Decapitated Man'. These sketches or playlets provided a narrative framework for magic effects, ranging from the poetic to the comic and the macabre – indeed often all of these combined. Transformations, disappearances, severed heads, skeletons and ghosts populated the world of Méliès's stage compositions; and after early open-air work in the same vein as the Lumières, they would become the staple of his films and their many imitations. The two main devices on which all such trick films depended were stop-motion and superimposition. By stopping the camera, and adding or subtracting something before continuing, 'magical' transformations could be performed without any of the subterfuge needed in the theatre. Equally, more elaborate sequences of transformation could be assembled, so that the early reproduction of a single stage routine developed between 1896 and 1900 into complex sequences of multiple transformation. This elaboration also depended on the trick film-makers' technique of re-exposing the same piece of film, superimposing layers of image that would register to the viewer as all part of the same scene. Maintaining this illusion required high precision and controlled conditions, which Méliès achieved by building a glass-house studio on the outskirts of Paris that would serve as the prototype of all such early studios.

Two contrasting types of film began to emerge from Méliès's studio. The most common was an elaborate form of fantasy, making full use of painted scenery, props and costumed performers, as well as stop-motion and superimposition, essentially to achieve the same effect as a pantomime or stage spectacle. *Cendrillon* (1899) ran for an unprecedented seven minutes and delivered, at least visually, what could only have been presented on stage by the largest city-centre theatres. Similar resources could also produce more futuristic and fanciful narratives, such as *Le Voyage dans la lune* (1902) and *Voyage à travers l'impossible* (1904), as well as working through the classic repertoire of pantomime subjects. The second new genre was the reconstruction of recent events, starting with a spectacular account of the Dreyfus affair that had split France since 1894. Controversy was at its height in 1899,

with the accused soldier brought back from Devil's Island for retrial, when Méliès made his longest film to date, *L'Affaire Dreyfus*. In this, and in *Le Sacre d'Edouard VII* (1902), Méliès turned his skill to creating plausible images that echoed (or anticipated, in the case of *Édouard VII*) contemporary illustrations of public events. What links these apparently different kinds of film is their construction as a series of self-contained tableaux, usually with printed titles. *Le Raid Paris–Monte Carlo en deux heures* (1904–5) was actually commissioned by the Folies Bergère to link sketches in a revue, then issued as an episodic film. Rather than look forward to the transitivity of narrative, Méliès remains within the semantic domain of illustration, expecting the audience to know the story already and enjoy its decorative elaboration. By 1905 his Star-Film had achieved international distribution and recognition, but this laborious mode of production, in which everything depended on the protean energies of Méliès himself, was already under threat from industrialised approaches to the medium.

Méliès's chief competitors were Charles Pathé and Léon Gaumont, both of whom entered moving-picture production in the late 1890s after experience of developing and selling the new photographic and sound-reproducing equipment. Both delegated the actual making of films to employees, and devoted themselves to the management of their rapidly growing business empires; but in doing so they also helped create new and influential kinds of film narrative. Although the large catalogues of these two companies would include many different kinds of film during the period up to 1914, certain genres become closely identified with the distinctive trademarks of Pathé's cockerel and Gaumont's daisy, notably the trick film and the chase comedy. Despite Pathé's extensive involvement in various trick-based films from as early as 1901, there is a history of all early conjuring films being automatically attributed to Méliès, as Paul Hammond (1981) noted in his shrewd analysis of this genre. Hammond explores how the Pathé version differed by comparing two typical productions from the year 1904: Méliès's *Le Coffre enchanté* and Pathé's *Japonaiserie*, the latter directed by another magician, Gaston Velle (and also known as *Magic Bricks*). Méliès's film uses a rapid succession of stop-action substitutions to weave variations on the traditional stage routine of disappearance and reappearance involving a woman and a trunk. The result, Hammond suggests, 'is a continuity that is both broken and not broken', essentially improving on – but not going beyond – the famous conjuror's illusion known as 'Pepper's Ghost' (Hammond 1981: 41–2). Pathé's *Japonaiserie* at first seems similar: a Japanese conjuror and assistants produce assorted mysterious objects, before the film's main spectacle is revealed. This is a wall of child's play bricks, on which various images magically appear and disappear as they seem to develop a life of their own. In Hammond's analysis, the Pathé/Velle film shows more interest in playing with the very notion of cinematic illusion than in the staged trick and, crucially, the film cuts to closer shots as its final subject becomes clear, losing the stage framing. Here we can see an important step from the 'cinema of attractions' represented by Méliès towards a form of narrative efficiency – in Burch's terms, a development within the 'primitive mode of representation' that presages the emerging 'institutional mode'.

Both Méliès and Pathé trick films would continue to develop in various ways until around 1910, putting illusion at the service of increasingly complex fairy-tale and fantastic narratives as audience interest moved beyond the simple stage-magic format. But during this period, Pathé was also developing a new form that would provide the basis for a more sophisticated understanding of 'real' space: the construction of 'point of view' by designating certain shots as subordinate to others. An early example of this occurs in *Ce que l'on voit de mon sixième* (1901), in which a middle-aged man is looking through a telescope from a balcony, while alternating shots show what he sees, framed by a circular mask. In this embryonic narrative, what arouses the protagonist's interest is the frisson of erotic discovery: after first spying a kissing couple, he scans the rooftops before discovering a woman about to undress. She, however, winks at the camera/audience before drawing her blind and the final shot is of the voyeur miming his, and by analogy the audience's, frustration. The crucial realisation, that such subjective or point-of-view images contain the seeds of narrative, was not unique to Pathé's film-makers – almost all such devices were

actually pioneered in England – but it was the French company that systematically developed them in the early 1900s. In its well-equipped studio, a staircase and landing set provided the essential device that allowed this discovery to become the underlying structure of many kinds of story film. A peeping tom could discover compromising scenes through the keyholes of a sequence of rooms; or in *Un coup d'oeil par étage* (1904) a concierge, also spying on tenants, could discover an apartment on fire and call the fire brigade, thus linking the 'keyhole' structure with another popular genre, the fire rescue drama. Soon fully fledged scenes within rooms would become the main dramatic content, and by 1907 coming and going on Pathé's staircase was a cliché, routinely removed by American distributors as 'padding', but it had served a vital transitional role in the international development of narrative grammar.

Léon Gaumont, Pathé's arch-rival, entrusted his early production to his secretary Alice Guy, and before the construction of a studio she had to make use of open-air settings, which resulted in her first film, *La Fée aux choux* (1897?), in which a voluptuous fairy produces babies in rapid succession from a cabbage patch, in naturalistic contrast to Méliès's theatrical fairy-tale style. Recent research has shown that many of Guy's subsequent films were actually remakes of Lumière subjects, such as *L'Arroseur arrosé* (1898) and *Les Cambrioleurs* (1898), with the latter using the same rooftop sets originally ordered for the Lumière production, *Poursuite sur les toits*, by Georges Hatot (McMahan 2002). The fact that Méliès also made a version of the same subject should underline how unwise it is to propose any radical opposition of 'styles' in this period. However, Guy seems to have retained a preference for street comedies, usually with a sharply satirical awareness of gender issues, as in *Madame a des envies* (1906), in which a visibly pregnant woman purloins vegetables from various shop displays and consumes these clearly phallic objects with relish in a series of interpolated close-ups that make this one of the earliest narratives in this form. Encouraged by Gaumont's frugality, later film-makers continued to improvise in the neighbourhood around the company's studios. Romano Bosetti's two street comedies of 1908, *Le Tic* and *Une Dame vraiment*

Musidora in *Fantômas* (Louis Feuillade, 1913–14)

bien, continue Guy's provocative theme: in the first, a peasant woman's uncontrollable winking invites endless attention, to the embarrassment of her husband; and the seductive lady of the latter turns so many heads that she has to be escorted home by two gendarmes, who also succumb. But more distinctive were Gaumont's comedies predicated on the dynamism of the chase. One of these, still widely quoted and illustrated, was *La Course aux potirons* (1908), in which a number of giant pumpkins fall off a cart in the city and appear determined to escape their owner, bouncing down streets and even into houses, before returning to the cart of their own accord.

This was not untypical of Gaumont's output – Guy's successor as head of production in 1907, Louis Feuillade, recalled 'eternal pursuits . . . with a constantly growing crowd that would be chasing a flying pumpkin or a postage stamp blowing on the

wind' – but *La Course aux potirons* also seems to illustrate the idea of a 'revolt of objects' so perfectly that it is not surprising to find a reference to it by the Surrealist poet Robert Desnos in 1923 (both quoted in Crafton 1990: 116, 326). A similar 'realism', which can easily become sur-real is apparent in other Gaumont trick-based comedies: *Le Ski* (1908), for example, combines the actuality of a factory chimney being demolished with a skier, apparently in mid-air, superimposed so as to imply that he has knocked it down. More bizarre, and characteristic of a fascination with 'body-altering' in the years before 1914, is *Le Bon invalide et les enfants* (1908), in which a group of boys are urged by an army veteran in a park to remove his limbs and head to play ball before returning them politely. The technical basis of this involves masking part of the frame with a matte, a device much used by Méliès, but here the tone is more pathetic than grotesque or merely farcical. As the single-reel film gave way to a two-reel standard, comedies and anecdotal dramas had to acquire more dramatic structure than a single conceit or trick to sustain their new length. One economical solution developed by Feuillade at Gaumont was to dispense with artifice and make a virtue of realism, which he did successfully in a series with the overall title *La Vie telle qu'elle est* (1911–13). In many respects, these can be seen as the vital prelude to Feuillade's most famous achievement, the crime series of the early 1910s: *Fantômas* (1913–14), *Les Vampires* (1915–16) and *Judex* (1916). Many myths have grown up around these talismanic works, some clearly inspired by the reproduction of striking images of hooded and cat-suited figures lying in wait for unsuspecting victims. In fact, these tableaux are relatively rare, usually marking the climax of an instalment, and the films' most striking feature is their muted suburban realism. When violence strikes, it is all the more shocking because of the mundane setting of familiar streets and villas. Nor are they cliffhanger serials, in the style of such American productions as *The Perils of Pauline* (1914), but actually prototype feature films, organised in self-contained parts. In this respect, they have more in common with the contemporary emergence of longer documentary-style crime films in the USA, such as George Loane Tucker's *Traffic in Souls* (1913) or Raoul Walsh's *The Regeneration* (1915).

Before pursuing the development of the longer film, it is necessary to turn back to two new forms of the late 1900s that would have important consequences in the decades to come. The first of these, the *film d'art*, is invariably associated with Pathé, who became its promoter after the collapse of a small company formed in 1908 by the Lafitte brothers with the aim of raising the cultural standard of cinema. Their first films, *L'Assassinat du duc de Guise* (1908) and *Le Baiser de Judas* (1908), set a high standard in all respects. Their literate scripts were performed in impeccable period settings by leading actors from the Comédie-Française, and both had dedicated musical scores: the former specially composed by Camille Saint-Saëns, and the latter drawing on Bach and Gluck. A series of equally cultivated subjects followed, *Carmen* (1909), *La Tosca* (1910), *Macbeth* (1910) and Sardou's

Madame Sans-Gêne (1911), before the company was taken over by Pathé and its model internationalised. Pathé now had branches throughout the world, and instead of these serving only to distribute French-made material, some were encouraged to mount 'local' *film d'art* productions. In at least one case, that of Russia, this resulted in several of the founding films of Russian cinema, with historical and literary subjects convincingly adapted for the first time. (Of equal international significance was Pathé's launch of a weekly multi-subject newsreel in 1910, which would stimulate rivals in many countries.)

Despite its clear importance, the *film d'art* episode was initially written into cinema history in almost uniformly negative terms. On the rare occasions that the films were seen (usually without their music), they were introduced as 'bad objects' – examples of where the emerging art of film began to go wrong, seduced by the trappings of theatre and bourgeois respectability. The source of this antagonism can be traced to the late-1920s purist tendency and its championing of filmic 'specificity'; and the fact that this was when synoptic cinema history began to be written has served to entrench disapproval of the *film d'art*. The legacy of the movement, however, is more complex, as its offshoots became a central feature of French production after 1909, bringing major theatre actors to the screen and creating a vogue for the adaptation of every kind of literature, ranging from Dumas to Zola. If the first *film d'art* productions seemed to aim primarily at theatrical reproduction, by the time of Henri Pouctal's stirring *Monte-Cristo* (1914–17) and his Zola adaptation *Le Travail* (1918), it had come to stand for the ambition to match classic literature's genre, whether melodramatic or naturalistic. It was again Sadoul who began to question the received verdict, noting that *L'Assassinat* set new standards of narrative economy and even suspense, as well as decor, and that its full commitment to authentic costume and setting ushered in what would soon become cinema's expected standard of design integrity (Sadoul 1951: 36–8). And no less a figure than Henri Langlois, founder of the Cinémathèque française and mentor of the New Wave, insisted that Lavedan actually demonstrated 'the cinema's first dramatic *découpage*-montage effect' in the sequence of shots that follow the Duke into the trap that the King has laid for him (Roud 1980: 401). Griffith and the Scandinavians learned from it and paid tribute, Langlois reflected, but French film-makers spurned it, to their later cost.

The other new development at the end of the century's first decade was less obviously a novelty. There had been knockabout physical comedy from the very start of moving pictures, often making use of established stage performers, even if these were at first usually anonymous in their screen appearances. By 1906, standardised series had become a feature of such large producers as Pathé, where André Deed became their first star comedian as 'Boireau', a clumsy blunderer. Many more such figures would follow, arguably keeping alive the music-hall tradition of the 'character' who remains always recognisable in spite of variations in his or her routine, and perhaps harking back to the fixed constellation of characters that made up the *commedia dell'arte* troupe. However, an innovation in this tradition appeared with the debut of Max Linder in, appropriately, *Les Débuts d'un patineur* (1907).

Linder had served his apprenticeship on the Paris stage and playing a variety of parts in Pathé films from 1905; but in this film he created the debonair young man, gallantly and sometimes foolhardily intent on impressing any pretty girl, who would recur in over 300 films before 1914. 'Max' rapidly became an international star, inspiring many imitators, after he took full control of his image and began directing all his films in 1910. His persona has been well described by Alan Williams as that of 'a distracted bourgeois dandy played with a real sense of what it means to belong to the bourgeoisie' (Williams 1992: 60). His dilemmas arise from attempting what is expected, or needed, to secure a conquest – trying to demonstrate a skill he does not have, whether skating or tossing pancakes, or playacting – with results that eventually end in comic chaos. In terms of form, the films show a development from the early physical comedy of 'action–reaction' towards an elaborated fusion of social comedy – manners, pretence, subterfuge – and an orchestration of social breakdown, often using either optical or physical special effects. The point has often been made that, while Max provided considerably more sophistication than most

film comedians of the era, he was still essentially two-dimensional compared with the most gifted of those he influenced, Charlie Chaplin. However, this is to ignore how successfully he pioneered the choreography of physical comedy and also the proto-Dada effect of the 'impossible' outcome, often motivated in the films' storylines by drunkenness or dreaming. Not only Chaplin but also Keaton, Sennett and many comedians of the later silent cinema would draw on his distinctive vein of trying to remain dignified amid disaster. In this way, the stylistic and formal innovations of French two-reel comedies in the pre-war years were to have far-reaching influence abroad.

WARTIME WINNERS AND LOSERS

It is convenient, although not necessarily correct, to treat World War I as a kind of interlude in the development of French cinema. As in almost all of the countries directly involved, the war had complex effects. While many kinds of film continued to appear without interruption, notably short comedies and longer melodramas, there were also patriotic films that often adopted a self-conscious rhetoric of nationalism – examples directed by Léonce Perret include *Mort au champ d'honneur* (1914), *L'Angelus de la victoire* (1915), *France et Angleterre for ever* (1915). Behind this relative normality, however, a major international realignment of the cinema industry was under way, which would leave most of Europe's national cinemas – and their international outposts, in the case of Pathé and Gaumont – severely weakened by the end of the war and America's worldwide export structure firmly established. The consequences of French cinema being forced by war conditions to become more reactive can be traced in a variety of ways. One of these was the evolution of the sensational crime genre already developed by several companies. Although Gaumont's *Fantômas* reached a new level of success in 1914, American serials began to dominate the market on both sides of the Atlantic and instead of the master-criminal motif that dominated in France, they offered a striking reversal of nineteenth-century melodrama's 'damsel in distress'. Pearl White in *The Exploits of Elaine* (1915) and Ruth Roland in *Who Pays?* (1916) were dynamic heroines, ready to tackle the criminals who had cheated, captured and often tortured them. It may be tempting to assume that this reflected different American attitudes towards femininity, or even a response to the new opportunities being created for women by the war; but we should be wary of jumping to simplistic conclusions. Francis Lacassin has suggested that the American serials represented a new way of catering for the desire to see virtue threatened and all but despoiled (Lacassin 1972: 133). Is not the all-American Pearl White, he asks, really de Sade's *Justine* in modern dress – an innocent ravaged by those who should protect her, in this case by the man who is, simultaneously, her cousin, tutor and fiancé?

Whether or not we follow Lacassin's reading, Gaumont quickly adopted the successful cliffhanger serial form and placed a woman effectively at the centre of their new crime saga. In *Les Vampires*, the black cat-suited Musidora as 'Irma Vep' created a memorable image of the modernised femme fatale, more powerful than her consort the Great Vampire and clearly attractive to the reporter-hero, especially when she kidnaps his wife. Even the obligatory restoration of conventional morality has a perverse twist, when the wronged wife shoots Irma Vep and her husband discreetly mourns his lost adversary. Subsequent wartime serials, however, would become more morally conventional, with the hero of *Judex* and *La Nouvelle mission de Judex* (1917) becoming a defender of the weak and wronged as he pursues his missions of revenge, occupying a place somewhere between Dumas's heroes and the 'caped crusaders' of the future. Ironically – or perhaps prophetically – the American serial that left its mark on the French crime adventure series, *The Perils of Pauline*, was actually produced by Pathé-Exchange, part of the French company's worldwide network of affiliates. And by an even more complex twist of transatlantic fate, the origins of the new Hollywood melodrama that would inspire France's post-war avant-garde can be traced back to the success of French imports into the USA. Adolphe Zukor's vast returns from the Film d'Art productions starring Sarah Bernhardt, *La Dame aux camélias* and *Elizabeth, reine d'Angleterre* (both 1912), led him to adopt a policy of quality production through his Famous Players company, which would become the main producer of Cecil B. DeMille's films in the mid-1910s. One

of these, *The Cheat* (1915), was greeted with such rapture in France that it has come to be regarded as a landmark in cross-cultural reception – the equivalent of Edgar Allan Poe's transformation into a Symbolist classic by his French translators, Baudelaire and Mallarmé. What impressed the French writers and future film-makers of 1916 was how *Forfaiture* (as *The Cheat* became) conveyed its brash interracial eroticism through a spare yet intense *mise en scène* that made full use of powerful new lighting equipment. The effect of silhouettes on paper walls in a Burmese ivory trader's house, and of deep chiaroscuro in the central drama between the trader and an American society lady who tries to renege on her contract with him would have echoes in the more self-conscious modernism and melodrama of the future French avant-garde.

Another important contribution to this new spirit of experimentation from the war years was the emergence of Abel Gance from the ranks of journeyman directors employed by the Film d'Art. An early example of Gance's formal innovation, *La Folie du docteur Tube*, was made in 1916 but withheld from immediate release in the belief that its eccentricity might prove uncommercial. By the mid-1920s, Gance's use of distorting mirrors to simulate a 'magic ray' effect would hardly seem unusual amid the profusion of Cubist and Dada films, but its presence within an otherwise conventional mad scientist drama pointed to the recurrent paradox of Gance's influence and status. The films that established his reputation, straddling the end

Ballet mécanique (Fernand Léger, 1924)

of the war, *La Dixième symphonie* (1918) and *J'accuse* (1919), contained passages of undeniable visionary power, such as the concert performance climax of the former and the eerie resurrection of an army of dead soldiers in the latter. But alongside such rhetorical triumphs, with their novel use of rapid intercutting and stylised tableaux, came an equally strong reliance on distinctly old-fashioned melodrama.

Gance, of course, was not alone in this confection of traditional melodramatic motifs with a visual rhetoric that increasingly seemed to chime with the geometric abstraction of developments in the visual arts. Film-makers in Italy, Germany, Russia and America were all reaching out during the late 1910s towards new expressive means, while continuing to base their films largely on traditional tales of passion, betrayal and hallucination. But it was Gance who offered perhaps the most provocative instance of this tension in his first post-war film, *La Roue* (1923). The sheer length of over five hours (later reduced) indicated an epic intention; and the film's major innovations were its 'mechanical' passages of virtuoso montage, derived from the narrative's railway setting. Gance was assisted in his editing by the poet Blaise Cendrars, and these elements of the film attracted the enthusiastic attention of the Cubist painter Fernand Léger, who hailed it as a veritable turning point in cinematic art: 'Close-ups, mechanical details, static and moving, projected with an accelerated rhythm which reaches a state of simultaneity, and which also rubs out, even eliminates the human object, reducing all interest in it' (Léger 1922: 55). Léger found these passages equivalent to his own radical research in painting, and they would inspire him to undertake a single pioneering venture into film two years later with *Ballet mécanique* (1924). But in 1922 he noted that the 'mechanical element which one sees disappear with regret and awaits impatiently is discrete; it appears like a series of projector blows within a vast, anguished drama that is otherwise unremittingly realist' (Léger 1922: 55).

The drama of *La Roue* may not seem realist compared with its near-contemporary, Erich von Stroheim's equally epic *Greed* (1924). Instead, its story of a proud engine-driver tortured by his love for an orphan girl he has raised and twice attempt-ing suicide before ending his days blind seems closer to the spirit of nineteenth-century tear-jerking melodrama, deployed on a grandiose scale. Bernard Eisenschitz compares it to the structural ambition of Griffith's *Intolerance* (1916), and suggests that it marks an advance by demonstrating 'that narrative and narration do not necessarily coincide ... that meaning is produced by the narrative process' (Roud 1980: 406). In fact, this apparently uneasy mixture of genres would give the emerging French film avant-garde its first indigenous masterpiece, and confirm Gance as its senior figure.

THE CHALLENGE OF THE AVANT-GARDES

By 1930, when Paul Rotha published his landmark international history, *The Film Till Now*, the French avant-garde had already become one of the pillars of cinema's claim to artistic achievement. Unlike the other major national schools of the 1920s, such as German Expressionism or Soviet montage, its significance tended to be seen in terms of experiment, with the short film shaped by a single artistic vision as its primary form. In many ways, this seemed to continue, or resume, the association between artistic innovation and the French capital that had developed during the 19th century:

> The experimental contribution of the French cinema will ever be present in Paris, which is a fitting locale for an avant-garde movement. The short capricious films of Germaine Dulac, Eugène Deslav, Georges Lacombe, Rougier, Man Ray, Kirsanov, Grémillon are always mentally stimulating in that they seldom end with themselves. They are continually suggestive of new ideas, new shapes and angles, that may be of significance to cinema proper. (Rotha 1930: 212)

Here is an early expression of the concept of an avant-garde as a laboratory, pioneering techniques and forms that may eventually be incorporated into the mainstream – in a contrary movement to Léger's appropriation of the avant-garde elements from Gance's heterogeneous masterpiece. Somewhat confusingly, the 1920s avant-garde has come to be known as 'impressionist', suggesting a continuity with the painting of the late 19th century and also some unity of aesthetic purpose. Yet its forms would range from large-scale modernist narratives to short abstract films that come close to the idea of moving paintings or sculptures, and include both documentaries and dream-based structures. What all of the new post-war generation of film-makers had in common was an impatience with the existing conventions of French mainstream narrative. As L'Herbier explained: 'None of us – Dulac, Epstein, Deluc or myself – had the same aesthetic outlook. But we had a common interest, which was the investigation of that famous "cinematic specificity" ' (Burch 1973: 69). The search for true or 'pure' cinema would lead in different directions, depending on the affiliation of individuals and groups in the fiercely partisan decade of the 1920s. However, setting aside these often vociferous disagreements, it is possible to trace three main strands of avant-garde production across the decade. First, the naturalistic narrative, usually set in rural landscape or beside the sea; second, the modernist, often reflexive narrative; and third, the 'film poem', which might be abstract, ironic or symbolic.

The new naturalistic narrative associated with the avant-garde's first leader, Louis Delluc, was born of several influences and impulses. As a critic and founder of one of the earliest specialist film journals, Delluc's enthusiasms included Thomas Ince and the Griffith of *Broken Blossoms* (1919), as well as the early Swedish masters Victor Sjöström and Mauritz Stiller. All of these made intensive use of landscape and atmospheric set decoration, both as indices of national identity and as structural features of their narratives, amplifying the emotions of their protagonists and correspondingly reducing the importance of plot. When Delluc turned to scriptwriting and direction only four years before his early death, his conception of a properly French cinema emphasised these elements. The Marseilles bar of *Fièvre* (1921), although created in the studio, defines the world of the trio of central characters; while the flat landscape of the banks of the Rhône plays an equally important part in *La Femme de nulle part* (1922) and *L'Inondation* (1923). Delluc was not alone in believing that the revival of French cinema needed to base itself on creating a physical image of France. When the great prophet of *fin de siècle* naturalistic theatre, André Antoine, turned to cinema for a brief period in mid-career, he filmed Zola's *La*

Terre (1919) in its original setting and went on to inaugurate what would become an important realist genre, the film of barge and canal life, with *L'Hirondelle et la mésange* (shot in 1920, but not edited until 1983).

Many others participated in this turn towards landscape, from the industry veterans Feuillade, Jacques de Baroncelli and Léon Poirier, to such avant-garde figures as L'Herbier and Jean Epstein. Among the reasons for this emphasis were no doubt a post-war desire to return to the roots of French national identity, often through adaptations of classic regional writers such as Daudet, as well as to provide exotic images for city-dwellers. The dramatic themes of these rural and coastal dramas deal with challenges to tradition, resisted or suffered, and with the appeal of an itinerant 'simple' life, as in Jean Grémillon's *Maldone* (1928), compared with life in upper-class society or in the city. They could be conservative and nostalgic, or, in the hands of Dulac, L'Herbier, Epstein and soon Jean Renoir and Jean Vigo, experimental in their handling of subjectivity through landscape and decor. And if the form of *plein air* naturalism seems not to be intrinsically avant-garde, then this may recall the ambivalence of an earlier Impressionism in painting and music – anti-academic and radical in its origins, yet later liable to recuperation by a sentimental nostalgia.

The second characteristic form associated with the 1920s avant-garde represents what was, and is, most closely identified with this movement: a genre of self-consciously modernist fiction that aims to disrupt the routine conventions of film narrative and draw attention to the specific signifying practices of cinema – not unlike the work of Proust, Joyce or Pirandello in literature. Other writers would provide subjects for films in this genre – Baudelaire's poem inspired Germaine Dulac's evocation of a failed romantic encounter in *L'Invitation au voyage* (1927) – but Pirandello was directly adapted by L'Herbier in *Feu Mathias Pascal* (1925). Here Pirandello's novel about a man who is falsely reported dead and so can enjoy a life of freedom becomes the basis for a form of modernist melodrama. Using stylised sets and superimposed images (now with quite a different purpose from Méliès), L'Herbier created with his lead actor, the émigré Russian Ivan Mosjoukine, what he termed 'a phantasmagoria with a realistic premise', in which the hero escapes from his provincial home to a vast apartment in Rome, where he faces a rival in love and a looming double of himself (Abel 1984: 416). Here, as in other films of this genre, ostentatious filmic devices mirror a sense of disorientation and of the insecurity of identity. L'Herbier had already made a conflation of two traditional myths, *Don Juan et Faust* (1923), in a film inspired by the stylised decor of Robert Wiene's *The Cabinet of Dr Caligari* (1919). Following this unsuccessful foray into period fantasy, he enlisted a group of leading modernist artists, including Léger, the architect Robert Mallet-Stevens and the composer Darius Milhaud, for a futuristic fantasy, *L'Inhumaine* (1924). Again, decor became a major protagonist, with a diva (Georgette Leblanc) living in an ultra-modern villa and the scientist who is her eventual saviour, after several resurrections, commanding an impressive laboratory. Essentially a reworking of two literary texts, Mary Shelley's *Frankenstein* (1910) and Villiers de l'Isle-Adam's *L'Eve future* (1886), L'Herbier's film marked the final frontier in France of a design-based approach to transforming narrative, with decor and costume acting as the main signifiers of modernity, before a climax that made use of Gance's *montage court*, or extremely rapid editing.

Few of the 'first' avant-garde could be considered modernist, and would be more accurately described as late Symbolists. But in this they fitted rather well with that trend in Symbolism that provided a sympathetic platform for the modernist break in mimesis through its self-conscious introspection. Thus, Epstein could follow his experiment in 'three-sided' narrative in *La Glace à trois faces* (1927), based on a contemporary story by Paul Morand, with an elaborately poetic adaptation of one of the original inspirers of French Symbolism, Edgar Allan Poe's *La Chute de la maison Usher* (1928). The ambience of the two films appears different, but the kaleidoscopic editing and 'simultaneism' of the former and the dreamlike slow motion of the latter can be seen as two sides of this avant-garde's belief in the power of cinema to create a kind of modern uncanny, which they termed *photogénie*. Whether it was achieved by elaborate decor and stylised acting, or by ostentatious filmic devices, such as swirling camera, rapid editing, slow motion

or extreme close-ups, these were seen as merely means to renew perception and enable cinema to penetrate 'the mystery of things'.

Another exotic factor which underpinned the symbolist–modernist axis of this avant-garde was the presence of a considerable Russian émigré group who had arrived in France after the Revolution. Although the producers Ermolieff and Kamenka did not confine their interests to the avant-garde – the Verne adaptation *Michel Strogoff* (Tourjansky, 1926) was only one of many commercial successes – this Russian presence seems to have actively supported a practice of marrying modernist elements to 'psychologised' melodrama, rather as Diaghilev had done a decade earlier in such modernised ballets as *The Rite of Spring*. This distinctive flamboyance can be seen to full effect in one of several films directed by the Russian star, Ivan Mosjoukine, *Le Brasier ardent* (1923), where an elaborate subjective structure justifies a stylistic tour de force that combined design, lighting and almost every filmic effect then available. Thanks to Mosjoukine's charisma, and his script's humour, the film also achieves greater dramatic unity than many other avant-garde works supported or influenced by the Paris Russians, including films by L'Herbier, Epstein and Gance.

The third generic strand from this period has probably earned a more permanent place than the others in cinema history, not least because of its connections with the major schools of modern visual art. Thus Clair's *Entr'acte* (1924), featuring such iconic artists as Marcel Duchamp, Man Ray and Erik Satie, has come to encapsulate the anarchic spirit of Parisian Dada. Likewise, *Ballet mécanique* relates to Léger's urbanist painting, as do *Retour à la raison* (1923) to Ray's experimental photography and *Anémic cinéma* (1926) to Duchamp's interest in kinetics and the machine. And yet, to see these now-famous works as simply part of the movements to which their makers have been assigned is to ignore how, before their canonisation, they also marked out a vital current of opposition to the dominance of the fictional narrative. In terms of form, it is significant that these were predominantly short films, ranging from a few minutes to around thirty minutes. Some were occasional pieces, intended to be shown as part of a composite event, such as *Retour à la raison* at a 1923 Dada performance evening, or *Entr'acte* within Picabia's provocative show *Relâche*. By the middle of the decade, specialist avant-garde cinemas had appeared, linked to a network of ciné-clubs, where short films could be seen alongside revived 'primitives'; and some avant-garde films from later in the decade, such as Renoir's *La Petite marchande d'allumettes* (1928), with its miniature artificial sets, were directly supported by this increasingly confident circuit.

The most distinctive form, however, was the film poem. Most of the 20th century's avant-garde movements were led by poets, even if they soon formed alliances with visual artists, and so it is hardly surprising that the idea of the 'film poem' should emerge as an alternative to the theatrical or novelistic film. One version of this was Ray's third film, *L'Étoile de mer* (1928), based on a poem by the Surrealist Robert Desnos. Another, more radical, version was championed by Henri Chomette in his *Jeux des reflets et de la vitesse* (1923–5) and *Cinq minutes de cinéma pur* (1925), aimed at freeing film from its narrative and representational associations through mingling diverse material according to a visual rhythm to create 'intrinsic, or pure cinema'. Denied 'the logic of events and reality of objects', the spectator would, it was hoped, turn from a passive acceptance of illusionism towards the process and material of film itself (Chomette in Christie 1979: 38). Chomette's other model, shared by Germaine Dulac, was the 'visual symphony'. Dulac demonstrated this musical analogy in several films that offered visualisations of pre-existing music, such as her 1928 *Disque 927* (based on Chopin's 'Raindrop' prelude) and 1929 *Arabesques* (to Debussy's 'Petite Suite'). Even if the ghost of Symbolism lies behind the concept of 'rhythm' running across different media, the idea of structuring film as music, whether abstractly or more often impressionistically, proved popular in France, as it did elsewhere.

More controversial as a structuring premise was the dream. This too had a considerable history as a formal motif, reaching back to the late romanticism of the *fin de siècle*, but it had been given new impetus by the growing popularity of psychoanalysis, with its clinical interest in dreams. Once the Surrealist group adopted its version of Freudianism, the stage was set for a series of confrontations over the

'poetics' of dreams. Dulac's attempt to deal with women's domestic subjugation in *La Souriante Madame Beudet* (1922) by visualising her heroine's dreams was condemned as naive; and her later realisation of Antonin Artaud's scenario *La Coquille et le clergyman* (1927) provoked an outright attack by Artaud and the Surrealists, who claimed that she had made this uncensored dream-material too 'dreamlike' in presentation. From a Surrealist perspective, the dream is 'real', and cinema should not seek to muffle its subversive impact by introducing stylistic dream effects. It was the Surrealists who began to revive the reputation of Feuillade's realist serials and Méliès's matter-of-fact supernaturalism; and their energetic promotion pitted these against the 'impressionism' of Dulac, Epstein and L'Herbier, as well as the dreamlike neo-classicism of Cocteau's first film, *Le Sang d'un poète* (1930). From a Surrealist perspective, the immediacy and apparent illogicality of the dream was better served by an erotic fable such as Georges Hugnet's *La Perle* (1929), or by Luis Buñuel and Salvador Dalí's deliberately scandalous and enigmatic *Un Chien andalou* (1928), which its makers claimed to be drawn directly from their own dreams.

BACK TO REALITY

The three main types of avant-garde production outlined above would all leave some mark on subsequent French cinema, and, in the case of the third, provide the founding canon of international artists' film-making. Amid the polemics between rival avant-garde groups, however, other important new currents of activity were also emerging, and it could be argued that an equal achievement from this period was the origin of documentary film. The very term 'documentary', although long associated with film-making in Britain after 1930, was already being used in France a decade earlier; and while there is no single line to trace, there are accumulating tendencies. As we have seen, the naturalistic dramas of Delluc and Antoine popularised filming on location in remote regions, often mixing professional with amateur actors. Other film-makers would be attracted to this *paysagiste* genre; and one, Léon Poirier, after making an outstanding story of the Breton salt-marshes, *La Brière* (1924), went on to film a whole series of semi-documentary location dramas in North and Central Africa and in the South Seas. While this might seem closer to Korda's 'imperial' cinema in Britain – and Poirier was an enthusiastic supporter of both empire and Vichy – it marked an important opening outward in a cinema that remained largely studio-bound, apart from the persistent and largely romantic appeal of canals and seacoast already noted.

An influential change of direction towards the centre was signalled by the Brazillian Alberto Cavalcanti with *Rien que les heures* (1926), which follows the life of tradespeople in Paris over twenty-four hours. This first full-scale social documentary established many of the parameters that would soon be adopted by Walter Ruttmann in Germany and Dziga Vertov in Russia (although it is unclear whether either saw it), and it underlines how much the portrayal of city reality was a priority for vanguard modernists. Cavalcanti's pioneering film led to his recruitment by John Grierson in 1934 to coordinate the fledgling British documentary group; but it was followed by what remains perhaps the most ambitious of all city films, André Sauvage's massive five-part *Études sur Paris* (1928–9). Sauvage's method is basically observational, but like Jean Vigo's contemporary *À propos de Nice* (1929), he articulates a point of view, by turns amused, affectionate and ironic. In France, as elsewhere at the turn of the decade, 'documentary' was by no means yet a fixed category, but offered the opportunity of making films that experimented with analysis and communication, rather than self-expression. So Vigo would make a film touched with fantasy about a swimming champion, *Taris* (1931), while Jean Painlevé would begin in the mid-1920s a long series of studies of underwater life that combined scientific precision with a Surrealist's eye for the incongruous.

To suggest, as many have, that the avant-garde of the 1920s collapsed in the face of synchronised sound is a convenient simplification. While the same anxiety and scepticism was recorded as in all other countries, the narrative avant-garde had already gone in different directions before sound-recording appeared; and some, such as L'Herbier and Gance, would embrace it enthusiastically, joined by figures such as Sacha Guitry. Other film-makers who had seemed uncertain of their direction

in the 1920s gained confidence and, like Clair and Renoir, made most of their best work with sound, laying the groundwork for France's distinctive school of Poetic Realism – itself a kind of avant-garde. And other prolific film-makers, who were never part of any avant-garde, continued to ply their trade, mainly in large-scale spectacle. These included Raymond Bernard, whose *Le Miracle des loups* (1924) and *Le Joueur d'échecs* (1927) had provided sophisticated period entertainment with export appeal; and Jacques Feyder, whose first version of the exotic adventure *L'Atlantide* in 1921 had given France its initial major commercial success after the war. Both would enjoy wide acclaim in the 1930s: Bernard for *Les Croix de bois* (1932), his French equivalent to the World War I memorials *Journey's End* (James Whale, 1930) and *All Quiet on the Western Front* (Lewis Milestone, 1930), and Feyder for the rich period detail of *La Kermesse héroïque* (1935).

However, one distinctively French form that had lasted through the previous decade, the *cinéroman* or multi-episode film, did come to an end in 1929, although it scarcely appears in most histories. Feuillade had coined the term to describe his adventure series *Judex*, to distinguish this from the rising tide of serials, and had established the basic idea of a film shown in episodes and accompanied by a popular newspaper serialisation. Between 1922 and 1929, the Cinéroman company directed by Jean Sapène, with Louis Nalpas as production supervisor, became the central force in mainstream French cinema. Working with a consortium of Paris newspapers that distributed their *feuilletons*, the company produced a steady stream of classic adaptations and new work, often using directors with an avant-garde background, including L'Herbier, Dulac and Epstein. The finale of this integrated enterprise came with a highly regarded version of *Monte-Cristo* in 1929 – a fitting end to the era of popular fiction that Dumas had originally done so much to create. The *cinéroman* was a uniquely French institution, although the links between press, publishing and cinema were becoming important everywhere, and this episode from the history of inter-war forms might serve to underline that film form is neither inherited nor autonomous, but always the product of multiple, shifting determinations.

Writing in 1919, Louis Delluc doubted that the French had 'any more feeling for cinema than for music', compared with other nations (d'Hugues and Marmin 1986: 168). If this now seems absurd, it is at least partly because Delluc set out to change what he saw as a national apathy that had developed during the decade since French film-makers had launched the innovative, yet contrasting, forms of *films d'art* and *scènes de la vie telle qu'elle est* ('life as it is'). Despite his early death, Delluc's initiatives prepared the ground for an equally influential series of new departures by the competing avant-gardes of the 1920s; yet by the beginning of the next decade, doubts were once again being openly expressed by key critics such as Jean-George Auriol about the competitive quality of French cinema in the new world of the talkies (Bordwell 1997: 20). And it was not until the late 1960s that Langlois, Burch and others succeeded in rehabilitating the long-neglected 'first wave' of Delluc and his followers. What this indicates is that the history of film form is as much in need of a history of taste as it is of more diligent technical analysis.

WORKS CITED

Abel, R. (1984) *French Cinema: The First Wave, 1915–1929*, Princeton, NJ, Princeton University Press.

Bazin, A. (1967) 'The Myth of Total Cinema', in Bazin, A., *What Is Cinema?*, vol. 1, Berkeley, University of California Press, 17–22.

Bordwell, D. (1997) *On the History of Film Style*, Cambridge, MA, Harvard University Press.

Burch, N. (1973) *Marcel L'Herbier*, Paris, Seghers.

Burch, N. (1990) *Life to those Shadows*, London, BFI.

Christie, I. (1979) 'French Avant-Garde Film in the Twenties: From "Specificity" to Surrealism', in *Film as Film*, London, Arts Council, 37–45.

Crafton, D. (1990) *Émile Cohl, Caricature and Film*, Princeton, NJ, Princeton University Press.

Gerstenkorn, J. (1999) 'Le mécano du "général": les pré-montages du catalogue Lumière', *L'Aventure du cinématographe*, Lyons, Aléas, 307–12.

Godard, J.-L. (1972) *Godard on Godard*, London, Secker and Warburg.

Hammond, P. ed. (1978) *The Shadow and its Shadow: Surrealist Writings on the Cinema*, London, BFI.

Hammond, P. (1981) 'Georges, this is Charles', *Afterimage*, 8–9, 39–49.

Haugmard, L. (1913) 'The "Aesthetic" of the Cinematograph', in Abel, R. (1988), *French Film Theory and Criticism: a History/Anthology 1907–1939*, vol. 1: 1907–29, Princeton, NJ, Princeton University Press, 77–85.

d'Hugues, P. and Marmin, M. (1986) *Le Cinéma français: le muet*, Paris, Atlas.

Lacassin, F. (1972) 'Pearl White ou les périls de Justine', in Lacassin, F., *Pour une contre-histoire du cinéma*, Paris, Union Générale d'Éditions, 127–46.

Léger, F. (1922) '"La Roue", sa valeur plastique', in Léger, F. (1997), *Fonctions de la peinture*, Paris, Gallimard, 55–60.

McMahan, A. (2002) *Alice Guy Blaché: Lost Visionary of the Cinema*, New York, Continuum.

Rotha, P. (1930) *The Film Till Now*, London, Jonathan Cape.

Roud, R. ed. (1980) *Cinema: A Critical Dictionary*, London, Secker and Warburg.

Sadoul, G. (1946) *Histoire générale du cinéma*, vol. 1, Paris, Denoël.

Sadoul, G. (1951) *Histoire générale du cinéma*, vol. 3, Paris, Denoël.

Williams, A. (1992) *Republic of Images: A History of French Filmmaking*, Cambridge, MA, Harvard University Press.

5 REPRESENTATIONS 1890–1930
Mutability and Fixity in Early French Cinema

Vicki Callahan

Cinematic representations from the 1890s to 1930 reveal France as a culture in transition with regard to questions of nationality, sexuality, ethnicity and class. France of the Third Republic was characterised by competing and often contradictory forces: between the secular and the religious, the republican and the autocratic, and in cultural terms between a modernist desire for mobility and transformation and a conservative impulse for fixity and identity. Significant changes in transportation (e.g. train, automobile, aeroplane) and communication (e.g. rise of mass press and the emergence of various popular entertainment forms, such as the cinema), along with new social categories (e.g. the urban working class, the modern woman), all put a strain on existing modes of representation. The cinema seemed especially well equipped to create a new visual language that might portray these conflicting cultural forces. It offered the possibility of new ways of thinking about change and representing identities. The new medium's ability to show the fixed and the mobile simultaneously (one frame followed by another) placed it in the unique position of indicating not only the dissonant impulses at work in the period but also the powerful desires and anxieties attendant upon these drives. This chapter will outline the successive representational strategies deployed by French cinema during this period, and will focus on the representation of the body, especially the emergence of the female body as a signpost for changing identities, as well as the role of narrative as the framing device for interpreting and controlling representation.

PERFORMANCE AND METAMORPHOSIS
The question of identity and its mutability is central both to the form and content of cinema right from its beginnings. We can see these conflicting motifs in the works of Lumière and Méliès, which have traditionally stood as the emblems of cinematic recording and transformation respectively. One of the Lumière brothers' comic films, *Chapeaux à transformations* (1895), which undoubtedly borrows from a stage routine and is filmed in one static medium long shot, shows a performer quickly moving through a number of characterisations with only the aid of make-up, costume and gesture. Although the image shows life as it is, with no cinematic effects or tricks, there is nonetheless a sense of fluidity and uncertainty – persons and events may not be as they appear. A similar concern may be seen as the central driving mechanism in many of Georges Méliès's films. Here the transformations are faster and more repetitive, and anyone and anything can change. The representation of gender is a frequent motif, and many of the transformations in the Méliès trick films are directed towards the female body, towards the creation and re-creation of an idealised object. In *Le Merveilleux éventail vivant* (1904), the leaves of an enormous fan metamorphose, or more accurately overlap and dissolve, into a group of beautiful women whose costumes and gestures are controlled by the wishes of the on-stage spectator, dressed in royal garb, and by the court's appointed magician.

More generally, Lucy Fischer (1983), a feminist scholar, points to the considerable violence directed at women's bodies in many of these works and argues that Méliès's magic films are indicative of male anxiety or even envy concerning female sexuality and procreative capacity. While gender is unquestionably an important factor in these films, a closer look reveals that the mutability of appearance potentially affects everyone, male and female alike. Linda Williams suggests that the conjuror films,

Jehanne D'Alcy in Georges Méliès's stage illusion 'Decapitation of a Woman'

which fragment and reassemble both male and female bodies, speak to an anxiety about the category of sexual difference itself (Williams 1987: 531). Thus the films do not so much situate the cinema as a male reproductive or procreative device as set in place the cinematic apparatus as the quintessential fetish object, which can infinitely control, albeit temporarily (hence the need for multiple restagings), concerns about gender distinctions. The male magician's central role in controlling this performance is indicative of these anxieties and also, ultimately, the need for mastery via the manipulation of woman's body.

However, while Méliès's trick films undoubtedly reflect the larger cultural anxiety of the era around gender roles, the extent of the processes of alteration in these films must be stressed: from animate to inanimate object, across animal and human forms, nothing is immune to transformation in Méliès's world. We can see some of this in *Les Cartes vivantes* (1905), a trick film in which a conjuror, played by Méliès, changes a large but blank canvas into an oversized playing card, the Nine of Spades, by progressively enlarging a normal-size version of the card until a stop-motion edit makes the enlarged card first disappear and then reappear on the canvas. Next, the magician produces a smaller Queen of Hearts card, which he rips apart and burns, thereby making the Nine of Spades into an oversized Queen of Hearts – all through the device of a dissolve. One more dissolve gives us a living, breathing version of the Queen (and subsequently changes her back to her inanimate form via the same technique). The pattern is then repeated as first the card of the King of Clubs is enlarged to fit on the canvas, followed by its human form, which, in turn, frightens the conjuror from the stage. The final trick comes from the unmasking of the King, who it turns out is, in fact, the conjuror in disguise. Even Méliès's own body and identity are caught up in this endless play of transformations.

It is important to note that the process of transformation in each of Méliès's trick films is formally quite different from the changes represented in the Lumière film *Chapeaux à transformations*. An examination of Méliès's *Le Roi du maquillage* (1904) is useful here. Again, we have a popular stage act, the quick sketch artist, being filmed. The act is usually

organised around the speed of the drawing or, in its cinematic variants, the sudden animation of the previously static drawing. However, in this instance, it is the artist who is changed in accordance with the image produced. Each alteration is produced with a costume change, as in the Lumière example, but the effect of this transformation is enhanced via the dissolve, so that we see the process of change unfold before us. The drawings stop and then we have a sequence of substitution for one character after another (from clown to sailor to devil). We have moved from the clever disguise to the troubling uncertainty of the very image and identity before us.

While a good deal of ink has been spilled over the differences between the Lumière brothers and Méliès, we now know that both worked in almost every conceivable genre of the early period and both incorporated staging throughout many of their works, as indeed should be clear from the careful compositions we find in both groups of films. Although film historians have dismantled the simplistic oppositions that used to categorise their films as documentary vs. fiction, science vs. magic, realism vs. fantasy, it is clear nonetheless that important differences remain between these two strands of French cinema and the representational strategies they employ. First, it is important to note that the films of Lumière and Méliès are in different ways essentially *cinematic*, i.e. their images revel in movement, even though both the relationship to the image and the function of movement are quite different. It is useful to cite here a review of the very first Lumière screening held in December 1895. The writer is enthralled with the new device:

> Photography has ceased to record immobility. It perpetuates the image of movement . . . When anyone can photograph the ones who are dear to them, not just in their immobile form, but with movement, action, familiar gestures, and the words out of their mouths, then death will no longer be absolute, final. (Toulet 1995: 130)

Although the writer highlights movement, we note too the emphasis on the photographic base of the new device and a certain fixing of the image, as if life itself might thereby escape alteration and even death. This desire to capture and freeze a moment, along with the almost nostalgic and mournful tone pervading almost all the Lumière films, points to a certain comfort and assurance that is being sought in the act of cinematic recording.

The fixing of the moment also implies an inscription of clear social and cultural distinctions, either around nationality and ethnicity (in the colonial travelogues) or class and gender (in the rendition of the domestic space as resolutely middle class and heterosexual, with working-class life represented generally outside the home, in work or play, or constrained by the factory gates). The continuous single shot captures the moment and at the same time guarantees the certainty of social distinctions based on fixed group identities. For Méliès, the attention is also on movement, but with the potential for discontinuity rather than continuity across the frames. As Tom Gunning notes, both Lumière and Méliès rely on the continuity of the single perspective (established by the predominance of the single shot), but what makes Méliès unique is the manipulation of that perspective through the 'substitution splice' or other editing techniques (Gunning 1990: 97–9). In other words, the emphasis in Méliès is on montage rather than the shot. Thus, his films could be said to heighten the larger sense of transformation and alteration at work during these first years of French cinema, whereas the Lumière films are a type of refuge against these inevitable changes. In time, both these representational strategies were superseded as new social changes occurred, and more explicit narrative codes eventually emerged in order to convey and contain the accompanying cultural anxieties.

To a great extent, the comic persona of France's first international star, Max Linder, was an embodiment of such concerns about the fluidity and fixity of social identity. Whether Max is described as a *rentier*, a dandy or even just a clown, it is the male body in this instance that represents the shifting rules around cultural categories in France at the turn of the century. While Linder appears to correspond to an established social type – looking like an impeccably groomed member of the bourgeoisie – his status is always uncertain and shifting before our eyes. Thus Richard Abel argues that Linder's early film persona seems to fit the somewhat blurred social category of the *rentier*, a person of independ-

ent means, or in Max's case 'a lower class bourgeois figure with pretensions to that status' (Abel 1998: 236). Max's uncertain class identity is typical of the *rentier*, which the historian Eugen Weber (1986) describes as an elastic category eluding the usual class boundaries and at best standing for someone with enough income to avoid work. This latter quality is certainly one that Max's character would aspire to attain. Indeed the vagueness and elasticity of Max's status makes him typically proto-modern and aspirational. What the character comically shows us is that the best start towards social advancement is the correct look and the proper accessories of the lifestyle. Thus, even by 1910, when Max appears more solidly outfitted in the trappings of bourgeois society (complete with servants and infinite leisure time), we are still not sure if this is due to good lineage or merely to good taste.

It is Max's uncertain social status and superficiality that have led two historians to label the character as 'a dandy and a marginal' (d'Hugues and Marmin 1986: 64), and another to see Linder as an essentially 'flat' persona without psychological depth (Williams 1992: 61). But these are perhaps the very qualities that make Max an emblematic figure for the cultural historian. However socially successful or disastrous, Max is all about style and performance. Unencumbered by intelligence or any discernible talent, but filled with unfailing optimism, Max pursues the good life relentlessly. His tickets to romance, respectability and leisure can all be traded or faked. In *Le Chapeau-claque* (1909), a romantic rendezvous is delayed when a succession of his top hats are destroyed and must be replaced before continuing on to his date. Another true romance is hindered in *La Petite Rose* (1909) by a girlfriend's demand that Max learn juggling before their courting ritual can resume; Max, of course, decides to take a short cut and hires a juggler to perform for him (with the aid of a strategically placed screen), but the woman quickly discovers the ruse. Perhaps most significantly, in *Victime du quinquina* (1911) the comic narrative concerns the true site of identity and respectability for a Frenchman in the Third Republic: the printed calling card. Here, a series of policemen misidentify a drunken Max and try to return him to his home address. Each policeman takes him to an address found on the numerous calling cards that he has, in fact, picked up on his drunken spree (the cards were given as reminders of his appointments to various duels the next morning). The cards, in conjunction with his dress (if not his behaviour), signify a gentleman, and thus, rather than spending a night in jail, Max is delivered to a succession of respectable homes (and in one instance he is even returned to a respectable wife in bed). Alongside their purely comic motivations, the narrative and performative strategies of Max Linder films play out important cultural anxieties about changing social status and structures.

DISGUISE AND CRIMINALITY

The era's suspicions about the authentic markers of class identity and the illusions of appearance come to the fore perhaps most dramatically in the series of crime films made during this period. Certainly the fascination with the crime figure had begun well before these particular films and can be traced back not just to popular novels at the turn of the century, but to a larger fascination with all aspects of criminality visible in the daily press and popular culture. Whether it was the individual crime of passion or the organised wrongdoings of anarchist gangs, the public faithfully followed the journalistic and cinematic representations of lawlessness. Intersections of these various media forms were not uncommon, as in Ferdinand Zecca's *Histoire d'un crime* (1901), which had been preceded by a waxworks version in the Musée Grévin. Its sensational narrative is conveyed through a series of tableaux outlining an individual outlaw's path from crime to punishment. Zecca's films were noteworthy for a certain realist style, and a number of them mixed documentary and melodramatic conventions to portray a life of crime or an existence at the margins of society: for example, *Les Victimes de l'alcoolisme* (1902), *La Vie d'un joueur* (1903), *Apaches de Paris* (1905) and *Les Exécutions capitales* (1904).

Covering similar ground was the detective film, which was also to be an important part of French cinema during this period. A number of series were organised around solo private investigators, such as Nick Carter, Nick Winter, Nat Pinkerton and Jean Dervieux. One of the earliest of these series, *Nick Carter* (1908), featured the eponymous gentleman detective, a character who demonstrated that clothes make the man, much like the Max persona did in a more comical vein (fittingly, there exists a *Max Linder contre Nick Winter* from 1911). Throughout these crime series, the strategy of disguise is often utilised by the detective to help solve a case. More generally, the recurrent theme of transposable and interchangeable identities reflects the nineteenth-century obsession with documenting and thereby recognising the modern criminal. Carter's disguise is a nice inversion of the fear that the criminal may be hiding among us with the aid of merely costume and performance. The idea of the urban space as a crime-filled arena was also present in the Éclair series, *Bandits en automobile* (1912), which presented fictionalised accounts of the criminal activities of a well-known anarchist group, the Bonnot gang.

Later variants of the crime genre, especially Louis Feuillade's *Fantômas* (1913–14) and *Les Vampires* (1915–16), simply expand the sheer range and scale of disguises and transformations, with criminals and detectives equally and interchangeably adopting outfits and assuming identities. Moreover, as Richard Abel notes, a very important transformation began around 1911–12, when the male hero shifted ground from representing the agent of the law to 'the master criminal of the modern city', beginning with the 1911 criminal series, *Zigomar* (Abel 1998: 355–8). In *Zigomar* and later in Feuillade's *Fantômas*, the reversal is complete as we move away from the gentleman detective to the elegantly dressed, but absolutely ruthless, 'gentleman bandit'. By *Les Vampires*, the criminal has mutated into a criminal gang, certainly as bloodthirsty as Fantômas, but now even more ubiquitous and polymorphous. The members of the criminal gang in the case of *Les Vampires* may appear anywhere at any time, and the outlaw may appear in any shape or form, as a guest at a society ball, a typist at a bank, a housekeeper in a journalist's home or a cab driver hailed in the street. There are many troubling qualities to these criminals beyond their omnipresence. There is a certain sense of randomness or unpredictability to their attacks, and the demographics point to an increasingly working-class character (e.g. the domestic servant, the urban labourer).

Nevertheless, these urban criminals, while clearly villainous, are not necessarily unsympathetic. One must not forget that early cinema audiences in France, from the exhibition sites of the travelling fair to the city movie palaces, attracted a diverse audience in terms of class and gender. Cinema was from its beginnings a mass art form with a mixed audience. So the figure of the criminal and the figure of authority are both often highly ambivalent characters, whose respective fates are played out to a range of class interests and identifications within the audience. Policemen in the *Fantômas* series, for example, are largely anonymous or even corrupt, with the exception of the detective, Juve, who is essentially ineffective and rather stodgy looking, so much so that it is his journalist friend, Fandor, who fulfils the role of the dashing young hero. But even the handsome and earnest Fandor is no match for the elegant and elusive bandit, Fantômas, whose seductive power is magnified by his invincibility – the very seriality of *Fantômas* and other crime films ensures that evil is never quite vanquished and will always return to haunt respectable society. Certainly crime films could be seen as playing off middle-class anxiety about crime while simultaneously providing a ghoulishly pleasurable scare, but this narrative paradox could also be understood as appealing to a broad range of the urban audience, some of whom would enjoy seeing the ruling class's sense of security and well-being briefly disturbed.

The simultaneous terror and pleasure of the crime serial can be seen in the central role played by humour in many of the Feuillade serials. Marcel Lévesque, one of the most popular French comic stars of the 1910s, had his own series of short films, but he was perhaps best known as the bumbling criminal-turned-detective of *Les Vampires*, *Judex* (1916) and *La Nouvelle mission de Judex* (1917). The case of *Les Vampires* is perhaps most instructive, as Lévesque, playing the character Oscar Mazamette, lives through a succession of changing social identities. From corrupt office worker and member of the Vampire gang of thieves, he becomes a diligent father and reformed new employee of a funeral parlour, and then aide to the intrepid journalist, Philippe Guérande (tracking the Vampire gang). This last occupation, perhaps most importantly, allows Mazamette to garner a large reward and alter his class and social status – which supplies a continuing source of amusement as he tries to be a soph-

isticated man of taste and leisure (although ultimately he marries one of the Guérande family's servants).

Another new trend in the crime series, less humorously represented, is the emergence of the female outlaw. The figure of the criminal woman needs to be understood in the context of the changes in women's roles during this time in France. As we can see from the very beginnings of French cinema, the Lumière brothers' *Sortie d'usine* (1895), women were now working in factories. This was not a condition unique to the establishment's hiring practices, but rather was indicative of the increased numbers of women working outside the home and in a variety of occupations associated with new urban space. The profound alterations in women's work experience, in conjunction with a whole range of political and cultural changes around issues of women's rights, provoked a debate about the new woman in France. However, this upheaval in women's status was not limited to the French context but was part of a larger international fixation on women's changing roles in the modern world, a phenomenon that the medium of cinema could only enhance with its global exchange of programmes and ideas. That women should start to appear as criminals in the films of the period may indeed reflect general anxieties about their changing position and unexplored potential in modern France.

Beyond these criminal roles, however, female characters are increasingly important and influential in film narratives. During the 1910s and early 1920s a number of films featured a central female protagonist who is crucial to the plot and action. Josette Andriot performed as the vengeance figure, Protéa, in a number of adventure films named after this leading character. The great silent star, Musidora, was an unambiguously evil character in two memorable crime series by Feuillade (*Les Vampires* and *Judex*). Her box-office nemesis, Pearl White, was perhaps a bigger star in France on the basis of a series of methodically marketed American films, beginning with *Les Mystères de New York* (1915–16). Unlike Musidora, Pearl is the personification of goodness and decency, so together they could be said to represent the contradictory feelings that surrounded the emergence of the new woman in

French society. Pearl White's films are much more in line with the conventions of melodrama, the narrative turning on the woman in peril, who must be rescued at the last minute from some disastrous physical threat. Pearl, however, is not so much of a victim as one might imagine from that description and in fact her 'rescues' are often results of her own efforts or even chance rather than the act of some virtuous male protagonist.

MELODRAMA AND COMEDY

World War I witnessed the growing importance of the melodrama, not only in the American-made Pearl White films but also in their French counterparts. In part we can explain this as the product of a more conservative political climate, but also by the effects of censorship on the crime film. Feuillade, who according to Francis Lacassin almost single-handedly prevented the collapse of the French cinema industry in the face of American imports during the war years, began to shift his films towards increasingly melodramatic modes of narrative and representation (Lacassin 1995: 210). Moreover, the female criminal, previously ruthless and enigmatic, is now explained and contained in these films through a medical discourse: her lawlessness is now accounted for via figures of hysteria, hypnosis or intoxication. These medical rationalisations also appeared in the popular and scientific literature of the period, which often tried to account for lawlessness through various physiological or sociological theories rather than political or economic analysis. This conservative shift in tone was matched by a cultural retrenchment in women's roles, especially during World War I, which saw a reinforced emphasis on motherhood and the family.

In a later crime serial by Feuillade, *Tih Minh* (1918), we can see how the terrain has altered. The melodramatic form fits the more conservative era, in that it draws the boundaries of the moral universe more distinctly and finitely into two clear spheres: good/evil, male/female, national/foreign. The dramatic attention is now clearly focused on the woman in peril, the lead character Tih Minh, who spends most of the film in an unconscious or semi-conscious state (whether through drugs or hypnosis) and is repeatedly kidnapped and returned while only dimly aware of what is happening to her. Tih

Minh's status as passive victim is aligned not only with her sexual but also her national and ethnic difference (her mother is Asian and her father French). Even Tih Minh's sometimes kidnapper and criminal double, Delorès (whose national identity remains unknown), would dearly wish to reform her bad behaviour. She agrees to undergo therapy, but when she realises it will fail, commits suicide. In part, the presentation of Tih Minh is consistent with a long-standing fascination with Orientalism in European culture. This is evident in French cinema from its earliest days, from the Lumière colonial treks to the numerous trick and *féerie* films that were dependent on exotic sets and scantily clad foreigners as part of the spectacle: Méliès's *Tchin-Chao* (1904), Pathé films such as *Ali Baba et les quarante voleurs* (1902), *Aladdin ou la lampe merveilleuse* (1907) and *Les Briques magiques* (1908), and Gaston Velle's invocation of the Chinese conjuror figure. But the emphasis on the foreign threat must also be situated within the international scope of World War I, and unsurprisingly the two main criminals in *Tih Minh* have Asian and German names: Kistna and Marx.

By the early 1920s the urban crime film – and with it the modern criminal woman – had all but disappeared (with an important exception, which we will discuss shortly), and the attention both culturally and cinematically had shifted definitively towards the family and romance. Melodrama became the preferred mode for both mainstream and avant-garde film. Feuillade moved on to make a number of tear-jerker serials organised around the victimised woman, epitomised by Sandra Milowanoff, the star who one critic labelled a 'touching heroine unendingly tortured by the undertakings of the wicked' (d'Hugues and Marmin 1986: 160). But a diverse range of film-makers also utilised melodrama in rather unconventional ways. In *Coeur fidèle* (1923), Jean Epstein mixed high melodrama, a gritty realist setting and experimental editing techniques in an effort to define characters and provide insights into their interior states and social conditions. On one level we follow the story of a romantic triangle involving a barmaid (Marie), who is trapped in a relationship with a drunken lout (Paul) but longs for a life with her true love (Jean). At the end of the film, the happy conclusion of the united lovers is tempered by the murder of Paul by a handicapped woman and the prospect of Jean and Marie's continued existence in an essentially bleak locale.

Similar strategies were employed by Germaine Dulac in *La Souriante Madame Beudet* (1922). Although *Madame Beudet*, like the Epstein film, provides subjective shots for multiple characters, the film is chiefly remarkable for its attention to the woman's point of view as she fantasises about a life outside her dull marriage in the provinces. Even more so than in *Coeur fidèle*, the unification of the romantic couple (the husband and wife) at the end of this film is not an occasion for joy, instead providing a decidedly grim resolution. The heterosexual couple fares little better in Charles Vanel's *Dans la nuit* (1929), another film mixing melodramatic, realist and experimental techniques, this time in order to show us a housewife's dream. The dream takes up most of the film and is ambiguously presented so it appears that we might be watching the wife's infidelity and attempted murder of her factory-worker husband. Once again, the happy ending is rather uncertain, since in her dream the wife accidentally kills her lover (believing it to be her husband), and the tension between the married couple only ends when the wife awakens and embraces her husband, who is returning from work.

This ambivalent representation of heterosexual romance and marriage is not limited to the 1920s melodrama; it can be found in a variety of styles and genres of the era. René Clair's comedies are particularly notable, in that the romantic couple in these films invariably requires an almost impossible setting for happiness. In *Le Voyage imaginaire* (1926), for example, the couple is formed in a fairy-tale setting (although this idyllic space is really the hero's dream). In *Paris qui dort* (1924), romance can only begin when the world stops moving, although here it is unclear whether this is not so much romance as boredom and male competition for the remaining two conscious females in the city. Even more sceptical about the subject of romance and marriage is Clair's *Un Chapeau de paille d'Italie* (1927). Here a bridegroom on his way to the altar accidentally encounters an adulterous couple. Despite her flagrant infidelity, the woman's respectability – and the bridegroom's wedding – can be saved only if the groom manages to replace the wayward wife's hat, which his horse has eaten. For the groom, it is not just his wedding that is at stake, it is also his whole bourgeois lifestyle. He is threatened with the destruction of his apartment and, in turn, the potential loss of his wedding presents. It is also interesting that only the hat, another commodity, can resolve this dilemma. As we noted in the films of Max Linder, the modern citizen and consumer (this time female) needs the correct costume to fulfil her performative role. When the hat is replaced at long last, but surely after all doubt as to the wife's integrity has been destroyed, the deceived husband accepts the symbolic proof of her faithfulness.

This negative image of the new woman as duplicitous and superficial can be read as symptomatic of cultural anxieties about the changing social identity of women in modern France and their as yet undetermined position in that society. No longer simply a wife or a worker, where does the new woman belong and what does she do? What role does she play as a modern consumer? What are her social and sexual desires? These questions are represented in two films, Jean Renoir's *Nana* (1926) and Augusto Genina's *Prix de beauté* (1929), with which we shall close this discussion. Set at the turn of the century, but very much a representation of the new woman, *Nana* uses its narrative's stage setting to highlight the theatrical nature of the lead character's desires. Nana is a prostitute-turned-actress, but most significantly she is an insatiable consumer (a former lover reprimands her that she thinks only of pleasure). Everything about her is excessive, as we see from her numerous and destructive affairs, her voracious desire for material goods and even her excessive performances on stage. Moreover, the actress playing the part of Nana, Catherine Hessling, doubles the excess of her character's histrionics, since her highly stylised performance does not match the other actors in the film. Our sense of Nana as out of control is thereby enhanced through this dissonance in acting techniques. In narrative terms, Nana must be punished for all this excess. Her death is quite horrific, as one might expect; most appropriately, her illness follows an evening of frantic revelry. When her large bracelets fall on the floor by her sickbed, Nana's death is confirmed, and a final link is made between the female performer and consumer.

Catherine Hessling in *Nana* (Jean Renoir, 1926)

The excess of Nana's life and death can be said to prepare us for its spectacular successor, *Prix de beauté*, which helps to mark the end of silent cinema in France (appropriately it is a type of hybrid film from this period, a post-synchronised, part silent and part sound film). *Prix de beauté* is in many ways a condensation of the multiple anxieties that we have tracked throughout this period. Louise Brooks, a major international star at the time (an American actress known particularly for her films in Germany), plays the role of Lucienne Garnier, a young office worker who enters the Miss Europe beauty contest. After winning the title, Lucienne's boyfriend presents her with an ultimatum and she gives up her glamorous lifestyle for a dreary existence with him. However, the desire to be a film star proves irresistible and Lucienne returns to the promoter who has promised her an opportunity in films. Lucienne's betrayal of her boyfriend is not just a professional choice, however, since the relationship between the beauty contestant and the film promoter is also explicitly sexual. Like Nana, Lucienne must be punished for her excessive desire, but in this instance her death will be staged as a specifically cinematic spectacle. Lucienne, dressed elegantly and accompanied by her new boyfriend and promoter, watches with delight a replay of her screen test. In the middle of the screening, however, Lucienne's ex-boyfriend, who has tracked her to the screening, abruptly shoots her. Lucienne's face as she dies is framed in a striking close-up, but her 'screen image' visibly and audibly plays on in the background.

In many ways the coming of sound, as represented in *Prix de beauté*, ends a kind of structural uncertainty brought about by the conditions and formal strategies of the silent era. The technology and the implementation of sound lent itself internationally – despite valiant attempts at experimentation – to increasingly homogeneous forms, especially with regard to questions of narrative, nationality and sexuality. It is perhaps fitting, albeit tragic and ironic, that one of the international symbols of the new woman, Louise Brooks, must die, glamorously, at the very moment when both she and the cinema begin to speak.

WORKS CITED

Abel, R. (1998) *The Ciné Goes to Town: French Cinema, 1896–1914*, Berkeley, University of California Press.

Fischer, L. (1983) 'The Lady Vanishes', in Fell, J. ed., *Film before Griffith*, Berkeley, University of California Press, 339–54.

Gunning, T. (1990) ' "Primitive" Cinema: A Frame Up? Or the Trick's on Us', in Elsaesser, T. and Barker, A. eds, *Early Cinema: Space–Frame–Narrative*, London, BFI, 86–103.

d'Hugues, P. and Marmin, M. (1986) *Le Cinéma français: le muet*, Paris, Atlas.

Lacassin, F. (1995) *Maître des lions et des vampires*, Paris, Pierre Bordas.

Toulet, E. (1995) *The Birth of the Motion Picture*, New York, Henry Abrams.

Weber, E. (1986) *France: fin de siècle*, Cambridge, MA, Harvard University Press.

Williams, A. (1992) *Republic of Images: A History of French Filmmaking*, Cambridge, MA, Harvard University Press.

Williams, L. (1987) 'Film Body: An Implantation of Perversions', in Rosen, P. ed., *Narrative, Apparatus, Ideology*, New York, Columbia University Press, 507–34.

6 SPECTATORS 1890–1930
The Cinemising Process: Filmgoing in the Silent Era

Elizabeth Ezra

In the Surrealist text *Nadja*, published in 1928, André Breton reminisces about going to the cinema with his friend Jacques Vaché:

> we would settle down to dinner in the orchestra of the cinema in the former Théâtre des Folies-Drama-tiques, opening cans, slicing bread, uncorking bottles, and talking in ordinary tones, as if around a table, to the great amazement of the spectators, who dared not say a word. (Breton 1960: 37)

When Breton recalled these youthful antics, which had probably taken place in the late 1910s or early 1920s, he characterised them as 'a question of *going beyond* the bounds of what is "allowed"', which, in the cinema as nowhere else, prepared me to invite in the "forbidden"' (Breton 1951: 44). Breton's remarks beg the following questions. How did such behaviour in a cinema come to be considered transgressive? How did the structures emerge that made it a transgressive act to speak or eat a meal in the cinema, to reject, in other words, the narrative absorption that had become a standard feature of the filmgoing experience?

The conventions that gave meaning to such forms of transgression emerged over the course of the silent era in what may be called, to adapt Norbert Elias's (1994) term, 'the cinemising process'. The earliest historians of cinema already relied heavily on a rhetoric of lost innocence (witness the multiple accounts of the first cinemagoers cowering under their seats in front of the Lumière brothers' film of a train pulling into a station); the cinemising process thus presupposes a 'golden age' of naive, uninitiated spectatorship followed by an evolution of audiences into worldy-wise creatures of habit. It is not the purpose of this chapter to condemn such nostalgia, but rather to examine its implications.

This nostalgia may or may not have been grounded in myth, but the fact remains that the establishment of cinema as a cultural force required and gave rise to new forms of sociability that characterised turn-of-the-century French culture. This sociability was shaped by codes of spectatorial behaviour that emerged as cinema became part of daily – or, at any rate, weekly – life in metropolitan areas. These new codes of spectatorship were not present from the very beginning, but developed over time, with the result that expectations about filmgoing behaviour at the end of the silent period differed significantly from those that had been in place at the inception of the medium.

In 1894, moving pictures had already been invented, but cinema was yet to be born. It is the social activity of spectatorship that turns moving pictures into cinema, and that differentiated Edison's kinetoscope from the Lumière brothers' historic Cinématographe exhibition at the Grand Café in Paris on 28 December 1895. As Jacques Audiberti has pointed out: 'Of all the aesthetic or intellectual objects of human contemplation, none quite like the cinema requires the presence, and indeed the collaboration, of the spectator' (Prieur 1993: 98). What, exactly, is the nature of this collaboration? As Miriam Hansen (1991) has argued, cinema, like any new technology, slotted into existing entertainment traditions before developing a network of consumer practices all its own. It adapted to – and was shaped by – these traditions, and retained a residue of the earlier practices from which it evolved. Thus, the cinema of attractions maintained within it the astonishing feats displayed in the live acts interspersed between films in early programmes, as if it had absorbed these character-istics metonymically. So, too, the musical, which grew out of the musical numbers featured in the café-concert – one of the first established cinematic venues in France – and which developed in two phases: first, around 1904, in the form of the filmed song (*chanson filmée*), a direct precursor of the music video, in which actors would lip-synch the words and act out the narrative of a popular song recorded on an accompanying disc; and then, with the advent of synchronised sound in France in the late 1920s and early 30s, in the form of the musical comedy with which we are familiar today. In the silent era, a live narrator, called alternatively a *bonisseur*, a *bonimenteur* or, in a more overtly pedagogical capacity, a *conférencier*, continued the role of the *raconteur* in a magic-lantern show (Restoueix 1996). Likewise, the trailers and advertisements that greet audiences as the lights dim in today's multiplexes, encouraging viewers to return and urging them to buy plenty of food at the snack bar, might be an after-image of the turn-of-the-century barker tempting members of the public to attend early film screenings.

IMMOBILISATION OF THE GAZE

There has been much discussion of the roots of cinema in *flânerie*, in the mobilised gaze of the nineteenth-century pedestrian out for a leisurely stroll across the urban landscape. Anne Friedberg writes that 'the same impulses that sent flâneurs through the arcades, traversing the pavement and wearing thin their shoe leather, sent shoppers into the department stores, tourists to exhibitions, and spectators into the panorama, diorama, wax museum, and cinema' (Friedberg 1993: 94). The work of Giuliana Bruno (1993) and Vanessa Schwartz (1995) has also emphasised the mobile nature of pre-cinematic spectatorship. But as cinema became an established and legitimate form of entertainment, the spectator's physical mobility was increasingly restricted: according to Friedberg, 'as the gaze became more virtually *mobile*, the spectator became more physically *immobile*' (Friedberg 1993: 61). Just as it is now taken for granted that cinemagoing in its beginnings was characterised by mobility, it is also widely accepted, especially since the work of commentators such as Jean-Louis Baudry, that one of the requirements, perhaps the central requirement, of classical cinema spectatorship is immobility. Certain physical constraints rendered spectators increasingly sedentary, but a whole

host of psychological factors also contributed to the reduction of spectatorial mobility. As Christian Metz wrote, 'the cinematic institution is not just the cinema industry, it is also the mental machinery – another industry – which spectators "accustomed to the cinema" have internalised historically and which has adapted them to the consumption of films' (Metz 1983: 7). It is this 'mental machinery' that is the key to film spectatorship in France. Just how did spectators become 'accustomed to the cinema' at the turn of the 20th century?

For one thing, before spectators could become accustomed to the cinema, they had to become accustomed to cinemas as fixed theatrical sites dedicated specifically to the new entertainment. For the first decade after their invention, films were shown largely at travelling fairs – Charles Pathé, we recall, started out as a fairground film exhibitor. Films were also shown at venues primarily devoted to other functions, such as cafés, department stores, music halls, variety theatres and museums (most notably the famous Grévin wax museum, but other museums as well, such as that of Porte Saint-Martin); even the Palais-Bourbon was transformed, during the summer recess of the National Assembly, into the Cinéma-Bourbon (Coissac 1925: 356; Meusy 1995: 154). Soon after the novelty of the medium itself wore off, films were incorporated into other spectacles as ancillary features, often as part of the decor. Footage of 'travel scenes' was used as a backdrop in lavish theatrical spectacles; footage of jungle scenery was projected onto a background behind animals at the zoo; and films of actual surgical procedures were shown at travelling fairs in rooms made to look like operating theatres, which were filled with wax anatomical figures, and into which spectators were led by actors dressed as nurses and hospital interns (Meusy 1995: 123–4).

Itinerant and incidental exhibition eventually gave way to permanent, purpose-built cinemas – at the very moment when, in an analogous shift, actuality footage shot by roving cameramen who travelled the world was supplanted as the main component of cinema programmes by fiction films, shot in the studio with an immobile camera (Abel 1990a: 87). Although the first permanent cinema in Paris, which opened in December 1906, was situated directly across from the Musée Grévin, it did not take long for cinema to leave behind its association with the kind of mobile spectatorship suited to viewing the displays in a wax museum. In October 1916, a regional newspaper, *La Petite Gironde*, could declare: 'The local, urban cinema has killed the fairground cinema' (Berneau 1988: 26). As cinemas became increasingly fixed, so did both spectators and conventions of spectatorship.

One of the most important contributing factors in the development of film spectatorship was the structuring of time. Adapting Giuliana Bruno's notion of 'film architecture', or the spatial conditions that determine the spectatorial experience, it is possible to identify temporal aspects of this experience in what might be called the temporal architecture of cinema (Bruno 1993: 56–7). This temporal architecture was first and foremost determined externally: the rise of cinema spectatorship was tied to the rise of leisure time in France. The six-day working week became law in 1906, and the growth of trade unions and the decrease in working hours (the eight-hour day was implemented in 1919) contributed to an increase in leisure pursuits (Forest 1995: 33). One poster, dating from shortly after the implementation of the six-day week, read: 'Hairdressers! Take advantage of the weekly day of rest to visit the Colour Cinema in Paris, at 104 rue de Vaugirard' (Meusy 1995: 167). Most working people had more time on their hands and more money in their pockets as the new century progressed. This link between leisure time and cinema spectatorship was suggested presciently in the Lumière brothers' first movie, *Sortie d'usine*, which showed workers leaving the Lumières' own photographic supplies factory after a day's work. Now that work is over, the movies can begin. Although Christian Metz observed that the cinema industry 'works to fill cinemas, not to empty them', the same industry seems to have successfully attempted to 'empty' spectators themselves. Thus, Metz famously

'They all take their children to the cinema!' (Cinéma Pathé poster, ca. 1907) (Coll. R. Abel)

compared moviegoers to fish watching other fish across a glass divide with helpless fascination: 'Spectator-fish, taking in everything with their eyes, nothing with their bodies: the institution of the cinema requires a silent, motionless spectator, a *vacant* spectator, constantly in a sub-motor and hyperperceptive state, a spectator at once alienated and happy' (Metz 1983: 7, 96). Full cinemas apparently required empty spectators. Such a vacancy presupposes an emptying out, an evacuation of the things that had previously occupied the blank space that Metz reserves for the film viewer: mobility and a voice.

THE MEDUSA EFFECT

The increase in free time for workers was accompanied by a reduction in temporal freedom at the cinema, or increasingly rigid temporal structures that placed limitations, however voluntary, on spectators' freedom to come and go as they pleased. A film programme in the early 1910s might advertise programmes from two o'clock to half-past six, without providing any indication of when individual films were to begin. Rather than planning their evening around the screening times at the cinema, as it is now necessary to do, viewers could enter and leave at any time during the long and varied programme. Other material factors also contributed to the more porous, unbound, active mode of spectatorship in the first ten to fifteen years of film exhibition. Richard Abel points out that 'specific conditions – frequent reel changes and the sometimes irritating flicker-effect of early film projection, caused by irregular perforations in the film stock and unsteady hand cranking – simply confirmed the established model of constant programme breaks' (Abel 1998: 25). One spectator, recalling viewing conditions in the first years of film projection (already a distant memory in the 1920s, when this *mémoire* was written), wrote: 'the projection trembled on the screen, slipped in and out of focus, flitted about feverishly, undulated, and made you dizzy and seasick; when you came out of these mysterious chambers, you would continue to tremble and quake' (Arnoux 1946: 27). This experience was such a widely recognised part of cultural life that it even inspired a popular song, 'La Cinématomagite', in 1907:

Dans le temps j'étais employé
Dans la cinématographie
Mais j'y ai bientôt attrapé
Un' drôl' de maladie
À force de voir trépider
Les vu's que l'on donne en séance
J'peux pas m'empêcher d'remuer
J'ai tout le temps quelque chos' qui danse
J'ai d'la ci-ci-ci-ci-ci
D'la cinématomagite . . .

[I used to work in the movies, but I quickly caught a curious affliction; after watching the flickering screen, I can't keep from flickering myself. My body is always doing a jerking dance; I have that moo-moo-moo-moo-movie bug, that moving picture bug . . .] (Meusy 1995: 134)

Advances in projection technology, however, soon drastically reduced the flicker effect, making it easier for spectators to settle in for an evening's entertainment without needing to rush out of the cinema to be sick. As well as the quality of the projection, a changing physical environment in which films were screened also imposed increasing limitations on spectatorial mobility. Room lighting greatly affected the attention that viewers directed toward the film. At first, films were often screened with the house lights on (in programmes advertised as '*projections en salle éclairée*'). A lighted room encouraged mobility, as an article about a travelling cinema in Bordeaux published in March 1910 suggested: 'Modern Electric Palace – Mr. Guillou presents his fairground show on a magnificent screen in a lighted room, which will prevent people from stumbling, which is a danger so prevalent in this type of establishment' (Berneau 1988: 25). Screening rooms in cinemas were eventually darkened, which not only presupposed or encouraged a certain degree of neighbourly trust on the part of the audience but also made it difficult for viewers to focus on anything other than the spectacle before them. Finally, the length of the films themselves played a pivotal role in decreasing viewer mobility. Between 1911 and 1913, average film length increased dramatically from fifteen minutes to an hour or more (Abel 1988: 16), which necessarily affected the spectatorial experience, making it more sedentary, with less frequent coming and going, and providing greater opportunities for narrative absorption (as well, surely, as naps). Broadsheet newspapers did not start listing film programmes until around 1913, as showings began to be organised around one or two featured films rather than a much larger number of very short films, none of which was emphasised more than the others (Meusy 1995: 283). Longer films meant captivated and, to a certain extent, more captive audiences. The moving pictures were turning all who gazed at them, Medusa-like, to stone.

THE DUMBING DOWN OF AUDIENCES

Just as their time outside of work was becoming more structured, so the range of possible (or, at least, socially acceptable) responses to what audiences saw was being restricted. In addition to being told when they could watch films, French audiences were also told how to watch them, as they were literally 'dumbed down', or silenced. By contrast, in the first years of the medium's existence, going to the cinema was a participatory activity. In 1946, Jacques Audiberti reminisced about cinema audiences of his youth:

Even in the time of the silent film, at least in the beginning, the cinema had a voice. In the auditorium, people made a racket. Half the room spelled out the intertitles aloud. There was always someone who would take it upon himself to explain what was happening on screen, even if it was obvious. 'He's going to his horse . . . He's climbing up . . . God help him if he ever runs into the police officer . . .' (Prieur 1993: 97–8)

Of course, there could be a certain amount of romanticised nostalgia here, a kind of exoticisation of the past in which 'now' and 'then' becomes the historical equivalent of 'the civilised' and 'the primitive', but similar accounts of early French cinema spectatorship proliferate. For example, writing of cinema's first mass audiences, Francis Lacloche notes:

The crowds that push their way into the travelling fairground cinemas are colourful and loud. The

screenings take place in an atmosphere of carnival. The band often hits false notes, and the audience whistles loudly. The film unleashes gibes, whistles, gasps of joy or tears, accordingly. (Lacloche 1981: 29)

Before the advent of intertitles around 1903, a narrator or film lecturer, often the exhibitor himself but sometimes an employee who also acted as a barker to draw customers in, was often required in order to elucidate the films' narratives, which might otherwise remain somewhat opaque. But as intertitles became widespread, the film lecturer became less common. After the decline of the lecturer but before the rise of talkies, many viewers in working-class or immigrant neighbourhoods where French literacy rates were low read intertitles aloud, either because they themselves were struggling with the language, or because they were assisting those viewers who could not read at all. In his autobiographical novel *Le Premier homme*, Albert Camus's character accompanies his illiterate grandmother to the pictures in French Algeria:

The films, being silent, contained numerous written titles intended to explain the action. As his grandmother could not read, Jacques's role was to read the titles to her. In spite of her advanced years, the grandmother was not deaf, but Jacques had to compete with the sound of the piano and the noise coming from the audience, who reacted vociferously to the film. Moreover, despite the extreme simplicity of the titles, many words they contained were not familiar to the grandmother, and there were even some that were completely foreign to her. (Camus 1994: 92)

Christophe Gauthier points out that in popular cinema magazines, 'exhortations and directives about the kind of behaviour to adopt in the cinema proliferated', and that heading the list was the injunction 'not to read the intertitles aloud' (Gauthier 1999: 261). Clearly, directives published in magazine articles were not aimed directly at the illiterate, but they did help to foster a general film-going culture in which the reading of intertitles aloud was frowned upon.

Although early French cinema audiences were not as predominantly working class as those in the USA in the same period, they still included a significant proportion of working-class viewers. Before about 1906, French audiences in urban areas were, according to Richard Abel, heterogeneous, but after the construction of permanent cinemas, they became, if anything, increasingly white-collar (Abel 1990b: 28). This was also the case in urban centres in French-speaking Canada (Gaudreault and Lacasse 1993: 24). The gentrification of cinema audiences corresponded to a concerted effort on the part of cinema exhibitors and producers to attract a greater proportion of higher-class customers. Advertisements and publicity posters featured well-dressed patrons from the middle and upper echelons of society, and playbills pointedly referred to the morally uplifting nature of the film programme.

The Film d'Art company, established in 1907, was an organised expression of this desire to attract audiences to the cinema who had previously been accustomed to going to the theatre. Middle-class spectators tended to behave as they did at the theatre or music hall, entertainment forms that they continued to frequent, while working-class spectators often whistled, cheered and hissed at characters on screen, because they were used to traditions such as Grand Guignol, where spectators were encouraged to participate actively in performances. It was the latter form of spectatorship that exhibitors discouraged, as they sought to bourgeoisify their clientele. Early film audiences had to be 'cinemised', taught how to be ideal spectators: taught, in other words, how to act middle class.

FROM THE IDEAL NARRATOR TO THE IDEAL SPECTATOR

Not only the external viewing environment but also the films themselves contributed to the development of a codified set of spectatorial conventions. Films functioned increasingly to hold spectators' attention, as they developed what has become known as a classical code of narration. André Gaudreault and Tom Gunning have written of how film evolved from the 'system of demonstrative attractions' characteristic of the years 1895 to 1908 to a 'system of narrative integration' in the period between 1908 and 1914. This evolution entailed the gradual suppression of visible marks of enunciation (perceptible signs of editing, visible narration in the form of playing to the camera, bowing, etc.), as

the storytelling process became hidden within the structure of the film in the form of an implied narrator 'whose existence is only theoretical but whose "voice" makes itself heard throughout the film by means of its structuring activities in the *mise en scène*, camera work and editing' (Gaudreault and Gunning 1989: 58).

There is a similar 'voice' constructed by the instructions and warnings that surround the moviegoer: the voice of the ideal spectator. It could be said that the process of suture between a film's implied narrator and the spectator also occurs at another level, between an ideal spectator and the real spectator. As narrative absorption, the product of evolving structures of narration within films themselves, became the rule, so this other form of suture emerged at the same time. Apparatus theory has attempted to deal with the physical presence of the spectator, the material conditions of spectatorship. Some theorists of the apparatus have spoken of the panopticon effect, referring to Michel Foucault's discussion of Jeremy Bentham's invention, which allowed a single prison guard to shine his searchlight at random into the cells of the prisoners that formed a circle around him. But they all locate the film viewer as the prison guard at the centre of the apparatus, shining his spotlight on the screen – that is, solely as the viewer, but never the viewed. Anne Friedberg, for example, writes:

> Like the central tower guard, the film spectator is totally invisible, absent not only from self-observation but from surveillance as well. But unlike the panoptic guard, the film spectator is not in the position of the central tower, with full scopic range, but is rather a subject with a limited (and preordained) scope. (Friedberg 1993: 20)

A further nuance may be added to Friedberg's refinement of the panoptical model, if we consider the spectatorial subject's status as the object of another – and, ultimately, its own – gaze. To extend Foucault's metaphor, the source of the prison guard's light is situated not with the spectator, but in the projection room, that is, in the cinematic apparatus itself, which necessarily sheds some light on the spectator as well as the screen. The early spectator was not exempt from the consciousness that he or she was being watched; on the contrary, this self-consciousness was the very prerequisite for the development of a classical code of spectatorship. Since subjectivity is by definition a function of splitting, the film viewer-subject is also, at some level, the viewed. The subject of the gaze in Lacan's model of subjectivity is also the object of one and the same gaze: what the infant sees in the mirror is itself being seen. In the cinema, it is not the film that is looking back: the spectator is 'watching' at least two dramas unfold, one on the screen, and one that has already been internalised, and whose protagonists are returning the gaze. The 'voice' of the ideal spectator, like the voice of the ideal narrator, was neither omnipresent nor eternal: it did not need to be. Just as film functions by means of 'images whose only duration is one of retinal persistence' (Virilio 1986: 29), so spectators only needed an occasional indication that they were being monitored before explicit articulation of this disciplining activity was no longer required, because it persisted in the social and indeed the bodily behaviour of audiences. The exhortations of popular film magazines, for example, advocated a neighbourly awareness of the collective: 'behave at the cinema the way you would want your neighbours to behave, and everyone will be happy' (Gauthier 1999: 261) – but such visible signs of spectatorial self-consciousness were, like narration within the film, eventually internalised by the spectator. The process of suture between the real and the ideal spectator worked to efface the particularity of real spectators, just as the real (or explicit) narrator was absorbed into the structure of the film with the development of a classical code of narration.

The effacement of heterogeneity effected in the first two decades of cinema in France found its logical extension in World War I, as excision and absence became part of daily life. After the outbreak of war, cinema itself was effaced from the cultural landscape, as many cinemas closed temporarily: in Bordeaux, for example, screenings were suspended for six weeks (Berneau 1988: 31). When cinemas reopened, filmgoing demographics reflected other absences. Wartime audiences were composed largely of women, children, invalids and the elderly: gone were the young men off fighting the war. This logic of gaps also extended to the media. Newspapers appeared with large blank spaces indicating articles that had been censored at the last moment. The gaps in what could be written were matched by gaps in what could be shown on screen, as films were censored for any content deemed too controversial. Of particular concern in 1914 was 'anything that could elicit painful emotions in the present circumstances or provoke violent reactions, notably scenes of war depicting enemy uniforms' (Meusy 1995: 415). Such concern over audience response at the beginning of the war suggests that the filmgoing public was still considered to be in need of monitoring.

By the 1920s, however, many aspects of the cinemising process were well in place. Spectators had internalised models of surveillance and discipline, and came to play the role expected of them, more or less (with exceptional acts of transgression, Surrealist or otherwise, proving the rule). Codes of spectatorship have been modified every so often to reflect changes in social and technological practices: trailers, advertisements and exhortations to refrain from smoking, all successfully internalised by viewers, have given way to admonitions to turn off our mobile phones in the theatre. Even in our homes, we are threatened with prosecution for 'unauthorised' use of the video we are about to watch. The emptying out of the spectator has come full circle, culminating (as it began) in the emptying out of the consumer's wallet. As filmgoing sprang from shopping, so shoppers in the 21st century are becoming as immobilised as filmgoers. We are becoming house-bound *flâneurs* as we watch and shop on television and the Internet. Customers no longer have to go out to shop for products, spectators no longer have to go out to see movies; products now shop for customers, as shopping and spectatorship come home. This, perhaps, is the end of the cinemising process, its final stage and ultimate purpose.

WORKS CITED

Abel, R. (1988) *French Film Theory and Criticism: A History/Anthology 1907–1939*, vol. 1, Princeton, NJ, Princeton University Press, 1907–29.

Abel, R. (1990a) 'Booming the Film Business: The Historical Specificity of Early French Cinema', *French Cultural Studies*, 1: 2, 79–94.

Abel, R. (1990b) 'The "Blank Screen of Reception" in Early French Cinema', *Iris*, 11, 27–47.

Abel, R. (1998) *The Ciné Goes to Town: French Cinema, 1896–1914*, Berkeley, University of California Press.

Arnoux, A. (1946) *Du muet au parlant, souvenirs d'un témoin*, Paris, La Nouvelle Édition.

Berneau, P. (1988) 'Les Débuts du spectacle cinématographique à Bordeaux', *1895*, 4, 18–32.

Breton, A. (1951) 'As in a Wood', in Hammond, P. ed. (1978), *The Shadow and its Shadow: Surrealist Writings on the Cinema*, London, BFI, 42–5.

Breton, A. (1960) *Nadja*, New York, Grove Press.

Bruno, G. (1993) *Streetwalking on a Ruined Map*, Princeton, NJ, Princeton University Press.

Camus, A. (1994) *Le Premier Homme*, Paris, Gallimard.

Coissac, G.-M. (1925) *Histoire du cinématographe*, Paris, Cinéopse.

Elias, N. (1994) *The Civilising Process*, Oxford, Blackwell.

Forest, C. (1995) *Les Dernières séances: cent ans d'exploitation des salles de cinema*, Paris, CNRS.

Friedberg, A. (1993) *Window Shopping: Cinema and the Postmodern*, Berkeley, University of California Press.

Gaudreault, A. and Gunning, T. (1989) 'Le Cinéma des premiers temps: un défi à l'histoire du cinéma?', in Aumont, J., Gaudreault, A. and Marie, M. eds, *Histoire du cinéma, nouvelles approches*, Paris, Sorbonne, 49–63.

Gaudreault, A. and Lacasse, G. (1993) 'Premier regard: les "néo-spectateurs" du Canada français', *Vertigo*, 10, 18–25.

Gauthier, C. (1999) *La Passion du cinéma: cinéphiles, ciné-clubs et salles specialisées à Paris de 1920 à 1929*, Paris, AFRHC/Écoles des Chartes.

Hansen, M. (1991) *Babel and Babylon: Spectatorship in American Silent Film*, Cambridge, MA, Harvard University Press.

Lacloche, F. (1981) *Architectures de cinémas*, Paris, Moniteur.

Metz, C. (1983) *Psychoanalysis and Cinema: The Imaginary Signifier*, London, Macmillan.

Meusy, J.-J. (1995) *Paris-Palaces, ou le temps des cinémas (1894–1918)*, Paris, CNRS.

Prieur, J. ed. (1993) *Le Spectateur nocturne*, Paris, Cahiers du cinéma.

Restoueix, J.-P. (1996) 'Le Bonisseur introuvable . . .', *Iris*, 22, 67–79.

Schwartz, V. (1995) 'Cinematic Spectatorship before the Apparatus: The Public Taste for Reality in Fin-de-Siècle Paris', in Charney, L. and Schwartz, V. eds, *Cinema and the Invention of Modern Life*, Berkeley, University of California Press, 297–319.

Virilio, P. (1986) 'The Overexposed City', *Zone*, 1: 2, 15–31.

7 DEBATES 1890–1930
Thinking about Cinema: First Waves

Monica Dall'Asta

In 1954, on the occasion of Jean Epstein's death, *Cahiers du cinéma* published an article in which the great French director and theorist was said to have been 'buried alive' by his contemporaries. Written by the curator of the Cinémathèque française, Henri Langlois, the article was overtly critical of *Cahiers* themselves, who were blamed for participating in the general amnesia regarding the significance of Epstein's contribution:

> Today for the first time, *Cahiers du cinéma* are taking an interest in Jean Epstein. Would it not have been more honest to have accorded him a few lines during his lifetime and to have insisted on the importance of his research? Was that not the role of the journal that claims to be devoted to the art of film and to be above the contingencies of commerce? But that would have required courage, and the vision to see beyond public opinion rather than following fashion while pretending to precede it. (Langlois 1986: 239)

It took many years for this amnesia even to begin to be cured. In 1968, *Cahiers* published a seminal essay in which Noël Burch and Jean-André Fieschi used Langlois's metaphor of a 'tunnel' to explore the idea of a secret link between the films of the first French avant-garde and the cinema of the New Wave (Burch and Fieschi 1968). But the theoretical relevance of the ideas elaborated in the context of what they called the 'First Wave' was not fully appreciated until many years later. The publication of Jean Epstein's *Écrits sur le cinéma* in 1974, for instance, had practically no impact in the field of film studies, which at this point were absorbed in discussions of structuralism and psychoanalysis. Moreover, the complete writings of Louis Delluc, the most important French film critic of the silent period, did not begin to be published until 1985. Only recently has an extraordinary body of material become available thanks to the work of Richard Abel, whose two-volume 1988 anthology of critical and theoretical texts provided the English-speaking public with a range of writings that were up to then unobtainable even in French, giving definitive evidence of the unique richness and diversity of French film debate during the silent period. Analogies between the two 'waves' are striking. In both cases we are presented with a somewhat heroic challenge to reinvent cinema from its roots after the shock of a world war, a passionate attempt to realise the immanent modernity of the medium on the part of a group of cinephiles in love with American films and profoundly dissatisfied with the state of French mainstream cinema. Similarly, in both cases the development of a new film praxis was fuelled by a combination of the intense activity of a network of film clubs and the production of theoretical discourses. It would even be possible to compare the respective roles played in the two movements by Ricciotto Canudo and André Bazin, two charismatic intellectuals whose contribution included not only the solitary work of writing but also the formation of true film communities through the creation of forums of debate such as journals and ciné-clubs.

Once discovered, this 'tunnel' begins to work on a theoretical level as well. As many have noted, Bazin's essay 'The Ontology of the Photographic Image' from 1945 shows a number of crucial similarities to Delluc's theory of *photogénie* some twenty-five years earlier. There is the same emphasis on the photographic base of the film image, the same insistence on filming as an automatic reproduction outside human control, as an unintentional revelation of 'a natural world we would not be able to see' (Bazin), a 'natural truth' that could never be created artificially but only 'stolen' by the camera

Cover of Jean Epstein's *Bonjour Cinéma* (1921)

specifically French genealogy of discourse. This genealogy, however, is perhaps less a tradition than the clandestine product of involuntary memory. For if Bazin and later the 'young turks' of the New Wave never explicitly referred to the experience of the First Wave, this is because, despite Langlois's reproach, they did more than just draw consciously from a tradition: in fact they gave this experience something like a posthumous life, repeating and reinventing the gesture of rupture that constitutes the cinema of modernity, or cinema *as* modernity.

PHOTOGÉNIE

Even if the term never appears as such in their writings, the concept of *photogénie* has been used frequently by the *Cahiers* critics, and in French discourse on film generally. Godard, for instance, called it 'the splendour of truth', while Barthes celebrated its power to displace codified meanings by calling it 'the obtuse sense' or 'the punctum'. *Photogénie* was one of the new words that began to circulate in the last part of the 19th century. In everyday language it was used to indicate the tendency of certain people to appear beautiful in photographic portraits. By the beginning of the 1920s, however, that simple concept had acquired an extraordinary complexity that writers such as Colette, Delluc, Vuillermoz and Epstein had come to identify with the specificity of the film image. Insistently associated with what was often described as the 'miracle' of cinema, *photogénie* was never defined in a rigorous way. For Blaise Cendrars, who once called it a 'precious hocus-pocus kind of word', it was the name of a 'great mystery' (Epstein 1974: 32). But to reject the early French writings on the topic as lacking in logic and consistency is to miss the point, namely that their lyrical, almost mystical character derived from the nature of *photogénie* itself, and offered the only possible expression for an experience that escapes, exceeds, or produces a crisis within language. As Epstein noted, 'one runs into a brick wall trying to define it . . . the words are lacking, the words have not been found to describe it' (Abel 1988: 243). The epiphany of film as sense, *photogénie* could not be signified through language but only expressed or translated into language, as an experience of language itself. It is no coincidence that some of the most remarkable contributions to

(Delluc). But Bazin's article also resonates profoundly with the ideas of Epstein and Canudo. The famous metaphor of film as 'the mummy of change' is an almost literal quotation of the 'mobile embalming' celebrated by Epstein in *Bonjour Cinéma* in 1921. And the description of the relationship between film and painting in terms of action and reaction, with painting finally 'achieving its aesthetic autonomy' when the advent of film relieves it from 'the obsession of realism', is clearly indebted to Canudo's earlier theories regarding the role of film within 'the system of the arts' and to his reading of abstraction as the result of the 'liberation' of the visual arts from 'representational competition'. To acknowledge the presence in Bazin's essay of so many motifs from earlier film theory does not diminish its originality. Rather, it makes it even more significant, for it allows us to situate his most famous text – which in its time served as a starting point for the thinking of a new cinema – in a the debate on film around 1920 were made by poets such as Cendrars, Aragon, Soupault and Cocteau.

Of course, what this mysterious word would try to name and express had little in common with the way it was used in everyday language. Its new intensity was especially evident in the writings of Delluc, whose 1920 book was particularly influential in establishing the centrality of the term. First of all, *photogénie* was no longer tied to a standard notion of beauty. Indeed the kind of decorative beauty that French directors tried to obtain by filming 'gracious' actors and actresses was harshly criticised by Delluc: 'If you aim for the *pretty*, you'll only get *ugly*,' he wrote. *Photogénie* had nothing to do with conventional beauty; rather, it was produced by the perception of singularities. What happened in the process of filming was an enhancement of the specific qualities of a given physiognomy:

A tiger or a horse will appear very beautiful in the light of the screen because they are naturally beautiful and there you will see their beauty displayed, as it were. An individual, whether beautiful or ugly, will keep his or her expression which the camera will intensify. (Delluc 1985: 35)

What cinema offered, then, was a kind of 'new beauty' that could be extracted even from ugliness through a sort of alchemy, as Epstein observed; a 'superior beauty' that resulted from the revelation of singularities. American actors were the most fascinating examples of the power that uncommon physiognomies could have on the screen. Sessue Hayakawa, the Japanese actor of Cecil B. DeMille's *The Cheat* (1915), was for Delluc a 'mask' that bore the imprinted signs of an 'implacable cruelty' and a 'mysterious brutality'; 'few things in the cinema reveal to us, as the light and silence of this mask do, that there really are *alone* beings' (Abel 1988: 139). But American cinema also showed to what extent the discovery of the poetry of singularity was dependent on the use of the close-up. In William Hart's Westerns, even objects revealed themselves to be endowed with character: 'Think of those two heavy leather cuffs, studded with copper and laced with savage stylishness, which one sees on William Hart's wrists. In close-ups, they sum up his power, anger, or sadness' (Abel 1988: 256). On the screen,

Aragon observed, 'objects that were a few moments ago sticks of furniture or books of cloakroom tickets are transformed to the point where they take on menacing or enigmatic meanings' (Abel 1988: 166). 'A close-up of a revolver', Epstein insisted, 'is no longer a revolver, it is a revolver-as-character, in other words the impulse towards or remorse for crime, failure, suicide . . . It has a temperament, habits, memories, a will, a soul' (Abel 1988: 317).

Photogénie was no longer associated by these writers with portrait photography. This is very important, because the experience of singularity was essentially conceived as a momentary and fleeting perception. 'I have never seen an entire minute of pure *photogénie*,' wrote Epstein (Abel 1988: 236). For this reason, the ideal medium of *photogénie* was not photography, but film. The long exposure times of studio photography resulted, in Delluc's words, in a 'petrifaction of life' that was completely at odds with the 'almost casual', contingent character of photogenic images. Film was a close relative of the snapshot, for in both cases what was rendered by the camera was a unique, unrepeatable event. 'The gesture caught by a kodak is never quite the gesture you wanted to fix. Generally that's a plus' (Delluc 1985: 33). If Delluc emphasised the role of chance, Epstein preferred to focus on movement:

The photogenic aspect of an object is a consequence of its variations in space-time . . . A moment ago I described as photogenic any aspect whose moral character is enhanced by filmic reproduction. I now specify: only mobile aspects of the world, of things and beings, may see their moral value increased by filmic reproduction. (Abel 1988: 315–16)

This fascination with the power of cinema to capture the mobility of a 'transient reality' was particularly elicited by non-fiction films. For Delluc, even the most anonymous documentary could reveal 'impressions of evanescent eternal beauty', or 'the beauty of chance' (Abel 1988: 137). Émile Vuillermoz, a prominent music critic and one of the earliest film reviewers in France, described the camera lens thus:

the multifaceted eye of a fly able to record all phenomena of life . . . It has no obstacle in time and space. It follows in all its stages the development of a chrysalis, the germination of a seed, the blossoming of a flower.

The techniques of scientific cinematography were a source of endless marvel. If the close-up allowed the magnification of space, fast and slow motion effected something like a magnification of time, offering what Epstein called a 'temporal perspective' that revealed a hidden world teeming with movement (Abel 1988: 316). Or as Cendrars described it:

a hundred worlds, a thousand movements, a million dramas . . . In fast motion, the life of the flowers is Shakespearean; in slow motion, everything classical is there in the flexing of a biceps . . . The least throb germinates and bears fruits. Crystallisations come to life. Ecstasy . . . All this is part of a living organism that we surprise, dislodge, and track, and which has never been seen before. (Abel 1988: 182–3)

At the very core of the debate on *photogénie*, then, rested an idea of film as the revelation of an otherwise imperceptible reality. In this, the French discourse on film showed an extreme consonance with the efforts of early twentieth-century philosophy to adopt a non-anthropomorphic stance as a way of overcoming the limits and illusions of natural perception and of gaining access to a more fundamental level of reality. What cinema offered was in a way an automatic realisation of the experience of evidence that Husserl was attempting to reach through his method of *epoché*, which posited the bracketing of all knowledge and prejudice as the preliminary condition for an immediate intuition of 'the things themselves'. It was precisely this condition that Epstein found automatically realised in the vision of the camera lens, which he described as an eye endowed with inhuman analytical properties:

It has no prejudices, no morals. Free from influences, in human faces and movements it sees features that we, with our burden of sympathies and antipathies, habits and reflections, are no longer able to see. (Epstein 1974: 137)

But the notion of *photogénie* was especially resonant with the philosophy of Henri Bergson, with his call

to a 'turn to experience' based on the apprehension of temporal duration, a pre-linguistic yet superior form of intellection that facilitated renewed contact with the real. As art historian Élie Faure wrote in 1922:

in the cinema, time clearly becomes necessary. Increasingly it forms a part of the always more dynamic idea that we are receiving about the object upon which we are gazing . . . Indeed I feel it as being part of myself, as enclosed alive, with the very space which it measures and which measures it, within the walls of my brain. (Abel 1988: 265)

Such was the 'miracle' of cinema: suddenly one could apprehend aspects and dimensions of life that the human eye had never seen before and that remained beyond the grasp of ordinary perception and the traditional art forms. In other words, cinema was celebrated as the instrument of a new encounter with the world that brought to an end the project of what German philosopher Odo Marquard (1989) has called 'the aesthetic art' of the 18th and 19th centuries. According to Marquard, the 'aestheticisation' of art had been a response to the 'modern disenchantment of the world' produced by the diffusion of scientific thought, which was no longer able to see the world as beautiful and conceived it instead only as 'useful'. Whereas in the ancient world beauty was an attribute of nature that could in no way be associated with the products of art, the disappearance of beauty from the disenchanted world of modernity meant that now it would have to be reintroduced through human work, as the creation of a 'genius' or a 'total work of art', in a process whose ultimate aspiration was to replace a dull, merely functional reality with the magic of art (an exemplary illustration of this paradigm can be found in Baudelaire's rejection of photography on the basis of a radical splitting between the 'beautiful' and the 'true').

This notion of art as compensation for a dull reality was precisely what *photogénie* came to displace. Contrary to the aesthetic resistance of modernity, *photogénie* signalled the possible poetic use of the scientific gaze, here represented by the camera lens. Turned into poetry, the scientific gaze no longer led automatically to the loss of the world;

it could lead instead to a new discovery of it, to an innocent perception that redeemed modernity from a merely instrumental vision of reality. As Canudo had first recognised, this implied a redefinition of the whole system of the arts, but some writers went even further. Delluc, for instance, saw film as a sensory form that went *beyond* artistic experience: 'Obviously, art would be utterly useless if each of us was capable of appreciating consciously the profound beauty of the passing moment ... The cinema is rightly moving toward the suppression of art, which reveals something beyond art, that is life itself' (Abel 1988: 137). In a similar way, Marcel L'Herbier argued that cinema was the 'opposite of an art', for art – to quote Oscar Wilde – was essentially 'the expression of beautiful falsehood' and cinema was instead a 'machine to imprint life', whose aim was 'to transcribe as faithfully and truthfully as possible . . . a certain phenomenal truth' and therefore to present 'exactly the opposite of what the consoling arts of unreality attempt to make manifest, in their desire for the absolute' (Abel 1988: 150). By recovering a non-aesthetic, because innocent gaze, modernity could suddenly appear to retrace the path to the classical. Canudo, for example, described the experience of film spectators as a 'new Festival', a sacred ritual in which the 'joyous unanimity' of Greek theatre was finally restored; and Delluc did not hesitate to compare the emotional intensity of William Hart's Westerns to the spirit of classical tragedy. Even more significantly, cinema seemed to foster a kind of primitive religiousness, a pantheistic belief in 'the spirit' or 'the religion of things', as Vuillermoz put it. 'I would even go so far as to say that the cinema is polytheistic and theogenic,' Epstein declared:

> Those lives it creates . . . are like the life in charms and amulets, the ominous, tabooed objects of certain primitive religions. If we wish to understand how an animal, a plant, or a stone can inspire respect, fear, or horror, those three most sacred sentiments, I think we must watch them on the screen. (Abel 1988: 317)

In a way, then, the mission of cinema was to present modernity with a new sense of the sacred that would bring to an end the dissociation between the 'beautiful' and the 'true', recovering the feeling of amazement that the modern subject had lost in relation to the world. But of course, this paradoxical re-enchantment of the world by means of technology could not happen in a straightforwardly realist mode of representation. The reality discovered by the camera eye escaped the definitions of common experience. It was something like a molecular level of reality, the inorganic life of matter, an 'optical unconscious', to borrow Walter Benjamin's phrase, that suddenly emerged to disclose unknown perspectives in the surface of things, showing the unreal at the very heart of the real.

'PURE CINEMA' AND SURREALISM

Interest in the cinema's power of transfiguration gradually shifted, during the 1920s, from the discussion of *photogénie* to a more articulated debate that focused on the creative possibilities of the moving image. If the raw material of film was not a product of invention, but the result of a mechanical operation, in what ways could cinema still preserve a creative, indeed artistic, character? Here we can identify three major responses to this question. At the most elementary level, Delluc insisted on the choice of the visual material. If film could still be considered an art, this was only in the sense of an art of seeing. The director's talent was basically an ability to select what to see, under what light and from what angle. This explains Delluc's special interest in the profilmic element of the cinema, from the choice of actors and settings to the selection of light. But the creative potential of the gaze could also emerge at the narrative level, for the ideal film story was nothing but the natural development of a particular setting, or the formal elaboration of the narrative possibilities that a sensitive eye had captured in it.

At the other extreme, a second response was proposed by the advocates of 'pure' or 'absolute' cinema. First introduced in 1914 by the painter Léopold Survage, this line of reflection was in no way interested in film as a reproduction of reality, but rather as a means of plastic composition. Central to this conception, which reached its high point between 1925 and 1927, was a fascination with the purely visual play of lines and shapes on the screen. If in the most radical cases this implied a rejection of representative images and an invitation to explore the possibilities of animated abstract figures (Henri Chomette, Louis Chavance), the notion of 'pure cinema' was usually employed to refer to the use of specifically cinematic means in the recording and the treatment of the images. These techniques ranged from montage to superimposition, and from slow motion to the deformations produced by certain types of filters and lens. In any case, the promise of pure cinema lay in the possibility of going beyond the narrative organisation of the images in favour of what was often described as a 'visual symphony', a metaphor first employed by Vuillermoz to indicate the role of rhythm and montage in the composition of a film. A decisive impulse towards a technical conception of cinematic specificity came in the winter of 1923 with the screening of Abel Gance's *La Roue*, which many writers praised for its 'plastic' sequences that suddenly erupted to punctuate or suspend the narrative, as in the rapid montage of the famous 'Symphony of the Wheel'. In the words of Fernand Léger:

> You will see moving images presented like a picture' centred on the screen with a judicious range in the balance of still and moving parts . . . a still figure on a machine that is moving, a modulated hand in contrast to a geometric mass, circular forms, abstract forms, the interplay of curves and straight lines . . . dazzling, wonderful, a moving geometry that astonishes you. (Abel 1988: 273)

This appreciation of the purely plastic value of the image had a number of different implications that varied from author to author. For painters like Marcel Gromaire and Fernand Léger, and for an art scholar such as Élie Faure, film was essentially an extension of painting in time and thus narrative was a mere accident that prevented the moving image from fully achieving its creative possibilities. For others (Pierre Porte, Germaine Dulac), the plastic nature of the film image was not necessarily at odds with the construction of a plot, but it could be used to integrate the narrative with 'sensations', with the description of subjective states of mind such as memories, dreams or fantasies. This last aspect of the debate seems particularly significant in light of the contemporary experiments by authors such as Gance, L'Herbier, Dulac, but also Delluc and

Epstein, and their attempts to use the film image as a visual objectivation of subjective states. The influence of Bergsonism, with its insistence on memory and lived experience, became evident in the increasing use of flashbacks and other mental images that no doubt were among the most characteristic traits of French cinema during the 1920s. 'The inner life made perceptible by images is, with movement, the entire art of cinema,' wrote Dulac. 'Movement, inner life. What is more mobile than our psychological life with its reactions, its manifold expressions, its sudden movements, its dreams, its memories? The cinema is marvellously equipped to express these manifestations of our thinking' (Abel 1988: 310). In this way, the exploration of the 'inner life' became a privileged field to test the creative possibilities of the film image and to delineate an auteurist view of the cinema. In fact, according to Dulac, it was especially in the description of the psychological world of the characters that the director could become a true 'creator', an artist who could compose a 'theme or a thought' by associating several 'isolated expressions'

Germaine Dulac, film-maker and theorist

according to his or her unique sensibility. In a similar way, in an article entitled 'Surrealism and Cinema', Jean Goudal invited French directors to open up their research to 'the regions of the dream', which he described as 'strictly personal' and therefore particularly suitable to reveal 'the individuality of the author' (Abel 1988: 359–60).

Despite its title, Goudal's article, although a classic reference work in the discussion of film and Surrealism, is only partially representative of the Surrealist conception of the cinema, which during the 1920s offered a third, quite original solution to the question of creativity in film. At the beginning of the decade, the advent of Surrealism had a strong impact on speculation about film, bringing many writers to explore the multiple affinities between dreams and the cinematic experience, an analogy first suggested by Robert Desnos in 1923. But in the majority of cases the reference to dreams had little to do with the authentic spirit of Surrealism. Many writers confined themselves to discussing the cinema's apparent inclination to translate dreams onto the screen, thus eluding or softening the subversive charge of André Breton's definition of *surréalité* as the fusion of dream and reality 'into a kind of absolute reality', a visionary experience in which the dualism between seeing subject and visible object was radically undermined. This 'domestication of the unconscious within a rational process of representation and perception' is well represented by a study entitled 'The Psychological Value of the Image', published in 1926 by one Dr Allendy, a well-known psychoanalyst who was then treating Antonin Artaud (Abel 1988: 337). In his study, Allendy evoked a kind of ultra-subjective film, in which 'real views of the objective world' would be continuously displaced by 'the subjective representation of this exterior world', or 'unreal creations of the imagination'. This reduction of the possibilities of vision to a purely psychological dimension was very far from the Surrealist concept of the cinema. As Alain and Odette Virmaux have noted, the Surrealists did not show any particular interest in those dreamlike eccentricities that were admired by so many critics in this period. Their preference was for the most trivial products of popular cinema such as comedies or serials, whose wild illogicality they celebrated as a spontaneous form of Surrealism. As Aragon and Breton wrote as late as 1928:

Soon people will understand that there was never anything so realistic and at the same time so poetic as the film-serial, which used to bring such pleasure to enlightened spirits. It's in *Les Mystères de New York* and *Les Vampires* that one will find the great truth of this century, beyond fashion and taste. (Virmaux and Virmaux 1976: 82)

But apart from their love for this or that film, actor or genre, what the Surrealists discovered as revolutionary in the cinema was the very experience of moviegoing, which they saw as an entirely new dimension of both urban life and artistic creation. Cinema was perceived as a kind of parallel universe that lay sunk in the folds of the real world – it was the unconscious of the city that only emerged into daylight through the multicoloured posters peering at the passer-by at the entrances to the theatres. In other words, cinema constituted something like a second world of images that were continuously available to the city's inhabitants, to whom they offered multiple, ever-changing possibilities of combination. As Breton and his young friend Jacques Vaché discovered in Nantes as early as 1916, a unique, perfectly unrepeatable film could be obtained by means of spectatorial montage, through the combination of several fragments of films seen during a whole day of aimless wandering through the city. They dropped into cinemas at random:

> when whatever was playing was playing, at any point in the show, and left at the first hint of boredom – of surfeit – to rush off to another cinema where we behaved in the same way, and so on . . . I have never known anything so magnetizing . . . (Breton 1951: 73)

A new version of nineteenth-century *flânerie* – the art of wasting time by roaming through the streets of Paris – this Surrealist moviegoing technique was meant to push to the extreme what Breton called 'cinema's power of disorientation', transforming a simple walk through the city into an almost trance-like experience and a new form of poetic creation.

In any case, what the Surrealists celebrated in the cinema was less its ability to extend the limits of representation to the regions of dream and imagination than its power to displace the visual subject from its pretension of control and self-control. The pleasure of cinema depended entirely on this loss of mastery that made the subject no longer the cause, but rather the *effect* of vision. Whereas such a loss of selfhood had been a central motif in Georges Duhamel's condemnation of cinema, 'no longer can I think about what I see, the moving images are replacing my own thoughts', Breton and his followers conceived the experience of automatic thought as the greatest contribution of film to the 'Surrealist revolution'. This notion was to find its most explicit formulation in the texts written by Antonin Artaud before his definitive break with Breton in 1928. Introducing his script for *La Coquille et le clergyman*, directed by Germaine Dulac in 1927, Artaud spoke of his work as an attempt to create 'an inorganic language that moves the mind by osmosis and without any kind of transposition in words', a new language made out of 'the human skin of things, the epidermis of reality' and whose aim would be to operate almost intuitively on the brain:

> We have yet to achieve a film with purely visual situations whose drama would come from a shock designed for the eyes, a shock drawn, so to speak, from the very substance of our vision and not from psychological circumlocutions of a discursive nature which are merely the visual equivalent of a text. (Abel 1988: 411–12)

Yet Artaud's reaction to Dulac's treatment of his script was totally negative and even violent. His harsh disappointment was represented publicly during the film premiere at the Studio des Ursulines on 9 February 1928, when a group of Surrealists managed to interrupt the screening, launching the worst insults against Dulac for her alleged betrayal of the original script. Their explicit reproach was that the text had been interpreted as a mere description of a dream, whereas Artaud's attempt was to achieve a 'pure play of appearances', a 'collision of objects, forms, repulsions, attractions', a 'visual cinema in which every psychology would be engulfed by actions' (Abel 1988: 411–12).

In fact, there is little doubt that the reason for Artaud's repudiation is to be found elsewhere, since a close comparison between the film and the script shows that Dulac had followed Artaud's text in great detail. More likely, his feeling of dissatisfaction was directed against the actor who had been chosen to play the leading role, one that Artaud had wished for himself and that in his eyes had been spoiled by the poor acting of Alex Allin. In any case, the controversy around *La Coquille* is certainly useful if we wish to grasp Artaud's conception of the cinema in all its singularity. Though his script does appear as the presentation of a dream, the re-creation of the oneiric experience was not its primary end. As Gilles Deleuze has shown, what was most interesting for Artaud was the contradictory, paradoxical relationship between film and thought, the cinema's power to transform the spectator into a 'spiritual automaton', or someone who thinks only to the extent that he or she is thought by the image and is 'robbed' of the possibility of thinking itself. Thanks to its power of 'osmotic' absorption, film could thus provide access to a new level of revelation, the sudden illumination of 'the impossibility of thinking that is thought' and the compulsion to think that which 'we are not yet thinking' (Deleuze 1989: 166–7).

In a sense, by taking the issue of revelation into the sphere of thought, Artaud was bringing the discursive tradition of French film theory to a turning point where the concepts elaborated during fifteen years of intense debate could acquire new meanings and a higher complexity. But the advent of sound forced the debate to follow a different line of development, in which the theoretical tradition of the silent period was rapidly forgotten. Once again, however, it did not disappear, it simply entered a tunnel from which it was to emerge after a gap of several decades. As Deleuze demonstrates in his profound reappraisal of Artaud and Epstein, the theoretical richness of the first wave of French cinema can still stimulate important reflections, and open up a new understanding of the film experience.

WORKS CITED

Abel, R. (1988) *French Film Theory and Criticism: A History/Anthology 1907–1939*, vols 1 and 2 Princeton, NJ, Princeton University Press.

Breton, A. (1951) 'As in a Wood', in Hammond, P. ed. (1978), *The Shadow and its Shadow: Surrealist Writings on the Cinema*, London, BFI, 42–5.

Burch, N. and Fieschi, J.-A. (1968) 'La Première Vague', *Cahiers du cinéma*, 202, 20–4.

Deleuze, G. (1989) *Cinema 2: The Time-Image*, London, Athlone.

Delluc, L. (1985) *Le Cinéma et le cinéaste: écrits cinématographiques*, vol. 1, Paris, Cinémathèque française.

Epstein, J. (1974) *Écrits sur le cinéma*, vols 1 and 2, Paris, Seghers.

Langlois, H. (1986) *Trois cents ans de cinema*, Paris, Cahiers du cinéma.

Marquard, O. (1989) *Aesthetica und Anaesthetica: Philosophische Überlegungen*, Paderborn, Schöningh.

Virmaux, A. and Virmaux, O. (1976) *Les Surréalistes et le cinéma*, Paris, Seghers.

Vuillermoz, É. (1917) 'Devant l'écran', *Le Temps*, 24 April, 3.

SELECTED FURTHER READING: 1890–1930

Abel, R. (1984) *French Cinema: The First Wave, 1915–1929*, Princeton, NJ, Princeton University Press. (Survey covering the cultural background, industry, forms and debates from World War I to the talkies.)

Abel, R. (1988) *French Film Theory and Criticism: A History/Anthology 1907–1929*, vol 1, Princeton, NJ, Princeton University Press (Translations of French critical texts up to the 1920s, with cultural context.)

Abel, R. (1994) *The Ciné Goes to Town: French Cinema 1896–1914*, Berkeley, University of California Press. (Survey covering the cultural background, industry, forms and debates up to World War I.)

Abel, R. (1999) *The Red Rooster Scare: Making Cinema American, 1900–1910*, Berkeley, University of California Press. (Study of the impact of Pathé films in the USA during the Nickelodeon era.)

Bordwell, D. (1980) *French Impressionist Cinema: Film Culture, Film Theory, and Film Style*, New York, Arno. (Study of 1920s forms and debates.)

Burch, N. (1990) *Life to those Shadows*, London, BFI. (Study of early cinema with extensive reference to French examples.)

Dahlquist, M. (2001) *The Invisible Seen in French Cinema before 1917*, Stockholm, Aura. (Study of the figure of invisibility in trick films, scientific films and crime series.)

Hammond, P. ed. (2000) *The Shadow and its Shadow: Surrealist Writings on the Cinema*, San Francisco, City Lights Books. (Selection of translated French critical texts, with cultural context.)

Kuenzli, R. ed. (1996) *Dada and Surrealist Film*, Cambridge, MA, MIT Press. (Collection including studies of 1920s French experimental cinema.)

Mannoni, L. (2000) *The Great Art of Light and Shadow: Archaeology of the Cinema*, Exeter, University of Exeter Press. (Survey of cinema's technological and cultural pre-history.)

Schwartz, V. (1998) *Spectacular Realities: Early Mass Culture in Fin-de-Siècle Paris*, Berkeley, University of California Press. (Historical background to early cinema.)

Slavin, D. (2001) *Colonial Cinema and Imperial France, 1919–1939*, Baltimore, Johns Hopkins University Press. (Study of colonial films and their ideological context.)

PART TWO

1930–60

INTRODUCTION 1930–60
Classicism and Conflict

Michael Temple and Michael Witt

The classical era of French cinema coincides with a historical period of unrelenting social upheaval, political division and military conflict. Even a cursory account of European history during these thirty years reveals a continent in crisis, deeply riven by economic depression and ideological extremism, almost destroyed by wars both within and beyond its frontiers, and completely recast in geopolitical terms by the rise or fall of Republics, Reichs, Blocs and Empires. France as a nation and as a colonial power felt the violent flux of these times as severely as any other European country, changing political regimes three times within the space of thirty years and experiencing a four-year occupation by a foreign power. The collapse of the Third Republic in 1940 led to the installation of a collaborationist state, under Marshal Philippe Pétain, during the German occupation; after the Liberation, the democratic institutions of the Fourth Republic were constantly undermined by colonial wars and political tensions, until the regime was eventually replaced by the Fifth Republic and the autocratic return of General de Gaulle in 1958. At the start of this period, in 1930, France was about to be hit by the full force of the global economic crash; at the end, in 1960, she was still caught in the middle of the violence and hatred unleashed by the Algerian war. During the turbulent intervening years, the French film industry had somehow struggled through the difficult conversion to sound, the economic depression of the 1930s, the penury of the Occupation, the post-war reconstruction in the face of US hegemony, and a series of new challenges posed by colour, widescreen and the ominous growth of television. And yet French cinema did much more than merely survive these historical upheavals and industrial changes.

In fact it prospered, and even excelled, both artistically and commercially. Some of its greatest films and best-known film-makers appeared and flourished at this time; and the public's desire for cinema during these difficult decades was surely never stronger. This enduring paradox of crisis and classicism raises some of the most interesting questions that we face in approaching the period from 1930 to 1960, notably the double challenge to relate these timeless classic films to the age of conflict and catastrophe in which they were made, and to negotiate the complex relationship between the story of French cinema and its broader historical context.

Between the culture shock induced by the conversion to sound and the descent of Europe into war at the end of the decade, French cinema of the 1930s produced a great variety of new trends and innovative practices: imaginative explorations of the possibilities of sound; growth in popular genre filmmaking; bold experiments associated with the left-wing Popular Front; and, perhaps most significantly in terms of critical resonance and subsequent influence, the series of dark French melodramas known to film history as Poetic Realism. The diversity and quality of French production during this decade has certainly bequeathed to film culture a substantial inheritance of popular gems and enduring masterpieces by directors such as Marcel Carné (*Quai des brumes*, 1938), René Clair (*À nous la liberté*, 1932), Pierre Colombier (*Ces messieurs de la santé*, 1934), Julien Duvivier (*Poil de carotte*, 1932), Jacques Feyder (*Pension Mimosas*, 1935), Sacha Guitry (*Le Roman d'un tricheur*, 1936), Yves Mirande (*Messieurs les ronds-de-cuir*, 1936), Marcel Pagnol (*La Femme du boulanger*, 1938), Jean Renoir (*La Grande illusion*, 1937) and Jean Vigo (*L'Atalante*, 1934).

Yet from the perspective of 1930, nobody would have predicted that the decade might one day be considered among the highpoints of world film history. For at the moment of the transition to sound, when French cinema found itself technically and artistically behind the pace, the pervasive mood was one of cultural pessimism and industrial panic. Numerous commentators, including some of cinema's most established names (Abel Gance, Marcel L'Herbier, even René Clair) viewed the arrival of sound less as a possibility for a fresh start than as the premature death of an art form still in its infancy. They were particularly concerned about theatrical and literary influences contaminating the 'purity' of the silent tradition; the increasing standardisation of film form resulting from the new technology and its uniform modes of production; the sudden decline in location shooting as filmmakers retreated to the controllable environment of the studio; and the general paralysis of camera and actor in response to the demands of the microphone and the dictates of the sound technician.

From an industrial viewpoint, the sense of panic is understandable, when we consider how unprepared the French industry was for the coming of sound. By late 1929, when almost half of the 20,500 cinemas in the USA were already equipped for sound, virtually none had been converted in France. The US and German companies moved swiftly to capitalise on the gap in the market, successfully driving the conversion of French theatres through the sale of their Western Electric, RCA and Tri-Ergon (Tobis-Klangfilm) systems. The investment required to convert studios and cinemas for sound recording and playback meant that only the larger well-established French companies, such as Gaumont and Pathé in their glory days, could have aspired to compete with the German and US conglomerates, but they were hampered throughout the decade by failed mergers and financial mismanagement. By the mid-1930s a more familiar picture of the French industry had emerged, with a variety of relatively small and under-capitalised businesses working in competition and combination with each other (see Chapter 9).

Given the industry's slow start, it is perhaps unsurprising that many early French sound films are often represented as neither very French nor very talkative. Thus *L'Eau du Nil* (Marcel Vandal, 1928) was shot as a silent and sonorised with a music track, as was *Le Collier de la reine* (Gaston Ravel,

1929), which also included a single section of dialogue; *Les Trois masques* (André Hugon, 1929), the film usually cited as the first French talkie, was shot in the Twickenham Studios in the UK, because the French studios were still inadequately equipped. Besides these technical and economic challenges, there was also a new problem of language: where silent films had communicated quite freely across linguistic barriers, the potential audience for dialogue in French (or any other single language) was necessarily limited. This led to the curious phenomenon of 'multiple-language versions' of the same film. Before dubbing became both technically and economically viable towards the end of 1931, the US company Paramount, for example, had experimented with multilingual film production at their Joinville base outside Paris, a studio famously called 'Babel-sur-Seine' by scriptwriter Henri Jeanson. Here as many as eight different linguistic versions of the same film were shot using the same sets and the same basic script but with different casts of actors, who all performed in their native tongues (Vincendeau 1999). An important by-product of this extraordinary system was the valuable practical experience that it gave to many young directors, such as Alberto Cavalcanti, Marc Allégret and Christian-Jaque, who were able to learn the new techniques of sound cinema by working on these multiple-language versions. In a similar vein, the Hollywood studios invited French acting and directing talent to make French-language versions of popular films in California; thus Claude Autant-Lara entered the sound era directing Douglas Fairbanks in *L'Athlète incomplet* (1930) for Warner Bros. (a French version of *Local Boy Makes Good*) and Buster Keaton in *Buster se marie* (1931) for MGM (a French version of *Parlor, Bedroom and Bath*) (Buache 1982: 14).

It would be tempting, but inaccurate, to portray French cinema as stuttering rather timidly into the sound era. In order to counter such a negative impression, we need only consider the response of those film-makers who welcomed the talkies as an artistic opportunity rather than as a regression in the art of film. Coming from the theatre, the playwright and entrepreneur Marcel Pagnol freely launched himself into the new format, at first as author and producer – *Marius* (1931), directed by

Alexander Korda, and *Fanny* (1932), by Marc Allégret – then as director with *Le Gendre de Monsieur Poirier* (1933), *Angèle* (1934), *César* (1936) and a host of other successes. Pagnol's status as a wordsmith and reputation as a polemical defender of 'canned theatre' have tended to obscure the real experimental and innovative qualities of many of these films, especially in their use of direct sound. Another successful playwright, also an actor, was Sacha Guitry, who (despite some initial scepticism about the talkies) soon entered the fray with *Pasteur* (1935), and then went on to write, direct and frequently interpret some of the most inventive (*Le Roman d'un tricheur*) and most successful (*Les Perles de la couronne*, 1937) sound works of the decade. As brilliant purveyors of the word, Pagnol and Guitry were very much the men of the moment, their genius entering onto cinema's stage with effective historical timing, but because their real achievements as film-makers were for years ignored by the anti-sound bias of many commentators, it is only with the passage of time that their popular success and commercial value have been reconciled with long-term critical recognition.

Conversely, one could argue that the critical fortunes of René Clair and Jacques Feyder have evolved in the opposite direction, insofar as their reputations were much higher between 1930 and 1960 than they have been since the New Wave. For decades, Clair's brilliantly playful and popular hits *Sous les toits de Paris* (1930) and *Le Million* (1931), with their magnificent sets by Lazare Meerson, were commonly promoted as the perfect defence and illustration of a typically French sound cinema, defined in double opposition to the technical homogenisation of the early talkies and the commercial dominance of Hollywood. The more socially conscious *À nous la liberté* was celebrated as a masterful combination of Clair's semi-musical experimentations with counterpoint and sound-orchestration, in which the spoken word played a fairly insignificant role, and a serious attempt to address the economic realities of modern industrial life and the impending political clashes between collectivist ideologies and democratic freedoms. Alongside these early French masterpieces, Clair's silent films, along with his English-language films and post-war career in France have largely been ignored. In a similar vein, Feyder's *Le Grand jeu* (1934) and *La Kermesse héroïque* (1935) were for many years evoked by historians as classic expressions of French artistic quality and cultural identity, and the director's return from Hollywood in 1933 was identified as a return to native soil and directorial form. Significantly, *Le Grand jeu* is set in colonial North Africa, an exotic but controlled environment for the imaginary expansion of French national identity; while *La Kermesse héroïque* reconstitutes in spectacle and costume a complex historical tale of sexual collaboration and national resistance in sixteenth-century Flanders, which some critics later interpreted as a predictive parable about the impending fate of Western Europe.

Just as Clair and Feyder are chiefly remembered for their work in the 1930s, so Julien Duvivier, despite a long and diverse career, is principally celebrated for the ingenious sound experiment *Allô Berlin? Ici Paris!* (1931), the dark Simenon adaptation *La Tête d'un homme* (1933) and the emblem of popular masculinity *La Belle équipe* (1936), while his output in other times or other countries has received far less critical attention (see Chapter 8). Among his most highly rated films of the 1930s, the fact that two are colonial tales (*La Bandera*, 1935; *Pépé le Moko*, 1937) again suggests a certain historical confluence between the identity of French classic cinema, both at the time and subsequently, and those filmic projections of imperial grandeur (perhaps inspired by the Colonial Exhibition of 1931) that together form a distinctive vein of the decade's production. These include comedies (*Bouboule 1er, roi nègre*, Léon Mathot, 1933; *Zouzou*, Marc Allégret, 1934), dramas (*Princesse Tam-Tam*, Edmond T. Gréville, 1935; *Un de la légion*, Christian-Jaque, 1936) and documentaries (*La Croisière jaune*, Léon Poirier, 1933; *La France est un empire*, Gaston Chelle *et al.*, 1939).

Closer to home, two important trends in 1930s French cinema addressed domestic issues and reflected national preoccupations: the films of the Popular Front and Poetic Realism. The term Popular Front designates the left-wing alliance of Communists, Socialists and Radicals, which briefly held power in France between May 1936 and October 1938. In those two and a half years, the Front introduced far-reaching economic, political and social reforms, including the forty-hour working week, paid holidays, union rights and wage increases. In film history, the period of the Popular Front is remembered for a flourishing of creative activity that produced a number of film-making collectives (e.g. Ciné-Liberté) and a string of collectively made documentaries, newsreels and fiction films, including Jacques Becker, Jean-Paul Le Chanois and Jean Renoir's celebrated *La Vie est à nous* (1936). In addition to Renoir's 1935 masterpiece, *Le Crime de Monsieur Lange*, many of the most familiar titles from the late 1930s are infused with Popular Front themes: *La Belle équipe, Le Temps des cerises* (Le Chanois, 1937), *La Marseillaise* (Renoir, 1937) and *Choc en retour* (Georges Monca, 1937).

In contrast to the political commitment and direct representation of society that we find in the cinema of the Popular Front, the films categorised as Poetic Realist reflect the spirit of the age indirectly and philosophically, often through dramatic storylines that the viewer is invited to read as an allegory of the times. This tendency is best illustrated through reference to the films of Marcel Carné, whose partnership with scriptwriter Jacques Prévert produced the doom-laden trilogy of *Quai des brumes, Hôtel du Nord* (1938) and above all *Le Jour se lève* (1939), in which the hapless Jean Gabin's wait for his inevitable death at the break of day is clearly an allegory for Europe's expectation of war after the Munich compromise with Hitler in 1938. These three films by Carné and Prévert are central to critical accounts of Poetic Realism, a genre whose main characteristics include working-class urban milieux, downbeat romantic narratives, bleak endings, intricate sets and magnificent cinematography (see Chapters 8 and 11). Many major directors contributed to this rich vein of 1930s film-making, including Raymond Bernard (*Faubourg-Montmartre*, 1931), Pierre Chenal (*La Rue sans nom*, 1933), Jean Grémillon (*Gueule d'amour*, 1937) and Renoir (*La Bête humaine*, 1938). The gloomy mood of these films and their pessimistic philosophy of human destiny has frequently been interpreted as an expression of the left's disappointment after the collapse of the Popular Front and, more broadly, as a prophetic vision of the inevitable drift towards war and the shameful years of the Occupation. Indeed, after the defeat of France

in 1940, the new collaborationist regime of Marshal Pétain readily accused these Poetic Realist films of expressing the defeatist attitude of a decadent nation, and consequently many of them were banned from French screens for the duration of the war.

Finally, in discussing the enduring appeal and permanent value of French classic cinema of the 1930s, it would be impossible to ignore the singular contribution of Jean Renoir, whose work for many observers both summarises the artistic evolution and excellence of the decade, and records for future generations a profound social image of the age. As Dudley Andrew puts it, Renoir can be viewed as 'a kind of institution set within the larger institution of the film industry' (Andrew 1995: 275). His entire corpus, stretching over more than four decades in France, the USA, Italy and India, has justifiably generated a voluminous body of critical writing. It is his prolific output of the 1930s, however, that forms the bedrock of his reputation, much as the 1960s work of Jean-Luc Godard will forever stand as the testament to an equally long, varied and exceptional career. The string of films that Renoir made in the decade before the war, from *La Chienne* (1931) to *La Règle du jeu* (1939), via *La Nuit du carrefour* (1932), *Boudu sauvé des eaux* (1932), *Madame Bovary* (1933), *Toni* (1934), *Le Crime de Monsieur Lange* (1935), *Une partie de campagne* (1936), *Les Bas-fonds* (1936), *La Grande illusion* (1937), *La Marseillaise* (1937), and *La Bête humaine* (1938), provides a roll-call of at least ten all-time classic films, without which (to rewrite Louis Delluc's formula) French cinema, in the eyes of the film world, would either not be cinema or would not be French. Among that list, one film in particular, *La Règle du jeu*, has been regularly elected as 'the greatest film of all time' by different generations of critics, historians and film-makers alike. Faced with these films' timeless appeal and Renoir's universal status, it is important to remind ourselves of the difficult circumstances and the conflictual times in which they were created. This is not to deny Renoir's eternal virtues; on the contrary it is a vital aspect of these works' classical qualities that they demand to be set in dynamic tension with the harsh and bloody history they have survived. On the eve of war, at the premiere of *La Règle du jeu*, some people in the audience were so incensed by the film's joyous depiction of French society dancing on the edge of disaster that, according to Renoir himself, they literally tried to set fire to the screen.

The German invasion of May 1940 had an immediate and drastic impact on all aspects of French society. In a cinematic context, it resulted in the abrupt shut-down of the industry, the interruption of all films in production and the closure of cinemas. Under the terms of the armistice signed at the end of June, France was partitioned between the German-occupied north and west (controlled from Paris) and the unoccupied so-called 'free' zone in the south-east, governed from the small town of Vichy under the leadership of former World War I hero Marshal Pétain. Until the free zone itself was occupied from November 1942 onwards, Vichy functioned as a semi-autonomous fascist state pursuing French 'National Revolution' under the banner of 'Travail, Famille, Patrie' ('Work, Family, Fatherland'). Following the armistice, the film industry in both zones was subjected to radical reorganisation along corporatist and racist lines: a strong framework of state regulation; the rational planning of production and resources; moral censorship over the content of films at all stages of production; the introduction of a professional identity card, whose prime purpose was to exclude Jews explicitly from every branch of cinema, both artistic and commercial (see Chapter 9). In the summer and autumn of 1940, cinemas gradually reopened and film production resumed; in 1941, sixty features were made, rising to seventy-eight the following year. Many film personnel gravitated to Marcel Pagnol's studios in Marseilles and to the Victorine studios in Nice; a minority fled the country for the USA (Clair, Duvivier, Renoir, Ophuls) or elsewhere (Chenal went to South America). Excluded from the industry, some Jews found work in clandestinity, for example the set designer Alexander Trauner and composer Joseph Kosma, whom Carné secretly employed for *Les Visiteurs du soir* (1942) (see Chapter 8).

In Paris, one of the most important production companies was the German-owned Continental-Films, established in 1940 under the directorship of former UFA producer Alfred Greven. By the time of the Liberation, the company had produced thirty titles, including the popular *L'Assassinat du Père Noël*

(Christian-Jaque, 1941), *Les Inconnus de la maison* (Henri Decoin, 1942), *Mam'zelle Bonaparte* (Maurice Tourneur, 1941), *Au bonheur des dames* (André Cayatte, 1943) and Henri-Georges Clouzot's enduringly controversial 1943 *Le Corbeau* (see Chapter 14). Far from being explicitly pro-Nazi or even pro-Vichy, Continental's output shares the main characteristics of the 220 features made during the Occupation. The majority are well-crafted 'quality' genre films (especially comedies, thrillers and women-centred dramas), made in the studio according to a tightly controlled script and budget, often drawing on literary and historical sources, and providing entertainment and distraction for audiences who, for obvious reasons, neither expected nor wanted an accurate representation of their lives or their country. The Germans were more concerned with controlling the press and the radio, and Vichy ideology was propagated through newsreels and documentaries, so the film industry was generally allowed the freedom of self-censorship.

For the captive audience, deprived of US films in the main, but delighted to have somewhere to go and something to dream about, the cinema was a reassuring source of comfort and distraction, and spectator numbers were healthy throughout the war (see Chapter 13). It is hardly surprising, therefore, that in later years many people who worked in the industry, as well as critics and historians, have remembered the Occupation as nothing less than a 'golden age' in artistic and popular terms. They draw attention to the disappearance of foreign competition, the orderly working environment, the consistently high quality of production and the absence of flagrantly fascist images and ideology on the screen (the more overtly Pétainist shorts and pro-German newsreels were soon forgotten after the war). Some even suggest that certain fiction films of the period carried secretly coded messages of national Resistance, most famously at the end of *Les Visiteurs du soir*, when the petrified lovers' beating heart defies the oppression of the foreign Devil. Interviewed in the 1980s, Marcel Carné summarised succinctly this sense of professional and national honour: 'We tried to regain by Art what we had lost through Arms' (*Arena* 1985).

Some historians have demonstrated significant cultural continuity between the 1930s and the

Michel Simon in *Panique* (Julien Duvivier, 1946)

Occupation, notably remarking that the Vichy regime merely realised the numerous protectionist and corporatist projects formulated before the war in response to Hollywoodian hegemony and the perceived threat of foreigners, especially Jews (Jeancolas 1983). Others have emphasised, on the contrary, the post-war legacy of Vichy film culture, especially the institutional environment of regulation, subsidies, training and censorship, which remained the basic model of the industry throughout the 1950s (Léglise 1977). The latter can also argue that just as the majority of post-war institutional and business structures – notably one of the mainstays of the industry to this day, the Centre National de la Cinématographie (CNC) – evolved directly out of the institutions of Vichy, so the personnel of French cinema went largely unchanged. In October 1944 the Comité de Liberation du Cinéma Français (CLCF) set out to identify and indict those who had collaborated with the Germans, focusing particularly on Continental. The committee's task was complicated, to say the least, by the fact that virtually everyone in the industry (including the members of the CLCF!) could be accused to some degree of 'collaboration', simply because most film people had kept their heads down and carried on working as best they could in the circumstances. In fact, many film-makers who were to rise to prominence in the 1950s had even taken the opportunity presented by the Occupation to establish themselves as recognised directors: Claude Autant-Lara, Jacques Becker, Robert Bresson, André Cayatte, Jean Delannoy, Louis Daquin, to name but a few. Ignoring such moral complexities, the CLCF's enquiries resulted in the temporary exclusion from the industry of about a thousand of France's 60,000 film personnel (Bertin-Maghit 1989: 430–6). This included a number of high-profile figures such as Arletty, Ginette Leclerc, Sacha Guitry and Henri-Georges Clouzot, whose crimes were as unexceptional as their punishment was symbolic.

Many film people had in fact led a double life during the Occupation, developing their careers while actively participating in the Resistance (Henri Alekan, Jacques Becker, Max Douy and many more). So from as early as 1943, the year that saw the start of clandestine activity on the part of the CLCF, some of them even started planning to record on film what they hoped would be the eventual Liberation of their country. Their collective efforts produced some powerful accounts of the rapidly changing historical situation: *La Libération de Paris* (1944), co-ordinated by the CLCF, showed street fighting in the capital; Grémillon's *Le 6 juin à l'aube* (1945) recorded two months of fighting along the Normandy coast; Robert Gudin and Albert Mahuzier's *Caméras sous la botte* (1944) was secretly filmed on the streets of occupied Paris; and Le Chanois's *Au coeur de l'orage* (1945) incorporates footage of the Resistance fighters in the Vercors. The Conseil National de la Resistance (CNR) itself commissioned two films: André Michel's short *La Rose et le réséda* (1945), based on a celebrated Resistance poem by Louis Aragon, and René Clément's *La Bataille du rail* (1945), prizewinner at the first Cannes film festival, which had veered from its initial documentary concept towards a semi-dramatised account of the French railway workers' heroic contribution to the war effort. Indeed, besides notable exceptions such as Carné's bleak 1946 portrait of life in post-war Paris, *Les Portes de la nuit*, which was poorly received by the public, films made in the immediate post-war era dealing with the Occupation tended to emphasise the strength and uniformity of Resistance over capitulation and collaboration. This has led historians to draw an unfavourable comparison with Italian neo-realism, which is generally held up as the great example of a national cinema redeeming and renewing itself both formally and ethically by confronting its historical responsibilities. By contrast, the French cinema of the 1950s is accused of failing to 'liberate itself' in the Italian manner, instead remaining an institutionalised code of representation, unable to engage imaginatively with the social problems and political tensions that contributed to the downfall of the Fourth Republic in 1958, and blind to the colonial conflicts in Indochina and Algeria that would ultimately redefine France's place and prestige in the world.

This harsh assessment, largely based on the 'quality' feature films of the 1950s, may be tempered to some degree if we consider the production of short films and documentaries during the corresponding years. This sector had experienced a boom during the Occupation, as a result of legislation that replaced the double-bill exhibition format of the late 1930s with programmes including a short film before the feature. The first documentary film congress was held in April 1943 and approximately 400 documentaries were made between 1939 and 1944 (Prédal 1996: 127). Although many of these shorts have the reputation as vehicles for Vichy propaganda, the change in legislation had created a culture in predominantly documentary short films, whose influence carried over into the post-war period. Exemplary in this regard is Georges Rouquier, who followed shorts such as *Le Tonnelier* (1942) and *Le Charron* (1943) with his influential study of rural life, *Farrebique*, shot between 1944 and 1945, released in 1947 and rewarded with the International Critics' prize at Cannes. In the late 1940s and early 1950s the shortdocumentary encompassed an impressive array of social and political topics: class struggle (*Vivent les dockers*, Robert Menegoz, 1950), colonialism (*Les Statues meurent aussi*, Chris Marker and Alain Resnais, 1953), militarism (*Hôtel des Invalides*, Georges Franju, 1951), film history (*La Naissance du cinéma*, Roger Leenhardt, 1946), sport (*Ski de France*, Marcel Ichac, 1947), ethnography (*Chasse à l'hippopotame*, Jean Rouch, 1946), underwater exploration (*Paysages du silence*, Jacques-Yves Cousteau, 1946), science (*Notre planète la terre*, Jean Painlevé, 1946), portraiture (*Colette*, Yannick Bellon, 1950), social commentary (*Aubervilliers*, Éli Lotar and Jacques Prévert, 1945), art (*Les Désastres de la guerre*, Pierre Kast, 1951), travel (*Terre Adélie*, Mario Marret, 1952) and urban life (*Désordre, vision de St-Germain des Près*, Jacques Baratier, 1949). In 1953, when approximately 400 shorts were being made annually, a further change in legislation proposed that exhibitors should no longer be required to include a short as part of the programme. By way of response, a number of interested producers, directors and technicians came together as the 'Groupe des Trente' (the 'Group of Thirty', whose membership quickly grew to over a hundred) and published a passionate manifesto in defence of the short film, whose status they equated to literary forms such as the poem, short story or essay (Porcile 1965: 17–32). Although they failed to prevent implementation of the new law, the ensuing debate about the values of the short film served to consolidate the group as a movement, and paved the way for initiatives such as the first short film festival in 1955. In the slipstream of the Groupe des Trente came another wave of film-makers eager to explore the short-film format and many of whose names and projects have tended to eclipse those of their predecessors and contemporaries: Jacques Demy (*Le Sabotier du val de Loire*, 1955, supervised by Rouquier), Jean-Luc Godard (*Opération béton*, 1954), Marcel Hanoun (*Gérard de la nuit*, 1955), Maurice Pialat (*Drôle de bobine*, 1957), Jean-Daniel Pollet (*Pourvu qu'on ait l'ivresse*, 1957), François Reichenbach (*Les Marines*, 1957), Jacques Rivette (*Le Coup du berger*, 1956), Éric Rohmer (*Bérénice*, 1954), Jacques Rozier (*Rentrée des classes*, 1955), Mario Ruspoli (*Les Hommes de la baleine*, 1956), François Truffaut (*Les Mistons*, 1957), Agnès Varda (*O saisons, O châteaux*, 1956), René Vautier (*Afrique 50*, 1951), Carlos Vilardebo (*Vivre*, 1958) . . .

One of the most important post-war developments was the signing of the 'Blum–Byrnes' agreements in April 1946. In exchange for cancellation of France's post-war debt to the USA ($1,800 million), and in anticipation of a further $500 million of credit, this free-trade agreement opened the French market to a flood of US imports. The number of visas granted to dubbed US films jumped from zero in 1945 to 92 in 1946 and 176 in 1947, by which time the overall audience share for French films had plummeted to 30 per cent (Darré 2000: 71–2; Billard 1995: 515). In the next ten years, the French industry responded by entering into international co-productions, especially with Italy, and above all by investing in carefully crafted quality domestic product. These classically composed, studio-based costume dramas and literary adaptations enjoyed great popularity with home audiences at a time when competition from television was still minimal (see Chapter 11). In 1952, in an article on Christian-Jaque's *Adorables Créatures* published in *Cahiers du cinéma*, Michel Dorsday announced the 'death of cinema', explicitly attacking the nefarious influence of the 'bonuses for quality' which the CNC had been awarding to selected films since 1949 (Dorsday 1952). A second attack came in January 1954, when François Truffaut proposed the label 'tradition of quality' as an ironic description of 'a certain tendency in French cinema', whose allegedly facile psychological realism, reductive scripts and hackneyed dialogue were exemplified by the works of film-makers such as Claude Autant-Lara and scriptwriters such as Jean Aurenche and Pierre Bost (Truffaut 1976). Whatever the rights and wrongs of Truffaut's famous polemic, the subsequent triumph of the New Wave, which defined itself precisely in opposition to the 'cinéma de papa' of the 1950s, meant that the popular cinema of the Fourth Republic was regularly denigrated or ignored by critics and historians for a number of decades. However, given the gradual fading of the New Wave's influence over academic film studies, and over French film culture in general, it may now be possible to address the 1950s mainstream on its own terms, and to start reconsidering its people, its forms and its audiences without the prejudices accepted by later generations.

Auteur theory, for example, is arguably not the best way of approaching the cinema of this period, not least because the concept of the film-maker as individual artist was developed precisely as a polemical weapon with which to attack the directors of the 'tradition of quality'. Rather than privileging solely those 1950s artists whose extreme singularity opposes them to the norm (Robert Bresson, Jean Cocteau, Jacques Tati), or indeed those directors who managed to develop a personal voice within the classical system (Jacques Becker, Jean-Pierre Melville, Max Ophuls), it is perhaps time to devote more concentrated attention to those mainstream film-makers who contributed to the diversity, as well as the majority, of the period's production. If we were willing to take a fresh look at the work of such forgotten or caricatured figures as Yves Allégret, Jacqueline Audry, Claude Autant-Lara, André Berthomieu, Bernard Borderie, Norbert Carbonnaux, André Cayatte, Christian-Jaque, Yves Ciampi, René Clément, Henri-Georges Clouzot, Louis Daquin, Henri Decoin, Jean Delannoy, Jean Dréville, and so on – as well as the neglected postwar careers of Marcel Carné, René Clair, Julien Duvivier, Sacha Guitry, Marcel Pagnol and even Jean Renoir – who knows what we might find? Maybe the 'mainstream' is more than just a monolithic backdrop against which to appreciate the unique work of the solitary genius. Such a reassessment of personality in relation to production could

then be extended towards a genre-based approach to the 1950s, for example by focusing on popular forms such as comedies, crime thrillers, costume dramas and especially the rich vein of adaptations from nineteenth-century and contemporary literature. This strategy could in turn lead to a further reconfiguration of the people of French cinema during this decade, if we were prepared to shift our attention from directors towards the other workers behind the camera, whether they be screenwriters (Aurenche and Bost, Jacques Companeez, Henri Jeanson, Louis Chavanne, Charles Spaak . . .), cinematographers (Henri Alekan, Roger Hubert, Christian Matras, Armand Thirard . . .), set designers (Jean André, Georges Annenkov, Léon Barsacq, Max Douy . . .), or producers (Georges de Beauregard, Raymond Borderie, Pierre Braunberger, Anatole Dauman, Georges Lourau, André Paulvé, Raoul Ploquin . . .).

Another vital category of film people that has still received relatively little serious critical attention are the actors and actresses, and above all the stars, of this period (see, however, Vincendeau 2000). Those big names and fascinating faces that appear on the screen not only served as points of recognition and sources of attraction for the contemporary public, they also remain as points of reference and recollection in the collective memory. One could surely therefore construct a convincing working model of 1950s French cinema around the films and performances, screen-personalities and public personae of stars such as Jean-Pierre Aumont, Brigitte Bardot, Bourvil, Martine Carol, Maurice Chevalier, Eddie Constantine, Danielle Darrieux, Fernandel, Jean Gabin, Michèle Morgan, François Perier, Gérard Philipe, Micheline Presle, Maria Schell, Michel Simon, Simone Simon and Charles Vanel . . . A star-based approach has the potential to provide a fresh way of considering the popular cinema of the Fourth Republic, especially in terms of what it meant to the millions of spectators who contemplated, inhabited and enjoyed the films of those times more regularly and in greater numbers than at any other period in the history of French cinema.

Finally, by turning our attention towards the audiences, to the people who contributed in a very real sense, not just commercially but also imaginatively, to the success of the classic French cinema as a whole, perhaps we will discover new strategies for thinking about the dynamic between cinema and History, between film history and cultural memory, throughout the period from 1930 to 1960. This may lead us to study that relationship less in terms of the direct representation of current and past events on the screen, and more along the lines of a history of mentalities and mythologies, a cultural memory of what people saw at the cinema and how they related it to their everyday lives.

WORKS CITED

Andrew, D. (1995) *Mists of Regret: Culture and Sensibility in Classic French Film*, Princeton, NJ, Princeton University Press.

Arena (1985) *Marcel Carné: The Classic Years*, BBC television.

Bertin-Maghit, J.-P. (1989) *Le Cinéma sous l'Occupation: le monde du cinéma français de 1940 à 1946*, Paris, Olivier Orban.

Billard, P. (1995) *L'Âge classique du cinéma français*, Paris, Flammarion.

Buache, F. (1982) *Claude Autant-Lara*, Lausanne, L'Âge d'Homme.

Darré, Y. (2000) *Histoire sociale du cinéma français*, Paris, La Découverte.

Dorsday, M. (1952) 'Le Cinéma est mort', *Cahiers du cinéma*, 16, 55–8.

Jeancolas, J.-P. (1983) *Quinze ans d'années trente: le cinéma des français 1929–1944*, Paris, Stock.

Léglise, P. (1977) *Histoire de la politique du cinema français*, vol. 2, Paris, Lherminier.

Porcile, F. (1965) *Défense du court métrage français*, Paris, Cerf.

Prédal, R. (1996) *50 ans de cinéma français*, Paris, Nathan.

Truffaut, F. (1976) 'A Certain Tendency of French Cinema', in Nichols, B. ed., *Movies and Methods*, Berkeley, University of California Press, 224–37.

Vincendeau, G. (1999) 'Hollywood Babel: The Coming of Sound and the Multiple-Language Version', in Higson, A. and Maltby, R. eds, *'Film Europe' and 'Film America': Cinema, Commerce and Cultural Exchange 1920–1939*, Exeter, University of Exeter Press, 207–24.

Vincendeau, G. (2000) *Stars and Stardom in French Cinema*, New York, Continuum.

8 PEOPLE 1930–60
Migration and Exile in the Classical Period

Alastair Phillips

French cinema of this period is commonly recalled for the singularly 'French' contributions of people such as the directors Marcel Carné, Jacques Becker and Jean Renoir, and performers Fernandel, Jean Gabin and Arletty. Films like Carné's *Hôtel du Nord* (1938), for example, seem to embody an era in which French cinematic identity rested on a skilful and knowing mixture of technique, wordplay and performance, and telling reference to the representation of place and national archetypes. During these decades, French audiences engaged with the cinema as a key site of nationally specific mass entertainment, spectacle and pleasure. It was also a period when official and popular explanation of the distinctive nature of the nation's cinema flourished in such diverse forums as the national fan press, new locally written film histories and the curatorial efforts of the Cinémathèque française. In this chapter, I wish to extend the boundaries of this picture in a number of directions. First, I want to challenge an overly determined definition of the 'French' nature of French film production by focusing on the contribution of many non-French émigré film-makers to the period's cinematic output. At a time when French cinema was indeed undergoing rapid official, commercial and popular redefinition, the influx of various European talents was of central significance. Second, I want to argue that the period in question was marked in part by a recurrent sense of instability regarding the nature of the boundaries of national identity. Due to various political and social tensions in the period leading up to and including World War II and its aftermath, questions of migration and national belonging had particular resonance for French film-makers working in France and elsewhere. Finally, I propose to supplement an understanding of the canon (and its fringes) by suggesting that we also need to examine

such under-explored roles as the cinematographer, producer and set designer in the making of French national cinema. I will focus on four individual case studies: the German cinematographer Curt Courant (formerly Kurt Courant) (1899–1968), the Russian set designer André Andrejew (formerly Andrei Andrejew) (1887–1966), the French producer Pierre Braunberger (1905–90) and director Julien Duvivier (1896–1967).

FRENCH CINEMA IN ITS EUROPEAN CONTEXT

French film production of the pre-World War II period needs to be placed within the broader context of the reshaping of cinematic relations across Europe as leading figures within the European film industry sought to counteract the increasing hegemony of the integrated production and distribution systems of Hollywood in the early sound era. During this period, the French capital became a crossroads for the many people who sought to take advantage of the existing network of interrelationships that had grown up between France and other European countries during the 1920s. In addition to the considerable numbers of Germans, Austrians and Hungarians should be added the significant presence of the Russian émigrés such as the director Fédor Ozep (formerly Fyodor Otsep), the set designer Lazare Meerson and the producer Joseph Lucachevitch. Many Italian figures like the directors Carmine Gallone and Augusto Genina also came to work in France for a time.

The conversion to sound is one of the critical points where European interests intersected with the industrial model of the USA. The Americans and the Germans used France as a staging post in the struggle for control of the lucrative market of Europe and its ancillary territories. A key component of the debate over the control of the production, distribution and exhibition of sound feature films was the issue of nationally specific cultural representation. The relative economic weakness of the French domestic infrastructure helped to facilitate a specific pattern of creative interrelationships between people in Berlin and Paris. These modes of exchange then served as a crucial formative context for the subsequent ways in which distinctive French cultural identities were soon to be pictured by foreign as well as French artistic talents. In 1929, for instance, the German company Tobis established its outlet in Paris as a subsidiary to its central operations in Berlin and recruited the likes of René Clair to develop prestious productions such as the hugely successful and influential *Sous les toits de Paris* (1930). The film is an interesting instance of the complexity of Franco-German film relations in the early sound period. Despite the fact that it was evidently a top-level project, with superbly designed sets of Paris by the Russian émigré set designer Lazare Meerson, it originally failed at the box office in its country of production. It was, ironically, only after a gala presentation in Berlin and positive critical reception from the Germans that it then reopened in Paris to lasting success.

Tobis was not the only foreign company to recognise the financial potential of the exchange of personnel in cross-European French film production. Between 1929 and 1930 the American studio Paramount spent $10 million equipping the Joinville complex in Paris with six sound studios ready for the production of the multilingual sound films shot in as many as nine languages, including French, German, Spanish, Italian, Hungarian, Swedish, Polish, Czech and Romanian. The multilingual film was a significant but short-lived method of overcoming the cultural and economic barriers presented by the arrival of sound in the global film marketplace. Usually shot simultaneously in different languages, for example at Joinville, these multilingual versions also consisted of projects that were 'made from the same source material, but with a short time gap' (Vincendeau 1999: 209) or even 'polyglot' films, such as Julien Duvivier's remarkable Berlin-based Tobis production *Allô Berlin? Ici Paris!* (1931) and G. W. Pabst's *Kameradschaft* (1931), in which each French or German actor spoke in his or her native tongue. For

French cinema they played a key role in the forging of links that would subsequently prove central to the broader phenomenon of the migration of European film-makers into the country over the rest of the decade.

One of the important and unexpected consequences of Paramount's project was the consolidation of relations between French film professionals and their German counterparts. This phase in the cross-cultural film relationship between the two countries prefigured the later wave of Berlin-based Europeans who arrived in Paris after the coming to power of the Nazis in 1933. As well as facilitating the number of German sound technicians who came to work in French studios, Joinville clearly led to a great deal of other contact between practitioners. What the Germans had to offer, in many cases, was the level of their technical expertise. As the former script-girl Jeanne Witta-Montrobert noted in her memoirs, the Germans were especially 'preoccupied with matters of technique' (Witta-Montrobert 1980: 36). This observation confirms Dudley Andrew's description of the lasting effect of Tobis and Paramount's presence was exactly in France:

> the opportunity and training they provided for hundreds of French artisans to learn a craft that they could then carry with them to the numerous feeble but native production companies that had inevitably sprouted on the newly bulldozed terrain of the French film industry. (Andrew 1995: 99)

Another port of call for European migrants to the French capital was the newly established production company owned by Adolphe Osso called Société des Films Osso. Osso had resigned from his influential position as chief administrator of Paramount Pictures in the USA at the beginning of the decade and returned to France, where, for a few years, his company sustained an ambitious programme of sound features, many of which were developed by émigré personnel. In May 1931, Noë Bloch was named director of production, and his links with the German film industry, via his previous partnership with the producer Gregor Rabinovitch, secured the recruitment of such names as the German directors Carl Lamac, Heinz Hilpert

Albert Préjean and G. W. Pabst during making of *L'Opéra des quatre sous* (Pabst, 1930)

Allô Berlin? Ici Paris! (Julien Duvivier, 1931)

and Max Neufeld. Bloch was also able to make use of family connections and, the same year, put his Russian nephew, Anatol (later Anatole) Litvak, under contract.

By the end of 1931, therefore, a significant number of foreign film-makers were operative in France. As well as the German, Italian and Russian names already mentioned, these included the Swiss Robert Wyler, the Czech Karel Anton and the Hungarians Alexander Korda and Paul Féjos. The number of overseas personnel working on French-language film production in France was regarded with consternation in some quarters. A shrill editorial in *La Cinématographie française* on 10 October 1931 entitled 'No More Foreigners in Our Country!' argued that although foreigners were providing an 'indispensable' service, there must be stricter regulation of the number of native French personnel working on any one production. For others, it was a case of the preservation of the right of the French to make films based on cultural properties of French origin. Yet, as we shall now see in more detail, the service provided by many of these film-makers working for such companies as Tobis, Paramount and Osso was indispensable precisely because of the fact that as foreigners they could enhance rather than subvert the needs of the French industry at a crucial period of transition in its cultural practice.

ÉMIGRÉ VISIONS I: THE CINEMATOGRAPHER

Curt Courant's first full-length film made in France was *Coeur de lilas* directed by Anatole Litvak for Osso in 1931, although he had worked on French-language films in Berlin after the coming of sound. He had started making films in 1917 and in Germany had worked with a number of directors such as Fritz Lang and Hans Steinhoff, both of whom would come to France following the rise of Hitler. Courant's time in France coincided with a concern in some professional circles that the rising number of émigré film-makers in France was posing a threat to native job prospects. In 1932, to circumvent criticism, Courant decided to make it clear in the French trade press that he always relied on native French technical support in his work. There was certainly a broadly held view that German cine-

matographers such as Courant, Eugen Schüfftan and Franz Planer were responsible for a specific German look. A review of Courant's *L'Homme qui assassina* (Kurt Bernhardt, 1931) in *La Cinématographie française* on 24 January 1931 maintained that if the film had a fault, it was because 'the atmosphere is too German, the photography has conceived both the interiors and the full daylight exteriors in *clair-obscur*'. Again and again, Courant's attention to the singular effects of lighting techniques was signalled by French commentators. Yet this 'German' visual style was to be one of the greatest contributions that the émigrés actually made to 1930s French cinema. In this sense, Courant was right to stress his affiliations with French film-making interests. He is a fascinating example of the way in which many of the European émigrés worked in Paris, fitting into the culture yet at the same time enhancing the development of native production by being different. Courant, like his other German compatriots, was different because of his technically astute understanding of the narrative possibilities of relating character, space and decor within the frame through the control and direction of lighting. As Philippe Roger (1991) has suggested, the key to this was the simultaneous concentration and dispersal of light within the shot. On the one hand, light was directed so that blacks and whites were reinforced at the expense of neutral and even lighting arrangements. Strong light sources created a kind of sculpting effect within the space of the image. This often produced harsh contrasts between illumination and ink-black darkness, so that the contours and outlines of facial features or objects were dramatically defined. On the other hand, light was carefully dispersed so that the direction of a particular light source was obscured in favour of a more diffuse and suggestive use of shadow. This offered multiple possibilities regarding the creation of space and depth in the image and the situating of the actor in relation to the design of the set in the studio. Courant himself was particularly known for the way he worked to soften the texture of this ambient light through the use of fine silk fabric attached to numerous small projectors.

Courant is especially interesting because of the important role he played in the future direction of

French film output. In particular, he was adept at playing a teacherly role to native cinematographers. The benefit of being considered German also meant that he could pass on the fruits of his own training. The relationship, for example, between the creative use of diffuse and pointed light sources was a particularly German characteristic partly because of the vast financial and material resources of the German studios. Industrial strength had led to a heightened degree of proficiency and expertise with the available technology. Lighting technology had developed rapidly in the late silent era and Berlin was able to invest in the skills needed to manipulate the various projectors now available. As well as knowing how to differentiate effectively between the older and stronger arc lighting and the softer potential of recent incandescent lamp sources, German technicians such as Courant were also skilled in the potential of new film stocks. The introduction of panchromatic film, for example, allowed a far more subtle palette of greys and washes, which proved to be of great potential regarding the illumination of the urban milieux favoured by populist French melodramas. The fame of the German camera operators in France was such that Courant's fellow future émigré Eugen Schüfftan was employed to advertise the new Eastman Kodak film alongside G. W. Pabst in the French film press. When the German lighting émigrés arrived in Paris to work, they were already also seen as in some way advantageous to the future growth of the industry. This pedagogical function was necessary because of the lack of artisanal studio-based learning along the lines of the model provided by the American corporations in Hollywood. Younger French cinematographers were obliged to develop their skills through temporary mentoring relationships that varied from one production to the other. Throughout the 1930s, before and after interludes spent in England between 1933 and 1936, Courant worked with French assistant camera operators such as Charles Bauer, Jacques Natteau, André Bac and Maurice Pecqueux. This amounted to a kind of informal schooling. Claude Renoir, for example, was Courant's assistant on Jean Renoir's celebrated adaptation of Émile Zola's *La Bête humaine* (1938). Here, the assistant might well have been impressed by the virtuoso way in which Courant modelled the

light for dramatic purpose. The cinematography in the film makes full use of the aesthetic potential of reflective surfaces like water, window panes, shiny black fabric and mirror glass, and at key moments in the narrative the key psychological tensions on the faces of its main protagonists are enhanced by expressive abstract patterning. In an important review of the film published in *Le Temps* on 14 January 1939, Émile Vuillermoz highlighted the way that Courant's 'Germanic' visual style actually served the purpose of such an ostensibly 'French' production, noting how the cinematography of the film reminded him of the work emanating from the Berlin studios in the late silent period. In his mind, however, this is appropriate, because 'the subject of the film is *noir*'. Indeed, '*noir* is currently the colour in fashion in our studios'. Vuillermoz then compares the success of this visual darkness and the novelistic qualities of the author on which the film is based, suggesting that 'the art of Zola itself is essentially cinematographic. His realism is exactly that of a cameraman.'

This equation between cinematographic and literary darkness is a central facet of Poetic Realism – one of the archetypal strands of French film culture of the period. Indeed, the sombre and melodramatic narratives of this mode of film-making may represent the kind of cinema that most explicitly benefited from the contribution of the European émigrés. Looking at *Coeur de lilas*, an early instance of the genre, we can see clear evidence of the ways in which Courant's abilities as an émigré cinematographer specifically helped to promote one of the directions that French sound cinema would take as an alternative to the model of more theatrically inclined filmed entertainment. Talking about the film at the time of its release in *Cinémonde* on 31 December 1931, Courant's collaborator Anatole Litvak argued that 'real cinema' should circumvent the pull of 'filmed theatre' through its attention to 'light, rhythm and images'. 'In *Coeur de lilas*, my cast only speak when the situation demands', he commented. 'I simply want to make cinema; nothing more, nothing less.' Reviews of Courant and Litvak's early work in the French film industry constantly praise the level of their technical prowess and the facility of their films to let the co-ordination of images speak at the expense of over-laboured dialogue. The director and cinematographer's use of extensive travelling shots and rhythmic editing are frequently singled out. Central to their concerns is the sense that the camera should create a spectatorial relationship that differed from that of the connection between a live theatrical audience and a stage play. Instead, we see repeated evidence that the partnership between the viewer and the screen could be as immediate and intense as the intimate bond created between the mind of a novelist and his or her reader. For these émigré film-makers, what clearly matters is the evocation of social atmosphere and detail over the sheer display and artifice of pure spectacle and performance.

ÉMIGRÉ FILM-MAKERS IN FRANCE AFTER 1933

With the coming to power of Hitler in March 1933, the influx of émigré film-makers into France became a veritable tide. Their movements were now motivated as much by political and moral concern as economic opportunity due to the newly pronounced anti-Jewish bias of the German film industry. The day after the infamous gathering of DACHO (the Association of German Film Producers), chaired by Goebbels at the Hotel Kaiserhof on 28 March, UFA had set about firing all its known Jewish employees. A formal national boycott of Jewish film-makers was also instituted on 1 April. The idea of hordes of people leaving on the first train out of Germany may be an exaggeration, but by the summer of the same year many leading European film-makers were in temporary residence and seeking work in the French capital. They can be distinguished under three main categories: Jews who were fleeing racial persecution, political opponents of the National Socialist regime and artistic or intellectual figures who refused to obey the terms of the new dictatorship. Apart from the émigrés already mentioned, these included the directors Kurt Bernhardt, Robert Siodmak, Billy Wilder, G. W. Pabst, Max Ophuls, Joe May, Robert Wiene and E. A. Dupont; the producers Seymour Nebenzahl, Eugen Tuscherer; the writers Hanns G. Lustig and Walter Reisch; the composers Franz Waxmann and Friedrich Hollaender; the cinematographers Otto Heller and Georg Krause; the editor Jean Oser; and the set designers Otto Erdmann, Ernö Metzner,

Hans Sohnle and Emil Stepanek. Several of these personnel were not of German origin but arrived in France after working in the Berlin studios.

This process of displacement had ramifications beyond the immediacies of national exile. Because of their outsider status, the émigré film-makers subsequently played a key part in the way notions of France's own film identity were discussed. From the perspective of the French film industry, the presence of foreign professionals working alongside French personnel on French-language productions was viewed with a certain ambiguity. On the one hand, foreign talent could help to forge a distinctively European alternative to Hollywood's sound output, but on the other, it threatened to dilute nationally specific cultural and working practices. In a report in *Pour Vous* on 26 January 1933, for example, Nino Frank acclaimed the potential benefits of political migration, suggesting that the French capital could soon amass a group of European talents that would be the envy of Hollywood. Articles also began to appear regularly in the French film press deploring the persecution of minorities in Nazi Germany, but at the same time emphasising the growing anxieties of native French film-makers. Some applauded the recent decision by the Employment Minister on 7 April to further regulate the proportion of foreign workers who were permitted to work on a single French film production. This decree followed previous versions issued on 10 August and 19 October 1932 and stated directly that no more than 10 per cent of the major artistic personnel, and no more than 25 per cent of minor staff members, on a single film project could be of foreign origin.

Throughout the summer of 1933, the Parisian film press was making sharper distinctions between genuine political refugees and those who were coming to work in France for economic reasons. In an article entitled 'The Great Exodus of Cinema Jews' published in *Cinémonde* on 25 May, Michel Gorel drew a line between the moneyed 'carpetbaggers' and the 'real victims of the Hitlerian terror'. 'Among these German Jews, I know two or three directors of real talent, a dozen excellent camera operators, several magnificent actors and a number of authors and scriptwriters of real sensibility,' he commented. 'We have to set them to work – and fast!' However, in an article bearing the headings

'The Overseas Invasion' and 'French Directors First' published on 30 June in *La Cinématographie française*, Lucie Derain pointed out that the employment of overseas talent such as Anatole Litvak and Kurt Bernhardt risked putting a French director out on the street. Similar arguments were consistently made to explain the number of French cinematographers facing unemployment. This point underlines the perceived strengths of the contingent of German émigrés, but it appears that little critical mention was made of the influx of Berlin producers who were in a position to galvanise their contacts and revitalise the French film industry. Derain's article, in particular, specifically bemoans the lack of native French talent in this domain to match the contributions of Germany and the USA. She was obviously yet to realise the impact that the likes of Seymour Nebenzahl, producer of several of Robert Siodmak's French features among others, would have on France's film production.

By 1934, as France's economic situation worsened, the film émigrés became the subjects of increasingly organised hostility from disenfranchised sections of the French film industry. Famously, the studios at which Robert Siodmak's prestige musical *La Crise est finie* (1934) was being shot were picketed by protesters bearing placards with the motto 'Siodmak Go Home!' In May, the Justice Minister specifically rejected requests that the émigré be naturalised, while the Employment Minister Adrian Marquet announced that no further work permits would be issued to foreign film personnel. Gaston Thiery captured the thinly veiled tone of antagonism in an article published in *Paris-Midi*, in which he noted that 'a film with a "truly French" subject and title is currently being shot in a Parisian studio, where the producer of this film is a Mr Apfelbaum (or some such name). If we think about this carefully, will this really be a French film?' (Jeancolas 1983: 115). This type of criticism was merely the polite manifestation of an increasingly harsh line of politically motivated rhetoric that held sway over segments of parliamentary discourse and more widely in the proliferating right-wing press. The pejorative term *métèque* (designating vaguely Mediterranean origins) thus began to appear more frequently in written articles, along with the potent suggestion of a foreign 'invasion'.

ÉMIGRÉ VISIONS II: THE SET DESIGNER

The figure of André Andrejew can be seen as another example of this cosmopolitan tendency in French film production. Unlike his Russian counterpart Lazare Meerson, who had exercised such a powerful influence on the look of French cinema from the late silent period onwards, Andrejew only came to Paris in the early 1930s after a lengthy and successful stint working and learning in the Berlin studios. During his time in France, he worked with a number of émigré directors, such as Pabst and Litvak, on a range of productions including the phenomenally successful *Mayerling* (Litvak, 1936). To an extent, the significance of his work has been overshadowed by the example of Meerson and perhaps also Alexandre Trauner (Meerson's assistant between 1929 and 1936), but he stands as a useful model for analysis, not least for the potential his work suggests in the level of creative interaction between émigré set design and cinematography. This articulation of the narrative and emotional potential of the delineation of space through a combination of light, shadow and three-dimensional design was a further way in which highly trained foreign personnel were able to fashion changes in the look of French cinema throughout the decade and beyond.

Andrejew was born in St Petersburg and trained in architecture and painting at the Academy of Fine Arts in Moscow. As a set designer in Berlin he collaborated with Pabst on *Pandora's Box* (1928) and *The Threepenny Opera* (also shot in a French version as *L'Opéra de quat'sous* in 1930). His tendency towards a heavily aestheticised depiction of the key features of a given social milieu was central to his impact on the visualisation of space in a number of French films. Unlike Meerson, who favoured a more even distillation of the matter-of-fact rendering of the ordinary contours of the real contrasted with the overtly stylised and expressive, Andrejew marked his set designs with a clear sense of how individual design features could resonate quite intense, even symbolic, meanings. 'What matters', Andrejew told *Pour vous* on 26 May 1932, 'is the spirit of the set design, its poetry, its inherent meaning. We have to remain faithful to the feeling of the project while doing what is asked of us in a material sense'. Dudley Andrew argues convincingly that it was Meerson's 'middle zone' approach to the depiction of a given social world that proved to be the dominant cinematic model for Poetic Realism. Yet, as he also points out, it was Andrejew's specific talent to be able to 'know how to isolate and exaggerate a single element to serve as the focus and filter through which even the most immense settings had to be moved' (Andrew 1995: 185). This concentration of effect is surely the hallmark of those émigré film-makers who came from Germany to France. It renders visible, in a related fashion, the same emphatic evocation of psychological feeling and social atmosphere remarked upon in the dramatic aims of Curt Courant.

This convergence of beliefs is consistent with a more general level of mixing between cinematographers and set designers in this period. The native French cinematographer Michel Kelber, for example, has underlined how he and other lighting practitioners benefited from their interaction with émigré set designers in the French studios:

> The decorator and the camera operator really worked hand in hand. Not least for the fact that at the time of black and white shooting in the studios, each aspect of the architecture had repercussions on the organisation of the lighting set-up. The camera operator could foresee his set-ups and effects just by looking at the models for the décor and the set designer participated in these preparations since the choice of lighting could highlight his own work. (Kelber 1981: 31)

In the case of Andrejew, and other non-native figures such as Trauner, he noted how the trained designer would divide a particular set into two zones to amplify a sense of spatial and expressive possibility. The rear area would be lit and painted to suggest depth and would be rarely entered by the actor, while the front section marked out the principal sphere in which the action would unfurl. This degree of attentive engagement spilled over into the physical texture of set design. The Russian set designer Georges Wakhevitch remembers Curt Courant showing him how to manage the shading and levels of darkness when painting a set: 'He taught me that a staircase is always slightly flattened by light and suggested that I paint the riser more

deeply to accentuate the shadow' (Wakhevitch 1982: 10).

This notion of the accentuation of shadow is crucial when it comes to the influential work of Rudolph Maté and Andrejew in *Dans les rues*, directed in 1933 by the Russian émigré Victor Trivas. The close links between the cinematography and set design in order to facilitate a psychological reading of the ordinary contours of space were commented upon in the press. The designer and the camera operator 'appear to be in the middle of developing a strange world which under the harsh light of the projectors is confounding the separation between fiction and reality', wrote a journalist in an early production report in *Le Courrier*. The correlation between Maté's modulated light and the distinctive space of Andrejew's street set is particularly noticeable in the treatment of the city at night. The film's spatial design privileges certain viewing relations regarding the world of the street. It features, for example, a number of high-angle shots looking down from the rooftops at the integrated milieu below. What is even more significant, however, is the way that relationships between domestic space and external street space are managed through the prominent incorporation of the staircase, which acts both as a symbolic dramatic device and iconographical element. Staircases also feature extensively in the Poetic Realist sections of another film designed by Andrejew, Fédor Ozep's *Mirages de Paris* (1932). Here, the interaction of the evocative set design, diffuse lighting and careful editing creates a deliberately menacing sense of suffocation and threat at odds with the more open scenes of plenitude and spectacle found in the backstage sequences of the film.

In his illuminating book on French set design, Léon Barsacq notes how Andrejew rejected any documentary approach as a hindrance to creative freedom (Barsacq 1976). He points out that in his preparatory charcoal and ink sketches, Andrejew would often reduce zones of the picture plane to pure shadow in order to emphasise the symbolic potential of a chosen object. While this process possibly led to some excessive tendencies, it is clear that, as in the case of many other émigrés, Andrejew also knew how to adapt to what was expected of him. His work on *Lumières de Paris* (Richard

Pottier, 1938), for example, is largely undramatic except for its self-conscious emphasis on the correlation between the artifice of the diegetic theatrical set design and his own work as a set designer in a number of sequences. In *Cette vieille canaille* (Litvak, 1933), another fascinating film from the period that appears to be predicated partly on the iconography of Poetic Realism, Andrejew seems particularly at home picturing the disjuncture between the seedy and atmospheric world of the fairground and the modernist trappings of the apartment of a wealthy surgeon. Thus the texture of the film is apparently marked by the same kind of heterogeneity indicated by the character of the personnel who worked on the production.

THE OCCUPATION

With the declaration of war between France and Germany on 3 September 1939, invasion ceased to be a metaphorical term. The period of the German occupation of France that followed the official signing of the armistice on 25 June 1940 clearly had a substantial effect on the nature of the Franco-German film relationship and led to a new sense of the processes of exile and emigration in French film culture. While the occupying authorities moved swiftly to build an institutionalised framework for the control and management of French film production, vast numbers of French film-makers fled the national capital. Their journeys were varied in terms of distance and the length of absence.

A large number of personnel headed south to spend time in what became the Vichy-controlled unoccupied zone. For many, this became a staging post for locations in the rest of Europe and the USA. Leaving France directly was not easy, due to the difficulties of obtaining official exit visas from the Vichy authorities, and people took circuitous routes via neighbouring countries such as Portugal and the North African territories. Max Ophuls, for example, now an émigré twice over, was forced to spend a year in Switzerland before being able to sail to America. The actress Françoise Rosay also spent time in Switzerland with her husband Jacques Feyder before moving to London, where she was employed by the BBC to broadcast Resistance messages. Hollywood was a natural destination for some, and over the course of the war a significant

number of French film-makers helped to swell the ranks of the large pre-existing French film community on the West Coast. The professional and social networks of the likes of the actor Charles Boyer and director Robert Florey, both of whom had worked in American film since the late silent period, facilitated the arrival of many prominent names, including the directors Jean Renoir and Julien Duvivier and the actors Jean-Pierre Aumont, Jean Gabin and Simone Simon (Phillips 2002).

Staying in France involved a complex negotiation between internal exile and provisional belonging, especially in the early years of the war when it was by no means certain that German occupation of France would be a temporary phenomenon. Some, like the screenwriter Charles Spaak and the director-to-be Jacques Becker, elected to return to Paris, uncertain about the professional possibilities in the unoccupied zone due to the scarcity of capital, film stock and studio space. With the immediate confiscation by the Germans of all American- and Jewish-owned businesses, a number of southern-based producers such as André Paulvé turned to the Italians for financial assistance. This trend would be maintained in the years after the war, and is yet another way in which the classical era in French cinema was marked by shifting definitions of European co-operation. Many, of course, could not return to the occupied zone and several Jewish film workers, notably the set designer Alexander Trauner and the composer Joseph Kosma, were shielded among the swelling ranks of internal émigrés based in the foothills of the Côte d'Azur. When Marcel Carné used Trauner and Kosma in his wartime production *Les Visiteurs du soir* (1942), he had to arrange fronts for their names (Georges Wakhevitch and Maurice Thiriet respectively) during the production and on the eventual credits. Several of these émigrés, such as the actor René Lefèvre and the cinematographer Claude Renoir, also played active combat roles in the Resistance during the war. Others, such as the Jewish cinematographer Henri Alekan, who had managed to obtain false papers claiming Catholic parentage, engaged in various clandestine activities.

The pattern of exchange and co-operation between Germany and France in the pre-war period had predictable consequences for the management of the French film industry in Paris during the war. On the one hand, it facilitated the sense of an organised transition in terms of supervision and personnel; on the other, it aided the pernicious realisation of the anti-Semitic rhetoric previously aired in French right-wing press and trade circles. When, for example, the authorities formed the Service du Cinéma on the 16 August 1940 to oversee industrial, censorship, legal and financial issues, they laid the framework foundations for the Comité d'Organisation des Industries Cinématographiques (COIC), which was to appear later on in the year. The first director of the COIC was Raoul Ploquin, who had been in charge of the many UFA French-language films made in Germany in the 1930s. Another former UFA contact, Alfred Greven, became head of the German government-sponsored production company Continental when it was formed on 1 October 1940 and therefore became a sort of émigré himself. Many of the French actors that Continental signed up, such as Danielle Darrieux, Albert Préjean and Pierre Fresnay, had already made films in Germany before the war and, in a sense, therefore simply continued a trend.

During the first autumn of the Occupation a raft of legislation and guidelines was enacted in order to legitimise the pre-existing tide of anti-Semitism in French film culture. These identified the Jewish proprietors of production, distribution and exhibition companies such as Jacques Haïk, Bernard Natan and the Hakim brothers, and forbade their further participation in French cinema. Known Jewish émigré film-makers such as Robert Siodmak were also banned, as well as other native French names like Marcel Dalio (because he was a Jew) or Michèle Morgan (because she was now an émigré based in Hollywood). As Evelyn Ehrlich (1985) makes clear in her study of the period, producers were faced with difficult immediate choices in these circumstances: either they could cut the relevant scenes in which such actors appeared, remove their names from the credits or simply reshoot scenes with new performers, which is what happened in the case of Dalio's role in Marc Allégret's *Entrée des artistes* (1938).

The tide of resentment against native and former émigré Jewish film-makers continued unabated after 1940. Right-wing journalists such as the notorious Lucien Rebatet were given critical licence to equate the cosmopolitanism of France's pre-war film culture with a decline in national moral and political standards. In his book on the 'corrupt' influence of the Jews on French stage and screen published in 1941, *Les Tribus du cinéma et du théâtre*, Rebatet denounced the

> 80 per cent of all kinds of film personnel who were Jewish, 10 per cent émigrés without papers, and 10 per cent French, but with Marxist or masonic links; and that's not counting the actors, of whom half are of foreign extraction – Russian, Rumanian, Italian, American, Swiss, Belgian. (Crisp 1993: 187)

The same year an exhibition sponsored by the German embassy at the Palais Berlitz on 'The Jew and the Cinema' actually proclaimed the advantages to the French film industry of the German authorities' racially motivated employment policies. An article published at the same time in the film weekly *Ciné-Mondial* listed all known Jews who had corrupted French cinema. Among the names featured was that of the celebrated producer Pierre Braunberger.

ÉMIGRÉ VISIONS III: THE PRODUCER

Braunberger had been a leading figure in international developments in French national cinema since the 1920s. He was in Berlin in the late 1910s and in 1923 had travelled to the USA, where he formed professional links with 20th Century-Fox and MGM. In 1924, as director of the Société des films Jean Renoir he arranged the Franco-German production of Renoir's adaptation of *Nana* (1926). As a producer, Braunberger had close links with Parisian avant-garde circles of the period, assisting the Brazilian émigré Alberto Cavalcanti on the city-symphony *Rien que les heures* (1926) and the American émigré Man Ray on *L'Étoile de mer* (1928). After the success of the early French-language sound film *La Route est belle* (Robert Florey, 1929), Braunberger became linked professionally with the distributor Roger Richebé, and the two formed the influential production company Les Établissements Braunberger-Richebé, which made a number of the major mainstream films of the early sound era.

Several of these made significant and influential use of émigré personnel. Braunberger, for example, hired the German cinematographer Théodore Sparkuhl to work on Renoir's *La Chienne* (1931) and the Hungarian Paul Féjos to direct an adaptation of *Fantômas* (1932). The German exile G. W. Pabst directed *Don Quichotte* (1933) for the company. By the end of the decade, Braunberger was also involved in Parisian exhibition.

Braunberger claims in his colourful autobiography that he had serious and well-evolved plans to assassinate Adolf Hitler after his rise to power in Germany in 1933. Whether this is true or not, it is fair to say that when war was eventually declared between the two countries, he was already in a position to take preventive measures as a prominent Jewish businessman. Originally, Braunberger had decided to 'Aryanise' his organisation by naming his colleague Roland Tual as managing director, but on 10 June 1940 he decided to close the offices of the Société du cinéma Panthéon, as his company was now called, and rent them out to another member of the organisation. By the end of the year, following investigation by the authorities, he was arrested and interned in the transit camp at Drancy with his brother who was a medical doctor. Miraculously, his brother managed to negotiate releases for himself and Pierre, and the two left the occupied zone immediately for the South of France having swiftly obtained sets of false departure papers.

Braunberger's war narrative is typical of that of many forced émigrés who remained in France during the Occupation. His interaction with other leading film and cultural figures reveals a shifting world of insecurity, frustration and various levels of professional and political engagement. For a few months, Braunberger was secretary to Edith Piaf on the Côte d'Azur before staying with his former colleague Marc Allégret and co-operating on a succession of unrealised script projects. He became aware of the dangers of staying in such an open community, however, and decided to move much further inland to the countryside in the Lot region. By now he had decided to sell his shares in the Panthéon cinema to former colleagues. In the spring of 1942 this transaction was annulled by the German authorities on account of the shareholders' previous association with Braunberger and the business was put on the open market. In the south-west of France, he became lightly involved with the activities of the Resistance having met the writer André Malraux, who was now an activist operating under the pseudonym of Colonel Berger. On one occasion, at the request of Malraux, Braunberger tried unsuccessfully to cross the border into Spain, along with his brother and the influential regional distributor Robert Dorfmann. His brother was arrested and later committed suicide in captivity. Dorfmann, partly as a result of his close association with Braunberger, went on to become an important producer in the French industry for such key postwar names as Jean-Pierre Melville. During the war, Braunberger remained constantly anxious about his fate and that of his remaining family. He was shot at by the Germans while escaping from the village in which he was staying and recounts his suspicions about the part played by the anti-Semitic director Claude Autant-Lara in the attempted arrest of his parents in Paris.

On account of his status, Braunberger played an active role in the re-assimilation of Jewish filmmakers in French film culture in the immediate aftermath of the Occupation. He was keen to denounce those responsible for creating a climate of such fear and distrust. As a commissioner in the Information Ministry in post-Liberation Toulouse, he enacted legislation to outlaw any films sympathetic to the Germans and was responsible for the arrest of a number of known anti-Semitic cultural journalists. At the end of 1944, along with the director Claude Heymann, he formed the Groupe Israélite de Renseignements et d'Actions (GIRA) to gather together all the producers and film-makers who had been affected by the policies of the wartime administration. This organisation sought to create a tally of all those in the French film industry who had behaved badly towards Jewish film personnel; not with the aim of denouncing them to a purging committee, but to circumvent any future professional misconduct. Braunberger's organisation also lobbied for formal recognition of the legal difficulties that returning film exiles would face in re-establishing themselves in the post-war period. This was a significant gesture, since those who had been in hiding for fear of their direct safety had inevitably experienced the Occupation very differently to the many French film-makers who had chosen to leave the country for broad political and professional reasons. In Braunberger's own case, he was able to resume his previous activities relatively easily and again became a driving force in what might be termed the cosmopolitanisation of the country's film culture. In 1945 he created his own studio, and in the next couple of decades became a central influence in establishing the younger generation of French film-makers such as Alain Resnais and Chris Marker. In the 1950s, he was involved with the return to French soil of the exiled Max Ophuls, and in the 1960s he produced major early New Wave films such as François Truffaut's *Tirez sur le pianiste* (1960) and Jean-Luc Godard's *Vivre sa vie* (1962).

RETURN FROM EXILE

There has been considerable debate as to whether the German occupation was a period of continuity and retrenchment for French cinema, or if it marked the emergence of new talent and long-lasting organisational changes. Both cases can be argued, but there is no denying the fact that during the war a significant number of leading French film-makers of all kinds had been unable to practise their respective crafts. Of all the Jews who lost their employment opportunities and businesses, for instance, Pierre Braunberger estimates that only one person managed to find work in the industry by fooling the Germans. Jean-Paul Dreyfus collaborated with Continental under the name of Jean-Paul Le Chanois and even worked as an informer for the Communist Party. According to Braunberger, Alfred Greven knew of Dreyfus's origins and activities, but kept quiet in order to protect himself after the war. Covering one's tracks and saying the right thing, which often meant not saying very much, was also part of the complex return to the ordinary circumstances of film production after 1945. Continuity was fairly rapidly re-established by producers, including Jews, as new businesses were formed or old ones recuperated. The Russian émigré Joseph Bercholz, who had made films with such leading French names as Sacha Guitry and Henri Decoin during the 1930s, returned to France from Hollywood and went on to work on many of Jean Delannoy's major films of

the 1950s. New émigré producers arrived, such as the Russian Alexandre Mnouchkine and the Romanian Henry Deutschmeister, who worked on many popular films of the 1950s directed by new names in French cinema like René Clément and Jacques Becker. As Colin Crisp notes, many of these people 'were notably less committed to the making of profits than their French colleagues, and thus tended to choose projects which appealed to them as worth making for their artistic or thematic value rather than their commercial viability' (Crisp 1993: 169).

In the case of the migration back to France of the actors and directors who had left the country, the picture is more mixed. The illusion that France as a whole had collectively resisted the Occupation forces was deemed politically expedient in the immediate aftermath of the years of resignation, collaboration and denouncement. This complicated the reception of those who had, for various reasons, not visibly been there at all. As Janet Bergstrom asks in her essay on the respective returns to France of Julien Duvivier, René Clair and Jean Renoir, were these figures now perceived as exiles or émigrés? That is, were they seen by the French public and the French film industry as having come back heroically after being forced out in the first place, or were they seen as returning to a country that thought it had been deserted once and for all? (Bergstrom 1998). It is perhaps no accident that in order to assuage these ambiguities, Clair's and Renoir's first post-war French films were both nostalgic representations of earlier, more innocent times: *Le Silence est d'or* (1947) and *Le Carosse d'or* (1953). The situation of successful pre-war director Pierre Chenal, who had previously changed his family name from Cohen on the advice of Jean Mitry, was complicated by his Jewishness. Chenal had taken refuge in the unoccupied zone after war was declared and crossed the border to Spain to obtain a visa to Argentina. After his return to France in 1946, his initial film *La Foire aux chimères* (1946) was a critical failure and his attempt to redefine his Frenchness with a screen adaptation of the popular comic novel *Clochemerle* (1948) suffered badly at the censors. Years later he argued that he had 'had the bad taste to come back. I was not cremated, I didn't disappear into thin air, something that the former collaborators didn't forgive me' (Williams 1992: 423). He left France again before his career picked up once more in the 1950s.

As for the acting fraternity who had spent the war years in the relative and lucrative safety of Hollywood, the level of disquiet varied according to circumstances and the prestige in which individual talents were held. Recalling the period of his return migration in his memoirs, the Jewish actor Marcel Dalio felt that although 'the Germans were gone, the Resistance continued'. He believed that many saw him as 'a living reproach for their work with Continental during the war' (Williams 1992: 423). Even the likes of Jean Gabin had initial difficulties establishing his post-exile career when he migrated back to France. Was this because in the mind of the industry and audiences alike, he could still be associated too closely with the dark, pessimistic pre-war tradition of films like Carné's *Le Jour se lève* (1939)? Such productions now seemed, in retrospect, either to confirm the political diagnosis of the right-wing or to remind others of a world perhaps best left behind.

ÉMIGRÉ VISIONS IV: THE DIRECTOR

One of the leading directors of this world of pre-war French cinema was the director Julien Duvivier, who during the 1930s had specialised in such expressive examples of Poetic Realism as *La Bandera* (1935) and *La Belle équipe* (1936). Critics have defined Duvivier's work as being marked by virtuoso treatments of lighting, camera angle and movement, along with a dense and sustained evocation of the materiality of space marked by close analysis of chosen social milieux. He was a natural cosmopolitan and had worked elsewhere in Europe, North Africa and the USA before his decision to spend the war years in Hollywood. Two of his most interesting films of the period, *La Tête d'un homme* (1933) and *Pépé le Moko* (1937), both, intriguingly, contain narrative figures of men in exile. Duvivier had been on his way to Southeast Asia on a film project when he heard that war had been declared between France and Germany. He hurried back and spent the ensuing months on *Untel père et fils*, a morale-boosting fiction about three generations of a French family's adversarial relationship with the Germans. The film, produced by the émigré Paul Graetz and shot in the Victorine studios in Nice, was not released in France until 1945, as Duvivier made the decision to leave his native country after the armistice. He fled to Portugal with his Jewish wife and arranged a passage to the USA.

On arrival in Hollywood, Duvivier was to face the same set of compromises he had experienced in the USA during the making of *The Great Waltz* (1938). Used to wide-ranging powers of delegation and management in the devising of creative projects within the looser constraints of the French production system, Duvivier had previously expressed disappointment to the French film press that the greater budgetary possibilities of American cinema were not matched with any significant power as a director. The same was true on his second visit. After the critical and commercial failure of his Merle Oberon vehicle *Lydia* (1941), Duvivier went on to work on two 'sketch films' composed of a set of interrelated narratives: *Tales of Manhattan* (1942) and *Flesh and Fantasy* (1943). The former was relatively successful, and the fact that Duvivier's émigré friend and compatriot Charles Boyer starred in one of its parts probably led to the French actor helping develop the second as a co-producer. It is worth remembering that Duvivier's sense of disempowerment was less keenly felt by émigré technicians and actors, although in the case of the latter, relative degrees of success and failure within the Hollywood system were strongly marked by the questions of the suitability of their accent and performance style and their placement within suitable genres. During a large part of his period of exile in the USA, Duvivier had to bear troubled comparison with two other French directors in Hollywood: Jean Renoir and René Clair. As Bergstrom reminds us, however, Duvivier and his fellow émigrés did share similar emotional and professional problems as outsiders. All three were largely unable to maintain any regular contact with mainland France following the suspension of the postal service between the two countries from 1942 to 1944. One way of keeping a sense of national identity was to assist in the war effort: Clair, who had now been legally stripped of his French nationality by the Vichy government, planned unsuccessfully to work for the Free French in North Africa, and Renoir and Duvivier both directed pro-French propaganda features. Duvivier's *The Imposter* was made in 1943 and featured the exiled Jean Gabin as a French convict released by chance in a German bombing campaign. The character then joins the French army under the assumed identity of a dead soldier. By the time the film was released in January 1944, the outcome of the war in Europe was not in any great doubt, and this must have been one of the contributing reasons for its failed reception at the American box office.

Duvivier returned to Europe in 1945 already aware that his wartime career had been singled out for critical attention in the French press by the likes of the producer and director Henri Diamant-Berger. According to Bergstrom, this negative reception was inevitable, since the director's French former colleagues had spent the war in the same state of ignorance about him as he had of them. Duvivier repudiated his detractors in an interview: 'It appears that Clair, Renoir and I have disowned our country! Absolutely untrue' (Desrichard 2001: 61). Stung by the remarks, he decided to leave again, this time to work for Alexander Korda in London, but a project with Vivien Leigh fell through. Eventually, he turned to a Georges Simenon adaptation, *Panique* (1946), which became a strong and memorable screen denunciation of the relations between French people in the confused aftermath of the war. *Panique* portrays the insidious ways in which a popular community in France turns on an elderly Jewish man, played by Michel Simon. It is a harsh but thoughtfully delineated portrait of a society riven by mistrust and suspicion. Responding to questions about his involvement in the project, Duvivier argued that 'we are far from people who love each other, who are the rage on the screens of Hollywood, but I have the strong impression that we are passing through a period where people do not love each other' (Bergstrom 1998: 97). His use of the collective pronoun 'we' touched a raw nerve in subsequent critical discourse and the film's contents were specifically described as misrepresenting the real characteristics of French society. The reaction also raises a broader issue relevant to the historical moment: could only someone returning from exile, like Duvivier, make a film that mainstream film-makers who had stayed in France during the Occupation seemed to disavow?

In an interview with the émigré director Kurt Bernhardt published in *Paris-Midi* on 19 June 1933, film journalist Henri Calef commented that 'the cinema is an excellent vehicle for the intensification of relations between two nations – it permits not only a richer mutual knowledge but also a greater mutual understanding'. Calef's utopian ideals were apparently matched by Bernhardt, who argued in *Cinémonde* on 29 June 1933 that the presence of foreign film-makers in France 'was the only means by which to achieve an international cinema'. This chapter has examined what happened to these aspirations in relation to the many waves of migration and exile within the French film industry during the classical era. We have seen that far from helping to create a completely new practice of internationalisation, many émigrés preferred to collude with French modes of cultural representation. In this sense, in terms of genre, narrative and the norms of music, gesture and voice, they adapted to, rather then deliberately reoriented, French film-making practice. Nevertheless, many émigré film-makers did inflect numerous productions with their particular awareness of the expressive possibilities of film form. In some cases, especially in the 1930s with Poetic Realism, this meant a new attention to the processes of filmic narration; in others, it involved a sophisticated handling of light and set design. Ironically, it was probably the very success of some of these films that lent weight to the outbreak of xenophobic French voices protesting the arrival of the post-1933 wave of migrants. The French right wing then turned what might just have been an economic argument into a critical and political dispute over the depiction of French identity. The repercussions of these debates were felt well into the period of the Occupation and its aftermath, resulting in a harsh and direct repositioning of the terms of exile and emigration within the country's film culture. If it can be argued that the whole classical era in French cinema was marked by chronic instability in terms of industrial organisation and financial management, the same is hardly less true in terms of the flux and exchange of personnel and the respective senses of belonging and disenfranchisement that came with that process.

The cosmopolitan nature of French film production in the classical period was forged by profound shifts in political and economic relations between France and its European neighbours. This chapter has concentrated on the period leading up to and including World War II, but Germans, Italians and Russians continued to work in the French film industry in various leading capacities throughout the 1940s and 1950s as European cultural production tried to respond to the increasing threat of the hegemonic position of Hollywood. The immediate post-war period, for instance, saw a new growth in co-productions between France and Italy, leading to new waves of exchange and co-operation. Many of the leading émigrés of the 1930s like Litvak and Ophuls also returned. What this suggests is that the French film industry was a continually internationalised site of activity, but that being European and being French were never necessarily the same thing at the same time. As Colin Crisp has argued, the many waves of interchanges between European film-making countries in the classical period raise important questions about the supposed specificity of national production systems (Crisp 1993: xv). As I also hope to have shown, the breadth of Crisp's assertion can be strengthened by nuanced micro-historical analysis, which is as alert to the specificities of individual case studies as it is to the shifting institutionalised frameworks of industrial practice.

I would like to acknowledge the kind assistance of Peter Graham and Ginette Vincendeau with sections of this chapter.

WORKS CITED

Andrew, D. (1995) *Mists of Regret: Culture and Sensibility in Classic French Film*, Princeton, NJ, Princeton University Press.

Barsacq, L. (1976) *Caligari's Cabinet and Other Illusions*, Boston, New York Graphic Society.

Bergstrom, J. (1998) 'Émigrés or Exiles? The French Directors Return from Hollywood', in Nowell-Smith, G. and Ricci, S. eds, *Hollywood and Europe. Economics, Culture, National Identity: 1945–1995*, London, BFI, 86–103.

Crisp, C. (1993) *The Classic French Cinema, 1930–1960*, Bloomington, Indiana University Press.

Desrichard, Y. (2001) *Julien Duvivier*, Paris, BiFi/Durante.

Ehrlich, E. (1985) *Cinema of Paradox: French Film-Making under the German Occupation*, New York, Columbia University Press.

Jeancolas, J.-P. (1983) *Quinze ans d'années trente: le cinéma des Français 1929–1944*, Paris, Stock.

Kelber, M. (1981) 'Michel Kelber', *Cinématographe*, 68, June, 29–33.

Phillips, A. (2002) 'Changing Bodies/Changing Voices: Success and Failure in Hollywood in the Early Sound Era', *Screen*, 43: 2, 187–200.

Roger, P. (1991) 'L'Obscure clarté de la lumière allemande du cinéma français', in Gassen, H. and Hurst, H. eds, *Tendres Ennemis: France–Allemagne*, Paris, L'Harmattan, 111–38.

Vincendeau, G. (1999) 'Hollywood Babel: The Coming of Sound and the Multiple-Language Version', in Higson, A. and Maltby, R. eds, *'Film Europe' and 'Film America': Cinema, Commerce and Cultural Exchange 1920–1939*, Exeter, University of Exeter Press, 207–24.

Wakhevitch, G. (1982) 'Georges Wakhevitch', *Cinématographe*, 75, February, 6–11.

Williams, A. (1992) *Republic of Images: A History of French Filmmaking*, Cambridge, MA, Harvard University Press.

Witta-Montrobert, J. (1980) *La Lanterne magique: mémoires d'une script*, Paris, Calmann-Lévy.

9 BUSINESS 1930–60
Anarchy and Order in the Classic Cinema Industry

Colin Crisp

The French film industry has received three major shocks in the course of its existence: first the dislocation of the World War I; second the economic impact of the introduction of sound; and third the takeover and restructuring introduced by the Germans in 1940. The first of these was the most devastating, since as a result of it Hollywood permanently dislodged the French cinema from its position as world leader in the production and distribution of films. The second and third factors, although almost as severe, were arguably more beneficial in the long run, since they were instrumental in forming an industry capable of once again competing with Hollywood as no other European film industry has done. It is these last two more ambivalent shocks that are crucial to the present chapter, since the industrial structure that they combined to establish conditioned the way in which classic French films came to be made, the way the personnel of the period related to one another and performed their tasks, and thus the range and nature of the films they made between 1930 and 1960.

THE INTRODUCTION OF SOUND

The introduction of sound was instrumental in inaugurating the period of classic French cinema. Originating in America in 1927, it was introduced in France two years later. Despite widespread expectations in the industry at the time that the production of silent films and sound films would proceed in tandem, it soon became apparent that silent films were no longer commercially viable, and that the industry must convert totally to sound. Inevitably this conversion dramatically disrupted the existing industrial structures, procedures and power relations, because it changed not only the nature of the market for French films but also the source and scale of the finances supporting the industry and the

nature of the technical competences and practices required of the personnel.

Although there had been French experiments in sound-film production, the critical sound patents were all held by American and German firms, which charged what the French considered exorbitant rates for the right to exploit the technology. The cost of sound production was further increased by the need to shield the relatively clumsy technology against ambient sound, which tended to confine production to the studio. Small production companies inevitably found it difficult to obtain the funding necessary to realise their projects, location shooting fell off and those larger firms that owned studios found themselves in a favoured position, provided they could afford the high cost of converting their studios to sound. But it was not only the studios that needed converting to sound. The cost of equipping the 4,000 cinemas in France for sound projection could seldom be borne by the individuals who owned them. Consequently a golden opportunity presented itself for those few well-capitalised corporations that had survived the 1920s to buy up the key cinemas in Paris and the provinces and to form chains of cinemas connected to production houses. The availability of finance became crucial in determining who would succeed and who would fail in the industry, and the urgent need for large-scale finance also ensured that the banking and financial sectors would wield an increasing influence in the film-making process, just at a time when the Depression was about to call into question the viability of those sectors. Finally, the higher cost of production meant that larger audiences were required to amortise the resultant films, which prejudiced the newly powerful financiers against experimental films.

In 1930, then, everything seemed to be pushing the film industry towards the creation of a few vertically integrated corporations producing accessible films aimed at the largest possible audience. This was, of course, precisely what had happened in America, where a small number of major players emerged to dominate the industry, and also in the UK and Germany, where the Rank Corporation and UFA came respectively to dominate. The same tendency is apparent in France between 1930 and 1934, when it might have seemed to contemporary commentators that the duopoly of Pathé and Gaumont was destined to dominate the industry, in conjunction with agencies of the German and American conglomerates. As it happened, this duopolistic tendency would be blocked by a series of financial scandals involving corruption, embezzlement and mismanagement: it was not a privileged few vertically integrated corporations that came to characterise the French industry, but an anarchic multiplicity of small under-capitalised production companies with no permanent production facilities or staff and no structural connection to the distribution or exhibition sectors.

At its most rationalised – in the year 1931–2, for instance – some five French firms and two foreign firms dominated production. Of about 70 films produced in France by French companies and in the French language that year, 20 were produced by Pathé-Natan, 12 by Osso, 9 by Haïk, 9 by Braunberger and 4 by Gaumont. To these one can add the Paramount subsidiary, which produced 25 French-language films in its Joinville studios (or Babel-sur-Seine, as it was sometimes known), and the Tobis French-language production in the Épinay studios (see Table 1: 'Sound Film Production 1929–59'). However, within a few years all the French firms listed above had either gone bankrupt or suffered financial problems that severely curtailed production. Moreover, once the technology was available to dub English-language films into any other language at a negligible cost, the elaborate multiple-language production unit established by Paramount at Joinville became superfluous, and was discontinued.

Although the two major conglomerates of the early 1930s, Pathé and Gaumont, were later refloated in a qualified way, their attempts to set up vertically integrated conglomerates on the standard capitalist model had proven unsuccessful, resulting in scandals and bankruptcies. Such financial scandals were of course characteristic of capitalist societies at the time, and particularly of France. The crisis of confidence (and distrust of financiers) that they generated was only heightened by the ineffectual nature of the government's response. Despite many inquiries and reports, the government proved reluctant to intervene. But then at the time, the film industry must have seemed one of its less urgent problems, since despite the crisis and numerous bankruptcies, it was one of the few sectors of the economy that still held out some hope of a profit on investment. If a third of producers went bankrupt each year, another third were making reasonable and even exceptional profits, which meant that the industry as a whole was arguably in profit. Yet the government did make gestures towards reform from time to time, inaugurating official reviews by Maurice Petsch in 1935 and Guy de Carmoy in 1936, and setting up the Renaitour Commission in 1937 to hear evidence from interested parties. But it was only in 1939 that it finally decided to regulate the finances of the industry, and by then it was too late – the war intervened and the government's proposals lapsed.

In sum, throughout the 1930s the industry appeared to be lurching from one crisis to another. In 1931 the larger production firms had been tending towards integration, a direction that by 1935 all of them had been obliged to renounce, and the industry settled into a structure that, while apparently chaotic, with progressively better administration and financing would prove enduringly productive. Essentially it consisted of the following: a large number of small and under-capitalised production companies each involved in producing relatively few films; a divorce between production companies and production facilities, which must usually be rented on credit; the lack of any large-scale vertical integration between the production, distribution, exhibition and manufacturing sectors; an unreliable funding base, which must often be renegotiated for each film and is mostly dependent on pre-production agreements with distribution companies; the absence of any ongoing contractual basis for most of the intellectual and technical personnel, who had to be hired anew for each new film. This situation would inevitably have consequences

Table 1 Sound Film Production (1929–59)

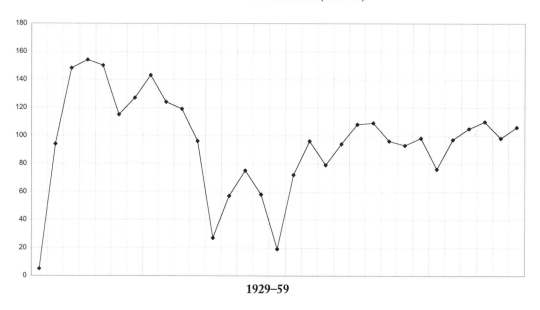

1929–59

Table 2 Audience Numbers (1929–60)

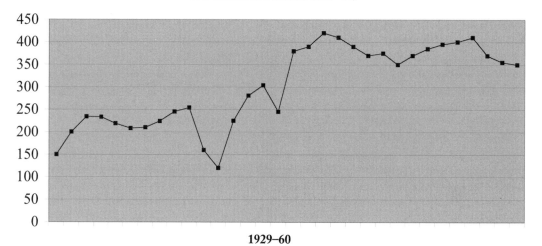

1929–60

All France (millions)

for other aspects of the cinema, since the industrial structure and funding was to determine what technology would be available, who was to use it and how. It would also determine how actors, directors and technical personnel saw their roles, what aspects of reality they would be able to represent, and how. In particular it would ensure that the economic disadvantage which the industry had suffered during the introduction of sound would be reproduced with each new advance in technology. This was not in any way due to a lack of inventiveness within the industry, since both sound itself and all subsequent advances – colour, relief and widescreen – had been developed previously or independently within the French industry. It was simply the case that the absence of any corporation in France with an adequate capital base, together with the relatively small clout that the French cinema had in the international arena, meant that it was impossible to industrialise French inventions and to oblige the international market to adopt them. Only the American giants proved able to do this, with the result that the French industry occasionally found itself in the position of buying back the right to exploit technological advances that it had itself originated, but which it had been forced to sell to American firms for development.

WAR AND OCCUPATION

Despite the apparent anarchy and constant financial crisis that reigned in the industry throughout the 1930s, the introduction of sound had by no means been an unmitigated disaster for the French cinema. After all, the sheer novelty of the new medium proved a significant attraction and audience numbers increased considerably (see Table 2: 'Audience Numbers 1929–60'). Competition from English-language cinemas, which had always been the principal commercial rival of the French cinema, was rendered significantly more complex by the introduction of talkies, and despite Paramount's Babel-sur-Seine and equivalent foreign-language production facilities in Hollywood, the American cinema was never again able entirely to overcome the obstacle created by linguistic and cultural boundaries. Moreover, the language-conscious French audience could now be provided with endless theatrical productions from the traditional classic and popular repertoires, translated into film form at a very moderate cost. These 'filmed plays' were severely criticised by contemporary commentators, who saw them as wordy and intrinsically un-cinematic, but arguably in economic terms they allowed the French sound cinema a crucial few years of low-cost but profitable productions, during which time it could find its feet and begin to explore the potential of the new medium.

Of course the protection provided by the national language still limited the French cinema to a relatively small audience, and French audiences would always be proportionally smaller than those of other European audiences, but by the end of the decade a spirit of optimism prevailed, as more and more of the films released each year were turning a profit. The industry attributed this to the higher technical quality of its productions, which in turn was due to increasing returns to producers. Foreign audiences confirmed this impression by their reception of French films in festivals and at the box office. Even the American market seemed to be opening up at last, with the success of such films as Jacques Feyder's *La Kermesse héroïque* (best film in USA, 1936), Anatole Litvak's *Mayerling* (1936) – twenty-four weeks in New York in 1937, taking $300,000 there alone – Jean Renoir's *La Grande illusion* (1937) – forty copies circulating simultaneously in USA in 1938 – Julien Duvivier's *Pépé le Moko* (1936) and *Un carnet de bal* (1937), Marcel Carné's *Quai des brumes* (1938) and *Le Jour se lève* (1939), and Sacha Guitry's *Le Roman d'un tricheur* (1936) – screened in 400 British cinemas – and *Les Perles de la couronne* (1937). Moreover, English-language versions of the most popular French films were being made regularly.

But just as a fragmented French industry was learning to cope with the emergence of sound film, it was devastated, as of course was the whole of Europe, by World War II. In the 1939–40 season, production, distribution and exhibition were all utterly disrupted. Key personnel were mobilised, air raids saw cinemas closed, then reopened to extremely restricted audiences, while fleeing populations had more pressing concerns to consider than which film to see next Saturday. The German invasion and occupation caused similar disruptions to the 1940–1 season, with many films banned, few new films released and production resuming only gradually, first in the south, then in early 1941 in the main Paris studios. The banning of Jews and other 'undesirables' caused a radical reduction in the available personnel. The continuing shortages of crucial material caused by the destruction of factories and by the demands of the war effort severely limited production throughout the war, and Allied air raids and subsequent advance on Paris progressively shut down the industry again in 1944.

This situation might at first appear even more disastrous than the chaos of the 1930s, yet in the course of the four years of the Occupation the industry managed to produce about 220 films of a surprisingly high quality, with relatively few concessions to the ideology of the occupier. Moreover, it underwent at the hands of the occupier an administrative overhaul that would in the long term prove extremely beneficial. Essentially the industry was restructured along the lines of the more general restructuring that was taking place in the whole of the French economy at that time, and was designed to ensure that the occupiers could effectively monitor and control all aspects of production. Ironically, many of these modifications were recognisably concordant with the reforms that had been recommended by the various experts and commissions appointed in the 1930s to review the industry.

First of all, such workers' and employers' organisations as existed were disbanded, and replaced by a Comité d'Organisation composed of members proposed by the various branches of the industry for the minister's consideration, and headed by a government-appointed commissioner. These committees were to produce statistical data, production schedules, legislative frameworks for the firms working within the industry and proposals concerning the price of goods and services. Overall control was exercised by the German Propagandaabteilung, which set up a German-controlled production company called Continental. The Propagandaabteilung's French counterpart, the Services du Cinéma, had three arms dealing respectively with the industrial sectors (production, distribution, exhibition, technical industries, import and export), censorship and propaganda, and legal and financial

matters (including the Jewish question). The Services du Cinéma set up an executive body, the Comité d'Organisation des Industries Cinématographiques (COIC), with the function of overall administration of the industry and of its personnel. It had five sub-committees, relating respectively to producers, artistic and technical personnel, distributors, exhibitors and manufacturers of cinema technology. All industrial activity was subject to control and monitoring from the moment a script was proposed through its production and distribution to the finished film's screening and export. Ticket prices were regulated and monitored, which meant that for the first time objective and authoritative figures became available on total audience numbers, receipts and the relative popularity of each film (though most of these data were never published, and seem to have been lost). Like all other areas of industrial production, this system was hierarchical, regulated, restricted to approved categories of personnel and subject to quantity and quality control.

It could easily have proved an excessively restrictive system for a film industry accustomed to extremes of laissez-faire. Fortunately it was administered by enlightened and experienced administrators who had considerable experience of both the French and German film industries as a result of their pre-war activities. Alfred Greven, who was appointed by Goebbels to oversee the French cinema industry, had been a producer for UFA in the 1930s. He was a francophile of long standing, and had had extensive contact with French personnel working in Germany. Guy de Carmoy, who was appointed as his French counterpart in charge of the Services du Cinéma, was able to introduce certain aspects of the reforms he had proposed in his 1936 report. He in turn recommended Raoul Ploquin as director of the COIC – a particularly appropriate appointment, since Ploquin had been director of production for Tobis's German production of French-language films and thus had forged extensive professional connections with the German film industry.

Under this committed group, French cinema was rapidly re-established, and within the limits of available material and personnel functioned in a surprisingly effective manner over the next four years,

Jean Renoir shooting *La Grande illusion*

as any list of the films produced would demonstrate: Marcel Carné's *Les Visiteurs du soir* (1942) and *Les Enfants du paradis* (1945), Jean Grémillon's *Le Ciel est à vous* (1944), Henri-Georges Clouzot's *Le Corbeau* (1943), Marcel L'Herbier's *La Nuit fantastique* (1942), Jean Delannoy's *L'Éternel retour* (1943), etc. The conditions under which these films were produced were fraught, not just because of the material difficulties but also because the need to obtain an official work-card in order to participate in the industry eliminated from the production system and from the ownership of cinema chains a number of individuals who had been central to the success of the industry in the 1930s. Many others – not just Jews, but also Communists and Resistance fighters – fled or went underground. Certain of them continued to participate clandestinely, occasionally even with the implicit blessing of the administration.

Nevertheless, a profound shift in personnel took place in the course of these years (though of a conservative nature, since responsibility devolved on 'dependable' existing personnel).

The work-card required to function in the industry was not, however, exclusively racist or even ideological in its criteria. For the first time technical competence became a crucial criterion for participation in the industry, and wartime production saw a formalisation of the pre-war tendency to promote the professionalism of French production and the quality of the resultant product. Only those production firms with a solid reputation for technical finish and with established financial backing were approved, ensuring the elimination from the system of that multitude of fly-by-night firms that had characterised the 1930s, and further guaranteeing 'a quality product'. Even the material restrictions had their positive aspect. The reduction in film stock meant that programmes had to be restricted to a single feature film, instead of the two, three or even six that had been the case in pre-war days, so returns to producers and exhibitors were significantly greater. Furthermore, the short films that were funded to supplement these feature films began to provide that semi-formal training ground for a new generation of film-makers that the introduction of sound had largely eliminated.

More importantly, since nearly all foreign films (and notably American films) were banned for most of the war in the occupied area, and for much of the war elsewhere in France, the local product was for the first time since World War I entirely free from the competition of its main rivals. The proportion of receipts returning to the French production system rose from its 1930s norm of 50 per cent to nearer 85 per cent. Moreover, these increased receipts were being earned by far fewer films than in the previous decade. This factor, combined with the boom in audience numbers as the population sought to escape the austerities of their everyday existence, produced a situation where nearly all films were profitable and the most successful of them returned astronomical profits. These profits allowed producers to contemplate superproductions with a cast of thousands and elaborate technical effects, as well as furthering the tendency towards a 'quality product'.

Finally it is worth noting that Continental, the production company established by the Germans, was allocated only 30 of the 220 films released during the war years, which makes it clear that the administrative bodies had no desire to see it dominate the marketplace. This was no doubt due in part to common assumptions by all those concerned that the industry would remain recognisably similar in structure to the one they themselves had known in the 1930s, but it was also due to the interests of the administrators themselves, since no fewer than six of the members of the COIC either already had or soon established their own small production companies. Consequently the industry continued to be relatively fragmented: in 1941, a year in which 47 films were produced (excluding those of Continental), 31 firms were active; in 1942 the 70 films were produced by 41 firms; while in 1943, the 49 films were produced by 34 firms.

THE POST-WAR PERIOD

The radical restructuring to which the wartime French film industry was subject has been seen by some as having no crucial or long-term effect, while others argue that it brought about fundamental changes that remain with it to this day. In my view the latter viewpoint is the more valid, since with strategic name changes for face-saving purposes the organisational reforms introduced by the Germans were perpetuated after the war, and had an enormous impact on the values and attitudes of those who worked in the industry. Nevertheless, it is certainly true that the basic industrial structure remained the same as during the 1930s: the annual output of about a hundred films was produced by a large number of small production companies that had to hire personnel and studios anew for each film and negotiate distribution and exhibition rights with firms over which they had no control. Indeed, in the post-war years the number of production companies was to sky-rocket, reaching 250 firms in 1947 (a year in which only 75 films were produced) and 463 in 1958. Nearly all of these were small under-capitalised firms. In 1954, for instance, when the average film cost 100 million francs, some 290 of the 300 production companies in existence had a capital base of less than 20 million francs. The great majority of these companies produced or co-produced a single film, and most of the rest no more than two.

Despite the continuing post-war fragmentation of the industry, it was no longer as threatened as it had been throughout the previous decade, since it was now run and monitored by competent administrators and financed in an open and accountable way by both subsidies and a startling increase in audiences. This administrative and financial prosperity continued throughout the 1950s, justifying the claim by commentators that the years from 1947 to 1957 could be seen as the good years. After the war, the COIC was replaced first by the Office Professionnel du Cinéma and then by the Centre National du Cinéma (CNC); but for better or worse, the cinema that this body now regulated and monitored was no longer the anarchic, unco-ordinated, unpredictable industry that had constantly lurched from crisis to crisis during the 1930s. Instead it had become, or was to become, a more formalised, unionised and professionalised industry, largely subsidised by a government that saw it as a means of re-establishing France's claim to cultural pre-eminence in Europe.

This evolution was by no means inevitable, and there was a brief period just after the war when the spectre of American domination reappeared. To an industry that had become accustomed to the protected environment of the war years, the post-war influx of a five-year backlog of Hollywood films recalled the American displacement of French cinema during World War I. The industry's anxiety was exacerbated when the French government signed the Blum–Byrnes agreement guaranteeing that 'no restriction of any sort whatever would be imposed on the import of American films into France'. Despite government protestations that, overall, this agreement provided a good deal for the French cinema – better than any other European cinema had won – all elements of the industry were outraged, and a highly political campaign was waged with a view to ensuring the cancellation of the agreement. Manifestos were published, public meetings were organised and well-known members of the profession toured the country speaking to audiences during the intermission. Finally the government felt constrained to renegotiate the agreement, notably reintroducing a quota of 121 visas per year for dubbed American films; and though this limit was not strictly observed, the number of American films on the French market dropped steadily from an annual high of 54 per cent in 1947 to an astonishing 28 per cent in 1960, at which point the number of French films entering the market, while lower than usual, nevertheless exceeded American films by 2 per cent.

The appearance of an industry united and acting in concert that this campaign generated soon proved illusory. Professional and class divisions rapidly made themselves apparent in all areas of industrial activity. Management practices and career paths produced a hierarchically organised and regulated industry of a neo-capitalist sort. Despite the intentions of its originators, the founding in 1944 of the Institut des Hautes Études Cinématographiques (IDHEC), a film school established in the south of France by film-makers displaced from Paris by the exodus of 1940, was ultimately to contribute to this tendency. Initially the IDHEC seemed to those

involved merely an extension of their exhilarating collective experience during the Resistance, yet within a few years it had produced a constricting and conservative formalisation of career paths. By 1950, for instance, it was almost obligatory to have completed the courses at the IDHEC in order to become an assistant cinematographer, and this in turn was a prerequisite to rising up the hierarchy towards the position of chief cinematographer. This formalisation of training and career paths was most marked in the field of set design, where the principal practitioners monitored or approved, and frequently themselves taught on, the IDHEC courses. Sets of guidelines and rules outlining what was considered appropriate professional practice were incorporated into these courses, and their implementation in the early stages of an initiate's career was carefully monitored as he or she progressed from set design assistant to architect-decorator.

Such practices were never enforced as systematically in the more literary field of scriptwriting or the more artistic field of directing, largely because the notion that these more artistic and literary vocations might be subject to rules that could be taught was anathema to those involved. This is not to say that cinematographers, set designers and other crew members did not consider themselves artists; simply, they were artists who recognised that the art forms they were defining were still emerging out of technical competences and artisanal tasks such as painting and carpentry. Consequently they still felt the need for degree courses from a formally recognised institution in order to establish their credentials.

Parallel to this formalisation of training, and arguably leading in the same direction, was the post-war unionisation of personnel. The spirit of collective action fostered by the Resistance led the left-wing sympathisers who were dominant in the immediate post-war years, to develop groups of workers affiliated to the Confédération Générale du Travail (CGT) that were not a world away from the workers' consultative groups established by the Germans during the war. The employers' groups also affiliated, generating a boss/worker mentality and a series of industrial confrontations analogous to those in any other capitalist industry. The contrast was marked between this militant confrontational situation and the chaotic and largely unregulated climate of the 1930s. Those who had experienced both systems often regretted the more spontaneous and companionable spirit of the 1930s, when films might be planned around a table in a brothel and it was quite common for producers to sleep with their stars. The transformation of working conditions was widely felt to have led to a degradation rather than an improvement in quality. For many, making films was no longer an intoxicating task in which those involved felt it a privilege to participate, but simply a nine-to-five job where you did what you were paid to do, then went home and watched television. For the bosses, cost-efficiency and productivity began to override fraternal considerations, while for the workers, improving their working conditions began to assume a primary importance.

In the immediate post-war years the state had nationalised certain elements of the industry – notably the Jewish-owned cinemas taken over by the Nazis in 1940, which then became the Union Générale du Cinéma (UGC). Rather than nationalisation, however, it was through subsidies that the state most effectively intervened in the activities of the film industry. A temporary law providing subsidies to both production and exhibition sectors, which was introduced in 1948 as a form of post-war rehabilitation for the shell-shocked industry and funded primarily by a surtax, turned out to be a semi-permanent feature of industrial existence. Outrageously protectionist in American eyes, this 'aid law' was nevertheless defended by various analysts as a necessary form of protection for any film industry based on a restricted language market, and was subsequently perpetuated in the face of considerable opposition during Common Market negotiations. At first a universal subsidy, it was limited in 1954 to 'those films which are of a nature to serve the cause of the French cinema, and to open new perspectives in filmic art, or to promote the great themes and problems of the French Union'. In 1959 the subsidy was transformed into a loan based on the quality of the proposed film, refundable if the film made a profit. By that stage state funding had already provided 21 per cent of total production costs over the previous decade, and an even greater sum towards the renovation of the exhibition sector.

Alongside this process of formalisation, regulation, professionalisation and subsidisation of the industry, a system of co-productions with other national cinemas developed. The main aim of this system was to counter the superproductions of the American film industry, with their cast of thousands and special effects. Despite the financial prosperity of the 1950s, the capital required to mount such productions was beyond the resources of any single European national cinema, but when two or more combined their capital and their technical and artistic personnel they could hope to mount more ambitious productions designed to attract the approval of each nation's funding authorities and audiences. Agreements were signed with a number of (primarily European) nations, and in the course of the 1950s these co-productions came to dominate the production system, if not in sheer numbers at least in financial terms. They regularly figured among the most successful films of the year, returning a reliable profit to producers willing and able to take the greater financial risk. Of about 1,000 films made in the 1950s, 382 were co-productions, of which 325 involved Italian participation.

The classic period of the French cinema is often said to have ended with a fourth shock – the advent of the New Wave. Usually represented as a purely aesthetic shock, it is generally seen as different in kind from the preceding three shocks. However, it is perhaps better to regard it as a logical consequence of industrial factors already at work in the classic French cinema. First, it was merely the latest of a series of waves that commentators had long come to recognise as typical of the French cinema, by means of which the ranks of directors were renewed every seven to ten years. Second, this was a wave for which the classic French cinema had been preparing the ground for some years: new technologies developed during the war had been steadily extending the potential practices and attitudes of the industry's personnel, as lighter cameras and more sensitive film stock permitted new liberties in the representation of time and space. Third, the abrupt decline in audiences from 1958 onwards, due to new leisure activities, the mobility afforded by the private car and the introduction of television, produced a climate that favoured innovation and the exploitation of niche markets such as art cinema and pornography.

Of course the New Wave was represented at the time as the courageous reaction by a band of inspired artist-directors against the industrialisation of the French film industry that had taken place during the 1950s, but nevertheless it has to be said that there had always been a cohort of directors in the classic cinema for whom film was primarily an art form, just as there continued to be a contingent of film-makers working parallel to the New Wave for whom the cinema was primarily an entertainment industry. This is still the case today. The diversity of its production is one of the great strengths of the French cinema.

10 TECHNOLOGY 1930–60
Imported Technologies in French Film-Making

Charles O'Brien

This chapter surveys film-historical change in France during the years from 1930 to 1960 and discusses the significance of French film-making for the historiography of film technology. Technology is generally understood as integral to a film industry's material infrastructure, part of the plant and equipment that makes film-making physically possible; in contrast, film style is typically conceived as directly determined by a film industry's industrial-technological base. It is argued here that an examination of the adaptation in France of technologies whose use was first industrialised elsewhere – notably in Germany and the USA, where many of the major technology patents were owned – reveals an important dimension of the style/technology relation that escapes the terms of this familiar deterministic model and invites an alternative conceptualisation. Throughout the period, the same technologies and techniques often functioned differently when transplanted into the French context, with important consequences for the look and sound of the films themselves. Although new film styles became possible – perhaps even necessary – in the wake of the industrialisation of certain film technologies, how these were used in film-making was dependent on local and changing circumstances.

FRENCH CINEMA AND THE HISTORIOGRAPHY OF FILM TECHNOLOGY

An emphasis on technology's effects on film aesthetics has been prominent throughout the history of French accounts of film-technological change, beginning with sound conversion and continuing through much later discussions of cinema's impending digitalisation (de Baecque and Jousse 1996). Indeed, as with discussion of digital cinema, early

commentary on sound film exhibited the expectation that technological change would fundamentally alter the cinema's artistic nature (Icart 1988). The introduction of synchronous sound brought with it a concrete and ubiquitous sense of artistic crisis; film style and industrial practice appeared to undergo a fundamental, irreversible transformation within only a few years. Aesthetic considerations were especially salient in France in light of the strong intellectual interest in film in Paris at the time of sound conversion. Stylistic differences between French-made sound films and the celebrated avant-garde and modernist films of the French cinema of the 1920s were particularly striking. Featuring popular stage actors, scripts based on hit plays and recorded songs that were also marketed through phonograph discs and radio broadcasts, the talkies appeared stylistically derivative, devoid of the silent cinema's uniquely poetic characteristics. For many influential commentators, synch-sound technology had reduced the cinema to a recording medium for musical and stage performances. In light of the commercial pressures, the sound cinema's distinctive artistic capacity – if it had one – was likely to remain untapped. At the same time, the cinema's conversion-era transformation appeared one-dimensional, with little likelihood of a return to the self-conscious explorations into the uniquely filmic aspects of cinematography and editing in the silent-era experiments of innovators such Abel Gance, Germaine Dulac, Marcel L'Herbier and Jean Epstein, whose films now appeared as masterpieces of the past rather than living exemplars for modern, sound-era film-makers.

The early sound years, both in France and other countries, have long been described as a period when film style had become a function of the available technology, with technical constraints ensuring a predictable, studio-bound approach to filming scenes. But what is meant by the claim that technology determines style? In the case of sound-era technological adaptation in France, where many of the technologies were imported, familiar notions of style as a function of technological constraint are both indispensable and problematic. On the one hand, an understanding of film-historical change in terms of a process of innovation and diffusion, whereby technologies invented in Hollywood ultimately became used in the French film industry, clearly captures an essential dimension of the French cinema between 1930 and 1960. On the other, such an understanding becomes problematic if the sequence of events is conceived deterministically and early uses of a technology are assumed to carry over into new contexts. With regard to historical method, a distinction is necessary between a technology per se and its aesthetic function; while a technology's physical properties impose limits on what is possible in terms of film practice and style, they do not determine their own application. Any such application must be seen as under-determined by the intentions of the technology's inventors, and also by earlier user groups – including film-makers in the technology's film industry of origin. Variations in application of the same technologies between national cinemas invite explanation through reference to myriad place-specific factors, including the state of the industrial infrastructure of the respective film industries and the innovative uses of technology in particular films. Between 1930 and 1960, certain films served to clarify a technology's artistic potential by disclosing new and unforeseen possibilities for film practice. In other cases, well-publicised but unsuccessful films demonstrated a technology's commercial and artistic limitations – even to the point of killing off any immediate film-industry interest in adapting the technology. In either event, films are best understood not as having been determined by technology but as exercising a determination of their own, altering how technologies were understood and used within the industry.

In the French film industry of this period, questions of technological adaptation must be seen in a context dominated by Hollywood's perceived centrality, which it could be argued defined the years from 1930 to 1960 as a distinctive period in the history of film technology in France. French films were systematically compared and contrasted to the Hollywood films that routinely outnumbered domestic product on French movie screens throughout the period, with the exception of the years of the German occupation, when Hollywood films were officially banned. In the film-industry trade press, technological modernisation was routinely invoked as necessary for improving the competitive position of the French cinema vis-à-vis Hollywood. Particularly significant for French film practice and style in the early sound period were unprecedented requirements relating to pre-production planning: new requirements for thorough and detailed methods of scripting, budgeting and planning powerfully affected what was possible during shooting and editing. Prior to sound conversion, the activities of planning and scripting had typically been minimal in France compared to the USA and Germany. Indeed, in France during the 1920s, the improvised redesign of a film's story during editing had been common practice (Thompson 1993: 388–92). During sound conversion, however, such established improvisatory practices came into conflict with new pre-production needs. It was not until the administrative centralisation of the French film industry under German control during the Occupation that intensive pre-production methods became institutionalised across the industry. In the face of unprecedented wartime restrictions relating to censorship and material deprivation, pre-production planning, including rehearsal of cast and crew, became essential to French film-making, and was imposed on virtually all films made during the period (Ehrlich 1985: 98–100).

At the same time, notwithstanding the general tendency towards increased planning, diverse forms of resistance to technological change ensured that film-industrial modernisation in France occurred selectively, in piecemeal fashion, according to local terms and priorities. In contrast to the familiar vision of the history of film-technological change as an industrial juggernaut, flattening local practices in its wake, the French case offers numerous examples of the stubborn inertia of local conditions. Crucial in this regard was the highly fragmentary nature of the French film industry: an ever-shifting patchwork of small- and medium-sized companies, even well into the post-war years, with minimal overall co-ordination among its various sectors. Factors inhibiting Hollywood-inspired technological modernisation ranged from local, company-specific methods of film-making to actors' preferences regarding shooting procedures, established hierarchies of film-production personnel and, beginning in 1934, union-protected workers' rights. As a consequence, the French film industry's sound-era modernisation remained selective, uneven and protracted during the period from 1930 to 1960. Hence the difficulty of characterising the industrial modernisation of French cinema in terms of an Americanisation of world film practice. While capturing the reality of Hollywood's technological dominance, to characterise French film-industrial history purely in terms of Americanisation can obscure the effects of local forces in conditioning how film-industrial modernisation touched ground, so to speak, as imported technologies became folded into distinctive local matrices of activity and commitment. Notwithstanding the French film industry's important technological links to the American film industry, French production methods remained singular in ways that proved decisive stylistically, as in the French preference for production practices that allowed for improvisation at various phases of a film's production, especially shooting.

MULTIPLE CAMERA SHOOTING AND SOUND RECORDING IN 1930s FRANCE

An example can be found in multiple-camera shooting. Although introduced in France in 1930, just as Hollywood began phasing it out, multiple-camera shooting endured within the French film industry throughout the 1930s and into the 1940s and 1950s, decades later than in Hollywood. An essential condition for this longevity was the technique's compatibility with established French work practices, and with the stage-derived skills of sound-era French film actors. Even under the pressure of the two- to three-week shooting schedules common in France during the early 1930s, multiple-camera shooting allowed for a considerable amount of on-set improvisation. In France, the majority of actors continued to work in theatre, and

were therefore accustomed to memorising lengthy passages of dialogue, and to enunciating clearly, in a manner appropriate for sound recording. Given their formidable stage training, French film actors often preferred recording scenes holistically, simultaneously with the other actors, in single takes, rather than having their performances broken up into numerous separately recorded shots and reassembled in post-production, as became common practice in Hollywood around 1931. In addition, the multiple-camera approach proved compatible with an established understanding of the dramatic scene familiar to European cinema since the 1910s: a performance staged for recording rather than an assemblage of shots.

In light of the unique conditions of its adaptation, multiple-camera shooting in France produced distinctive stylistic effects. In contrast to the visual monotony associated with multiple-camera shooting in Hollywood, whereby scenes unfold according to a predictable sequence of master shot, medium shot and close-up, French films employing the technique made a more anarchic or ludic impression. One factor was the extraordinary variety of camera placements in multiple-camera French films, which often exhibit indifference to Hollywood's 180-degree rule. In some cases, frequent reversals in screen direction serve to keep the viewer perceptually off-balance, uncertain about the framing of the next shot in a scene. Examples can be found in numerous films made at the Joinville production complex of Pathé-Natan, French cinema's largest conversion-era production company. Indeed, in the case of films such as Pierre Colombier's *Le Roi du cirage* (1931) and René Guissart's *Prince de minuit* (1934), the total reversals in screen direction occur so frequently as to appear systematic. Such cases suggest a distinctive local approach to filming a scene, rather than a bungled attempt at continuity editing. In this context, rather than speak of the Americanisation of French cinema, it would be more appropriate to refer to a domestication of Hollywood's technologies and methods, whereby a familiar technique, transplanted into and indigenised within the matrix of French film-making, acquired a novel artistic function.

The peculiarities of technological adaptation in French film-making ensured that French films of the

1930s would amount to an artistic hybrid, exhibiting both evident similarities and differences with films from other countries. Differences in representation in French films – featuring French settings, cultural allusions and speech accents – were complemented by distinctive stylistic variations. In comparison to Hollywood films, for instance, French films exhibit fewer close-ups, a slower cutting pace, greater use of staging in depth and a preponderance of ensemble compositions, whereby the nature of a dramatic event becomes manifest less through editing than through the actors' positions relative to one another within a common, simultaneous *mise en scène* (Crisp 1993: 400–14; Vincendeau 2000: 7–10). In contrast to the forward-directed narration associated with continuity editing, French films offered the perceptual stimulation of ensemble compositions crowded with visual activity.

Supporting this distinctive visual style was an approach to sound-recording that differed fundamentally from the Hollywood approach, with French films implying a conception of film sound that privileged a sound's fidelity to its source over its intelligibility as representation. In Hollywood, beginning in 1931, with the industry-wide adoption of multitrack recording and mixing, all sounds, with the exception of dialogue, were recorded separately and then mixed into the soundtrack during post-production. In France, however, beginning in 1930 and continuing into the 1940s, voices and ambient sounds such as footsteps or doors closing were typically recorded together, at the same time as the image. Although multitrack technologies had been introduced in France as early as the summer of 1933, until the 1940s they were used only intermittently – on an ad hoc basis, when budgets and film-makers' preferences allowed. As a consequence of the routine use of the simultaneous recording of sound and image, scenes in French films tend to show up as recordings of actors' unique performances, captured live, so to speak, as they had occurred on a sound stage. Conversely, French films often also exhibit a relatively weak diegetic illusion. Rather than incarnate fictional characters, actors in French films appear to play themselves, as if bypassing the mediation of the film's story-world and addressing their fans directly (Lagny, Ropars and Sorlin 1986: 177–214;

Andrew 1995: 116–21). In enhancing the impression of French films of the early 1930s as the recordings of actors' performances, multiple-camera shooting and other techniques relating to direct-recorded sound helped establish the reputation of the French cinema of the decade as an actor's cinema.

FILM STYLE AND TECHNOLOGY AFTER 1940

If the introduction of recorded sound opened a new period in the history of French film style, then the emergence of France's 'tradition of quality' in the 1940s could be said to have brought that period to a conclusion. In affirming French literary and artistic traditions while simultaneously exhibiting a high degree of technical finish, quality cinema marked the French film industry's domestication of sound-era technology within an industry-wide artistic project. In effect, quality cinema implied a reconciliation of artistic and technical demands that had been in sharp conflict during the early sound years. In contrast to the stage-performance style of the films of the early 1930s, the quality films of the 1940s and 1950s offered a strong diegetic illusion. Rather than foreground actors' performances, knowingly played to an implied collectivity of fans, the quality cinema rested on a narration emphasising novelistic shifts in character point of view, as if trading the externality of staged performances for the character interiority of psychological realism. In the 1950s, quality cinema's status as an artistic culmination rather than a new beginning became evident with a further reconfiguration of the film-technological field. Especially noteworthy were two distinct developments. First, beginning in 1948, Hollywood began standardising colour and widescreen, thereby initiating the first major change in cinema's basic technological parameters since the introduction of synchronous sound in the late 1920s. The impact on film criticism and film theory in France was far-reaching. Generating a context for rethinking technology's impact on the history of film art, Hollywood's post-war industrialisation of colour and widescreen enabled a fundamental reinterpretation of the film-historical significance of synchronous sound. In particular, it became possible to see recent film-historical developments as continuous with aspects of silent-era practice. Countering the notion that synchronised sound had produced a complete break from the cinema's past, critics and theorists from André Bazin to Georges Charensol, writing after the war, redefined sound conversion in terms of artistic continuity across silent and sound eras, proposing a reconsideration of the entirety of film history in terms of an aesthetic of film realism (Bazin 1967: 23–4; Charensol 1949: 54). From the post-war standpoint, film-technological changes associated with synchronous sound, colour, widescreen and 3D became understood less in a strictly aesthetic context and more in socio-psychological terms, as a progressive technology-driven increase in humankind's mimetic capacity.

In the 1950s, a second major film-technological change occurred with the availability of new, lightweight technologies for image and sound recording, including portable, battery-operated magnetic tape recorders, professional-quality 16mm cameras and film stocks, zoom lenses and transistorised cables enabling the synchronised linking of camera and sound-recorder. Developed outside the film industry – in some cases for wartime purposes, in contexts unrelated to cinema – these devices proved highly consequential in enabling alternative film styles based on location shooting, such as the cinéma vérité associated with film-makers like Jean Rouch. Moreover, in contrast to the introduction of recorded sound, which in France had seemed instantly and dramatically to reduce the cinema's stylistic potential, the new portable technologies allowed for a retrieval of the artisanal methods characteristic of the small-scale independent film-making practised by the modernists and avant-gardists of the 1920s. Hence, the prevalence in post-war France of references to the post-war cinema of personal expression as a new avant-garde. Notable examples include experiments with location filming in the post-war work of independent film-makers such as Alexandre Astruc and Jean-Pierre Melville, which anticipated practices that would define the New Wave of the late 1950s and early 1960s. Location-shooting practices also became prominent in mainstream French film-making, which appears to have been especially receptive to the new technologies; according to one

report, more than one-third of French films made in 1960 were filmed virtually entirely in exterior locations (Courtade 1978: 274).

A new period in French film history is often said to have begun around 1960, as the major technological changes of the past fifteen years seemed to culminate with the international critical success of the New Wave. While certain Hollywood superproductions, based on familiar, star-oriented formulae, failed to draw audiences, the New Wave's low-tech films became artistic exemplars for a new generation of film-makers throughout the world, including Latin America, Asia and Africa. Many of these film-makers worked independently, outside the domain of studio film-making. At this point, at the close of what Colin Crisp refers to as the French cinema's classical period, a shift in national artistic status could be said to have occurred. As Hollywood entered a state of artistic crisis, the contemporaneous French cinema garnered international critical acclaim – including in Hollywood, where director Vincente Minnelli praised the New Wave's refreshing primordial quality and director John Huston characterised it as a liberation from the formulaic methods of big studio film-making.

COLOUR AND WIDESCREEN

Despite their small numbers relative to Hollywood films, French films consistently ranked highest in popularity among French viewers throughout the period from 1930 to 1960. At the same time, French films were understood in relation to films from other countries, especially the USA and Germany, which served as principal technology suppliers for the French film industry. The German cinema proved uniquely important to the French cinema between 1930 and 1932, when the German film industry functioned as Hollywood's main international competitor, with France serving as the principal export market for German films. The German–American rivalry was particularly salient in France, where German and American companies competed for dominance in the licensing of sound-film technologies, and operated major production subsidiaries such as Paramount-Paris and Tobis Films Sonores. With an emphasis on quality over quantity in its export productions, the conversion-era German cinema was known in France for its

Gérard Philipe in *Fanfan la Tulipe* (Christian-Jaque, 1952)

careful approach to scripting and rehearsal, and to exemplary methods pertaining to film-music recording.

During the first years of sound conversion in France, the German cinema's presence came mainly in the form of so-called multiple-language films: German-made sound films that had been released in France in special French-language versions, using the same scripts, sets and production crews as the German originals, but starring popular French actors/entertainers such as Henri Garat, Albert Préjean and Annabella. Although the German film industry also produced versions of its film operettas in English, Spanish and other languages, nearly two-thirds of its multiple-language films were made for the French market (Garncarz 1999). French-language operettas such as Max de Vaucorbeil and Wilhelm Thiele's *Le Chemin du paradis* (1930) attracted extraordinary critical and commercial success in France. Although the German film industry had retreated from the international film market by 1933, France's geographical proximity to Germany ensured that relations between the French and German film industries remained close throughout the rest of the decade and into the Occupation. In many cases, film-makers who emigrated from Germany in the 1930s ended up working temporarily in Paris; conversely, during the 1930s and the Occupation, French actors, directors and technical personnel routinely journeyed to the German studios to make films.

The German cinema's significance in France in the domain of film technology was intermittent, peaking during conversion and the Occupation, and then fading quickly with Germany's military defeat. An exception, however, concerned technologies and techniques of film colour, which had become a central topic in film aesthetics in France during the 1940s. Certain historical parallels between colour and sound were evident. As with synchronous sound, French film companies had pioneered the industrialisation of film colour in the decade prior to World War I. By the 1920s, however, as Pathé, the largest French film company, pulled back from investment in film production, French inventors struggled for the entrepreneurial capital needed to commercialise their inventions. Nonetheless, the sound-era shift from orthochromatic to panchro-matic film facilitated the development of new colour processes. During the 1930s, small French companies attempted to market various colour systems, such as Rouxcolor (1932), Lumicolor (1932), Thomsoncolor (1935), Dufaycolor (1935), Dugromacolor (1937) and Francita-Realita/Opticolor (1939) (Noël 1995: 163–9, 172). In the wake of the cinema's sound-era industrialisation, however, film-technological change had become increasingly dependent on corporate funding and industrialised forms of technological innovation. By 1950, French-made colour technologies found only limited and sporadic use in industrial film production. As with synchronous sound two decades earlier, technologies owned by large German and American firms, and already industrialised in their film industries, had become central in world film practice and also in French discussions of film-colour aesthetics.

From the standpoint of the film community of post-war France, the German use of Agfacolor was significant largely for its evident differences from Technicolor. Hollywood films featuring Technicolor had been screened in Europe since the 1920s. By the 1940s, Technicolor had become associated with a distinctive, trademark approach to colour technique. This distinctiveness rested on unusual control over usage of the technology: film-makers were required to use Technicolor's special film stock, its patented beam-splitter camera and also the expertise of its colour consultants during preparation and shooting and its laboratory technicians during developing and printing. In France, Technicolor's trademark consistency provided the background for Agfacolor's emergence as the principal film-colour aesthetic alternative. A relatively new stock, Agfacolor was first used for feature-film production in 1941. When in October 1942 Germany imposed a blockade in France against the importation of American and English films, German Agfacolor films opened up a context in France for rethinking the possibilities for film colour. Immediately after the war, companies in Belgium, Italy, the USA and other countries marketed the Agfacolor process under new names.

There were indeed important differences between the two technologies, and also between how film-makers were using them, with films made in Agfacolor (or in the various post-war Agfacolor clones) reportedly exhibiting greater stylistic variety. Concerning the wartime German films, Barry Salt claims that their use of colour 'was bolder than in any Technicolor films made up to that time'; examples include experiments with 'large areas of half-light in the interiors, which was something that was avoided in Technicolor', and monochromatic scenes employing 'shots lit entirely by light of various single colours' (Salt 1992: 228–9). In the context of post-war French film culture, what might appear to have been Agfacolor's technical limitations looked like positive aesthetic attributes. Thus Agfacolor's limited brightness, evident in its brick reds and undifferentiated shades of green, showed up as a high-art alternative to Technicolor's bright, cartoon-like saturation (Andrew 1985: 67–9). After the war, Agfacolor-based processes became the major colour technology in Europe. By 1953, according to one report, a quarter of French films were made in colour, with the majority of these films featuring Gevacolor (1945), a Belgian-made derivative of Agfacolor (Courtade 1978: 252).

Colour-film production in France increased throughout the 1950s, as did the production of big-budget historical films, which became a major genre of the French cinema of the time. But with films shot in colour in France costing more than twice as much, black and white remained a viable option even for period spectacles such as Christian-Jaque's *Fanfan la Tulipe* (1952). In any case, the French film industry faced less pressure to adopt photographic colour and widescreen than it had in 1929 to make sound films. The major factor was the cinema's position relative to other entertainments, with the French situation differing significantly from that in the USA. Most notably, television's diffusion occurred less rapidly and evenly in France, with television ownership in France totalling only 125,000 in 1955, the figure quadrupling to one million in 1959 (Courtade 1978: 258). Moreover, with competition in France between film and television hindered by laws restricting television stations from broadcasting films, the French film industry was under less pressure to emulate Hollywood's recent efforts in big-screen spectacle. Thus, the cinema's basic technical parameters of the late 1920s – black-and-white panchromatic cinematography, 35mm film and the 1.33:1 academy ratio

screen dimension – endured in France throughout the 1950s, more than a decade after Hollywood's standardisation of colour and widescreen.

The case of widescreen in 1950s France raises questions about the impact of exemplary films on aspects of film culture other than film-making, such as film theory and criticism. Until the late 1950s, widescreen was used infrequently in French film production, as French film producers waited until French exhibitors equipped theatres for the screening of widescreen Hollywood films. As during the early sound years, theatre conversion occurred slowly and unevenly – first in the large theatres in the urban centres and then later in smaller cities, big-city neighbourhoods and finally, much later, in the rural provinces. Comprising mainly one-off experiments, notable French widescreen films of the mid-1950s include Marcel Ichac's short film *Nouveaux horizons* (1953), which appeared on the first French CinemaScope programme in December 1953; Bernard Borderie's *Fortune carrée* (1954), allegedly the first CinemaScope feature film made in France; and *Lola Montès* (1955), Max Ophuls's auteur masterpiece, likewise made in CinemaScope. Notwithstanding its slow adaptation in France, the use of widescreen in Hollywood's big-budget narrative films affected film theory and criticism in France, as a new generation of French critics began examining film history in terms of a progressive, technology-based movement towards improved mimesis. Essential conditions for the re-examination included basic national differences in how the technology was used. Although 20th Century-Fox's CinemaScope technology employed patents deriving from French inventor Henri Chrétien's anamorphic 'Hypergonar' lens (1927), Hollywood's approach to widescreen differed radically from earlier French experiments. In contrast to Abel Gance's famous three-panel images in *Napoléon* (1927) or Claude Autant-Lara's *Construire un feu* (1929), whose innovations included multiple movie screens arranged in a giant cross-like shape, Hollywood, some twenty-five years later, adopted widescreen according to its established norms of story construction. From the standpoint of the French film-critical vanguard of the 1950s, Hollywood films served to redefine widescreen's significance for film history, transforming it from an experimental special effect or technological wonder to another item in the mainstream cinema's panoply of narrative-defined film techniques.

This examination of the adaptation of foreign technologies in French film-making has attempted to open up an alternative to the tendency within film historiography to see film style as determined by industrial and technological conditions. In France during this classical period, film-making amounted to much more than the product of technological causes; instead, the films clarified and exemplified a technology's artistic significance. By changing the way critics, viewers, and film-makers' understood the artistic potential of technologies of sound, colour and widescreen, individual films effectively transformed these technologies, enabling unexpected stylistic developments while simultaneously pushing certain established styles to the film-cultural margins. Transformations of this sort proved uniquely relevant to French film-making during the period from 1930 to 1960. Notwithstanding the use in France of imported technologies, native film-makers inevitably adapted the latter within a matrix of activities and concerns unique to indigenous film culture, as became evident in the distinctive look and sound of French films.

WORKS CITED

Andrew, D. (1985) 'The Post-War Struggle for Color', in De Lauretis, T. and Heath, S. eds *The Cinematic Apparatus*, New York, St Martin's Press, 61–75.

Andrew, D. (1995) *Mists of Regret: Culture and Sensibility in Classic French Film*, Princeton, NJ, Princeton University Press.

de Baecque, A. and Jousse, T. (1996) *Le Retour du cinéma*, Paris, Hachette.

Bazin, A. (1967) 'The Evolution of the Language of Cinema', in *What Is Cinema?*, vol. 1, Berkeley, University of California Press, 23–40.

Charensol, G. (1949) 'Le Film Parlant', in Marion, D. ed., *Le Cinéma par ceux qui le font*, Paris, Fayard, 51–65.

Courtade, F. (1978) *Les Malédictions du cinéma français*, Paris, Alain Moreau.

Crisp, C. (1993) *The Classic French Cinema, 1930–1960*, Bloomington, Indiana University Press.

Ehrlich, E. (1985) *Cinema of Paradox: French Film-Making under the German Occupation*, New York, Columbia University Press.

Garncarz, J. (1999) 'Made in Germany: Multiple-Language Versions and the Early German Sound Cinema', in Higson, A. and Maltby, R. eds, *'Film Europe' and 'Film America': Cinema, Commerce and Cultural Exchange, 1920–1939*, Exeter, University of Exeter Press, 249–73.

Icart, R. (1988) *La Révolution du parlant vue par la presse française*, Toulouse, Institut Jean Vigo.

Lagny, M., Ropars M.-C. and Sorlin, P. (1986) *Générique des années trente*, Vincennes, Presses Universitaires de Vincennes.

Noël, B. (1995) *L'Histoire du cinéma couleur*, Paris, Press'Communication.

Salt, B. (1992) *Film Style and Technology: History and Analysis*, London, Starword.

Thompson, K. (1993) 'Early Alternatives to the Hollywood Mode of Production', *Film History*, 5: 4, December, 386–404.

Vincendeau, G. (2000) *Stars and Stardom in French Cinema*, New York, Continuum.

11 FORMS 1930–60
The Art of Spectacle: The Aesthetics of Classical French Cinema

Ginette Vincendeau

This chapter examines the aesthetic features of the classical French cinema from the coming of sound to the modernist break of the New Wave. During these three decades, 3,094 feature films were made in France: 1,305 in the 1930s, 807 in the 1940s (including 220 during the Occupation) and 982 in the 1950s (see Chirat 1975, 1981; Sabria 1987). This vast corpus is usually divided into three historical tranches: the 1930s, the period of the German occupation (1940–4) and the years running from the Liberation in 1945 to the New Wave (1959/60). This temporal division, which structures much writing on French cinema, has long coloured aesthetic judgments. The 1930s, dominated by Renoir and Poetic Realism, have been seen as a golden age (Martin 1983). The less well-known wartime cinema has been regarded as an oddity because of the extraordinary circumstances of the German occupation; critics accordingly have emphasised its 'ambiguity' (Ehrlich 1985; Siclier 1981). As for the post-war cinema, it has been analysed (and often despised) retrospectively as the era of the conservative 'tradition of quality', especially the psychological and costume dramas that would 'mercifully' be blown away by the New Wave, according to François Truffaut's polemical article 'A Certain Tendency of French Cinema' and much of the historiography that followed in its wake (Truffaut 1976). This periodisation has been challenged in various ways. Jean-Pierre Jeancolas argues for strong continuities between the 1930s and the war years, while André Bazin sees the break taking place in 1941 rather than 1945, considering the new generation who rose during the war while some of the giants of pre-war cinema, such as Jean Renoir, René Clair and Julien Duvivier, had fled to Hollywood. Jeancolas and Bazin's differences are partly predicated on their approach: the former

identifies mainly ideological continuities from the 1930s through the war years, while the latter defines the post-1941 generation chiefly in aesthetic terms (Jeancolas 1983; Bazin 1983). But their divergences are also indicative of the complexities of the period under examination, as more local studies reveal, for instance François Garçon's *De Blum à Pétain* (1984), on the late 1930s/early 1940s juncture. A number of studies, however, have begun to embrace the whole of the 1930–60 period as the classical age, both in France (Pierre Billard, who places the 'golden age' between 1935 and 1945) and outside, notably Colin Crisp's industry study (Billard 1995; Crisp 1993). Noël Burch and Geneviève Sellier (1996) have explored the period from the point of view of gender representations.

The focus of this chapter is on the continuities and the breaks that characterise French cinema during the eventful years from 1930 to 1960, a period troubled socially and politically (the world economic crisis, the Popular Front, World War II, the Cold War), and book-ended by two technological innovations with important aesthetic repercussions: the coming of sound in 1929 and the arrival of colour in the 1950s. The period under study was one during which cinema in France was the dominant popular art form, reaching peaks of annual box-office sales in 1947 (423 million) and 1957 (411 million), and in which the split between auteur cinema and mainstream cinema was not particularly relevant in terms of the institution and the audience, although the distinction was crucial to the emerging post-war critics, from André Bazin to the writers of *Positif* and *Cahiers du cinéma* (Vincendeau 1995). Although undoubtedly some film-makers experimented with the medium in more original ways than others, this chapter will give as much weight to 'ordinary' films as to masterpieces, and will reclaim the despised musical comedies and 'filmed theatre' alongside the acknowledged triumphs of Poetic Realism. Throughout this chapter, the expression 'classical French cinema' is used to refer to a set of common practices understood by both practitioners and audiences and applying mainly to mainstream fiction feature films (excluding documentary, avant-garde and experimental cinema). In this respect 'classical French cinema' obviously shares aesthetic features with classical Hollywood cinema as defined by Bordwell, Staiger and Thompson in their 1985 study. Hollywood films were widely seen in France (apart from during the war years when they were banned), while many French film-makers – Maurice Tourneur, Clair, Renoir, Duvivier and Henri Verneuil, to name a few – spent periods in America. Like Hollywood movies, the majority of classical French feature films are narrative fictions built around characters placed in recognisable milieux, whose trajectory is clearly motivated and who normally provide figures of identification. The avant-garde experiments of the 1920s noticeably retreated with the coming of sound and, with exceptions, did not return until the more experimental side of the New Wave (Godard, Rivette, Marker). Though it is the auteur cinema that has been celebrated (Renoir, Feyder, Bresson), genres such as comedy, romance, musicals, thrillers and costume films were the mainstay of film production in French as in American cinema, and French cinema evolved its own star system (Vincendeau 2000). Continuity editing, eye-line matches and a combination of long shots, medium shots and close-ups defined the basic grammar of film language in France as elsewhere. Although location shooting took place, the majority of films made between 1930 and 1960 were shot on studio sets. France followed Hollywood, albeit belatedly, and introduced colour in the 1950s, though at the turn of the 1960s the majority of films were still in black and white.

Yet, there were also enormous differences between classical French and Hollywood cinemas. Some, relating to industry practices, personnel and representations, are considered elsewhere in this book, whereas this chapter will discuss aesthetic/formal differences. The discussion will concentrate on three areas of distinctiveness that, without flattening out the differences between individual films and film-makers, together form a representative and informative picture of classical French cinema that I call 'the art of spectacle'. It is my contention that spectacle remains the basis of classical French cinema long after the early 'cinema of attractions' supposedly gave way to the 'cinema of narrative integration' (Gunning 1986). These three areas are, first, sound (especially music and dialogue) and performance; here the focus will be on musicals and 'filmed theatre'. Second, image – and notably the question of a specifically French use of camerawork and editing. Third, realism as an audiovisual construction, from 1930s Poetic Realism to 1950s noir and crime dramas.

AN ALL-TALKING, ALL-SINGING CINEMA

The coming of sound was initially a disaster for the French film industry in terms of patents, equipment and then as a barrier to export (Andrew 1980, 1995; Gomery 1980; Crisp 1993). Yet the novelty of sound was also a godsend for French cinema: the ability to hear its own language spoken and its songs and music performed proved a source of unending pleasure for French audiences. It also provoked intense controversies among the filmic avant-garde and its supporters, who were largely hostile. With the reproduction of the human voice, cinema seemed to regress towards a simple imitation of reality, and to be doomed to terminal decline as a specific art form. According to Clair, who was one of the clearest exponents of this attitude, 'with speech and sounds, the spectator has lost the dreamy feeling that silent images created' (Clair 1953: 68). As soon as sound film reigned, claims of cinema's imminent demise evidently became absurd. The specificity debate was replaced by that of cinema vs. theatre, in the face of the huge number of play and operetta adaptations. 'Filmed theatre' was attacked from all sides, including by theatre people, but especially by film purists. Playwright-turned-film-maker Marcel Pagnol provocatively entered the fray in Les Cahiers du film on 15 December 1933, hailing the birth of 'canned theatre' and claiming that the image was subservient to dialogue and performance: 'any sound film which can be projected silently and remain

The comic performer Fernandel

comprehensible is a very bad film' (Lapierre 1946: 293). When the dust settled, however, Pagnol and Clair led the growth of French sound cinema – Clair with his 'musical' *Sous les toits de Paris* (1930) and Pagnol with his filmed play *Marius* (1931, technically directed by Alexander Korda). Sacha Guitry followed suit a few years later. The common link between these film-makers, and many lesser-known ones such as Yves Mirande, Jean Choux, Pierre Colombier and Christian-Jaque, was the harnessing of the new technique of sound cinema to the 'old' live entertainment forms: theatre, song, cabaret, *café-concert* (or *caf'conc'*), music hall, operetta. From this partnership they fashioned a distinctive popular film aesthetic for the decades to come. Musicals and filmed theatre dominated the first half of the 1930s; they evolved and waned somewhat in later years, yet formed the backbone of a major trend in French classical cinema.

The first French sound films, *L'Eau du Nil* (Marcel Vandal, 1928), *Le Collier de la reine* (Gaston Ravel, 1929) and *La Route est belle* (Robert Florey, 1929), were little more than upgraded silent films with song and music. With their hold on sound patents and superior financial means, American and German studios developed the musical into a high-profile genre, with elaborate ensemble dancing and stunning decor. Although the French stage music hall was at that time developing its own *grand spectacle*, very few French films could follow this route. Traditional French popular dances – *java, valse-musette* – were small-scale community-based forms that did not lend themselves to either the virtuoso displays of American films or the grand-scale Viennese waltz. Consequently, 'French dancing' is found in populist films where, in dance halls and open-air *guinguettes*, it serves as decor and metonymic indication of a community spirit – among many such films, examples include: *Coeur de lilas* (Anatole Litvak, 1931), *Quatorze juillet* (Clair, 1932), *Jenny* (Marcel Carné, 1936), *Hôtel du Nord* (Carné, 1938) *Prisons de femmes* (Roger Richebé, 1938), *Circonstances atténuantes* (Jean Boyer, 1939). As for the filmed versions of the lavish shows featuring stars such as Mistinguett, Tino Rossi, Josephine Baker and Maurice Chevalier, they look small-scale and lack-lustre in, respectively, *Rigolboche* (Christian-Jaque, 1936), *Lumières de Paris* (Richard Pottier,

1938), *Zouzou* (Marc Allégret, 1934) and *L'Homme du jour* (Duvivier, 1936). Musicals with high production values were French versions of German films, such as the hugely popular *Le Chemin du paradis* (William Thiele, 1930) and G. W. Pabst's *L'Opéra de quat'sous* (1930), or films shot in German studios, like *Adrienne Lecouvreur* (Marcel L'Herbier, 1938).

Alongside operetta, the nineteenth-century French vaudeville, a fast-moving farce with songs, provided another important source of musicals. Vaudeville ensured the predominance of comedy, and structurally dictated the way songs were inserted in films, as loosely connected and sometimes barely justified moments of pure spectacle. In *Dactylo se marie* (René Pujol, 1934), the actor Armand Bernard suddenly sings the only song in the film. Similarly, in *Messieurs les ronds-de-cuir* (Yves Mirande, 1936), a piano just happens to be in an office, the excuse for a few songs and a number with chorus girls. Further examples of impromptu singing are Jean Gabin in the crime thriller *Pépé le Moko* (Duvivier, 1937) and the realist drama *La Belle équipe* (Duvivier, 1936), or Fernandel in the military vaudeville *Ignace* (Pierre Colombier, 1937). While *Ignace* was the most popular French film of 1937 (along with Renoir's *La Grande illusion*), it baffled Graham Greene, who wondered in his review, 'I cannot understand why the middle of the film should be filled with lovelies and a stage show and Fernandel dressed as a Mexican blundering on to the stage' (Greene 1980: 246). What the latter example indicates is that by the mid-1930s, French spectators, familiar with the theatrical forms and the performers, had become attuned to the rules of this heterogeneous genre. Many actors, such as Fernandel, Albert Préjean, Arletty, Gabin and Florelle, had started on the stage and some pursued parallel careers. *Caf'conc'* comics Georges Milton and Bach enjoyed a late flowering of their careers through a highly successful series of vehicles, in which comic turns and songs rupture loosely organised narratives, for example Milton's *Le Roi des resquilleurs* (Colombier, 1930) and Bach's *Bouboule 1er, roi nègre* (Léon Mathot, 1933). In turn, star singers such as Tino Rossi and Charles Trenet began in the mid-1930s a series of successful vehicles in which a romantic plot is intertwined with a backstage narrative where they end up as stars (e.g. Rossi's *Marinella*, 1936, and Trenet's *Je chante*, 1938).

Across these varied manifestations of the French musical of the 1930s, some common points emerge. Theatricality is always consciously foregrounded. Several films, including Éric Charrell's *Le Congrès s'amuse* (1931) begins with shots of a proscenium arch and a curtain. Most numbers are filmed straight, as if on stage, and singers address the audience directly. Artificiality is both acknowledged and celebrated. This approach informs most variations on the French musical genre, which, unlike Hollywood, never developed its integrated version. For instance, *La Vie parisienne* (Robert Siodmak, 1935) also opens with a view of a stage. Throughout the film, a stage version of Offenbach's eponymous operetta is the bridge between diegetic events set in 1900 and those set in 1936, providing a *mise-en-abyme* of the Parisian myth and of the genre itself. There is thus a double, and somewhat paradoxical, movement. On the one hand, the films 'quote' songs and numbers in a direct, unsophisticated manner, akin to the cinema of attractions, often in blatant defiance of narrative logic or verisimilitude. On the other hand, a high degree of self-reflexivity and sophistication is in evidence in the films' celebration of their own artificiality. This point contrasts quite markedly with the approach of René Clair, the only canonical French film-maker to have made musicals. Clair's five French films of the early 1930s divide into two thematic clusters: the comic/poetic evocation of the 'little people' of Paris in *Sous les toits de Paris*, *Le Million* (1931), *Quatorze juillet* (1933), and social satire in *À nous la liberté* (1932) and *Le Dernier milliardaire* (1934). All, however, are consistent in their treatment of music and spectacle. R. C. Dale rightly notes that *Sous les toits de Paris* is structured like a song, consisting of melodies connected by refrains (Dale 1986: 143). The same could be said of all Clair's early 1930s films, where whole sequences are music-led and dialogue is kept to a minimum. As Bazin points out, this downplaying of dialogue helped Clair's international career (Bazin 1983: 25). In this structural sense, Clair's films are more 'musical' than other French musicals. Yet, and despite Clair's stated desire to reach the widest audience, they did not do all that well at the French box office. In my view this is connected to their

ironic slant towards the popular entertainment forms they depict, not, as is often stated, because the irony was too subtle for the popular audience, but because it was too obvious – hence the initial Parisian resistance to *Sous les toits de Paris*. Whereas performers in the *caf'conc'* and operetta adaptations use direct address to the spectator, those in Clair's films are mediated through the gaze of the camera, as for instance in the celebrated crane shot that opens *Sous les toits de Paris*. Where operetta-type films embraced the frivolity of their material, and Bach, Milton and Fernandel squarely endorsed the vulgarity of their *caf'conc'* origins, Clair kept his distance.

FILMED THEATRE IN THE 1930s

The delight induced by song and music in French cinema of the 1930s was paralleled by an enthusiasm for language. Its vernacular variations, its poetry, its accents (especially Parisian and southern) are a key to the cinema of the period. This was reflected in the special status of the new brand of scriptwriters, adapters and dialogue-writers who emerged at the coming of sound, ranging from playwrights (Marcel Achard, Tristan Bernard) to journalists and writers (Charles Spaak, Henri Jeanson) and poets (Jacques Prévert). 'Filmed theatre' refers to films based on boulevard plays (as opposed to classical drama), a mostly comic genre, which includes the work of playwright-turned-directors Achard, Verneuil and Yves Mirande (among others), as well as Pagnol and Guitry, although there were exponents of the genre in a serious mode, such as Henri Bernstein. Its hallmarks are a bourgeois milieu depicted satirically, salacious situations (from adultery to suggested incest) and an emphasis on witty repartee. Mirroring and underlying the sparkling language was the performance of brilliant actors (including Raimu, Harry Baur, Arletty, Jules Berry, Louis Jouvet and Michel Simon) who, like the *caf'conc'* and operetta singers, often conducted parallel careers. Filmed theatre was adored by the audience and did much to shore up a specifically French cinema in the face of Hollywood. Traditionally considered socially and aesthetically worthless, filmed theatre constitutes a fascinating testimony to the period, not least in its satire of institutions. Historians Bardèche and Brasillach are characteristic of the critical disparagement of the genre when they say that 'as for the general public, all they wanted on the screen was theatre and bad theatre at that. They certainly got a lot of it' (Bardèche and Brasillach 1948: 411). Jean-Pierre Jeancolas much later echoed their view: 'French films of the 1930s talk too much: they recite tirades already worn out on the stage by one, and sometimes two, generations of actors' (Jeancolas 1983: 144). Too wrapped up in their dislike of filmed theatre, critics and historians do not stop to ask what pleasures these films, like the musicals, hold for spectators, thus writing off the majority of mainstream films of that era. Boulevard theatre and vaudeville on stage already dramatised highly codified character types and situations. The same obtains for the films. The point was not what the characters' trajectory would be, since that was already familiar – as signalled by fairly basic titles such as *Les Maris de ma femme* (Maurice Commage, 1936), *Mon député et sa femme* (Commage, 1937), *Nicole et sa vertu* (René Hervil, 1931) – but how they would do it, and how they would say it. The soaring success of the southern films after 1930, as Claudette Peyrusse (1986) shows, owed much to sound media (radio, records) because it foregrounded the picturesque quality of the accent. But in the rest of France too, not only could the great stars of the Paris and Marseilles stage reach the far corners of the country, but sound cinema also showcased the declamatory and rhetorical tendency in French culture. How did it affect the *mise en scène* of filmed theatre?

In filmed theatre the camera frequently takes the place of the fourth wall, as if looking from the rows of spectators. A majority of frontal two-shots and ensemble shots in medium close-up (rather than cross-cutting) creates a series of tableaux with little attempt at continuity editing between the tableaux or between long shots and close-ups (hence the accusations that the films are 'uncinematic'). Decors favour theatrical spaces: the village square or harbour, the church, the café, the dining table, with other characters acting as diegetic audiences. Scenes are frequently excessive in length in relation to the overall narrative. For example, Pagnol's *Le Schpountz* (1937), a satire of the film milieu starring Fernandel as the eponymous 'village idiot', begins in a shop run by Fernandel's uncle, who is played by Fernand

Charpin. Nephew and uncle are having a row, watched by aunt and brother. The scene has little impact on the main narrative; apart from anchoring the film in the Pagnol genre, its real function is to give Charpin and Fernandel time to do their 'routines' with florid language and gestures. There are many two-shots of the two stars, with the back of the other two in silhouette in the bottom corners of the frame. Later on in the film, Fernandel has been picked up by a Parisian film crew, who mercilessly mock him. Asked to display his acting talent, he reads a phrase adopting different tones (sad, fearful, comic). This scene, though shot outdoors, is emblematic of filmed theatre's drive to privilege spectacle and performance over narrative development. As Fernandel begins his recitations, the camera moves increasingly closer, isolating him so that his acting for the crew becomes a direct address to the camera. This is by no means rare. Guitry, for instance, frequently used direct address, winking at the spectator during his parade in several disguises in *Le Roman d'un tricheur* (1936). In his seventeen-minute take of a telephone conversation in *Faisons un rêve* (1936), he also addresses the camera on several occasions with remarks like: 'I was dead right to speak when I did, wasn't I?' In another scene from the same film, Raimu pauses after a line, looks at the camera, and says: 'Quite an amusing expression, that was.' In this way, Pagnol and Guitry (and many others) incorporated the essence of live performance into the film experience. At these moments, another feature of the genre is that the actor takes over the character. In *Le Schpountz*, as the camera frames Fernandel triumphing with his comic version of his phrase, we are watching 'Fernandel' the great comic star rather than the inept 'schpountz'. The self-consciousness of the moment, apart from Fernandel's helpless laughter, is highlighted by a microphone ostensibly appearing in shot and one of the members of the diegetic audience (Pierre Brasseur) wielding a camera. As for the musicals, episodic or cyclical narratives are designed to accommodate actors' routines and the showcasing of dialogue rather than the development of characters. *Le Roman d'un tricheur* and *Le Schpountz*, in this instance, are typical of many other films. Erich von Stroheim's biographer, Peter Noble, recalls that when the star was approached to act in *L'Alibi*

(Pierre Chenal, 1937), a thriller, he found himself in opposition to the scriptwriter, Jacques Companeez:

> The latter had turned out a scenario which contained a number of thin situations overloaded with thick layers of dialogue. Stroheim, with his cinematic mind, invariably saw scenes in which the characters expressed themselves pictorially, rather than verbally. Inevitably, star and scenarist clashed. (Noble 1950: 117)

Thus the word-driven nature of filmed theatre permeated all classical French cinema, across filmmakers and genres. Beyond questions of genre (and personal taste), it is important to see the theatrical tradition in French cinema not as a technologically based limitation or poverty of imagination, but as a powerful intertextual determinant.

THE SPECTACULAR GENRES BEYOND THE 1930s

What I have been defining so far is a French golden age of spectacular genres, which is very different from the critically sanctioned golden age of Poetic Realism. Unlike the Hollywood spectacular based on large-scale action and landscapes (e.g. the Western), it was based on the performance of song, music and language, through an array of formal strategies, from quotation to self-reflexive incorporation. The filmed operetta began to wane in the mid-1930s (in France as elsewhere), as did the films of performers such as Fréhel, Josephine Baker, Mistinguett, Maurice Chevalier and comics Bach and Milton – those in fact who corresponded to an older, nostalgic era of live entertainment that was gradually disappearing. The popularity of Fernandel continued but in comedy rather than musicals (the *Don Camillo* series in the 1950s). The musical performers who survived into the 1940s and 1950s cinema, namely Tino Rossi, Charles Trenet and the Ray Ventura band, represented a more forward-looking type of music, often incorporating jazz (Trenet, Ventura), and whose popularity had been mainly propelled by radio and recordings rather than the stage (Rossi and Trenet).

During the war years, the German-controlled company Continental was advised by Goebbels to produce 'light, superficial and entertaining films'

(Billard 1995: 380). Although only 30 of the 220 wartime films were made by Continental, many other light, entertaining (if not necessarily superficial) films were produced. Critics have noted the emergence of new genres in French cinema of the Occupation: in particular, a fantastic tendency, with *Le Baron fantôme* (Serge de Poligny, 1942) and *Les Visiteurs du soir* (Carné, 1942), and the rise of women-centred melodramas and comedies, such as *Le Voile bleu* (Jean Stelli, 1942) and *L'Honorable Catherine* (L'Herbier, 1942) (see Ehrlich 1985; Siclier 1981; Burch and Sellier 1996). Another notable trend is the rise of crime films, which I will come back to later. But the musical, comic and spectacular dimension of French cinema endured, despite the poverty of means suffered by the industry in the war years. Several major singing stars stayed in France during the German occupation. In particular, Trenet made three wartime films, including *La Romance de Paris* (Boyer, 1941), and Rossi five, including *Le Chant de l'exilé* (André Hugon, 1942) and *L'Île d'amour* (Maurice Cam, 1943); both continued in the post-war period. Édith Piaf's short film career took off during the war years, with *Montmartre-sur-Seine* (Georges Lacombe, 1941) and *Étoile sans lumière* (Marcel Blistène, 1945). But the war years are notable for the pervasiveness and success of costume films, partly prompted by the need to evade contemporary topics and thus censorship, but also because of the strong basis in spectacular cinema established in the 1930s. Among the most famous are *La Duchesse de Langeais* (Jacques de Baroncelli, 1941), *Mam'zelle Bonaparte* (Maurice Tourneur, 1941), *Le Destin fabuleux de Desirée Clary* (Guitry, 1941), *Le Capitaine Fracasse* (Abel Gance, 1942), *Félicie Nanteuil* (Marc Allégret, 1942), *Carmen* (Christian-Jaque, 1943), *Au bonheur des dames* (André Cayatte, 1943) and *Le Bossu* (Jean Delannoy, 1944). The best-known war-time French costume films is of course *Les Enfants du paradis* (1945), which is usually cited as the culmination of Poetic Realism but is also, indeed primarily, a spectacular costume film.

The importance of the costume film during the war years endured. It is therefore not surprising that, apart from the continued success of comedy and the rise of the *policier*, the defining genre of the late 1940s and 1950s was the so-called tradition of quality, which consisted of well-made literary adaptations, both the psychological dramas attacked by Truffaut and sumptuous costume dramas. Both these sub-genres were underpinned by a new generation of scriptwriters, in particular Jean Aurenche and Pierre Bost (who worked as a team), and Michel Audiard. Virtually all directors worked in costume film, from mainstream (Christian-Jaque, Jacqueline Audry) to auteurs (Renoir, Clair, Ophuls), including archetypal noir director Henri-Georges Clouzot with *Miquette et sa mère* (1949). Pierre Billard, who calls the tradition of quality 'neo-classicism', discusses even a contemporary film like *La Symphonie pastorale* (Delannoy, 1946), from a novel by André Gide, as based on the idea of performance, pointing also to the expert craft in decor, lighting, music, actors and dialogue. Although Billard also disparages many costume dramas, he puts his finger on two key aspects of these films: performance and craft (Billard 1995: 539). Indeed the tradition of quality foregrounds the craft of studio set designers and cinematographers, and star performances. These aspects place them in the spectacle tradition of the 1930s and 1940s. But they departed from them in other ways, in particular in the source literature, shifting from boulevard theatre to literary classics, a move which turned a domestic genre into an exportable one. Contents also changed, from the satire of institutions to sex and nostalgic celebrations of historical figures. In the first category are the risqué Martine Carol costume films like *Caroline chérie* (Pottier, 1950) and *Nana* (Christian-Jaque, 1955) and Jacqueline Audry's Colette adaptations such as *Minne, l'ingénue libertine* (1950). Former Hollywood exiles Clair and Renoir made nostalgic spectacle films such as *Le Silence est d'or* (1947), *Les Belles de nuit* (1952) and *Les Grandes manoeuvres* (1955); and *Le Carrosse d'or* (1953), *French Cancan* (1955) and *Élena et les hommes* (1956) respectively. Also part of this flourishing tradition are the women-centred French films of Ophuls, *La Ronde* (1950), *Le Plaisir* (1951), *Madame de . . .* (1953) and *Lola Montès* (1955); Guitry's historical pageants, *Si Versailles m'était conté* (1953), *Napoléon* (1954), *Si Paris nous était conté* (1955); and adventure films like Christian-Jaque's *Fanfan la Tulipe* (1952). Musicals such as the filmed operetta *Violettes impériales* (Pottier, 1952) and the backstage musicals *Folies-Bergère* (Henri Decoin, 1956) and *French Cancan* are now on a much bigger scale and in colour. The majority of popular hits, however – Christian-Jaque's *Fanfan la Tulipe*, *Les Grandes familles* (Denys de la Patellière, 1958), *Le Salaire de la peur* (Clouzot, 1952), *Les Diaboliques* (Clouzot, 1954), *La Vache et le prisonnier* (Verneuil, 1958), *La Traversée de Paris* (Claude Autant-Lara, 1956) – were still in black and white. Widescreen was also a rarity. The first films in this format, Bernard Borderie's *Fortune carrée* (1955) and Yves Allégret's *Oasis* (1955), made little impression; *Lola Montès*, a critical landmark, was a box-office failure.

The accent placed on performance, craft and language in this cinema of spectacle made it a particular target for the New Wave critics, with exceptions such as Ophuls and Renoir, whom they admired. Obviously there were major differences in the way the films related to the spectacle at their heart, as in the 1930s. Some used plain 'quoting' (*Folies-Bergère*), while others also provided a sophisticated reflection on the artistic process itself (*French Cancan*). Yet, from the artistic heights of Renoir's *French Cancan*, to the work of critically ignored directors of the time, such as Autant-Lara (*Douce*, 1943), Jacqueline Audry (*Olivia*, 1950), Christian-Jaque (*Nana*) and many others, costume films display a wealth of detail in decor, lighting and costume, well served by dynamic and sometimes virtuoso camerawork, belying the frequent accusations of a 'moribund' and 'stilted' cinema. Bazin, trying to find a common ground between the films of the 1940s and 1950s, suggested 'intellectuality frequently reinforced by the literary origin of scripts' (Bazin 1983: 28). He thus identifies what led French critics to accuse this cinema of being dry and unemotional, as opposed to the lyricism of American cinema and the spontaneity of Italian neo-realism. Yet, this supposed intellectuality did not prevent most of these films from being extremely popular. It would appear then that for the audience of the time, as in the 1930s, language was still a spectacle, especially when spoken by great theatre stars – such as Gérard Philipe in *Le Rouge et le noir* (Autant-Lara, 1954), Gabrielle Dorziat and Jean Marais in *Les Parents terribles* (Jean Cocteau, 1948) or Edwige Feuillère in *Olivia* as she gathers her students together to read Racine aloud. Across very disparate films, the performance and celebration of text and music formed the basis of a rich and popular classical vein in French cinemagoing that stretches back to the early 1930s.

FRAME, SPACE, EDITING: A DIFFERENT PACE

If French films unarguably place more emphasis on dialogue than Hollywood movies, they also differ in their slower editing rhythm, use of long takes and framing. Distinctions have often been made along these lines in an impressionistic fashion, contrasting mainstream Hollywood and French auteur cinema, Renoir in the 1930s and Ophuls in the 1950s being prime examples. Barry Salt (1992) and Colin Crisp (1993) have both widened this remit by introducing more systematic measurements, for instance of average length of takes and percentage of camera movements. Neither entirely escapes the mainstream Hollywood/French auteur dichotomy, as their French sample is biased towards auteur films, and yet their work is important in moving issues of authorial signature into a more contextualised field. The work of Renoir in the 1930s has indeed been celebrated for its extensive and striking use of long, often mobile, takes and staging in depth. The scenes of the arrival of guests at the chateau and their antics in its corridors in *La Règle du jeu* (1939) are frequently quoted examples of this use of the camera, exceptional in relation to Hollywood's faster cutting. But the fact is that long and mobile takes were common in 1930s French cinema and many directors used longer takes than Renoir, from well-known directors like Duvivier and Pierre Chenal, to run-of-the-mill film-makers, including Pierre Colombier and Roger Richebé. Films such as *Crime et châtiment* (Chenal, 1935), *La Belle équipe* and *Ces messieurs de la santé* (Colombier, 1933) all contain many shots over two minutes, with multiple reframings and complex negotiations of cinematic space and decor.

Average shot length (ASL) is a crude measurement – it hides differences between groups of very short takes and a few exceptionally long ones, as well as camera mobility. It still, however, gives us an indication of a film's pace. Renoir's *Boudu sauvé des eaux* (1932), for example, has an ASL of 13 seconds, which is lower than many of his other films, yet still higher than the Hollywood average of 8–9

seconds. Crisp, however, is not entirely right to assert that Renoir systematically has a slower editing rhythm than anyone else in France in the 1930s (Crisp 1993: 404). For instance, *Les Rois du sport* (Colombier, 1937), a comedy, has an ASL of 21 seconds, *Le Mensonge de Nina Petrovna* (Victor Tourjansky, 1937), a costume drama, 22 seconds, *Le Dernier tournant* (Chenal, 1939), a film noir, 27 seconds. Through the 1940s and the 1950s, the editing rhythm dropped from around 15 seconds in the mid-1930s to below 10 seconds in the 1950s. While this downward curve in ASL was marked, the costume films of the 1950s bucked the trend somewhat, modifying Crisp's conclusions. Whereas the ASL of Renoir's *French Cancan* is 10.2 seconds, other films move way out of this range – Audry's *Olivia*, 15.9 seconds, Clair's *Les Grandes manoeuvres*, 13.3 seconds, *Les Misérables* (Jean-Paul Le Chanois, 1958), 18 seconds, and even a film noir like *Une Si jolie petite plage* (Yves Allégret, 1948), 14.8 seconds. This also contradicts Salt's point that the failure of Ophuls's *Lola Montès* can be ascribed to his 'continuing on his commercially dangerous course of using very long takes (ASL = 18 sec.)' (Salt 1992: 312), since Le Chanois's *Les Misérables*, with the same ASL, was one of the greatest hits of the decade. There are economic and technological reasons why French films tended towards longer takes. To take an extreme example, Guitry shot some of his 1930s films in a few days, sometimes during one afternoon. Where days or weeks of shooting could be 'canned' in an afternoon, savings obviously were made. Crisp also links this to technology, in particular the reduced number of cameras and the lack of modern editing equipment, especially the automatic numbering machine that allowed the editing of a higher number of shorter takes (Crisp 1993: 405). But there are also aesthetic determinants as well as consequences that have to do with a different relation between cinematic space and performance.

The classical French style of longer takes was developed partly in response to the theatrical/musical tradition discussed in the first part of this chapter. The theatrical style determined a slower rhythm and a different kind of framing in its need to respect a particular tradition of performance. This goes back a long way. Historians of early cinema acting have identified a move from a melodramatic and pictorial style (emphatic, based on particular poses) to a more realistic or naturalistic style, aiming at verisimilitude. Ben Brewster and Lea Jacobs further argue for a French/European specificity and relate editing styles to performance, compared to American rapid cutting: 'Given their lengthy takes and tendency to employ deep staging in long shot, European films of the 1910s necessarily relied more upon the actor and the acting ensemble to provide dramatic emphasis'; and in Europe, 'film-makers were more likely to retain the long-shot framings in which actors were shown full figure' (Brewster and Jacobs 1997: 111, 120). The use of longer takes and staging in depth certainly distinguishes classical French cinema, as we have just discussed. I would in fact reverse the terms of Brewster and Jacobs's argument and suggest that performance determined cinematography rather than (or at least as much as) the other way round. With the advent of sound, the importance of dialogue entailed wider shots and longer takes to display actors interacting with each other, and, as in silent film, to allow the spectator to see the entirety of their bodies and gestures.

Thus the slower rhythm of French cinema during the classical period stages an interplay between actors that is both visual (gestures) and aural (dialogue), and tends to place stars among an ensemble of actors rather than isolate them with close-ups. Attention is given to decor, atmosphere and to ensemble playing rather than to foregrounding individual stars. Indeed, the latter is considered as an American practice designed for 'selling female flesh' (Crisp 1993: 384). The quality costume dramas of the 1950s all feature major stars (for example Gérard Philipe and Michèle Morgan in *Les Grandes manoeuvres*; Jean Gabin and Maria Felix in *French Cancan*) but they make remarkably little use of close-ups of the stars' faces. Cinematic framing and pace in the classical period worked in symbiosis with performance, as confirmed (albeit negatively) by film-maker and editor Henri Colpi, who complained that 'the rhythm is no longer imposed externally, by the editor, but internally, by the acting and directing' (Crisp 1993: 408). For example, in the comedy *Les Rois du sport*, many of the interactions between the stars Raimu and Jules Berry occur in takes over one minute long, during

which the two actors shake hands, circle around each other, sit down, get up, zip across the frame in several directions, etc. By contrast, as Kristin Thompson has observed, Hollywood actors often 'sit or lean casually against things so that they are kept in fixed spots for shot/reverse shots' (Thompson 1988: 234).

Also linked to filmed theatre is the use of predominantly eye-level camera positions and a majority of two-shots or three-shots – for instance, of two or three people having a conversation – rather than the Hollywood practice of shot/reverse shot exchanges of close-ups. Extreme, tilted angles are unusual. They are notoriously used by Ophuls in baroque films such as *La Ronde* and *Le Plaisir* but also by Cocteau in the more intimate *Les Parents terribles*. The latter falls into the category of filmed theatre, since Cocteau shot it with the cast who had been performing his play on stage, yet the many short takes and striking camera angles place it in a very different realm from the Pagnol and Guitry adaptations of the 1930s. The cinematography of *Les Parents terribles* is, however, still at the service of the actors' internalised, psychologically charged performance, where Guitry's had served the flamboyant boulevard gestures of his actors, including himself.

Prisons de femmes, directed by Roger Richebé in 1938, can be considered an emblematically 'ordinary' film of the period. This was one of the top box-office successes of that year, but it has received virtually no critical attention. It deserves a reappraisal, since *Prisons de femmes* sums up many of the points I have made so far about the classical French cinema, both in terms of a cinema of spectacle and of cinematography. The story follows Juliette Régent (Renée Saint-Cyr), a rich woman blackmailed by pimp Dédé (Georges Flamant) through his girlfriend Régine (Viviane Romance), a caf'conc' singer who knew Juliette in prison. Juliette's husband Max (Jean Worms) finds out, when Juliette is shot accidentally in a fight between Régine and Dédé. The past is evoked in a flashback narrated by the writer Francis Carco playing himself (*Prisons de femmes* is adapted from one of his novels). The narrative and visual style of the film is based on the contrast between the wealthy world of Juliette and the seedy working-class/underworld that Régine and Dédé inhabit, with Carco as mediator. The first sequence takes place at the Régents' luxury residence, where a high-society reception is in full swing. Language is refined, music jazz-inspired. All is order, wealth and glitter in an exaggeratedly large apartment. Lighting is high key and white surfaces (women's satin evening dresses, flowers, curtains) dominate. By contrast, Dédé's telephone call to Juliette in mid-party takes us to a working-class *caf'-conc'*, the Paradis, where decor and lighting dramatically change. We are now in a noir environment of contrasted, expressionist lighting. It is tempting to see the scenes at Juliette's as Hollywood-derived (the iconography is reminiscent of the Astaire and Rogers musicals and of screwball comedies), and the working-class/underworld scenes as French, in the idiom of Poetic Realism. To some extent this is true, yet it is also the case that both worlds are depicted in similar ways in terms of cinematography and editing, the classical French style cutting across disparate genres (the heterogeneous nature of the film is itself typical of the 1930s; for instance, there are also documentary elements in the film with the scenes in the women's jail). In both sequences described above, two-shots, three-shots and ensemble shots predominate over close-ups and shot/reverse-shot cutting. Framing is predominantly frontal and eye-level; one exception is a couple of shots of Viviane Romance on stage taken from the point of view of the audience below. In both cases, establishing shots are followed by series of ensemble shots rather than classical Hollywood's progressive penetration of space. Takes are often long: the ASL for the whole film is 14 seconds, though in the two opening sequences it goes up to 22 seconds, no doubt because of the need to establish the spaces of the Régents' apartment and of the Paradis – in both sequences there are lengthy lateral tracking shots across the space. The pace generally is slow, and the film exhibits the persistence of tableaux shots in the tradition of the cinema of attraction: views of the audience at the Paradis, for instance, not to mention Romance's singing. Whether in the bourgeois world or the underworld, the emphasis is on the representation of communities, illustrating Crisp's point about the resistance in 1930s French cinema to what he calls the ideology of individualism (Crisp 1993: 383). But where Crisp sees this gradually eroding through the classical period, in a move towards individual drama, I would argue that some genres, especially the 1950s costume drama, show the survival of the cinema of spectacle, which is by necessity more communal.

DESIGNS ON REALITY: THE CENTRALITY OF POETIC REALISM

The term 'Poetic Realism' was originally applied to literature; in the cinema it was allegedly first used about Chenal's *La Rue sans nom* (1933). Often seen as related to the political context of the time, especially the Popular Front (1936–8) and the menacing pre-war years, Poetic Realism was rather the product of a long French cultural tradition, which included nineteenth-century classics (Balzac, Eugène Sue, Zola), crime literature (Georges Simenon), populist novels of the 1920s and 1930s (Eugène Dabit, Pierre MacOrlan, Francis Carco) and popular songs, magazines and photography (Cartier-Bresson, Brassaï). Cinematically, antecedents can be found in French and German cinema, especially the *Kammerspielfilm* and the *Straßenfilme*. Although only one important trend among many in French 1930s cinema, Poetic Realism caught historians' attention internationally not only for its formal visual beauty (whereas the attractions of dialogue travel less well) and cultural prestige but also because it formed such a strong contrast to Hollywood. As a result it dominates conventional histories of French cinema of the classical period, to the detriment of the light, musical and theatrical 'art of spectacle' discussed so far.

Poetic Realism is a critical construction with blurred edges – terms such as 'populist melodrama', 'the social fantastic', 'noir realism', 'romantic pessimism', 'magic realism', etc. have been at various times substituted for it. As with American film noir, there is uncertainty about whether it designated a genre, a mood or a visual style. But however hazy, the expression 'Poetic Realism' is evocative. It designates pessimistic and nostalgic urban dramas, usually set in Paris (though there are colonial examples) in working-class and artisan communities. Its doomed romantic narratives focus on tragic proletarian heroes, best embodied by Jean Gabin. The latter evolved a minimalist type of performance, radically opposed to the dominant theatrical aesthetics of the filmed theatre evoked above, and thus contributed to the sense of authenticity in

Poetic Realism. The supreme examples are the films of Marcel Carné and Jacques Prévert – *Quai des brumes* (1938), *Le Jour se lève* (1939) – but the canon also includes Carné's *Jenny* and *Hôtel du Nord*, Jean Vigo's *L'Atalante* (1934), Renoir's *La Bête humaine* (1938), Jacques Feyder's *Le Grand jeu* (1933) and *Pension Mimosas* (1935), Duvivier's *La Bandera* (1935), *La Belle équipe* and *Pépé le Moko*, Jean Grémillon's *Gueule d'amour* (1937), Marie Epstein and Jean Benoît-Lévy's *La Maternelle* (1933), Raymond Bernard's *Faubourg-Montmartre* (1931), several films by Chenal and large sections of *Prisons de femmes*, as we saw above. As its name suggests, Poetic Realism proposes a duality between the everyday and the lyrical/emotional, poetry arising precisely from the everyday. This key aspect was brilliantly analysed by Bazin in relation to *Le Jour se lève*. In an introduction to the film, Bazin examines the role of objects surrounding the hero François (Gabin) as he spends his last night trapped in his bedroom: a teddy bear, a bicycle, a mirror, a brooch, cigarettes (Bazin 1983: 53–69; see also Andrew 1995, 328–32). These humble objects signify the hero's everyday life but they also bridge 'poetically' the gap between denotation and connotation, between present and past (Turim 1990). Graham Greene, who loved French cinema of the 1930s for knowing 'the immense importance of the careful accessory', wrote of *Hôtel du Nord*:

> we believe in the desperate lovers and the suicide pact on the brass bed in the shabby room, just because of the bicyclists on the quay, the pimp quarrelling with his woman in another room, and the First-Communion party. (Greene 1980: 229–30)

Poetic Realism thus lifts the quotidian into a lyrical, almost abstract dimension while retaining the surface depiction of the everyday world. The focus on working-class milieux places Poetic Realism within earlier traditions of realist cinema, including early Pathé dramas, some Feuillade films and André Antoine's *L'Hirondelle et la mésange* (1920). These, however, were mostly shot on location; a defining characteristic of Poetic Realism, on the contrary, is the reconstruction of reality in sets.

Poetic Realism is a stylised visual construction created, beyond individual directors, by an exceptional ensemble of craftsmen and artists: the decors of Alexandre Trauner, the photography of Jules Kruger, Eugen Schüfftan, Curt Courant and Claude Renoir; and stars like Gabin, Arletty, Jules Berry, Charles Vanel and others. Sound is also important: the dialogues of Prévert, Charles Spaak and Henri Jeanson are key to Poetic Realism, as is the music of Maurice Jaubert and Joseph Kosma. As argued in the first part of this chapter, dialogue and music are at the centre of the whole of classical French cinema. Thus, although the visual aspect of Poetic Realism is particularly arresting, its sound (dialogue, music) and performative dimensions should not be forgotten as linking these films – as also do the actors – to the rest of the French classical tradition. The look of Poetic Realism is indebted to the Expressionist lighting of German cinematographers such as Courant and Schüfftan, who taught the subsequent generation of French directors of photography. Yet, it is different from German Expressionism. Coupled with the panchromatic film stock introduced in the late 1920s, which enabled a softer graduation between black and white (Crisp 1993: 381), the French Poetic Realist look was thus a hybrid, able to shape figures in everyday settings and produce strong, expressionist lighting effects. Such hybridity is in evidence in most of the films: in *La Bête humaine*, for example, Renoir and his cinematographers Curt Courant and Claude Renoir switch from Gabin driving his train on location or interacting with colleagues in fairly high-key lighting, to highly dramatic scenes such as Gabin's murder of Séverine (Simone Simon) shot with violent light and dark contrasts. Although some pessimistic dramas in the classical period are shot on location, such as Renoir's *Toni* (1934) and Grémillon's *Lumière d'été* (1942), the realism of classical French cinema is mainly reconstructed in sets, built by Lazare Meerson and his pupils, Alexandre Trauner, Georges Wakhevitch and Eugène Lourié, who would continue the tradition until the late 1950s at least. These sets proposed a minutely observed yet abstract vision of cityscapes (usually the *faubourgs* of Paris), moulded and enhanced by lighting. It is the interaction of lighting, set and camerawork that characterises Poetic Realism. A good example is *Hôtel du Nord*. Its superb set designed by Trauner is a replica of a segment of one side of the Canal Saint-Martin (in north-east Paris), with apartment blocks, hotels, shops, quayside and bridges, punctuated by location shots of the canal and barges. The set is plainly artificial, yet still a vibrant metonymy of Paris. In their sophisticated symbiosis of sets, camera and lighting, Poetic Realist films construct an aesthetics of visual control. The sets are often of enclosed spaces within the city, such as hotels, courtyards, staircases and rooms; these act as metonymies of the city and metaphors of the closed, warm, nostalgic community, as in Renoir's *Le Crime de Monsieur Lange* (1935). But increasingly in the 1940s they are used to evoke the inward-looking, small-minded communities, even the rejection of strangers: this is evident in the courtyard where the main characters live in Clouzot's *Quai des Orfèvres* and in Duvivier's *Panique* (1946), where outsider Michel Simon is

ostracised and eventually lynched. The achievement of Poetic Realism was to film authentically connoted characters as connected to an environment that, despite the obvious artificiality of the sets, possessed enough symbolic charge to stand for reality. This was partly because of the accumulated visual capital of the city of Paris in painting, photography and film, and partly because of the evocative poetry of the sets and lighting. As in the famous scene in *Hôtel du Nord*, the key word was 'atmosphere'.

REALISM BEYOND POETIC REALISM

While Carné and Prévert's *Les Enfants du paradis* is considered the culmination of Poetic Realism, by the mid-1940s this type of film had become, as Dudley Andrew puts it, 'codified and citable' (Andrew 1995: 321). The war years tended to

Jean Gabin in *Touchez pas au grisbi* (Jacques Becker, 1954)

eschew the realist genre, although a number of films used its visual idiom, for instance Albert Valentin's *Marie-Martine* (1942), and there were attempts to replace Gabin (who had gone to Hollywood), for instance with René Dary in a number of populist movies such as *Forte tête* (Mathot, 1942) and *Port d'attache* (Jean Choux, 1942). At the Liberation, René Clément's *La Bataille du rail* (1945), a tribute to the Resistance shot on location with railway workers, raised hopes of a French neo-realism. Although Clement's work in particular continued this trend towards location shoots, with *Au-delà des grilles* (1948), *Jeux interdits* (1951) and *Monsieur Ripois* (1953), most films quickly returned to the studios, as symbolised by Carné and Prévert's epitaph to Poetic Realism, *Les Portes de la nuit* (1946). In this context, Poetic Realism mutated into 'realist' genres of two kinds: noir psychological drama on the one hand and the *policier* on the other. The first category includes the films of Clouzot, Yves Allégret, Verneuil, Autant-Lara. These films became excessively dark, both literally and metaphorically, especially Allégret's *Une Si jolie petite plage* and *Manèges* and Clouzot's *Manon* (1948) and *Les Diaboliques* (1954), with a focus on the psychology of the – frequently criminal – individual. We were still in the popular *faubourgs* of the city on the whole, but the main difference was that, unlike Poetic Realist films like *Le Quai des brumes*, *Le Jour se lève* and *Hôtel du Nord*, love no longer had any redeeming power. Bazin saw the change as a movement away from the 'poetic' towards the 'realist', and as a loss of spirituality, towards a cinema in which 'the *mise en scène* no longer tries to create through the expressionism of lights and décor a transcendent metaphysics of disaster which pre-exists the script' (Bazin 1983: 22). Without necessarily following Bazin down the spiritual route, it is the case that the increased cynicism of the films' contents is echoed by their more polished yet gloomier and in some cases sordid set designs.

The noir Poetic Realist idiom also, importantly, fed into the expansion of the *policier*, helped by the success of crime literature in the post-war period (the *série noire*) and of Eddie Constantine's series of spoof thrillers. From numerically modest though qualitatively important beginnings in the 1930s, for example Renoir's *La Nuit du carrefour* (1932) and

Duvivier's *La Tête d'un homme* (1933), among others, the *policier* went through an important renaissance during the war, with Becker's *Dernier atout* (1942) and Clouzot's *L'Assassin habite au 21* (1942), and several Simenon adaptations. But it is Becker's *Touchez pas au grisbi* (1954), followed by Jules Dassin's *Du rififi chez les hommes* (1955) and Jean-Pierre Melville's *Bob le flambeur* (1956), that truly launched a renaissance of the genre, in which ageing gangsters (typically Gabin or Lino Ventura) and their male 'families' roamed the cobbled streets of Montmartre in black Citroëns. From Poetic Realism the *policier* took the urban, usually Parisian, topography and, until the late 1960s, the black-and-white photography. The working-class/criminal milieu of Poetic Realism has become a more hermetic underworld that, paradoxically, also becomes more bourgeois, as signified by the gangsters' luxury apartments and glamorous nightclubs. This evolution can be traced concretely by taking films from each decade: for example, *La Tête d'un homme*, *L'Assassin habite au 21* and *Maigret tend un piège* (Delannoy, 1958). All three concern the exploration of specific areas of Paris, with a policeman/detective figure as guide (in the first and last, Simenon's Inspector Maigret). *La Tête d'un homme* is situated in Montparnasse, in a bohemian, cosmopolitan community. Maigret (Harry Baur) is a world-weary but benign figure who takes the spectator through an exciting artistic underworld, in a visually highly expressionist film, both in terms of sets (art deco brasserie, crooked staircase) and lighting. *L'Assassin habite au 21* (Pierre Fresnay as detective), made during the war, figures a thoroughly mediocre petit-bourgeois community where everyone is a suspect. Although some scenes use expressionist lighting – including a remarkable street scene in which the assassin's murderous cane and the use of subjective camera prefigure Michael Powell's *Peeping Tom* (1960) – most are flatly lit in sober decors. When we get to *Maigret tend un piège* (Gabin as Maigret), communities are still explored (as in the Simenon novel), but the drama has shifted to a small core of individuals, especially a bourgeois couple who have fled the popular Marais area for the wealthy sixteenth arrondissement.

Finally, another way to look at the evolution from Poetic Realism to gangster film noir is to trace the difference from *Pépé le Moko* to *Touchez pas au grisbi*. Both star Gabin as the head of a gang. But where the young Pépé and his motley crew are romantic outsiders, outlaws in Algiers' Casbah (Vincendeau 1998), Max in *Touchez pas au grisbi* has become a champagne-drinking, bourgeois gang-leader, fighting his rivals in luxury surroundings. At the same time, the memory of the young Gabin inhabits the older star, the warm Montmartre community evoked in *Touchez pas au grisbi* is a distant echo of the Casbah of *Pépé le Moko*. Other 1950s gangster films, such as *Du rififi chez les hommes* and *Bob le flambeur*, exhibit similar features, whereas the post-New Wave gangster films will evolve in different directions.

THE END OF CLASSICAL FRENCH CINEMA

All dominant systems can incorporate marginals, exceptions and mavericks. In the post-war period, several figures worked on the margins of the industry, producing work that was often starkly different from the traditions discussed in this chapter: Agnès Varda's *La Pointe courte* (1956), Alain Resnais's *Van Gogh* (1947), *Les Statues meurent aussi* (co-directed with Chris Marker, 1953), *Nuit et brouillard* (1955) and *Toute la mémoire du monde* (1956), Melville's *Le Silence de la mer* (1949), Robert Bresson's *Le Journal d'un curé de campagne* (1951) and many others. These directors were disparate aesthetically and ideologically, but they were united in their difference from the mainstream. Their independence, their emphasis on personal vision and the relative austerity of their practice marked them as auteurs, the precursors and models for the New Wave. Auteur cinema was increasingly recognised by the French film industry as a vital aesthetic and marketing category, offering an alternative to Hollywood just as the tradition of quality did on a different terrain. Their location shooting, refusal of stars and less scripted dialogue produced a novel aesthetic and, so the story goes, prompted the end of the classical era of studio shooting.

But the reality is more complex. On the one hand, as Crisp shows, the New Wave emerged from practices and infrastructures already in place in the industry of the classical period (Crisp 1993: 415–22). On the other hand, classical French cinema did not come to an end in 1959. It continued as a parallel strand manifest in popular genres such as comedy, adventure films – now more frequently located in contemporary settings, such as the Belmondo hit *L'Homme de Rio* (1963) – and the *policier* in the 1960s and 1970s, increasingly shot on location. Studio work and large-scale costume productions returned with a vengeance in the 1980s with the *cinéma du look* and heritage cinema. The editing rate of mainstream French cinema has continued to decrease, yet it still remains slower than the American rate (this is perceptible, for instance, when comparing French films with their American remakes). One reason for this is the continued greater importance given to dialogue and performance over action and character development. We are a long way from the early 1930s when critic Benjamin Fondane wrote in typically negative terms that with sound 'in French cinema the importance of rhythm – i.e. montage – loses all meaning and allows dialogue, song, dance, to take complete possession of space, to mark it by their takeover, and even to immobilise it' (Abel 1988: 51). Yet dialogue still remains in many genres a key *mise en scène* determinant and a mark of national identity. Classical French cinema has privileged self-conscious yet sensual spectacle, a feast for the emotions and the intellect, divorced from, or at least as important as, action and goal-orientation. French cinema has lost a sizeable share of its popular audience to Hollywood since the 1960s. The fact that it has done so far less than other European national cinemas is usually attributed to the state support it has been given since the war. While this is true, it is equally a tribute to the continued success of indigenous popular genres. Box-office hits at the turn of the 21st century, such as Francis Veber's *Le Dîner de cons* (1998) and *Le Placard* (2001), Thomas Gilou's two *La Vérité si je mens* films (1997 and 2001), Jean-Pierre Jeunet's *Le Fabuleux destin d'Amélie Poulain* (2001) and François Ozon's *8 femmes* (2002) – notwithstanding their different visual idioms that range from filmed theatre to post-modern fantasy, and different degrees of reference to American cinema – show the continued importance of language, music, and song to the construction of French national identity through the cinema and the perenniality of the classical tradition.

WORKS CITED

Abel, R. (1988) *French Film Theory and Criticism: A History/Anthology 1907–1939*, vol. 2: 1929–39, Princeton, NJ, Princeton University Press.

Andrew, D. (1980) 'Sound in France: The Origins of a Native School', *Yale French Studies*, 60, 94–114.

Andrew, D. (1995) *Mists of Regret: Culture and Sensibility in Classic French Film*, Princeton, NJ, Princeton University Press.

Bardèche, M. and Brasillach, R. (1948) *History of the Film*, London, Allen and Unwin.

Bazin, A. (1983), *Le Cinéma français de la Libération à la Nouvelle Vague*, Paris, Cahiers du cinéma/Éditions de l'Étoile.

Billard, P. (1995) *L'Âge classique du cinéma français*, Paris, Flammarion.

Brewster, B. and Jacobs, L. (1997) *Theatre to Cinema: Stage Pictorialism and Early Feature Film*, Oxford, Oxford University Press.

Burch, N. and Sellier, G. (1996) *La Drôle de guerre des sexes du cinéma français, 1930–1956*, Paris, Nathan.

Chirat, R. (1975) *Catalogue des films français de long métrage, films sonores de fiction, 1929–1939*, Brussels, Cinémathèque Royale de Belgique.

Chirat, R. (1981) *Catalogue des films français de long métrage, films de fiction, 1940–1950*, Luxembourg, Imprimerie Saint-Paul.

Clair, R. (1953), *Reflections on the Cinema*, London, Kimber.

Crisp, C. (1993) *The Classic French Cinema, 1930–1960*, Bloomington, Indiana University Press.

Dale, R. C. (1986) *The Films of René Clair*, Metuchen, NJ, Scarecrow Press.

Ehrlich, E. (1985) *Cinema of Paradox: French Film-Making under the German Occupation*, New York, Columbia University Press.

Garçon, F. (1984) *De Blum à Pétain: cinéma et société française (1936–44)*, Paris, Cerf.

Gomery, D. (1980) 'Economic Struggle and Hollywood Imperialism: Europe Converts to Sound', *Yale French Studies*, 60, 90–3.

Greene, G. (1980) *The Pleasure Dome: Graham Greene, The Collected Film Criticism, 1935–40*, Oxford, Oxford University Press.

Gunning, T. (1986) 'The Cinema of Attractions: Early Film, its Spectator and the Avant-Garde', *Wide Angle*, 8, Autumn, 63–70.

Jeancolas, J.-P. (1983) *Quinze ans d'années trente: le cinéma des Français, 1929–1944*, Paris, Stock.

Lapierre, M. ed. (1946) *Anthologie du cinéma*, Paris, Nouvelle Édition.

Martin, J. W. (1983) *The Golden Age of French Cinema, 1929–39*, Boston, G. K. Hall.

Noble, P. (1950) *Hollywood Scapegoat: The Biography of Erich von Stroheim*, London, Fortune Press.

Peyrusse, C. (1986) *Le Cinéma méridional 1929–1944*, Toulouse, Éché.

Sabria, J.-C. (1987) *Cinéma français, les années 50, les longs métrages réalisés de 1950 à 1959*, Paris, Éditions du Centre Pompidou/Économica.

Salt, B. (1992) *Film Style and Technology: History and Analysis*, London, Starword.

Siclier, J. (1981) *La France de Pétain et son cinéma*, Paris, Henri Veyrier.

Thompson, K. (1988) *Breaking the Glass Armor: Neoformalist Film Criticism*, Princeton, NJ, Princeton University Press.

Truffaut, F. (1976) 'A Certain Tendency of French Cinema', in Nichols, B. ed., *Movies and Methods*, Berkeley, University of California Press, 224–37.

Turim, M. (1990) 'Poetic Realism as Psychoanalytical and Ideological Operation: Marcel Carné's *Le Jour se lève* (1939)', in Hayward, S. and Vincendeau, G. eds, *French Film, Texts and Contexts*, London, Routledge, 103–16.

Vincendeau, G. (1995) *The Encyclopedia of European Cinema*, London, Cassell/BFI.

Vincendeau, G. (1998) *Pépé le Moko*, London, BFI.

Vincendeau, G. (2000) *Stars and Stardom in French Cinema*, New York, Continuum.

12 REPRESENTATIONS 1930–60
The Geography and Topography of French Cinema

Keith Reader

Why interrogate French cinema between 1930 and 1960 through the varying topographical and geographical representations of France that it offers? There are two main reasons for my choice of this approach. In the first place, it provides a convenient way of thinking about a massively heterogenous body of work, which from the introduction of sound at the beginning of our period to the arrival of the New Wave at its end underwent immense changes. The major upheaval in French society during this period, of course, occurred during the war years, but it was not until the 1970s that the traumas of that period were to be confronted in the cinema. The more piecemeal and less dramatic changes that took place over thirty years – the shift from a predominantly agricultural to an industrial economy, the increased mobility made possible by the motor car, the introduction of the forty-hour week and paid holidays – do, on the other hand, figure importantly in the films made during this period, and topography can often provide a helpful way of thinking about them. Thus, Renoir's *Une partie de campagne* (1936) reflects the increased importance of leisure in the wake of the Popular Front legislation of that year giving workers the right to paid holidays, while Jean Boyer's 1939 comedy *Circonstances atténuantes* derives much of its humour from the consequences of a motor-car breakdown, which forces the pompous lawyer Le Sentencier (Michel Simon) into unwonted proximity with a ruffianly group, including a forward, and somewhat tarty, Arletty. Both films take respectable Parisians – the ironmonger Monsieur Dufour and his family and Le Sentencier and his wife respectively – and bring them into contact with somewhat less respectable, or at least less self-righteous, inhabitants of the area surrounding Paris (the amorous boatmen in *Une*

partie de campagne, the denizens of the café in *Circonstances atténuantes*). Thus themes of topographical displacement and social mobility appear closely intertwined.

Second, a focus on the represented rather than the representation, however theoretically unsophisticated it may at first appear, has the merit of drawing attention to films and film-makers whose work may often be neglected. Canonical giants such as Jean Vigo, Marcel Carné and Jean Renoir have a tendency to commandeer critical attention, and this combines with the wider visibility of their work to relegate perhaps less outstanding but still significant directors such as René Clair or Jean Grémillon to relative undeserved obscurity. This is particularly marked with the cinema of the Fourth Republic (1945–58), which is tarred with the brush of Truffaut's denunciations of the *cinéma de papa*. Directors such as Christian-Jaque and Claude Autant-Lara were important chroniclers of the France of their time, and a topographical approach provides a framework for considering their work side by side with that of more prestigious and familiar figures. This is what we shall try to do in the following discussion.

The gulf that above all characterises French society is, of course, the split between Paris and the provinces – or as the planner Jean-François Gravier put it in 1947, 'Paris and the French desert'. This stems primarily from the post-1789 concentration of French institutional life in the capital, where the Revolution had started and the place that was deemed by the Jacobins to be their safest stronghold. Transport, administrative, intellectual and cultural networks all converge on Paris in a way that has no equivalent in other major European countries, where the most important city may not be the capital (Amsterdam), may have a significant counterweight or rival (Milan, Barcelona) or may encounter other factors inhibiting its sway (the post-war partition of Germany, the UK's peculiar 'federal' structure). Neither the Fifth Republic's administrative division of France into a number of large provinces nor the Socialist government's 1981 introduction of elected regional assemblies has significantly undermined the hegemony of Paris, evidenced in the commonly used phrase 'la France profonde' (the depths of France) to refer to those rural provinces in which it would be thought delightful to own a second home, as many Parisians do, but hell on earth to live permanently. Despite its continued dominance, however, we should not forget that the cultural topography of Paris has changed almost beyond recognition even since the end of our period. The erstwhile heartlands of 'le titi Parisien' – the Parisian 'cockney', most memorably incarnated by Jean Gabin but most authentically perhaps by the character actor Carette – still house examples of the genre, but their dominance has been challenged by on the one hand large ethnic communities such as the North Africans of Belleville, on the other the middle classes who now inhabit the Bastille area, once a stronghold of the skilled artisan. Paris-set films of our period undoubtedly derive much of their fascination, for a French audience at least, from their evocation of a bygone era, as in Renoir's *Le Crime de Monsieur Lange* (1936) or Carné's *Hôtel du Nord* (1938). Jean-Pierre Jeunet's *Le Fabuleux destin d'Amélie Poulain* (2001) enjoyed such enormous box-office success at least in part because of its harking back to what Ginette Vincendeau calls 'the look and sensibility of the Poetic Realism that flourished in French cinema in the 1930s' (Vincendeau 2001: 23). Finally, it should be pointed out that the setting of a film, for the purposes of this chapter, refers to what is depicted on the screen, not to where the shooting actually took place. Carné's *Les Enfants du paradis* (1945) was shot in the Victorine studios in Nice, but it would be absurd to think of it as anything but a 'Parisian' film. The relative place of studio and location shooting in French films of this period in particular is a fascinating area for research, but one that we shall not have the space to touch on here.

MEMORIES OF THE CITY THAT NEVER WAS

The Paris that will above all interest us here is 'le Paris populaire', the working-class Paris that survives in the memories of sentimentalists and - nostalgia-hounds largely through its cultural and textual reproductions during the period under discussion. Novelists such as Francis Carco, whose work is often set in the bygone world of Les Halles, where food and human flesh formed the staple objects of trade, or Pierre MacOrlan, whose 1927 novel *Le Quai des brumes* is set in Montmartre (he was displeased at Carné and Prévert's 1938 relocation of it to Le Havre), rank alongside singers such as Fréhel and Mistinguett – giants of the music hall – as important figures in this respect. The world they evoke is one of poverty and violence – Mistinguett's man, in her most famous song 'Mon homme', regularly beats her – coexisting with tenderness and solidarity. A world far removed from the intellectual sanctuaries of the Latin Quarter and Saint-Germain-des-Prés, popular Paris is more closely associated with the Right Bank, notably the environs of the Canal Saint-Martin (*Hôtel du Nord*) or the then still ungentrified Marais (*Le Crime de Monsieur Lange*; Autant-Lara's 1956 *La Traversée de Paris*). Among major films of the pre-war years, only Renoir's *Boudu sauvé des eaux* (1932) takes us into the milieu of the Left Bank bourgeoisie, whose pretensions are sardonically lampooned in the person of the fundamentally benign but do-gooding and hypocritical bookseller Lestingois. The world of working-class Paris has of course its counterpart in representations of many capital cities, as Brecht's Berlin or even Pasolini's Rome may suggest. Because Paris ranks second only to New York as the most widely represented of world cities in the cinema, 'le Paris populaire' provides a particularly vivid and tenacious example of urban representation. This was inflected in a heavier, more sinister direction after the war by the arrival of professional gangsters – descendants or reincarnations of the black marketeers such as Bourvil's Marcel Martin in *La Traversée de Paris* – frequently played by Jean Gabin, whose earlier roles for Renoir, Carné and Duvivier thus appear even more benign in retrospect, as though to illustrate Adrian Rifkin's assertion that 'memories of the city that never was are more perfect than those of a city lived but changing' (Rifkin 1993: 1).

René Clair's *Sous les toits de Paris* (1930), probably the first French musical comedy, is an early sound example of popular Paris on screen, revolving around the friendship of a street-singer and a pedlar. The romantic (though in reality doubtless squalid) garrets of *Sous les toits de Paris* are to be found too in *Le Crime de Monsieur Lange*. Renoir's only film scripted by that best-loved of Parisian bards, Jacques Prévert, is set around a courtyard in the Marais area of Paris. The lower floor is occupied by a laundry and a magazine publisher's-cum-printing-works, the latter of which is taken over by the workers and run as a co-operative when its owner, the villainous Batala, absconds. Solidarity is a leitmotif both of the film's narrative and its visual organisation, most famously exemplified by the 360-degree pan around the courtyard immediately before Lange shoots Batala at the film's dramatic climax (see Bazin 1973: 40–8). The courtyard, like many such in the Paris of its day, is the focus of the characters' work and of their personal lives (Lange and Valentine live in the building in which they work), so that the film gives us a strong sense of popular urban community actualised in the setting-up of the collective. Renoir and Prévert were, however, too politically astute to present this community as in any sense untroubled or Arcadian. Its financial and institutional precariousness is underlined by Batala's confident assertion that the profits generated by the collective during his absence legally belong to him. Indeed a possible source of conflict has already been identified in the concierge, whose old-soldier racism and slavish readiness to obey his masters' orders mark him out as what would once have been called a 'class collaborator'. The communitarian romance with which *Le Crime de Monsieur Lange* is suffused, and hence the film's view of Paris, is far less idyllic than it might at first appear.

Nineteen thirty-six – year of the Popular Front government and of *Le Crime de Monsieur Lange* – also saw the release of Duvivier's *La Belle équipe*, which focuses on a group of unemployed workmen who win the national lottery and decide to set up a riverside bar-cum-restaurant or *guinguette* beside the Marne. It is easy to forget that the Seine is not the Paris area's only river; for the working classes who traditionally lived on the eastern side of the city, the Marne was the traditional playground, whose bars and restaurants provided the destination for many a Sunday outing. Carné's 1929 silent documentary *Nogent, Eldorado du dimanche* is an affectionate presentation of the proletariat at play beside the river, which 'arouses nostalgia like that produced by the tableaux of painters such as Renoir, Sisley, or Pissarro' (Turk 1989: 21). The *guinguette* set up by Duvivier's five workmen is an apparently idyllic escape from the misery of their pre-lottery existence in a squalid lodging-house – never more so than when Jean (Jean Gabin), cloth cap at a particularly jaunty angle, leads a riverside chorus of the song 'Quand on se promène au bord de l'eau' ('When you're walking along the riverside'), extolling the joys of semi-bucolic life. But tensions within the group, especially between Jean and Charles, who are rivals for the fickle Gina, lead to murder and tragedy – in one of the alternative endings shot by Duvivier. The more upbeat ending, in which the two men spurn Gina and reassert the values of male bonding and the camaraderie of work, is the more convincingly written and acted, but the earlier problems the group has encountered, notably the deportation of one of its number who is an illegal immigrant, are enough to offset any suggestion that afternoons by the river offer an unproblematic cure for the strains of urban life. The Marne plays an important role too in Renoir's *Une Partie de campagne* (1936, though the action is set in 1860), where it is the setting of the Dufour family's Sunday excursion, culminating in the seduction of Madame Dufour and her daughter Henriette by two smooth-talking boatmen. The Dufours are of solid bourgeois stock (Monsieur Dufour is an ironmonger), which emphasises how wide a clientele the Marne appealed to in its heyday. Renoir himself has a cameo role as the innkeeper who serves the family their lunch, and the film's costumes and decor quite clearly recall, like *Nogent, Eldorado du dimanche*, the paintings of Renoir's father, Auguste, and the other Impressionists for whom the river was such an important source of inspiration. Having been safely married off to her father's assistant, Henriette returns to the *guinguette* some years later, to come face to face with her one-time lover in a moment steeped in melancholy and nostalgia. More

Maurice Bacquet and Nadia Sibirskaïa in *Le Crime de Monsieur Lange* (Jean Renoir, 1936)

unequivocally than in *La Belle équipe*, Paris (not depicted on screen) is associated with a world of harsh and depressing realism, from which the river provides a momentary but essential escape.

Vigo's *L'Atalante* (1934), by contrast, gives us a Paris at once enticing and dangerous. The newly-weds Jean and Juliette spend their 'honeymoon' on the barge that Jean skippers, sailing up the Seine – the river of work – to deliver a consignment of goods to Le Havre. When they dock in Paris, the mate Père Jules (one of Michel Simon's greatest performances) promptly absconds in search of sexual and alcoholic booty. Juliette, frustrated by having to remain on board, plays truant in her turn, but the city she discovers is one where luxury – the goods in shop windows at which she can only stare – coexists with misery, not least in the guise of the lines of unemployed workers that anticipate *La Belle équipe*. When her purse is stolen at the railway station, she is stranded, returning to the claustrophobic but reassuring security of the barge only when tracked down by Père Jules. Love may conquer all in *L'Atalante*, but the conflicts and dangers of urban life are nonetheless plain to see. It is also worth noting that the Canal Saint-Martin, in the north-east of the city, where Père Jules miraculously finds Juliette, is traditionally the workaday artery of popular Paris par excellence; and although it was later to be greatly gentrified, it is still one of the few Parisian areas to house a significant working-class population. The Canal Saint-Martin's best-known cinematic appearance, however, remains Carné's *Hôtel du Nord*. The eponymous hotel still looks on to the canal, and until the late 1980s it functioned as a flophouse much as it does in the film, though with a largely North African clientele. *Hôtel du Nord*, scripted by Henri Jeanson and Jean Aurenche, brings together an array of working-class Parisians – two young lovers tired of their difficult life and determined to end it all; the hoteliers Monsieur and Madame Lecouvreur who preside over the hotel's surrogate family, the homosexual confectioner Adrien; the golden-hearted prostitute Raymonde (Arletty) and her pimp Monsieur Edmond (Louis Jouvet). Attempts at breaking out of this world are generally unsuccessful. Edmond's decision to go fishing on his own rather than on holiday with Raymonde leads to a quarrel, during which Raymonde

delivers the celebrated line: 'Est-ce que j'ai une gueule d'atmosphère?' ('Do I look like an atmosphere?'). Edmond also plans to leave for Egypt with Renée (one of the young lovers), but this too comes to nothing. His departure from what he perceives as the claustrophobic world of the hotel occurs only at the end, when he allows himself to be gunned down by a former underworld sidekick. Raymonde's sharp repartee and the somewhat saccharine portrayal of the young lovers – who needless to say live happily ever after – may tend in retrospect to occlude some of *Hôtel du Nord*'s harsher, less sanguine aspects. Popular Paris of the pre-war years was not always an easy place to live.

Under German occupation, of course, that reality became significantly more harsh, although strict censorship meant that the Paris of those years did not figure prominently in the cinema until after the Liberation. Carné's *Les Portes de la nuit* (1946) begins with an encounter between a young worker (Yves Montand in his first lead role) and a tramp claiming to represent Destiny. They meet under the overhead Métro at Barbès – on the edge of Pigalle and Montmartre and never regarded as one of Paris's most salubrious areas. The film's insistently gloomy tone was not what French audiences wanted as they emerged from the dark years of the Occupation, and it marked the final Carné–Prévert co-operation; but the depiction of a post-Liberation Paris in which collaborators cling to their ill-gotten gains while former Resistance fighters eke out a difficult life remains extremely telling.

A decade later, Autant-Lara tackled the dark themes of the Occupation in *La Traversée de Paris*, whose eponymous crossing brings together the taxi-driver and part-time black marketeer Marcel Martin (Bourvil) and the successful artist Grandgil, played by Gabin in one of his best-known post-war bourgeois roles. They smuggle a contraband pig, fortunately dead and concealed in four suitcases, across the city, starting out in the Rue du Faubourg du Temple – later to become a centre of gay and artistic chic, but back then well and truly part of popular Paris. The metaphor of the pig's crossing of Paris illustrates Autant-Lara's perception that 'there are no valiant exploited poor and wicked rich exploiters, but only individuals giving themselves away through their day-to-day acts' (Bellinger 1990:

919), a cynicism that foreshadows, from a right-wing viewpoint, the calling into question of the myth of Resistance that began in the late 1960s with *Le Chagrin et la pitié* (Marcel Ophuls, 1971). A blind man playing 'La Marseillaise' is another particularly telling detail of *La Traversée de Paris*. The people of Paris are not the fundamentally benign, poor-but-happy community of legend, but a more complex and troubling phenomenon altogether.

PROVENÇAL MIRTH, BRETON STORMS AND DARK SATANIC MILLS

Turning now to the provinces, it is easy to concur with René Prédal's assertion that only Brittany and Provence in the period from 1930 to 1960 enjoyed 'a relatively satisfactory cinematic portrayal', for these are the two regions with the most recognisable images both inside and outside France (Prédal 1972: 78). Brittany's rugged, often rainswept coastline, its inhabitants' reputation for stubbornness and its Celtic romanticism stand in contrast to the jovial, sun-soaked Mediterranean bonhomie so often perceived as characteristic of Provence. It is significant that both provinces have had somewhat equivocal relationships with the France of which they form part, Provence having been finally united with France only in 1486 and Brittany always having harboured regionalist and separatist movements. These geographical and institutional differences have their linguistic counterparts too. Almost half of Brittany's inhabitants spoke Breton with some degree of fluency in 1952, while although the Provençal language is far less widespread, Provençal-accented spoken French, with its sing-song intonations and nasal diphthongs, is strikingly recognisable. The defining characteristics of these two provinces – favourite holiday destinations that maintain often contentious relations with their 'mother-state' – made them propitious terrain for film-makers, both during our period and subsequently. Renoir's *La Marseillaise* (1937), a re-enactment of the origins of the 1789 Revolution, begins in the hills where Provençal working men fleeing persecution have taken refuge before joining in the revolutionary movement, first in Marseilles and then in Paris. This provided Renoir, anxious to show in the contemporary context of the left-wing

Popular Front government he supported that fundamental social change had to come from the people as a whole, with an adroit means of 'sidestepping the cliché of the violent Parisian crowd' (O'Shaughnessy 2000: 132). On their march to Paris the Marseillais strengthen their bond with one another, as they later do with a Breton contingent that has arrived in the capital at the same time. Neither group, at the time when the film is set, would have had French as its native language – a way of reinforcing the film's view of France as an amalgam of once disparate cultural groups, and also perhaps of subtly contradicting the sometimes condescending exoticism that can inflect literary and cultural portrayals of the two provinces. Brittany was of course a bulwark of Catholic anti-revolutionary, pro-monarchist feeling at the time of the Revolution, as Balzac's early novel *Les Chouans* (1829) demonstrates, so that Renoir's decision to include a group of Breton revolutionaries has a marked polemical relevance.

Long before Provence became the holiday and second-home destination of choice for the educated bourgeoisie, its cinematic reputation was firmly established. The work of Marcel Pagnol played the key role here, capturing on film the intonation and locutions that also characterise his novels, and making the tubby Toulonnais Raimu a star through the trilogy of *Marius* (directed by Alexander Korda in 1931), *Fanny* (Marc Allégret, 1932) and *César*, which Pagnol himself directed in 1936. Pagnol's Provence is an easy-going place largely immune to the problems and tensions of the wider society, in which even Raimu's cuckolded baker in *La Femme du boulanger* (1938) is eventually able to forgive and forget. Pagnol was among the first major French directors to shoot extensively on location, and it is largely thanks to this that his cinematic image of Provence is such an influential and enduring one. Yet that Provence, as the baker's misery when his wife elopes with a shepherd suggests, is not simply an idyllic, because anachronistic, Arcadia. Pagnol's *Regain* (1937), based on a Jean Giono novel and set on the Haute-Provence plateau, centres on the love triangle between a nearly destitute poacher, the brutish knife-grinder Gédémus (played by Fernandel in an unusually dramatic role) and the failed actress Arsule. We are closer here to the world of

Jean Gabin and Michèle Morgan in *Remorques* (Jean Grémillon, 1941)

Fellini's *La Strada* (1954) – or to Sandrine Veysset's much later *Y aura-t-il de la neige à Noël?* (1996) – than to the 'Provençal mirth' beloved of Keats.

It was Pagnol who produced Renoir's first Provence-set film, *Toni* (1934), whose central characters are Italian and Spanish immigrants working in a quarry. The title role is played by Charles Blavette, as important a character actor in Provençal roles as Carette was in Parisian ones, and indeed arguably after Raimu the period's leading Provençal performer. There is joviality and conviviality among *Toni*'s nationally mixed community; but there is also homicidal love rivalry and a sense of great material precariousness, almost like a version of *La Belle équipe* transposed to the south. The film's tragedy is rooted in 'an inherently unstable collision between rural tradition and urban industrial modernity' (O'Shaughnessy 2000: 88) prophetic of much social change and conflict to come.

That sense of material precariousness is of course still more marked in the opening sequences of *La Marseillaise*. Whereas *Toni* displays an awareness of the wider contemporary political sphere through its depiction of transnational and working-class relationships, *La Marseillaise*, as we have seen, transposes that political sphere back in time, with a view to emphasising the continuity between the French nation forged in the struggle of 1789 and that seeking to emancipate itself in the 1930s. In that respect it echoes André Hugon's little-known film *Gaspard de Besse* (1935), which tells the story of a Provençal 'Robin Hood' of the pre-Revolutionary years, who is eventually caught and hanged along with his closest ally, played by Raimu. Like *La Marseillaise* a few years later, the film has evident contemporary political relevance, which was noticed by reviewers at the time. Provence here, once again, functions less as exotic scenic backdrop than as wild guerrilla terrain. However, it is neither of those things in Jean Grémillon's two major Provence-set films – *L'Étrange Monsieur Victor* (1938) and *Lumière d'été* (1942). Monsieur Victor (Raimu) is an outwardly respectable Toulon tradesman who doubles as the leader of a gang of thieves, and is willing to see a poor but honest cobbler go to prison in his stead. He is exposed at the end, leading Claudette Peyrusse to conclude that 'the world of Southern France is once more a world of transparency' (Peyrusse 1986: 147) – that transparency and luminosity for which Provence in particular is a scenic byword. *Lumière d'été*, set in the Provençal Alps, makes great visual play with those qualities, and like *L'Étrange Monsieur Victor* ends with the uncovering (here the violent death) of its villain, the landowner Patrice (Paul Bernard). As in *Toni*, we are reminded that Provence is an important industrial area as well as a magnet for the wealthy, for contrasted to the film's idle rich are the clean-cut workers who are building a dam nearby, and whose supervisory engineer – almost a benign antidote to the grasping Albert in *Toni* – rescues the heroine Michèle (Madeleine Robinson). The complexity of the province emerges more fully in the films that represent it during this period than a purely 'Pagnolesque' view of it might suggest.

Brittany is the setting for two important Grémillon films, *Remorques* (1941) and *Pattes blanches* (1949). *Remorques* brings together Jean Gabin and Michèle Morgan from *Le Quai des brumes*, inevitably once again playing star-crossed lovers. Gabin is a tugboat captain in Brest, passionately attached to his calling and to the stormy ocean as the archetypal Breton is supposed to be. Even the retirement home of which he dreams will have a sea view. There are numerous shots of stormy seas and a constant stress on the male bonding at the heart of the sailor's work, as if to illustrate the remark made at the wedding banquet that opens the film: 'Every sailor has two wives – his own and the sea.' This chimes with the long-standing romantic regionalist view of Brittany as the maritime province par excellence, but at the same time represents an opening up of the cinema to the world of often newly mechanised work characteristic of many films of the period. As Gilles Deleuze wrote of Grémillon, 'few directors have filmed man's work so well, even discovering in it the equivalent of a sea' (Deleuze 1986: 78–9); and *Remorques* is the outstanding example of this in his oeuvre. By contrast, *Pattes blanches* recalls the decadent provincial aristocratic world of

Lumière d'été, in its tale of the doomed passion of the landowner Keriadec for the femme fatale Odette, whom he eventually strangles and throws over a cliff. The world of work is much less marked here than in *Remorques*, for although the village is peopled by fishermen, they 'play no part in the story other than as spectators or consumers' (Sellier 1989: 252). Brittany is an exotic backdrop that lies all but outside historical time, more untamed and inward-looking than its Provençal counterpart, as conducive to involuted and excessive passion as Daphne du Maurier's Cornwall in Hitchcock's *Jamaica Inn* (1939) and *Rebecca* (1940). No other French province could have fulfilled that role in quite the same way.

Another province widely depicted in the cinema, though in a considerably less flattering light than either Brittany or Provence, is the 'Nord' – the north-eastern area centring on Lille, one of France's industrial heartlands and, ever since Zola's novel *Germinal* (1885), a byword for 'dark satanic mills' and social exploitation. This has been especially marked in later films, such as Claude Berri's 1993 adaptation of *Germinal*, Eric Zonca's *La Vie rêvée des anges* (1998) and Bertrand Tavernier's *Ça commence aujourd'hui* (1999), but the stereotype goes back to the cinema of our period. For example, the region provides the setting for the framing narrative of *Le Crime de Monsieur Lange*, after Lange and Valentine have made their escape to the Belgian border. The clearly working-class drinkers in the bar where the couple takes refuge listen to their tale sympathetically and, with one exception, they refuse to denounce the lovers to the police. This instance of working-class solidarity echoes the sense of community that we see developing around the Paris courtyard in the film's main narrative.

However, the other occurrences of the north in the cinema of our period are distinctly short on such solidarity. Yves Allégret set *Une Si jolie petite plage* (1948) in a rain-sodden northern seaside resort off-season. The opening shots of a mournful, fog-shrouded landscape make the irony of the film's title almost oppressively clear, as does the progress of Gérard Philipe's central character towards the suicide on which the film ends. One character in the hotel bar even says 'Berck, berck, berck!' – at once the French word for 'Ugh!' and the name of a seaside resort on the Pas-de-Calais coast. Robert Bresson's *Le Journal d'un curé de campagne* (1951) is set in a small village in the poor agricultural country near Arras. The young priest's crushing spiritual isolation is reinforced by his inability to establish good relationships with most of his parishioners, from whom he becomes increasingly alienated as the film goes on. Yet solidarity, as the bar-room scene in *Le Crime de Monsieur Lange* shows, is not completely evicted from films set among the working-class communities of the north. Louis Daquin, the French Communist Party's film-maker-in-chief, shows in *Le Point du jour* (1949) how it is attained in a mining community (though only after a potentially disastrous accident). Likewise, Louis Terme and Jacques Morin's *La Fille de la route* (1959), shot in Lille using local, non-professional actors, depicts the day-to-day life of young women commuting by coach from mining villages to the textile factories in Roubaix. The combination of grim living conditions and a strong sense of community in these films is reminiscent of the British 'kitchen-sink' texts – both novels and films – that came to prominence at about the same time and correspondingly depicted the themes of social change seen from a provincial viewpoint.

The topography and geography of France through its films is such a potentially vast field of enquiry – no mention has been made of the colonies, for example – that this chapter can only pretend to have begun to map out the terrain. So if certain provinces have been excluded, it does not mean that their cinematic representation is non-existent. The provincial 'depths' of France, peasant-infested and the butt of countless Parisian jibes, are strikingly represented, for example, in Jacques Becker's *Goupi mains rouges* (1942), set in the westerly province of Charente, where an almost Balzacian drama of greed, theft and murder unfolds. Another case would be Normandy, closer to Paris than Brittany and thereby less exotic, which provides the backdrop for Carné's *Quai des brumes* and *La Marie du port* (1949), set in the port-cities of Le Havre and Cherbourg respectively. The reconstruction of Le Havre is particularly striking, since it was all but bombed flat in the war, so what we see is a studio representation of a city that no longer exists. Finally, Lyons, hub of the silk industry for so many years, is the setting for Christian-Jaque's *Un revenant* (1946), in which Louis Jouvet's character returns to take delicious revenge on the family who many years before exiled him for marrying beneath himself. The film's opening shot of a smoky and fog-wreathed Lyons could almost delude us that we are in northern France, while the prominence it gives to the world of work and to issues of social class clearly reflects the social changes in France during the period under discussion. It is the depiction of diversity and change, along with the rediscovery of so-called minor film-makers, that most recommends a topographical approach to the question of representation in French cinema during this period. Although a great deal of work remains to be done on how different cities and regions are represented, and what they connote, this chapter may at least have suggested some of the possible uses and developments of such an approach.

WORKS CITED

Bazin, A. (1973) *Jean Renoir*, New York, Simon and Schuster.

Bellinger, G. (1990) 'La Traversée de Paris', in Tulard, J. ed., *Guide des films*, Paris, Bouquins.

Deleuze, G. (1986) *Cinema 1: The Movement-Image*, London, Athlone.

O'Shaughnessy, M. (2000) *Jean Renoir*, Manchester, Manchester University Press.

Peyrusse, C. (1986) *Le Cinéma méridional, 1929–1944*, Toulouse, Éché.

Prédal, R. (1972) *La Société française à travers le cinéma, 1914–1945*, Paris, Armand Colin.

Rifkin, A. (1993) *Street Noises: Parisian Pleasures, 1900–1940*, Manchester, Manchester University Press.

Sellier, G. (1989) *Jean Grémillon*, Paris, Méridiens Klinksieck.

Turk, E. (1989) *Child of Paradise: Marcel Carné and the Golden Age of French Cinema*, Cambridge, MA, Harvard University Press.

Vincendeau, G. (2001) 'Café Society', *Sight and Sound*, 11: 8, August, 22–5.

13 SPECTATORS 1930–60
The Golden Age of Spectatorship

Gregory Sims

This period is justifiably characterised as the golden age of cinema attendance in France. From the introduction of sound in the late 1920s, attendances increased substantially, although it should be said that in 1930 only 1,100 of the 4,500 cinemas in metropolitan France were actually equipped for sound projection, 150 of which were in Paris, and even as late as 1934 there were still 1,590 cinemas that remained unequipped. A good indication of sound as a major new attraction can be gained from William Wellman's *Wings* (1928), which easily exceeded all attendance records when released at the Paramount cinema in Paris in November 1928, taking 650,000 francs per week. *The Jazz Singer* (Alan Crosland, 1927), released at the Aubert-Palace in Paris in January 1929, drew more than 540,000 spectators at this one cinema in just under a year. And when Robert Florey's *La Route est belle*, one of the first French talkies, was released at the Capitol in Marseilles in 1929, it almost doubled the previous attendance record. Over the next thirty years, attendances grew fairly steadily: 220 million in 1930, 234 million in 1931, 220 million in 1938, 304 million in 1943, peaking in 1947 at 423 million, slipping back to 360 million in 1952 before recovering to 411 million in 1957, at which point the decline began, falling to 354 million by 1960.

The cinema's dominance of mass entertainment was particularly strong during the Occupation, with attendance during this bleak period averaging nine entries per year per head of population. Such dominance is understandable: the choice of films may have been narrow as a result of the restricted film market (although there were frequent violations of the bans placed on British and American films, and the many 'immoral' French films from the 1930s), but the public's need for imaginary escape from

hardship was stronger than ever. The cinemas were heated in the winter, and other forms of entertainment and distraction were severely limited, since many bars, dance halls and restaurants were closed down, cafés were required to shut at ten o'clock and weekend trips to the country became impossible. After the war, the return of American films to the French market (77 in 1946, 175 in 1947, 169 in 1948, similar figures to those of the mid-1930s) led to a further boom in audience numbers, which reached a historic peak in 1947. Even if attendances in the 1950s remained fairly healthy, it is clear that by the end of our period a dramatic and irreversible decline had begun. This fall coincided with an important shift in the socio-demographic profile of cinema audiences. People on more modest incomes were drifting away from the cinema, significantly altering their leisure priorities and spending more of their income on consumer goods and services, which, with the advent of mass production and mass marketing, were becoming progressively more affordable and desirable to the ordinary citizen. Thus, cinemagoing as the dominant pastime for almost all social classes was slowly transformed with the advent of the consumer society into a cultural pursuit for the well-heeled and, increasingly, for younger people. As we shall also discover, from the early 1950s the nature of cinemagoing had begun to change, since many cinemas were demolished or renovated, and the viewing experience they offered the spectator was duly redesigned and standardised. Given this general picture of steady growth followed by the beginnings of a historic decline in audiences, the following discussion will examine in detail some significant trends and influences throughout the period from 1930 to 1960, such as geographical variations, new forms of leisure, questions of class and the modernisation of cinema design.

GEOGRAPHICAL VARIATIONS IN ATTENDANCE

The most prominent variation in geographical terms is the clear dominance of the major towns. A study carried out by the Centre National de la Cinématographie (CNC) in 1950 revealed that the 54 towns with a population of 50,000 or more comprised 21 per cent of the total population and 20 per cent of the cinemas, but the attendance figures were 50 per cent of the total for metropolitan France, and the takings an even more disproportionate 60 per cent. The trend is stronger if the statistics are limited to the 22 towns of 100,000 or more, which had a mere 15.7 per cent of the total population, but provided 42 per cent of the total attendance and 52 per cent of the total takings (*Film français*, June 1951). Ten years later, there were 28 centres of 100,000 or more, representing 25 per cent of the total population, 21.8 per cent of the number of cinemas, 30.7 per cent of the number of seats, 47.3 per cent of the total attendance and 55 per cent of the total takings.

If the cinema was primarily an urban phenomenon, Paris and its suburbs stand out especially, audiences remaining more robust compared to other cities and towns, and its market share disproportionately high, in spite of average ticket prices being 35 per cent to 38 per cent higher than the rest of the country as a whole (*Bulletin du CNC*, August 1960). Paris had a higher attendance rate (30 visits per year per inhabitant in 1949–50) than the rest of the country, although some of the larger cities were not far behind: Lille (28), Marseilles (21.9), Nice (25.6), Strasbourg (25.5), Metz (31). Compared to most towns, Paris had an attendance rate between three and six times greater, depending on the region, and a clear dominance of the market. While the national takings for 1931 were estimated at around 1 billion francs, the city of Paris alone had takings that year of 300 million francs, almost a third of the total, with only 10 per cent of the total number of seats and 2.5 per cent of the total number of cinemas. In 1949, Paris had 30.5 per cent of takings with 22.88 per cent of spectators; in 1959, these percentages had slipped slightly, to represent 26 per cent of takings with 19 per cent of spectators. The importance of Paris is underscored by the concentration of high-earning

cinemas. In 1959, of the 133 cinemas nationally (2.3 per cent of the total) taking more than 60 million francs, accounting for 24 per cent of the national takings, 65 of these were situated in Paris. René Bonnell gives various explanations for this, including the considerably higher density of cinemas, the much wider choice of films (making it possible to attract all segments of the potential market) and a disproportionately high concentration of middle and upper-level managers, professionals, intellectuals and single people (Bonnell 1978: 37).

After Paris, the next most important centre was Marseilles. For example, the figures relating to 1955, show 8 per cent of spectators and 7 per cent of takings for Marseilles, followed by Lyons (5.07 per cent of spectators and 4.98 per cent of takings), Nice (3.27 per cent and 3.15 per cent), Lille (3.39 per cent and 2.8 per cent), Bordeaux (2.99 per cent and 2.88 per cent), Strasbourg (2.72 per cent and 2.19 per cent) and Metz (1.54 per cent and 1.18 per cent) (*Bulletin du CNC*, February 1957 and December 1960). Nevertheless, this relative strength in urban centres did not prevent a general drop in attendance rates after 1957, with a dramatic fall of 16 per cent, for example, in Paris. Rural areas show a less sudden decline, the drop in attendance in less densely populated regions being explained by the decrease in the overall number of cinemas, and thus of programme choice, and by the spread of automobile ownership, allowing rural dwellers, especially younger people, better access to cinemas further away from home. The decline in average attendance in the larger urban centres was linked to the migration of rural populations to the cities and large towns. This migration increased the total urban population, but the newcomers often settled on the suburban fringes, which had fewer cinemas and were increasingly better served by television in terms of proximity to transmitters and ownership of sets. This last point is crucial to an understanding of audiences during the period from 1930 to 1960, since the final years of the period coincide with the spread of television, which was a significant factor in declining attendances, especially influencing those who stopped going to the cinema altogether (*Bulletin du CNC*, August 1958).

NEW FORMS OF LEISURE

From its inception, television caused concern to cinema proprietors, who in May 1950 in Paris organised an international conference of European cinema proprietors to discuss the problem. The Germans had introduced television to France as early as 1943. The station Fernsehsender Paris used a transmitter on the Eiffel Tower to broadcast between three and five hours of programmes each day to approximately 300 television sets in Paris's military hospitals (Kubler and Lemieux 1990). Television was relaunched after the Occupation in October 1948, but at that stage only a few thousand Parisians owned a set. Among the larger urban centres, Lille had television from April 1950, Strasbourg from October 1953, Marseilles from September 1954, Metz from January 1955, Nancy from May 1955, Grenoble and Reims from November 1955, Lyons from December 1955, Mulhouse (Alsace) from January 1956, Neuvy-Deux-Clochers (Bourges/Sancerre) from May 1956. By June 1956, about one-fifth of the country was covered by television transmitters, serving potentially 40 per cent of the population, although a much smaller percentage actually had access to a television set. According to the RTF (Radio-Télévision Française), there were some 204,000 sets in service in 1955, and in May 1956 there were 340,934 sets registered with the central licensing service. Four years later, the number of sets had risen exponentially to around 2 million (one set for every 22.5 inhabitants, as compared to one set for every 4.6 inhabitants in Great Britain at the same time). There were 15 hours of weekly broadcasts in 1948, 20 in 1950, 25 in 1951–2, 34 in 1952–3, 40 in 1954 and 48 on average in 1956. As the *Bulletin du CNC* of June 1956 put it: 'Given this situation, aren't there grounds for wondering whether television isn't on the way to becoming one of the cinema's most serious competitors?'

But the arrival of television was merely one aspect of a much larger set of economic and cultural changes that were steadily overtaking the cinema. An editorial in *Film français* from March 1957 proclaimed that 'cinema programming must adapt to changing life-styles', arguing that, given the disturbingly weak average occupancy rate of 30 per cent for first-release cinemas in Paris, proprietors must take into account the changes in the working hours and leisure habits of consumers generally, and remarking that sessions timed to coincide with the end of the working day for white-collar workers were increasingly well attended, simply because many people faced long commutes and were more likely to go to the cinema before returning home to dine later in the evening. More generally, patterns of consumption were rapidly changing in the post-war years. Escape from work and the routines of everyday life was no longer afforded exclusively by the cinema, which found itself being overtaken by a range of distractions and pastimes: travel, sporting events, camping and other outdoor activities, the purchase of records and record players, cameras, portable radios, tape recorders and, of course, television sets. Car ownership grew rapidly in France at this time, along with motorcycles and scooters, which were especially popular among younger people. This was a major worry for cinema proprietors and industry commentators, since the fifteen to twenty-five age group represented such a crucial segment of the market. According to *Film français* in March 1959, 88 per cent of young French people between the age of fifteen and twenty-five went to the cinema on average forty-two times a year. A letter from a cinema proprietor published in the *Bulletin du CNC* in September 1954 illustrates the point:

> Over the last three years, we've reached the point where all French people seem to be motorised: you only need to consider the sheer number of mopeds, scooters and the like on the roads. Since it is young people under thirty who make up the cinema's main clientele, and since it is these same young people who are acquiring all these two-wheeled, motorised forms of transport, it is obvious that they can't be simultaneously out touring around the countryside and at the cinema.

The industry reacted to these profound changes by making the cinema experience bigger and better for its diminishing clientele. It introduced CinemaScope and other large-screen formats, such as Vistavision, Cinerama and Franscope, the first projection of a CinemaScope film (*The Robe*, directed by Henry Koster) taking place in Paris at the Rex and the Normandie on 4 December 1953. Indeed, the number of widescreen films released in Paris rose by almost 100 per cent between 1955 and 1956 (from 54 to 102, an increase from roughly 19 per cent to 30 per cent of the total). There was a concomitant emphasis on programming spectacular, big-budget films. According to an article entitled 'The Turning Point' in *Film français* from February 1958, television meant that 'cinema is obliged to fall back on its most invincible, its most formidable asset: sheer spectacle'. It explains that Hollywood is using the profits from sales of films to television to finance the manufacture of 'war-machines':

> blockbusters, a specific kind of cinematic production, costly, high-profile, providing the spectator with grandiose vistas. There are already numerous indications that the industry is coming to realise that the only way it will survive is through ambition and grandeur. We will therefore see budgets escalate and takings increase.

One year later, another article in *Film français* observes that, even though overall attendance continued to fall quite dramatically, large-scale spectacle and real entertainments remain attractive to the public, with certain films attracting record numbers of spectators: *Bridge on the River Kwai* (1.5 million spectators in Paris and the seven major provincial towns), *War and Peace* (805,000 spectators), *Mon oncle* (793,000), *The Ten Commandments* (784,000) and *Around the World in 80 Days* (730,000).

French co-productions became an important part of the counter-offensive. These were big-budget films that targeted large audiences. Co-productions (mostly Franco-Italian) accounted for one-third of the overall takings for the period from 1953 to 1955, the numbers of co-productions growing from 21 in 1952 to 98 in 1961 (Bonnell 1978: 168). However loosely defined, French films performed strongly in the marketplace, as an analysis of the performance of all films released in France in 1955 shows. Over a four-year period, 107 French films, out of a total of 459, garnered just under half the total takings, with 31 per cent going to American films. In the upper reaches of the market, French films were very clearly in the ascendant,

with 52 films grossing more than 200 million francs, a feat managed by only 19 American films. Roughly half of the 56 most successful films of the period from 1950 to 1959 were French, successfully competing against major Hollywood productions. In order of success, we have, for example: *Si Versailles m'était conté* (Sacha Guitry, 1954), *Bridge on the River Kwai* (David Lean, 1957), *Les Liaisons dangereuses* (Roger Vadim, 1959), *Orfeu Negro* (Marcel Camus, 1959), *Les Tricheurs* (Marcel Carné, 1958), *Le Retour de Don Camillo* (Duvivier, 1953), *Mon oncle* (Jacques Tati, 1958), *Le Petit monde de Don Camillo* (Duvivier, 1952), *The Ten Commandments* (Cecil B. DeMille, 1958), *War and Peace* (King Vidor, 1956), *Limelight* (Charlie Chaplin, 1952), *Les Grandes familles* (Denys de la Patellière, 1958), *Le Salaire de la peur* (Henri-Georges Clouzot, 1953), *Notre-Dame de Paris* (Jean Delannoy, 1956), *The Greatest Show on Earth* (DeMille, 1953) and *Around the World in 80 Days* (Michael Anderson, 1957).

The emphasis on spectacle led to a particularly lopsided market. In 1955, 10 of the 110 French films released accounted for 25 per cent of the total takings of French productions (Bessy and Chirat 1995: 18). In other words, fewer films were claiming the lion's share of the takings. The figures for first-release cinemas in Paris over the period from 1957 to 1960 show, for example, that the number of films attracting between 100,000 and 200,000 spectators was in decline (dropping from 40 out of a total of 52 to 26 out of a total of 43), while the number of films in the 200,000 to 700,000 range was increasing (from 12 out of 52 to 17 out of 43). This evolution accompanies the concentration of takings in a small number of cinemas, with 10 per cent of the cinemas accounting for half of the global takings (Bessy and Chirat 1995: 20). It also confirms the movement towards selective consumption of individual films rather than cinemagoing as a part of everyday life:

> There was a time when the spectator went to the cinema regularly, automatically, once or twice a week, depending on his income; that time is over. The cinema is no longer seen, as it was for years, as the only spectacle. Increasingly, the spectator goes to the cinema to see a film that he has specifically chosen.

Box-office hits in the 1950s, *Si Versailles m'était conté* (Sacha Guitry, 1954) (top) and *La Vache et le prisonnier* (Henri Verneuil, 1958) (bottom)

He keeps himself informed, reads the newspapers, asks his friends, and, if he's not convinced, he decides against going. (*Film français*, Autumn, 1952).

BOURGEOIS AND POPULAR AUDIENCES

The cinema in France during this period was overwhelmingly an urban entertainment, as we have seen. However, there is a distinction to be made between the better-off clientele who frequented the 'salles d'exclusivité' or first-run cinemas, especially in Paris, and the more modest clientele of the 'salles de quartier' or local cinemas, with marked variations in average ticket price. The figures for Paris in 1957 show that the average ticket price for the 77 first-run cinemas was 270 francs, while for the 265 local cinemas it was only 130 francs. The distinction between bourgeois and popular audiences is clear in a report in *Film français* from April 1959, describing the opening of a Parisian cinema equipped for the projection of Kinopanorama (a Russian version of Cinérama):

The Kinopanorama – formerly the Splendide – is located on Avenue de La Motte-Picquet in the fifteenth arrondissement, one of the Parisian neighbourhoods considered to be off the beaten track and working-class. Ticket prices don't go beyond 225 francs, and the bourgeois clientele from the Champ-de-Mars in the seventh arrondissement never crosses the border constituted by the Avenue de Suffren. Thus, the gala openings attract a gigantic crowd of locals who, night after night, go into raptures, displaying very provincial astonishment and curiosity at the dazzling spectacle of all the stars and celebrities.

Towards the end of the period under study, it is this popular clientele that begins to go to the cinema less often. Given the weight of their numbers (representing 67 per cent of total spectators in Paris in 1957, according to the *Bulletin du CNC*, December 1958), this phenomenon could not fail to have an effect on attendances, even if, as a result of the disproportionate share of the market held by first-run cinemas (35.5 per cent of the total spectators in Paris in 1959, representing 53.4 per cent of the takings in the capital), the drop in attendance did not immediately show in the actual takings, which remained stable and even showed a slight increase at the end of the 1950s.

All commentators agree that, especially in the glory days of the immediate post-war years (1946–52), the cinema was a truly popular form of entertainment, penetrating almost all social classes. With the decline in attendance in 1957–8, audiences began to be dominated by the middle and lower middle classes, with those at the upper and lower extremes of the social hierarchy noticeably under-represented in percentage terms. According to René Bonnell, 'the crisis in the cinema from 1957 puts an end to equality of access to the 7th art, which becomes a privilege transmitted by sociocultural inheritance' (Bonnell 1978: 154). This opinion is echoed by Joëlle Farchy, who argues that in the early 20th century, the cinemagoing public had closely resembled the theatregoing public of the 16th and 17th centuries, with lots of working-class and family groups. But in the second half of the century, 'the cinema becomes a class-based form of leisure, meeting the same economic fate as all other cultural activities: consumption for the well-heeled' (Farchy 1992: 61). This is confirmed by a 1958 CNC survey, which revealed that with the increase in ticket prices in the second half of 1957, those who reduced their attendance most were people at the bottom end of the social scale: the group classified 'D' (the unemployed, the under-employed, retired working people and so forth), 28 per cent of whom declared that they now went less often, while a much lower percentage (12 per cent) of those in the classification 'C' (workers, employees, lower-level public servants, artisans, farmers, agricultural labourers and small-business proprietors) claimed to go less often.

The changing socio-economic profile of cinemagoers is revealed by looking at ticket prices. For example, figures from 1956 show that 70 per cent of spectators fell into the lower-level price range (up to 129 francs); this tendency is even more marked in the numbers of cinemas, 90 per cent of which charged admission prices of less than 130 francs. The statistics for 1954–9 (see Table 3: 'Spectators and Takings in Relation to Ticket Prices') show a sharp decline in the market share of tickets up to 160 francs (the CNC's 1958 survey shows that 153 francs was considered to be the average ticket price for a local cinema and 290 francs for a first-run cinema). In 1954, this cheaper end of the market accounted for a full 97.5 per cent of the cinemas (with 82 per cent of these charging less than 130 francs), 90 per cent of the spectators and 82 per cent of the takings. Five years later (after the 1957 price increases), there were still 82.3 per cent of cinemas charging up to 130 francs for a seat, but they were now attracting only 59.3 per cent of the spectators and 44.9 per cent of the takings. Accordingly, at the other end (160 francs and above), market share went from 2.4 per cent of the cinemas, 10 per cent of spectators and 18 per cent of the takings in 1954, to 17.6 per cent of the cinemas, 40 per cent of the spectators and a massive 55 per cent of the takings in 1959 (thus tripling their market share in five years), with a mere 1.08 per cent of cinemas at the highest end of the market (300 francs and above) garnering a hugely disproportionate 12.2 per cent of the takings for that year.

A study published in the *Bulletin du CNC* in December 1958 shows geographical variations here: the smaller the city, the narrower the range in ticket prices. Thus Paris had 10.7 per cent of the total number of spectators paying prices over 130 francs (bringing in 18.5 per cent of the total takings for France), with 9 per cent of total numbers of spectators paying less than 130 francs (bringing in 7.6 per cent of the total takings), while Marseilles had 6 per cent of spectators paying more than 130 francs, bringing in 7 per cent of the total takings, with 8.1 per cent paying below 130 francs, and bringing in 6.6 per cent of the total takings. The narrowest range of ticket prices was found in Nancy, with only 0.5 per cent of the total numbers of spectators paying more than 130 francs, and 2.6 per cent of the total paying less than 130 francs. The figures for France as a whole clearly show that those paying more than 130 francs (35.5 per cent) bring in proportionally much more (47.27 per cent of the takings) than those paying less (64.47 per cent who bring in 52.76 per cent of the takings). In the centre of the market, where ticket prices ranged from 100 francs to 130 francs, and which accounted for 40 per cent of the total number of spectators, there was a close correlation between takings and numbers (43 per cent of the total takings). Even more revealing are the figures for the handful of first-run cinemas charging between 200 and 500 francs: 81 cinemas out of 5,210 (1.5 per cent) were bringing in 12.3 per cent of the total takings. This is no doubt one reason for the steady increase in average ticket prices after the war, quadrupling at all price levels between 1947 and 1958, with the largest increase (ranging from 10 per cent to 40 per cent, averaging around 20 per cent) in late 1957.

MODERNISATION AND STANDARDISATION OF CINEMAS

Having considered geographical and demographic factors, as well as changes in leisure patterns, we shall now turn to the cinemas themselves. Pierre Billard describes the transformation of certain Parisian *cafés-concerts* and vaudeville theatres into well-known cinemas, arguing that the cinema at the start of this period tends to replace traditional popular entertainment (theatre, music hall, *café-concert*) physically as well as culturally: 'talkies didn't complement the popular theatre, they displaced it' (Billard 1995: 125). Likewise in Lyon, according to Bernard Thaon, sites previously occupied by brasseries, music halls, cafés, theatres or even casinos were turned into cinemas, which necessarily retained many traces of their architectural origins and functions: 'The installation of projection facilities in theatres, music halls or brasseries contributed, in certain respects, to the tendency to preserve these architectural forms, creating a certain vagueness as to the specific function of such theatres' (Thaon 1995: 73). These spaces are by nature ephemeral, springing up, evolving and often disappearing in accordance with the dictates of the market. From the early 1930s, there was a demand for grander, purpose-built cinemas, such as Le Rex, opening in Paris in 1932 with 3,200 seats. Paris also had the enormous Gaumont-Palace, with 4,670 seats, while Marseilles boasted two cinemas with 2,000 seats, the Rex and the Variétés, and three with 1,500–2,000 seats. In Lyons, it was the Pathé-Palace, built in 1929, that met this demand, with 1,800 seats in a 750m^2 space. Toulouse was the only other major town equipped with cinemas of similar size: the Variétés (2,100 seats), the Plaza (1,800 seats) and the Gaumont (1,680 seats). And other major towns, such as Bordeaux, Lille, Nancy,

Table 3 Spectators and Takings in Relation to Ticket Prices (1954–9)

%		<100F	100F–130F	130F–160F	Total >> 160F	160F–200F	200F–300F	300F>	Total 160F >>
Cinemas	1954	67.19	24.73	5.64	**97.56**	1.41	0.82	0.21	**2.44**
	1955	61.15	29.75	6.3	**97.20**	1.69	0.81	0.3	**2.80**
	1956	54.26	35.3	7.38	**96.94**	1.94	0.73	0.39	**3.06**
	1957	33.55	52.22	9.55	**95.32**	3.12	1.03	0.53	**4.68**
	1958	7.38	58.01	21.67	**87.06**	7.41	4.74	0.79	**12.94**
	1959	5.88	53.35	23.13	**82.36**	10.27	6.29	1.08	**17.64**
Spectators	1954	37.2	37.97	15.65	**90.82**	4.26	3.57	1.35	**9.18**
	1955	32.64	39.7	16.9	**89.24**	5.54	3.45	1.77	**10.76**
	1956	27.23	42.73	18.8	**88.76**	6.14	2.83	2.27	**11.24**
	1957	14.56	50.23	19.77	**84.56**	9.51	3.1	2.83	**15.44**
	1958	3.17	35.32	28.88	**67.37**	14.38	13.69	4.56	**32.63**
	1959	2.67	31.68	24.95	**59.30**	18.76	16.72	5.22	**40.70**
Takings	1954	27.46	35.83	18.91	**82.20**	6.39	7.63	3.78	**17.80**
	1955	23.86	36.43	19.74	**80.03**	7.92	6.98	5.07	**19.97**
	1956	19.7	38.52	21.44	**79.66**	8.55	5.6	6.19	**20.34**
	1957	10	43.09	21.26	**74.35**	12.39	6.63	7.63	**26.65**
	1958	1.8	25.87	25.74	**53.41**	15.93	19.55	11.11	**46.59**
	1959	1.43	22.16	21.32	**44.91**	19.87	23	12.22	**55.09**

Nantes, Nice and Strasbourg, all had 1,000–1,500-seater cinemas. Just after the war, the cinema architect Maurice Guidaine claimed that 'cinemas will have to seat more people, assume larger proportions. In the future, small cinemas will, I suppose, rarely be built. We need cinemas able to accommodate 1,400, 1,800 and 2,000 people' (*Film français*, August 1946).

Apart from their sheer size, the cinemas in the 1920s and 1930s showed a tendency towards luxuriousness and extravagant decoration, no doubt in order to attract more spectators from the bourgeoisie. As Jean-Marc Ivanovitch says:

Architecturally, this meant impressive high façades, with large windows and often a glass canopy and an elaborate sign displaying the name of the establishment and announcing the feature film. These façades were often highly decorative, with mouldings, statuettes, small columns and medallions more or less inspired by Antiquity. In short, everything was designed to capture the client's eye. Inside, the dream was pursued: a vast lobby to welcome the crowds, magnificent staircases leading to the upper levels, long corridors, bars, smoking rooms and balconies, private boxes so as to be seen, just as if one were at the theatre, all this with a heavy overlay of gilding and colours. (Ivanovitch 1998: 24)

The emphasis on monumental size and decoration did not sit easily with the advent of sound, when many cinemas obviously had to be redesigned in order to ensure acceptable acoustics throughout. This meant soundproofing by adding sound-absorbent materials and abandoning relief decors and mouldings, while ceilings needed to be vaulted in order to facilitate sound circulation. Since larger theatres did not lend themselves especially well to sound projection, smaller theatres were initially preferred.

The drive for the modernisation of cinemas began after the war, when many cinemas had been damaged or destroyed. From the late 1940s, hardly a week passed without news of cinemas being modernised, part of an increasing emphasis on the importance of the theatre itself as a key attraction. The overriding concern was to eliminate ornament and decoration, to move towards uncluttered functionalism, towards clean, modernist lines. 'At the Montrouge Palace, the columns and the flowers took up as much space as the screen,' explains a 1951 article in *Film français* about the various renovations undertaken by Georges Peynet, perhaps the highest profile cinema architect in France during the 1950s. The photos accompanying the text show a completely streamlined space, with a much larger screen, a higher, ovoid ceiling and a concern to eliminate the impression of corners and angles. The same transformation can be seen with the Voltaire Gaumont in Paris: 'At the Voltaire the screen was, like the advertising materials on the outside of the building, dominated by useless decoration' (*Film français*, Autumn, 1951). Here the decorative façade of the cinema has been stripped bare, the old-fashioned effect of the lettering eliminated in favour of functionalism, with the emphasis no longer on the arabesque, but on rigorously straight lines and purified forms. A further striking example is provided by the renovation of the Empire in Nancy in 1952. A photo in *Film français* from Autumn 1952 shows an ornate theatre with a decorative ceiling and lots of woodwork, the screen forming part of a stage that betrays the theatrical origins of the performance space. The second photo shows a space entirely modernised: the balcony and the boxes have been eliminated in favour of a single level of seating; all ornament has been removed, the lighting concealed except for two designer lamps, one on each side; and the screen is now the centrepiece, with all traces of the stage removed.

The cinemas were redesigned to make sure that the spectator had the sense of participating in the performance, of being 'in on the action', as Georges Peynet puts it. The overriding concern was to eliminate as much as possible any distinction between the surrounding architectural framework and the screen itself, to make sure that 'nothing separates the spectator from what is happening on the screen' (*Film français*, Winter, 1955). The spectator should be able to project him or herself onto or into

the screen in the same way that the film itself was projected. The spectacle of the architecture must not overshadow or detract from the spectacle on the screen. The goal is, spatially, to abolish the distinction between real life and fantasy, to allow for a seamless transition between the two:

> A cinema remains a place of public gathering, of collective pleasure. Its function is to bring together a large number of spectators and to offer them to varying degrees, a spectacle that affords oblivion and pleasurable sensations; its goal is illusion. A cinema is a closed vessel on three sides and wide-open on the fourth. (*Film français*, Winter, 1955)

Thus there appears to be a tendency towards the standardisation of cinemas, accompanied by a standardisation of the conception of the spectator. The regional or local specificity of the cinema as an architectural site, an organic part of the local town or cityscape, gradually disappears in favour of universal design standards, driven by a new conception of spectacle as pure absorption. Likewise decor is standardised according to a middle-class conception of domestic comfort and streamlined, hygienic luxury, the kind of clean taste that is satirised in Jacques Tati's *Mon oncle*. It is what the historian Kirstin Ross has described as 'functionalist luxury: a total system made up of the set of integers that, taken individually, mean very little but together equal perfection' (Ross 1995: 193). In conclusion, we can give the last word to Bernard Thaon:

> It would be interesting to observe the parallels between the graph tracing the multiplication and then the rarefaction of cinemas (the turning point situated, depending on the town, at the beginning of the 50s or the 60s) and the graph delineating the transformation of a form of sociability and the establishment of a standardised form of leisure. (Thaon 1995: 71)

WORKS CITED

Bessy, M. and Chirat, R. (1995) *Histoire du cinéma français: encyclopédie des films 1951–55*, Paris, Pygmalion.

Billard, P. (1995) *L'Âge classique du cinéma français*, Paris, Flammarion.

Bonnell, R. (1978) *Le Cinéma exploité*, Paris, Seuil.

Farchy, J. (1992) *Le Cinéma déchaîné: mutation d'une industrie*, Paris, CNRS.

Ivanovitch, J.-M. (1998) 'Les Salles de cinéma dans l'entre-deux-guerres', in *Le Nord et le cinéma*, Paris, Le Temps des Cerises, 21–31.

Kubler, T. and Lemieux, E. (1990) *Cognacq-Jay 1940: la télévision française sous l'Occupation*, Paris, Plume.

Ross, K. (1995) *Fast Cars, Clean Bodies: Decolonization and the Reordering of French Culture*, Cambridge, MA, MIT Press.

Thaon, B. (1995) 'Architecture, cinéma', in Dureau, J.-M. ed., *Les Cinémas de Lyon 1895–1995*, Lyons, Archives Municipales, 71–3.

14 DEBATES 1930–60
Critical Debate and the Construction of Society

Christopher Faulkner

Debates about French cinema justify to an unusual degree the precept that aesthetic conditions of possibility are always social conditions of possibility. Critical debate about film for its own sake has never meant very much in the course of the history of French cinema. This chapter argues that throughout the period from 1930 to 1960, the major critical debates are inevitably the conduct of social and political dispute by other means. In a word, they all return to the social and/or political question of 'Frenchness'. While no single debate, nor all of the debates taken at once, can simply be reduced to the question of French national identity and what it means to be French, the issue remains a constant across these thirty years – whether the matter debated be aesthetic, cultural, moral or philosophical. What is always in contention is who or what shall represent the idea of Frenchness and how that shall be defined, what inclusions and exclusions shall be practised and what interest such discriminations may serve. From the beginning of the sound period to the arrival of the New Wave a number of institutional and textual practices proved to be the focus for debates about the question of Frenchness and the construction of a national imaginary: sound; realism; censorship; film criticism and film history itself. Attention to these issues will permit a rough chronology from 1930 to 1960 that acknowledges the changing historical negotiation of Frenchness, but does not preclude a synchronic understanding as well.

SOUND AND THE EARLY 1930s

At the end of the 1920s and the beginning of the 1930s, the film press and the review columns of daily newspapers were filled with polemical essays, audience surveys, questionnaires and interviews with film personnel, all of which examined the new place of sound, and especially speech, in the cinema. But the debate often masked a social unease about the pressures of difference (of class, region or gender) in French society. 'Do you believe that the sound film has a future?' *Mon Ciné* asked of directors, actors and critics, week after week from January to March 1929, i.e. before the French had made any sound films of their own. As though in condemnation of modernity itself, and of film's role in the documentation of modern life, Marcel L'Herbier replied: 'It's of little interest to me. The faithful reproduction of the words of an actor or the arrival of a locomotive in a station have no real artistic value' (Icart 1988: 139). To the contrary, Jacques Feyder asserted without hesitation: 'I believe in the talking picture' (Icart 1988: 143). For Jean Renoir, in these early days, it was all a mixed blessing that might work for sound effects but certainly not for speech (Icart 1988: 158).

Film history has crystallised the debate about sound as an opposition between René Clair's refined plea for a 'cinéma pur' (pure cinema) and Marcel Pagnol's heavy-handed claim on behalf of a 'théâtre de conserve' (canned theatre). Clair was prepared to concede the stylisation offered by sound effects and music, if contrapuntal to the image-track, but not speech. Films were not literary texts, they were written by the camera under the eye of an author-director. For his part, Pagnol achieved notoriety by saying to the critic Roger Régent in *La Cinématographie française* of October 1933 that he welcomed the talking cinema because it could serve as the publishing house of the theatre. Their debate intersects with general concerns about the theatricalisation of French cinema at the expense of its plastic qualities. Critics and film-makers alike worried that films would talk too much, and talk too much like the stage. Had playwrights like Sacha

Guitry, Yves Mirande and Pagnol suddenly become the new 'authors' of the cinema, supplanting the visual imagination of the director? In September 1933, *La Cinématographie française* published a statistical analysis of the numbers of literary adaptations at the origin of French films made since the beginning of the talkies and reported that 171 were from plays, 100 from novels and only 113 were original subjects. The alarm that this provoked led to a denunciation of adaptations and a call in the same issue of the magazine for 'a return to realism'.

But there are more disturbing issues at work here than the simple explanatory possibilities offered by casting the debate in straightforward aesthetic terms. Not only is the debate between Clair and Pagnol a debate between an avant-garde and a populist role for cinema, between a director's and a writer's cinema, between a high and a vernacular modernism, it is also a social conflict between Clair's Paris (at the centre, the metropolis) and Pagnol's Marseilles (at the periphery, in the regions). The voiceless cinema of Clair lays claim to the idealism of a universal language, allegedly the basis of silent cinema; whereas the accents and vocabularies of Pagnol's characters unfold through the specificities of historical place and time. Clair's transhistorical, disembodied spectator is opposed by the affective, grounded spectator of Pagnol. With the arrival of speech, spectatorial relations changed fundamentally and irrevocably. Through their adversarial uses of sound, the narrative cinemas of Clair and Pagnol made social relations differently intelligible to audiences. Indeed, with the talking cinema, a diverse and fragmented listening public could find pleasure in hearing itself for the first time, and spectators could fully internalise their identification with their likenesses up on the screen. 'We can write a scene in whispers, and make it understandable to three thousand people, without changing the pitch and tone of the whispering,' said Pagnol (Abel 1988: 56). With this new, intersubjective experience lies the modest beginnings of a politics of the voice which clearly worried Clair:

> in London it can be observed that the Americans were not exaggerating when they told us about the extraordinary attraction the talking picture has for the masses. From noon to eleven at night, one group of

spectators replaces another and the houses are always full. A few months ago the sound of American slang elicited smiles, but today no one is surprised at it any more, and tomorrow it may affect the speech of Londoners. (Clair 1972: 135)

The varieties of the human voice connote a cultural and social heterogeneity that shapes contradictory desires and projections, and can in turn arouse unpredictable attitudes and behaviours.

What Clair and Pagnol both admit, in their contrary ways, is that sound could produce new knowledge. Furthermore, Clair's anxiety about speech conceals a deeper fear about its social and political potential. Speech brought to the screen a new signifier of social class, gender and regional identity, challenging normative and hegemonic definitions of Frenchness (bourgeois, masculine and metropolitan). As André Rigaud expressed it:

> The talking cinema is the most realistic art there is. People in films speak the living language, and that's how we identify with them. The most striking sign of this is that a slang, which would be intolerable when written, works very well and no longer shocks when it is spoken. (Rigaud 1930: 33–4)

This acknowledges speech in the movies as a fully discursive rather than a merely phenomenological practice, carrying potentially disruptive social and political consequences. Interestingly, therefore, one of the contradictions to be faced by the fascist emphasis on national interests was precisely the socially heterogeneous nature of speech and its democratising effects: talking film exposed the right-wing myth of an inevitable conformity between linguistic purity and national identity.

REALISM AND THE POPULAR FRONT

As with speech, the importance of the realist enterprise – especially Poetic Realism – lies with its historical specificity and not with its purely formal or representational characteristics. 'The principal merit of the young French school is to have ripped the set open,' Georges Sadoul declared in 1936 (Abel 1988: 219). Realism could show contemporary social life in its immediacy and topicality, particularly the urban environment and the hardships of working people, and could deploy the speech of the streets rather than the language of the salon. In the first half of the decade the historical context for this new realism, and occasionally its subject matter, was the Depression, unemployment, the immigration of foreign workers and the movement of peoples from the countryside to the city. Thus in 1931, Marcel Carné praised Renoir's *La Chienne* for its 'realistic and brutal slice of life' (Carné 1931a: 64), and found that Pagnol's *Marius* 'breathed the most genuine air of everyday life in Marseilles' (Carné 1931b: 63).

Critics who objected to this new realism in subject matter were inclined to occupy the moral high ground and condemn such works on the supposition that the film-makers' motives were sensational and dishonest, that the films catered to baser impulses and were not suited to refined tastes. Realism, however, was always contested in French cinema for political as much as moral reasons, with the latter often acting as a screen for the former. As early as 1932 Carné was arguing that it was the responsibility of the cinema of France to show 'the profound unrest of our time, the urgent problems at hand', specifically 'the unemployed masses' and other 'phenomena of a social or collective order' (Abel 1988: 103–5). The political import of the Poetic Realist film comes precisely from its representation of the frustrations and ambitions of a historically marginalised urban underclass and its milieu. This was cause for either celebration or anxiety, since political developments, particularly the election of the Popular Front government under the Socialist Léon Blum in 1936, suddenly made the easy reproduction of existing social relations a matter of contention. The extreme polarisation of political life brought to the fore the question of how the nation was to be imagined. Would the problematisation of class relations, of the current property structure and the role of capital put the existing nation at risk, and extend the definition of Frenchness to the previously disavowed and disenfranchised? Would solidarity among the international working class challenge the monological ambitions of the European fascist states? And what was the role of film to be in this revolution?

For the Communist Georges Sadoul, the way was clear:

Realism implies an understanding of the world that is ours, an acknowledgment that this world contradicts the highest aspirations of man and particularly the engaged artist, a sense of revolt against the society which has produced this inhuman world, and hope in the people who wish to free mankind. (Abel 1988: 220)

By contrast, the realism of *Quai des brumes* (Carné, 1938) was deplored as 'a sordid adventure which breathes blood and fear, and which can only stage cowards, larvae, instinctive, sadistic, and asocial creatures', according to *La Cinématographie française* of May 1938. The dangers of realism were no less clear to the fascist critic François Vinneuil, who made explicit his objection to the political convictions it implied:

I'm getting a little tired of dealing with the subject of this cinema of blood, of fog, and of mud. In the last two weeks, coming after so many others, one counts *Le Dernier tournant* by Pierre Chenal and *Le Jour se lève* by Carné. These films have been reproached on moral grounds. With good reason. It seems not to have been observed, furthermore, that the genre blossomed at the same time as the Popular Front, that it only began to arouse protests with the decline of said Front, and that its principal representatives, such as Pierre Chenal and Carné, don't hide their Marxist convictions. These films are unfortunate because they attach a sordid label to French cinema. (*Je suis partout*, 16 June 1939)

Such strong opinions are a reminder that one's identity (national, social or personal) is not a fixed state of being, but a condition that is always in dispute and subject to representation and interpretation.

Critical to the politics of cultural work throughout the 1930s, therefore, were the film columns of the popular film press, the thirty or so daily or weekly Parisian newspapers and the monthly journals. Reviewers' columns became the locus for debates about whether the scriptwriter or the director was the true 'author' of a film; about the cottage nature of the French film industry; the virtues of dubbing; the impact of American cinema; as well as for judgments of individual films. They were also most obviously platforms for political opinion, since there was no newspaper that was neutral or disinterested, no critic and few film-makers who did not take sides and no issue that escaped ideological inflection. French and European politics of the mid-1930s put popular culture on the ideological agenda as never before. Debate flourished about whether film work should be organised collectively or led by an individual; about the merits of independent political film-making as opposed to commercial cinema; about alternative means of production, distribution and exhibition. On the extreme right, newspaper reviews become an outlet for an explicit racism and xenophobia and for expressions of anxiety about the linguistic and artistic 'corruption' of French cinema by Jewish and foreign influences. We return, then, in another and more extreme guise, to the anxieties about difference and identity that fuelled critical and public debate at the beginning of the decade.

CENSORSHIP AND THE OCCUPATION

Under the German occupation and the Vichy government, essentialising definitions of Frenchness were organised around a state-controlled dichotomy of inclusion and exclusion. The political, social and cultural engineering of Frenchness became the *raison d'être* of the new 'National Revolution' headed by Marshal Pétain. In reaction to the left's attempt at internationalising working people in the 1930s, the French right produced its programme for nationalising the masses on a platform of 'Work, Family, Fatherland': social regeneration through hard labour, a Catholic moral order and a cult of the native soil.

If the possibilities for Frenchness were reduced and constrained by a fascist politics mobilised for war against its own citizens, so the opportunity for debate about the place of culture was inevitably circumscribed. To ensure that debate could not flourish in the open, cultural works were banned and

Pierre Fresnay in *Le Corbeau* (Henri-Georges Clouzot, 1943)

withdrawn, publications suspended and outlawed, professional organisations and unions dissolved. Legally, under Vichy, the film industry was made an arm of the state. *La Cinématographie française, Ciné-monde, Ciné-Miroir, Pour vous* and all left-wing papers and journals ceased publication in June 1940. *Le Film* became the new, official organ of the French film industry and the only source of information about current production. Some opportunity for debate was opened up in the clandestine pages of the Communist *L'Écran français*, which first appeared in the underground *Les Lettres françaises* in December 1943. However, the only serious matter to be debated was whether wartime films were susceptible to pro-Resistance or collaborationist interpretations. Two films that focused this debate, both at the time and again after the war, were *Le Corbeau* (Henri-Georges Clouzot, 1943), made by Continental, the German-financed wartime production company, and *Le Ciel est à vous* (Jean Grémillon, 1943). Clouzot was condemned in *L'Écran français* on the 10 March 1944 for his sordidly realistic portrayal of petit-bourgeois hypocrisy and the effect that a string of anonymous poison-pen letters has on the inhabitants of a small provincial town. Grémillon's provincial story of a couple who sacrifice everything for the wife's personal dream of a world aviation record was celebrated in the same article for its image of French heroism:

> To the crippled, the amoral, the corrupted, which dishonour, in *Le Corbeau*, one of our provincial towns, *Le Ciel est à vous* opposes characters full of French sap, of true courage, of moral health, in whom we rediscover a national truth which will not and cannot die. (Barrot 1979: 14–15)

In contrast to the early 1930s, the left now occupies the moral high ground and condemns the deleterious effects of cinematic realism. After the war, the positions of *Le Corbeau* and *Le Ciel est à vous* were reversed, as some critics saw the former as an anti-collaborationist critique of informing and the latter now as Pétainist for its small-minded patriotism! Meaning is a function of the needs of historically specific interpretive communities; in the case of the debates around these two films, those needs were entirely ideological.

THE POST-WAR DISCOURSES OF FILM HISTORY AND FILM CRITICISM

The years after the war through to the New Wave were distinguished by a preoccupation with the discourses of film history and film criticism. Writing about cinema became self-conscious and self-reflexive in a way that it never had before. It became, as André Bazin wished, and in large measure because of his influence, 'a criticism of criticism' (Bazin 1981: 56). Indeed, many of the first films of the New Wave, between late 1958 and 1961, are themselves the fulfilment of this critical and historical enterprise. Following a period of state-controlled film history (the suppression of some texts; the authorisation of others) and film criticism (single-minded ideological judgment and value), it was understandable that those writing about cinema should reflect upon the practice of their craft, their responsibilities and their objectives. As the first order of business, the theoretical and critical debates that informed the late 1940s and early 1950s addressed the reclamation of a French national cinema following the collaboration with Nazi Germany. France was the only country to have signed an armistice with the Germans and to have made active collaboration a matter of official government policy. In the interests of papering over the cracks that divided the French from themselves, Charles de Gaulle created the post-war myth of a France uniformly resistant, a France united against a common enemy, an idea of Frenchness that was to endure for the next twenty-five years. This raises a question about the extent to which discursive possibilities for talking about cinema and culture were determined by the post-war Gaullist mythology.

If there were a few post-war films that took the Resistance as their subject, most famously *La Bataille du rail* (René Clément, 1945), there were none that addressed French collaboration with fascism. More telling than the films themselves, however, was the post-war reconstruction of the history of French cinema. This was carried out in curatorial and institutional form – the rehabilitation of Jean Vigo, the inauguration of the international Cannes film festival (1946), the creation of the Fédération Française des Ciné-Clubs (1945) – as well as in the newly written film histories. Roger Régent's *Cinéma de France* (1948) provides the model for an oft-repeated periodisation of French film history, which treats the years from 1930 to 1944 as one continuous block of meaning, stylistically, thematically and institutionally. The period break is always 1945, never 1939 or 1940. Another contemporary example, *Sept ans de cinéma français* (1953), with contributions from Henri Agel, André Bazin and Jacques Doniol-Valcroze, discusses the filmic output of the seven years from 1945 to 1951. The war years are consistently consigned to a past that is not the responsibility of the present. As for the political divisions of the 1930s, on the extreme right, the 1948 and 1954 editions of *Histoire du cinéma* by Maurice Bardèche and Robert Brasillach (the latter had been executed for collaboration) endeavoured to sustain a pre-war political discourse, with their unrepentant anti-Semitism and blunt ideological judgments. At the same time, the cachet earned by its clandestine beginnings and a strong Communist presence in the immediate post-war enabled *L'Écran français* to carry the torch for the political left, until it ceased publication in 1953. However, ideological criteria as a basis for judgment or value, whether mobilised from the right or the left, were quickly overwhelmed by a preferred aesthetic discourse, and the dominant voices in critical debate from the 1950s consciously avoided the political.

The brief return of Jean George Auriol's pre-war journal *La Revue du cinéma* from 1946 to 1949 set the dominant tone, with its organised devotion to the work of major film artists. Alexandre Astruc, in a piece entitled 'The Birth of a New Avant-Garde: The Camera-Pen', published in *L'Écran français* in March 1948, convincingly laid out the case for the authorial role of the director as the basis for a theory of cinema as an art of individual expression:

Specifically, the cinema is quite simply in the process of becoming a means of expression, a form in which and through which an artist can express his thought, however abstract it may be, or translate his obsessions, exactly as is the case today with the essay and the novel. Better, there will no longer be screenwriters, because in such a cinema the distinction between author and director no longer makes sense. The author writes with his camera as the writer writes with a pen. (Barrot 1979: 236–40)

And when the first issue of *Cahiers du cinéma* appeared in April 1951, edited by Joseph-Marie Lo Duca, Jacques Doniol-Valcroze and André Bazin, it proudly took up the artistic discourse of *La Revue du cinéma* and the Romantic theory of authorship advanced by Astruc. True cinephiles, its young critics – especially Éric Rohmer, François Truffaut and Jean-Luc Godard – became adept at *mise en scène* criticism, able to perform virtuoso analyses of composition, editing, camera, costumes and lighting, both within and between films, and across the spectrum of art films and popular cinema. French film criticism had seen nothing like it. In January 1954, the *Cahiers du cinéma* theory that the director was the true author of the film – known as 'la politique des auteurs' (author policy) – achieved notoriety with Truffaut's 'A Certain Tendency of French Cinema', a much more famous and polemical essay than Astruc's earlier piece. It finally resolved, in the director's favour, a dispute about film authorship dating back to the 1920s. For his pains, Truffaut was attacked for being anti-French and pro-American. In May 1953, Jacques Rivette's 'The Genius of Howard Hawks' had already extended the case for the author-director beyond the art cinema to the commercial cinema and, more especially, to the Hollywood cinema. The young critics who would become the New Wave feasted on the consumer culture of the 1950s, adored the contemporary American cinema and brought to the discussion of French cinema a new critical – but non-political – internationalism that would become a fertile intertextual practice when they got to make their own first films.

In the face of *Cahiers du cinéma*'s enthusiasms, the only serious opposition came from *Positif*, first published in Lyons in 1952 and edited by Bernard Chardère, a critic with a social conscience interested in reaching a mass audience (although this attitude did not extend to writing about the immensely popular films of Bourvil or Louis de Funès). *Positif* did not so much question *Cahiers du cinéma*'s auteurist position – it liked Renoir too – as it took exception to the exclusivity of its aesthetic discourse. Given *Cahiers du cinéma*'s mania for Hollywood cinema and its promotion of selected French and European auteurs, *Positif* was left to take up the cause of those cinemas that could not

Theorist and film critic André Bazin, 1950s

be found along the Euro-American axis, for example the cinemas of Latin America and the Third World. *Positif* also gave generous space to other practices that challenged dominant cinema, both stylistically and ideologically, such as experimental and Surrealist films and film-makers. In contrast to the apolitical virtuosity with which the *Cahiers du cinéma* critics performed their stylistic analyses of mainstream cinema, *Positif* offered a measure of counter-cultural dissent and political discussion, recognising that there was a world outside the cinema, dominated by the Cold War, and that the French themselves were involved in a series of 'hot' wars with their former colonies in Southeast Asia and Algeria. The one subject that neither *Positif* nor *Cahiers du cinéma* would touch was the Occupation, particularly France's collaborative role in the Holocaust. Perhaps the overriding enthusiasm in both journals throughout the 1950s for a critical discourse to do with individual authorial agency and formal and stylistic analysis at the expense of historical determinations is consistent with the post-war avoidance in France of collective responsibility for collaboration with Nazism. The ahistorical nature of auteurism and the apolitical practice of *mise en scène* criticism may be taken as the critical or theoretical displacement of a national forgetfulness, the equivalent of a historical amnesia about the war.

It was left to André Bazin to combine the discourses of film history and film criticism in a sophisticated synthesis. Until his death in 1958, Bazin's singular preoccupation was to understand the 'nature' of film, and in order to do this he developed a theory of realism. Unlike the theories of realism that provoked debate in the 1930s, however, Bazin's theory had neither a moral nor a political basis, but – influenced by the philosopher Maurice Merleau-Ponty – a phenomenological one. Bazin conferred upon cinema the distinction of being the least mediated of the arts in its relationship with reality, and referred to it as 'objectivity in time' (Bazin 1967: 14) and as a 'virtual metaphor' (Bazin 1945: 130). Reality for Bazin has a prior ontological existence, that is to say, it exists and has meaning prior to the presence of any human observer. As he famously wrote about Jean Renoir:

He forced himself to look back beyond the resources provided by montage and so uncovered the secret of a film form that would permit everything to be said without chopping the world up into little fragments, that would reveal the hidden meanings in people and things without disturbing the unity natural to them. (Bazin 1967: 38)

Consequently, Bazin's preference was for a film practice that would reveal these 'hidden meanings' to maximum effect, and to that end he praised a cinema of long takes, mobile camera and depth of field, at the expense of what he took to be the more interventionist and manipulative practices of montage or standard psychological editing. However, realism is not an autonomous aesthetic practice, and any theory of realism is the product of a historically specific set of relations. So even though Bazinian realism may be philosophically an idealism, it can still be read in the context of post-war nation-building. Thus, in his celebration of Renoir, Bazin not only centred *La Règle du jeu* (1939) within the corpus, and situated the film within the history of a privileged realist style, he also made Renoir the most French of French film-makers. In Bazin's genealogy of a realist film practice, Renoir becomes France's principal representative, the heir of an earlier international tradition of silent realism. This move conveniently bypasses the Occupation and the political cinema of the 1930s. Bazin's nationalistic claims on behalf of Renoir suit a vision of French film practice, and French cultural patrimony, as a historical continuity, in which the dark years of the war are seen merely as an unfortunate hiatus.

However, Bazin could be said to have invented a Renoir who would confirm his theories of criticism and of history. Like all of the *Cahiers du cinéma* critics, he studiously ignored Renoir's political engagement in the 1930s and consistently de-historicised and de-politicised his films. For example, instead of discussing the possibility of a radical politics at the time of the Popular Front, what Bazin offers us with *Le Crime de Monsieur Lange* is an analysis founded on 'the pure spatial expression of the entire *mise en scène*' (Bazin 1973: 46). Similarly, Italian neo-realism was famously 'an aesthetic of reality', which Bazin celebrated for its humanism at the expense of its historically situated origins and political significance: 'Is not neo-realism primarily a kind of humanism and only secondarily a style of film-making? Then as to the style itself, is it not essentially a form of self-effacement before reality?' (Bazin 1967: 29). In both instances, Bazin repressed the specific historical conditions within which the realism that he admires was originally produced and received. Bazinian realism was unquestionably a matter of ethical, or even spiritual, good faith, but it was certainly not a politically grounded social criticism. Perhaps such a development was inevitable in the forgetful atmosphere of the immediate post-war years. It would be left to the next generation of critics, in the 1960s and 1970s, both to re-politicise discussion of the cinema and to turn from a theory of film as an organ of perception to a theory of film as a system of signification.

WORKS CITED

Abel, R. (1988) *French Film Theory and Criticism: A History/Anthology 1907–1939*, vol. 2: 1929–39, Princeton, NJ, Princeton University Press.

Barrot, O. (1979) *L'Écran français 1943–1953*, Paris, Éditeurs Français Réunis.

Bazin, A. (1945) 'À propos de *L'Espoir*, ou du style au cinéma', *Poésie 46*, 26–7, August–September, 125–33.

Bazin, A. (1967) *What Is Cinema?*, vol. 1, Berkeley, University of California Press.

Bazin, A. (1973) *Jean Renoir*, New York, Simon and Schuster.

Bazin, A. (1981) *French Cinema of the Occupation and Resistance*, New York, Ungar.

Carné, M. (1931a) 'Les Films du mois: *La Chienne*', *Cinémagazine*, 11: 10, October, 64–5.

Carné, M. (1931b) 'Les Films du mois: *Marius*', *Cinémagazine*, 11: 11, November, 63.

Clair, R. (1972) *Cinema, Yesterday and Today*, New York, Dover.

Icart, R. (1988) *La Révolution du parlant vue par la presse française*, Toulouse, Institut Jean Vigo.

Rigaud, A. (1930) 'Dialogues', *Cinémagazine*, 10: 11, December, 33–4.

SELECTED FURTHER READING: 1930–60

Abel, R. (1988) *French Film Theory and Criticism: A History/Anthology of 1929–1939*, vol. 2, Princeton, NJ, Princeton University Press. (Translations of 1930s French critical texts, with cultural context.)

Andrew, D. (1990) *André Bazin*, New York, Oxford University Press. (Study of the influential French film theorist, with cultural background from the 1930s to 1950s.)

Andrew, D. (1995) *Mists of Regret: Culture and Sensibility in Classic French Film*, Princeton, NJ, Princeton University Press. (Survey of 1930s cinema, mainly thematic and stylistic, with cultural context.)

Bazin, A. (1967), *What Is Cinema?*, vols 1 and 2, Berkeley, University of California Press. (Translations of major theoretical essays from the 1940s and 1950s.)

Bazin, A. (1981) *French Cinema of the Occupation and Resistance*, New York, Ungar. (Critical essays on 1940s films.)

Buchsbaum, J. (1988) *Cinema Engagé: Film in the Popular Front*, Urbana, University of Illinois Press. (Study of left-wing film-making in the mid-1930s.)

Crisp, C. (1993) *The Classic French Cinema, 1930–1960*, Bloomington, Indiana University Press. (Survey of the period, covering industry, technology and working practices.)

Crisp, C. (2002) *Genre, Myth, and Convention in the French Cinema, 1929–1939*, Bloomington, Indiana University Press. (Study of key social themes, genres and stars in 1930s films.)

Ehrlich, E. (1985) *Cinema of Paradox: French Film-Making under the German Occupation*. New York, Columbia University Press. (Study of the period from 1940 to 44, especially the cultural and political context.)

Hillier, J. ed. (1985) *Cahiers du Cinéma: The 1950s*, vol. 1: 'Neo-Realism, Hollywood, New Wave', London, Routledge/BFI. (Translations of 1950s critical writings from the influential film journal.)

Martin, J. W. (1983) *The Golden Age of French Cinema, 1929–39*, Boston, G. K. Hall. (Survey of 1930s films, mainly stylistic and thematic.)

Ross, K. (1995) *Fast Cars, Clean Bodies: Decolonization and the Reordering of French Culture*, Cambridge, MA, MIT Press. (Cultural history from the post-war years to the early 1960s.)

PART THREE

1960–2004

INTRODUCTION 1960–2004
A New World

Michael Temple and Michael Witt

'Does a New Wave Really Exist?' This question was posed to a variety of French film-makers – Alexandre Astruc, Claude Chabrol, René Clair, Georges Franju, Louis Malle, Jean Renoir, Jacques Tati and Roger Vadim – in a series of interviews published in *Le Monde* in August 1959 (Frodon 1995: 23). Their unanimous answer was a resounding 'no'. The response of this illustrious line-up of film-makers reminds us that a convenient definition of the 'New Wave' has never been easy to achieve, not least among those, such as Chabrol, generally considered central to the movement. First used in 1957 in the magazine *L'Express* to describe the generation born between the wars, the term 'Nouvelle Vague' (New Wave) came to be associated with a loose-knit grouping of film-makers, many of whom were among the ninety-seven first-time directors who released a feature between 1958 and 1962. Three groups of film-makers are usually included under the New Wave banner. First, there is the group of young critics writing for *Cahiers du cinéma* in the 1950s. Their astute commentaries on Hollywood genre cinema and critical attacks against the psychological realism of the post-war French mainstream cinema, the so-called 'tradition of quality', were cautiously encouraged by André Bazin, the highly influential film theorist and spiritual father of the New Wave. The *Cahiers* group made two major contributions to critical thinking about cinema: realist film theory, primarily associated with Bazin, and *la politique des auteurs* or 'auteur theory' (see Chapter 14). Ardent cinephiles and passionate critics, they were also making short films with the ambition of breaking into the industry. Their early films may be viewed as extensions of their criticism: audiovisual essays on the nature and potential of cinema as art. The best-known of these critics-turned-film-makers, in terms of the impact of their early films and the length of their illustrious careers, are Claude Chabrol (*Le Beau Serge*, 1959; *Les Cousins*, 1959), Jean-Luc Godard (*À bout de souffle*, 1960; *Le Petit soldat*, 1961), Jacques Rivette (*Paris nous appartient*, 1961), Éric Rohmer (*Le Signe du lion*, 1962) and François Truffaut (*Les 400 coups*, 1959; *Tirez sur le pianiste*, 1960). Also contributing to *Cahiers* in this period were Jean Douchet, André S. Labarthe and several slightly older critics, including Alexandre Astruc (*Une Vie*, 1958), Jacques Doniol-Valcroze (*L'Eau à la bouche*, 1959) and Pierre Kast (*Le Bel âge*, 1959).

Second, there is the so-called 'Left Bank' group. This includes Chris Marker (*Description d'un combat*, 1960; *¡Cuba, sí!*, 1961), Alain Resnais (*Hiroshima mon amour*, 1959; *L'Année dernière à Marienbad*, 1961) and Agnès Varda (*La Pointe courte*, 1956; *Cléo de 5 à 7*, 1962). Their interests in documentary, left-wing politics and the literary experimentation of the *Nouveau Roman* (New Novel) sets them somewhat apart from the *Cahiers* group. Third, we can identify a number of important satellite figures, sympathetic to the aspirations of the New Wave: Jacques Demy (*Lola*, 1961), Louis Malle (*Ascenseur pour l'échafaud*, 1957), Jean-Daniel Pollet (*Méditerranée*, 1963) and Jacques Rozier (*Adieu Philippine*, 1963).

In 1959, with the example of the New Wave in mind, the Minister of Culture, André Malraux, introduced the *avance sur recettes* ('advance on receipts', operative since 1960), a system of state-funded interest-free loans designed to encourage the production of artistically adventurous projects and to cultivate the emergence of young talent (see Chapters 9 and 16). Paradoxically, the New Wave auteurs were comparatively unsuccessful in securing these loans: the most regular beneficiaries between 1960 and 1968 were three of the decade's most

Brigitte Bardot and Jeanne Moreau in *Viva Maria!* (Louis Malle, 1965), scenario by Jean-Claude Carrière

commercial directors: Robert Enrico, Yves Robert and Claude Lelouch (Prédal 1996: 264). Many of the early New Wave films were cheap, semi-improvised and shot on location by small crews. They also profiled a new generation of actors whose unaffected performance style reflected the liberated tone of the films: Stéphane Audran, Gérard Blain, Jean-Claude Brialy, Anna Karina, Bernadette Lafont, Jean-Pierre Léaud and Emanuelle Riva. A minority, notably Brigitte Bardot, Jean-Paul Belmondo and Jeanne Moreau, became major mainstream stars. Key points of reference, especially for the *Cahiers* group, included cinema of the silent period (especially the French avant-garde of the 1920s, Soviet montage cinema and German Expressionism), Italian neo-realism, post-war Hollywood genre cinema, Orson Welles, French live television drama of the 1950s and a select pantheon of French precursors, including Robert Bresson (*Le Journal d'un curé de campagne*, 1951), Jean Cocteau (*Les Parents terribles*, 1948), Roger Leenhardt (*Les Dernières vacances*, 1947), Jean-Pierre Melville (*Bob le flambeur*, 1956), Jean Renoir (*French Cancan*, 1954), Jean Rouch (*Moi, un noir*, 1958) and Jacques Tati (*Jour de fête*, 1949). In his seminal 'essay on the young French cinema', André S. Labarthe identified the dissolution of boundaries between documentary and fiction as a defining characteristic of the movement (Labarthe 1960: 49). Backed by adventurous producers (Pierre Braunberger, Georges de Beauregard, Anatole Dauman), the New Wave certainly developed a fresh synthetic form through which to tell tales of modern youth against the backdrop of General de Gaulle's nascent Fifth Republic. As has frequently been remarked, these stories focus mainly on the loves and lives of young middle-class characters, while the working class, which had been a strong motif in earlier periods of French film-making, was largely excluded from New Wave imagery.

Despite these evident limitations, the young French cinema's combination of narrative energy, technical daring and formal insolence became a cultural force that influenced a string of national cinemas (Polish, Czech, Yugoslav, Hungarian, Brazilian, Belgian, Italian, Swiss, German, American . . .) and installed the New Wave as a permanent landmark in French and world film history.

Ever since the 1960s, it has remained an inspiration to film-makers and a mainstay for film students and cinephiles. However, this hallowed status has led to a number of negative effects and critical responses. The most obvious drawback of the movement's success has been an unfortunate tendency to reduce French film-making of the 1960s, sometimes French cinema in its entirety, to the sole contribution of the New Wave. As Serge Daney observed in his 1984 essay 'Surviving the New Wave', it sometimes feels like a full understanding of the intricacies and significance of those 'heroic times' has become a prerequisite for an appreciation of all subsequent French cinema (Daney 1998: 62). Such cultural hegemony has of course been repeatedly challenged and reappraised from a number of angles over the years. 'It's very vague and not that new', was the claim of the film journal *Positif*, who ferociously attacked what they saw as the aesthetic posturing and political irresponsibility of the *Cahiers* film-makers (Borde, Buache and Curtelin 1962). Many historians have described the New Wave as a triumph of marketing over substance; some have questioned its historical significance by demonstrating the basic industrial continuity in French cinema from the 1950s to the 1960s (Crisp 1993: 415–22); others have criticised its representation of gender (Sellier 1999). In Chapter 18 of *The French Cinema Book*, Nicole Brenez challenges the orthodox positioning of the New Wave at the heart of post-war French film history, by giving the political and experimental film-making traditions an equally important role in her highly original account of 'Forms' since 1960.

Between the New Wave and May 1968, we can identify a number of key trends in French film production of the 1960s. In the wake of the New Wave, the *Cahiers* film-makers pursued divergent paths: Godard (*Les Carabiniers*, 1963; *Weekend*, 1967) and Rivette (*L'Amour fou*, 1968) gravitated to the experimental end of the art-cinema spectrum; Chabrol (*Landru*, 1963) and Truffaut (*La Peau douce*, 1964) quickly joined the mainstream; and Rohmer combined exemplary low-budget film-making (the 'Six Moral Tales' series, 1962–72) with work for educational television. Hot on the heels of the *Cahiers* group came a second wave of directors associated with the journal: Jean Eustache (*Le Père Noël a les yeux bleus*, 1966), Luc Moullet (*Brigitte et Brigitte*, 1966), Barbet Schroeder (*More*, 1969) and Paul Vecchiali (*Les Ruses du diable*, 1965). Moreover, a number of the New Wave's inspirational precursors went on to produce some of their strongest work in this decade. Rouch, whose pioneering post-war cinematic ethnography and improvised fictions of the late 1950s had provided one of the movement's richest sources of inspiration, pursued his bold experiments in cinéma vérité (*Chronique d'un été*, 1961) and narrative technique (*Gare du Nord*, 1965); Melville extended his highly personal exploration of the crime film, notably in *Le Samouraï* (1967); and Bresson made a series of minimalist masterpieces, including *Au hasard Balthazar* (1966) and *Mouchette* (1967). In a parallel development, the Left Bank group continued their social commentary on life under Gaullism, including the representation of taboo subjects such as the Algerian war in Marker's *Le Joli mai* (1963) and Resnais's *Muriel* (1963). Another alternative to the New Wave was offered by the first films of certain writers associated with the New Novel, notably Alain Robbe-Grillet (*L'Immortelle*, 1962) and Marguerite Duras (*La Musica*, 1966, co-dir. Paul Seban). In a more classical mode, a number of mainstream directors employed the traditional formulas (studio, stars, careful story-boarding, popular genres) to produce a variety of formally tired if sometimes thematically adventurous films: André Cayatte (*Les Chemins de Katmandou*, 1969), René Clément (*Paris brûle-t-il*, 1966) and Henri Verneuil (*Cent mille dollars au soleil*, 1964). Veteran Claude Autant-Lara – one of the film-makers targeted by the *Cahiers* critics in the 1950s – made a dozen films in the 1960s before ending his career working for television in the 1970s, fulminating to the end against the talentless New Wave upstarts whom he blamed for ruining the industry. Finally, alongside these established figures there appeared a younger generation of directors happy to serve the mainstream market, including Pierre Grenier-Deferre (*Les Aventures de Salavin*, 1963), Gérard Oury (*La Grande vadrouille*, 1966), and Paul Vecchiali (*Les Ruses du diable*).

The late 1960s witnessed a ferment of political activity that increasingly influenced French cinema, for example the collaborative film *Loin du Vietnam* (1967), a display of solidarity on the part of 150 film workers addressed to the embattled people of Vietnam. In February 1968, when André Malraux tried to sack the popular and symbolic figure of Henri Langlois from his position at the head of the Cinémathèque française, the film world rose up in arms, forming a 'Committee for the Defence of the Cinémathèque' (including Bresson, Carné, Godard, Rivette and Truffaut, presided over by Renoir) and organising a series of high-profile public demonstrations by cinephiles, critics and film-makers. This eventually led to Langlois's reinstatement in April, but by May a much more widespread discontentment with the Gaullist regime had crystallised around three main issues: protest against war in Vietnam; the monolithic media structures of press, radio and television; and above all the ossified and inadequate education system. Deep-rooted student unrest at the beginning of May culminated in a violent rout by police on 10 May (the celebrated 'Night of the Barricades'), which was followed by a series of massive strikes, factory occupations and university sit-ins. By 24 May approximately 10 million workers were on strike. Drawing on the informal network established among the film community during the Langlois Affair, the Union of Film Production Technicians brought together actors, students, technicians and directors, under the banner the 'Estates General of Cinema' (États Généraux du Cinéma, or EGC), and initiated a debate about how the film and television industries might be reconceived along more egalitarian lines. Nineteen far-reaching projects were discussed at the general assembly of the EGC in early June. On 18 May, at a press conference devoted to the Langlois Affair at Cannes, a group of film-makers – Godard and Truffaut prominent among them – declared solidarity with the striking students and workers and succeeded in closing down the festival.

Godard's trajectory during this period may serve to illustrate the impact of these events on cinema: having explored increasingly essayistic forms and political themes in the second half of the 1960s (*Deux ou trois choses que je sais d'elle*, 1966), and produced a number of prescient visions of the concerns and confusion of May (*La Chinoise*, 1967), he temporarily withdrew from the industry into the anonymity of the Groupe Dziga Vertov, where he made a series of collaborative militant 16mm tracts funded by foreign television companies (*British Sounds*, 1969, co-dir. Jean-Henri Roger; *Pravda*, 1969, co-dir. Roger and Paul Bourron), before returning to 35mm film-making with the commercially disastrous *Tout va bien* (1972, co-dir. Jean-Pierre Gorin). These audiovisual experiments reflected a wider theoretical exploration of the politics of representation, which continued through the early 1970s in the newly politicised *Cahiers du cinéma* and other left-wing film journals such as *Cinéthique*. The post-1968 period also saw the introduction and expansion of film studies as an academic discipline in France, a move heavily influenced by the pioneering semiological studies of Raymond Bellour (2000) and Christian Metz (1974a and 1974b).

In response to the events of May 1968, General de Gaulle had dissolved the National Assembly, and the legislative elections in June resulted in an overwhelming reaffirmation of support for the Gaullist regime. This popular victory laid the ground for a further decade of conservatism: De Gaulle (until 1969), Georges Pompidou (from 1969 to 1974) and Valéry Giscard d'Estaing (from 1974 to 1981) would continue to rule France, while French cinema enjoyed one of its most volatile and varied periods of film production. In the domain of popular genres, the 1970s were particularly rich years for film comedy, primarily due to cross-fertilisation between feature films and the anarchic *café-théâtre* comic tradition. Bertrand Blier's work in particular is marked by libertarian satire of social and sexual mores, notably *Les Valseuses* (1973), which stars *café-théâtre* veterans Patrick Dewaere and Miou Miou alongside Gérard Depardieu. The field of auteur cinema saw a number of figures emerge in this period: Alain Corneau (*France S.A.*, 1974), Jacques Doillon (*L'An 01*, 1973, co-dir. Resnais and Rouch), Philippe Garrel (*Le Berceau de crystal*, 1976), Claude Miller (*La Meilleure façon de marcher*, 1976), Maurice Pialat (*La Gueule ouverte*, 1974) and Bertrand Tavernier (*L'Horloger de Saint-Paul*, 1974). But the most significant film of the early 1970s is Jean Eustache's 1973 masterpiece, *La Maman et la putain*, a film without which, as Serge Daney put it, the generation of May 1968 – 'lost and prematurely aged' – would have remained almost faceless in cinema (Daney 1986: 54).

An important new trend emerging in this decade was feminist cinema, which played a significant role in the campaign to legalise abortion: for example, Marielle Issartel and Charles Belmont's documentary *Histoires d'A.* (1973), a film about women's experiences of illegal abortions, was widely distributed despite an initial ban. The work of three influential women film-makers took a more explicitly feminist turn in this period – Yannick Bellon (*La Femme de Jean*, 1974), Duras (*Le Camion*, 1977), Varda (*Réponse de femmes*, 1975) – while a new generation was emerging with directors such as Chantal Akerman (*Je tu il elle*, 1974), Nelly Kaplan (*Néa*, 1976), Diane Kurys (*Diabolo menthe*, 1977), Coline Serreau (*Mais qu'est-ce qu'elles veulent?*, 1975) and Nadine Trintignant (*Ça n'arrive qu'aux autres*, 1971). The end of the decade saw the foundation of a woman's film festival in Sceaux, now the largest such event in the world (held annually in Créteil).

By contrast, the 1970s also saw a marked escalation in the production and consumption of pornography, especially between 1973 and 1978. The relaxation of censorship by the Giscard administration coincided with the enormous success of the first *Emmanuelle* (1974), and this was followed in 1975 by the uncensored mainstream release of a compilation of hard-core shorts. In 1974 and 1975, pornographic films accounted for almost half of all French production, and soon Giscard himself was expressing concern at the proliferation of 'violent and perverse' imagery (Courtade 1978: 344). The following year, new legislation and increased taxation were introduced to return pornography to the margins of the industry. But this brief exposure opened up the possible conjugation of pornographic forms and figures with those of other genres, and pornography's influence can be seen in the more explicit treatment of sex and sexuality in mainstream and auteur cinema since the 1970s, for example in Catherine Breillat's *Une vraie jeune fille* (1976, released 2000), *36 Fillette* (1988) and *Sex Is Comedy* (2003).

Another significant development in the 1970s was the reinterpretation of contemporary French history through documentary cinema and archive films. The post-1968 period witnessed a major documentary renewal, most famously with Marcel Ophuls's

Le Chagrin et la pitié (1971), which confronted the Gaullist myth of French Resistance during the German occupation. Together with André Harris and Alain de Sédouy's critical account of France's role in World War I and the Algerian war, *Français si vous saviez* (1972), the historical documentary paved the way for the fictional treatment of sensitive topics such as the Occupation in works like Louis Malle's *Lacombe Lucien* (1974) and Joseph Losey's *Monsieur Klein* (1976).

Finally, in this eventful decade, a major change occurred in the relationship between cinema and television. The French Television Act of 1974 ended the monopoly hitherto enjoyed by the state broadcasting organisation, the ORTF (Office de Radio-Télévision Français). From 1975, it was replaced by seven separate bodies, including the new Institut National de l'Audiovisuel (INA). The reforms had a profound long-term impact on French cinema. Television quickly became a major exhibitor of old films and a significant producer of new ones; indeed the investment of television's money in film production would remain a key factor in the modern economic model of the French industry. At the same time, INA, under the guidance of Manette Bertin, embarked on a remarkably ambitious policy of co-productions and commissions involving film-makers, including Akerman (*News from Home*, 1976), Edgardo Cozarinsky (*Mary McCarthy*, 1982) and Varda (*L'Une chante, l'autre pas*, 1975). Of particular note was the exploitation of the national audiovisual archive as the basis for the production of new experimental television series, notably *Hiéroglyphes* (1975), *Rue des archives* (1978–81) and *Juste une image* (1982), all produced by Thierry Garrel and Louisette Neil (Forbes 1984).

In 1981, the left took power in France for the first time since 1936. The election of François Mitterrand as President generated considerable optimism among film people, who hoped that political change would stimulate a renaissance of French cinema. Under the influence of Jack Lang, Minister of Culture, the Socialist government introduced extensive reform in the realm of cultural politics and far-reaching initiatives to bolster the film industry during the 1980s and early 1990s (see Chapters 16 and 20). Lang's principal strategies involved a challenge to Gaumont-Pathé's near-monopoly on distribution; a number of decentralising measures (renovation of the regional cinema network, development of a regional training infrastructure, facilitation of the distribution of first-run films to the regions); initiatives to foster script development; and the establishment of new funds to stimulate production (Hayward 1993). By the early 1990s, however, these policies to revitalise the industry appeared to have had little impact on escalating competition from Hollywood. Nor did they counter the relentless fall in audiences figures from 1982 to 1992 (see Chapter 20), which was influenced by the massive increase in the availability of films on television and the expansion of the video market. This downward trend continued a general decline in cinemagoing that had begun in the late 1950s and a corresponding rise in television ownership, which had increased from 1 million households in 1959 to 11 million in 1970, and had reached almost every household by 1975.

But the relationship between cinema and television is not just a question of statistics. From the 1950s, a certain cultural condescension, on the part of the more established medium, successively evolved into suspicion in the 60s, panic in the 70s and crisis in the 80s, when cinema suddenly found itself a relatively minor feature in what was becoming known as the 'French audiovisual landscape'. Cinema's changing representation of television during this period illustrates the point clearly: the innocuous sets that usually remain dormant in the corner of New Wave films (Chabrol's *Les Bonnes femmes*, 1960) flicker into life and acquire a more sinister presence in the mid-1960s (the outsize screens and forest of television aerials in Truffaut's *Farenheit 451*, 1966), and by the mid-1970s they occupy the cinematic image from within (Godard and Anne-Marie Miéville's *Ici et ailleurs*, 1975). From this moment, coinciding precisely with the dissolution of the ORTF, television became the single most important element in film production, notably through advance sales of broadcasting rights and its investment in co-productions. Throughout the 1970s and 1980s, the critic Serge Daney's duel with television and his running commentary on the televisualisation of film form produced the most profound body of critical writing in the post-New Wave era (see Chapter 21). In 1985, another major step was taken with the beginning of the deregulation of French television, resulting in the privatisation of TF1, a proliferation of new channels and a corresponding increase in television's stake in film production and exhibition. The subsequent multiplication of specialist cable and satellite film channels servicing the cinephile market effectively turned television into a non-stop electronic cinémathèque. In the new deregulated environment, it appeared as though television had effectively taken over film production, since it was partially financing over 60 per cent of films by the early 1990s.

Given television's gradual annexation of cinema, accompanied by the rise of big-budget international co-productions promoted through saturation marketing (*L'Ours*, Jean-Jacques Annaud, 1986; *Le Grand bleu*, Luc Besson, 1988), it is perhaps unsurprising that many commentators have identified the premature death of François Truffaut in 1984 as the symbolic demise of a certain idea of auteur cinema. While many key auteurs continued to produce strong work – Akerman (*The Golden Eighties*, 1986), Godard (*Je vous salue, Marie*, 1983), Marker (*Sans soleil*, 1982), Pialat (*À nos amours*, 1983), Rivette (*Hurlevent*, 1985), Rozier (*Maine-Océan*, 1986), André Téchiné (*Rendez-vous*, 1985), Varda (*Sans toit ni loi*, 1985) – the main trends of the Mitterrand years were emerging from elsewhere. First, there is the *cinéma du look*, which was initially associated with Jean-Jacques Beineix's *Diva* (1981), but soon came to designate a loose grouping of films and film-makers, including other work by Beineix (*37°2 le matin*, 1986), Besson (*Subway*, 1985) and Leos Carax (*Mauvais sang*, 1986). Common features include studio shooting, high production values, romantic plots, symbolic use of colour, explicit borrowings from advertising and pop videos, and an emphasis on spectacle over characterisation. Valued by some for its dazzling experiments in neo-baroque aesthetics and subtle reflections of the unconscious of the 1980s, the *cinéma du look* was dismissed by others as a series of irretrievably vacuous exercises in the exploitation of the youth market.

The second important trend is the 'heritage' film, which in many ways can be considered an updating of the costume drama and *film historique*, a genre dating back to the 1900s. Certainly French cinema of the 1980s and 1990s saw many of these big-budget, broad-canvas period dramas, usually employing major stars and based on famous novels. They were explicitly encouraged by Jack Lang as part of his vision of a popular and exportable modern national cinema. Examples of the genre are Claude Berri's two Pagnol adaptations, *Jean de Florette* and *Manon des sources* (both 1986), which deploy Daniel Auteuil, Emmanuelle Béart and Yves Montand in the Provençal countryside, evoking a nostalgic idyll of French rural life and cultural homogeneity. Successful at home and abroad, their sentimental synthesis of history lesson, tourist brochure and melodrama may be seen as the culturally acceptable face of the neo-nationalism that was gaining political ground during this time.

By contrast, a fresher vision of France was provided by so-called *beur* cinema. The slang term *beur* derives from a reversal of the syllables of the word 'arabe', and is generally used to describe the generation of 'immigrant' film-makers whose parents arrived in mainland France from Morocco, Tunisia and Algeria during the 1960s. In the late 1970s, a number of *beurs* began to make films, often using non-professional formats in the context of community groups; by the mid-1980s, a handful had secured a foothold in the industry. Early *beur* films include Abdelkrim Bahloul's *Le Thé à la menthe* (1984), Rachid Bouchareb's *Bâton rouge* (1985) and Mehdi Charef's *Le Thé au harem d'Archimède* (1986). In a political atmosphere marked by the popularity of the racist Front National, the emergence of *beur* cinema provided an important space for the representation of working-class youth culture in multiethnic France (Bosséno 1992; Tarr 1993).

Another positive development was the steady increase in the number of female directors, who significantly moved from the margins to the mainstream during the 1980s and early 1990s. Thus women have been responsible for such box-office hits as Serreau's 1985 *Trois hommes et un couffin* (which reached over 10 million spectators) and Josiane Balasko's 1995 *Gazon maudit* (almost four million). These successes are indicative of a much deeper transformation, which today sees many female directors equally pursuing careers as auteurs or working in mainstream genres: for example, Vera Belmont (*Marquise*, 1997), Catherine Corsini (*Mariées mais pas trop*, 2003), Claire Denis (*Trouble*

Every Day, 2001), Nicole Garcia (*Place Vendôme*, 1998), Zaïda Ghorab-Volta (*Jeunesse dorée*, 2001), Jeanne Labrune (*C'est le bouquet!*, 2001), Tonie Marshall (*Vénus beauté*, 1999) and Yolande Zauberman (*La Guerre à Paris*, 2001). Films directed or co-directed by women rose to 6.4 per cent of total output in the 1980s, then to 13.7 per cent in the 90s, a marked increase but still a small proportion of the whole (Tarr with Rollet 2001: 3).

The second presidential term of François Mitterrand came to an end in 1995. Whereas his fourteen-year rule had begun in a mood of great optimism for the people of the left, it finished in a depressed climate of ideological confusion and political scandal, which the subsequent election of Jacques Chirac as the new right-wing President did little to improve. For French cinema, the 1990s pivoted on an unexpected diplomatic coup at the 1993 Uruguay round of the negotiations for the General Agreements on Tariffs and Trade (GATT). In the run-up to the talks, the French had made clear their deep-rooted suspicion of American financial and cultural imperialism: 'Who', asked Mitterrand, 'can be blind today to the threat of a world gradually invaded by a uniform Anglo-Saxon culture, under the cover of economic liberalism?' (Miller 1996: 72). On the question of audiovisual free trade, there appeared to be an intractable disagreement between the American negotiators, who argued that use of state subsidies and import quotas to protect national industries contradicted the very spirit of the GATT, and a broad coalition of countries led by the French, who contended that since audiovisual media were 'culturally specific' to each nation state and inextricably bound to national identity, they should be treated as 'cultural exceptions'. At the last minute, in the interests of saving the GATT from total collapse, it was agreed to grant cinema and television this exceptional status. Given the French fear that audiovisual free trade would have opened their markets to a glut of foreign (i.e. American) products, quite possibly leading to the obliteration of the national film industry, the 'cultural exception' was celebrated in France as a major diplomatic victory.

To the astonishment of many observers who had experienced the hazardous 1980s, the French film industry began to regain confidence in the post-GATT period, buoyed by fresh talent and supported by a complex production model based on a new relationship with television (see Chapter 16). Whereas the latter had long been demonised for its supposedly negative impact on cinema in the 1970s and 1980s, the positive role of the younger medium has been perceived since the mid-1990s as vital to the health of the film industry. As Jean-Pierre Jeancolas puts it succinctly, 'television needs films; cinema lives off television's money' (Jeancolas 1995: 91). An example of this newfound harmony and productive symbiosis is the autobiographical film series *Tous les garçons et les filles de leur âge*, commissioned by the Arte television channel and broadcast in 1994, which featured contributions from established directors such as Akerman and Téchiné alongside an emerging generation of auteurs, including Olivier Assayas (*La Page blanche*), Émilie Deleuze (*L'Incruste*), Laurence Ferreira-Barbosa (*Paix et amour*) and Cédric Kahn (*Bonheur*). Following the success of the series, Arte repeated the experiment in 2003 around the theme of *Masculin/féminin*, with contributions from some of the same directors (Deleuze, Ferreira-Barbosa) and a range of less familiar names: Mathieu Amalric (*La Chose publique*), Nabil Ayouch (*Une Minute de soleil en moins*), Nadia Farès (*Anomalies passagères*) . . .

Such an atmosphere has even inspired some critics to speak of 'the return of cinema' (de Baecque and Jousse 1996), while others have identified the latest in a long line of 'new New Waves', this time calling it 'the young French cinema' in a deliberate echo of Labarthe's 1960 essay (Marie 1998). Like the participants in the original New Wave, many of France's young film-makers have been criticised for drawing too heavily on their own backgrounds and experiences at the expense of political vision. Although this critique is not entirely without foundation, it is worth recalling that in 1997 the major protest against the proposed 'Debré law' on immigration (which sought to oblige citizens to denounce illegal immigrants) was spearheaded by just such a group of young film people. While a total of fifty-nine film-makers signed a collective call to civil disobedience, the short protest film, *Nous, sans-papiers de France*, was co-ordinated by Nicolas Philibert, with the support of 175 directors and technicians, and rapidly distributed in several hundred cinemas. Another positive sign of recent French cinema's social concerns is the so-called *cinéma de banlieue* (cinema of the suburbs), which emerged in the 1980s and 1990s alongside *beur* cinema and provided a reflection of multiethnic France in the poorer suburbs of its major cities. Unfortunately, the media prominence of Mathieu Kassovitz's *La Haine* (1995) has sometimes obscured the real extent and authenticity of this phenomenon, which includes films by Ahmed Bouchala (*Krim*, 1995), Malik Chibane (*Hexagone*, 1994), Karim Dridi (*Bye Bye*, 1995), Thomas Gilou (*Raï*, 1995) and Jean-François Richet (*Ma 6-T va crack-er*, 1997).

In terms of creative diversity and independence, then, as well as its relatively strong economic health, French film culture is looking fairly well equipped to negotiate the beginnings of the 21st century. Certainly there are few nations outside France and the USA that enjoy a film industry capable of sustaining both popular genre production and the diversity of forms and themes characteristic of the young auteur cinema: Tran Anh Hung (*Cyclo*, 1995), Xavier Beauvois (*Nord*, 1992), Lucas Belvaux (*Pour rire!*, 1996), Christine Carrière (*Rosine*, 1995), Arnaud Desplechin (*Comment je me suis disputé . . .*, 1996), Bruno Dumont (*La Vie de Jésus*, 1997), Pascale Ferran (*L'Âge des possibles*, 1995), Noémie Lvovsky (*La Vie ne me fait pas peur*, 1999), Laetitia Masson (*La Repentie*, 2002), Gaspard Noé (*Irréversible*, 2002), François Ozon (*8 Femmes*, 2002), Manuel Poirier (*Les Femmes . . . ou les enfants d'abord*, 2002), Sandrine Veysset (*Martha . . . Martha*, 2001).

The health of contemporary cinema in France is partly a result of this balance between popular filmmaking and art cinema, partly of that between the creative activity of emerging film-makers and the strength of the projects pursued by established auteurs. Rivette's later films, for instance, have continued his rich exploraion of the overlap between theatre, cinema and life (*Va savoir*, 2001). Other well-known figures have engaged with new technologies and forms: Rohmer (*L'Anglaise et le duc*, 2001) and Godard (*Éloge de l'amour*, 2001) have both embraced the painterly potential of digital post-production; Varda has pursued the semi-autobiographical strand to her work through digital video (*Les Glaneurs et la glaneuse*, 2000); and Marker has opted latterly for new media (the CR-Rom

Immemory, 1997) and the gallery installation format (*Silent Movie*, 1995). But of all the directors of the modern period, only one has acquired truly iconic status: Jean-Luc Godard. The last of the *Cahiers du cinéma* critics to make the transition to feature filmmaking in the late 1950s, Godard's name and work have ultimately eclipsed those of his contemporaries, including Truffaut. Unfortunately, revilement or quasi-deification of the person have often taken precedence over an adequate critical response to the films. In fact to call Godard a film-maker in the conventional sense is something of a misnomer: he is better described as a multimedia essayist or critic who has traversed and blended different media throughout his career to produce features, shorts, sketches, essays, poems and collages in a variety of formats: 35mm, 16mm, U-matic video, video 8, photography, photocopier, typewriter, pen and paper and museum installation.

Godard's unique position in contemporary cinema is the result of a combination of factors. First, there is the brilliance and force of much of the work, plus its sheer volume (his filmography currently includes nearly ninety titles). Second, there is Godard's adeptness at using his star status to stimulate discussion of his films or to intervene in topical debates (as he did alongside the young film-makers in protest against the proposed 'Debré law'). Third, as this introduction has indicated, his work has been at the vanguard of French cinema not just once, but at successive key moments in its evolution: the burst of New Wave creativity from 1959 to 1965, producing a string of palyful masterpieces from low-budget tongue-in-cheek gangster films (*À bout de souffle*; *Bande à part*, 1964) to bittersweet romance in widescreen colour (*Le Mépris*, 1963; *Pierrot le fou*, 1965); the latter half of the 1960s, with a sequence of barbed neo-Brechtian critiques of what Guy Debord termed the 'Society of the Spectacle' (*Deux ou trois choses que je sais d'elle*, *La Chinoise*, *Weekend*) then in the wake of May 1968, the influential exploration of oppositional 16mm political filmmaking; followed by collaboration with the INA in the 1970s, resulting in one of the most beautiful experiments in televisual composition ever attempted, the twelve-part series *France/tour/détour/deux/enfants* (1977–8, co-dir. Anne-Marie Miéville); and lastly, the monumental eight-part videographic history of cinema, *Histoire(s) du cinéma* (1988–98), whose intense, crystalline forms outshine Godard's melancholic vision of cinematic decay and the bloody history of the 20th century.

Finally, French cinema in the last ten years has witnessed a strong renewal of interest in the documentary tradition. While some film-makers like Nicolas Philibert (*Qui sait*, 1998; *Être et avoir*, 2002) have chosen to focus exclusively on documentary practice, others move easily between documentary and fiction, such as Claire Simon (*Sinon, oui*, 1997) and Dominique Cabrera (*Nadia et les hippopotames*, 1999). Many young French directors cite as major points of reference not only the realist dramas of precursors like Maurice Pialat but also the politically charged work of documentarists like Denis Gheerbrant (*Et la vie*, 1989–91). It is worth noting that television is again largely responsible for reinvigorating this branch of French cinema in the early 21st century. Back in the mid-1980s, documentary slots on television were slashed, funding virtually disappeared and production ground to a halt. A decade later, the proliferation of subscription, satellite and cable channels had created extensive new funding sources and the fate of documentary was spectacularly reversed. In 1995, the pan-European cultural channel, La SEPT/Arte, alone bought or co-produced 135 hours of new original documentaries. By the end of the decade, documentary film production had overtaken that of fiction for the first time.

Central to this renaissance, indeed to documentary film-making in France over the past three decades, has been the work of producer Thierry Garrel at INA, La SEPT/Arte. In 2000, this contribution was honoured in Paris by a major retrospective at the Jeu de Paume, a rare, perhaps unique, occurrence for a documentary producer. What Garrel calls the 'new documentary school' stems from the unlikely conjunction of two historical forces: the neo-liberal deregulation of television in the 1980s and the belated coming of age of the Estates General of Cinema of May 1968. Many of the directors and producers at the forefront of the current renaissance can be traced back to the radical film-making collectives of the post-1968 period: Jean-Michel Carré, director of over twenty films, including *Les Trottoirs de Paris* (1994), is a former

member of the 'Grain de Sable' collective; 'Les Films d'Ici', one of the most prominent and prolific production companies of the contemporary era, is run by three former activists (Richard Copans, Yves Jeanneau, Serge Lalou); Jean-Louis Comolli, co-editor of *Cahiers du cinéma* in the 1970s, has directed numerous films, including an extraordinary ongoing portrait of political life in Marseilles since 1989. In this context, it is far from accidental that one of the most exciting programming initiatives to have emerged alongside the documentary revival should have adopted as its title 'Estates General of Documentary', an event staged annually in the village of Lussas in the Ardèche, which is not just a festival but a 'centre of information, a site of reflection and a forum for debate' (Michelson 2000: 141). The Estates General of May 1968, with its slogan of 'The Cinema Is Rising Up', may well have taken a long time to mature, but its belated crystallisation in the late 20th and early 21st centuries has had a massive impact on the new documentary school and on young French cinema as a whole.

WORKS CITED

Bellour, R. (2000) *The Analysis of Film*, Bloomington, Indiana University Press.

Borde, R., Buache, F. and Curtelin, J. (1962) *Nouvelle Vague*, Lyon, Serdoc.

Bosséno, C. M. (1992) 'Immigrant Cinema: National Cinema – The Case of *Beur* Film', in Dyer, R. and Vincendeau, G. eds, *Popular European Cinema*, London, Routledge, 47–57.

Courtade, F. (1978) *Les Malédictions du cinéma français*, Paris, Alain Moreau.

Crisp, C. (1993) *The Classic French Cinema, 1930–1960*, Bloomington, Indiana University Press.

Daney, S. (1986) *Ciné journal 1981–1986*, Paris, Cahiers du cinéma.

Daney, S. (1998) 'Survivre à la Nouvelle Vague', *Cahiers du cinéma*, special issue: 'Nouvelle Vague: une légende en question', 62–6.

de Baecque, A. and Jousse, T. (1996) *Le Retour du cinéma*, Paris, Hachette.

Forbes, J. ed. (1984) *INA – French for Innovation: The Work of the Institut National de la Communication in Cinema and Television*, London, BFI.

Frodon, J.-M. (1995) *L'Âge moderne du cinéma français*, Paris, Flammarion.

Hayward, S. (1993) 'State, Culture and the Cinema: Jack Lang's Strategies for the French Film Industry 1981–93', *Screen*, 34: 4, 380–91.

Jeancolas, J.-P. (1995) *Histoire du cinéma français*, Paris, Nathan.

Labarthe, A. (1960) *Essai sur le jeune cinéma français*, Paris, Terrain Vague.

Marie, M. ed. (1998) *Le Jeune Cinéma français*, Paris, Nathan.

Metz. C. (1974a) *Film Language: A Semiotics of Cinema*, Oxford, Oxford University Press.

Metz, C. (1974b) *Language and Cinema*, The Hague, Mouton.

Michelson, A. (2000) 'The Estates General of the Documentary Film', *October*, 91, 141–8.

Miller, T. (1996) 'The Crime of Monsieur Lang: GATT, the Screen, and the New International Division of Labour', in Moran, A. ed., *Film Policy*, London, Routledge, 72–84.

Prédal, R. (1996) *50 ans de cinéma français*, Paris, Nathan.

Sellier, G. (1999) 'Images de femmes dans le cinéma de la Nouvelle Vague', *Clio: femmes, histoire et société*, 10, 216–32.

Tarr, C. (1993) 'Questions of Identity in *Beur* Cinema: From *Tea in the Harem* to *Cheb*', *Screen*, 34: 4, 321–42.

Tarr, C. with Rollet, B. (2001) *Cinema and the Second Sex: Women's Filmmaking in France in the 1980s and 1990s*, New York, Continuum.

The Other Auteurs:
Producers, Cinematographers and Scriptwriters

Alison Smith

Ever since the New Wave, French cinema has been perceived as auteur-based. Although frequently questioned, this notion of the director as the single artistic personality behind the film has proved durably convenient. Indeed it has often served as a symbol of the very difference between European cinema culture and the American film industry. Yet it is obvious that a film has multiple creators, all those working individuals who contribute to the process and the product, in different ways and to different degrees. The aim of this chapter is not to deny the importance of the director, however, it is rather to rethink and extend the category of 'auteur'. What the French concentration on the director has obscured, for example, is the important creative roles played by the producer and the screenwriter. These functions have more readily been associated with the Hollywood system in the case of the producer, and the French system pre-1960 in the case of the screenwriter. Furthermore, the auteurist assumption that cinema is a form of personal artistic expression has elided the specialised contributions of the set designer and the composer, as well as the more technical and uniquely cinematic contributions of the editor and the cinematographer. Among the many 'other auteurs' whose input contributes to the finished film, this chapter will focus on three figures who have a strong claim to be considered as at least co-auteurs: one who 'conceives' the work; one who 'makes' the work; and one who 'writes' the work. We shall thus look in turn at the changing function and role of the producer, the cinematographer and the screenwriter, from the arrival of the New Wave to the present day.

PRODUCERS: 'NO PRODUCER, NO FILM'

Alexis Bernier places producers among the 'holy trinity of cinema – actor, director, producer', but notes that they receive much less media attention than the other two (*CinémAction* 1990: 18–21). Almost certainly, the low profile of French producers comes from the perception that their function is necessarily tainted by money. The cinema is both art and industry, and the producer links the individual artwork to the industry from which it comes and the world into which it will be launched. This could be seen as a highly 'creative' function, but in the eyes of a primarily art-oriented critical establishment the producer usually represents constraint and compromise. Film-makers would ideally be their own producers, conceiving themselves and negotiating their entry into the world. Distrust of the producer in post-New Wave France was also based on a false comparison with the classical Hollywood studio system, in which the producer had reigned supreme. Such tyranny had never really existed in the French industry, where production was usually undertaken on a smaller scale, and producers were individuals endowed with an interest in cinema and a certain amount of private capital. The New Wave at its outset depended on this kind of small-scale production system, the film-makers developing individual relationships with enlightened producers such as Georges de Beauregard, Pierre Braunberger, Mag Bodard or Anatole Dauman. Combining affection and cynicism, the New Wave generation always located the producer squarely on the artistic side of the cinema, not as an auteur perhaps, but certainly as the director's friendly collaborator, and with the same priorities. As Godard expressed it in 1962:

> At heart producers are like us – people who don't have money and want to make films. I have never met a producer who didn't love his profession. He is an entertainment contractor, a showman, so whatever else he's a kindred spirit. And he works. (Godard 1972: 226)

Some New Wave directors became producers themselves, as if the auteur could absorb a potentially rival role. Thus Truffaut's Films du Carrosse, Agnès Varda's Films Tamaris and Rohmer's Films du Losange, the latter becoming a major player in the independent sector long after the New Wave had come and gone. Certainly the artisanal approach of the key New Wave producers seemed to be effective. As Truffaut noted in 1962:

> The two most New Wave directors in Paris, Braunberger and de Beauregard, continue to do business, while elsewhere we are witnessing some strange occurrences: the imminent closure of Cinédis, the biggest French group and distributor of big budget films; reduction of personnel at Pathé; an agreement between Gaumont and MGM; the fading away of Cocinor. (Truffaut 1999: 157)

Although associated chiefly with the New Wave, this model of the independent producer, functioning through personal relationships with directors, has remained a distinctive feature of French cinema throughout the period, even within the more recent context of a French film industry aspiring to imitate, if not rival, the always dominant American mega-industry.

During much of the 1970s, production might be described as a forgotten function. The post-1968 film culture was profoundly anti-commercial, and so production – except the 'alternative' production of politically involved collectives – was not discussed. It was late in the decade before the specialist press (other than *Le Film français*) began to show much interest in the producer's function again. When in 1981 *Cahiers du cinéma* decided to devote its June issue to a major enquiry into the state of both production and cinematography in France, Serge Toubiana declared: 'in the last decade, production has been the missing link, or at least the weakest link, of French cinema' (*Cahiers du cinéma* 1981: 5). This is not, of course, wholly accurate. Critical and theoretical interest may have been minimal, but to reach the market films needed a producer, and throughout the 1970s, film production had continued for better or for worse. The map of the French cinema had grown increasingly divided, however, with a thoroughly

commercial, although not yet vastly ambitious, output of comedies and thrillers existing alongside a mostly low-budget 'young' cinema financed in large measure by the 'advance on receipts'. A steep decline in audience figures had also increased the risks of an already hazardous profession. Small-scale production was beginning to look impractical, while the distribution and exhibition sectors were reacting in their turn to hard times with a demand for involvement in production. The future dominance of the television companies was already becoming apparent: at the very least, no producer could afford do business without them. In his editorial, Toubiana claimed that the age of the auteur–producer dialogue was past. The industry had taken over and instigated 'a dialogue without artists or behind their backs, a dialogue between money and money' (*Cahiers du cinéma* 1981: 10).

Nonetheless, an examination of the pattern of production through the 1970s reveals a preponderance of small, privately run companies, and the dominance of individuals over the major institutional players, although the big companies, such as Gaumont, increased their involvement very rapidly from about the middle of the decade. Gaumont found it advantageous to play along with the system, dividing its interests in the films it produced across a number of small subsidiary companies whenever its participation exceeded about 50 per cent. As Daniel Toscan du Plantier expressed it: 'With Fellini, it's 100 per cent. It never looks that way, you'll see lots of names of companies, but they are all ours. For *The City of Women* there are four names but in fact it's one company' (*Cahiers du cinéma* 1981: 29). These subdivisions were not just accounting fictions. Gaumont's strategy was to employ semi-independent producers to work on individual films, because 'a director needs someone he knows on the set, someone he knows that he can speak to and shout at. Otherwise it's too bureaucratic' (*Cahiers du cinéma* 1981: 30). These independent units were to some extent still being deployed in support of the auteur-director, but here, particularly, Gaumont's company policy in 1981 is divided against itself. Fellini is one thing, according to Toscan du Plantier, new auteurs quite another:

There is a lack of auteurs, it's been the case for some time. It takes time to make an auteur . . . I've invented a house-style which has made up for the lack of auteurs, in fact I'd be tempted to say that the only auteur I've discovered is me. (*Cahiers du cinéma* 1981: 33).

If *Cahiers du cinéma*'s enquiry proves anything about the role of the producer in the early 1980s, it is that the contradictions inherent in Gaumont's position were generalised across the sector. On the whole, the director's place is still unchallenged, although the role is now seen as primary rather than supreme, and there is a strong current of protest against the 1957 legal requirement that he or she should always have the final cut. What is clear, however, is that for the vast majority of the survey's interviewees (Toscan du Plantier, Marin Karmitz, Margaret Ménégoz, Alain Poiré, Albina de Boisrouvray, Pierre Héros and Jacques Hinstin, Raymond Danon, Claude Nedjar, Hélène Vager, Yves Rousset-Rouard, Gérard Beytout, Paul Vecchiali), the prevailing production model in the French industry is still small scale and the producers are correspondingly implicated on a daily basis in every aspect of the film-making process. Claude Nedjar expresses clear support for that model: 'We need a lot of producers each producing few films, taking care of everything from preparation to production' (*Cahiers du cinéma* 1981: 68). But a significant proportion of respondents express fears that scale is beginning to pose practical problems, as larger players make their presence felt at other levels of the industry. Notably Héros and Hinstin feel that the power of a small producer is negligible when confronted with the increasing star-power of the best-known actors and their agents on the one hand, and the demands of the television companies on the other. Interestingly, there is widespread agreement, even among the most independent and auteurist of the interviewees, that the system of state subsidies as it existed in 1981 should be rejected, and that relations with the Centre National de la Cinématographie (CNC) were appalling: Hélène Vager describes them as a 'cold war' (*Cahiers du cinéma* 1981: 69).

When in 1987 *Cahiers du cinéma* picks up its enquiry into French production again, the trends noted in 1981 had become for the most part more pronounced. Although Yannick Flot remarks that in 1986 there were some 800 production companies in France, only 170 of them were active, which suggests that the profession was still small scale and probably in a real sense inefficient (Flot 1986). But television's role in film production had become notably decisive, and with it had come the media barons as investors and the imperative to find international markets to match the arrival of international capital. Not that, from the *Cahiers du cinéma* perspective, this had led to a complete eclipse of the director as creator of a film: indeed they see a tendency towards a greater degree of individuality in the commercial sector, when compared with the previous decade. Toscan du Plantier, the only producer interviewed both in 1981 and 1987, had in the meantime left Gaumont to set up independently, and his comments on his role reveal that he perceives the need to protect the existence of individual creativity, be it in production or direction. In that regard he is still somewhat contradictory: 'A producer is someone who has a style. I like people with a recognisable manner, auteur-producers.' But he adds:

> The actor is closer to the auteur. Between them there's a real complicity that gives birth to films. As producers we are there to organise their coming together: that they love each other, that they are reconciled. In the hope that they'll call us back another time. (*Cahiers du cinéma* 1987: 15–18)

Furthermore, he notes the rise of directors who are themselves oriented to a primarily commercial logic, with enough expertise to work out their own finances and to let that govern the content of their films (his example is Jean-Jacques Annaud). Although he cites other reasons for leaving Gaumont, one cannot but wonder whether the contradictions that were already showing in 1981 may have played a part in his departure. He subsequently spent fifteen years as president of Unifrance, the French film promotion agency, until his death in 2003.

Since the 1990s, several strong tendencies have become apparent. First, the undeniable importance of investment drawn from television. As the independent producer Patrick Godeau, whose company made *Le Bossu* (Philippe de Broca, 1997) and *Les Morsures de l'aube* (Antoine de Caunes, 2000), declared to *Film français* in March 2001:

> For a number of years now I only contact television companies to finance my films, never the cinema groups. The money of the cinema groups goes into their catalogues and their theatres, whereas the television companies are looking to make a profit from the money they are legally obliged to invest in cinema production.

Second, it is clear that a form of vertical integration of production and distribution has become a necessity for the world of 'art-house' production. Thus Films du Losange, certainly the most durable of the auteur-based production companies of the New Wave, has taken on a distribution function separate from its production activities, and for a successful young company such as Haut et Court – the producers of *Ma vie en rose* (Alain Berliner, 1997), for example – an early entry into distribution was an important factor in their success. Other independent producers enter into more or less temporary partnerships with larger production groups, including the media companies, in order to negotiate distribution deals from a position of relative power. Such partnerships obviously carry their share of risk, since it is a small step from a successful long-term partnership to actual merger and the absorption of the independent producer into a larger corporate structure.

And yet, despite protests, conflicts and critical arguments, it seems that the symbolic status of the director-auteur still remains the basis for the relations of production in French cinema, whether we are talking about small companies such as Haut et Court or the members of the 'Club des Cinq' (ARP, Diaphana, Losange, Pyramide, Rezo), large production companies like Téléma (directed by Charles Gassot, one of the major names in French production in the last thirty years) or even UGC France. Indeed, perceived from abroad, one of the attractions of the French production sector may still be its residual auteur structure. For example, Tarak Ben Ammar, talking about a recent transatlantic project with Brian de Palma, declared to *Film français* in April 2001 that the freedom offered to a major American director by a European company

goes some way to outweighing the attractions of Hollywood budgets: 'The American system was beginning to annoy him, and I offered him the budget of a major without the interference from the executives.' It could be argued of course that such projects should be placed outside the ambit of 'French' film entirely: the company concerned, Quinta Communications, was acting in conjunction with Berlusconi and the Kirsch group, and its main interest was in working with English-language directors (Paul Verhoeven and Ridley Scott were also mentioned). But this example of ambitious cross-border and cross-media financing in fact illustrates another strong tendency in contemporary 'French' film production, an approach that is being followed even by such important players as Alain Sarde, whose name seems ever more inevitable on quality international productions, whatever their origin, in the early 21st century.

A MAJOR INDEPENDENT: MARIN KARMITZ

Marin Karmitz is one of the most important contributors to French cinema of the past forty years. First as director, then as producer, distributor and exhibitor, his career has been devoted to the promotion of alternatives and countercurrents to the main flow of film output. His consistent dedication to international cinema and art cinema has played a not inconsiderable part in ensuring that the variety of films available to audiences in France is perhaps unequalled anywhere in the world. Karmitz has combined this uncompromising fidelity to an independent ethos with an approach to the film business more typical of a large mainstream company. In this way he has come to occupy a unique, perhaps precarious, but certainly exemplary position in the French production system. Romanian-born, Karmitz came to France in 1947 to study at the IDHEC film school. After his studies he found a place as assistant director on several films, including Agnès Varda's *Cléo de 5 à 7* (1962), and in 1966 he directed his own first film, a version of Samuel Beckett's *Comedy* produced in close collaboration with the author. Very experimental in form, it was an early sign of Karmitz's independence and his desire to discover new possibilities for the cinema. In the aftermath of May 1968, and the climate of intense debate about the political potential of cinema to which those events gave rise, Karmitz made two films that caused a stir, *Camarades* (1969) and *Coup pour coup* (1972). The latter was a genuine attempt to put into practice the much-discussed ideal of passing the camera to the people whose struggles are filmed, in this case the striking workers at a textile factory. *Coup pour coup* received praise but also such savage attacks that, as Jill Forbes put it, 'it gave Karmitz a reputation which prevented him from ever directing another fiction film' (Forbes 1992: 24). So Karmitz, to keep working in cinema, turned his attention to distribution, using the contacts that he had made in the world of underground, radical cinema. At first he bought films to be programmed in the Latin Quarter, but his ambitions were broader, and in 1974, in partnership with François Maspéro, he bought a former restaurant just off the Place de la Bastille and transformed it into the '14 juillet MK2' cinema, the first of what was to become a successful chain.

Karmitz and Maspéro had two main aims: the first was to reverse the decline of the neighbourhood cinema by setting up their business in what was then still a working-class area. The second was to show something different from the usual fare available outside the Latin Quarter, in particular foreign-language films and, especially at the beginning, politically committed work that could be coupled with debates. Rather than a cinema, the MK2-Bastille was a small arts centre, with a bookshop, social spaces and a programme of events connected with the films. It proved extremely successful, and it was not long before Karmitz was able to open another centre. His activity as a distributor was primarily aimed at supplying his cinemas, and it was for the same reason that he ventured into production, supporting in the early years Marco Bellocchio, Jean-Louis Comolli and Jean-Luc Godard. Karmitz's choices of production projects and distribution deals proved singularly effective. In 1977, he acquired distribution rights to

Marin Karmitz's *MK2 Bibliothèque*, next to the new Bibliothèque Nationale in Paris (Photo: M. Tinel)

the Taviani brothers' *Padre Padrone*, just before it won the Palme d'Or at Cannes, and the resultant profits were ploughed back into the company. In 1982, the company presented ten films at Cannes, and came away with the Palme d'Or for *Yol* (Yilmaz Güney), the Special Jury Prize for *The Night of San Lorenzo* (Paolo and Vittorio Taviani), the Caméra d'Or for *Mourir à trente ans* (Romain Goupil) and the Prix du scénario for *Travail au noir* (Jerzy Skolimowski). In the early 1990s Karmitz produced Krzysztof Kieślowski's influential *Three Colours* series, and later he worked with Abbas Kiarostami (*The Wind Will Carry Us*, 1999), Claude Chabrol (*Merci pour le chocolat*, 2000) and Michael Haneke (*Code inconnu*, 2000).

Thus, MK2 provided an example of vertical integration in the independent sector, which now appears ahead of its time, indeed until the late 1990s Karmitz was unique in combining in one independent company all the functions relating to the production, distribution and exhibition of a film. Furthermore, given that a large proportion of the films supported by MK2 have achieved a critical reputation that might class them as 'modern classics', it is not surprising that the expansion of the video and DVD market has been of particular significance for the company's fortunes. Thus Karmitz seems to have been remarkably far-sighted when, asked by *Cahiers du cinéma* in 1981 whether he felt quick returns or the construction of a catalogue should be a producer's main priority, he opted for the latter, whereas all the other producers interviewed, except Margaret Ménégoz, thought that quick returns should come first. This choice has been a factor in the survival and success of both MK2 and Films du Losange.

By 1998 MK2 had 150 employees and a turnover of 196 million francs. It had seven cinema complexes in Paris, some of which were in very prestigious areas cinematically (Odéon, Montparnasse). But Karmitz had not abandoned his commitment to restore cinemas to less culturally privileged areas, and in 1998 he opened a cinema and cultural centre in the nineteenth arrondissement, beside the Bassin St-Martin. This scale of operations, while not approaching the level of Gaumont or UGC, is nonetheless considerably more important than the activities of most independent players. Having said that, Karmitz was well aware of the contradictions involved in this position. In a 1998 television interview, he described his activity as 'the Research and Development arm' of cinema:

> Producing films by creative people means in fact to create against the institutions, against the established order, against the system in place; in order to do this, I am obliged to behave like everyone else, i.e. to work within the market, to work in the industrial system of cinema. But when I have to choose, I almost always choose in favour of creativity. (*Les Rendez-vous de l'entreprise* 1998)

Creatively, Karmitz's stance has indeed been uncompromising, although the days of political debates and revolutionary films from Latin America are long gone. As a production and distribution company, MK2 has an international reputation that is a major business asset, resulting ironically from Karmitz's decision to support 'marginal' films from across Europe and the rest of the world. As an exhibitor, MK2's activities are, by deliberate choice, restricted to Paris, but within the capital its visibility is extremely high. It has become higher still since the opening in February 2003 of Karmitz's 30-million euro 'city of image and sound', MK2 Bibliothèque, on the Avenue de France directly adjacent to the Bibliothèque Nationale de France (French National Library) and just across the Seine from the planned national Maison du Cinéma (House of Cinema). The monumental MK2 Bibliothèque – which incorporates a fourteen-screen multiplex, shops, restaurants and space for exhibitions, debates and even musical experiment – declares itself by its title a centre of film culture comparable to the centre of written culture next door. The complex stands as concrete evidence of Karmitz's move from the margins to the centre of the French cinema system.

CINEMATOGRAPHERS: ARTISANS OR ARTISTS?

What is a cinematographer? As the review *Ciném-Action* makes clear in its survey of the profession published in 1990, the term 'cinematographer' covers two technical functions: the *chef-opérateur* (or *directeur de la photographie*) responsible for lighting and overall control of the image quality, and the *cadreur* or *caméraman*, who actually takes up the position behind the camera, places it appropriately in each scene and executes the movement. The *cadreur* is a subordinate function, under the orders not only of the director but also of the *chef-op*. In fact, it is quite common for one person to take on both roles, although a majority of cinematographers prefer working with the light, since it is in this part of their work that they are most independent from the director. There is another sense in which the cinematographer's functions may be described as split: creative yet technical, autonomous yet subordinate to the director, he or she is both an artist and an artisan. Thus the stars of the profession, in demand nationally and internationally, are free to choose their projects and they develop a personal style out of their accumulated experience. Raoul Coutard, Henri Decaë and Nestor Almendros have become part of the story of the New Wave along with the directors they worked for, and the deaths of two of the most prominent cinematographers of post-war French cinema, Henri Alekan and Sacha Vierny, drew the kind of media attention that only a select few French directors might expect to receive. On the other hand, the cinematographers are trained to be technicians for hire, offering a precise and semi-scientific expertise; and, at least below the very top levels, they are inserted into a highly regulated, union-based industrial structure from which directors are by and large excluded or exempt. This contradiction can create internal conflict: it may be one reason for many cinematographers' ambivalence towards attempts to raise them to the status of auteurs. It may also account for the practical difficulties faced by the newly trained cinematographer. Repeatedly, the cinematographers interviewed in *CinémAction*'s survey return to the paradox whereby the only way to get work as a cinematographer is through personal relations, despite the training in technical expertise: 'It's a question of establishing a clientele from acquaintances and recommendations. You never make an application. The directors have to come and get you' (*CinémAction* 1990: 57). So speaks Patrick Blossier, *chef-op* to Varda, Alain Tanner and Costa-Gavras. Charlie van Damme, another ex-collaborator of Varda, puts the dilemma succinctly: 'I think

there's only one way. You have to be known. To be known you have to have done something. To have done something you have to be known' (*CinémAction* 1990: 62).

Despite a continual development of new technologies, the essential features of the role of the cinematographer seem to have remained very much the same from the time of the New Wave. It would probably be fair to say that the New Wave imposed a greater and more sudden change on the profession of cinematographer than any other that occurred in the subsequent forty years. The almost total desertion of the studio, and the concomitant change in emphasis from elaborate manipulation of highly variable sources of light, to an ability to create effects with natural light and an increased emphasis on framing, required a genuine change in the conception of the role, thereby relegating some of the greatest of the established exponents to a period of obscurity – Henri Alekan being the most obvious example. The re-emergence of Alekan in the early 1980s was in fact read by many as symptomatic of a return to the studios, and of a less naturalistic, more ambitious, approach to film lighting. Such a return was welcomed by many who considered that the overall effect of the New Wave had been to impoverish the range and potentialities of the film image. For example, Nestor Almendros, despite being one of the star cinematographers of the later New Wave, gives a very critical verdict on the effect of the movement on his profession:

> That shadowless light always shining down from a strange sky (the ceiling), by day or by night, had eventually destroyed visual atmosphere in modern cinema. We had moved from old conventions to new ones, but unfortunately these new conventions were oversimplified, impoverished. (Almendros 1984: 7)

However, although the absolute hegemony of the naturalistic may have been somewhat reduced, there has been no sudden or wholesale reaction, and it is striking on reading interviews with cinematographers across the forty years since the New Wave that their preoccupations and their position on the set seem to have changed little from the 1960s and 1970s. Alekan himself, during the period when he was perhaps less in demand for work on films, taught at the national film school, IDHEC and became the patron and mentor of a new generation. Even the New Wave at its most revolutionary could not dispense with the cinematographer. Perhaps they needed cinematographers even more than their predecessors in the 1950s, since the whole New Wave ethos assumed that technical experience was no substitute for visual imagination in the process of making a film. Rather than downgrading the cinematographer's role to that of adjunct at the service of the director, the arrival of directors without technical experience often valorised it. On the whole, the new generation of directors had no illusions at the beginning of their careers about their need for technical guidance; they were on the other hand entirely convinced of the primacy of image (and sound in its most general sense) over dialogue and narrative in defining the essential characteristics of cinema. The cinematographer therefore became the primary partner, adviser and second-in-command to the director, a role that became a constant of French cinema culture long after the New Wave. With a few very rare exceptions, such as Alekan, the star cinematographer in France is a phenomenon of the post-1960 period.

Nonetheless, descriptions of the actual activity of the cinematographer make it clear that almost all have experienced their role as something more active than a simple submission to the requirements of the director. When Claude Berri engaged Bruno Nuytten to work on *Tchao Pantin* in 1983, Nuytten acted as a permanent consultant on location and lighting long before shooting began. Pierre-William Glenn's experience of regular active input led him to move into film directing on his own account, albeit with limited success: 'I've always collaborated intimately on the mise en scène. So at a certain point you think that your own dreams are as valid as those of the people you're working for as cinematographer' (*CinémAction* 1990: 64). Whether or not a cinematographer should allow themselves a personal style seems sometimes to be a question of professional morality. Interviewed by *Cahiers du cinéma* in 1983, Sacha Vierny declared:

> All cinematographers will tell you that you just have to ask and they'll do whatever style you want. We're all liars, it's certainly not true. The proof is that direc-

tors choose one cinematographer rather than another for a particular film. (*Cahiers du cinéma* 1983: 51)

In other words, there is a widespread ideal of technical competence and adaptability, but real experience suggests that accomplished cinematographers are likely to be auteurs despite themselves. As a result perhaps, both cinematographers and directors insist on the absolute necessity that they should be compatible, and on both sides there is emphasis on the choice of collaborators and also sometimes of projects. As Caroline Champetier puts it: 'We all have a note. If a film-maker assembles an orchestra, he has several instruments at his disposition and I am one of those instruments. I have my own note' (*24 Images* 1992: 28).

The role of the cinematographer has traversed the years since the New Wave with an unchanging, broadly traditional structure perpetuated through a system of semi-apprenticeship. However, one important change, which may not be entirely separable from technical developments, is the increasing presence of women behind the camera. The importance of women in non-acting roles in the cinema industry has been a subject of debate since the 1970s, and not only in France. Most interest has inevitably concentrated on the existence of women directors, who were still exceptions to the rule until the 1990s. On the other hand, the production function in France has been accepted and carried out successfully in France by a surprising number of women, certainly since the period of the New Wave, and not always at the smaller-scale end of the market. Similarly, there have been and still are a fairly large number of successful women screenwriters, not to mention other creative functions such as designers and, perhaps especially, editors. In cinematography, however, the same quite definitely did not apply. Until the 1990s there have been remarkably few women cinematographers, and the star cinematographers were without exception men. In part, the male domination of this particular function may genuinely have been due to technical factors – or at least the perception of technical factors. The physical manipulation of cameras in the 1960s and 1970s was heavy work, and even a director such as Agnès Varda, while fully and deeply committed to expressing female experience in the

cinema, recognised early in her career that one of
the problems for a woman director was the absolute
dependence on the cinematographer that the
weight of the equipment imposed. That said, Varda
was one of the earliest directors to form a lasting
partnership with a woman cinematographer, Nurith
Aviv, who became one of the pioneers of female
camera operation. The technical limitation was, in
all probability, largely a myth, maintained by a
degree of machismo within the profession. What is
clear, however, is that by the 1990s the male domination of this field had significantly diminished.
Agnès Godard, Caroline Champetier and Jeanne
Lapoirie have become some of the star names in
the profession. This development has not taken
place without discussion: Agnès Godard recalled in
an interview with *Positif* that when Alekan
arranged an engagement for her with Wim Wenders, he considered it necessary to check first that
the director would accept a woman, a precaution
that she accepted as natural. According to Godard,
the situation in France is quite exceptional: 'Elsewhere, I've always felt a sort of testing out, a reti-
cence about the idea of these jobs being performed
by women' (*Positif* 2000: 132). The feminisation of
French cinema at the practical level is not, of
course, confined to cinematography. The stream of
new women directors in the 1990s has been much
commented on, and some have shown an inclination to engage women as cinematographers – one
of the best-known examples of such collaboration
would be Claire Denis's work with Agnès Godard,
to whom we shall now turn.

THE NEW FEMALE *CHEF-OP*: AGNÈS GODARD

Agnès Godard describes herself as one of the
second generation of women to enter the traditionally male-dominated world of cinematography, following the pioneers of the 1970s and early 1980s
such as Nurith Aviv and Dominique le Rigoleur.
Since her debut on Varda's *Jacquot de Nantes* in
1991, she has established herself as one of the most
respected cinematographers in France, especially –
but not exclusively – through her close association
with Claire Denis, starting with *J'ai pas sommeil*
(1994). Denis's reputation as one of the most visually inventive French film-makers working today

Agnès Godard was cinematographer for *Beau travail* (Claire
Denis, 1999)

can be attributed at least in part to Godard's expertise. Her career has taken on the typical profile of a
star cinematographer, in which a strong association
with a successful director has led to the development of an identifiable personal style. Evolving
from the partnership between director and cinematographer, the style is then modified, while still
retaining both technical mastery and some elements
of its own character, in the course of high-profile
work with other directors, such as Erick Zonca for
La Vie rêvée des anges (1998) or Catherine Corsini
for *La Nouvelle Ève* (1999). As a student at
IDHEC, which she entered in 1976, she had the
opportunity to experiment with all aspects of film
production, and following a year's practical experience as production assistant on the set of Danielle
Jaeggi's *La Fille de Prague* (1979), she decided to
become a cinematographer – although she was fas-
cinated by editing and claims to have spent nine
months editing her graduation film. At the end of
her studies, the entry into the profession came
through the time-honoured route of work as an
apprentice to an established cinematographer, in
Godard's case no less a figure than Henri Alekan,
who had taught her for a while at IDHEC.
Alekan's support in the early stages of her career was
vital: his confidence in her was such that he offered
her the job of camerawoman/assistant for Wim
Wenders's *The State of Things* (1982) when her total
experience, she claims, amounted to twelve days,
eight of them using 16mm film. After *The State of
Things* she continued to work with Alekan, and also
with Sacha Vierny, who offered her the job of

cadreuse on Peter Greenaway's *Belly of an Architect* (1987). The transition from *cadreuse* to *chef-op*, the final consecration of a career, could easily have taken place in 1988 with Claire Denis, who requested her services on *Chocolat*. According to Godard, it was the producers who blocked this idea, a sign of continued resistance to the employment of women in the role, even though Godard claimed that, at least in France, such discrimination was almost a thing of the past: 'when I was assistant camerawoman, there were already a lot of girls in that job' (*Positif* 2000: 133). The two women's first real collaboration on a fiction film did not take place until 1994, when she was already an established cinematographer. However, prior to that, and indeed prior to *Jacquot de Nantes*, Godard had taken full responsibility for the image, both lighting and framing, in Denis's well-known two-part television portrait of Jacques Rivette, *Jacques Rivette, le veilleur* (1990).

Since *Jacquot de Nantes*, Godard has combined the functions of *chef-op* and *cadreuse*, a decision that she shares with many, probably most, of today's cinematographers. In common again with the majority of the profession, she insists on the necessity of adapting oneself to the style of particular directors, and denies that she has a confirmed style of her own: 'As technicians, we should be chameleons and adapt ourselves to each person's method' (*Positif* 2000: 133). However, when she talks about her work, her particular attitude to the material before her camera becomes apparent. It is characterised above all by sensuality, even tactility: 'I like filming the body, the skin, you feel like you're in contact with something secret. How does the light fall on people, how does it fall on the skin? It's tactile' (*Positif* 2000: 133). It is this element of Godard's work that Yannick Lemarié describes as a respect for objects and for the faces and bodies of the actors, which 'draws new vitality from the materiality of things' (Lemarié 2000: 128). Lemarié's analysis supports the idea that a cinematographer can be said to have a personal style; its stance is very close to auteurism, since it attributes to the cinematographer not only the choice of lighting and precise framing but also decisions regarding the general content of the frame, for example a fondness for close-ups on apparently banal objects, which thus

acquire unexpected significance. Lemarié finds examples of such choices in films by different directors on which Godard has worked, thus adding weight to the argument for a coherent cinematographic style.

This sensual, tactile aspect to Godard's relationship with her subjects creates an interesting contrast with Caroline Champetier's description of the ambiguous position of a woman behind the camera. Champetier clearly perceives her position as gendered, implicitly masculine, and her response is to take a critical distance from the camera itself:

> I am not a man, a camera is not at all a phallic object for me. It's an object I find dangerous, awkward, disagreeable, and I'd like to be rid of it sometimes. A camera isn't the centre of anything, the centre is certainly not there . . . It's quite nice, even if a bit old-fashioned today, not to exaggerate the importance of the camera. (*24 Images* 1992: 31)

Godard on the other hand has said that the camera, especially the hand-held camera, gives 'a central vision, which functions like a magnet, you're either drawn to it or repelled' (*Positif* 2000: 134). But she does not perceive her position as gendered. 'I think that if we see differently, then the look is different because of the person, not because one is a man and one is a woman,' she declared to the Canadian Society of Cinematographers website in 2000, recognising at the same time that the directors she works with are more often women than men: 'I don't know why but maybe it is because I did my first film with Claire Denis and this set a standard' (*CSC* 2000). This is in fact a common pattern for women currently working as cinematographers in France. It is also worth noting that those women, Godard included, have largely been restricted, or perhaps have restricted themselves, to the art-house sector. Godard is consistently optimistic in interviews about the prospects for women in the profession, but even she admits that 'there are a lot of productions which never hire women' (*CSC* 2000). In the meantime, she has contributed a great deal towards gaining visibility and professional respect for the abilities of women as the technicians of image-making.

THE SCRIPTWRITERS: AUTHORS BUT NOT AUTEURS?

Prior to 1957, French law considered the scriptwriter to be the author of a film. The law of 11 March 1957, regulating authorial rights and intellectual property, broadened the term and opened the legal way to a concept of auteur cinema. But it still seems to give priority to the written sign. Article 14 states that 'the following shall have the status of author of a cinematographic work: the author of the scenario, the author of the adaptation, the author of the spoken text, the author of the musical compositions, the director'. It is perhaps small wonder that the New Wave reacted against the inflation of the role of the scriptwriter in the name of image and sound. Christian Salé has described the 1960s as 'the crossing of the desert' for scriptwriters, and remarked that even in the late 1970s a student at IDHEC might be taught every other cinematic profession by practitioners and experts, but not scriptwriting: 'The scenario? I had never met even the ghost of a scriptwriter or a script. Our films were made from an idea, a decision, a few typed pages' (Salé 1981: 6). Even if this was not quite the norm in the established professional echelons of the cinema, there was, in the aftermath of the New Wave, an increasing sense that the scenario was not an autonomous part of the film. Preferably, a director should be capable of writing his or her own script, and at the very least a professional scriptwriter was not expected to dictate to the director regarding the image, as had happened in the bad old days of the 'cinema of quality'.

But inevitably there was a reaction later in the period, starting in the 1980s and reaching a climax in the 1990s. Thus in 1991 *CinémAction* published a special issue on the status of the scriptwriter, which reveals how much, by the beginning of the 1990s, scriptwriting had become the focus of the crisis that the French cinema was experiencing with respect to its American competitor. The sense of inferiority is such that the whole legacy of the New Wave is called into question: 'We must consider the problem of the New Wave which destroyed the process of identification and all the techniques of classical narration. The taste for telling stories seems to have disappeared' (*CinémAction* 1991: 13). A few years later,

the celebrated actress of the New Wave, Jeanne Moreau, as head of the committee allocating the 'advance on receipts', lamented again the lack of scriptwriting ability in France, famously proclaiming that 'if carpenters made chairs in the way that screenwriters produce scripts, we would all be sitting on the floor' (Finney 1996: 16). A scriptwriting panic took hold of the French cinema of the 1990s. A host of practical guides to scriptwriting suddenly appeared in specialist bookshops, as well as *Synopsis*, a film magazine devoted entirely to the topic. Seminars on scriptwriting were established – one of the most high-profile examples being founded by Moreau herself – and courses were instituted, while the statements from within the industry seemed sometimes to imply that scriptwriting had been non-existent in the French cinema from 1960 until the mid-1980s, and that the source of salvation lay wholly in the encouragement of better screenwriting habits. In reality, the situation is much less clear-cut. What does seem true is that the French cinema post-New Wave – and to some extent also before it – has maintained a hysterical relation with the concept of the screenwriter, where the role is imagined to be everything or nothing, and its real contradictions are ignored. In fact, scriptwriters continued to exist and to find employment throughout the heyday of the New Wave and even the more dogmatic 1970s, while the difficulties of the position, although real enough and exacerbated by the wild oscillations in its status, were probably comparable to those that obtained in other national film industries.

The problem facing the scriptwriter, in fact, seems to be the transitional position that he or she inevitably occupies. Working with words on paper to circumscribe the imagination, the process has something in common with the work of the novelist, and several prominent writers, and a great many others of lesser reputation, have produced scripts at some time or other. On the other hand, the scenario of a film is never likely to be more than a recipe for a film to come, and the New Wave's theoretical insistence on the visual could not but impress indelibly on the minds of potential scriptwriters the secondary role of literary and dramatic techniques. Caught between two art forms that both hold out the prospect of real authorship, it hardly seems surprising that scriptwriters who show complete commitment to the function are rarer than in the other major creative roles of the cinema. An exploration of the most prominent French scriptwriters of the last forty years reveals how large a proportion either came from a literary background and remained primarily active as writers (Marguerite Duras, Jean Cayrol, even Jorge Semprun, one of the most prolific scriptwriters of the 1970s), or moved from scriptwriting to directing as soon as resources and confidence permitted. Some did both, such as Duras, using the experience of scriptwriting as a bridge from one kind of authorship to another. These patterns are by no means unique to France, and in all probability they are both inevitable and relatively healthy. On the other hand it is true that the particularly high profile given to Jean-Luc Godard's and Jacques Rivette's improvisatory script habits led to a New Wave myth, the idea that a film could, in normal circumstances, be elaborated from a few sketchy typewritten pages. This was an idea that naturally appealed to newly trained film students, especially since training in scriptwriting was not provided at IDHEC. The mounting panic in the industry at the end of the 1980s seems to have arisen from a sense that the new generation of filmmakers – urgently necessary for the survival of the French cinema – was taking the line of least resistance regarding forward planning. But the panic was also due to the increasing pressure of globalisation in the film industry. When the mechanisms of film funding are working on an international scale, the power of personal contacts and personal confidence necessarily diminishes, and the need for ideas to be thoroughly worked out on paper for the satisfaction of decision-makers who cannot be expected to trust their originators becomes paramount.

A crisis in screenwriting probably did exist in the French cinema in the 1980s. However, the way in which it has been presented by the industry has involved some rewriting of history. Jean-Claude Carrière commented on the scenarios of the classic Tati films (which he read in the 1950s): 'If the advance on receipts had existed at the time, Tati's scenarios wouldn't have had a chance. Nobody would have got it anyway, the scenarios were all unreadable' (Salé 1981: 53). This contradicts the rather vague golden age of the French scenario evoked by Olivier Gassot, one of the most import-

ant producers in France, in a television interview: 'French cinema has never been as good as when there was a producer, a director and scriptwriters. So we're trying to recreate this deadly trio in order to increase our share of the market' (*Absolument cinéma* 2001). It is not at all clear when this idyllic system is supposed to have been in perfect working order, but the New Wave did not sign the death-warrant of the scripted film, despite its rhetoric. Some directors – notably Alain Resnais – made a point of their refusal to write their own scripts; indeed Resnais offered almost equal auteur status to the writers he worked with, who usually had considerable literary reputations. Others, including the *Cahiers du cinéma* team themselves, collaborated with each other on scripts, and that pattern has never disappeared, particularly in small-scale French production where personal contacts still count for a great deal. Several *Cahiers du cinéma* critics of the subsequent generation experimented with screenwriting, and Pascal Bonitzer, for example, has become one of the most consistent professionals working at what might be called the intellectual end of the market. Some directors were quite genuinely able to write convincing scenarios and needed no support. The New Wave directors did for the most part use scriptwriters – although certainly collaborating on the writing themselves. In 1991, Valérie Villeglé compiled for *CinémAction* a list of 1,200 active scriptwriters in France, many with long filmographies to their credit: a reference to this list should be sufficient to prove that scriptwriters were far from unemployed in the 1960s and 1970s.

However, even if the scriptwriting function persisted, its status declined with the New Wave, and its attractiveness to potential recruits suffered. The active scriptwriters of the 1970s and 1980s, even those who chose the profession and considered it as their primary activity, express a certain frustration. The *CinémAction* dossier provides a few examples. Jacques Audiard, at this stage in his career a young scriptwriter who considers himself a specialist in this field and is pleased to note that he can earn a comfortable living from it, nonetheless declared: 'It's a question of lack of consideration on the part of the directors and producers. That's why I understand the bitterness of the scriptwriters' (*CinémAction* 1991: 149). It was not long before Audiard's interests would turn to directing. Simon Michael commented: 'When the American scriptwriters went on strike, the French said they could go on strike for ten years and nobody would notice!' (*CinémAction* 1991: 165). Luc Béraud felt that the lack of respect was reflected also in the payment available: 'Contrary to what people believe, in France there are plenty of scriptwriters but they don't get paid properly. Apart from five or six stars, it's a weekend job' (ibid.: 210). This complaint about money is not borne out by all his colleagues, but they do express a certain bitterness about a perceived lack of respect, underlining the ambiguous status of scriptwriters as authors who are not auteurs. However much they may enjoy collaborating on others' films, therefore, almost all the interviewees express a wish either to direct or to turn to novel-writing. It is noticeable too how many of these scriptwriters had close prior ties with the industry. Neither Danièle Thompson, daughter of Gérard Oury, Jacques Audiard, son of Michel, nor Bonitzer the established critic are idealistic newcomers and they are prepared to take a niche where they can find it. All three later became directors.

In the 1990s, discussion about the state of French cinema turned decisively in favour of screenwriting, if not perhaps the screenwriters themselves. It is a little unfortunate that the terms of this debate have often been dictated by the post-GATT pursuit of competitive advantage over the American industry. Direct comparison between the French and the American approaches to the scenario has led to a tendency to import the American model, given the aforementioned perception of French inferiority. This is also true in relation to training, for example in the renowned workshops sponsored by Jeanne Moreau under the name of Equinoxe. The principle of the Equinoxe workshops is that young scriptwriters with a project are given the chance to meet more experienced international colleagues in order to polish the project over a week. This is sponsored by a Franco-American foundation, and while it is not always the case that the consultants are American and the consulters European, in the case of contrasting national approaches the recent terms of the debate seem to have ensured that the French position is placed at a disadvantage. This is notably the case with regard to the French

'individual' versus the American 'team'. A French participant in a television debate on this subject in 2001 stated: 'I think there's something a bit perverse about the idea that adding contributors to a scenario necessarily makes it better'; while on the same programme a representative of an American production company spoke unequivocally in favour of teamwork, even presenting it as necessary (*Absolument cinéma* 2001). Ten years earlier, Jacques Fieschi had identified in this 'team' system one reason why the American scriptwriter was less likely to consider him or herself as a frustrated director (*CinémAction* 1991: 235). Teamwork would seem to be the very antithesis of the auteur system, and the enthusiasm for it needs to be seen in the context of a general re-evaluation of the screenwriter's role. However, judging from the results that have sprung from the Equinoxe workshops and the system still at work in the French cinema, there seems no great hurry to put such teamwork into place. The most likely outcome of the current revalorisation of the scenario would seem to be the adoption of a somewhat more professional and structured approach to the issue by new film students, who will still, eventually, want to move on from writing scripts to direction.

THE PROFESSIONAL SCRIPTWRITER: JEAN-CLAUDE CARRIÈRE

In 2003, the list of films for which the Internet Movie Database credits Jean-Claude Carrière as scriptwriter (including television work) contained some 106 titles. Best known as Buñuel's French collaborator, Carrière's other credits reveal him as a force behind the development of a resurgent 'tradition of quality' throughout the 1970s and 1980s, including a number of landmark films, highly successful in France and abroad, that extracted maximum value from his ability to construct a tight and inventive script. Much of his work has involved adaptation, from Patrice Chéreau's *La Chair de l'orchidée* (1974), based on James Hadley Chase, to *Le Hussard sur le toit* (1995), based on Jean Giono, with along the way ventures into such apparently cinematically resistant texts as Rostand's *Cyrano de Bergerac* (Jean-Paul Rappeneau, 1990) and even Proust's *Un Amour de Swann* (Volker Schlöndorff, 1984). He has worked with some of the most highly reputed auteur-directors of the second half of the century. Apart from Buñuel, the list includes Louis Malle's *Viva Maria!* (1965) and *Milou en mai* (1989), Godard's *Sauve qui peut (la vie)* (1980), Andrzej Wajda's *Danton* (1982) and Nagisa Oshima's *Max, mon amour* (1986). His scriptwriting career has included non-French-language films, notable examples being Schlöndorff's adaptation of Günter Grass, *The Tin Drum* (1979) and Hector Babenco's *At Play in the Fields of the Lord* (1991). At the same time his name has become indissolubly linked with the theatre of Peter Brook, with whom his collaboration has been as close as with any film director. In addition to film scripts, he has had a consistent, if discreet, career as a writer, in the course of which, apart from his own novels and plays, he extended his collaboration with Buñuel by giving final form to the director's recollections in the famous autobiography, *My Last Breath* (1982).

Carrière's connection with film began when, at the age of twenty-five, he won a competition that, paradoxically, required him to draw a literary text from a pre-existing filmic one, Jacques Tati's *Les Vacances de M. Hulot* (1953). As a result, he met Tati, 'my first master' as he calls him in his interview with *CinémAction* in 1991, and worked with him on the translation from film to paper of *Les Vacances de M. Hulot* and then *Mon oncle* (1958). It was Tati who introduced the young writer to Buñuel, Peter Brook and Pierre Étaix, for whom he wrote his first scenario. These meetings marked a decisive turn in Carrière's career: in the late 1950s he had published a number of thrillers under the pseudonym of Benoît Becker, but from 1962 onward the increasing demands of screen and theatre writing progressively eclipsed all other literary production until the 1990s.

The conversion to cinema was not simply a matter of experimenting with another form of writing. Tati's welcome to his new collaborator, in fact, took the form of an intensive course in filmmaking, about which the young Carrière – although strongly cinephile from a spectator's point of view – knew almost nothing. He had not been engaged to write scripts for Tati, but the ten-day apprenticeship in film technique formed an approach to scriptwriting that never allows itself to forget that the destiny of a film script is not literary. Carrière's interviews

and descriptions of his art give the highest priority to the visual: 'Working with Jacques Tati taught me to look at the world differently,' he told the website of *Le Routard magazine* in 2001. 'Sitting down, watching people, but watching them in a certain way, imagining that a detail of their clothing or their behaviour might later become part of a scene' (*Le Routard magazine* 2001). This desire for observation has led him on several occasions to go location-seeking in the close company of the director, for example in Mexico for *Viva Maria!*, or in Amazonia for *At Play in the Fields of the Lord*. He has said that he would be unable to write about such places without seeing and experiencing them first hand. He also works with actors prior to shooting, and, if he claims to avoid being present during the actual shoot, he also observes the editing process 'as often as possible because that's where you rediscover the scenario' (*CinémAction* 1991: 132). Such active participation in the film's creation is not universal among scriptwriters, but Carrière clearly conceives the script as an organic part of the whole film, neither a negligible shackle on the director's creativity – as the stereotype of the New Wave would have it – nor an autonomous entity: 'There has to be a very subtle and lasting marriage between a script and a film, one is like the caterpillar that gives birth to the butterfly' (*CinémaAction* 1991: 131). Or, more trenchantly: 'I fail to see how you can dissociate a screenplay from a film, and appreciate them separately' (Carrière 1995: 147).

His dedication to the art of film, and the thought he has given to its visual and technical elements, leaves one a little surprised that he has not been tempted to move into directing as so many scriptwriters have done. He would seem to be highly qualified for it – his identification with the film world, and his profile in it, was indeed so high that in 1984 he was appointed to the presidency of the FEMIS film school, and remained at its head until the mid-1990s. And yet he has only directed one film in his career, a short called *La Pince à ongles* (1969), in collaboration with Milos Forman. Nor do his interviews and writings suggest that he has ever been strongly drawn to directing. The possible frustration inherent in the screenwriter's position is something that Carrière accepts easily: 'A screenwriter has to make do. He must accept the fact that the public gives the director credit for ideas and intentions that are often his own. Basically, as we know full well, it is all just a matter of vanity' (Carrière 1995: 177). The motivating force of his work, he has said, is the desire to tell stories, 'the desire to share with people a story that I love' (*CinémAction* 1991: 132). 'The art of telling stories', this was the sub-title that René Prédal gave his book-length study of Carrière, surely a unique example of a monograph devoted to a scriptwriter in Europe (Prédal 1994). Through telling stories, in a medium he defines as intrinsically disposable, Carrière has achieved a uniquely distinguished position in the world of French cinema.

In conclusion, we can say that while the 1960s and 1970s marked a period in which the director was perceived as all-powerful in the creative process around a film, from the 1980s onward the contributions of other major collaborators have increasingly been rehabilitated and their functions studied. The intense debates around the state of the film industry have served to raise the perceived importance of producers – able to dictate, up to a point, the pattern of national film output – and of screenwriters. Increased status and critical attention for non-directorial positions has to some extent increased their attraction for a new generation. This is certainly true of screenwriting, in which a wide variety of training is now available. A new generation of cinematographers is likely to find a much less closed profession than hitherto, although the unpredictable effects of digital techniques will undoubtedly change the nature of their craft. While there remains a consensus in all parts of the French industry that the director, although neither omniscient nor omnipotent, really does have a privileged role in the construction of a film, a role that neither producers, cinematographers nor screenwriters seem inclined seriously to contest, the names of the most influential players in all these fields are, to an ever greater extent, becoming known to the general public and recognised as personalities in the cultural profile of French cinema.

WORKS CITED

Absolument cinéma (2001) La Cinq, transmitted 15 April 2001.

Almendros, N. (1984) *A Man with a Camera*, London, Faber and Faber.

Cahiers du cinéma (1981) special issue: 'Spécial situation du cinéma français 2', 325.

Cahiers du cinéma (1983) 'Entretien avec Sacha Vierny', 345.

Cahiers du cinéma (1987) special issue: French film production, 395–6.

Carrière, J.-C. (1995) *The Secret Language of Film*, London, Faber and Faber.

CinémAction (1990) special issue: 'Les Métiers du cinéma, de la télévision et de l'audiovisuel', Paris, Corlet-Télérama.

CinémAction (1991) special issue: 'Les Scénaristes français', Paris, Corlet-Télérama.

CSC (2000) 'Interview with Agnès Godard by Zoe Dirse', Canadian Society of Cinematographers website <www.csc.ca>, September 2000.

Finney, A. (1996) *The State of European Cinema*, London, Cassell.

Flot, Y. (1986) *Les Producteurs: les risques d'un métier*, Geneva, Hatier/5 Continents.

Forbes, J. (1992) *The Cinema in France after the New Wave*, London, Macmillan/BFI.

Godard, J.-L. (1972) 'Interview with Jean-Luc Godard', in *Godard on Godard*, London: Secker and Warburg, 171–96.

Lemarié, Y. (2000) 'A propos d'Agnès Godard et de quelques autres', *Positif*, 471, May, 128–30.

Positif (2000) 'Agnès Godard: regarder jusqu'à vouloir toucher', *Positif*, 471, May, 131–6.

Prédal, R. (1994) *Jean-Claude Carrière, scénariste. L'Art de raconter des histoires*, Paris, Cerf.

Les Rendez-vous de l'entreprise (1998) Interview with Marin Karmitz, TF1, transmitted 16 May 1998.

Le Routard magazine (2001) 'Le Monde selon Jean-Claude Carrière', <www.routard.com/mag>.

Salé, C. (1981) *Les Scénaristes au travail*, Geneva, Hatier/5 Continents.

Truffaut, F. (1999) 'Entretien avec les *Cahiers du cinéma*', in *La Nouvelle Vague*, Paris, *Cahiers du cinéma*, 153–92.

24 Images (1992) 'Mémoires d'aveugle: entretien avec Caroline Champetier', 61, Summer, 28–31.

16 BUSINESS 1960–2004
A Certain Idea of the Film Industry

Laurent Creton and Anne Jäckel

The relatively healthy state of contemporary French cinema is often attributed solely to protectionism. It is true that French cinema owes its survival, both as a going concern and a cultural force in the modern world, to a strong regulatory framework with a well-established support system covering the production, distribution and exhibition sectors. It also enjoys a financing model based on collaboration between cinema and television, and on diverse forms of international co-operation. However, France's regulatory and financing systems cannot wholly explain its healthy film business. This chapter will argue that other factors must be taken into account, such as the exceptional status that cinema holds in French culture; the continued vitality of older players in the market; the development of innovative business strategies; and the emergence of new major and independent players.

Historically, the privileged situation of French production in the film world can be traced back to three steps taken in the immediate post-war years. First, the creation of the Centre National de la Cinématographie (CNC), the institution responsible, under the aegis of the Ministry of Culture, for the collection and allocation of the monies of the *fonds de soutien*, the cinema support fund; second, the introduction of quotas to protect French cinema from the invasion of Hollywood films after the lifting of the bans on foreign films during the Occupation; and third, the establishment of selective and automatic aid mechanisms in the 1950s. Other forms of support to all sectors of the industry followed, and these were regularly amended according to the changing economic and social situation of the country. Certainly the business of cinema as a whole has experienced highs and lows during the period under consideration. With the emergence of a new consumer society enjoying more forms of leisure,

the number of admissions fell sharply from the late 1950s onwards. From over 371 million in 1958, it dropped to 182 million in 1969 and 116 million, a record low, in 1992. However, the advent of multiplexes in 1993 has largely contributed to a rise in admissions since then (from 133 million in 1993 to 185 million in 2001). Another long-standing concern has been the declining market share of French films compared to American movies, as shown in Tables 4 and 5 ('Market Share of Films in Distribution in France According to Nationality'). However, in spite of these two broadly negative trends, the figures for French film production have remained fairly stable, as we can see in Tables 6 and 7 ('French Film Production'). This relative stability in the number of films produced, as well as in the number of screens available (4,857 in 2,901 theatres in 1983, 5,103 in 2,164 in 2000), is only partly due to government intervention.

Along with the existence of a remarkable regulatory system, the good health of French cinema over the last decades owes much to more broadly cultural factors. Among these we could mention a well-established film culture sustained by an intellectual and artistic tradition and witnessed in the vitality of public debates about cinema; the existence of creative and artistic talent; the emergence of entrepreneurs who are encouraged to take risks; an industry made up of a myriad of companies that have been able to maintain a certain level of activity; a passion and an involvement from all sectors of the industry as well as from the general public, the media and politicians. All this has contributed to give cinema a special status in France. It also explains how 'a certain idea of cinema' has developed in which 'the profitability of the sector has remained secondary' (Frodon 1995: 141). But does this all amount to a system of

Table 4 Market Share of Films in Distribution in France According to Nationality (1960–80)

Year	French Films	American Films	Italian Films	British Films	German Films	Others
1960	51.21	28.46	4.36	5.5	5.28	5.19
1961	51.18	27.57	6.17	4.48	4.67	5.93
1962	50.9	29.56	6	3.05	3.42	7.07
1963	48.77	30.69	7.18	3.81	2.36	7.19
1964	48.8	30.4	7.25	5.78	1.88	5.89
1965	52.23	26.97	5.97	7.76	1.47	5.3
1966	50.96	28.07	6.41	7.74	1.64	5.18
1967	52.13	27.53	6.69	6.47	1.18	6
1968	49.98	26.23	8.74	6.08	2.81	6.16
1969	46.33	26.11	11.59	7.54	2.36	6.07
1970	49.03	25.98	12.03	5.53	2.36	5.07
1971	52.99	24.79	8.83	5.49	2.86	5.04
1972	53.51	24.32	8.77	5.04	3.29	5.06
1973	58.32	19.72	7.73	4.135	3.14	6.955
1974	53.87	21.28	6.87	4.09	2.87	11.02
1975	50.64	26.94	4.86	4.04	2.82	10.7
1976	51.12	27.71	5.52	5.33	1.65	8.67
1977	46.53	30.38	8.56	6.25	1.34	6.94
1978	46.02	32.55	8.58	4.23	1.38	7.25
1979	50.11	29.32	6.34	5.08	1.66	7.47
1980	46.9	35.21	5.11	3.99	1.8	6.93

Source: CNC

cultural as well economic protectionism? Describing the French system, Martine Danan has made such a claim:

in France the encouragement to both national mass culture through automatic subsidies, and to high culture through selective aid schemes should not be viewed as a contradiction but rather as the necessary means to maintain the vitality of the closed national system. (Danan 1996: 75)

While this description rightly emphasises the centrality of automatic and selective aids to the health of French cinema, its evocation of a subsidy-reliant 'closed national system' is less accurate. First, the French government is not a financier but an initiator, a regulator and a moderator (Jeancolas 1993). As

industry professionals are eager to point out, film-financing in France does not come directly from the public purse. It is drawn from the wider national regulatory framework, for example the redistribution of a tax on cinema tickets and the requirement introduced by the French government in the 1960s for broadcasters to undertake a financing programme for film. Second, the French system may well be 'national', but it is certainly not closed. Paris is probably the most openly cinephile capital in the world and France has a long tradition of welcoming foreign film-makers and of collaborating with foreign partners through co-production agreements and co-financing arrangements. Culturally and economically, the evolution of cinema in France both as an art form and an industry has always been open to international influences and developments.

Table 5 Market Share of Films in Distribution According to Nationality (1981–2001)

Year	French Films	European (non-French) Films	American Films	Films from Other Countries
1981	49.5		30.8	19.7*
1982	53.8		30	16.2*
1983	46.7		35	18.3*
1984	49.4	10.5	36.9	3.2
1985	44.5	11.3	39.2	4.9
1986	43.7	10.2	43.3	2.8
1987	36.2	11.2	43.7	9.0
1988	39.1	10.3	45.7	4.8
1989	34.2	7.2	55.5	3.1
1990	37.5	5.7	55.9	0.9
1991	30.6	10.0	58.0	1.4
1992	35.0	4.7	58.2	2.2
1993	35.1	4.4	57.1	3.4
1994	28.3	8.7	60.9	2.0
1995	35.2	8.4	53.9	2.4
1996	37.5	6.2	54.3	2.0
1997	34.5	10.0	52.2	3.3
1998	27.6	7.6	63.3	1.6
1999	32.4	11.1	53.9	2.6
2000	28.5	6.0	62.9	2.6
2001**	41		49	10*

Source: CNC
* Data include European (non-French) films
** Estimates

THE FRENCH REGULATORY FRAMEWORK

It is through a comprehensive and regularly amended regulatory framework that France has succeeded in sustaining a relatively strong film industry and film culture, enabling new talent and new entrepreneurs to emerge over the years. Introduced before the 1960s, the automatic and selective aid mechanisms may no longer represent a major source of revenue for the cinema support fund, but they remain a key element of the system. Most films are now financed from a variety of sources, but those with some form of funding already in place stand a better chance of attracting further investment. Yet the role of automatic and selective aids is still far from negligible. After the record-breaking success of Ridley Scott's *Titanic* in 1998, the French econ-omist Éric Dubet estimated that five or six French films could have been made with the tax raised on the box-office results of the American blockbuster alone (Dubet 2000: 128). Particularly significant is the selective aid known as *avance sur recettes* (advance on receipts), which only goes to projects that arguably could not be financed without public funding: first and second films and works with 'cultural ambitions' (*art et essai*, auteur films). Projects are assessed by committees and the 'advance on receipts' takes various forms corresponding to the different stages in the production of a film. In theory, the loan is repayable but, in practice, only around 10 per cent of films are successful enough at the box office to repay the loan (for an illustration of the system in the 1960s and 1970s, see Wilson 1978–9). After regulatory measures were introduced

Table 6 French Film Production (1960–91)

Year	French Films Agreed	French-initiated Films	Totally French Films	Majority French Co-prod.	Minority French Co-prod.	Total Co-prod.
1960	158	119	79	40	39	79
1961	178	108	69	39	70	109
1962	150	82	45	37	68	105
1963	161	87	37	50	74	124
1964	161	95	45	50	66	116
1965	151	90	34	56	61	117
1966	130	95	45	50	35	85
1967	120	87	47	40	33	73
1968	117	92	49	43	25	68
1969	154	119	70	49	35	84
1970	138	110	66	44	28	72
1971	127	102	67	35	25	60

Source: CNC

Table 7 French Film Production (1972–2000) Showing First Films

	French Films Agreed	French-initiated Films	Totally French Films	Majority French Co-prod.	Minority French Co-prod.	Total Co-prod.	ECO* Films	First Films ()**
1972	169	120	71	49	49	98		32
1973	200	153	97	56	47	103		33
1974	234	182	137	45	52	97		38
1975	222	197	160	37	25	62		37
1976	214	190	170	20	24	44		41
1977	222	209	190	19	13	32		43
1978	160	135	116	19	25	44		47
1979	174	152	126	26	22	48		33
1980	189	160	144	16	29	45		37
1981	231	208	186	22	23	45		36
1982	164	149	134	15	15	30		26 (11)
1983	131	118	101	17	13	30		31 (17)
1984	161	136	120	16	25	41		34 (21)
1985	151	131	106	25	20	45		23
1986	134	112	97	15	22	37		32 (12)
1987	133	113	96	17	20	37		29 (13)
1988	137	115	93	22	22	44		26 (11)
1989	136	101	66	35	35	70		27 (13)
1990	143/146	106	81	25	37	62	3	26 (12)
1991	144/156	108	73	35	36	71	12	34 (16)
1992	144/155	113	72	41	31	72	11	39 (19)
1993	137/152	101	67	34	36	70	15	39 (21)
1994	111/115	89	61	28	22	50	4	22 (11)
1995	129/141	97	63	34	32	66	12	33 (19)
1996	131/134	104	74	30	27	57	3	37 (13)
1997	158/163	125	86	39	33	72	5	46 (14)
1998	180/183	148	102	46	32	78	3	58 (21)
1999	181	150	115	35	31	66		62 (21)
2000	171	145	111	34	26	60		53 (19)
2001***	204	171	124	47	33	80		56

Source: CNC (NB: Between 1974 and 1982, figures are inflated by a large number of pornographic films.)

* Films made with the support of the Fund for co-productions with Central and Eastern Europe countries.

** Of which films beneficiary of the 'advance on receipts' aid.

*** CNC Estimates.

to direct television financing into films, the French government played a lesser role in cinema in the late 1960s and 1970s. By contrast, during the following decade, the Socialist government of François Mitterrand was at the forefront of initiatives for fostering credit and investment in all sectors of the audiovisual industries. They include the Institut pour le Financement du Cinéma et des Industries Culturelles (IFCIC) and the Sociétés de Financement de l'Industrie Cinématographique et Audiovisuelle (SOFICAs). The former was created in 1983 to provide, by means of a guarantee fund with mixed capital, a wide range of financial measures including a venture capital fund for start-up and development capital in films and film companies and a completion guarantee for co-productions. The latter, a tax shelter scheme designed to introduce private funds into film and television production, was introduced in 1985. The SOFICAs have a highly regulated status. They can only finance productions that have received CNC approval or that are made by French producers, and they are obliged to invest a minimum of 35 per cent of funds raised in the independent sector. Critics of the system, however, say that SOFICAs take few risks with projects and prefer to invest in large-budget productions with well-known stars, because they are private funds whose aim is to create a profit for their shareholders.

In absolute terms, investments in film production greatly increased during the 1980s and 90s. After a rise of over 220 between 1981 and 1991, they have doubled between 1991 and 2000. However, sources of financing have changed. In 1981, for example, contributions raised from theatrical exhibition, via the Taxe Spéciale Additionnelle (TSA), covered three-quarters of the French share of production costs, whereas ten years later they had fallen below 20 per cent. It is television broadcasters who have become the most important source of film financing, their contributions representing over 40 per cent of total investments in French film production (see Table 8, 'Financing of French-Initiated Films'). They are encouraged to invest at an early stage as co-producer status allows them to show films earlier. Since 1990, the law requires that five terrestrial television channels (TF1, France 2, France 3, M6 and La SEPT/Arte) must invest at least 3 per cent of their turnover in film production. In order to ensure the independence of producers from broadcasters, the channels can only co-produce through a subsidiary dedicated to such activities, and their contribution cannot exceed 50 per cent of the film budget or of the French share of the budget. In 2000, for example, the French terrestrial channels invested 561 million francs in ninety-five French films. Since 1993, taxes have also been imposed on the distribution of films released on video and on blank videotapes, and these are fed into the cinema support fund. A separate feature-film investment law applies to the pay-TV channels Canal Plus and TPS (La Télévision par Satellite). Canal Plus invests around 20 per cent of its turnover in film acquisition. Its contribution to cinema rose from a mere 9 per cent in 1991 to 20.6 per cent in 1996 (20.5 per cent in 1999). In 2000, total investments in the 171 films produced or co-produced by French producers were estimated at 5.26 billion francs. Canal Plus invested 954.4 million francs in 115 of those films. Its rival TPS (in existence since 1997) invested 114 million francs in nineteen films. Since 1993, 60 per cent of the sums Canal Plus spends on acquiring rights is to be dedicated to European works (45 per cent of which goes to French-language films). In the last decade, Canal Plus has pre-bought 80 per cent of French-initiated films (70 per cent in 2000) and almost all films with a budget over 13 million francs. (Under a 'diversity clause', the broadcaster is obliged to dedicate 45 per cent of its investments in French production to films with a budget of less than 35 million francs.)

In France, all broadcasters invest in first feature films as well as large-budget pictures. The price paid by broadcasters for films varies between 500,000 francs and over 30 million francs. In the late 1990s, TF1, France 2 and Canal Plus were reported to pay between 3 and 4 million francs for the rights to one broadcast of recent French films with strong potential appeal (Creton 1997). Private broadcasters are more likely to co-produce films with a strong popular appeal, making substantial investments in the most expensive productions. In 1999, TF1 contributed 22 million francs to the 200 million franc budget of Gérard Depardieu's vehicle, *Vatel* (Roland Joffé, 2000), and in 2000, 33 million francs to the 113 million franc budget film, *Le*

Table 8 Financing of French-Initiated Films (1986–2000) (in percentages)

Year	French Producers	SOFICAs	Automatic Aid	Selective Aid	Television		Distributors France	Foreign Input
					Co-prod.	Pre-buy		
1986	42.2	4.8	6.5	5.2	4.6	7.1	18.8	8.8
1987	40.3	10.5	4.2	4.5	7.6	13.4	7.3	11.5
1988	39.7	8.9	7.6	4.1	4.7	14.5	5.6	14.2
1989	38.0	7.5	9.5	4.7	3.6	14.2	1.9	20.6
1990	42.4	6.7	7.6	5.4	3.9	15.9	2.8	15.3
1991	33.7	5.9	7.6	4.7	4.6	18.9	4.4	20.2
1992	36.5	6.1	5.8	4.6	5.4	24.7	5.4	11.5
1993	33.4	5.2	7.7	5.5	5.6	25.2	5.1	12.3
1994	29.3	5.3	7.5	6.7	6.5	27.4	5.0	12.3
1995	26.8	5.6	8.7	5.7	6.8	30.1	4.0	12.3
1996	24.3	4.8	8.3	4.9	7.7	34.3	5.5	10.2
1997	33.4	4.5	7.7	5.2	7.2	28.7	3.5	9.8
1998	27.9	4.3	7.8	4.4	7.0	31.5	6.8	10.3
1999	28.0	4.4	6.8	4.4	6.0	34.2	8.8	7.5
2000	31.9	5.7	6.6	3.6	9.0	31.2	5.5	6.5

Source: CNC

Prince du Pacifique (Alain Corneau, 2000). However, of the twenty-one films in which the private channel invested, ten were directed by first-time film-makers. French broadcasters also invest in other European countries' films and increasingly in English-language films. Special mention should be made of Arte, the cultural channel funded by the French and German governments at the initiative of President Mitterrand and Chancellor Kohl in 1990. Through its support for 'a cultural cinema' and its investments in European co-productions, Arte has acquired a well-established reputation as a of purveyor of quality film producing (Jäckel 1999).

Fostering a diverse production of films is only one of the aims of French film policy. With half the resources of the cinema support fund going to exhibition and distribution, it also aims at encouraging professionalism in all sectors of the business as well as modernising the exhibition sector. France operates various selective and automatic aids to film distribution and exhibition. The selective aid supports the smaller operators and helps to launch French and foreign films that involve a certain risk. Although France's automatic aid generally tends to

serve the distribution arms of the French conglomerates backing the more commercial films, the various selective aids are more generously accorded to independent companies. This reflects the CNC's wish to maintain a certain equilibrium between the small and medium-sized distribution and exhibition companies and the larger groups. It has also helped keep in business those companies more inclined to specialise in the distribution of films for the art-house cinemas. In areas of low-density population, cinemas are maintained by public authorities. The arrival of multiplexes in France was delayed until 1993 as local authorities can object to their construction on the outskirts of cities, on the grounds that this increases the ongoing economic deterioration of the city centres. French policy in this domain is 'both an economic and a social policy' (London Economics and BIPE Conseil 1994: 7).

CO-PRODUCTIONS AND EUROPEAN INITIATIVES
The widespread misconception that the French system is a 'closed national system' is unfortunately encouraged by the discourses of both politicians and

industry professionals. One only has to think of the speeches made by Jack Lang about the need to protect the national film industry and culture against American imperialism in the early 1980s or during the 1993 GATT negotiations. Yet France has one of the most comprehensive and sophisticated systems of collaboration with film-makers from all over the world. This includes special measures to help film-makers who find it difficult to make films in their own country, as well as co-financing arrangements and bilateral and multilateral co-production treaties. Mergers and alliances on a global scale may have altered the nature of the film business but films made through inter-governmental co-production agreements continue to represent a substantial percentage of French film production. France has co-production agreements with over forty countries on every continent. First set up in the late 1940s, bilateral treaties have traditionally required that each co-producer's financial participation be matched by an equivalent artistic and technical participation. Despite strict nationality criteria requirements, co-production agreements have been subject to many abuses (Gili and Tassone 1995; Jäckel 1996). Over the years, they have also been subjected to a number of amendments – sometimes due to the politics of the time but more often because of the strength of the French film lobby and/or changes in the wider international audiovisual environment. Occasionally, the CNC has intervened to ensure that co-producers abide by the rules. In 1995, for instance, considering the imbalance between French and British investments in co-productions made under the France–UK agreement, co-productions between the two countries were put on hold temporarily as the CNC insisted that the concept of 'reciprocity' be strictly applied. By contrast, under the terms of two special funds, Fonds Sud and Fonds ECO, reciprocity is not a requirement. Created in 1984 with funding from both the Ministry of Culture and the Ministry of Foreign Affairs, the Fonds Sud encourages co-productions made between France and countries in the African and South American continents, as well as with the former French colonies of South-east Asia. The now-defunct ECO Fund (Fonds d'aide aux coproductions avec les pays d'Europe Centrale et Orientale) was set up in 1990 in order to help the rapidly disappearing film industries of the countries in the former Eastern bloc. With an annual budget of around 10 million francs, it contributed to the making of sixty-five feature films between 1990 and 1997. Almost all were shot on location in the country of the director and in a language other than French. For many film-makers from the countries of Central and Eastern Europe, the Fund represented a precious source of financing at a critical time in the history of their film industry (Jäckel 1997).

As for the European Union, France has always hoped that its highly regulated model would be adopted more widely, and it was at the forefront of the various European (MEDIA, EUREKA) and pan-European (Eurimages) programmes. Eurimages, for example, is a French initiative that fosters the co-production and distribution of cinematographic works between European partners by grouping public funding from the member states. A proponent of a strong European cinema, France has always requested more money than the finally approved budgets of the MEDIA programmes, and the French position has often been challenged by those member states favouring a more liberal approach, particularly the UK. Although France's traditionally defensive stance may now be developing into a more aggressive and expansive strategy, its commitment to cultural diversity and pluralism continues to shape a significant number of MEDIA initiatives.

NEW CHALLENGES, NEW STRATEGIES

Along with the existence of a strong institutional framework and regular contacts and exchanges at industry level with other countries, the vitality of French cinema owes much to the balance between a handful of large and well-established players and a myriad of small and medium-sized dynamic companies, largely under independent ownership. In the past, France's few vertically integrated groups, Gaumont, Pathé and UGC, by investing heavily in both French film production and distribution, have played an important role in the promotion of French cinema. Since the 1980s, in order to remain competitive, the French conglomerates have forged closer links with broadcasters and financial institutions, and have made deals with foreign partners,

Christophe Gans's *Le Pacte des loups* was a domestic and international hit in 2001

including American companies. For example, GBVI is an alliance between Gaumont and Buena Vista (the American distributor of Disney, Touchstone and Hollywood Pictures), while France's UFD is the joint distribution venture between UGC and 20th Century-Fox. Through acquisitions, mergers and alliances, the larger French companies have now become global players. Canal Plus has been the most ambitious in the 1990s, moving into production and/or distribution in other European countries (both in the West and in the East) as well as in the USA. The importance of industrial policy issues in France is much greater than it would appear from official statements and positions on cultural and artistic causes. Given the construction of the European Union and the global orientation of the economy, regulations, quotas and other forms of protection can no longer guarantee the development of economic activities. Putting into practice the theses of American economist Robert Reich (1991), France has adopted a new policy encouraging French companies with global aspirations. In the late 1990s, French policy seemed to focus on providing the conditions for those large entities to retain their centre of gravity at home, for example the acceptance by the Conseil Supérieur de l'Audiovisuel (CSA) of the constitution of the Vivendi-Universal group in 1999. In the case of Canal Plus, it seemed particularly important, as it is largely on the model of public/private duopoly (CNC/Canal Plus) that French cinema has developed over the last fifteen years.

Faced with a relatively limited domestic market, the French are using a number of new strategies to improve their position in the international market. One of them is to encourage the production of films with strong export potential. While comedies, the most popular genre in the domestic market, on both large and small screens, continue to play an important part in sustaining the viability of the French film industry, they have not exported well in the past (Jeancolas 1989). The trend is now to make ambitious comedies that cross borders, such as the *Astérix et Obélix* films of 1999 and 2002. The French have also resumed the practice of making lucrative sequels, for example *Les Visiteurs 2* (Jean-Marie Poiré, 1998) and *La Vérité si je mens 2* (Thomas Gilou, 2001). Traditionally, two categories

of French films, auteur films and large-scale co-productions – so-called 'euro-puddings' – have found it easier to appeal to foreign distributors and audiences abroad. The former – best illustrated by Rohmer's work – are appreciated as 'typically French' by a small but reliable audience of cinephiles who attend art houses and film festivals. The grand co-production is best represented by historical films such as Régis Wargnier's *Indochine* (1992) and *Une Femme française* (1995) or Patrice Chéreau's *La Reine Margot* (1994). Films shot in English and directed by 'international' film-makers like Milos Forman's *Valmont* (1989), Roman Polanski's *Bitter Moon* (1992) and *The Ninth Gate* (1999), as well as Jean-Jacques Annaud's *The Bear* (1984), *The Name of the Rose* (1986) and *The Lover* (1991), can also be included in this category. As shown by the poor results of the English-language film of Philippe Rousselot, *The Serpent's Kiss* (1992), their box-office performance can sometimes be disappointing.

In response to the changing economic environment, CNC rules for accessing French sources of funding have changed (to accommodate English-language films, for example), and production and promotion budgets have soared in the last few years. French investments in French-initiated films rose from 2 billion francs in 1990 to 4.1 billion francs in 2000. A significant number of French films can now claim a budget worthy of Hollywood. While until 1987, only four French-initiated films a year had a production budget exceeding 50 million francs, ten years later, there were twenty-two such films. In 2001, eleven films had a budget over 100 million francs. In 1999, *Astérix et Obélix contre César* (Claude Zidi) was promoted as 'the most expensive film made in the French language'. Claiming a 270 million franc budget and boasting an international cast led by Gérard Depardieu and Roberto Benigni, the film is a French–German–Italian co-production. Its 2002 sequel, *Astérix et Obélix: mission Cléopatre* (Alain Chabat) had a 327 million franc budget. The record to date in France belongs to Luc Besson's English-language films *The Fifth Element* (1997) with 493.3 million francs and *Joan of Arc* (1999) with 360 million francs. In order to compete with Hollywood films made for a global audience, French cinema is also putting more emphasis on marketing. If, until the mid-1990s, an emphasis on the market, the consumer and profitability was anathema to many film professionals, and the application of marketing tools and techniques to cinema looked upon with suspicion in France (Creton 1994), this is no longer the case today. While it is true that massive releases and marketing deals with mass-product chains such as McDonald's restaurants continue to reinforce fears of 'American cultural hegemony' and arm the protectionist lobby in France, attitudes have changed. French distributors are now fully engaged in massive promotion deals, and policy-makers and film producers acknowledge the importance of marketing strategies. Investments in the promotion of films in France increased from 278.7 million francs in 1992 to 842 million francs in 1998, with the top five distribution companies (representing 75 per cent of admissions) spending 55 per cent of all monies invested in film promotion that year (Lafontaine 1998: 15).

Those who invest in large-budget films now leave little to chance, as the promotion of *Le Pacte des loups* (2001) illustrates. Released on 31 January 2001 on 725 prints, this gothic martial arts fantasy was launched as a film event. Its marketing campaign (trailers, Internet site, wide distribution of luxury brochures, publication of stills in film magazines, special radio and television programmes) had been in place months before its release. Shooting problems and the delay in releasing the 200 million franc film were integrated in the marketing strategy and merely contributed to the mystery surrounding the film. In spite of its length (140 minutes) and a 12-certificate, *Le Pacte des loups*, with almost two million admissions in its first week, claimed one of the best starts of the season. By the end of the year, it had reached over five million entries at home. The film was sold throughout the world and, with a little help from Unifrance, the organisation responsible for promoting French films abroad, also proved an international success.

The commercial success of films as diverse as *Le Pacte des loups*, *La Vérité si je mens 2* as well as *Taxi 2* (Gérard Krawczyk), *Le Placard* (Francis Veber), *Le Fabuleux destin d'Amélie Poulain* (Jean-Pierre Jeunet) and *Sous le sable* (François Ozon) certainly shows that the decline in the share of the French market is not irreversible. These films all contributed to a rise in the market share of French films to 41 per cent in 2001. But a different mentality is also required to survive in the contemporary capitalist economy. In response, the French are openly adopting offensive competitive strategies and creating new synergies. It is almost possible to talk about a new generation of professionals (directors, producers, distributors, exhibitors, technicians, special effects specialists, etc.), who recognise and integrate the important legacy of the New Wave, but refuse to be limited by it and are prepared to go beyond it to promote superior levels of economic performance. All sorts of partnerships are now flourishing: several independents have formed alliances with the larger players; others prefer to form joint ventures with like-minded people to achieve economies of scale. For instance, the 'Club des Cinq' was created in 2001 to obtain 'a special status for independent distributors'. It brings together five of the most important independent distribution companies – including Diaphana, Pyramide and Les Films du Losange. Yet, the demise of many independents remains a major concern. The development of French cinema has largely been conditioned by the existence of an interwoven system of independent production, distribution and exhibition companies. In the 1990s, the emergence of powerful entities in the wake of mergers and alliances, combined with the advent of multiplexes, has had major effects on the independent sector. Notwithstanding French legislation that requires the larger players, including broadcasters, to commission and distribute independent work, a significant number of small independent companies are struggling to remain in business. The situation is particularly critical in the distribution and exhibition sectors, as the major groups not only obtain the more commercial products and control the best locations but also get hold of the more promising art-house titles (e.g. the UGC Ciné-Cité in Paris). The mass-consumption ethos embraced by the larger operators is best reflected in the introduction of loyalty cards in the year 2000. First used by UGC, this practice was soon adopted by its competitors, including Marin Karmitz's 'independent' company, MK2. At the 2000 Cannes film festival, the Minister for Culture Catherine Tasca declared the distribution sector one of the most vulnerable in the film business – and promised to introduce new measures. Announced in 2001, one of these is related to the introduction of loyalty cards: should financial losses occur, the more powerful players will have to compensate the smaller operators; another requires broadcasters to invest an additional 0.2 per cent of their turnover in the theatrical distribution of European and French films.

Faced with a global market economy, French producers have a number of options. First, they can resist by developing France's traditional strengths, a specificity that has enabled French cinema to exist, to be recognised and appreciated by a small number of cinephiles worldwide, allowing it both to become an alternative model and to maintain a certain diversity in the world of film-making. Second, they can play the same game as the most powerful players in a global market, although they risk thereby losing part of French cinema's identity – the increasing role of marketing in the business of film is part of a concentration trend in which investors are privileged to the detriment of creators, which encourages standardisation and uniformity rather than diversity, not only in programming but also as far as audiences are concerned. Third, they can attempt to reconcile both strategies, using them together in the hope that they can combine creativity and diversity on the one hand and financial, industrial and commercial power on the other – this presupposes the retention of a strong regulatory framework that creates and guarantees the necessary conditions for the two models to coexist. Worldwide, the gap is widening between a single mega-economy and many micro-economies, between large and small players. Inflated promotion budgets (including an ever-increasing number of prints) along with more films in distribution (in France 350 feature films in 1995, 535 in 1999 and 607 in 2000) tend to widen the gap between successes and flops as well as between conglomerates and independents. An emerging two-tier system – the global-commercial vs. the individual-cultural – will always carry the danger of collapsing the aesthetic into the economic and commercial.

WHAT FUTURE FOR THE FRENCH MODEL?

Allen Scott concludes his study of contemporary French cinema by saying that 'the regulatory system which has maintained the French film industry so forcefully as it has as a bastion of alternative cinematic culture to Hollywood represents a service whose benefits resound well beyond the frontiers of France' (Scott 2000: 31). In the film business, success is relative and uncertain. It can always be questioned and must never be attributed to a single factor. The French model is neither perfect nor universal, but it still offers an alternative to the dominant model and, as we have seen, it has the capacity to change. Its survival will depend on its ability to combine a number of factors operating at different levels (economic, cultural, social, artistic, political, etc.) with the action of various players (majors, independents, private and public, mainstream and cultural television channels) in a coherent regulated environment in which all social forces can play a part and to which most political parties can commit. The challenge for the French regulatory system is to take account of current developments without losing its own characteristics, to develop in such a way that other countries in Europe and elsewhere can find in it a conceptual model and business practices that will also allow them to retain cultural and aesthetic values in the face of a concentrated industrial system. This entails acknowledgment of the market (in this case, an uncertain space where the supply economy and the tastes of audiences meet – often unpredictably), as well as acceptance of the need to be competitive in terms of new economic strategies. However, without rules and regulations, the market is subjected to concentration and exclusion trends that are contradictory to the development of a diverse and pluralistic cinema. As Pierre Chevalier, the head of fiction at Arte, has observed, financial and technological upheavals brought about by globalisation tend to force national institutions 'to play the role of observer and monitor, and therefore a regulatory role rather than one of incentive and action'. In response, he suggests that 'the institutional should perhaps become more political, less on the defensive, more assertive of the absolute prevalence of creation over the economy of the market, while soaking up the latter's energy and enthusiasm' (Garbaz 2001: 20).

In France, cinema still occupies an important place in the symbolic order of cultural values. But in the real world of business and finance, there is always the danger that this micro-sector of the economy – which relatively speaking is all that cinema represents – may disappear in the negotiation of international trade agreements. Jean-Michel Frodon argues that the survival of the French model 'depends on its ability to contaminate its various partners in Europe' (Frodon 1995: 815), but in many European countries cinema does not enjoy the same status nor provoke the same passion as it does in France. Consequently, the risk is high that a European consensus may produce a regulatory framework based on the lowest common denominator. The challenge today is, on the one hand, to avert a deregulatory trend that would merely subjugate creativity and diversity to financial interests and, on the other, to avoid a return to the excessive bureaucracy and protectionism of the past. What is required is an ambitious and demanding agenda able to guarantee the integrity of a diverse and plural cinema without falling into an unproductive and oppressive dualism between regulatory control and liberal innovation. In the contemporary environment, the sooner France can convince its European partners to adopt such an agenda, the better chance the French model stands of continuing to be, in Scott's words, a bastion of alternative cinematic culture and a service whose benefits resound well beyond the frontiers of France.

WORKS CITED

Creton, L. (1994) *Économie du cinéma, perspectives stratégiques*, Paris, Nathan.

Creton, L. (1997) *Cinéma et marché*, Paris, Armand Colin.

Danan, M. (1996) 'From a "Pre-national" to a "Post-national" French cinema', *Film History*, 8: 1, 72–84.

Dubet, É. (2000) *Économie du cinéma européen: de l'interventionnisme à l'action entrepreneuriale*, Paris, L'Harmattan.

Frodon, J.-M. (1995) *L'Âge moderne du cinéma français*, Paris, Flammarion.

Garbaz, P. (2001) 'What Future Is There for a Creative Industry?', *Label France*, 44, July, 20–1.

Gili, J. and Tassone, A. eds (1995) *Paris–Rome, cinquante ans de cinéma Franco-Italien*, Paris, Éditions de la Martinière.

Jäckel, A. (1996) 'European Co-Production Strategies: The Case of France and Britain', in Moran, A. ed., *Film Policy*, London, Routledge, 85–97.

Jäckel, A. (1997) 'Cultural Co-Operation in Europe: The Case of British and French Cinematographic Co-Productions with Central and Eastern Europe', *Media, Culture and Society*, 9: 1, 111–20.

Jäckel, A. (1999) 'British and French Broadcasters' Involvement in Cinematographic Co-Productions', in Scriven, M. and Lecomte, M. eds, *Television Broadcasting in Contemporary France and Britain*, London, Berghahn Books, 175–97.

Jeancolas, J.-P. (1989) 'Un cinéma inexportable?', unpublished conference paper, Popular European Cinema conference, Warwick University, 14–17 September.

Jeancolas, J.-P. (1993) 'Le Mode de production français en 1992: péril en la demeure', *Nottingham French Studies*, 32: 1, Spring, 1–9.

Lafontaine, T. (1998) '+18.2% pour les investissments publicitaires en 98', *Le Film français*, 2769, 16 March, 13–15.

London Economics and BIPE Conseil (1994) *White Book of the European Exhibition Industry*, vol. 2, Milan, MediaSalles.

Reich, R. (1991) *The Work of Nations: Preparing Ourselves for Twenty-First Century Capitalism*, New York, Simon and Schuster.

Scott, A. (2000) 'French Cinema, Economy, Policy, and Place in the Making of a Cultural-Products Industry', *Theory, Culture and Society*, 17: 1, 1–38.

Wilson, M. H. (1978–9) 'Défense et illustration du système français des avances sur recettes', *FilmÉchange*, 4, 64–71; and 5, 56–69.

17 TECHNOLOGY 1960–2004
From Images of the World to the World of Images

Laurent Jullier and Lucy Mazdon

Recent decades have witnessed a terminological shift in French and English: the term 'technique' has gradually been replaced by 'technology'. This apparently minor change reflects a much more significant social mutation: technique governs the production of goods in industrial societies where products circulate; technology – literally 'discourse on technique' – accompanies consumer societies where information circulates. At a local level, this substitution reflects the major changes in film technique in France in the period from 1960 to 2004, in particular the redirection of the focus of research and development from hardware to software. The French word for software, *logiciel*, is etymologically related to 'technology' via the Greek word *logos*, meaning both 'discourse' and 'logic'. Techniques for the mechanical and chemical recording of traces of the world have been progressively replaced by technologies for the arithmetic generation of images.

The design and use of film technology in France in the past four decades is best understood in relation to the enduring tradition of Bazinian realism. As Serge Daney noted, French cinephilia has accorded 'an almost metaphysical importance to the truth of the recording and the recording of the truth' (Daney 1988: 192–3). It is worth recalling in this context that the term 'profilmic' to describe objects whose imprints are recorded on exposed film stock – a notion with a distinctly Bazinian flavour – is French in origin and comes to us from the phenomenologists working at the École de Filmologie in 1949 (Souriau 1953). Roland Barthes summarised the Bazinian position succinctly: when we look at an image, we look with the irrefutable knowledge that what we see was present at the time of recording (Barthes 1980: 122). Since the 1950s, it is a view that has guided not only a succession of critics but a string of key inventors whose work is

central to this chapter: Albert Lamorisse, André Coutant, Jean-Pierre Beauviala, Jean-Marie Lavalou and Alain Masseron. The machines made by designers such as these all reflect Bazin's advice to film-makers: place yourselves at the service of the world, *render* rather than *signify*. But a new generation of designers working with digital technology has reversed the terms of Bazin's brief and sought to signify through the creative alignment of pixels rather than re-present the world as accurately as possible. This chapter examines how these two tendencies – 'images of the world' and 'the world of images' – have come to coexist in France.

THE CAMERA AS ORSTHESIS

A number of myths have taken hold regarding the New Wave, especially in relation to topics such as improvisation, direct sound and lightweight shooting material. The powerful Commission des Demandes d'Agrément (Committee for Requests for Approval) at the Centre National de la Cinématographie (CNC) would never have endorsed amateurish, improvised practices at the time of the New Wave. Technicians on these shoots were highly qualified card-carrying professionals, fully skilled in the operation of their machinery (Gimello-Mesplomb 2000: 158–61). Similarly, while 16mm has come to exemplify in film history many of the qualities associated with the movement – low weight, manoeuvrability, direct synchronised sound – the early New Wave features were all shot using the only legitimate format for professional fiction film-making at the time: 35mm. As Alain Bergala notes, following calls in the 1940s by the twin 'Uncle Jeans' of the New Wave, Rouch and Cocteau, for the use of 16mm on the grounds of its liberating flexibility – both explored the possibilities of the format in this period, in *Au pays des mages noirs*

(Jean Rouch, 1946) and *Coriolan* (Jean Cocteau, 1949) respectively – the New Wave film-makers were eager to cut their teeth on 16mm in their 1950s shorts (Bergala 1998: 36–8). But as Bergala goes on to show, a sensitivity to criticisms of amateurism and caution regarding potential marginalisation within the industry effectively meant they had to wait a full decade before the 35mm equipment began to approximate the proportions and weight of 16mm.

The inventor who rose to the challenge of developing lightweight machines capable of responding quickly and simply to the ephemeral present was Jean-Pierre Beauviala, an electronics lecturer at the University of Grenoble. Following a period as an advisory engineer at Éclair, where he was instrumental in developing the Éclair ACL 'single system' 16mm camera capable of recording sound on a magnetic strip on the film stock at the time of filming, Beauviala founded Aäton in 1967 (Frodon 1995: 323–6). Jean-Philippe Carson, the American agent for Éclair and a documentary film-maker linked to the Black Panthers, instigated the development of lightweight weather-resistant equipment easily operable by non-specialists. The aim of this so-called 'Cinéminima' project was the production of a robust 'agricultural camera' and 'bush projector'. Carson died in an accident in 1974, but Beauviala pursued work on two other cameras conceived as orsthetic extensions of the human hand: the 1973 Aäton 7A 16mm, known as the 'Cat on the Shoulder' (*Chat sur l'épaule*), followed by a miniature 10-ounce video camera – approximately the size of a microphone, and linked directly to a video monitor – dubbed the *Paluche*, an old French slang term meaning 'hand'. These cameras were not intended for use on tripods; on the contrary, they were designed to be held and handled, to register the movement and tremors of the human body, to produce 'Bonnardised' images, as Beauviala put it, through reference to the style of the Impressionist painter. In 1979, Jean-Luc Godard commissioned a compact 35mm camera from Beauviala, whose size was allegedly inspired by the interior dimensions of the glove compartment of his car. Godard wanted a lightweight camera that could be operated quickly, without technical assistance, to produce high-quality silent 35mm images. As Beauviala explained,

commercial production of a compact camera to these specifications proved economically unviable (Beauviala and Godard 1983). The commission resulted, however, in the Aäton 35-8 (the 8 refers to the small size and low weight of Super-8) – a prototype of which Godard used for *Sauve qui peut (la vie)* (1980) – and the slightly larger and heavier Aäton 35 that he used for the celebrated shots of the sky in *Passion* (1981).

The exploration of 16mm in France in the 1950s derived much of its impetus from professional ethnography, especially in the guise of the pioneering ethnographic film work of Jean Rouch. Gilles Marsolais dates the technological–aesthetic 'break' in French cinema not to the New Wave, but to the rapid growth in semi-professional 16mm film-making by ethnographic film-makers inspired and supported by the International Ethnographic and Sociological Film Committee at the Musée de l'Homme (Museum of Mankind) in Paris, a body established by Rouch and André Leroi-Gourhan in 1952 with the express aim of preserving, distributing and producing ethnographic films (Marsolais 1974: 212). Following this lead, and in step with parallel trends in Canada and the USA, many non-New Wave film-makers in France embraced 16mm in the early 1960s – a period that saw the proliferation of silenced lightweight hand-held 16mm synchronised sound cameras – as the most direct route to filming real people in real locations. Developed more or less simultaneously in the USA, it was the French deployment of the technology that was to have a profound impact on indigenous film-making. A key figure in these developments was André Coutant, who had already designed the groundbreaking 35mm Caméflex camera for the Éclair laboratory in 1948. The innovative shape of the Caméflex facilitated steady hand-held shooting and was famously used by cinematographer Raoul Coutard to shoot Godard's 1960 New Wave manifesto, *À bout de souffle*. The fresh visual look of this film was due in large part to Godard and Coutard's daring in stringing together 17.5-metre reels of Ilford HPS still camera film stock to make up motion-picture-length reels of film, which they then ran through the Caméflex (Coutard 1965–6). A very light (8lb) prototype of Coutant's design for a synchronised sound 16mm camera, the revolution-

AATON 35 mm & 16 mm

Ferco   Camera Mart   Victor Duncan
New York   New York   Dallas
San Francisco   Chicago Detroit

Aaton Cameras Inc.
1697 Broadway New York N.Y. 10019 (212) 541-8181

The exciting future developments of Aaton's innovations in 35 mm should not, however, overshadow its proven achievements in the 16 mm field. The Aaton LTR has now shown itself to be a reliable instrument, with over 400 sold in Europe in the last few years.

Below, Dedo Weigert, « shooting » a film on location in Java Indonesia, with camera number 54. One of the early cameras to come out of Aaton, Dedo also took it with him for extensive filming in the jungles of the Amazon; with up to 100 % humidity, and condensation dripping in the lens, he shot 60,000

feet without so much as a single scratch, or any other problem.

Neither the very low noise level of the LTR (average : 26 dB) nor its excellent image steadiness and sharpness are compromised to make it a rugged and reliable tool for work in expedition type settings. The Aaton LTR is at home in the icy chill of Lapland*; it has proven itself problem free in the muggy humidity of the African jungle (see A.C. Aug. '79). And in the torrid dust storms of the Iranian desert too, the Aaton 16 mm camera has been shown to be robust and

dependable (A.C. June '77). It is established as a camera that can brave the wilds with ease, and bring it all back on film.

The LTR magazine is simple to load : with gloves in cold climes, or with hot and sticky hands in the tropics. And the aperture gate can be checked and cleaned effortlessly with the magazine off the camera.

The Aaton LTR is now available in the U.S. Rapid maintenance and turn-around are ensured through Aaton's New York operation.

* Remember, when working in sub-zero temperatures, it is best to leave the camera in the cold at all times. And to keep it up in the cold as well.

Aaton 35 mm

Aaton makes J.-L. Godard a 35 mm camera. Ultimate steadiness.

111 ⁰
OCT 03 1979

Two years ago, the well known film director, J.-L. Godard, commissioned Aaton to make a 35 mm camera. He wanted to combine the advantages of the quantity of information contained in a 35 mm film image, and the ease of handling and unobtrusiveness of super 8 cameras. The first prototype has been in use since April 1979, and the results are more than encouraging.

The Aaton 8-35 is handheld, and has instant magazines; until now, the only 35 mm camera with instantmags has been the Cameflex (1946), which is extremely noisy.

The noise level of the 8-35 is 33 dB. Without any sound absorbing material, the prototype runs at 35 dB ; two decibels less is realistic with damping. 33 dB appears quite acceptable in light of the fact that a non-optimum self-blimped 16 mm camera can run in that area.

The steadiness is excellent ; it is ensured by the same claw movement system (U.S. patent 3806016) that has made a name for the Aaton 16 mm LTR. The pulldown of the strike is absolutely linear, with the dead point in the film plane. Willy Lubtchansky, J.-L. Godard's cameraman, contends that the 8-35's steadiness is comparable to that of a Mitchell. On double exposure tests, no visible sign of any movement whatsoever can be observed.

An original feature : a second electric motor in the camera body drives the

60 m and 120 m magazines through an independant drive clutch.

The 8-35 is small, and light; it weighs in at around 5 kg, with 60 m mag — slightly less than the Aaton LTR 16 mm camera.

This camera is meant to be a companion to the Panavision or Arri 35 BL : it is easy to handle, unobtrusive, mobile. For certain films, it may even be the only camera; with a soft blimp, the sound level could be made acceptable for indoor work.

The first pre-series of some twenty cameras will be launched early in 1980. Many well-known cameramen and directors have already spoken for theirs by putting down 50 % payment (in the order of $ 10,000 to 15,000); delivery will be early 1981.

'Aäton makes J.-L. Godard a 35mm camera. Ultimate steadiness.' (Aäton)

ary KMT Coutant-Mathot Éclair – originally developed with the support of Éclair's managing director, Jacques Mathot, for use in military satellites – was produced in 1960. With slight modifications, the KMT could be made to operate on batteries and pilot a Nagra tape recorder. According to filmmaker Mario Ruspoli, the combined weight of the camera, recorder, microphone and battery for this prototype 'Coutant-Mathot-Nagra' unit came to around 20lb and was easily handled by two people:

> For the first time, in France, sound and picture 'stroll along' arm in arm with the characters in motion. The light-weight KMT which Michel Brault manipulated unflaggingly with acrobatic skills 'lives' with the characters, 'sculpts' them as it circumambulates them, explores them and spies out their secrets with the steady gaze of a living person . . . The light-weight camera, continuously carried, becomes part of the cameraman's body, replacing his eyes by a sort of extra

organ which enables him to record everything he experiences and sees, to grasp and record reality. (Ruspoli 1964: 10, 14)

Early use of the KMT prototype by the director-cinematographer mentioned here by Ruspoli, the Canadian Michel Brault (who shot films for both Ruspoli and Rouch), revealed the camera to be still somewhat noisy and, due to poor weight distribution, difficult to handle over long periods of time. In an exemplary instance of the symbiosis in this period between inventors, practitioners and the development of new modes of film-making, it was a meeting in March 1963 between Coutant and Rouch, Ruspoli, Brault and Richard Leacock – four film-makers who were all to play a major role in the development of new forms of documentary cinema in France, Canada and the USA – that led to the refining of the prototype. Éclair, however, apparently considered the KMT too 'primitive' to compete with the new generation of 16mm cameras being manu-factured abroad (Ruspoli 1964: 19). As Barry Salt explains, the subsequent version of the camera produced by Coutant for Éclair, the Éclair 16 (Coutant-Mathot), commonly known outside France as the Éclair NPR (NPR standing for 'Noiseless Portable Reflex') – commercially available from 1963 and adopted widely throughout the industry thereafter – was significantly different in design to the prototype and, at 19lb, considerably heavier, although the added weight was more efficiently distributed (Salt 1992: 256). As Marsolais notes in his overview of the rapid changes in 16mm camera technology in this period, no fewer than four updates on the original Éclair KMT prototype were released, culminating in 1971 with the comparatively cheap and very lightweight (8.5lb) Éclair ACL (Marsolais 1974: 220–3).

In the summer of 1960, the KMT Coutant-Mathot Éclair prototype was used by Brault, Coutard, Roger Morillère and Jacques Tarbes to shoot one of the landmark films of the period: Jean Rouch and Edgar Morin's *Chronique d'un été* (released 1961), the first full-length film to be shot in synchronised sound in France using the emerging generation of lightweight equipment. Two years later, cinematographers Pierre Lhomme and Denis Clairval used it again (together with a 16mm Arriflex) to shoot Chris Marker's *Le Joli mai* (1963). While formally quite different from *Chronique d'un été* – Marker's use of a narrator to reflect on the images might be seen as an implicit criticism of Rouch and Morin's method – these two experiments in documentary form were cornerstones of the new style of film-making known as cinéma vérité. Documentary film practice was especially influenced by experiments in cinéma vérité in France and in direct cinema in Canada and the USA in the early 1960s. But as Ruspoli argued, following completion of his study of the poor peasants of the Lozère region, *Les Inconnus de la terre* (1961, shot by Brault and Morillère), the new technology had the potential to transform all cinema (Collomb and Patry 1995: 87). Cinéma vérité certainly had a profound impact on fiction film-making in France, including the New Wave, and it is important to view the development of the two movements as occurring in tandem and involving significant cross-

fertilisation. The impact of Rouch's experiments on the New Wave at both a technical and aesthetic level, especially on Godard, is inestimable. Whereas in 1958 French feature films were generally still shot on 35mm with sound added later in the studio, by the early 1960s a significant number were being shot on location in synchronised sound using 16mm or Super 16mm. Cinéma vérité may have remained an acquired taste, the domain of a relatively small group of cinephiles, but the innovation provoked by these films, coupled with the visual and narrative experimentation of the New Wave, was to have a profound and lasting impact on French cinema in its broadest sense.

SYNCHRONISED SOUND

Following Bazin, whose eulogies to the mimetic precision of neo-realism had conveniently overlooked the fact that the films were post-dubbed (sometimes with the voices of actors other than those depicted in the images), the early New Wave features were usually shot silent, or at least without synchronised sound. Although Truffaut used synchronised sound for a number of localised sequences in his early films, sound was generally only recorded by the New Wave directors in the late 1950s and early 1960s in the form of ambient sound on a guide track for use in post-production (Douchet 1998: 222–31; Marie 2003: 95–7). Throughout the shooting of one of the key films of the New Wave, *Adieu Philippine* (shot 1960, released 1963), Jacques

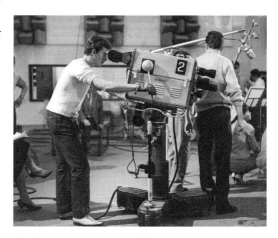

Representing television in Jacques Rozier's *Adieu Philippine* (1963)

Rozier went as far as to record dialogue and ambient sound himself without the aid of a sound technician on an unsynched tape recorder. Most of the dialogue proved inaudible, and to the exasperation of producer Georges de Beauregard, Rozier devoted the next five months to painstakingly reconstituting the actors' semi-improvised banter by lip-reading the rushes and, eventually, post-dubbing the film (Zand 1963: 33). Godard was the first to experiment systematically with synchronised sound, notably on *Une femme est une femme* (1961) and *Vivre sa vie* (1962). As Jean Collet recognised at the time of the release of *Vivre sa vie*, sound engineer Guy Villette's radical experiment in the live location recording of sound and voice on a single track throughout the shoot represented a milestone in the use of sound in cinema (Collet 1972). Others followed from the mid-1960s: Jacques Rivette shot his first full film in synchronised sound in 1965 (*La Religieuse*), Truffaut in 1966 (*Farenheit 451*) and Éric Rohmer in 1969 (*Ma nuit chez Maud*) (Bergala 1998: 38–9).

For Rohmer, who considered actors to be more at ease in the post-synchronisation studio than on set, the choice of post-dubbing was primarily an aesthetic one. More often, however, the decision was dictated by technical constraints: the recording of optical sound required vast unwieldy machines. Although portable magnetic tape recorders such as the highly regarded Swiss-made Nagra II were available from 1953, it was following the development of cable-based and then cordless systems for the maintenance of synchronisation between image and sound during recording and – through the use of electronic synchronisers known under brand names such as Fairchild, Néopilotton, Pilotton and Rangerton – during playback and editing that shooting with lightweight 35mm synchronised sound equipment finally became a reality. Coutant's Éclair NPR, for instance, came supplied with an optional crystal oscillator-controlled motor allowing cordless synchronisation with a portable tape recorder that was also fitted with a crystal oscillator (Salt 1992: 256). As Barry Salt notes, the successor to the Nagra II, the Nagra III, developed in Switzerland by Stephan Kudelski, was launched in 1959 to great acclaim and commercial success. Its slightly larger, heavier French rival, the Perfectone,

was launched the same year but failed to seriously challenge the Nagra on performance. Being slightly cheaper, however, the Perfectone was adopted by a number of television companies (Salt 1992: 264).

Cordless or not, none of these synchronised sound systems guaranteed perfect synchronisation, and technicians invariably had to address slight discrepancies between image-track and soundtrack during post-production (Villeval 2000). Jean-Pierre Beauviala became aware of the inconsistencies and limitations of synchronised sound while working on a documentary about Grenoble in 1967. He was interested in particular in the question of how to synchronise several Nagras with the single Arriflex camera on his shoulder as he walked down the street. His technical solution exemplifies his neo-Bazinian investment in the truth of the trace of the moment of recording: time code. In 1967 he took out a patent for Aäton's RealTime recording system, more commonly known as AätonCode, an in-camera time-recording system that stamps a unique and definitive ninety-one-bit time code on the exposed film stock and magnetic tape during shooting – including the date and exact time – and so guarantees perfect synchronisation during editing. Besides providing a 'birth certificate' for each image and sound, AätonCode dispenses with the intrusive noise of the traditional clapper-board and allows the operator to turn the camera on and off during recording to save film while recording audio continuously and maintaining synchronisation throughout (for detailed technical information, see <www.aaton.com>). The new system was built into Aäton 16mm and 35mm cameras from 1981. As with Beauviala's 'orsthetic' cameras, a link is retained to the human body: while all other time-code systems on the market rely on bar codes, AätonCode – in the interests of 'editors in love with their craft' – remains legible by the naked eye (Beauviala 1978: 17). By facilitating the exact reconstitution of the simultaneity of events separated during shooting, Beauviala's work on time code revolutionised working practices relating to directing and editing and redefined the meaning of 'recording' for modern cinema (Frodon 1995: 324).

The question of exhibition, in particular of the sound–image relationship during playback in the theatre, was revisited by engineers Elisabeth Löchen and Pascal Chédeville in 1990. Their LC-Concept digital sound system separated the soundtrack to be broadcast in the theatre from the image-track: sound was located on a separate hard disc and activated by a series of bar codes on the filmstrip. As with DVDs, the disc was capable of storing several soundtracks, thus allowing distributors to move from the original language track to a range of dubbed versions without the need for a different set of reels. The system was first used for the Paris release of Jean-Paul Rappeneau's *Cyrano de Bergerac* in 1990. The film was released initially in March in analogical format, then three months later in digital LC-Concept at one of Paris's best-equipped theatres, the UGC-Triomphe. Despite being adopted for the Paris release of films by directors such as Jean-Jacques Annaud, Jean-Jacques Beineix, Alain Corneau, Claude Lelouch and Roman Polanski, the system failed to sell and disappeared quickly from the marketplace. This economic failure was perhaps partly ideological in nature: to separate sound from image so categorically represented a return to the distant experiments of Edison (the Kinetophone) and Gaumont (the Chronophone), and undermined the reassuring homogeneity of image and sound now widely familiar from domestic technologies such as camcorders and DVDs. Meanwhile Chèdeville and Löchen successfully sued the manufacturers of a rival system, Digital Theater Sound (DTS), launched in 1993 with *Jurassic Park*. Although not identical – DTS sound is located on the filmstrip rather than on a separate disc – the system was strongly inspired by the LC-Concept. The DTS version of *Jurassic Park* was duly banned in France, and a Dolby version distributed there instead. The patent for the LC-Concept was eventually sold to the USA and led to belated international recognition for the system by way of a Hollywood Technical Achievement Award in 1996.

CAMERA MOVEMENT AND REMOTE CONTROL

A number of significant French inventions have been inspired by the quest to regulate camera movement. The tracking system developed in 1946 by Durin and Chapron employed a revolutionary system of wheels mounted on a bogy similar to that of a railway carriage – Chapron had previously worked as a mechanic for the French state railway – to minimise jolts, allow the dolly to negotiate corners and generally execute long complex movements fluidly. Claude Lelouch used the 'Durin and Chapron' in 1973 on the shoot in Turkey of *Toute une vie*, notably to film what was at the time the longest travelling shot on tracks in the history of French cinema: 110 metres, including a 30-metre level differential. Following the closure of the 'Auto-Travelling Durin' company in 1975, another manufacturer, André Bouladoux, took over production of the equipment using lighter materials and removable wheels and continues to supply the industry today (Collomb and Patry 1995: 284–5).

In a similar vein, albeit this time underwater, Coutant and Mathot had taken out a patent in 1948 for the Aquaflex, a 35mm camera for underwater filming fitted with stabilisers to ensure smooth movement and used to shoot one of Bazin's favourite films, Jacques-Yves Cousteau and Louis Malle's *Le Monde du silence* (1955) (Bazin 1985: 35–40). Looking to the air, director, cinematographer and former photographer Albert Lamorisse developed the Hélivision in 1955 with the aim of minimising the effects of vibration when filming from helicopters. His anti-vibration helicopter mount isolated the camera from the unwanted movements of the aircraft through the use of a gimbal and counterweight to keep it stable and free of the effects of gravity and centrifugal force. Lamorisse first used the system on *Le Ballon rouge* (1956), a short film scripted largely with the display of the spectacular possibilities of the Hélivision in mind. *Le Ballon rouge*, again enthusiastically received by Bazin (1967: 41–52), was awarded the Prix Louis Delluc in 1956 and the Oscar for best original screenplay in 1957, but the technique itself only attracted widespread international attention in 1965 as a result of its use for the opening aerial sequence of Robert Wise's *The Sound of Music*. Lamorisse, who pursued his interest in aerial filming throughout his career, was killed in a helicopter crash while shooting a documentary on Iran in 1970. His rushes were assembled and released posthumously in 1979 under the title *Le Vent des amoureux* to considerable acclaim, earning him an Oscar nomination for best documentary feature.

Lamorisse's pioneering work on the Hélivision has since been pursued by a new generation of inventors set on extending the boundaries of aerial cinematography, notably through the use of remote control. The Belgian Emmanuel Prévinaire, the first (in 1988) to attach a 35mm film camera to a radio-controlled miniature helicopter, went on to found the company Flying Cam. He has since been joined by Frédéric Jacquemin's Birdy Fly venture in France. However, the most influential remotely controlled film-making device to have been developed in France in recent decades is the Louma. In 1970, while working as camera operators on a documentary set largely on the bridge of a submarine, Jean-Marie Lavalou and Alain Masseron were faced with the problem of how to achieve intricate smooth camera movements in extremely cramped conditions where there was no room for a tripod, let alone a dolly, and indeed where there was seldom space for the camera operator (Collomb and Patry 1995: 279). Their solution, the prototype for what later became known as the Louma crane ('Louma' being an acronym of the technicians' names), was to fix a Caméflex to a gyroscopic pan-and-tilt head on the end of a pole, connected to a tripod mounted on a dolly, and to improvise a system for operating the camera's zoom and focus rings remotely. Following a series of improvements and intermediate versions, the technicians took out a patent in September 1975 for the influential and much imitated modular remote-control camera crane, the Louma 4: a lightweight crane mounted on a dolly supporting the camera on a mobile pivot at the end of a telescopic arm, all of which can be controlled remotely using a joystick. Focus and framing are controlled via a video link, and the Louma head adjusts itself automatically to compensate for vertical movements of the crane, thereby ensuring that the camera itself remains horizontal at all times. Since its widespread adoption within the television industry, the characteristic arabesques and vertiginous swoops of the Louma have redefined the aesthetic of the pop video, televised concert and talk show. Lavalou himself continues to operate the crane regularly on programmes for the popular subscription channel, Canal Plus. Having founded their own company, GTD (Grue Téléscopique Démontable), Lavalou and Masseron went on in 1987 to patent an even more sophisticated programmable telescopic lightweight crane that has the added advantage of being easy to dismantle, transport and reassemble in otherwise inaccessible locations (Collomb and Patry: 283).

In December 1974, Aäton, who had also been investigating the boundaries between profilmic, camera and operator, unveiled a ground-breaking viewfinder system for relaying the image seen through a 16mm film camera directly to a video monitor. The camera itself was widely adopted for use in television while the system set the agenda for the film industry and foresaw the widespread introduction of 'in-built video assist' over the ensuing years. But the motivation behind the development of this 16mm camera with video tube was quite different to that driving the Louma: where the aim of the Aäton was essentially a democratising one (to redistribute some of the power of the camera operator among other members of the crew), the Louma, by distancing body from machine and maximising camera autonomy, flew in the face of the neo-Bazinian 'orsthetic' tradition. In a review in *Le Monde* on 26 May 1976 of the first film where the Louma was used to its full effect, Roman Polanski's *Le Locataire* (1976, shot by Sven Nykvist), Jacques Siclier expressed concern at where such displays of technical wizardry might lead. As time has shown, the Louma has gone on to thrive in the age of digital imagery. Just as computer-game players explore virtual 3D environments, so the Louma glides through space and takes the camera through openings where a human operator could never follow. As such, it has proved the natural choice on numerous big-budget post-modern superproductions, including Spielberg's *1941* (1979), for which the inventors received a scientific and engineering award at the 1980 Oscars.

DIGITAL CINEMA

French CGI studios have enjoyed significant success in the international marketplace since the mid-1980s. The largest studios are Mac Guff Ligne, Buf Compagnie, ExMachina, Duran-Duboi, Gribouille and Mikros Image. All work across media (cinema, television, advertising, CD-Roms, video games, theme parks) and service a variety of clients around the globe. In a cinematic perspective, Buf provided special effects for *Les Visiteurs* (Jean-Marie Poiré, 1993), clouds for *Batman and Robin* (Joel Schumacher, 1997) and composite imagery for New Wave veteran Éric Rohmer (*L'Anglaise et le duc*, 2001). ExMachina has worked with film-makers from Philippe de Broca (*Le Bossu*, 1997) to Leos Carax (*Pola X*, 1999); Gribouille on superproductions such as *Vatel* (Roland Joffé, 2000) and intimate projects such as *La Ville est tranquille* (Robert Guédiguian, 2000). Mac Guff Ligne (MGL, founded in 1986), one of the best known of the studios, is credited with the production of the world's first entirely 3D CGI television series, *La Vie des bêtes* (1988). Composed of forty 20-second episodes in which imaginary creatures evolve in an environment drawn by one of France's highest-profile designers, Philippe Starck, the series exemplifies many of the characteristics of first-generation CGI: the design and movements of the creatures are a direct effect of the possibilities and limitations of the software; narrative is less significant than the display of striking visuals; and the project was designed from the outset for worldwide distribution (it was immediately bought and broadcast on MTV under the title *Animals*).

Although in terms of overall financial revenue, French CGI companies lag well behind the USA, the UK and Australia, they have developed a reputation for highly creative personnel and have successfully maintained a significant profile in a notoriously competitive marketplace. According to Hervé Lecoz at Duran-Duboi and Olivier Gilbert at Buf, economic and creative factors are ultimately less significant in the success of the French CGI studios than a combination of sheer technical quality bolstered by enduring myths of 'old European know-how' and 'French artistic chic'. Contrary to received wisdom, the French studios are no cheaper than their American counterparts. Indeed according to Olivier Gilbert, when the Hollywood majors turn to them, it is essentially for the specialised treatment of a limited number of shots or as a result of a temporary glut of work. But there is perhaps a further reason: the willingness of the French studios to innovate and exploit limited resources to the full. For Nicolas Trout of MGL, this openness to improvisation provides a direct link to the Méliès tradition and distinguishes the French studios from their Hollywood counterparts; without the resources available to the American majors, the French are constantly obliged to devise comparatively cheap, creative solutions to technical problems while maintaining optimum image quality. The French studios have also come to be associated with distinctive modes of production. Computers excel at generating clean, geometric representations. One of MGL's aims when developing their own software was to reintroduce chance and irregularity into the world of CGI. Eighty per cent of their output relies on the company's in-house 'Symbor' and 'Trukor' software, the former for modelling and animation, the latter for composite imagery, morphing, warping and the production of cinematic grain effects.

Digital technology is now integral to much film production in France. For Lecoz, the runaway success of big-budget special-effects superproductions such as *Le Fabuleux destin d'Amélie Poulain* (Jean-Pierre Jeunet, 2001), *Astérix et Obélix: mission Cléopatre* (Alain Chabat, 2002) and *Le Pacte des loups* (Christophe Gans, 2001) – all reliant on digital post-production – marks a turning point in French cinema. In 2003, his company Duran-Duboi was working on the most ambitious special-effects film to blend live action and animation yet made, the film adaptation of Enki Bilal's comic-strip adventure fantasy *La Femme piège*. The first film to integrate a computer-generated figure into an analogical environment was *Young Sherlock Holmes* (Barry Levinson, 1985); the first computer-generated feature was *Toy Story* (John Lasseter, 1995). In the context of this lineage, Pitof's *Vidocq* (2001) – the first 'entirely' digital-film, in that the shots into which the computer-generated figures are inserted were themselves all digitally coded from the outset – might be considered the latest phase in an ongoing game of technical/aesthetic one-upmanship with Hollywood. One should beware, however, of simply equating the spread of CGI with the disappearance of the profilmic or the end of the tradition of the 'truth of the trace' identified by Daney. While CGI designers no longer seek merely to optimise the accuracy of their recordings of the world, they still require real-life objects to scan or simply as inspiration for their digital shapes. Digital special effects are a direct extension of cinema's long-standing relationship with magic and spectacle; Méliès after all began his career as a conjurer at the Robert-Houdin Théâtre. There are plenty of revolutionary CGIs outside cinema, but once transferred to film, the highest-tech digital creation is materially equivalent to a Méliès stucco moon.

In David Fincher's *The Panic Room*, made in a French CGI studio in 2002, the passage of the camera through a keyhole combines and takes to their logical conclusion the 'scopic drive' theorised by Jacques Lacan and the 'telescopic desire' that produced the Louma. The price we pay for the realisation of this voyeuristic ambition is the disappearance of the camera altogether: the background was scanned and the movement generated digitally. As it abandons all links to the mechanical principal at the origin of its development – the ratchet wheel – cinema is finally leaving the 19th century. The LC-Concept already represented a significant step towards the 'dematerialisation' of the image. But despite the dissociation of the camera from the eyes and hands of the operator, even an inventor as attached to the logic of the 'trace' as Jean-Pierre Beauviala is prepared to recognise a residual gestural beauty in the shots of the Louma: at least someone, present at the moment of filming, was controlling the machine and – like their prehistoric ancestors who painted on the walls of caves – has left their fingerprints on the image. As film is superseded by 'ecinema' and movies on hard disc, cinema is facing a major material and conceptual mutation. When the cinematic image is divided into billions of 0s and 1s from the time of shooting onwards, any attempt at the genetic decipherment of the inscription of the body in the image becomes futile. Future reconciliation of the two traditions is, however, imaginable: the development of the genetic reading skills of a generation of viewers raised on digital cinema, to the point where they are able to appreciate the beauty of the gesture of a programmer in the same way that their predecessors recognised and appreciated the beauty of the gesture of a camera operator.

Many thanks to the following for responding to our enquiries: Jean-Pierre Beauviala (Aäton), Olivier Gilbert (Buf Compagnie), Frédéric Jacquemin (Birdy Fly), Hervé Lecoz (Duran-Duboi) and Nicolas Trout (Mac Guff Ligne).

WORKS CITED

Barthes, R. (1980) *La Chambre claire: notes sur la photographie*, Paris, Cahiers du cinéma/Gallimard/Seuil.

Bazin, A. (1967), *What Is Cinema?*, vol. 1, Berkeley, University of California Press.

Bazin, A. (1985), *Qu'est-ce que le cinéma?*, Paris, Cerf.

Beauviala, J.-P. (1978) 'Le Maillon central', *Cahiers du cinéma*, 288, 16–21.

Beauviala, J.-P. and Godard, J.-L. (1983) 'Génèse d'une caméra: premier épisode', *Cahiers du cinéma*, 348–9, 94–111; 'Génèse d'une camera: deuxième épisode', *Cahiers du cinéma*, 350, 45–61.

Bergala, A. (1998) 'Techniques de la Nouvelle Vague', *Cahiers du cinéma*, special issue: 'Nouvelle Vague: une légende en question', 36–43.

Collet, J. (1972) 'An Audacious Experiment: The Sound Track of *Vivre sa vie*', in Brown, R. ed., *Focus on Godard*, Englewood Cliffs, NJ, Prentice-Hall, 160–2 (first published in *La Revue du son*, 1962).

Collomb, J. and Patry, L. (1995) *Du cinématographie au cinéma 1895–1995: 100 ans de technologies cinématographiques françaises*, Paris, Dixit.

Coutard, R. (1965–6) 'Light of Day', *Sight and Sound*, Winter, 9–11.

Daney, S. (1988) *Le Salaire du zappeur*, Paris, Ramsay.

Douchet, J. (1998) *French New Wave*, New York, Distributed Art Publishers.

Frodon, J.-M. (1995) *L'Âge moderne du cinéma français*, Paris, Flammarion.

Gimello-Mesplomb, F. (2000) 'Enjeux et stratégies de la politique de soutien au cinéma français. Un exemple: la Nouvelle Vague, économie politique et symboles', unpublished doctoral thesis, University of Toulouse II Le Mirail/Maison de la Recherche CNRS/UTM Toulouse.

Marie, M. (2003) *The French New Wave: An Artistic School*, Oxford, Blackwell.

Marsolais, G. (1974) *L'Aventure du cinéma direct*, Paris, Seghers.

Ruspoli, M. (1964) *The Light-Weight Synchronized Cinematographic Unit*, Paris, UNESCO.

Salt, B. (1992) *Film Style and Technology: History and Analysis*, London, Starword.

Souriau, E. (1953) *L'Univers filmique*, Paris, Flammarion.

Villeval, A. (2000) 'La Synchronisation de l'image et du son au cinéma', <www.cst.fr/dtech/25-mai00/index.html> (CNC *Dossier Technique* No. 25).

Zand, N. (1963) 'Le Dossier Philippine', *Cahiers du cinéma*, 148, 32–9.

'For It Is the Critical Faculty That Invents Fresh Forms' (Oscar Wilde)

Nicole Brenez

To the staff of the Cinémathèque française

With a few remarkable exceptions (Jean Mitry, Jonathan Rosenbaum, Noël Burch . . .), the history of cinema has mainly been recounted from the industry's point of view. May this contribution to a history of forms help us to escape such a dominant ideology and reconsider the works and the artists from a different perspective. Today the violence of the cultural industry is so cynically triumphant that it is possible to establish a law of inverse proportions between the social visibility of a film and its real eminence. So the reader should not feel reassured: the less familiar the names and titles mentioned in this essay may appear, the more important they are in reality. But the author of these lines is far from sure of herself: prey to the intuition that she still knows nothing of all that remains to be done in this field, and aware that it will require a vigilant, collective and infinite effort.

FALSE OPPOSITIONS AND REAL DIVISIONS

The 1960s begin in 1957. At least three events of that year now appear highly symptomatic of the creativity and crises that were to follow. The Situationist International is founded in Cosio d'Arroscia, a movement whose theoretical reflection and strategic example prefigure the radical film collectives that will appear all over Europe some ten years later. In Venice, Jean Rouch receives a prize for *Les Maîtres fous*, a film that politically forces the Western world to look at its own image as a colonial oppressor, while formally announcing the critical ethnology that will influence so much of the cinema of the 1960s and beyond. And in Paris that year, a polemical exchange took place between André Bazin and Jean Carta in the pages of *Esprit* that

illustrates precisely how a radical challenge to the false distinction between formal experiment and political content was to set the filmic agenda for the whole period covered in this chapter. In an article entitled 'The Resignation of French Cinema', Carta had attacked Jean Renoir's *Élena et les hommes* (1956) for portraying the love life of a proto-fascist general when French cinema as a whole lacked the courage to fight political censorship and address contemporary issues such as the war in Indochina, the Suez crisis or the Algerian question (Carta 1957: 494–7). In response, Bazin penned his last published essay, 'Cinema and Commitment', arguing that a film's importance should not be judged by its content alone but also by its aesthetic rigour and ambition (Bazin 1957: 681–4). This polemic is important because, stuck in a Cold War confrontation, both protagonists are right: Bazin recommending that cinema be pushed to its limits within a given economic system, Carta calling for an alternative cinema that would help to build a different future. The history of French cinema since 1960 is the story of the more or less abrasive or conciliatory responses to a fundamental split around this question: 'What is cinema – doing in the world?'

The division is therefore between two conceptions of the real, rather than between content or form, experiment or commitment. On the one hand, there is the Bazinian conception of the world as already there, always given, a 'seamless robe of reality' that cinema can approach but never touch, and in relation to which the essence of cinema becomes a critical engagement with the forms of representation. Developing the models of Robert Bresson and Roberto Rossellini, this line of figurative investigation has proven to be the most prodigious in modern French cinema, notably in the work of Marcel Hanoun, Jacques Rozier, Jacques

Rivette, Jean-Marie Straub and Danièle Huillet, Jean Eustache, Philippe Garrel, Maurice Pialat, Christian Boltanski, Ange Leccia ... But there exists another conception of the world that sees the real as never definitively given, a real that remains to be decided and that cinema can precisely help to transform. Whereas the first notion of the real-as-given addresses the moral consciousness of the spectator, this second conception of the real-to-change addresses the spectator as citizen, capable of political action. This real-to-change has produced two further vital tendencies in modern French cinema. First, there is a political cinema of contestation, of counter-information, of 'social intervention', to use René Vautier's expression, a cinema that engages with the world in a historical struggle whose outcome it believes it can influence. Second, there is a vein of 'useless' experimentation, to use Jonas Mekas's term: in other words a cinema that is unruly and asocial, irretrievably committed to ever more radical research, as if by defying all the formal conventions and institutional demands of its time, a purely experimental cinema could already assert the existence, here and now, of another world. Since 1960, therefore, three equally rich areas of experimentation have existed side by side: figurative investigation; social intervention; and irreconcilable research. As we shall now see, however, the most significant works of the last forty years have transgressed such boundaries in order to create their own legitimacy. In the following pages, it is above all their story that this history of forms will endeavour to record and relate.

CINEMA RIPPED FROM THE REAL

According to a convenient misconception, politically committed cinema, because it is caught up in the practical necessities of history, remains indifferent to questions of form. This betrays a purely decorative understanding of formal issues, since on the contrary the cinema of intervention exists precisely in order to pose the most vital questions about cinema's presence in the world. Why make an image, which one and how? With whom and for whom? If it is the image of an event (the death of a man, a war, a massacre, a struggle, an encounter), how should one then edit it, in which context should one place it? To which other images is it

opposed? In terms of the story, which images are missing and which are indispensable? Who should be given the right to speak, and how do you assert that right if it is denied you? Why do we want a history and which history do we want? All these questions materially inform the project of René Vautier, each of whose films is an instance of cinematic thought in action. Through specifically filmic means, each work reflects on the place and responsibilities of cinema in the world. Above all the film-maker's role is to realise those images that the political context forbids and forgets. As Vautier often says, 'you can't allow governments to write history'.

In the course of his lifelong investigation into the necessity and relativity of images, Vautier has explored a vast array of different possible articulations between visual document and visual argument. Here is a crude taxonomy of his creative range: documented fiction, e.g. *Avoir 20 ans dans les Aurès* (1971) and *La Folle de Toujane* (with Nicole Le Garrec, 1974); didactic fable, e.g. *Les Ajoncs* and *Les Trois cousins* (both from 1970); allegorical pamphlet, e.g. *Le Remords* (1974), a highly burlesque satirical assault in which Vautier himself plays the role of a film-maker who has succumbed to self-censorship like so many others; documentary poem, e.g. *J'ai huit ans* (1961, with Yann and Olga Le Masson) and *Le Glas* (1970); documentary polemic, e.g. *Transmission d'expérience ouvrière* (1973) and *Quand les femmes ont pris la colère* (with Soizig Chappedelaine, 1977), *Marée noire et colère rouge* (1978) and *Hirochirac* (1995); methodological enquiry, e.g. *Mourir pour des images* (1971), a piece about the links between those who film and those who are filmed. This latter question is further examined in the theoretical essay, *Vous avez dit français?* (1985), which traces an alternative history of France through successive phases of immigration, and questions the notion of collective identity; and more recently in the work in progress *Dialogues d'images en temps de guerre*, which demonstrates practically the need to produce and compare images of all the parties concerned in a conflict, whether it be local or national, and is thus primarily a history of political, military and economic censorship, informed by Vautier's experience in this matter.

Sometimes his films become pure testimony, as in the case of *À propos de l'autre détail* (1988), which presents a series of interviews with the Algerian victims tortured by Lieutenant Jean-Marie Le Pen (long before he became a presidential candidate) and which was actually used as evidence in a real trial. This rawness of the document could hardly be more poignant than in the case of *Destruction des archives* (1988), which shows Vautier himself walking among the remains of his films and archives after they had been covered in petrol and partially destroyed by an as yet unidentified assailant. Filmed by Yann Le Masson, *Destruction des archives*, in its absolute factual simplicity, sums up the fate of political cinema today: dispersed, destroyed, shredded in the memories of those younger generations for whom it sought to build a better future. A similarly emblematic quality can be seen in the poetic essay, *Et le mot frère et le mot camarade* (1995), which explores the function of writing and especially poetry in the history of the French Resistance during World War II. Taken as a whole, then, Vautier's work of the last fifty years constitutes the backbone of French cinema understood in terms of its ethical and political responsibility. In the process, it has expanded more than any other single work the range of cinematic forms of critical investigation.

In spite of their stylistic differences, there exist many points of contact between the works of René Vautier and Chris Marker. Products of the same political culture of Resistance and Communism, they have both explored the relationship between a cinema of factuality (producing concretely the image that official history does not authorise) and a cinema of methodology (reflecting on the functions of images in history). They share a political commitment to collective action (Vautier founding the Britanny Cinema Production Unit, Marker establishing the group Slon/Iskra) and to the political struggles against colonialism in Africa and for the working class in France. They also have in common a love of Dziga Vertov and Eisenstein, and a stylistic preference for essay and argument, both of which derive from the same formal principle of 'images in dialogue', to use Vautier's expression. They are also to be found at the origin of two great polyphonic films of cinema history: in Vautier's case, *Peuple en marche* (1962), a film about the first year of Algerian independence; in Marker's case, *Loin du Vietnam*

(1967), which in the service of the Vietnamese cause brought together 150 film-makers and technicians, among whom were Jean-Luc Godard, Alain Resnais, Joris Ivens, Agnès Varda and William Klein.

In the conception of these two collective projects, it is possible to see a clear distinction between Vautier and Marker's methods: the former opts for a fusional polyphony, i.e. the sequences filmed by different film-makers and cameramen remain unsigned and are edited together (in the same way that to this day Vautier freely gives away his images and films to whoever might need them); whereas Marker prefers a differential polyphony, i.e. each autonomous episode is signed by its creator. This reflects a more general difference between the two figures: while Vautier proclaims a committed partiality, notably taking sides with those who do not have the right to images, Marker always tends to the problematics of subjectivity. Point of view, memory and amnesia, the workings of the psyche in general, these are Marker's concerns, each film dealing with the representation of consciousness, the ways in which the mind associates or separates phenomena, organises them in networks, in layers, knots and loops. If Marker's early films are constructed as subjective cartographies, e.g. *Description d'un combat* (1960) and *¡Cuba si!* (1961), after *La Jetée* (1962) the task of description becomes increasingly complex and problematic, until we reach the haunted structure of *Sans soleil* (1982), where the actual film merges into a pure hypothesis of a film. Such labyrinthine cartographies, serial inventories and visibly embroidered montage in fact constitute the emblematic forms not just of Marker's work, from *Olympia 52* (1952) to *Level Five* (1996), but also those of the other so-called 'Left Bank' film-makers: Resnais, from *Hiroshima mon amour* (1959) to *L'Amour à mort* (1984), and Varda, from *L'Opéra-Mouffe* (1958) to *Les Glaneurs et la glaneuse* (2000). Although Marker's cinema explores the movement of the image through the twists and turns of thinking, the folds and recesses of memory, it never becomes mere subjectivism. However intimately melancholic and utopian it may appear, history for Marker remains collective, and the intellectual internationalism that he invented provides us with a record of the successive states of universalism in the 20th century.

In the late 1960s and early 1970s, Vautier and Marker participated in a common political experience, the emergence of the Medvedkine groups, which involved teaching workers how to use film equipment so that by and for themselves they could describe the conditions of their lives and their struggles. Thanks to Marker's initiative, and the logistical and material support of Vautier, Ivens, Godard, Mario Marret, Bruno Muel, Antoine Bonfanti, Jacques Loiseleux, Michel Desrois and many others, a number of brilliant and violent film-pamphlets appeared from 1967 onwards, initially made by the workers of the Rhodiacéta factory in Besançon, then by the workers of the Peugeot factory in Sochaux. The names of these unknown film-makers, who are the pride of French cinema, deserve to be cited: Georges Binetruy, Christian Corouge, Georges Maurivard, Henri Traforetti, and many more . . . Their films, such as *Classe de lutte* (1969), *Images de la nouvelle société* (1969–70) and *Sochaux 11 juin 68* (1970), fully realise the project defined by Bruno Muel in these terms: 'to show the cultural taboos that must be overcome, the knowledge that must be usurped, in order to give oneself the means to struggle on equal terms against those who believe that everyone should remain in their place' (Muel 2000: 23). Formally diverse and inventive – featuring rapid montage and long takes; flickers, zooms and slogans; quotations from the discourse of the authorities contrasted with direct testimony; a loving use of music and songs; the systematic working with collage – these Medvedkine films, which refer directly to the 'laboratory-studios' invented by the soviet Proletcult, today appear even more precious than their model because of their purely critical character. The simple description of facts is a form of protest, just as information is a call to arms, not so much propaganda as a permanent feeling of revolt. The experience comes to an end in 1974 with a masterpiece by Bruno Muel, *Avec le sang des autres*, an implacable essay on the everyday despair of working life in a controlled society.

Prefigured by the experience of the Newsreels collective in the USA, active since 1966, as well as by the example of *Loin du Vietnam* in France, the era of the film collectives began in the wake of an extraordinary historical event, the Estates General of Cinema, in May 1968. The Estates General

'The Cinema Is Rising Up', Estates General of Cinema (1968)

brought together 1,500 people, professionals and non-professionals, who wanted to 'make political films politically' and who were ready to reconsider all aspects of film practice, whether it be production, direction or distribution. The Estates General serve as a reference point in one of the most formally inventive periods of film history, with the propagation of what might be called the Grand Revolutionary Style, one of whose essential components was its internationalism. Inspired by Soviet examples, by the Frontier Films of Paul Strand and Leo Hurwitz, by Santiago Alvarez in Cuba or Fernando Solanas and Octavio Getino in Argentina, inspired more profoundly by the heroic example of the Vietnamese people, a common style of protest spread across the world, adapting itself to local political conditions.

These counter-information films are generally made like tracts, foregrounding the lived experience of protagonists rather than elaborate argumentation, and featuring constructivist graphics, the use of the caption-stand, rapid montage, pop music, the iconography of the struggle and the irrepressible urgency of the here and now. Each collective adapts these common stylistic features to its own ends: an investigation, a documented pamphlet, a theoretical demonstration. The *ciné-tracts*, for example, a collective enterprise again inspired by Marker and bringing together many protagonists of the French avant-garde such as Godard, Resnais, Guy Chalon, Hélène Chatelain, Loiseleux and many more, constituted a simple form of visual report. Predominantly silent and shot in black and white, each work was made by refilming photographs of May 1968 and of current events in the world, in order to create a brief visual collage three minutes long. According to their own anonymous and undated protocol, the *ciné-tracts* must 'contest-propose-shock-inform-question-assert-convince-think-shout-laugh-denounce-cultivate' in order to 'inspire discussion and action'. The *ciné-tract* numbered '1968' known as *Le Rouge*, a collaboration between the painter Gérard Fromanger and Jean-Luc Godard, was the film version of a poster created by Fromanger for the Popular Workshops of the School of Fine Arts, the source of the most famous emblems of May 1968. In *Le Rouge* we see the red of the French tricolour spreading out onto the other two colours of the flag until it covers the whole screen. It is both a powerful visual conceit and a humorous response to other committed painters such as Pommereulle, Erro and Stämpfli, who in 1967 had organised an exhibition entitled 'Painting in Action', where instead of displaying canvases they had projected films by Lang, Eisenstein . . . and Godard. In 1969, at the request of Marin Karmitz, Fromanger produced a second version of *Le Rouge* that served as the trailer for Karmitz's film *Camarades*, the story of a young worker who comes to Paris and discovers the necessity of revolutionary struggle. Fromanger uses the same motif of the flag, adding a soundtrack recorded in the Renault factory at Boulogne-Billancourt and a series of silk-screen prints that he describes as 'ten images of righteous working-class anger faced with police brutality and ten images of flags that burst through the wall just as a hard and beautiful image bursts though the screen at the cinema' (Danet 1996: 167).

The *ciné-tracts*, along with other collective series such as *On vous parle de . . .* (1968–71) and *Images de la nouvelle société*, return to the inventive practices of agit-prop, of Vertov's Kino-Pravda, Alexander Medvedkine's agit-films, and in this sense we can say that the 1970s reinvent the 1920s for different times with different needs. Many individual artists disappear into the anonymity of the collectives, at least temporarily (Godard of course, but also Muel, Dominique Dubosc, Jean-Pierre Thorn), while others emerge as artists from these groups: Tobias Engel, Nicole and Félix Le Garrec, Jean-Louis Le Tacon. Still others work tirelessly for the cause, filming, producing, distributing, maintaining the link between the different collectives, artists and media (photography, film, television, newspapers): Marker and Roger Pic are exemplary in this regard. As for Philippe Garrel, he makes what Godard called 'the best film about May 68', in 35mm, although unfortunately it is lost today (Godard 1989: 6). Among all this creative activity, three types of initiative can be traced, although they are by no means exclusive: first, to encourage the autonomy of the protagonists in the struggle by training them in the use of film equipment (the Medvedkine Groups, the Peasant Front); second, to work on the description of conflicts (the Brittany Cinema Production Unit and Slon/Iskra, but also Cinéma Libre, Cinélutte, les Cahiers de Mai, le Grain de Sable, Cinéma Politique); third, to invent and enrich the cinematic forms of questioning and argumentation (the Dziga Vertov and Cinéthique groups). In this latter vein, several essays are devoted to a political analysis of cinema itself: for example, *Quand on aime la vie, on va au cinéma* (1975) by the Cinéthique group is an implacably concrete analysis of the ideological determinants underlying the mass production of stereotypes ('not a single image, nor a single sound, that is not linked to reality from a class point of view'); as well as the films of the Dziga Vertov group, which develop the line of research started by Godard in the 'Camera-Eye' episode of *Loin du Vietnam* and in *Le Gai savoir* (1968). Taken as a whole, the period of the film collectives from 1967 to 1975 represents perhaps a unique case in French history, where future researchers will one day be able to establish the truth based on audiovisual sources that for once will not have been dependent on any economic or state power. Rarely has cinema collectively developed its descriptive and analytical powers to such an extent, and if Saint-Just could write of the 18th century that 'it should be placed in the Panthéon', then the avant-garde cinema of this period, thanks to its cult of critical reason and its aspiration to social justice, must certainly merit the same recognition.

Whether working alone, or in dialogue with Jean-Pierre Gorin in the context of the Dziga Vertov group, or with Anne-Marie Miéville in the context of Sonimage, or indeed with the great ghosts of the history of cinema in, precisely, *Histoire(s) du cinéma* (1988–98), Godard has essentially developed a poetics of the missing image. Whereas René Vautier rips the image from the real, paying the price with injuries, condemnations, imprisonments and hunger-strikes, and Chris Marker travels the world highlighting and commentating on the links that secretly exist between one phenomenon and another, Godard collects already existing images in order to observe their relationships, their powers and their limitations. All the texts, sounds, shots and cuts in his work are citational and, if they ever appear original, it is simply because we have not yet come across the reference. But his general project, enriched by the formally sumptuous manner of the invocation, remains totally original, indeed it is the greatest systematic interrogation of the image undertaken by cinema in cinematic terms. Explicitly present, therefore, in Godard's work are the three characteristic formal traits of what he calls 'modern cinema': the negative; the heterogeneous; and the critical. He has worked on these through six decades of incessant invention, always renewed, always inspired, always at the vanguard not only of cinema but of art in general.

The first trait, identified by Godard as early as 1958, is the incorporation of the negative, which results from the conflict between his original classic cinephilia and his apprenticeship in the values of Bazinian cinema. The negative appears in the first instance as the opposite of mastery, as the cinema of fear:

> After all, if a modern novel is fear of the blank page, a modern painting fear of the empty canvas, and modern sculpture fear of the stone, a modern film has the right to be fear of the camera, fear of the actors, fear of the dialogue, fear of the montage. (Godard 1972: 75)

Therefore each shot, each cut, each filmic phenomenon in Godard's work must take the risk of starting cinema from zero, in the name of an ideal called firstly 'truth' (the 1960s, *Pierrot le fou*), then 'reality' (the militant years), then 'the Real' (in the Lacanian sense, during the 1980s and 1990s), and finally 'History' (the project of a lifetime). It is a fundamental principle of Godard's cinema that representation must always confront that which it cannot represent, a great alterity that relativises its powers, informs it with its absence, threatens it at all times with disappearance (as in the broken ending of *Soigne ta droite*, 1987), and yet justifies its efforts precisely in terms of the most fragile, uncertain and naked qualities that it nonetheless conveys.

The second principle is therefore an imperative need for heterogeneity: since no image, whether it be vision, word or sound, will ever be sufficient, it will never be too much to summon all images, taken from the vast web of their links and their differences. On this point, the work of Godard continues the tradition of German romanticism, of Schlegel and Novalis, about whose work Benjamin wrote, 'the infinity of reflection is not an infinity of progression but an infinity of connection' (Benjamin 2001: 57). In *The Old Place* (2001), Godard described this labour of linking as 'the constellation' and he thus rediscovers the formula of Hölderlin, 'to connect infinitely (exactly)'. At the same time, this principle of heterogeneity determines first the most consistent feature of his work, which is the bringing together of the two most distant images possible in order to produce a third image, or what Alain Bergala describes very well as 'the cinema of the greatest gap' (Bergala 1999: 82–5); and secondly the most dynamic element, since these constellations evolve from one period to the next, always producing new forms of confrontation and discontinuity: jumping (e.g. the initial jump-cut of *À bout de souffle*, 1960), irruption (the flashes of *Le Mépris*, 1963), interruption (the black screen and the prophylactic soundtrack of the militant years, 'a healthy sound over a sick image'), suspension (the endings of *Je vous salue, Marie*, 1983 and *Soigne ta droite*, 1987), pure conflict (the flickering of opposites), crossing (the superimpositions), stratification (the multiple superimpositions of sound as well as image in the videographic works).

This constantly creative dialectic between continuity and discontinuity leads to the third trait of Godard's work, his profound belief that cinema is invested with a critical mission. Over the decades, there are few powers that Godard has not attributed to cinema, and its mission has variously been to tell the truth, to restore people's dignity, to produce the image of a nation, to find a cure for cancer, to divide, disturb, frighten, even to haunt the universe with a solitary and orphaned history of mankind . . . In what sense is this messianic torment to be considered modern? It is that cinema is never a response but rather a question addressed to History, a permanent laboratory of understanding and exchange with phenomena, the place where we can see most clearly human thought at work, in its obscure stumblings, in the impatience of its efforts, its tensions and its ironies. Across the range of forms that he has explored or invented – fables, pamphlets, tracts, songs, reports, sketches, frescoes (as in *Histoire(s) du cinéma*) – Godardian cinema remains *poiesis*, creation, in the sense that no manner of totalisation can exhaust its possibilities, nor can any critical accomplishment deny the promise of a new beginning.

SINGULAR EXPERIENCES AND SOLITARY WORKERS

Each in their own manner, the projects of Vautier, Marker, Godard and the film collectives have consistently and coherently developed the critical forms of French cinema. There also exist isolated experiments in this field that are nonetheless important, in some cases astonishing: *Vite* (1970), for example, by the artist Daniel Pommereulle is a dance of execration during which the artist travels through worlds symbolically opposed to the West, in search of gestures and rhythms, connections and sensations that no longer have anything to do with rationalism: exorcism, repetition, discontinuity, access to the impossible. If the poet Arthur Rimbaud had made films in Abyssinia, he would have created *Vite*. Two further unique instances of critical protest bring to its culmination the polemical experimentation typi-

cal of the 1970s: namely *Yaa Bôe* (1975) by Dominique Avron and Jean-Bernard Brunet, a joyous little pamphlet demonstrating through the sheer force of its formal invention the predatory character of the cinematic apparatus as a powerful Western technique for the visual conquest of the world; and also *Ali au pays des merveilles* (1976), a film about Algerian immigration in Paris, whose authors Djouhra Abouda and Alain Bonnamy confront the official denials of racism with the brilliant eloquence of a documented conflict, a political struggle between shots, sounds and discourses, producing a general conflagration whose symbolic violence constitutes a proportional response to the oppressive violence of the social reality.

Another highly individual form of protest cinema, the psychedelic autobiography, can be traced back to the mid-1960s. This is no longer a question of presenting a critical vision of the world, but rather the creation here and now of a visionary reality, starting from a unique and singular point of view that is capable of rebuilding a human community. With *Voyageur diurne* (1966), *Homéo* (1967) and *Chromo Sud* (1968), the French Canadian Étienne O'Leary inaugurates the flamboyant tradition of hedonist and utopian filmed journals. His example inspires Pierre Clémenti's *Visa de censure n° X* (1967) and *New Old* (1978), Alain Montesse's *U.S.S.* (1970) and *Les Situs heureux* (1970–6), and Ahmet Kut's *Pour faire un bon voyage prenons le train* (1973) . . . All use the same technique, the daily filming of the everyday, in 16mm or Super-8, employing rapid montage and multiple superimpositions, often with saturated colours, sumptuous graphic effects and lots of music, sometimes created by the film-maker himself (e.g. Pierre Clémenti playing live accompaniment to the projection of his films). Two crucial works mark the historical and formal limits of this tradition: Clémenti's *Visa de censure n° X* in 1967 and *Ixe* by Lionel Soukaz in 1980. In an intimate mode of expression, these two artists take up the protest against social censorship and private self-censorship: both exposing their lives and their bodies in the smallest details of their pleasure and their pain; both pursuing an aesthetic of collage, flashing montage and generous doses of pop music; both following the same ethical 'appeal to disorder', a call to live (as proclaimed by the poster of the Kurosawa film *Live* [1952] that we see on the walls of Lionel Soukaz's room), according to Rimbaud's 'scrambling of all the senses'. Certain social changes of the 1970s are summed up in the difference of tone between these two otherwise very similar works. In 1967, Clémenti's euphoric psychedelia incorporates images of death, struggle and exorcism into a radiant, densely mystical energy that absorbs those images and transposes them into a love song. But thirteen years later, in Soukaz's work, despite the love, the beauty and the corrosive laughter, an irresistible movement now carries the protagonist towards death, pleasure becoming convulsion, the flashes becoming atomic explosions, the sampled songs becoming a sardonic snigger. *Ixe* wipes out the 1970s and announces prophetically the different pandemics (including AIDS) that would only be identified from 1985. Between 1967

and 1980, sexual desire has been cruelly transformed from the driving-force of liberation into a deadly game of chance, and in the following decades all that remained was for it to be reduced to a mere advertising strategy. We can be sure that this tragic trajectory will one day be visible in Soukaz's filmed journal, *Les 1001 heures, journal/annales*, a fascinating work in progress since 1991 that has yet to be shown publicly.

Finally, in this section, French cinema has always been rich in solitary pamphleteers, some of whom have preferred to work in the context of industrial cinema and even genre cinema, far from the collective movements of social protest. This reclaiming of a genre by a critical spirit has given us some masterpieces, each of which represents a brilliant formal proposition. First, there is the great Jacques Tati, whose *Playtime* (1967) and *Trafic*

The modern world seen by Jacques Tati in *Playtime* (1967)

(1971) are critical essays of a supreme stylistic elegance about the supposedly advanced features of a consumer society. In *Amours collectives* (1976), Jean-Pierre Bouyxou subverts pornographic cinema by crossing a sense of burlesque improvisation with a veritable passion for the human body. Jacques Demy with *Une Chambre en ville* (1982) and Chantal Akerman with *Golden Eighties* (1986) each pay homage to the most unreal of genres, the musical comedy, by linking it to the most concrete of real problems, the class struggle. With *Ma 6-T va cracker* (1997), Jean-François Richet, a great admirer of Soviet cinema, crosses the ethnographic cinema of Jean Rouch with the action films of John Woo, and frames the result with revolutionary music videos: political analysis and unreasoning rebellion, sentimental identification and formal distanciation, alternate, accumulate and merge into a cinematic proposition with an energy unmatched in French cinema.

If Richet is today the only film-maker directly representing the collectivity with motifs of crowds, tribes and class, other artists are renewing genre cinema by working with individual characters: a French teen-movie, Patricia Mazuy's *Travolta et moi* (1994), by introducing discontinuity everywhere, between people, between shots, between types of images, draws the ultimate portrait of adolescence hallucinated by the absolute, whether it be love (for the heroine, Christine) or freedom (for the hero, Nicolas). In surely the most corseted of genres, the historical reconstitution of *Saint-Cyr* (1999), Mazuy again succeeds in profoundly questioning the strange workings of rationalisation: rather than employing the usual techniques of modernist distanciation, she develops a critical construction from the scenario, in the manner of Rossellini and Francesco Rosi, so we have to deduce the film's proposition from the crossing of the characters' trajectories (the sympathetic little girl rebels, the rebellious girl wears herself out). In another move, *Baise-moi* by Virginie Despentes and Coralie Trinh-Ti (2000) imports into France a minor American genre, the rape revenge movie: the film proclaims loud and clear its formal nudity and invents an intransigent irony that makes it one of the most violent and idealistic films about power ever made. Gaspar Noé's *Seul contre tous* (1998) articulates both

gore film and visual essay, and its descent into the psyche of a fascist butcher admirably expresses the autism of hatred. All of the above examples are rare and solitary films that nonetheless transform the most restrictive and widespread aspects of cinema (genre and stereotype) into formal treasures. They are the authentically popular films of that 'missing people' identified by Carmelo Bene and later by Gilles Deleuze (Deleuze 1989: 215–24).

ALWAYS AT THE VANGUARD OF THE AVANT-GARDE!

On 9 January 2002, coming out of the Trois Luxembourg cinema, André S. Labarthe turned to Maurice Lemaître and declared: 'That's what will remain of cinema when everything else has been destroyed.' He was referring to the projection of *Un soir au cinéma* (1962), which Lemaître, its indefatigable creator, had typically just transformed into a live performance. The exchange is significant for this history of forms. For here were the two great branches of modern cinema in France, the New Wave and Lettrism, speaking to each other again after decades of rivalry and mutual incomprehension. And yet in the 1950s they had sat alongside each other at the Cinémathèque of Henri Langlois, whom they had also jointly defended in the demonstrations leading up to the revolt of May 1968. However, whereas the project of the New Wave was to invade the mainstream by various means (notably by creating independent economic structures, like Rohmer and Truffaut), the strategy of the Lettrists was, on the contrary, to refuse any compromise whatsoever with the film industry or the art market. The result of their refusal is that, fifty years after *Le Traité de bave et d'éternité* by Isidore Isou and *Le Film a déjà commencé?* by Maurice Lemaître (both 1951), we can observe the exceptional phenomenon of an avant-garde movement that has lasted half a century, and still continues today, without losing any of its radical aesthetics and ethics (two synonymous terms in the context of Lettrism). So although 1960 is an important date in the cultural memory of French and world cinema because of the New Wave, one could equally argue that 1951 marks the real break and renewal in terms of formal history, since with those two films Isou and Lemaître established a profound inversion of formal values that has characterised a certain tendency in French experimental cinema for the last fifty years. All the essentials are present in these two works: the privileging of critical reflexivity, of unfinished work, of destruction; an aesthetic of discontinuity, negativity and appropriation; and a possible fusion of art and life via the creative disruption of the parameters of the film apparatus (what the Lettrists called 'syncinema', later to be known as 'expanded cinema').

After *Le Traité de bave et d'éternité*, Isou more or less abandons cinema, but from 1962 Lemaître takes up the initiative in this field and since then his filmic creations have never ceased. For Lemaître, each film work must be simultaneously a new formal proposition (about the relationships between image and sound, image and body, or film and projection); an invention in aesthetic terms (on the status of the work in life); and an assertion about the history of art (its so-called 'meca-aesthetic dimension'). Let us cite, among the forty films catalogued that by definition do not cover the whole corpus, a selection of works that Lemaître has made on the basis of these three requirements: *Chantal D, Star* (1968), *Le Soulèvement de la jeunesse* (1969), the series of *Six films infinitésimaux et supertemporels* (1967–75), *Un Navet* (1976), *50 bons films* (1977), the hyperautobiographical series *Vies de M.B.* (1985–90), especially the sixth episode *Tunisie, Tunisie*, the homage to *Erich Von Stroheim* (1979), *L'Ayant-droit* (1991) . . .

One day, alas, Lemaître's films will be shown without their necessary link to live performance: the presence of the artist, the participation of the spectators, the general displacement of the film apparatus. According to syncinema, every material element of cinema can and must be brought to life: the traditional white screen is replaced by a human screen (*Un Soir au cinéma*, 1962), by a screen of flames (*Montage*, 1976), by sheets of paper distributed to the audience . . . The spectator must become a creator, either by participating in the show, or by making the work himself (supertemporal cinema), or by being prevented from making it himself (anti-supertemporal cinema) and therefore being obliged to free himself (anti-anti-supertemporal cinema). Cinema leaves the film theatre, and the film is projected onto buildings, the sky, anywhere and everywhere. The film can be projected intermittently,

shown (in the cans) but not projected, constructed during the course of the show. It can equal the sum of the images that the spectators have in their heads, or are carrying on their person, or are capable of making on the spot . . . The film show is transformed into a happening, a lucky dip, a critical discussion. It can sometimes not take place at all, or it can happen anywhere and at any time, or it can be the meeting of the film-maker and the spectator on the street, or the simple fact of thinking about it . . . With the Lettrists (Isou, Lemaître, but also Roland Sabatier and many others), the cinema becomes an infinite expansion of possibilities organised with one simple aim in view: namely that art should be fused with life, that it should not remain the property of a few but should contribute to the liberation of everyone. In the great tradition of Dada, Lettrism has practised the cult of creativity against the cult of the object, of art as the deathly emblem of fetishism.

While the creative rigour and polemical virulence of the Lettrists protect them from any institutional recuperation, their vehemence has also been exerted against those film-makers who, consciously or not, have worked on similar formal questions: the desynchronisation of sound and image ('discrepancy'), the material destruction of the photogram ('chiselling'), graphical research ('hypergraphy'), the absence of the image, appropriation, expanded cinema . . . In turn, Godard, Resnais, Marguerite Duras, Alain Robbe-Grillet and many others have been attacked as crooks and plagiarists. But the most fratricidal polemic took place between the Lettrists and their principal dissident branch, the Situationists. As far as cinema is concerned, Guy Debord, at first very close in the 1950s to the abstract and destructive aesthetic of François Dufrêne, Gabriel Pomerand and Gil Wolman, adopted another style in the 1960s and 1970s: *Critique de la séparation* (1961), *La Société du spectacle* (1973) and *In girum imus et consumimur igni* (1978) today represent the classic form of the film essay. This is for three related reasons: first, Debord's use of visual appropriation expresses his cinephile's contempt for the cinema, since in 'the society of the spectacle' it is no longer possible to make images innocently; second, the soundtrack, almost entirely occupied by the voice of Debord and punctuated by sad and beautiful musical extracts, never diminishes the speculative demands particular to critical theory; and third, the whole accords a new importance to the expression of sentiment in thinking. Whereas the Lettrists are always seeking more artistic radicality in order to open up more formal and conceptual inventions ('Always at the vanguard of the avant-garde until paradise and beyond!', to quote Lemaître's formula), Debord explores a single and simple form, the essay-pamphlet, ever more profoundly. His films are the hypothetical product of an impossible encounter: a simplified Lettrist montage crossed with a text written by the philosopher Adorno that somehow has been translated by the eighteenth-century moralist La Rochefoucauld. Their beauty stems from this tension between the elegant irony of a heteroclitic visual collage and the apodictic character of the commentary, which is in turn underlined by the perfect calm of the diction. Like the Dadaists and the Lettrists, Debord conceives his work in an afterlife of art, formally seeking to satisfy two negative criteria: that art should no longer be a symptom of the division between life and creation, nor a simple instrument for the destruction of a divided society. For Debord the solution consists in inflecting critical theory ('the negation of negation') towards melancholic meditation. The essay can thereby become the site of a subjective assertion of self, even in the 'false world' of Adorno, where everything is working towards depriving the individual of himself and teaching him merely to understand his unhappiness. In this regard, it is in Debord's work – and Lemaître's *Tunisie, Tunisie* – that we find a unique formal rehabilitation of feeling: far from any arbitrary pathos, sentiment for Debord no longer represents the obscure origin of an individual expressivity, but results logically from a revindication of speculative sovereignty and a fiercely defended critical dignity.

THE GREAT EXCHANGE OF CINEMA

The readymade is well known as one of the most radical forms of modern art. The second half of the 20th century saw a proliferation of filmic readymades, such as *Une Oeuvre* by Lemaître (1968), the films or performances of Giovanni Martedi and

Nicolas Villodre, but also the appearance of its dysphoric version, the 'readystroyed' (if we may introduce the term). Whereas the Duchampian readymade, by the sheer force of its modest presence, quietly induces the collapse of an institution (the Museum) upon its very foundations (the fetishistic conception of art), the 'readystroyed' film adds to the refusal of fabrication implied in the found object by further refusing to preserve the film's integrity. With *Graphyty* (1969), Jean-Pierre Bouyxou establishes the epitome of the readystroyed: during a year he edits together found images in an aleatory fashion, then paints them, scratches them, adds different soundtracks to them in performance, and simultaneously attends to the decomposition of his film in the course of its projection-cum-performance. Of a maximum length of forty-five minutes, the film today lasts twenty minutes; a generalised destruction of forms, of syntax, of any ideal of self or art, it is twenty minutes of pure infantile beauty, convulsive and enraged. As is always the case, we realise only in retrospect that the destiny of the arts was played out precisely in those forms, which at the time were experienced as peripheral or ignored as extravagant. Thus the Lettrist proposition of syncinema, which simply involves respecting the heterogeneous nature of the cinema apparatus and enriching it with multiple crossovers, notably from live performance, has today become an institutional reality. In museums today, films are hung on the wall like paintings; in galleries, video manipulates film as if it were a natural substance; and in films themselves the different technologies and formats are superimposed, like so many coats of paint, to produce new textures and forms. On this last point, certain contemporary masterpieces belong just as much to the history of video as they do to the history of cinema: *Sombre* (1998) by Philippe Grandrieux, *Île de beauté* (1996) and *Gold* (2000) by Ange Leccia and Dominique Gonzalez-Foerster, *Il n'y a rien de plus inutile qu'un organe* (1999) by Augustin Gimel, *My Room le Grand Canal* (2002) by Anne-Sophie Brabant and Pierre Gerbaux, *High* (2000) by Othello Vilgard, *Samouraï* (2002) by Johanna Vaude, *Histoire(s) du cinéma* and the end of *Éloge de l'amour* (2001) by Godard . . . Film shoots become exhibitions, as when Philippe Jacq invites the visitors to a Contemporary Art Fair to watch the making of his film *Ophélie et Marat* (2001). Or the film's projected version is adapted into an installation, as in Akerman's *D'Est* (1993). For the last thirty years, the work of Maria Klonaris and Katerina Thomadaki has practised these disciplinary hybridisations, between film, video and the visual artists. Their films, installations and performances, organised into grand cycles and closer to architectural frescoes than to episodes or chapters, such as *Tétralogie corporelle* (1975–9), *Cycle de l'Unheimliche* (1977–82), *Cycle des hermaphrodites* (1982–90) or the current *Cycle de l'ange*, employ the full range of artistic instruments in their studies of the body, especially the female body.

At the start of the 21st century, cinema has become a disciplinary interchange; constantly exporting itself beyond its frontiers, it has invaded the other visual arts and collects all their artistic grafts. In fact, the material medium of cinema has never been as determined or determinant as people like to pretend. From the chronophotographs of Étienne-Jules Marey in the 1880s to the multimedia installations of Chris Marker, in particular *Silent Movie* (1995), the cinema has not been subordinated to projection any more than to celluloid. We could rather consider it, more generally, as the art of organising or disorganising all its component parts, as the art of montage understood in its broadest sense. Today there is more cinematic commerce in *Aveugle* (2000) by Régis Cotentin, *Pulsar* (2002) by Maria Klonaris or the films of Dominik Barbier, which are all made on video, than there is in the majority of films projected in commercial theatres. Does this mean that cinema, once 'an impure art', has now become dissolute? Have we entered a platinum age, corresponding to the golden age of the 1920s? Does the White Ball, with Man Ray projecting Méliès's colour films onto dancers, transformed into mobile screens, provide the model for Visual Jockeying and other contemporary forms of audio-visual performance? Or are we now witnessing a final firework show before celluloid is devoured by digital? And will cinema leave to the collective imaginary something more than an industrial iconography? We believe that, to use Eisenstein's expression, its legacy will comprise both the instruments and examples of an art of movement, as well as the keys and principles of the movement of

art (Eisenstein 1980). Certainly the work of great film-makers, from René Vautier to Lionel Soukaz, from Jean Rouch to Maria Klonaris and Katerina Thomadaki, from Robert Bresson to Christian Boltanski, authenticates Adorno's belief that 'cinema enlarges the field of art' (Adorno 2002: 73).

MIMESIS AS THE ART OF RUPTURE

In France, two related strands of figurative investigation, minimalism and naturalism, have explored the problematics of cinema as mimesis or the representation of the real. Minimalism is essentially an aesthetic of trauma, stripping representation down to its barest essentials, as in the works of Jean-Pierre Melville, Alexandre Astruc, Robert Bresson, Jean-Marie Straub and Danièle Huillet, Philippe Garrel, Sylvina Boissonnas, Yvan Lagrange, Jean-Pierre Lajournade, Christian Boltanski, Chantal Akerman, Gérard Blain, Jacques Doillon, Claude Lanzmann. Naturalism is not so much the opposite of minimalism as its continuation by other means: in the works of Maurice Pialat, Jean-François Stévenin, Patrick Grandperret and Claire Denis, mimesis is the bare presentation of everyday reality rather than the codified universe of conventional realism. All of these film-makers have worked on mimesis as the art of rupture, clearing the path of all superfluities, in the case of minimalism, and accepting only the sublime, even if it is a sublime of the ordinary, as in the case of naturalism. Although the greatness of these works stems from their extreme singularity, we can identify common traits that characterise this particularly fertile area of formal experimentation. They all use mimesis, explicitly or in effect, as a critique of the verisimilitude of orthodox realism. They also share a common aesthetic horizon: absolute exactitude, whether this be thought of as the truth, as the Real, or as the unnameable. Three principal sources inform their aesthetic project: the decisive historical trauma of World War II; the powerful model of high French classicism, which Paul Bénichou (1948) called 'the morality of the Great Century', derived from Racine, Pascal and La Rochefoucauld; and a constructivist imperative that each film must discover its own form, rather than obey the iconographic, narrative or plastic conventions currently in force. We can survey this field under five major headings: litotes (understatement); syllepsis (the use of the same term to two different effects); inductive logic (arguing from the particular case to the general truth); discordance (the incompatibility of elements); and the architectonic sublime (a unique structure for each work).

Two fundamental texts, Robert Bresson's *Notes on the Cinematographer* and Marcel Hanoun's *Cinéma cinéaste: notes sur l'image écrite*, both in turn drawing on Pascal's *Pensées*, mark out the ethical necessity and the material means of this art of exactitude. 'They lack poverty,' says Bresson (1997: 44) citing Mozart; 'the film is constructed by cutting back images and sounds,' says Hanoun (2001: 22). According to litote, when everything else has been removed, that which remains is unquestionable. In order to reach that state, two approaches are possible: either pure factography, a descriptive literalness that presents the event in all its factual cruelty, like the partisans' bodies that are bound hand and feet and thrown into the river Po at the end of Rossellini's *Paisà* (1946); or a strategy of confirmation, like the voice-off that confirms the image in Bresson's *Le Journal d'un curé de campagne* (1951) and *Pickpocket* (1959). For more than twenty years, from the end of the 1950s to the early 1980s, the great factographic films invented new combinations of these two seminal approaches. In Marcel Hanoun's *Une Simple histoire* (1958), which in turn develops the model of Francesco Maselli's *Histoire de Catherine* (1952), there is a system of exact duplication between on-screen dialogue and voice-off, which describes to the last franc the protagonists' gradual descent into destitution. We find the same extreme approach to the documentary function in Maurice Pialat's *L'Amour existe* (1960), where the soundtrack announces in descending order a list of statistics regarding poverty in France: 'The number of germs per square metre inhaled by a shop-girl: four million. The annual number of keys struck by a typist: fifteen million. Percentage of working-class students at university: three. The number of theatres outside Paris: zero . . .'. And we find the same idea in Christian Boltanski's *L'Essai de reconstitution des 46 jours qui précédèrent la mort de Françoise Guiniou* (1971), in which the voice-off describes with an objectivising precision (since it delineates the facts as well as the unfolding of the film) the actions of the people filmed without sound, a profound silence that provides an equivalence to the absence of response and love that is slowly killing them: 'The Jean Jaurès housing-project was constructed in 1933. Here they come up the stairs and go into the apartment. Here they are in the kitchen . . .'. And finally in Straub and Huillet's *Trop tôt, trop tard* (1981), we hear a voice reading the enumeration of taxes, of the poor and the dead, established by Engels in *The Peasant Question in France and Germany* (1894), which informs the landscapes we see filmed in long sequence-shots.

One of the obvious strengths of this pure literalness is that, far from being univocal, it leads to forms of syllepsis (the same element used twice in different ways), which can describe the real precisely in its complexity. At the start of Jean-Pierre Melville's *Le Cercle rouge* (1970), for example, we see two men get into a train. Similarly dressed, they also have the same blank facial expression, they make the same gestures, without exchanging a word. Are they accomplices, colleagues, friends, brothers? They go into their compartments and we discover that they are joined together by a pair of handcuffs. But the twin-like prologue lends a human fraternity to their social antagonism. Certain films maintain the syllepsis throughout: for example, Christian Boltanski's *L'Essai de reconstitution des 46 jours qui précédèrent la mort de Françoise Guiniou* transposes the enforced seclusion of Anne Frank into the suicidal seclusion of Françoise Guiniou. But the latter is probably no less constrained by emotional and economic factors than the former, so the current-day story of Françoise Guiniou is also and simultaneously part of a collective historical mourning. In similar fashion, Philippe Garrel's *Le Berceau de cristal* (1975) portrays mainly in long takes a series of characters isolated from each other: Garrel himself, Tina Aumont, Margareth Clémenti . . . and above all Nico. She dreams, writes, composes, and on her monumental face we witness the temporality of the creative act, as if we were entering the spiritual world of Sappho or a mythological poetess. But in the final shot, Nico picks up a gun and shoots herself in the head. What we understood as creative meditation must now be rethought as preparation for death, the work as testament, the portrait as a *memento mori*.

Whether it be in the works of Bresson, Melville, Pialat, Garrel or Boltanski, why are they peopled by all these obstinate, fierce, solitary characters, blinded by their passion? What is the 'reason for these effects', as Pascal would say? What infinite powers must we infer from this art of understatement? In modern cinema, there are three types of infinity we can establish by induction, although they may often appear superimposed or, with certain film-makers, mixed together. The first is transcendence, as in the great tradition of Bresson, who considers any figurative universe as a negative anthropology. The second infinity is the historical trauma of World War II, which determines in particular the aesthetic of Melville, as Olivier Bohler has demonstrated: whether cops or gangsters, partisans or gamblers, the characters survive the trauma according to a code of behaviour derived directly from the Resistance, and founded upon clandestinity, moral rigour and sacrificial loyalty, which are totally incompatible with the industrial modernity of the so-called 'thirty glorious years' of post-war economic prosperity. According to Bohler, Melville invented the contrary of the archetype, the telotype, in other words 'a figure neither living nor dead, inheriting a past that is definitively extinguished, and for whom there is no future' (Bohler 2004). While maintaining the anachronistic values of the Resistance, and investing them in figures as apparently different as a partisan leader or a Samurai, Melville affirms the presence of an irreparable trauma at the heart of a modernity that is less interested in treating the wound than in dramatically forgetting or foreclosing it. Only Pialat, in L'Amour existe, L'Enfance nue (1970) and La Maison des bois (1971), and Christian Boltanski in his entire filmic and artistic output, have recorded with such implacable constancy the forms of survival, in the industrial world, of the disasters of war.

The third infinity, rarely commented upon, is economic oppression, Adam Smith's 'invisible hand' as defined by Hegel: 'an alien power over which man has no control . . . a scarcely knowable, invisible, and incalculable power . . . this unconscious and blind fate' (Hegel 1979: 169–70). This is the most frightening infinity of all, because it is the most banal and ineluctable, yet it structures the formal invention of Bresson, Hanoun, Pialat,

Jean-Pierre Melville in his burned-down studios in rue Jenner, Paris, 1967

Garrel, Jean Eustache and Jacques Doillon. Bresson's character Mouchette epitomises the figure of the pariah: despite her total emotional destitution, distraught solitude and economic misery, which place her beyond the bounds of the village and transform her into a sexual prey, she manifests nonetheless a fierce class solidarity with her rapist when, against all the evidence, she declares to the bourgeois women who come to her assistance that 'Monsieur Arsène is my lover'. Rather poverty, rather emotional confusion, rather rape and death than accept the false charity of wealthy old women. Such is Mouchette, the figure of political intransigence who does not need anyone or anything to remind her where justice resides. The female protagonist of Hanoun's Une Simple histoire obeys the same logic: descending into poverty, she does not even think about asking for help from anyone, because this is still a time when women have interiorised the laws of oppression to such an extent that they only have duties but no rights. The difference between Bresson's Mouchette and Hanoun's character Micheline Bezançon lies in the treatment of interiority: whereas Mouchette's intuition does not vary one iota, Micheline goes deeper into the experience of disaster, and through her we understand more painfully the way in which poverty affects human relations and the relationship to the world. When, from the depths of her despair that renders everything opaque and incomprehensible, she says, 'I went by a tunnel where cars were going in and coming out further on', we realise that, unlike the cars, fragile human beings do not always re-emerge from the shadows. However, it is the same world that we must infer both from the off-screen space of *Mouchette* (1967), where cars constantly pass but never stop, and from the suburban waste-lands of *Une Simple histoire*, where women end up abandoned: it's a world where to be poor is to be guilty.

Where Bresson represents the infinity of earthly evil in the form of an event, and Hanoun represents it as a process of psychological interiorisation, Maurice Pialat proceeds in the same inductive manner to extend this observation onto a class level and to describe self-deprivation as a condition accepted by the majority of people, and the absence of self as an active principle of socialisation. The silent shots of the miners' demonstration at the start of *L'Enfance nue*, the distant allusions to unemployment in *Passe ton bac d'abord* (1979) – and the same is true of the financial impossibility of Daniel continuing his education in Eustache's *Mes Petites amoureuses* (1974) – all designate an economic context that is never treated other than in terms of its effects and whose

Jean Eustache and Maurice Pialat making *Mes Petites amoureuses* (Jean Eustache, 1974)

relationship to events is never presented as direct or even certain. In *L'Enfance nue*, perhaps it is poverty that obliges François's mother to abandon her son, but perhaps she is also an unworthy mother. In *Passe ton bac d'abord*, a common resignation is transmitted from generation to generation: emotional relation-ships get worse and worse, nobody learns anything at school, the working-class woman sleeps with the bar-owner out of pure emotional lack, the mines close, people have to go to Paris to find work. But none of this is experienced as scandalous, the every-day is saturated with familial and tribal gestures and it provides a thick, ultimately protective, barrier between the adolescent apprenticeship of selfhood and the harsh economic realities. As it is said in *L'Amour existe*, 'this is the time of civil barracks, of prison-camps financed on the instalment plan, of town-planning conceived in terms of refuse-collection, and cheap materials worn out before the building is complete'. Having stated head-on this collective suffering, Pialat's work explores those individual resources that allow human beings to endure the violence they must suffer without even having the means to account for what is happening to them.

What characterises the relationship between effect and cause, event and origin, personality and environment is discordance, a dissonance between the powers of the world and our powers of under-standing. Discordance may take the form of an excess, an event that is unassimilable by fiction, for example the reappearance of the supposedly dead gamekeeper in *Mouchette*. But more generally it takes the form of an absence, a lack, because what remains incomprehensible and unacceptable is the inaccessibility of other people. The great modern characters are figures of abandonment: Mouchette, Françoise Guiniou, Micheline Bezançon, François in *L'Enfance nue*, Hervé in *La Maison des bois*, the child in Garrel's *Le Révélateur* (1968), who is pur-suing his own abandonment, or the protagonist of Sylvia Boissonnas's *Un Film* (1969), played by the film-maker herself, cloistered in her barrel into which are poured sand, like tons of despair, and water, like floods of tears. These constructions deal head-on with the impossibility of finding a corre-sponding counter-shot, a space that is exterior to the shot, some kind of a response. The perfect illustration of this is Pialat's *La Maison des bois*, in which war produces a mass of children who have lost their parents, but also, and even more tragically, just as many parents who are desperately searching for their children. When they do exist, even the closest relationships – whether blood-ties (legitimate children) or emotional bonds (orphans, lovers, husband and wife) – are destroyed by collective history (Pialat, Eustache). But more often they are not even possible, and the films become rituals of lamentation and mourning (Boltanski, Boissonnas, Garrel), or denial (as in Doillon's *Ponette*, 1996). The third type of discordance, the most astonishing, concerns those films that are trying to find forms of healing, ways of getting over the trauma, of bringing experience back into the realm of understanding, or of discovering a route to the inaccessible: but then nothing is more painful than the healing process. In Hanoun's *L'Authentique procès de Carl Emmanuel Jung* (1967), for example, a fundamental essay on barbarism, there is the shot of the torturer Jung finally screaming his guilt, a shot that is realised but at the same time is explicitly signalled as impossible. In Hanoun's *L'Été* (1968), there is the final undecidable shot where we perhaps hear the man murmuring to the woman 'I've come to get you'. In Bresson, there is the shot of Mouchette in tears, exhausted, beside her dying mother and almost appearing to breast-feed her younger brother, thereby offering a poignant image of what she will no longer be and what she will never become, neither daughter, wife nor mother. Symmetrical to this image we can place that of Françoise Guiniou, who has just strangled her daughter and is offering her breast to her older son. Or there is the elegiac 'Deutschland über Alles' that we hear at the end of the third episode of Pialat's *La Maison des bois*, accompanying a forward tracking-shot that instead of finishing on the corpse of a German moves slowly towards the face of a surviving French soldier. Finally there are the adolescents at the end of Doillon's *Les Doigts dans la tête* (1974) who have lost everything, family, work, love, but who sing their total and unconditional freedom at the top of their voices. All these moments represent acts of symbolic healing in respect of collective suffering and private pain, and although there is something necessarily impossible about these acts, they do constitute

modern cinema's response to Pascal's expression of fear as 'suffering this pain and abandonment in the horror of the night'. They are consciously working against the evidence of despair.

The final important form is the architectonic sublime. From the pure seriality of Sylvia Boissonnas's *Un Film* to the fragmentary sketches of Godard's videographic essays, there is no preconceived composition, the films invent their own rules of construction. Sometimes the scaffolding is left visible, as in Hanoun's *Octobre à Madrid* (1964), sometimes it is all that is visible, as in Hanoun's *Un Film* (1983), whereas in other cases the films enact their own destruction and extinction, like the admirable libertarian films of Jean-Pierre Lajournade, *Cinéma cinéma* (1969), *Le Joueur de quilles* (1969) and *La Fin des Pyrénées* (1971). One artist, Philippe Garrel, reinvents the rules of construction in every film, as is readily visible in his films of the 1970s and 1980s, where the motifs are always the same (portraits, especially of women), the sequences are always serial, but the architecture is different each time. *Un Ange passe* (1975), for example, exposes in a profound and disturbing way the powers of parallel editing. Two types of sequences are alternated throughout the film: on the one hand, portraits of Nico, on the other, dialogues between the actors (Laurent Terzieff, Maurice Garrel, Bulle Ogier, Jean-Pierre Kalfon). These two sides of the film never meet, their relationship remains implicit, mysterious, suspended. What is happening, however, on each side of this schism? It is essentially a formal question, the question of creation. What is the relationship between Nico's face and her music? Is she remembering, preparing, contemplating her music? Is she letting it take her over or is she taking a rest from it? Symmetrically, the spoken sequences with the actors represent all the possible forms of the sketch, they show the actors at work, getting ready to perform, in performance, improvising and in full flight. In this way, the timeless, indescribable and enigmatic link between Nico and her song, the sublime link of creation, is displayed in its clear, material, concrete forms by the actors, who remain in a perpetually formless time of work-in-progress. Thus *Un Ange passe* proposes two endings, the first is classical, like a fairy-tale, in which the fairies are the modern forms of poetry, with Nico playing in concert, far off, on the distant stage, caught in an immense beam of white light; she becomes the syncretic image of poetry, musician, poetess, actress, priestess. As for the second ending, with the actors, its incompleteness is made sublime by a falling away: starkly shot against the devouring light of an immense bay, Laurent Terzieff and Maurice Garrel speak to each other, reciting the German poet Rilke and the shortest haiku in the world: 'A man falls. The sound of water.' To reach this point, Garrel has had to invent a new structure, which shows at the same time the profound silence presiding over the demiurge, as well as the concrete, sometimes faltering, inspiration – nurtured by hesitations and anxieties – that characterises the working of art.

QUESTIONS OF FORMAL NEGLIGENCE

In contrast to the inventive and experimental qualities that distinguish the films discussed in this chapter, what should we say, in conclusion, about the formal negligence in mainstream cinema? What is there to say about purely conventional forms? Is it just a question of formlessness? Is it perhaps an eternally fixed formal repertory? Or maybe it is a continual bastardisation of older forms, and if so which ones? Does the process have a history? Do we really need to analyse it, or does the corpus by definition contain no surprises and nothing that we do not know already? For the moment, then, we simply propose to replace this vast and exciting historical project by an enjoyable projection of Maurice Lemaître's *Un Navet* . . .

(. . . And then there all the lost films.)

WORKS CITED

Adorno, T. (2002) *L'Art et les arts*, Paris, Desclée de Brouwer.

Bazin, A. (1957) 'Cinéma et engagement', *Esprit*, 4, April, 681–4.

Bazin, A. (1967) *What Is Cinema?*, vol. 1, Berkeley, University of California Press.

Bénichou, P. (1948), *Morales du Grand Siècle*, Paris, Gallimard.

Benjamin, W. (2001) *Le Concept de critique esthétique dans le romantisme allemand*, Paris, Flammarion.

Bergala, A. (1999) *Nul mieux que Godard*, Paris, Cahiers du cinéma.

Bohler, O. (2004) *Vestiges de soi, vertiges de l'autre: l'homme de l'après-guerre dans l'oeuvre de Jean-Pierre Melville*, Pertuis, Rouge Profond.

Bresson, R. (1997) *Notes on the Cinematographer*, Copenhagen, Green Integer.

Carta, J. (1957) 'Démission du cinéma français', *Esprit*, 3, March, 494–9.

Danet, L. (1996) 'Gérard Fromanger', in Bouhours, J.-M. ed., *L'Art du mouvement*, Paris, Centre Georges Pompidou, 167.

Deleuze, G. (1989) *Cinema 2: The Time-Image*, London, Athlone.

Eisenstein, S. (1980) *Le Mouvement de l'art*, Brussels, Complexe.

Godard, J.-L. (1972) *Godard on Godard*, London, Secker and Warburg.

Godard, J.-L. (1989) 'Préface', in Buache, F. (1990), *Le Cinéma français des années 70*, Paris, Hatier/5 Continents, 5–7.

Hanoun, M. (2001) *Cinéma cinéaste: notes sur l'image écrite*, Crisnée, Yellow Now.

Hegel, W. F. (1979) *System of Ethical Life and First Philosophy of Spirit*, Albany, NY, SUNY.

Muel, B. (2000) 'Les Riches heures du Groupe Medvedkine', *Images documentaires*, 37–8, 23.

19 REPRESENTATIONS 1960–2004
Parisian Images and National Transformations

Naomi Greene

No city, perhaps, symbolises a nation as surely as Paris does France. In the words of French historian Maurice Agulhon: 'Paris is a symbol of France, doubtlessly more than Rome is of Italy and, certainly, much more than Madrid is of Spain or Berlin of Germany' (Agulhon 1992: 869). Not surprisingly, as the cultural as well as the political capital of the nation – the centre of power and knowledge for the last three centuries – Paris has long held a privileged role in French cinema. From early films by Georges Méliès and Louis Feuillade to the *cinéma du look* of the 1980s or the *banlieue* films of the 90s, filmic representations of Paris have reflected deep currents of national life. The edgy metropolis of Jean-Luc Godard's *À bout de souffle* (1960) and *Alphaville* (1965) speaks of post-war social dislocations and anxieties just as surely as *banlieue* films of the 1990s suggest the changing face of the nation's cities and the increasingly diverse nature of her population. Keeping in mind this broader climate, this chapter will look at some of the portraits of Paris offered by films from these four decades. Providing a dramatic visual record of the physical changes that have transformed the nation's capital in this period – the gentrification of working-class neighbourhoods; the growth of affluent suburbs as well as the rise of desolate housing projects; the influence of globalisation and of the kind of consumerist culture associated with the USA – these filmic portraits also suggest the complex range of economic and social changes that have taken place not only in Paris but in France itself. Qualifying this period as one of 'anxiety and doubt', historian Robert Gildea claims that the French 'have had to come to terms with the legacy of the Occupation, with the loss of empire, with the influx of foreign immigrants, with the rise of Islam, with the destruction of traditional rural life, with the threat of Anglo-American culture to French

language and civilisation' (Gildea 1997: 1). As we shall see, virtually all these important changes are refracted in the cinematic portraits of Paris that emerge from films of the period.

Looking back at the evolution of French society since 1945, observers invariably stress the pivotal role played by the 1960s. It was at this time that the post-war economic expansion – in the course of which France was transformed from a largely rural, traditional society into an urbanised, industrialised one – reached its peak. The period often referred to as 'thirty glorious years' of expansion, stretching from the end of World War II to the oil-induced recession of 1974–5, saw the weakening of traditional social values and customs as well as a transformation in long-standing economic and ideological divisions. Observing that this period witnessed the collapse of the great social structures of the 19th century, French sociologist Henri Mendras maintained that the years from 1965 to 1984 experienced nothing less than a 'second French Revolution' (Mendras 1988). This internal revolution, moreover, was accompanied by dramatic changes abroad. That is, France's long reign as a colonial power came to an end when, in 1962, treaties according Algeria its independence were signed. Undermining a sense of national prestige, the end of empire had important internal repercussions. Kristin Ross argues that during these years France transformed an imperial concern with order, technology and discipline in the colonies into an infatuation at home with technology and machines (automobiles, household appliances, factory production) (Ross 1995); François Loyer points out that the vast building projects that changed the face of Paris in the 1970s and 1980s might well be seen as compensation for lost imperial glory (Loyer 1991). But the most important legacy of the nation's imperial role was, certainly, the influx of foreigners who came to metropolitan France from her former African colonies. Adding to the diversity of her population, their presence has consistently fuelled political controversies and sparked debates about what it means to be French in a country marked by different ethnic groups with their own culture and religion. Along with these momentous internal and external changes, the decade of the 1960s, in particular, also saw the coming of age of a new generation. Unscathed by the wartime memories of their parents, this generation grew up in a new world – one characterised not only by the weakening of traditional social patterns and structures but also by a virtual revolution in mass communications and popular culture. Often seduced by the new culture coming from the other side of the Atlantic, the young people growing up at this time found it logical to pursue an 'individual happiness' that, as French historian Michel Winock writes, 'would have seemed unimaginable to the workers of previous generations':

> It was in the 1960s, he continues, that industrial and urban civilisation took over in a France which had for so long remained agricultural: the reign of fathers and patriarchs came to an end. The so-called nuclear family (father-mother-children) often imposed a painful confrontation between two generations without shared experiences. (Winock 1985: 308)

CHANGING IMAGES, IMAGES OF CHANGE

Virtually all these critical changes resonate, directly or indirectly, in the portraits of Paris offered by French films of the 1960s. In the best-known films of the decade – those of the so-called New Wave – this resonance is largely indirect. Still, there is no question that films such as Godard's *À bout de souffle*, François Truffaut's *Les Quatre cents coups* (1959) and Claude Chabrol's *Les Cousins* (1959) reflect changes that were transforming the tenor of French life. Keenly aware of themselves as a new generation of film-makers in rebellion against their predecessors, the young directors of the New Wave also enjoyed a productive relationship with Paris. If, as legend has it, they were initially inspired to make films by a desire to shoot on the city streets – the

New Wave, observed Éric Rohmer, 'was born from the desire to show Paris, to go down into the street, at a time when French cinema was a cinema of studios' (Rohmer 1981: 34) – it is also true that, for them, Paris seemed to embody the rapid changes taking place around them. Marked by incessant traffic and speed – created by camerawork and editing as well as by protagonists who are constantly on the run and by cars that zoom through the city streets – the Paris that emerges from early New Wave films is marked by a newfound affluence and cosmopolitan edge. Americans, in particular, are everywhere – from the young expatriate of Jacques Rivette's *Paris nous appartient* (1961), to the young people who frequent the Left Bank haunts of *Les Cousins*, to the female protagonist of *À bout de souffle* who hawks copies of the *New York Herald Tribune* along the Champs-Élysées. So, too, are reminders of American culture – refracted by film posters, advertising images and popular music – omnipresent. The very fact that much of Godard's first feature takes place along the Champs-Élysées is telling. Associated with American rather than French images of Paris – 'one rarely sees', remarked Godard, 'the Arc de Triomphe in films except in American ones' (Marie 1985: 52) – this tourist zone of neon lights and fast-food chains is in sharp contrast with the iconic Paris portrayed in an earlier tradition of French films.

Not surprisingly, even as this Paris became less French, it also saw the dissolution of conventional mores and of the long-standing social ties provided by friends and family, by neighbours and work. Relentlessly pursuing the individual happiness described by Winock, the young people in New Wave films exhibit a disregard for the social conventions – particularly those governing sexuality – that marked their parents' generation. But this pursuit, this new freedom, it was clear, had its price. Like the doomed gangster of *À bout de souffle*, or the country cousin of *Les Cousins*, who is destroyed when he comes to the big city, the characters in these films are often vulnerable and alone. Nowhere are the currents of alienation that pervade these works more visible than in the first features of Éric Rohmer and Jacques Rivette. In Rohmer's *Le Signe du lion* (1962), the protagonist – locked out of his apartment at the start of a long summer weekend –

wanders anonymously through steaming and desolate streets anxiously searching for help that is not forthcoming; in Rivette's *Paris nous appartient*, a deserted Paris seems to harbour vast conspiracies that threaten to encircle and destroy the hapless protagonists.

While New Wave features such as these captured the emotional tremors of France's second Revolution, it was left to other directors – notably so-called Left Bank and cinéma vérité film-makers such as Agnès Varda, Chris Marker and Jean Rouch – to investigate the larger social and historical context surrounding the rapid changes overtaking the nation. Unlike their contemporaries associated with the *Cahiers du cinéma* branch of the New Wave, these directors were decidedly on the left of the political spectrum; their films displayed a concern with issues related to social justice, to the legacy of colonialism and to the dark underside of the new affluence and consumerism that were rapidly gaining ground in France. For them, alienation and marginality were embodied not in romantic individuals (like the gangster of *À bout de souffle*) but, rather, in social groups ostracised by poverty and racism. Similarly, the 'foreigners' that mattered to them were not a few rootless American expatriates wandering the streets of the Left Bank but, rather, the large numbers of foreigners arriving in France, especially those from the former colonies. To some extent, of course, a film like *Paris nous appartient*, with its sense of hidden menace and its allusions to right-wing figures like McCarthy and Franco, does hint at a larger political context. One might even see its dark and claustrophobic mood as an indirect reflection of the climate of censorship and repression that surrounded the actual struggle that was tearing France apart at this time: that is, the bitterly divisive war the nation was waging in Algeria. But, significantly, Rivette's film contains no direct allusions to the Algerian war nor to its repercussions at home – repercussions that included demonstrations that were brutally repressed by the Paris police. In contrast, the controversies and brutalities engendered by the Algerian war are very much in evidence in both Jean Rouch's *Chronique d'un été* (1962) and in Agnès Varda's *Cléo de 5 à 7* (1962). A film composed largely of interviews with a wide range of Parisians, *Chronique d'un été* contains an important sequence in which interviewees angrily debate the war that one of them deems 'absurd'. In Varda's film, the presence of the Algerian war is filtered through the experiences of its protagonist, a young Parisian singer named Cléo. At one point, as Cléo rides through Paris in a taxi, she hears a radio broadcast referring to events in Algeria and to protests in Paris; still later in the film, the war intersects with her own life more directly when she strikes up what appears to be a romance with a young soldier about to return to the front.

If the Algerian war makes itself felt in certain sequences of *Chronique d'un été* and *Cléo de 5 à 7*, it moves to the very heart of the urban landscape that emerges from *Le Joli mai* (1962), Chris Marker's highly personal documentary about Paris and its people. The very title of the film, in fact, refers to what many perceived as the nation's first springtime of peace in many years. Using a voice-over commentary that offers facts and philosophical musings about Paris, *Le Joli mai* mixes interviews with ordinary Parisians and documentary footage as it explores some of the repercussions of 'the events' (as the Algerian war was euphemistically called). Interviews suggest the climate of repression and censorship that surrounded the war as well as, perhaps, a deeper social disaffection, a turning away from issues affecting the nation. That is, many interviewees – including, in one case, a soldier about to leave for the front – display a kind of selfish narrowness or complacency: they tell us that they are not interested in politics or even that they dare not let themselves speak, or sometimes think, about outside events. (A number of women even declare that women are too emotional to vote and that politics should be left to men.) Such attitudes are all the more dismaying when contrasted with the historical and social awareness implicit in the remarks made by two young men from former French colonies in Africa – a young black student from Dahomey and a skilled Algerian worker. While their very presence points to the changing nature of the nation's population, their observations about the racism they have endured first in Africa and then in France raise the spectre of the xenophobic currents that would eventually turn France's far right Front National into the largest neo-fascist party in Europe.

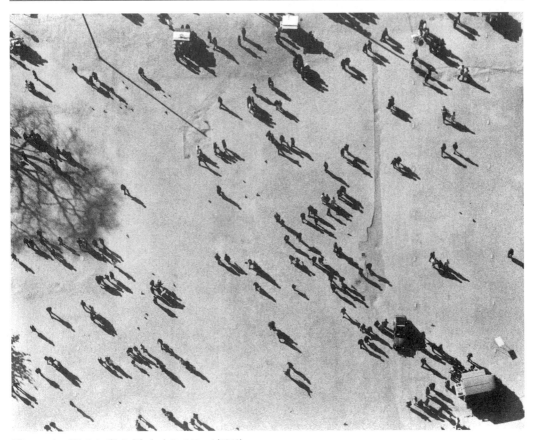

The people of Paris in Chris Marker's *Le Joli mai* (1962)

Colonialism and racism are not, moreover, the only social ills implicitly denounced in *Le Joli mai*. The film also turns a critical eye to some of the more disquieting repercussions of France's second Revolution. No less than the New Wave films, *Le Joli mai* displays the most visible tremors of this revolution: the frenetic traffic in Paris, the post-war infatuation with machines and appliances (in one sequence, a salesman demonstrates the use of washing machines), the pursuit of an individual happiness that prompts young people to endlessly dance the twist in a Paris nightclub. But, unlike New Wave films, *Le Joli mai* also seeks to go beyond these outward manifestations of newfound affluence and to see how it has affected the national soul. Thus, several of the interviews suggest the ways in which an obsession with money has been accompanied perhaps generated by, a spiritual and emotional emptiness – what Marker calls a new solitude. In the opening interview, for example, a harried shopkeeper emphatically observes that he is only happy when making money. All he asks from life, he insists repeatedly, is to eat, sleep and make money; he has no interest in politics, nor in the kind of 'difficult' movies – such as Alain Resnais's *Hiroshima mon amour* (1959) – that the interviewer mentions to him. Looking at the kind of selfish complacency displayed by the shopkeeper from a broader perspective, the film implicitly denounces the enormous gap that still exists between rich and poor. One sequence underscores this gap through a contrast between sound and image: as the camera wanders through the crumbling streets of an urban slum, the soundtrack carries an advertisement for luxury housing. Given Marker's obvious concern with social justice, it is hardly surprising that what may be the most moving interview in the film is with a worker-priest, who quietly tells us that he was forced to leave the Church to devote himself to the struggle against class exploitation and oppression.

FROM REVOLUTION TO NOSTALGIA

It is clear that *Le Joli mai* touched upon some very raw nerves in French society. The cracks that Marker sensed below the surface of French life exploded in May 1968 when student radicals denounced the kind of narrow smugness and selfishness displayed by so many of those interviewed in *Le Joli mai*. But above and beyond the drama of May 1968, the film seemed to foreshadow the widespread sense of spiritual emptiness, the growing national malaise, which overtook France in the course of the following decade. In part, of course, this malaise had economic roots. As the post-war economic boom ground to a halt with the recession of 1974, France had to face a variety of woes: high unemployment (particularly among young people), the rigours of global competition, the decline of the working class, together with the fear that traditional left-wing solutions and goals (like those embraced by the worker-priest in Marker's film) were no longer viable. Even as ideological certainties wavered, economic difficulties gave rise to new patterns of social exclusion, as the homeless, the chronically unemployed, the addicted and the depressed became as marginalised as criminal gangs and illegal immigrants on the edges of society. Commenting on these changes, Michel Winock observed:

> the demographic decline of France and Europe, the constraints exerted on the job market by economic mutations, the end of the great movements of secularisation and urbanisation that began at the end of the nineteenth century – all these factors create anxiety in a population which has been struck by unemployment (or the fear of unemployment), stripped of protective structures (the village community, the church, the patriarchal family), and which lacks a collective agenda. (Winock 1990: 39)

From a still broader perspective, the loss of empire meant that the long decades of French grandeur had come to an end. France was now merely an average power dwarfed by the superpower on the other side of the Atlantic. Moreover, the looming spectre of the European Union as well as the growth of immigration from former French colonies in Africa exacerbated fears that national identity – traditionally based on the notion of a shared culture and religion – would be lost. Not surprisingly, anxieties about the contours of national identity, about the loss of French prestige and power, about economic stagnation and unemployment, appeared to fuel an ever-growing nostalgia for the past. Analysing this complex mood of fear and nostalgia, historian Michel Wieviorka writes:

> Massive urbanisation is perceived as having destroyed everything; consumer society and television have done the rest. A deep sentiment of decadence and degeneration is mixed with fear and the theme of insecurity. The past is perceived as a golden age, and discourses feed upon the image of a multifaceted crisis. (Wieviorka 1992: 16)

It is precisely this sense of crisis and nostalgia that reverberates throughout some of the most significant French films of the 1980s and 1990s. Just as surely as New Wave and cinéma vérité films bore witness to the second French Revolution of the 1960s, those of subsequent decades reflect the climate of doubt and anxiety that had begun to haunt French consciousness in the 1970s. Once again, as in the case of the New Wave, their portrayal of Paris – the 'symbol' of the nation – says much about the temper of the times. Not unexpectedly, these portraits vary greatly. While the post-modern *cinéma du look* of the 1980s depicts a Paris that could hardly be more glossy or unreal, the so-called *banlieue* films of the 1990s view the French capital through a lens of gritty realism. Yet despite such profound differences, virtually all these portraits point to what has been described as a mood of national malaise and crisis. In an article published in 1983, French critic Alain Bergala makes a critical distinction between directors of the New Wave and those associated with the *cinéma du look* or, as it was also called, the 'new New Wave' of the 1980s. He observes that while New Wave directors were concerned with a search for 'truth' – obsessed by the need to breach the wall between the image and the real – directors such as Jean-Jacques Beineix, Luc Besson and Leos Carax embraced the 'untruth' of cinema even as they sought to create films based on what he calls the 'pure and simple forgetfulness of the principle of reality'. They begin, he writes, 'with the same logic: if the image is ontologically false, there is no point resisting this falseness. You may as well make the most of it, and get the best out of it – that is, its theatricality' (Bergala 1983: 5).

In one sense, Bergala is absolutely correct. Films such as Beineix's *Diva* (1981), Besson's *Subway* (1985) and Carax's *Les Amants du Pont-Neuf* (1991) are clearly built on what might be called an aesthetic of the false. Marked by one-dimensional characters and artificial plots, these works incorporate Paris itself into a world of images even as they drain the real world of weight and substance. To this end, they may replace an actual place, like the bridge in *Les Amants du Pont-Neuf*, with an obvious replica or shoot familiar places, like the metro stop in *Subway*, in such a way that they appear strange and unrecognisable. But in another sense, Bergala

does not go far enough. For just as New Wave films could never reach reality – 'it's not a just image, it's just an image', as Godard and Jean-Pierre Gorin expressed it in *Vent d'est* (1969) neither can directors such as Carax and Besson simply forget reality. For one thing, their very embrace of the image seemed to confirm fears that the contemporary world was falling sway to the images of advertising and the media. For another, their images of a false Paris suggests, perhaps, the forces of globalisation that threatened to eclipse the essential Frenchness of the capital. Lastly, and less speculatively, even the false images of their films hint (albeit in a stylised and allusive way) at some of the pressing social problems that were fuelling the nation's sense of doubt and anxiety. Indeed, French writer Raphaël Bassan suggests that critics do not usually want to go below the glossy and unreal surface of these works precisely because they hide such a 'pessimistic vision of the society of the 1980s' (Bassan 1989: 48).

This pessimistic vision bears eloquent witness, for example, to the new patterns of exclusion that

Juliette Binoche and Daniel Buain in *Les Amants du Pont-Neuf* (Leos Carax, 1991)

had begun to come into sharp focus at this time. The Paris depicted here is a city of lonely, marginalised individuals who are stripped of family and friends. Like the strange punk band living beneath the Parisian metro in *Subway* or the homeless lovers who find shelter on the bridge in *Les Amants du Pont-Neuf*, the characters in these films seem to come from nowhere, to live in makeshift dwellings cut off from the city as a whole. Confined to the edges of society, these hapless beings find themselves confronted, moreover, by an urban landscape punctuated by a new kind of casual violence: murders (*Diva*, *Subway*), accidents and drug- or alcohol-induced frenzies (*Les Amants du Pont-Neuf*) are everyday occurrences. Given their circumstances and surroundings, it is hardly surprising that these characters seem prone to numbness and despair. The gangster hero of *À bout de souffle* may proclaim his weariness, but he is a complex human being still capable of dreams and desire. Those who haunt the *cinéma du look*, in contrast, seem to have renounced all hope: they are as paralysed and devoid of emotions as the robotic characters imagined by Godard in the futuristic vision of Paris he had created in *Alphaville*. Most importantly, perhaps, the Paris that surrounds these pathetic beings seems to share, to underscore, their lethargy and sadness. But if the falseness of this world is a source of the melancholy it exudes, there are other factors at work. For, as depicted here, Paris is strikingly desolate, deprived of life and vibrancy. Just as the characters lack a sense of energy, so the city, as if in the wake of some disaster, appears lifeless and paralysed. When, for example, the principal couple of *Diva* walk through the pre-dawn streets of Paris, they see no one: the public gardens are as empty and quiet as the monuments and plazas they stop to admire. In *Les Amants du Pont-Neuf*, too, Paris is hushed and desolate. Although the Pont-Neuf bridge is in the virtual heart of Paris, in Carax's film it appears, as Graeme Hayes notes, 'cut off from the rest of Paris, placed outside the time and the space of the city' (Hayes 1999: 20). Even on Bastille Day, when Paris is invariably thronged with crowds and merrymakers, Carax's lovers see no one else: the presence of the holiday is made known by the explosive noise and the reflections of firecrackers.

Informed by the sense of crisis that haunted the nation in the 1980s, the films of the *cinéma du look* also suggest the growing nostalgia of those years. This nostalgia is evoked principally by the many allusions to classic French films of the 1930s that punctuate works such as *Diva* and *Les Amants du Pont-Neuf*. In this respect, it is telling that while New Wave directors waxed nostalgic for a lost tradition of Hollywood films, directors like Carax and Beineix look back, instead, to classics of French populist cinema such as René Clair's *Le Million* (1931), Jean Vigo's *L'Atalante* (1934) and Marcel Carné's *Hôtel du Nord* (1938). In evoking memories of these beloved classics, they pay homage, of course, to a great moment of French cinema. But, at the same time, they also call to mind the image of Paris – seen as a city of family and friends, of small tradesmen and charming neighbourhoods – so central to populist films of this era. Inevitably imbued with the desolating and deeply nostalgic contrast between past and present, these filmic echoes evoke a time when the French capital was still vibrant and alive – a time when it had not yet been reduced to lifeless images and simulated icons. This nostalgia is, in fact, explicitly acknowledged as such in the final sequence of *Les Amants du Pont-Neuf*. In this scene, the lovers, who have endured a long separation, once again meet on the bridge: joyful at their reunion, they jump about and ultimately fall from its parapets into the Seine. There, they wind up in an embrace that inevitably recalls a famous scene from *L'Atalante*, in which a young husband – whose wife has disappeared following a quarrel – dives into the Seine, where he sees a surreal, sensuous image of his beloved. Rendering Vigo's dreamlike scene totally concrete, Carax follows it with an even more explicit allusion to *L'Atalante*. For when the lovers rise to the surface of the Seine, they see a barge named – what else? – 'L'Atalante'. Its captain good-naturedly fishes the lovers from the river and, as *Les Amants du Pont-Neuf* comes to an end, the barge, with the lovers safely aboard, steams away from view. As the modern-day lovers leave the bleakness of contemporary Paris for the warmth and comfort of a remembered past, they illustrate not only the emotional charge of cinematic images but also the depth of the nostalgia that turned the French past, in Wieviorka's words, into a 'golden age'.

NEW REALISM, NEW REALITIES

If Paris is bathed in melancholy and nostalgia in certain films of the 1980s and 1990s, a different strand of contemporary cinema has shed the harshest of lights on the French capital at the end of the 20th century. These films are not set in the luminous areas of the city like those surrounding the Pont-Neuf but, rather, in squalid, crime-ridden back alleys and in bleak suburbs or *banlieue* on the outskirts of the city. Here, vague allusions to contemporary woes were replaced by an unrelenting look at one of the most pressing issues confronting the nation: the cluster of social problems – racism, violence, crime, social disaffection – associated with France's so-called 'immigrant' communities. Not surprisingly, some of these films belonged to a genre that had long reflected the dark underside of French society: the *policier* or crime film. In works such as Bob Swain's *La Balance* (1982), Maurice Pialat's *Police* (1985) and Bertrand Tavernier's *L626* (1992), the never-ending war between the police and the Parisian underworld so often portrayed in this genre assumes a strikingly contemporary cast. Here, the 'underworld' is composed largely of North Africans who are frequently no more corrupt or violent than the policemen who seek to punish them. Later works, deemed *banlieue* films, were set in the impoverished suburbs that ring many of France's major cities. Populated largely by people descended from France's former African colonies, the desolate housing projects or *cités* of these suburbs are a breeding ground for anger, violence and crime. The social problems associated with these modern-day ghettos, as well as the 'otherness' of their inhabitants – who are perceived as different by virtue of religion (many are Muslim) as well as colour – have tended to fuel racist sentiment and misinformed debates about the very nature of French identity. The best-known film of the period to portray the ghetto-like world of the deprived suburbs was Mathieu Kassovitz's *La Haine* (1995). Focused on three young friends (a Jew, an Arab and a Black) who live in a project outside Paris, *La Haine* paints a devastating portrait of a social and economic prison from which few escape. The world of these three young men is one of broken families, violent confrontations (with the police as well as with racist right-wing skinheads), drugs and dreams of revenge and escape. In terms of distance, Paris is not far from the devastated *banlieue* they call home. But the contrast between the civilised and affluent heart of the city and the harsh conditions of the *cité* – which resembles a war zone after a night of protests, looting and wanton destruction – could not be more stark. This is made very clear in one sequence in which the three protagonists take the train to the centre of the city. As they step from one world into another, they might be visitors from another planet. And when they return to the *cité* and see the Eiffel Tower gleaming in the distance, it seems to be the symbol of a world – not only that of Paris but of France itself – to which they do not, or cannot, belong.

The invisible walls ringing the ghetto – walls both social and psychological – are at the heart of another 1996 film, *Salut cousin!*. Made by Merzak Allouache, *Salut cousin!* belongs to the growing ranks of films that bring an insider's eye to bear on the problems faced by those in the communities resulting from earlier immigration. Within the film, these problems are filtered through the experiences of two young cousins: Mok, a Parisian-born Algerian who dreams of becoming a rock star; and Allio, his naive cousin from Algeria who is in Paris on a work-related errand. The choices they face are not enviable ones: to work (as does Allio) for a pittance amidst the dangers and violence of Algiers; to be regarded (like Mok) as alien or foreign in the country of one's birth. In fact, the intensity of Mok's desire to be seen as 'French' rather than Algerian has given rise to a host of pathological symptoms: a compulsive liar and gambler, he is estranged from loving parents, who continue to inhabit the despised *cité* where he spent his youth. In an ironic final twist, Allio remains in France while Mok is summarily deported to Algeria – a land that he has never seen. He ignored, it seems, a law that required him, as the son of immigrants, to actively request French citizenship.

In some ways, *Salut cousin!* might be likened to Chabrol's second feature, *Les Cousins*, made several decades earlier. Both films deal with fateful visits paid by naive country cousins to their sophisticated relatives in the city. But the differences between the two films speak volumes about fundamental social changes. Set in a milieu that is intensely French and very bourgeois, *Les Cousins* is a psychological study of individuals, in which the dangers of the big city assume a melodramatic cast infused with echoes of Balzac, whose presence is felt throughout the film. Here, as in Balzac's novel *Les Illusions perdues* (1843), the young provincial student must guard against the lure of the city, seen as an amoral place of sex and sin. In *Salut cousin!*, psychology – particularly the cluster of symptoms surrounding Mok's desire to reject his Algerian roots – is rooted less in melodrama than in very real social conditions. And the urban dangers portrayed by Allouache – that is, racism, the threat of deportation, social alienation, sub-standard housing – speak not of vice and virtue but of the difficulties faced daily by the cousins and thousands like them. Given such differences, it is hardly surprising that the Paris that surrounds Allio and Mok bears little resemblance to the alluring city of *Les Cousins*. While Chabrol's film takes place in the venerable streets and chic clubs of the Latin Quarter, in *Salut cousin!* Allio follows a trajectory that takes him from his cousin's squalid tenement to the barren projects on the outskirts of the city and to the streets, lined with strip clubs and drug dealers, around Barbès. Jostled by crowds and beset by noise, the cousins might well be living in a Third World metropolis rather than in the 'city of lights'. In fact, when the naive Allio first sees the run-down alley that leads to Mok's apartment, he remarks with surprise, 'it's just like Algiers'. Significantly, the only moments of liberation or escape are those linked to speed and flight. In the most striking of these, the two cousins are riding a motorcycle through the streets of Paris when, suddenly, their cycle begins to lift off the ground. As they see the city spread out below them, Paris once again becomes the city of sparkling lights and infinite promise, 'la ville lumière'. But the moment is brief. And even as their latter-day magic carpet makes its brutal descent, we are reminded of the seismic changes that have altered the face of Paris – and, indeed, of France – in the closing decades of the 20th and opening years of the 21st century.

WORKS CITED

Agulhon, M. (1992) 'Paris', in Nora, P. ed., *Les Lieux de mémoire*, Paris, Gallimard, 3: 3, 869–909.

Bassan, R. (1989) 'Trois néo-baroques français', *La Revue du cinéma*, 449, 45–53.

Bergala, A. (1983) 'Le Vrai, le faux, le factice', *Cahiers du cinéma*, 351, 4–9.

Gildea, R. (1997) *France since 1945*, Oxford, Oxford University Press.

Hayes, G. (1999) 'Representation, Masculinity, Nation: The Crises of *Les Amants du Pont-Neuf*', in Powrie, P. ed., *French Cinema in the 90s*, Oxford, Oxford University Press, 199–210.

Loyer, F. (1991) 'Préface', in Fermigier, A., *La Bataille de Paris*, Paris, Gallimard.

Marie, M. (1985) 'Les Déambulations parisiennes de la nouvelle vague', in Hillairet, P., Lebrat, C. and Rollet, P., *Paris vu par le cinéma d'avant-garde: 1923–1983*, Paris, Paris Expérimental, 51–5.

Mendras, H. (1988) *La Seconde Révolution française: 1964–1984*, Paris, Gallimard.

Rohmer, É. (1981) 'Entretien avec Éric Rohmer', *Cahiers du cinéma*, 323–4, 29–39.

Ross, K. (1995) *Fast Cars, Clean Bodies: Decolonization and the Reordering of French Culture*, Cambridge, MA, MIT Press.

Wieviorka, M. (1992) *La France raciste*, Paris, Seuil.

Winock, M. (1985) 'Années 60: la poussée des jeunes', in *La France de 1939 à nos jours*, Paris, Seuil, 304–21.

Winock, M. (1990) *Nationalisme, antisémitisme et fascisme en France*, Paris, Seuil.

20 SPECTATORS 1960–2004
The Decline, Fall and Rebirth in Cinemagoing

Sue Harris

The final four decades of the 20th century witnessed a protracted decline in the number of spectators in French cinemas (see Table 9; 'Audience Numbers 1960–2002'). By the time the Socialist government seriously addressed the question of falling audiences in the 1980s, the total annual number of spectators had more than halved in just twenty years. Audience figures since 1995 indicate a long-awaited reversal of this long downward trend. This chapter examines the decline and rebirth in cinemagoing since the 1960s through reference to a series of key factors: limited support from government, growth in the domestic audiovisual market, expansion of aesthetic trends in 'difficult'

areas of cinematic production (avant-garde experiment, political cinema, erotic cinema) and the dramatic reorganisation of exhibition sites. It concludes with an analysis of the socio-demographic profile of those on whom the future viability and vitality of the industry depends: twenty-first-century audiences.

THE END OF THE GOLDEN AGE

Between the years 1945 and 1960, total annual attendance at French cinemas never fell below 350 million, and frequently surpassed the figure of 400 million tickets (Prédal 1996: 838). Thus the 1960s began on the cusp of a 'golden age', energised by the project and

Table 9 Audience Numbers (1960–2002)

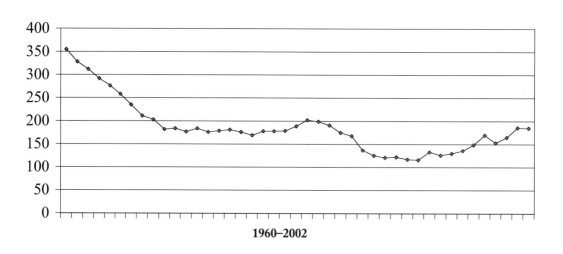

1960–2002

—◆— All France (millions)

innovations of the New Wave, and buoyed by the active participation of a dynamic ciné-literate audience base. In 1959, state interest in the cinema was transferred from the Ministère de l'Industrie et du Commerce to the newly formed Ministère de la Culture, headed by André Malraux until 1969. This dedicated Ministry of Culture was created to cement the state–culture relationship across a range of arts and activities, and Malraux's associations with literary culture rather than with institutional politics, together with his personal involvement in the 1930s with a range of left-wing causes (including the Popular Front, the Spanish Civil War and Communism) made him a popular candidate for the post of first national cultural administrator. Throughout the 1960s, support for the arts was channelled through this new Ministry according to criteria that were largely determined by Malraux himself. Although sympathetic to the needs of the cinema industry (one of the first measures to be implemented was the introduction of the *avance sur recettes* in 1959), there was little practical recognition on the part of the Ministry of the significance of contemporary popular culture as represented by film. For Malraux, the democratisation of culture meant facilitating access to existing high cultural artefacts and institutions, not the consolidation of audiences or the promotion of what he perceived as leisure pursuits. The cinema and the wider apparatus of the mass media were, for him, the stuff of the commercial rather than the cultural sphere, regardless of the exceptionally high numbers of the population that participated in these activities. This lack of a progressive interest in cinemagoing at a crucial political juncture is something from which the industry to date has never fully recovered. The year 1960 therefore announced the end of the golden age and the beginning of a protracted period of slow decline in spectatorship that would be compounded by the eventual deregulation of the broadcasting industry and by significant development in the domestic audiovisual market. Forty years later, government reports estimated that the average French person sees up to 250 films per year on television, compared with an average of only three at a cinema hall, a complete transformation of habits within a single generation. For today's French spectator, 'film culture is acquired primarily via the small screen' (*Développement culturel* 2000: 5).

René Prédal has described the crisis in spectatorship that ensued in the 1960s as an irreversible catastrophe in which French cinema sustained the most enormous loss of audience in its history: almost 150 million spectators in only ten years (Prédal 1996: 249–50). This was not immediately apparent to cinemagoers, who found themselves exposed to a range of cinematic forms, genres, styles and national cinemas that had simply not been available to them a decade earlier. Indeed, the early 1960s are notable for the rapid growth of the *ciné-club* movement, which boasted a record 8.2 million participants in 1964, and for the continued expansion of the art-house cinema (*art et essai*) network, which had been established with only five cinemas under the auspices of the AFCAE (Association Française des Cinémas d'Art et d'Essai) in 1955, but was already fifty-strong in 1962 (Prédal 1996: 250). Nevertheless, investment in the exhibition infrastructure in general was low, a factor that could only impact disadvantageously on the potential audience base. Films may have looked different to the 1960s viewer, but the experience of cinemagoing was still either tied to old-fashioned and poorly equipped, often pre-war theatres, or was very much constrained by unimaginative urban planning: many of the new housing estates, such as that built at Sarcelles in northern Paris, were constructed without any thought to the desirability, or indeed necessity, of commercial and leisure facilities. Poor transport links only compounded the physical and cultural isolation in which these new peripheral communities found themselves. But perhaps even more significantly, cinemagoing became an increasingly costly pastime. As Jean-Michel Frodon notes, the relative price of cinema tickets increased at almost twice the cost of living in the period between 1960 and 1970, and multiplied almost seventeen fold over the period from 1960 to 1990, against only a seven fold rise in the average cost of consumer goods (Frodon 1995: 137).

By 1965, *Cahiers du cinéma* took the step of devoting a whole issue to the crisis in French cinema, in which the question of falling audiences was paramount. As the years went on, this problem was compounded by a further realisation: the remaining audience base was increasingly shunning the domestic in favour of the international film, and demonstrating a clear preference for popular commercial films over traditional French art-house movies. In the watershed year of 1968, for example, France found itself projected onto the global stage, confronting civil unrest in its capital city and political contestation in its factories and universities. The public's viewing preferences, however, tell a story of very different preoccupations: the top three films of the following winter were Disney's *Bambi* (David Hand, 1942), the home-grown *bande dessinée* spin-off *Tintin et le temple du soleil* (Eddie Lateste, 1969) and the latest in the British 'James Bond' series, *On Her Majesty's Secret Service* (Peter R. Hunt, 1969). We might assume perhaps that politico-reflective domestic fare had more success later in the season, once the events and their impact had been better digested, but this was not the case: the biggest box-office hit of the 1968–9 season was another Disney product, *The Jungle Book* (Wolfgang Reitherman, 1967), which achieved close to 15 million entries nationally, and record attendance figures of 20,000 in a single day at the Rex in Paris (Bosséno 1996: 110).

French industry statistics from the mid-1950s onwards reveal a similar pattern of national viewing that has not changed significantly since, despite major social change on both national and global levels. Events, personalities and movements have all come and gone, but the calendar of attendance, together with a national preference for certain genres, has remained constant for the French public. At the beginning of the 1960s, the situation was highly typical: *Le Film français*, in its annual assessment of the state of the industry, noted that the highpoint of attendance in 1959 was week fifty-two, that is the Christmas/New Year holiday week, which saw occupancy rates peak at 42.5 per cent in a year in which rates averaged 24.2 per cent. The least successful week for attendance was week twenty-nine (the week of 15 July), which achieved only 14.4 per cent occupancy. The figures for this lowpoint in 1959 reflect the impact of the national holiday (14 July), as well as a heatwave across France, where temperatures of up to 32 degrees centigrade were recorded. The figures recorded by *Le Film français* relate specifically to Paris in this case, but investigation of the archives shows that these results are indicative of trends across the whole of France. Again, at the time of the French

Presidential elections of May 1981, a moment that saw the triumphant return of the left to power for the first time in forty-five years, the French viewing public sought escapism in its preferred choice of film: the re-release of Disney's *Sleeping Beauty* (Clyde Geronimi, 1959) dominated the April box office in Paris and surrounding areas, as well as cinemas in Bordeaux, Grenoble, Lille, Lyons, Marseilles, Metz, Montpellier, Nancy, Nice, Nantes, Rouen, Strasbourg and Toulouse. The evidence of other less politically 'significant' years is consistent with this pattern, leading us to conclude that the French are, in the main, a representative example of the global cinematic public: as elsewhere in Europe, the Disney hits *Dumbo* (Ben Sharpsteen, 1941), *The Aristocats* (Wolfgang Reitherman, 1970), *101 Dalmations* (Clyde Geronimi, 1961) and *The Lion King* (Roger Allers and Rob Minkoff, 1994) all topped the French box office in the year of their French release. Interestingly then, for a public with an international reputation for favouring avant-gardist cinematic pursuits, the French are really not so different from the majority of Western spectators when it comes to their Saturday-night and holiday viewing.

The 1970s witnessed a further culture shift in matters of genre and style that did little to stem the haemorrhage of audiences from French cinema halls. Valéry Giscard d'Estaing abolished censorship in 1974, opening the floodgates for the saturation of the French market by erotic films: during the period 1975–9, this accounted for around half of all French production screened in France (Hayward 1993: 244). The sheer visibility and weight (in production terms) of difficult or previously marginal modes of representation was, in the long term, extremely damaging to French cinemagoing habits. Adolescent and family audiences were marginalised both by the reduction in the range of choice of films and by the impact of this production on venues and their management. As films like *Emmanuelle* (Just Jaeckin, 1974) topped the annual box office, so a marked segregation of exhibition sites ensued (mainstream/marginal; adult/youth), resulting in the creation of 'porn only' cinema districts in many towns, where cinema halls in close proximity exhibited similar kinds of films: the reinvigoration of the Pigalle area in Paris in the early 1970s would be an example of this. The restrictions that these changes placed on particular segments of the potential audience, together with the high level of production of specifically adult material resulted, by the end of the 1970s, in the decimation of the French audience base. Guy-Patrick Sainderichin, writing in the second part of a special edition of *Cahiers du cinéma* published in 1981 remarked of contemporary audiences that 'the public is essentially young: 4/5 of spectators are under 35, and fall into the category of frequent or regular cinemagoers, attending at least twice a month' (*Cahiers du cinéma* 1981: 13). By dint of age, lifestyle and politics, this group was understandably the most receptive to the trends in film-making outlined above. However, as a percentage of the total population, this was much lower than in previous years: by this time, the total annual audience had fallen to a mere 179 million, its lowest point for forty years, and approximately half that recorded in 1960. In the midst of the most buoyant period of production since World War II – 209 films were produced in 1977, against an average of 100–10 in the 1950s (Prédal 1996: 836) – French cinema was indeed deep in crisis.

In 1981 a Socialist President and government came to power after nearly forty-five years in the wilderness. This administration, which swept to power on a wave of national optimism, immediately sought to address the institutional problems outlined above by prioritising legislation that promoted new conditions of 'citizenship', much of which had a direct impact on both leisure time and access to cultural venues and activities. Thus, early in the regime, the French population found itself benefiting from a reduced working week (the thirty-nine-, then later the thirty-five-hour week), the security of minimum-wage legislation (raised by 10 per cent in the first year of Socialist office) and increased vacation entitlement (raised to five weeks per annum in the first year of the administration). The conditions for more frequent participation in non-labour-specific activity were therefore established. Alongside this social legislation, the regime invested heavily in the cultural infrastructure of the country in ways that were economically and politically unprecedented. The support for the cinema industry in particular was phenomenal: as the culture budget was doubled almost overnight from 2.96 billion

(0.47 per cent) to 5.99 billion francs (0.75 per cent) (Loosley 1995: 80-1), so overall subsidies to the film industry increased by an incredible 600 per cent between 1981 and 1983 (Safran 1994: 312). In 1982, the budget for the *avance sur recettes* alone was increased from 27.7 million to 72 million francs, and was thereafter increased from year to year.

Therefore, 1981 should have been the year in which the French cinema began to experience a renaissance of creativity and attendance. More films were supported by more money, and political logic dictated that more people, with more time on their hands should have flocked to the cinema, and shared proudly in the experience of their own national creativity. Increased participation, so it went, would reinvigorate the economy, as well as teach the French something about their own culture, history and society. As Jack Lang, Mitterrand's flamboyant Minister for Culture, famously put it: 'Culture, economy: same battle' (Collard 2000: 44). Thus, even when faced with the fallout from the oil crisis of the mid-1970s and the effects of the global recession of the 1980s, French politicians exempted cultural affairs and spending from the otherwise dominant politics of austerity that France was forced to espouse. The Socialist cultural project was vigorously pursued, to the extent that by 1993, the Ministry of Culture allocation had reached the symbolic figure of 1 per cent of the total state budget (equivalent to $2.8 billion, resulting in a phenomenal per capita spending of $41 compared with $1.43 in the USA) (Safran 1994: 327 n.27).

However, the desired transformation in cinemagoing habits did not happen, and the effects of massive state investment in the cinema were exposed as negligible. Instead of increasing the audience base in France, attendance figures in fact continued to fall dramatically between 1980 and 1989, from 179 million to only 121 million by the end of the decade (Prédal 1996: 448). This demise was most marked in terms of young spectators, with cinemagoing in the fifteen-to-twenty-four age group falling by 42 per cent in only five years (1983–8) (Frodon 1995: 628). And even more incredibly, the domestic product, that is French films made in France with French money and stars, lost more than one-third of its audience in the space of just five years (1982–7), compounding trends set in motion in the 1960s.

This decline continued on into the 1990s: in 1982 French films were seen by 53.4 per cent of cinemagoers compared with only 30.1 per cent for US films, but by 1995, the figures were practically reversed: 35.4 per cent for French films, against 54.2 per cent for US films (Prédal 1996: 833).

The paradox of why such a heavily subsidised and fiercely protected modern industry should be so unsuccessful in attracting large numbers of its national audience has been the subject of much debate. Scholars and critics have analysed the quality of the product, but generally agree that this factor in itself is not likely to account for such a substantial loss of audience. Indeed, modern French films often have very extensive budgets, on the Hollywood model; production values are generally high, and talented domestic stars inspire immense loyalty among the population. Content and genre have also been queried with rather more success: government subsidies prioritise certain types of 'prestige' cinema, most notably what could still be considered as auteur cinema or semi-didactic, 'edifying' cultural cinema, such as the heritage film and literary adaptation. A comparison of two of the biggest commercial successes in France in the 1990s is revealing: at a time when the average grant amounted to 2.49 million francs, Jean-Marie Poiré's *Les Visiteurs* (1993) received a meagre 300,000 francs of government money; Claude Berri's *Germinal* (1993), on the other hand, received local and national subsidies to the tune of nearly 15 million francs (Prédal 1996: 715, 729–30). However, Centre National de la Cinématographie (CNC) statistics reveal that attendance figures for the two were 13 million and less than 6 million respectively, and that the films were ranked 9th and 103rd respectively in the overall league of 1945–2001 box-office receipts. The French state has had to learn the hard way that, laudable though its efforts may have been to extend the cultural possibilities of the average citizen, one cannot legislate for preference and taste.

NEW TOPOGRAPHIES OF SPECTATORSHIP

With the progressive loss of audience since the late 1950s has come a steady erosion of the number of venues on the French mainland, and this topographical change has impacted considerably on the habits of the cinemagoing population. Although the number of active cinema screens fell by only about 20 per cent over a twenty-four-year period (there were 5,834 in 1959, compared with 4,857 in 1983), the global number of seats fell by close to 50 per cent: the 1959 figures relate to nearly 3 million seats, a figure which, in line with audience numbers, had more than halved by 1983 (Prédal 1996: 448, 835). By 1995 there remained a comparable number of screens (4,614), but significantly fewer seats (992,023), all of which were centred on only 2,113 sites (Prédal 1996: 835). This reorganisation of the infrastructure impacted most seriously on local and small-town cinema halls (Bosséno 1996: 84). Frodon assesses this reduction as a fall from an average of 62 seats per 1,000 of the population in 1960, to a mere 18 per 1,000 in 1990 (Frodon 1995: 138). In the main, this reduction in capacity was an effect of necessary modernisation measures and a desire to increase spectatorial comfort. Nevertheless, the reality was that geographically, as well as spatially, options for access to cinema halls over a forty-year period were significantly reduced. Paradoxically, venues in rural areas were largely exempt from this practice. Instead, rural sites benefited considerably from the establishment in 1983 of the 'Agence pour le Développement Régional du Cinéma', an association that aimed not only to modernise but also to protect vulnerable rural economies, and saw the creation of new venues as a priority (Prédal 1996: 448). Furthermore, the introduction of financial aid packages such as the 1989 'Plan d'aide à l'ouverture et à la rénovation des salles' – which sought to support a programme of cinema construction and renovation – ensured that by 1991, 'the re-opening rate of cinema halls has overtaken the closure rate, and France has easily the highest number of cinema halls in Europe' (Prédal 1996: 828). Thus, in European terms, the French cinema network was the largest and most modern of its kind, well placed to attract spectators, even if its overall capacity could never equal that of 1960.

As the landscape of cultural consumption in France was radically transformed in the space of a few years, so existing modes of distribution and exhibition were inevitably modified. Multi-screen sites in town centres were a feature of French life from the early 1970s, and responsible to some extent for the compression of available seats noted above. These *multisalles* were not purpose-built, but were essentially conversions of formerly prestigious single-screen establishments such as the Paramount Opéra in Paris (1,920 seats in 1971, divided into two screens in 1973, and further divided into five screens in 1975), the Cézanne in Aix-en-Provence (nine screens by 1975) or the Gaumont Palace de Toulouse (five screens in 1975) (Bosséno 1996: 85). These were soon to be complemented, and to some extent replaced, by the US-style multiplex, offering a minimum of ten screens in purpose-built entertainment and leisure complexes. The 'multiplex theatre' as such did not exist in France until 1992, when the first venue was built in Toulon. However, the growth of these sites has been very rapid, with sixty on the French mainland at the turn of the century. Indeed, by 2001, forty-seven French *départements* boasted at least one multiplex cinema, compared with only eight equipped *départements* in 1996. Building programmes continue, and these venues have now become a permanent feature of French cultural life. Audiences tend to be metropolitan, with the highest concentration in urban areas with populations of over 100,000. This is unsurprising given that the best-equipped *départements* are those with high population centres (the Paris region, Nord, Gironde, Bouches du Rhône, Rhône) and those on the Atlantic and Mediterranean coasts that experience a significant influx of tourists in the summer months. Fifty-three per cent of multiplexes are concentrated in only five regions: Île de France, Nord-Pas-de-Calais, Provence-Alpes-Côte d'Azur, Rhône-Alpes, Pays de la Loire, with 43 per cent of art-houses concentrated in only three (Île de France, Provence-Alpes- Côte d'Azur, Rhône-Alpes). The least well-equipped, and consequently those where there is consistently a low attendance, are rural areas such as Lozère, Creuse and Corsica. Nevertheless, in 2001 provincial communes experienced an increase of 20.7 per cent attendance on the previous year, a fact that is attributed to the unusual commercial success of a series of domestic films: *Le Fabuleux destin d'Amélie Poulain* (Jean-Pierre Jeunet, 2001), *La Vérité si je mens 2* (Thomas Gilou, 2001), *Le Pacte des loups* (Christophe Gans, 2001) and *Le Placard* (Francis Veber, 2001).

The multiplex has been a key factor in further modifying patterns of French spectatorship. First, it is not an indigenous form. Based on the US model, it implies the US package: out-of-town location, an environment of restaurants, parking facilities and proximity to other leisure facilities such as shops, ice rinks and bowling alleys. But the facilities are crucially not those that French families traditionally patronise: restaurants in this case does not mean brasseries, but McDonald's, Burger King or Le Quick. The target market for such venues is inevitably the younger cinemagoer, long the backbone of French audiences, who is invited to experience film culture in the multiplexes in ways that break with previous French modes of consumption. Programming too is of a particular kind: US products account for up to 80 per cent of films shown, supplemented by popular domestic comedies such as *Gazon maudit* (Josiane Balasko, 1995) and *Un Indien dans la ville* (Hervé Palud, 1994). Auteur cinema, and non-US foreign films are rarely screened, but instead find their audience at the 941 art-house cinemas scattered around the country. The programming of multiplexes is of course intrinsically linked to the regular audience base, and distribution practices underline this. As Prédal points out:

> The decisions taken at the Wednesday 2 o'clock screening, that is the first weekly screening of new releases, are crucial to the fate of many films. From 2.15pm, audience numbers are calculated, and distributors then decide how the film will be exploited in the weeks to come. (Prédal 1996: 715)

Wednesday afternoons in France are traditionally free from school commitments, and the chances of this session being other than a predominantly teenage audience are slim. This new trend is consistent with previous analyses of audience composition: throughout the period from 1960 to 2001, eleven to twenty-four year-olds – made up mainly of school pupils and students – have consistently registered the highest share of market penetration.

Even so, we might consider to what extent the impact of investment in the material landscape of cultural consumption has had a democratising effect in terms of emerging patterns of spectatorship. Certainly, the installation of multiplexes in urban suburbs has facilitated access to leisure amenities for those social groups who traditionally live on the physical as well as material margins of French society, especially immigrant and working-class populations. The economic investment of the cinema industry in neglected city spaces has also been beneficial to local economies in terms of the provision and convenience of facilities. Furthermore, the loss of any real system of 'exclusivity' (although the term is still used in measuring Parisian attendance figures) means that films now tend to be released nationally at all venues in a given distribution network: provincial spectators see the latest big release at the same time as Parisians and those in other major French cities. Thus, we might conclude that urban renewal of the cinema industry and its sites of distribution has allowed for an acculturation of sorts that has not necessarily affected the public in other arts and media, such as print journalism, theatre and music. The democratisation of the internal space that these establishments have

engendered is equally of note: since the *multisalles* refurbishments of the 1970s, cinema architecture has taken a significantly more functional turn, forgoing the ornate finery of theatre halls in favour of streamlined purpose-built space. With the imposition of a modernist rather than traditional baroque aesthetic has come a dilution of the rituals and conventions so encouraged by traditional Italianate performance and viewing spaces. Indeed, the reality of French multiplex venues – like those elsewhere in the world – is that they can routinely accommodate 2,000, even 4,000 spectators while offering high levels of comfort, ease of access, pre-booking and allocated seats. The experience of cinemagoing may have become rather blander and less socially 'exciting' than at earlier stages in its history, but the result is an experience that is more predictable and arguably more 'pleasant' for the spectator.

These establishments also promote variety of choice. While the Kinépolis de Lille, with its

One of the most successful French films of all time, *Les Visiteurs* (Jean-Marie Poiré, 1993)

twenty-three screens, is evidence for some of a profound loss of quality – too many low-budget or hastily made films in circulation to fill screens; reduced screen size and poor sound quality in order to accommodate the maximum number of halls – one could also argue that, in theory at least, there is now far more scope for the average viewer in terms of choice of genres, star vehicles, level of production values and imported films. The downside of this is that films distributed simultaneously across France – anything between 300 and 500 copies can be in circulation at the launch of a major film – tend to have shorter runs than previously, compelling spectators to participate in the experience on distributors' terms rather than their own. The homogenisation of the sites has had further benefits for the industry in general, notably that of movement of spectators between forms and venues. While the growth and popularity of the multiplex appear to signal an inevitable erosion in the health of the alternative art-house circuit, this has not proved to be the case. *Art et essai* cinemas accounted in 1995 for 18.2 per cent of the total venues, against 15.8 per cent in 1987: the increase is only slight, but significant enough to indicate that the alternative circuit is in good health. Arguably, the expansion of the market may have made consumers of spectators, but these consumers exercise choice. As Jean-Max Causse of the Action network puts it: 'The public has changed: a few years ago, serious cinema buffs would never have gone to a commercial venue, but today we share the same clients' (Bosséno 1996: 114).

TWENTY-FIRST-CENTURY AUDIENCES

A survey of the cultural practices of the French published by the Ministry of Culture and Communication towards the end of 2000 (*Développement culturel* 2000), together with the official statistics gathered in the 1999 census, have brought a degree of relief and reassurance to policy-makers and industry commentators. These have indicated a tentative rise in spectator numbers since 1995, a trend confirmed by 2002 figures produced by the CNC. In 2001, 186 million cinema tickets were sold in France (an increase of 12 per cent on 2000), of which a total of 77 million were for French-made films (a market share of 41.5 per cent compared with 28.5 per cent in 2000). The average per capita number of visits to a cinema was 3.18, compared with 2.92 in 2000. Surveys use a series of categorisations of spectators: *les occasionnels* (occasional attenders, at least once a year); *les habitués* (habitual attenders, at least once a month); *les réguliers* (regular attenders, at least once a month, but less than once a week); *les assidus* (frequent attenders, at least once a week). The last three categories represented 41.2 per cent of the public in 2001, and accounted for nearly 78 per cent of ticket sales. Young people remain the most assiduous attenders: up to 70 per cent of cinemagoers are situated in the fifteen to forty-nine age bracket, with the fifteen to twenty-four age group representing more than a third of total annual spectators, and accounting for 40 per cent of all ticket sales. Indeed, more than 89 per cent of eleven to twenty-four year-olds went to the cinema once in 2001, as did 92 per cent of twenty to twenty-four year olds. Attendance is currently higher among men (51.2 per cent male against 48.8 per cent female) even though women represent the majority in the population (52 per cent). In terms of educational level, the cinema is a preferred leisure pursuit of those who are professionally categorised as 'skilled', 'managerial' or 'students'. Indeed, 76 per cent of the population categorised as 'CSP+' (a social category that includes the professional classes, equivalent to 'ABC1') attended at least once in 2001. While this population represents only 25.2 per cent of the entire population, they account for 32.5 per cent of the cinemagoing public, with a market penetration of 79.8 per cent.

In 2001, French cinema experienced an exceptional year, achieving the highest box-office figures for twenty years. This development, however, must be tempered against the realisation that this is a predominantly young audience with a preference for US-style action thrillers, complete with glamorous young stars and Hollywood-style special effects. Luc Besson's *The Fifth Element* (1997) is a case in point: made in English, starring Bruce Willis, Gary Oldman and Milla Jovovich, screened in French multiplexes, dubbed into French, to record audiences. That such a film, alongside James Cameron's *Titanic* (1997), and a score of domestic comedies should top the box office at the end of the 1990s is not especially surprising given current audience composition, but must nevertheless give cause for concern to cultural policy-makers in France. The phenomenal success, in France and abroad, of the home-grown *Le Fabuleux destin d'Amélie Poulain* may well be evidence at last of a renaissance in French cinema's popular appeal, but this is yet to be proved.

Figures used in this chapter are based on Institut National de la Statistique et des Études Économiques (INSEE) census statistics as recorded annually in the industry journal *Le Film français*, and on annual statistics produced by the CNC. These can be found in: 'La Culture cinématographique des Français', *Développement culturel* 135, September 2000 (Ministry of Culture and Communication); 'La Géographie du cinéma', *CNC info 281*, 2002; 'Les Films en salles', *CNC info 283*, May 2002.

WORKS CITED

Bosséno, C.-M. (1996) *La Prochaine séance: les français et leurs cinés*, Paris, Gallimard.

Cahiers du cinéma (1965) special issue: 'La crise du cinéma français', 161–2.

Cahiers du cinéma (1981) special issue: 'Situation du cinéma français 2', 325.

Collard, S. (2000) 'French Cultural Policy: The Special Role of the State', in Kidd, W. and Reynolds, S. eds, *Contemporary French Cultural Studies*, London, Arnold, 38–50.

Développement culturel (2000) 135, September.

Frodon, J.-M. (1995) *L'Âge moderne du cinéma français*, Paris, Flammarion.

Hayward, S. (1993) *French National Cinema*, London, Routledge.

Loosley, D. (1995) *The Politics of Fun: Cultural Policy and Debate in Contemporary France*, Oxford, Berg.

Prédal, R. (1996) *50 ans de cinéma français*, Paris, Nathan.

Safran, W. (1994) *The French Polity*, New York and London, Longman.

21 DEBATES 1960–2004
The Exercise Was Beneficial, Monsieur Daney

James S. Williams

Of all the major figures in French film theory and criticism since 1960, Serge Daney, by profession a journalist and, by his own account, an intellectual amateur, may well turn out to have been the pivotal agent of film debate in France during the second half of the 20th century. When he died tragically in 1992 from AIDS at the age of forty-eight, Daney became the object of unanimous adulation in France, his greatness immediately recognised in the French daily newspaper *Libération* as well as in a special issue of *Cahiers du cinéma*. In 2001, the popular cultural magazine *Les Inrockuptibles* described Daney as nothing less than 'the cinema incarnate', and the film journal *Trafic* devoted to him an almost totally uncritical special issue. In addition, the first two parts of a mammoth four-volume edition of his work entitled *La Maison cinéma et le monde* began to be published (Daney 2001, 2002). Without doubt, Daney was one of the most intelligent thinkers of film, a stylist and essayist who decoded and demystified the mythologies of cinema in the manner of early Roland Barthes. He was also an eloquent public speaker and debater, possessing great wit and charisma. In recognition of his remarkable range and status, Godard has described him as part of an illustrious line of French art critics beginning in the 18th century with Denis Diderot and featuring Charles Baudelaire, Élie Faure, André Malraux, André Bazin and François Truffaut.

In the context of his own generation, Daney was entirely representative of its gradual drift away from high political and psychoanalytic film theory during the 1970s back towards a more accessible cinephile approach informed by questions of history and culture. For this reason, by following the particular twists and turns of his career and essentially employing his story as a narrative pretext, we shall be able to review and assess the key moments and trends of film debate in France during the period under consideration. Such an approach is justified, moreover, by the paradox of Daney's relative invisibility in the English-speaking world in comparison with the exposure of Christian Metz during the 1970s and 1980s and Gilles Deleuze in the 1990s and beyond. The aim of this chapter, however, is not simply to commemorate Daney as some kind of immaculate *critique maudit* or 'melancholic hero' (Jean-Michel Frodon) caught in the shadow of death that haunts French film criticism and mirrors the intrinsic martyrology of French cinema (both Metz and Deleuze took their own lives, for example). What made Daney so unique and special, and why he is the central focus of this chapter, is that he was always able to see the wider picture and to conceive of film affirmatively in its complex relation to the personal, social, historical and political. Indeed, Daney was crucial in the way that he shifted the very nature and location of film debate in France, and his later work, a form of personal criticism that also directly addresses issues of gender, constitutes a particular and crucial challenge for current and future thinking about film.

FROM CINEPHILIA TO RADICAL THEORY

Daney's first published article was on John Ford's *Rio Bravo* in 1962 for a fanzine that he created with Louis Skorecki entitled *Visages du cinéma*. He then followed in the footsteps of Truffaut, Godard, Rivette and Rohmer at *Cahiers du cinéma*, which by the early 1960s was firmly established as an international crucible for film interpretation. Not untypically for *Cahiers du cinéma*, he celebrated classical Hollywood (e.g. Hawks, DeMille, Ford, Sturges, Preminger, Wilder, Cukor, Ray) while promoting modernism (notably Lang, Godard, Rossellini, Pasolini, Oliveira and his one abiding and unconditional love, Mizoguchi). By resisting any temptation to make films himself (he would always retain to his benefit the 'primary' position of spectator), Daney fashioned his critical style into something at once subtle and rigorous, elliptical and rich, lyrical and contestatory. Reading the first volume of *La Maison cinéma et le monde*, one is struck by the elegant clarity and boldness of Daney's method. One brief but instructive example is his 1966 overview of Orson Welles entitled 'Welles au pouvoir' ('Welles in Power'), which typically brings together Daney's ethical and aesthetic concerns. He proceeds carefully from the specific (the parallel fates of Kane and Falstaff) to the more general – Welles's desire to begin at the point where other films end, i.e. where everything is now to be lost because already gained. Like Shakespeare, Daney claims, Welles offers a reflection on the very nature of Power, the fact that, for instance, absolute power destroys real power. The article then returns to the particular to make a subtle distinction between Falstaff and Kane: Falstaff's death is neither legendary nor mysterious but rather a lacklustre, even 'naked' event that bespeaks the end of the world. To formalise the recurring theme of betrayal and abuse of trust in Welles, Daney then refers to other films, such as *The Lady from Shanghai* (1947) before closing with a consideration of the various existential and political choices facing the future Henry V in *Chimes at Midnight* (1965). It is this rare combination of wide intellectual interest and human concern that will characterise Daney's critical work, as does his pedagogical ambition to start from the evidence of the visible in order to speculate and ultimately declare his hand on ethical and aesthetic matters.

Although *Cahiers du cinéma* had already begun at this point to question the *politique des auteurs*, it was not until much later in the 1960s that it veered towards politics proper, influenced particularly by Godard's practice and thought around the time of *La Chinoise* (1967). And then history took over. We shall not rehearse here the well-established narrative of events leading up to May 1968, from the Langlois Affair to the peremptory halting of the Cannes film festival and the brief formation of the Estates General of Cinema, which entailed the closing down of the major studios and the occupation of IDHEC and the CNC. Suffice to say – and to Daney's eternal regret – almost no films of the May events were made at the time, with the exception of the collectively made *ciné-tracts* and 16mm documents such as William Klein's *Grands soirs et petits matins* (1968–78). *Cahiers du cinéma* had been galvanised into action, however, and it attempted to establish political platforms in order to define both revolutionary cinema and revolutionary criticism. This necessitated an analysis both of the economic means of production and distribution, and of the ideological effects of form (montage, framing, etc.).

Such broad theoretical aims matched those of engaged film-makers like Godard, who sought to discover how to make films politically, rather than simply how to make political films. The key points of reference were Marx and Lenin, particularly as interpreted by Louis Althusser, who argued that notions of base and superstructure had to be rethought in terms of practices – economic, political and ideological. This approach was informed in different ways by structuralism and semiotics (notably Metz, who used the linguistics of Saussure to analyse film as a structure of signification and proposed 'the great syntagmatic chain'), Lacanian psychoanalysis and the deconstructionist insights of Derrida and Foucault. By affirming the centrality of the dialectic between ideology and representation, *Cahiers du cinéma* was orienting itself towards a theory and politics of representation. Its fundamental aim was to disqualify the institution of classic representation with its mere appearance of reality (or 'Realism') and in the process help to transform society. Every film was therefore political, and if bourgeois cinema and classic Hollywood were to be studied, it was above all for the formal 'cracks' and 'fissures' that somehow escaped the dominant ideology.

Daney was joined at *Cahiers du cinéma* in this radical 'scientific' – as opposed to simply aesthetic – task by Jean-Louis Comolli and Jean Narboni (the mainstay of the editorial board up to 1972), Pascal Bonitzer, Sylvie Pierre, Serge Toubiana, Jacques Aumont and Bernard Eisenschitz. It was a period marked by the retrieval of Eisenstein and his framework of dialectical materialism. A project to translate his writings covered fifteen instalments from February 1969 to February 1971 and included a special Eisenstein issue in January–February 1971. Issues were also devoted to Revolutionary Russian film culture in May–June 1970, featuring texts by – and commentary on – Vertov, Lenin, Eisenstein, Mayakovsky, Meyerhold and Kuleshov. In March 1970, the first major 'reading' of the newly reconstituted *Cahiers du cinéma* was a collective analysis of Renoir's militant film *La Vie est à nous* (1936), based upon an understanding of the social and historical context of France during the Popular Front. At the same time, the journal pursued a critique of classic American cinema (Ford, Sternberg, Cukor, Griffith), articulated through the twin master discourses of historical materialism and psychoanalysis. The title of one famous article by Daney and Jean-Pierre Oudart – 'Travail, lecture, jouissance' ('Working, Reading, Coming') – captures the heady mix of Althusserian Marxism spiced with Lacanian psychoanalysis.

BETWEEN CINEMA AND TELEVISION

During the heyday of radical theory in the early 1970s, the study of mainstream narrative cinema had virtually vanished from film debates. Indeed, cinema as a living art form was barely discussed. While *Cahiers du cinéma* certainly did its best to keep pace with feminist 'counter-cinema' – the work of Agnès Varda, Coline Serreau, Chantal Akerman and above all Marguerite Duras, who experimented uncompromisingly with the cinematic apparatus eventually to the point of its negation – the only contemporary film-makers deemed truly worthy of its consideration were the Dziga Vertov group and the team of Jean-Marie Straub and Danièle Huillet. As Daney later acknowledged, *Cahiers du cinéma* became completely absorbed by the need to pursue a strict party line, even if in January 1972 it finally cut itself loose from the French Communist Party and aligned itself more generally with Maoism. An important parallel can be drawn here with the evolution of Metz, who in 1975 changed course with his essay 'Le signifiant imaginaire'. Now he deployed Lacanian psychoanalysis to theorise the cinematic apparatus itself and with it the physical and ideological conditions of spectatorship. Metz faithfully assumed all the consequences his approach entailed, including the very dissolution of

the sovereignty of the cinematic apparatus, since cinema had effectively been 'taken out of itself'. All hinged on one key point: the cinema screen is never a mirror (of the self, for instance), and imaginary presence in the image should be regarded as the result of a signifier standing for something absent.

But the problem was not simply that the 'savage' application of political theory untainted by literary or theatrical models had deleterious, even 'terroristic' effects on film thinking, and effectively evacuated the study of film *qua* film. The prose of *Cahiers du cinéma* had itself become increasingly hermetic and rebarbative, and almost nobody wanted to read it any more. For Daney, who had originally been attracted to *Cahiers du cinéma* by its writerly style, the journal had reached a creative dead-end. When in 1974 he became chief editor, he penned with Toubiana an editorial entitled '*Les Cahiers* aujourd'hui' in which he bravely admitted as much. Mindful no doubt of the recent launch of two other determinedly cinephile film journals, *Écran* (edited by Guy Hennebelle) and *Cinématographe* (by Jacques Fieschi), Daney realised that the priority was to return to a more straightforward discussion of film that both reached out to a diverse viewer and provided some kind of continuity with what had come before, notably the inheritance from André Bazin. Choosing not simply to abandon the many substantial findings of *Cahiers du cinéma*'s theoretical work but rather to build on them at a more accessible level, Daney managed during the mid to late 1970s to steer the journal back to its roots in cinephilia and open it up to the study of photography, video and television. It would now feature a newspaper-style 'chronicle' and commit itself to the production and distribution of videotapes and monographs on film. Among many enterprising initiatives, he invited Godard to be guest editor and designer of the special 300th issue in May 1979, and he personally assisted Duras on one of the most beautiful double issues of *Cahiers du cinéma* entitled 'Les Yeux verts' in June–July 1980, which brought together the political and philosophical, journalistic and epistolary, photographic and poetic.

Given the nature of these changes, it was perhaps unsurprising that in 1981, the year when the Socialists finally came to power, Daney joined *Libération* to write both on film and television. Not only did this give him the opportunity to engage with, and forge, a much wider form of readership beyond the institutional walls of film theory; it also allowed him to move freely as a self-styled *passeur* (boatman/smuggler) between television and what he called its 'occupied territory', cinema. Influenced in no small measure by Godard's recent experiments in video and television, as well as by Guy Debord's Situationist account of the 'society of the spectacle', Daney was the first critic in France to attempt to formalise thoroughly the complex relations between television and cinema. His chief objective was to confront the 'image' of cinema with what he called 'the visual', i.e. all those forces such as television, advertising and music videos that together absorb, deform and transfigure the physical experience of vision. Television, he argued, was a matter of 'diffusion' and thus the reverse of projection, that is to say, the *pro*-jection of a creative act as originally found in the cinema and other art forms. Yet Daney never demonised television as such. In an early article for *Libération* entitled 'Du grand au petit écran' ('From the Big to the Small Screen'), Daney had also recognised that now films were actually seen, or rather glimpsed, mainly on the small screen, and that the desire to 'zap' between programmes and, as it were, 'deprogramme' the schedules in order to recuperate the odd fleeting 'image', was something to be valued. New thinking on the image could be generated in this way, in particular regarding cinema's ethnographic function as a record of social reality. This is a prime example of Daney crossing different fields and media in order to resituate the very parameters of film debate in France, now back firmly in the public domain. With his daily forum, film became a serious, live issue for the educated masses and no longer one of purely academic interest. This is in marked contrast to so much of the later work on television by 'mediologists' like Régis Debray and engaged sociologists such as Pierre Bourdieu, who actually deal very little with the medium itself and opt instead for an often scathing and defeatist critique of its manipulative functions, dismissing out of hand any capacity television might have to generate a critical or analytical discourse. With his remarkable talent always to think through the medium and, as the film and critical theorist Raymond Bellour has stated, to attend to every sign of what cinema was and still is, Daney might even be described as a type of film visionary.

This was certainly the view of the philosopher Gilles Deleuze, who in his preface to Daney's collection of articles for *Libération* from 1981 to 1986, hailed his underlying mission to establish the links between cinema and thought and so retain the 'grand conception of cinema's first age' (Daney 1986: 7). In this respect, of course, Daney and Deleuze were kindred spirits. In his pioneering two-volume study, Deleuze constructed the first taxonomy of film by concept (as opposed, say, to genre), embodying each concept in a name or figure, work or body of works (Deleuze 1986, 1989). By employing Henri Bergson's various theories of movement to develop a fundamentally new way of understanding the mutation of classical into modernist cinema, that is to say, the passage from a 'movement-image' inscribed in the truth of action to its disintegration in a 'time-image', Deleuze renewed a concern in film studies with philosophy and aesthetics, one that continues strongly in the work of Hubert Damisch, Jacques Rancière, Clément Rosset and Bernard Stiegler. For Deleuze, World War II and the birth of Italian neo-realism was a crucial turning point, and, as we shall see shortly, the same was true for Daney who, during the 1970s and 1980s, increasingly viewed cinema as part of the cultural work of mourning following the Holocaust.

It was while working on *Libération* that Daney found his true critical voice, since the daily pressure for copy suited his desire to convey in writing the immediate present of the viewing experience. The stakes of his critical enterprise were invariably high and required all the resources of language at his disposal, including extensive word-play and neologisms. This is why his written style often possesses the power and rhythm of speech, however dense and allusive it may at first appear. It may also explain why Daney could be so withering when polemical and on the attack, as for example when he famously described Jean-Jacques Annaud's crass adaptation of Duras's autobiographical novel *L'Amant* (1991) as a work by the world's first 'postfilm-maker'. At times it seemed like Daney's column was transforming itself into a public court of law. In 1992, however, sensing that his work for

■ **Serge Daney** *Journal de l'an passé* ■ **Giorgio Agamben** *Notes sur le geste* ■ **Jean Louis Schefer** *De la vie des mutants* ■ **Leslie Kaplan** *Children, Children : depuis longtemps déjà nous ne naissons plus de pères vivants* ■ **Roberto Rossellini** *Une lettre* ■ **João Cesar de Monteiro** *Que Dieu me vienne en aide* ■ **Sylvie Pierre** *Le mystère et la vie passionnée* ■ **Jean-Luc Godard** *La paroisse morte* ■ **Raymond Bellour** *La mort inassouvie* ■ **Robert Kramer** *Going (back) to Vietnam* ■ **Elias Sanbar** *Vingt et un ans après* ■ **Bill Krohn** *Lettre d'un ami américain* ■ **Jean-Claude Biette** *A pied d'œuvre* ■ **Pierre Legendre** *Eloge du titre*

HIVER 1991   **REVUE DE CINÉMA. P.O.L**

Cover of the first issue of Serge Daney's *Trafic*, 1991 (P.O.L.)

Libération might itself be a lost cause due to the paper's compromised position within the network of multimedia, and still feeling on a personal level dismayed at its lack of editorial support when Claude Berri took legal action against him for his pugnacious review of *Uranus* (1990), Daney founded with Bellour the quarterly film journal *Trafic*. They conceived of it both as a means of 'traffic' between critics of different generations and disciplines, and as a calm, individual means of resistance against the mass media and the dominant theoretical discourses. Resolutely devoid of illustrations, the journal marked a deliberate attempt by Daney to position cinema within the general body of history and culture. It also exemplified his receptiveness to the voices of others, his genuine internationalism and above all his literary sensibility – the fact that cinema could also be an extension of literary discourse just as it had once been for Jean Epstein and Louis Delluc. The first issue, in which Daney defended the cinephile's 'love' against the combined forces of broadcasting, information and communications, included extracts from his own journal, a poem by Godard entitled 'La paroisse morte' ('The Dead Parish'), personal reflections from João César Monteiro and Robert Kramer, and letters from Rossellini and Bill Krohn. Since Daney's death in 1992, *Trafic* has continued to exemplify this sober and heterogeneous approach.

VOICES FROM BEYOND

Daney's posthumously published works remain relatively unknown, even in France, yet they are arguably his most significant. The first, *L'Exercice a été profitable, Monsieur* (1993), was presented by the editors as the autobiography that Daney hoped one day to write, and what strikes the reader immediately is its extremely personal tone (the title is a remark by the child John Mohune in Fritz Lang's *Moonfleet*, 1954, a film from deep within Daney's childhood). It might best be described as a stream of theoretical consciousness taking the form of a diary divided chronologically into four chapters covering the years 1988 to 1991. In his intimate and self-reflexive late critical manner, Daney continually runs the risk of narcissism and of troping on himself one phrase too far, yet this constitutes an almost baroque move on his part both to dazzle and involve the reader intimately in the multi-perspective, filmic present of his text. While a breathless flow of ideas on film, politics and philosophy, relayed in shorthand style, gives the work its force and beauty, it is the predominantly elegiac mood of nostalgia and loss that establishes its cohesion and singularity.

The second posthumous work, *Persévérance* (1994), comprises an extended interview with Serge Toubiana arranged in sections that relate cinema to history, cinephilia, travel and Communism. It also features one of Daney's most extraordinary critical performances, a piece originally published in *Trafic* entitled 'Le travelling de Kapo' and which showcases the versatility of his method. Focusing first on Rivette's coruscating 1961 review 'De l'abjection' of Gillo Pontecorvo's *Kapo* (1960), a melodrama about the concentration camps that Daney admits never having seen, he weaves an intricate web from twentieth-century history, the history of cinema and film criticism, as well as his own personal story, turning these associations around and over and against each other to forge a tightly argued dramatic whole. The approach is both anecdotal and axiomatic, the tone both sharp and melancholic. Again, Daney invokes his 'naive' position as impassioned cinephile, and, always aware of the importance of dates, points out that he was born in 1944, the year of the discovery of the camps and also when Rossellini shot *Rome, Open City*. For Daney, whose own father was deported and most probably died in the camps, the year represents an ambivalent locus of loss and affect. However, by bringing the figure of his father directly into the discussion at this point, Daney is also seeking, as it were, to retrieve the corpse of cinema, in order to pay belated homage to both. For in this unusual form of textual cure, cinema and the father have become one. The conclusion Daney reaches, not simply that cinema is an art that can afford access to the truth of the world (his long-standing and fundamental belief) but that cinema enables a personal understanding of the Other, is articulated with genuine pathos: 'I see clearly why I adopted cinema for it to adopt me in return. For it to teach me to touch with my gaze, again and again, that point in the distance where the Other begins' (Daney 1994: 39).

What is particularly significant about Daney's posthumous work and its intense emphasis on the self is that for the first time he writes explicitly as a gay man, overcome by the sensation of being alone in a darkened auditorium and encountering what he calls his 'secondary world', or the temporary escape into identification and projection. He obliges his reader to imagine a range of erotic, aesthetic and political connections in cinema that, he believes, still has the artistic power to signal human togetherness. Even Rossellini is reappraised in this light, at one point downgraded in *L'Exercice* as a 'hetero-hetero' film-maker. Daney reminds us, too, that one of the major reasons why he left *Cahiers du cinéma* was precisely because he found the journal oppressively straight. The more mixed and relaxed daily experience of *Libération* provided a form of personal release (for the record, Daney insisted, unlike some public figures in France, notably Foucault, that the cause of his death should not be covered up). Hence, despite its tantalisingly unfinished state, Daney's posthumous work, and *L'Exercice* in par-

ticular, presents one of the most original aspects of Daney's project: the possibility of a gay French cinephilia.

The unfortunate fact that there is no other immediate '*ciné-fils*' in France to carry such a project forward makes his absence all the more significant. Indeed, there remains in French film debates a woeful lack of interest in matters of gender and sexual difference, and critical writing directly informed by either feminist or gay/queer theory is relatively rare. The work of Geneviève Sellier and Noël Burch (1996), in particular their study of gender and cultural representation in wartime and post-war cinema, is one exception that proves the rule. Morever, feminist thought often finds itself in France cast under the still suspicious imported term of 'cultural studies' (there still exists in France no equivalent to the American feminist journal *Camera Obscura*). It was certainly no surprise that on the fortieth anniversary of the New Wave, major French critics such as Antoine de Baecque, Jean Douchet and Michel Marie, while honouring the movement as a decisive formalist break effected by male heterosexual directors bent on sacralising the status of the auteur, deliberately downplayed the more mundane yet equally important factors of society, politics and gender. This state of affairs is even more regrettable in view of the continuing proliferation of information and discourse on film at all levels of the specialist and popular media (television, websites and of course print journalism, from the highbrow *Vertigo* and *Cinémathèque* to the explicitly commercial *Première* and *Studio*). Of much greater weight in France are the more 'serious' debates on the development of new media and technologies, or the old chestnut of French cinema's crisis in the face of Hollywood and television (most visibly during the 1993 GATT talks).

Yet it would be a mistake to view this prevailing lack of concern with matters of gender and sexuality as somehow permanent. If we associate Daney's jubilant return to the self with Deleuze's general theoretical aim to retrieve the body in cinema, we can appreciate better his strategic role and importance within contemporary debates. In 1993, a year after Daney's death, in a valuable overview of contemporary French film theory that directly mentions *L'Exercice*, Nicole Brenez argued convincingly that the body lies at the root of a new theoretical articulation: 'the description of the unknown relations that the cinema installs between the subject and its experience (of the world, of others, of the image) (Brenez 1997: 6). For Brenez, as for Daney, modern theories of cinema must always return to the basic question: that of the body, and how and where to find it. She offers by way of example the work of Jean-Louis Schefer (1980), in particular his highly influential autobiographical study *L'Homme ordinaire du cinéma*, which proposes movement in film as a kind of anamorphosis (the frequency of deformed, freakish or burlesque figures in cinema, for example); and also Bellour's *L'Entre-images: photo, cinéma, vidéo* (1990), which interrogates three terms of the body's identity: face, portrait and self-portrait. She concludes that the primordial subject of cinema remains a 'creature haunted by heterogeneity that, more than knowing itself, prefers to verify that something else is still possible (a body, a friend, a world)' (Brenez 1997: 16). In her own pioneering study, a work Deleuzian in nature insofar as it treats bodies in the cinema as a figure of thought, Brenez (1998) uses corporeality as represented in film to elaborate a dense network of cinematic figuration. Rather than classifying films according to genre or historical period, she proposes two major cartographies: one that remaps cinema by grouping films according to their treatment of bodies, and another that charts the relations between the body and the artist. Her method of figural analysis is consequently one that treats films as forces rather than effects, and as a form of knowledge rather than expression. Encompassing not only French cinema but also Rossellini, Lang, Fassbinder, Eisenstein, Hawks, Ferrara, Cassavetes, among many others, Brenez's study initiates new paths for thinking through the body as aesthetic effect, and in this sense she continues the work of the illustrious corpses – Metz, Deleuze and Daney – who have come before her.

We have effectively come full circle, arriving with Brenez at a contemporary blend of the ethical and aesthetic criticism found in so much of *Cahiers du cinéma* during the 1960s and in Daney's work throughout (with the noted exception of the immediate post-1968 period). Such an outcome is due in major part to the availability and reach of Daney's constantly evolving cinephile project committed to exploring alterity and the responsibilities of form and address. We discover with Daney that just as the study of cinema cannot be studied in isolation either from its various audiences or from other forms of visual culture and communication, so gender and identity as overlapping paths of enquiry make full critical sense only when linked to questions of ethnicity, history and culture. For these reasons, his work offers a fertile and dynamic basis upon which to engage with contemporary film practice in France, which, although not overtly political, provides new representations of gender and sexuality that challenge sexist, racist and heteronormative forces within the culture. However, to genderise and elaborate the cinematic body in its multiple aspects and forms, French film studies will also need, in the open and capacious spirit of Daney, and with equal honesty and sensitivity, to embrace other contemporary approaches and methodologies. One example of such an exchange would be the feminist and psychoanalytic readings in film by Kaja Silverman, whose development has itself been so profoundly influenced by modern French thought and whose 1992 study re-examines the categories of masculine and feminine, as well as ideology and authorship, across a range of cinematic, literary and theoretical texts, notably the cinema of Fassbinder. Such a reciprocal move will enhance the vital international traffic between different fields, disciplines and critical traditions that Daney epitomised and promoted. The once imperial age of French film theory may be definitively over, but the defiant call for independent and creative thinking on film – let us call it 'the Daney effect' – will continue to resound.

WORKS CITED

Bellour, R. (1990) *L'Entre-images: photo, cinéma, vidéo*, Paris, La Différence.

Brenez, N. (1997), 'The Ultimate Journey: Remarks on Contemporary Theory', <*www.latrobe.edu.au/screeningthepast/reruns/brenez.html*>, 1–16 (originally published in *Art Press*, special issue 14, 1993, 65–72).

Brenez, N. (1998) *De la figure en général et du corps en particulier: l'invention figurative au cinéma*, Brussels, De Boeck.

Burch, N. and Sellier, G. (1996) *La Drôle de guerre des sexes du cinéma français, 1930–1956*, Paris, Nathan.

Daney, S. (1986) *Ciné journal 1981–1986*, Paris, *Cahiers du cinéma*.

Daney, S. (1993) *L'Exercice a été profitable, Monsieur*, Paris, P.O.L.

Daney, S. (1994), *Persévérance: entretien avec Serge Toubiana*, Paris, P.O.L.

Daney, S. (2001) *La Maison cinéma et le monde*, vol. 1: 'Le Temps des *Cahiers* 1962–1981', Paris: P.O.L..

Daney, S. (2002) *La Maison cinéma et le monde*, vol. 2: 'Les Années Libé 1981–1985', Paris, P.O.L..

Deleuze, G. (1986) *Cinema 1: The Movement-Image*, London, Athlone.

Deleuze, G. (1989) *Cinema 2: The Time-Image*, London, Athlone.

Schefer, J.-L. (1980) *L'Homme ordinaire du cinéma*, Paris, Gallimard.

Silverman, K. (1992) *Male Subjectivity at the Margins*, London, Routledge.

Selected Further Reading: 1960–2004

Austin, G. (1966) *Contemporary French Cinema: An Introduction*, Manchester, Manchester University Press. (Survey of key trends from the early 1970s to the mid-1990s.)

Austin, G. (2003) *Stars in Modern French Film*, London, Arnold. (Study of a selection of stars from the 1950s to the 1990s.)

Forbes, J. (1992) *The Cinema in France after the New Wave*, London, Macmillan/BFI. (Survey of selected film-makers, genres and trends from May 1968 to the early 1990s.)

Grantham, B. (2000) '*Some Big Bourgeois Brothel*': *Contexts for France's Culture Wars with Hollywood*, Luton, University of Luton Press. (Study of 1993 GATT negotiations in the context of wider Franco-American cultural relations.)

Greene, N. (1999) *Landscapes of Loss: The National Past in Postwar French Cinema*, Princeton, NJ, Princeton University Press. (Study of the representation of history in post-war French cinema, especially the work of Resnais and Tavenier.)

Harvey, S. (1980) *May 68 and Film Culture*, London, BFI. (Study of the impact of May 'events' on film-making and political film theory.)

Marie, M. (2003) *The French New Wave: An Artistic School*, Oxford, Blackwell. (Study of the New Wave in terms of production, technology and representation.)

Mazdon, L. ed. (2001) *French on Film: Reflections on Popular French Cinema*, London, Wallflower. (Collection of interpretive essays on selected films from the 1990s.)

Neupert, R. (2002) *A History of the French New Wave*, Madison, University of Wisconsin Press. (Study of key New Wave film-makers.)

Powrie, P. (1997) *French Cinema in the 1980s: Nostalgia and the Crisis of Masculinity*, Oxford, Oxford University Press. (Essays discussing selected heritage, *policier* and comic films of the 1980s.)

Powrie, P. ed. (1999) *French Cinema in the 1990s: Continuity and Difference*, Oxford, Oxford University Press. (Collection of essays on selected films from the 1990s, with cultural context.)

Tarr, C. with Rollet, B. (1992) *Cinema and the Second Sex: Women's Filmmaking in France in the 1980s and 1990s*, New York, Continuum. (Thematic and generic discussion of films made by women in the 1980s and 1990s.)

Wilson, E. (1999) *French Cinema since 1950: Personal Histories*, London, Duckworth. (Discussion of

Selected On-Line Resources

SOURCES FOR BUYING VIDEOS AND DVDS

FRANCE

Alapage: <www.alapage.com> (On-line shop. In French.)

Amazon: <www.amazon.fr> (On-line shop. In French.)

CPEDERF: <www.cpederf.com> (Paris-based company servicing the academic community outside France. Can supply university students or teachers with any video or DVD commercially available in France. Site is in English. All staff are bilingual.)

FNAC: <www.fnac.com> (On-line shop. In French.)

Médiathèque des Trois Mondes: <www.cine3mondes.com> (Extensive video and DVD catalogue of a Paris-based organisation specialising in francophone cinema from around the world. In French.)

Re-Voir: <www.re-voir.com> (Paris-based company specialising in experimental cinema on video. Site in English and French.)

UK

Amazon: <www.amazon.co.uk> (On-line shop.)

British Film Institute video and DVD publishing: <www.bfi.org.uk/bookvid> (Catalogue includes a selection of French videos and DVDs.)

Grant and Cutler: <www.grantandcutler.com> (Supplier of foreign-language materials. Video and DVD catalogue includes many French films.)

MovieMail: <www.moviem.co.uk> (On-line video and DVD store with an extensive French film list.)

USA

Amazon: <www.amazon.com> (On-line shop.)

CineFile video: <www.cinefilevideo.com>. (On-line store specialising in hard-to-find and out-of-print videos and DVDs. Includes many French titles.)

Facets: <www.facets.org> (On-line store with an extensive French film list.)

Milestone Film and Video: <www.milestonefilms.com> (Catalogue includes a subtitled DVD of *Le Chagrin et la pitié*.)

New York Film Annex: <www.nyfavideo.com> (Video store with an extensive French film list. Titles include numerous rare and experimental works.)

US Videoflicks: <www.videoflicks.com> (On-line shop with a good French film list.)

JAPAN

Amazon: <www.amazon.co.jp> (On-line store offering many videos and DVDs not available elsewhere. Note that your computer must be able to read Japanese script to negotiate this site.)

CD Japan: <www.cdjapan.co.jp> (English-language website specialising in Japanese DVDs. List includes many titles not available elsewhere.)

SELECTED REFERENCE SITES

Centre National de la Cinématographie: (CNC) <www.cnc.fr> (Site of the National Centre for Cinema. Invaluable source for data relating to the contemporary industry. Also gives access to detailed technical dossiers. In French.)

Internet Movie Database: <www.imdb.com> (Useful general film reference guide.)

Stars of French Film: <www.shef.ac.uk/french filmstars> (Database of French film stars, including short biographies and filmographies.)

SPECIALIST LIBRARIES

British Film Institute National Library: <www.bfi.org.uk> (Access to the BFI book library catalogue.)

Bibliothèque du Film: <www.bifi.fr> (Access to the catalogue of the principal specialist cinema library in Paris. In French.)

AUDIOVISUAL ARCHIVES

Bibliothèque National de France (BNF): <www.bnf.fr>
   (Catalogue of the French National Library. Gives
   access to details of audiovisual materials available for
   viewing at the BNF in Paris. In French.)

Forum des Images (aka Vidéothèque de Paris):
   <www.forumdesimages.net> (Gives access to details
   of the large collection of video copies of films set, or
   partially set, in Paris and available for viewing at the
   Forum des Images, Paris. In French.)

French Ministry of Foreign Affairs Film Library:
   <www.diplomatie.gouv.fr> (Access to the catalogue
   of the large government-sponsored collection of
   films and videos available for distribution abroad.)

Institut National de l'Audiovisuel:
   <www.ina.fr/inatheque> (Site of the National
   Audiovisual Institute, whose collection is accessible
   to researchers in the National Library in Paris.)

Médiathèque of the Institut Français, London:
   <www.ifl.agate-fr.net> (French Institute library
   catalogue. Library holds books and a substantial
   collection of French films on video that can be
   borrowed by members.)

MAGAZINES AND JOURNALS

Le Film français: <www.lefilmfrancais.com> (Site of the
   weekly industry journal. In French.)

Les Inrockuptibles: <www.lesinrocks.com> (Site of the
   popular weekly cultural magazine. In French.)

Première (France): <www.premiere.fr> (Site of the
   popular monthly film magazine.)

ACADEMIC ASSOCIATIONS

Association Française de Recherche sur l'Histoire du
   Cinéma (AFRHC):
   <www.dsi.cnrs.fr/afrhc/pub_home-e.htm> (English-
   language site of a French academic association
   devoted to the study of French cinema history. The
   association publishes the journal *1895*.)

Studies in French Cinema:
   <www.ncl.ac.uk/crif/sfc/home.htm> (UK-based
   academic association devoted to the study of French
   cinema. The association publishes a journal of the
   same name.)

Further Reading on Films and Film People

This is a selection of English-language books relating to individual films and film people. It is divided into four sections: (i) studies of film-makers; (ii) writings by film-makers; (iii) writings by other creative personnel; (iv) studies of individual films.

STUDIES OF FILM-MAKERS

CHANTAL AKERMAN

Foster, G. ed. (1999) *Identity and Memory: The Films of Chantal Akerman*, Trowbridge, Flicks Books.

Margulies, I. (1996) *Nothing Happens: Chantal Akerman's Hypperrealist Everyday*, Durham, NC, Duke University Press.

JEAN-JACQUES BEINEIX

Powrie, P. (2001) *Jean-Jacques Beineix*, Manchester, Manchester University Press.

LUC BESSON

Hayward, S. (1998) *Luc Besson*, Manchester, Manchester University Press.

BERTRAND BLIER

Harris, S. (2001) *Bertrand Blier*, Manchester, Manchester University Press.

ROBERT BRESSON

Quandt, J. ed. (1998) *Robert Bresson*, Toronto, Cinémathèque Ontario.

Reader, K. (2000) *Robert Bresson*, Manchester, Manchester University Press.

MARCEL CARNÉ

Turk, E. (1989) *Child of Paradise: Marcel Carné and the Golden Age of French Cinema*, Cambridge, MA, Harvard University Press.

CLAUDE CHABROL

Austin, G. (1999) *Claude Chabrol*, Manchester, Manchester University Press.

RENÉ CLAIR

Dale, R. (1986) *The Films of René Clair*, Metuchen, NJ, Scarecrow Press.

McGerr, C. (1980) *René Clair*, Boston, Twayne.

JEAN COCTEAU

Gilson, R. (1969) *Jean Cocteau: An Introduction to His Films and Philosophy*, New York, Crown.

ÉMILE COHL

Crafton, D. (1990) *Émile Cohl, Caricature and Film*, Princeton, NJ, Princeton University Press.

MARGUERITE DURAS

Günther, R. (2002) *Marguerite Duras*, Manchester, Manchester University Press.

ABEL GANCE

King, N. (1984) *Abel Gance: A Politics of Spectacle*, London, BFI.

Kramer, S. and Welsh, J. (1978) *Abel Gance*, Boston, Twayne.

JEAN-LUC GODARD

Brown, R. ed. (1972) *Focus on Godard*, Englewood Cliffs, NJ, Prentice-Hall.

MacCabe, C., Mulvey, L. and Eaton, M. (1980) *Godard: Images, Sounds, Politics*, London, BFI.

Temple, M. and Williams, J. eds (2000) *The Cinema Alone: Jean-Luc Godard 1985–2000*, Amsterdam, Amsterdam University Press.

Temple, M., Williams, J. and Witt, M. eds (2004) *For Ever Godard: The Work of Jean-Luc Godard*, London, Black Dog Publishing.

ALICE GUY BLACHÉ

McMahan, A. (2002) *Alice Guy Blaché: Lost Visionary of the Cinema*, New York, Continuum.

KRZYSZTOF KIEŚLOWSKI

Wilson, E. (2000) *Memory and Survival: The French Cinema of Krzysztof Kieślowski*, Oxford, Legenda.

DIANE KURYS

Tarr, C. (1999) *Diane Kurys*, Manchester, Manchester University Press.

ÉTIENNE-JULES MAREY

Braun, M. (1992) *Picturing Time: The Work of Étienne-Jules Marey (1830–1904)*, Chicago, University of Chicago Press.

GEORGES MÉLIÈS

Ezra, E. (2000) *Georges Méliès*, Manchester, Manchester University Press.

Frazer, J. (1979) *Artificially Arranged Scenes: The Films of Georges Méliès*, Boston, Twayne.

Hammond, P. (1974) *Marvellous Méliès*, London, Gordon Fraser Gallery.

JEAN-PIERRE MELVILLE

Vincendeau, G. (2003) *Jean-Pierre Melville, An American in Paris*, London, BFI.

MAX OPHULS

Willemen, P. ed. (1978) *Ophuls*, London, BFI.

Williams, A. (1980) *Max Ophuls and the Cinema of Desire, 1948–1955*, New York, Arno.

G. W. PABST

Atwell, L. (1977) *G. W. Pabst*, Boston, Twayne.

MARCEL PAGNOL

Caldicott, C. (1977) *Marcel Pagnol*, Boston, Twayne.

JEAN RENOIR

Bazin, A. (1973) *Jean Renoir*, New York, Simon and Schuster.

Faulkner, C. (1986) *The Social Cinema of Jean Renoir*, Princeton, NJ, Princeton University Press.

O'Shaughnessy, M. (2000) *Jean Renoir*, Manchester, Manchester University Press.

Sesonske, A. (1980) *Jean Renoir: The French Films,*

1924–1939, Cambridge, MA, Harvard University Press.

ALAIN RESNAIS

Armes, R. (1968) *The Cinema of Alain Resnais*, London, Zwemmer.

Monaco, J. (1978) *Alain Resnais*, London, Secker and Warburg.

ALAIN ROBBE-GRILLET

Armes, R. (1981) *The Films of Alain Robbe-Grillet*, Amsterdam, John Benjamins.

ÉRIC ROHMER

Crisp, C. (1988) *Éric Rohmer: Realist and Moralist*, Bloomington, Indiana University Press.

JEAN ROUCH

Eaton, M. ed. (1979) *Anthropology, Reality, Cinema: The Films of Jean Rouch*, London, BFI.

COLINE SERREAU

Rollet, B. (1998) *Coline Serreau*, Manchester, Manchester University Press.

JACQUES TATI

Chion, M. (1997) *The Films of Jacques Tati*, Toronto, Guernica.

Harding, J. (1984) *Jacques Tati: Frame by Frame*, London, Secker and Warburg.

FRANÇOIS TRUFFAUT

de Baecque, A. and Toubiana, S. (1999) *Truffaut*, New York, Knopf.

Holmes, D. and Ingram, R. (1998) *François Truffaut*, Manchester, Manchester University Press.

Insdorf, A. (1995) *François Truffaut*, Cambridge, Cambridge University Press.

AGNÈS VARDA

Smith, A. (1998) *Agnès Varda*, Manchester, Manchester University Press.

JEAN VIGO

Salès Gomès, P. (1998) *Jean Vigo*, London, Faber and Faber.

Simon, W. (1981) *The Films of Jean Vigo*, Ann Arbor, MI, UMI Research Press.

WRITINGS BY FILM-MAKERS

Bresson, R. (1997) *Notes on the Cinematographer*, Copenhagen, Green Integer.

Buñuel, L. (1994) *My Last Breath*, London, Vintage.

Clair, R. (1972) *Cinema, Yesterday and Today*, New York, Dover.

Cocteau, J. (1954) *Cocteau on the Film*, London, Dobson.

Cocteau, J. (1972) *Beauty and the Beast: Diary of a Film*, New York, Dover.

Debord, G. (1994) *The Society of the Spectacle*, New York, Zone Books.

Godard, J.-L. (1972) *Godard on Godard*, London, Secker and Warburg.

Guitry, S. (1935) *If Memory Serves: Memoirs of Sacha Guitry*, New York, Doubleday.

Léger, F. (1973) *Functions of Painting*, New York, Viking.

Nogueira, R. ed. (1972) *Melville on Melville*, New York, Viking.

Pagnol, M. (1960) *The Days Were Too Short*, London, Hamilton.

Renoir, J. (1974) *My Life and My Films*, London, Collins.

Renoir, J. (1989) *Renoir on Renoir: Interviews, Essays and Remarks*, Cambridge, Cambridge University Press.

Rohmer, É. (1989) *The Taste of Beauty*, Cambridge, Cambridge University Press.

Rohmer, É. and Chabrol, C. (1992) *Hitchcock: The First Forty-Four Films*, Oxford, Roundhouse.

Rosenbaum, J. ed. (1977) *Rivette: Texts and Interviews*, London, BFI.

Truffaut, F. (1978) *The Films in My Life*, New York, Simon and Schuster.

Truffaut, F. (1984) *Hitchcock by Truffaut: The Definitive Study*, London, Paladin.

Truffaut, F. (1987) *Truffaut by Truffaut*, New York, Abrams.

Vadim, R. (1976) *Memoirs of the Devil*, London, Hutchinson.

Vigo, J. (1983) *The Complete Jean Vigo*, Godalming, Lorrimer.

WRITINGS BY OTHER CREATIVE PERSONNEL

Almendros, N. (1984) *A Man with a Camera*, London, Faber and Faber.

Aumont, J.-P. (1977) *Sun and Shadow*, New York, Norton.

Barrault, J.-L. (1974) *Memories for Tomorrow: The Memoires of Jean-Louis Barrault*, New York, Dutton.

Barsacq, L. (1976) *Caligari's Cabinet and Other Grand Illusions: A History of Film Design*, Boston: New York Graphic Society.

Carrière, J.-C. (1995) *The Secret Language of Film*, London, Faber and Faber.

Chevalier, M. (1949) *The Man in the Straw Hat: My Story*, New York, Crowell.

Dauman, A. (1992) *Pictures of a Producer*, London, BFI.

Lourié, E. (1985) *My Work in Films*, New York, Harcourt Brace Janovich.

Morgan, M. (1978) *With Those Eyes*, London, Allen.

Préjean, A. (1956) *The Sky and the Stars: The Memoirs of Albert Préjean*, London, Harvill.

Signoret, S. (1976) *Nostalgia Isn't What it Used to Be*, New York, Harper and Row.

STUDIES OF INDIVIDUAL FILMS

Affron, M. and Rubenstein, E. eds (1985) *The Last Metro*, New Brunswick, NJ, Rutgers University Press.

Andrew, D. ed. (1995) *Breathless*, New Brunswick, NJ, Rutgers University Press.

Andrew, G. (1998) *The 'Three Colours' Trilogy*, London, BFI.

Bordwell, D. (1973) *Filmguide to La Passion de Jeanne d'Arc*, Bloomington, Indiana University Press.

Boston, R. (1994) *Boudu Saved from Drowning*, London, BFI.

Braudy, L. ed. (1972) *Focus on Shoot the Piano Player*, Englewood Cliffs, NJ, Prentice-Hall.

Brownlow, K. (1983) *Napoléon: Abel Gance's Classic Film*, New York, Knopf.

Brunette, P. ed. (1993) *Shoot the Piano Player*, New Brunswick, NJ, Rutgers University Press.

Crittenden, R. (1998) *La Nuit américaine (Day for Night)*, London, BFI.

Forbes, J. (1997) *Les Enfants du Paradis*, London, BFI.

Guzzetti, A. (1981) *Two or Three Things I Know about Her: Analysis of a Film by Godard*, Cambridge, MA, Harvard University Press.

Hammond, P. (1997) *L'Âge d'or*, London, BFI.

Heath, S. (2004) *César*, London, BFI.

Jones, K. (1999) *L'Argent*, London, BFI.

Kaplan, N. (1994) *Napoléon*, London, BFI.

Kear, J. (1999) *Sunless*, Trowbridge, Flicks.

Kinder, M. ed. (1999) *Luis Buñuel's The Discreet Charm of the Bourgeoisie*, Cambridge, Cambridge University Press.

Leutrat, J.-L. (2001) *L'Année dernière à Marienbad*, London, BFI.

Showalter, E. ed. (1993) *My Night at Maud's*, New Brunswick, NJ, Rutgers University Press.

Vincendeau, G. (1998) *Pépé le Moko*, London, BFI.

Warner, M. (1993) *L'Atalante*, London, BFI.

Wexman, V. ed. (1986) *Letters from an Unknown Woman*, New Brunswick, NJ, Rutgers University Press.

Wills, D. ed. (2000) *Jean-Luc Godard's Pierrot le fou*, Cambridge, Cambridge University Press.

Wood, M. (2001) *Belle de jour*, London, BFI.

Index

Notes: Page numbers in *italics* denote illustrations; those in **bold** type indicate detailed analysis.